ALEXANDRIA
THE SUBMERGED ROYAL QUARTERS

ALEXANDRIA

THE SUBMERGED ROYAL QUARTERS

Franck Goddio

André Bernand, Etienne Bernand,
Ibrahim Darwish, Zsolt Kiss, Jean Yoyotte

Periplus

London

First published in 1998 by
Periplus Ltd
4 Bedford Row
London WC1 R 4DF

Editors: Leonard Harrow and Danièle Juncqua-Naveau
Translation by Ludwig von Bomhard and Leonard Harrow
Assistant editor Alan Ball
ISBN 1 902699 00 9

Origination by Walden Litho Plates, England
Printed and bound in Spain by SYL, Barcelona

This archaeological project was made possible
with the support of

HILTI F O U N D A T I O N

(Principality of Liechtenstein)

and of

Discovery Communications Inc
(Bethesda, USA)

We wish to express our thanks particularly to Monsieur Jean Yoyotte, Professeur Honoraire au Collège de France, Directeur d'Études EPHE, for his tireless assistance and great efforts of co-ordination without which it would not have been possible to have completed this publication in the time available.

Editor

Since Napoleon Bonaparte's French conquest of Egypt nearly thirty plans of Ptolemaic or Roman Alexandria were made by modern scholars, historians or archaeologists. All these plans were inaccurate, particularly regarding the harbours, as archaeologists were unaware of the shore level since the great earthquake which destroyed the famous lighthouse, the Pharos.

Franck Goddio, with the help of a skilled team of divers and sophisticated equipment, has drawn for the first time with the utmost accuracy the submerged eastern part of the Eastern Harbour of Alexandria. This plan conforms, to the minutest detail, with the description of an eyewitness, Strabo the Geographer, who visited Alexandria around 25 BC: the promontories which issue from the ancient submerged coast, the reefs, the ancient ports including the hidden Royal Harbour, the submerged island of Antirhodos with the location of the palace in which Cleopatra VII lived, the jetty which Antony built, the location of his Timonium and of the temple of Poseidon and part of the Basileia and Emporium.

Most important of all is the discovery of a light wood landing place on the island of Antirhodos dating from the 5th century BC, thus before the founding of the city by Alexander the Great. The squared plan of the third harbour looks like a coffer, a *kibotos*, as well as the hieroglyphic sign for 'house' (*per*).

Hundreds of submerged artefacts, including fine sculptures and important inscriptions dating from Pharaonic times up to the Roman period, were also located and photographed. In short the IEASM's work in this area is of the utmost scientific importance for the history and archaeology of Egypt.

Fawzi El Fakharani

Professor Emeritus of Archaeology
Alexandria University

PARTICIPANTS

Project Co-Directors:

Ibrahim Darwish, Director of the Department of Underwater Archaeology
Franck Goddio, Director of the Institut Européen d'Archéologie Sous-Marine

Scientific Committee:

Prof. Jean Yoyotte
Prof. André Bernand
Prof. Etienne Bernand
Prof. Fawsi Al Fakahani
Prof. Manfried Clauss
Prof. Aziza Said
Prof. Emily Teeter

Archaeologists of the Supreme Council of Antiquities:

Mohammed Abd El Hamid
Alaa El Din Mahrous
Ashraf Abd El Rahouf Raghed
Abd El Hamid Abd El Magid
Mostapha El Dissouky
Magdy Gazala
Ibrahim Ahmed Metwaly
Ehab Fahmy
Usama El Nahas
Ahmed Omar Shoukry
Mohammed Mostapha
Ahmed Samah

L'Institut Européen d'Archéologie Sous-Marine:

Gérard Schnepp
Jean-Jacques Groussard
Jean-Claude Roubaud
Jean-Paul Blancan
Daniel Visnikar
Bernard Camier
Fernando Pereira
Philippe Rousseau
Alain Peton
Nicolas Ponzone
Susan Hendrickson
Eric Smith

Pablo Rodriguez
Alain Denaix
Grégory Dalex
Frédéric Osada
Patrice Sandrin
Stéphane Brousse
Georges Broccot
Lionel Julien
Roland Savoye
Pascal Morisset
Gérome Delafosse
Christoph Gerigk

Hilti Foundation:
Michael Hilti
Georg Rosenbauer
Hans Saxer

Discovery Communications Inc.
Judith McHale
Mike Quattrone
Dara Altman

Administration:
Jean-Louis de Talancé
Tatiana Michel-Curchod
Gertraud Walch
Amani Mohammed Badr
Sahar Hassim
Yassin Aly
Selim Said Sidim

CONTENTS

I **Preface**
Franck Goddio, Director of IEASM

II **The Topography of the Submerged Royal Quarters of the Eastern Harbour of Alexandria** 1
Franck Goddio and Ibrahim Darwish, Director of the Department of Underwater Archaeology, Egyptian Supreme Council of Antiquities

A 20th Century Engineer's Viewpoint of the Eastern Harbour of Alexandria 53
Antoine de Graauw, Marine Engineer, SOGREAH Ingénierie, Grenoble, France

III **Testimonia selecta de portu magno et palatiis Alexandriae ad aegyptum e scriptoribus antiquis excerpta** 59
(Selected Accounts on the Great Harbour and Palaces of Alexandria ad Egytptum according to ancient writers)
André Bernand, Professeur émérite des Universités

IV **Epigraphical Documents and Caracalla in Egypt** 143
Etienne Bernand, Professeur honoraire des Universités
Greek and Latin Inscriptions in Alexandria
Caracalla in Alexandria According to the Inscriptions
Caracalla in Alexandria According to the Sources

V **The Sculptures** 169
Zsolt Kiss, Professor at the University, the Centre for Mediterranean Archaeology and the Academy of Sciences, Warsaw

Priest Bearing an 'Osisris-Canopus' in his Veiled Hands 189
Françoise Dunand, Professor at l'Université des Lettres et Sciences Humaines de l'Université de Strasbourg

A Colossal Sphinx with Falcon's Head 195
Jean Yoyotte

VI **Pharaonica** 199
Jean Yoyotte, Professeur honoraire au Collège de France, titulaire de la Chaire d'Égyptologie, Directeur d'Études
I. Reflections concerning Alexandria's *pharaonica.*
II. The Egyptian Inscriptions 221

VII Epilogue 245
Franck Goddio et Jean Yoyotte

Chronological Outline 255

Abbreviations 259

Selected Bibliography 261

Photographic Credits 269

List of Illustrations, Figures and Maps 271

PREFACE

The undertaking to find the submerged royal quarters of ancient Alexandria, to map them and carry out archaeological excavations at strategic locations was an ambitious one. The success of such an enterprise could only be founded on experienced teamwork. The most sophisticated survey techniques, on the contrary, did not reduce at all the human factor. The knowledge gained by the numerous electronic surveys made during the last fifteen years by our Institute in this area was vital and avoided many mistakes. The different electronic data and its application to maps allowed our team of archaeologists and divers experienced in archaeology to reach with great effect in a few months a stage that seemed to many to be impossible. The quality of the scientific work was only made possible thanks to valuable assistance of eminent scholars who guided it, such as Professor Fawzi El Fakharani, who devoted much time and great energy to our work. Such work can only be justified when the results are published to make them available to the scientific community. This important work could not have proceeded without the invaluable assistance of Professor Jean Yoyotte who generously put at our disposal his immense knowledge and who skilfully co-ordinated this publication. His advice, allied to that of Professors André and Etienne Bernand enabled the teams on site to gain a deeper understanding on many important points, thus producing an exemplary interaction between excavation and scientific analysis, which was reinforced by the expertise of Professors Françoise Dunand and Zsolt Kiss and M. Antoine de Graauw, a marine engineer. The expertise that Professors Aziza Said, Manfred Clauss, Emiy Teeter and Grzegorz Majcherek brought to our work was much appreciated and shaped the direction of our research.

I wish to thank the Egyptian authorities for the confidence shown in allowing us the opportunity to resurrect from the past this sunken area of the history of mankind. I will not forget the enthusiasm for this project shown by H. E. Farouk Hosni, the Minister of Culture, when I had the honour of presenting to him the objectives of our project in 1990. Professors, Mohammed Bakr and Abd el-Halim Nour el-Din, Presidents of the Egyptian Organisation for Antiquities, Aly Hassan and Gaballah Aly, General Secretaries of the Supreme Council for Egyptian Antiquities have every year since that date renewed with confidence and granted the excavation permits for the Eastern Harbour of Alexandria to the Institut Européen d'Archéologie Sous-Marine.

The assistance of the military authorities, as well as the Coast Guard, who were responsible for the areas we were working in, was always outstanding and greatly helped our work which was followed with kindness by the Directors of the Graeco-Roman Museum of Alexandria, Madame Doreiya Said and Dr. Ahmed Abd el- Fatah. The constant support of the Services du Ministère Français des Affaires Etrangères, both in Paris and Cairo, has also been for us an invaluable contribution.

The main results of our work have already been made available to the general public thorough the usual means of communication. The time has now come to reveal and show in detail our methods and conclusions. This volume, devoted to the submerged royal quarters of ancient Alexandria, describes and comments on the zones, the works of art and the remarkable inscriptions on which our conclusions and hypotheses are based in order to allow historians of the ancient world to assess and discuss them in full knowledge of the facts.

We acknowledge first and foremost those through whom this scientific undertaking was made possible and primarily the Hilti Foundation which has participated generously in this scientific adventure on the recommendation of the late Martin Hilti and Mr. Michael Hilti.

We extend our thanks to H. E. M. Aly Maher El Sayed, Ambassador of the Arab Republic of Egypt in France, H. E. the French Ambassador in Spain and Madame Patrick Leclercq, the late M. Ahmed Sidky, former Ambassador of the Arab Republic of Egypt in France and Madame Magda Sidky, who have followed and assisted our enterprise with great kindness.

We wish to express our gratitude to the following persons and institutions who have made possible and facilitated our work:

Guy de Casteja
Josseline de Clausade
Bertrand Defline
Mostafa el-Abbadi
Hassan el-Bana
Paolo Gallo
Amar el-Gaya
Gilles Gauthier
Jean-Claude Jacq
Muriel Juncqua-Moity
Sherif Kabbabe
Nabil Kassim
Kadiga Lamlou
Zizi Louxor
Alexandra Maiers
Bernard Malauzat
Claire Mugnet-Pollet
Francine d'Orgeval
Charro Palacios de Montarco
Nadine Sauneron
Yves Saint-Geours
Yann Streiff
L. A .R. Pce. Hussein and Pcesse Mounira Toussoun
Anne-Sophie von Bomhard
Ludwig von Bomhard
François de Wissocq
The library staff of the Institut d'Egyptologie du Collège de France
The Centre for Mediterranean Archaeology of the Polish Academy of Sciences, Alexandria
The Polish Centre for Mediterranean Archaeology of the University of Warsaw, Cairo
The Department of Archaeology and the Faculty of Arts, Alexandria
The Archaeological Society of Alexandria

) ROYAL QUARTER

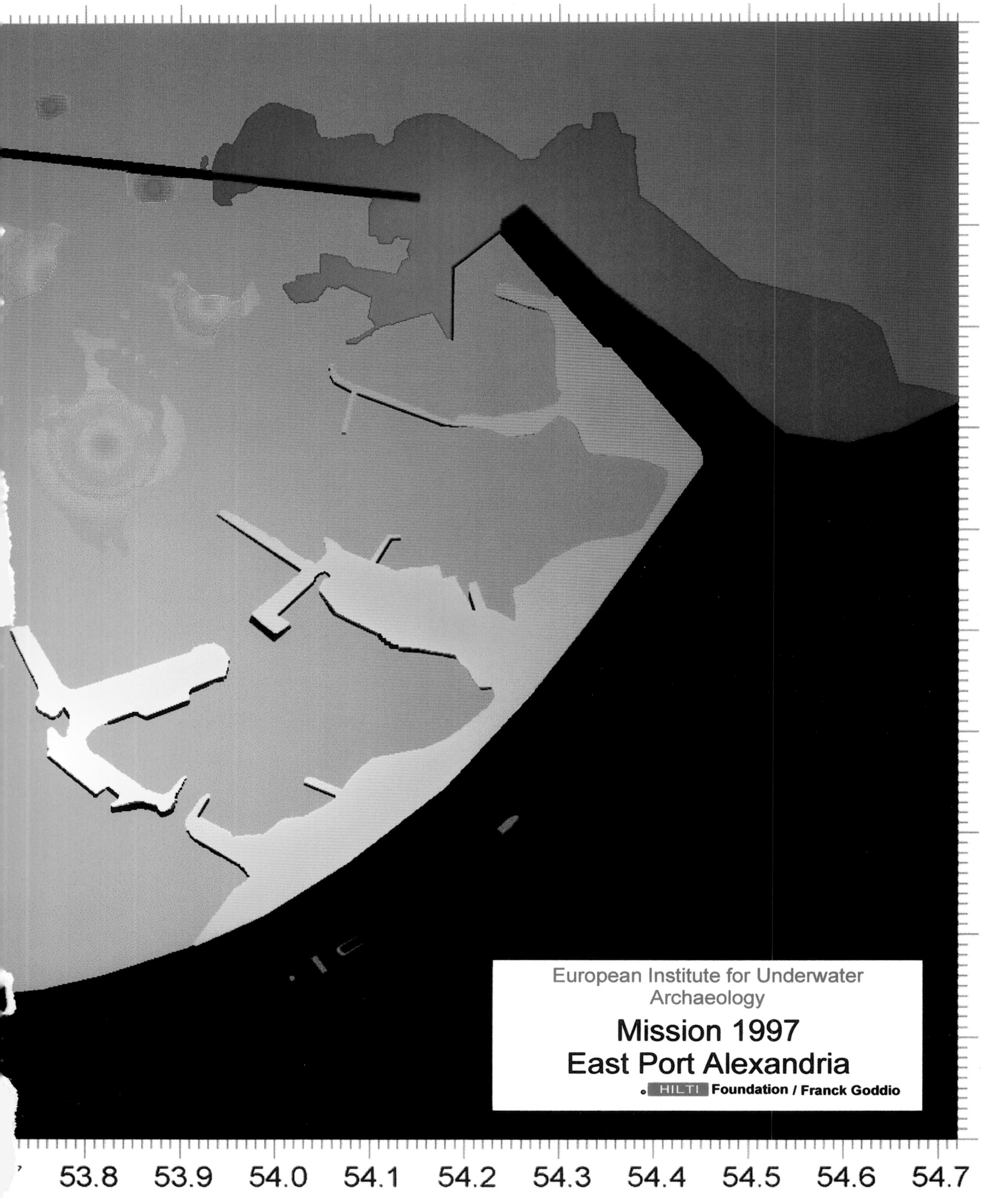

THE SUBMERGED

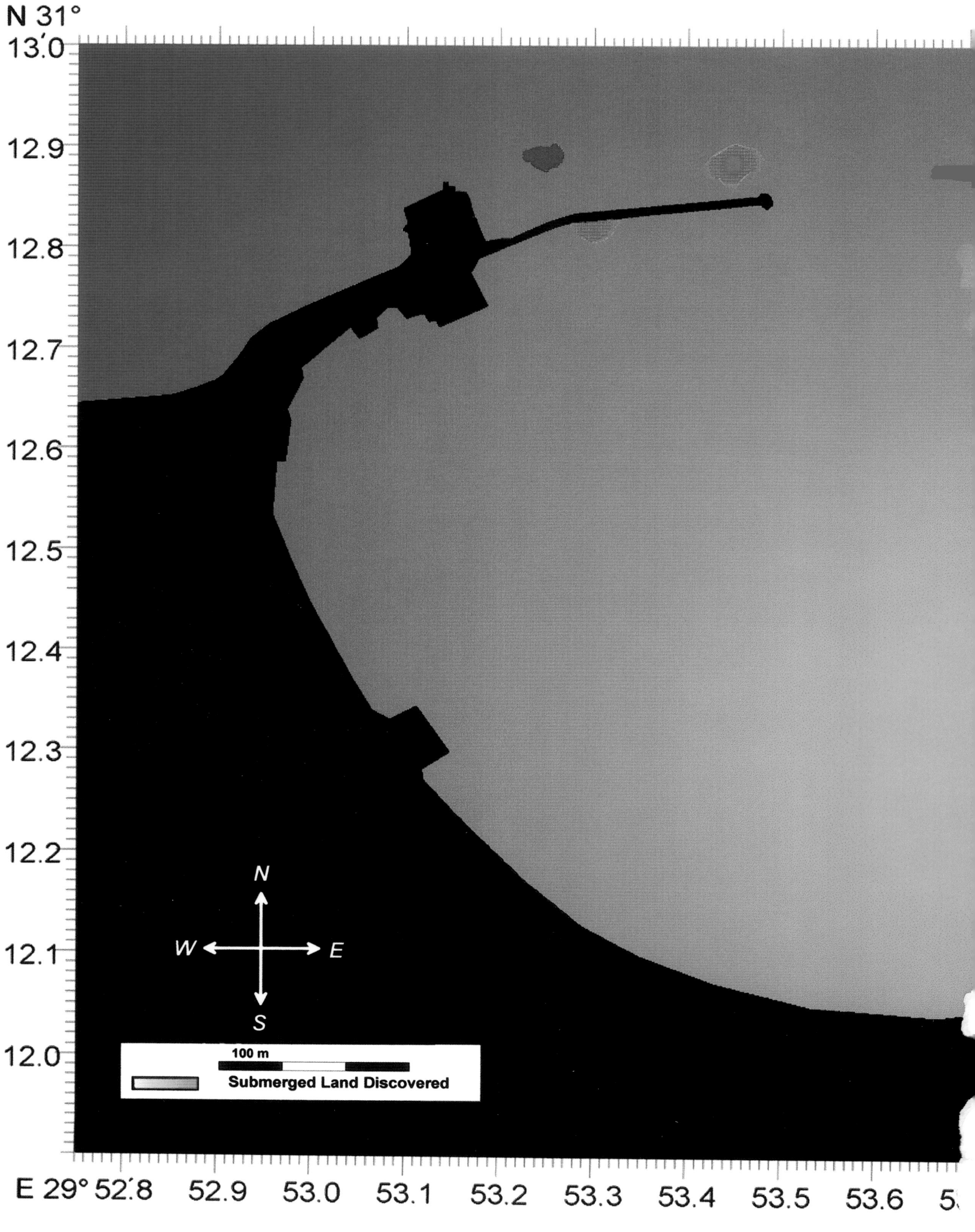

THE TOPOGRAPHY OF THE SUBMERGED ROYAL QUARTERS OF THE EASTERN HARBOUR OF ALEXANDRIA

Franck Goddio
Ibrahim Darwish

1. Aims of the topographical survey project and the archaeological excavations in the East Port of Alexandria[1]

The Institut Européen d'Archéologie Sous-Marine (IEASM) has been engaged for five years in topographical surveys and archaeological excavations in the East Port of Alexandria in co-operation with the Egyptian Department of Underwater Archaeology under the Supreme Council of Antiquities.

The main objective of the project, led by IEASM since 1992, in the eastern harbour of Alexandria has been to establish the topography of the submerged area, the royal buildings and harbour installations of the ancient town which were probably swallowed up by the sea towards the end of the 4th century AD.[2]

Since a large part of the royal quarter had in effect been destroyed and overwhelmed by a catastrophic subsidence of the coast probably caused by sundry earthquakes and tidal waves, until the present we only had a theoretical knowledge of the topography of this quarter.

This knowledge was based on the interpretation of classical texts[3] describing the town, or on various details gleaned from works about events at Alexandria, albeit incomplete, of observations made at the port from 1872.

Numerous maps, based upon the interpretation of these ancient texts have shown the topography of Ptolemaic and especially that part of the Magnus Portus now lost beneath the sea and of the royal quarter which bordered it. The following list is not exhaustive:

—*Aegyptus Antiqua*, par Abraham Ortelius, made in 1570, published in Antwerp in 1603 in *Theatrum orbis terrarum*.

—*Plan d'Alexandrie (cartouche: Alexandria)*, by M. d'Anville *(Mémoire sur l'Egypte ancienne et moderne*), Paris, 1776.

—*Plan of Alexandria*, by Sir Gardner Wilkinson, London, 1843.

—*Carte de l'antique Alexandrie et de ces faubourgs*, by Mahmud Bey al-Falaki. Map made in 1866 and published at Copenhagen in 1872.

—*Plan comparatif du Port Oriental d'Alexandrie sous les Ptolémées et à l'époque actuelle*, H. de Vaujany, Paris, 1888.

—*Carte de l'ancienne Alexandrie*, by G. Botti, 1898.

—*Karten des Alten Alexandria*, by Wilhelm Sieglin, Leipzig, 1907.

—*Alexandrie, plan de la ville ancienne et moderne*, by Ev. Brecchia in *Alexandrea ad Aegyptum*, Bergama, 1914.

All these maps are quite similar, especially those which come after the publication of the map by Mahmud Bey al-Falaki.

Recent works on the topography of Alexandria refer to these maps.

2. Survey undertaken in 1992

An electronic survey was undertaken in 1992 thanks to the assistance of the Elf Group. This bathymetric and magnetic survey was carried out by the IEASM team using the research catamaran *Kaimiloa*. The magnetic detectors used were nuclear magnetic resonance magnetometers (RMN), developed by the Commissariat à l'Energie Atomique, of which IEASM has the exclusive use for archaeological research.

---

[1] 'Alessandria e il mondo Ellenistico-Romano', *Atti del II congresso internazionale Italo-Egiziano*, Alessandria, Nov. 1992. F. Goddio, 'Cartographie des vestiges archéologiques submergés dans le Port Est d'Alexandrie et dans la rade d'Aboukir', *L'Erma di Bretschneider*, Roma, 1995.

[2] It is known, for example, that a tidal wave ravaged the coast of the southern Mediterranean on 21 July 365. Cf. F. Jacques-B. Bousquet, 'Le raz de marée du 21 juillet 365', *MFRA*, 96, 1984.

[3] See A. Bernand, , '*Testimonia …*' *infra.*

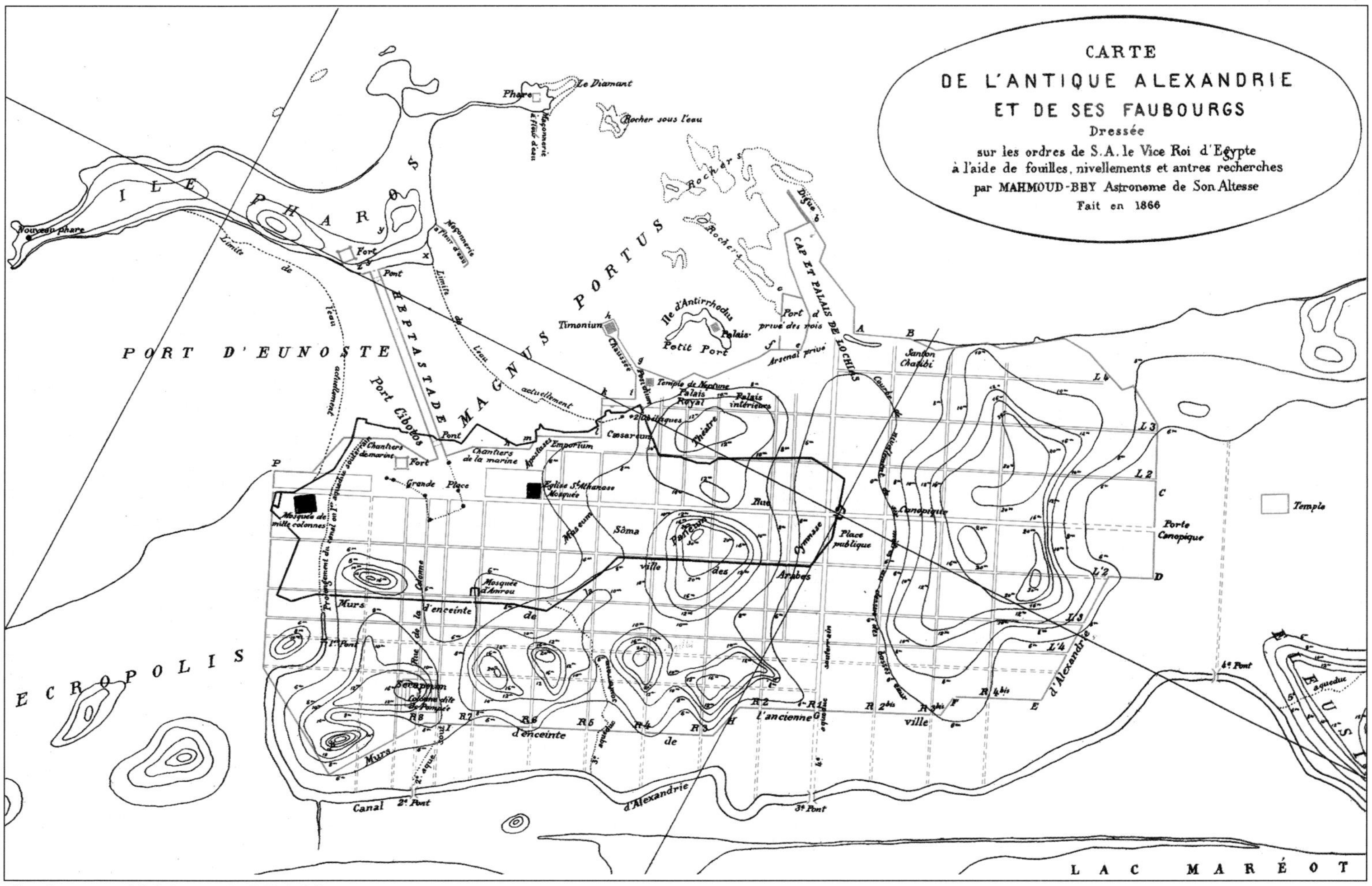

Fig. 1: map of Mahmoud el-Falaki

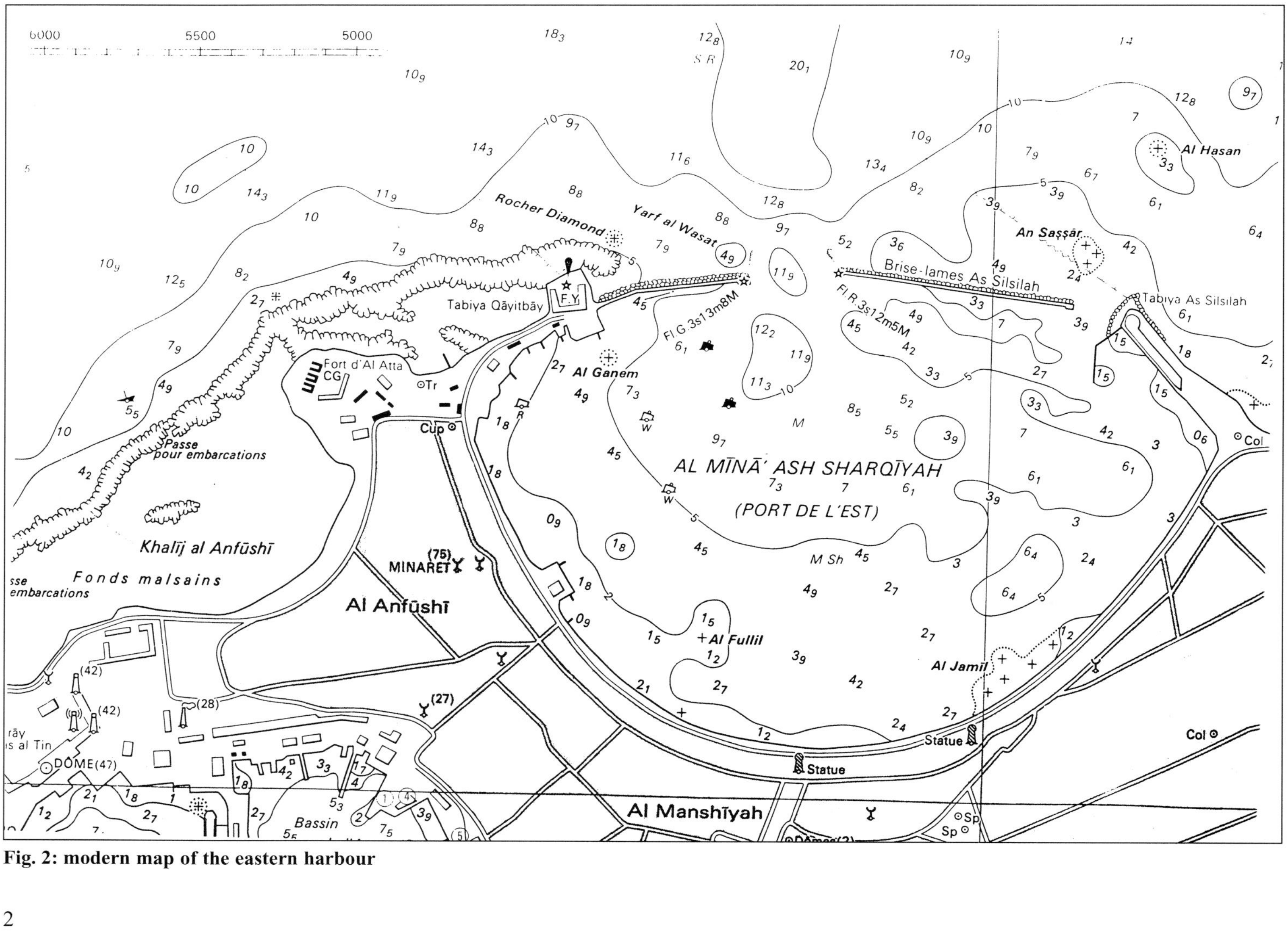

Fig. 2: modern map of the eastern harbour

The terrestrial magnetic field is set on a series of complex spatial and temporal phenomena; the geology of the earth's crust, the dynamo effect, the interaction of the sun and the earth, the movement of ionospheric currents and oscillations. The geomagnetic field can be thought of as a bi-polar magnetic field with a value between 20,000 gammas at the equator and 60,000 gammas at the poles, to which should be added worldwide anomalies to the order of 10,000 gammas, anomalies in the magnetic field due to local geological conditions and transitory phenomena of some dozens of gammas per day.

When investigating objects buried or submerged, the extent of the magnetic anomalies should be added to those anomalies with a natural source and to the magnetic disturbances related to human activity (at Alexandria, for example, the tramway and vehicular traffic on the boulevards than skirt the port). The three magnetometers towed by the catamaran form the most important factor in differential magnetometric survey. The position of these receptors is fixed by an acoustic system relative to the survey vessel. This vessel is itself located geographically in real time. The receptors measure continuously the absolute value of the earth's magnetic field to an accuracy of a few thousandths of a gamma.

The intrinsic sensitivity of the magnetometers and the continuous measurement of the local magnetic gradients (the difference between the two receptors) enable us to identify buried archaeological remains, thanks to the magnetic variations between these remains and the sediment.

The geographical position of the survey vessel and thus of the receptors was established by the use of three electronic beacons set up ashore (the Motorola Trisponder system). Using the principle of triangulation between a moving beacon aboard the vessel and the three beacons ashore, this high frequency radio system was able to produce continuous and accurate measurements.

Photo 1: survey equipment on the research vessel

The inner and outer areas of the east port were divided up into a rectangular grid north-south and east-west at 10 metre intervals by magnetic detection and bathymetric recording devices.

The bathymetry which consists of identifying precisely and continuously the depths of the water along the lines of any survey would enable us to appreciate the topology of the site and to sketch the main lines of buried remains. We had attached to the sounding devices our nuclear magnetic resonating magnetometers (RMN).

The interpretation of all the data led to the need to supplement this information by a campaign of systematic surveys in order to reconnoitre visually the bottom.

In fact the important magnetic interference from the modern town sometimes adversely affected the data and made their interpretation less coherent, or at least insufficiently precise.

It seemed, however, that the area to the east of the port presented some remarkable anomalies both on the depth and the magnetic chart.

Thus an important archaeological campaign was launched in 1996 with the support of the Hilti Foundation.

Photo 2: Fort of Qait-Bey from the eastern harbour

Photo 3: the 'Corniche' along the eastern harbour

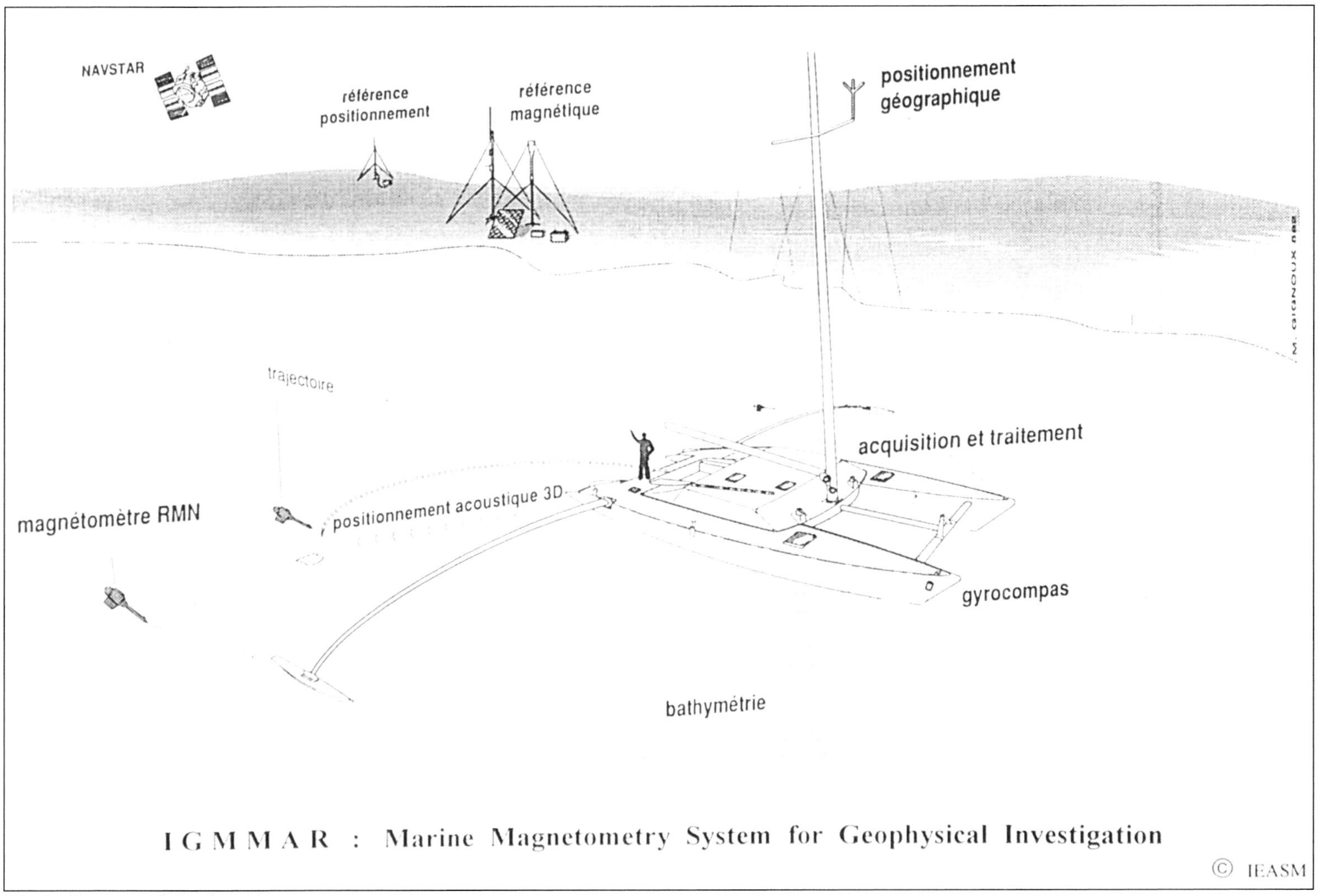

Fig. 3: diagram of the detection process

Photo 4: the magnetic detectors seen from the research vessel

Photo 5: GPS magnetic reference and positioning beacon on the fort of Qait-Bey

The Peninsula
Bathymetry 1997

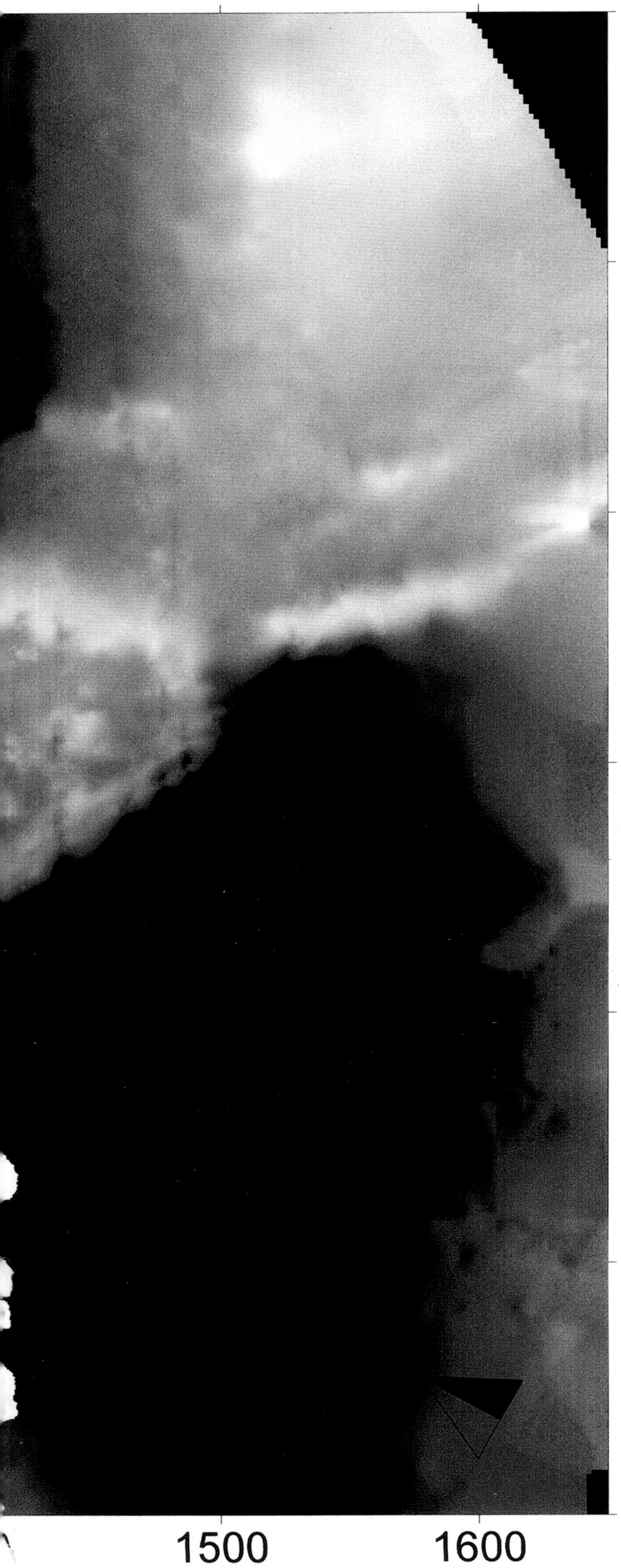

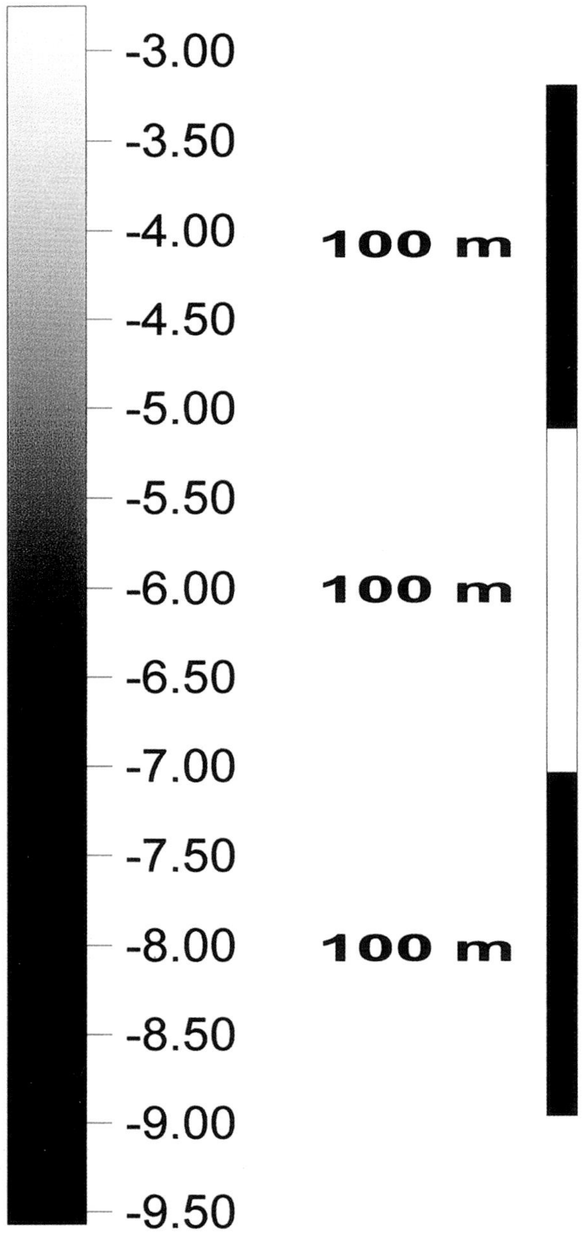

European Institute For Underwater Archaelogy

1997 Mission
East Port of Alexandria

© HILTI Foundation/ Franck Goddio

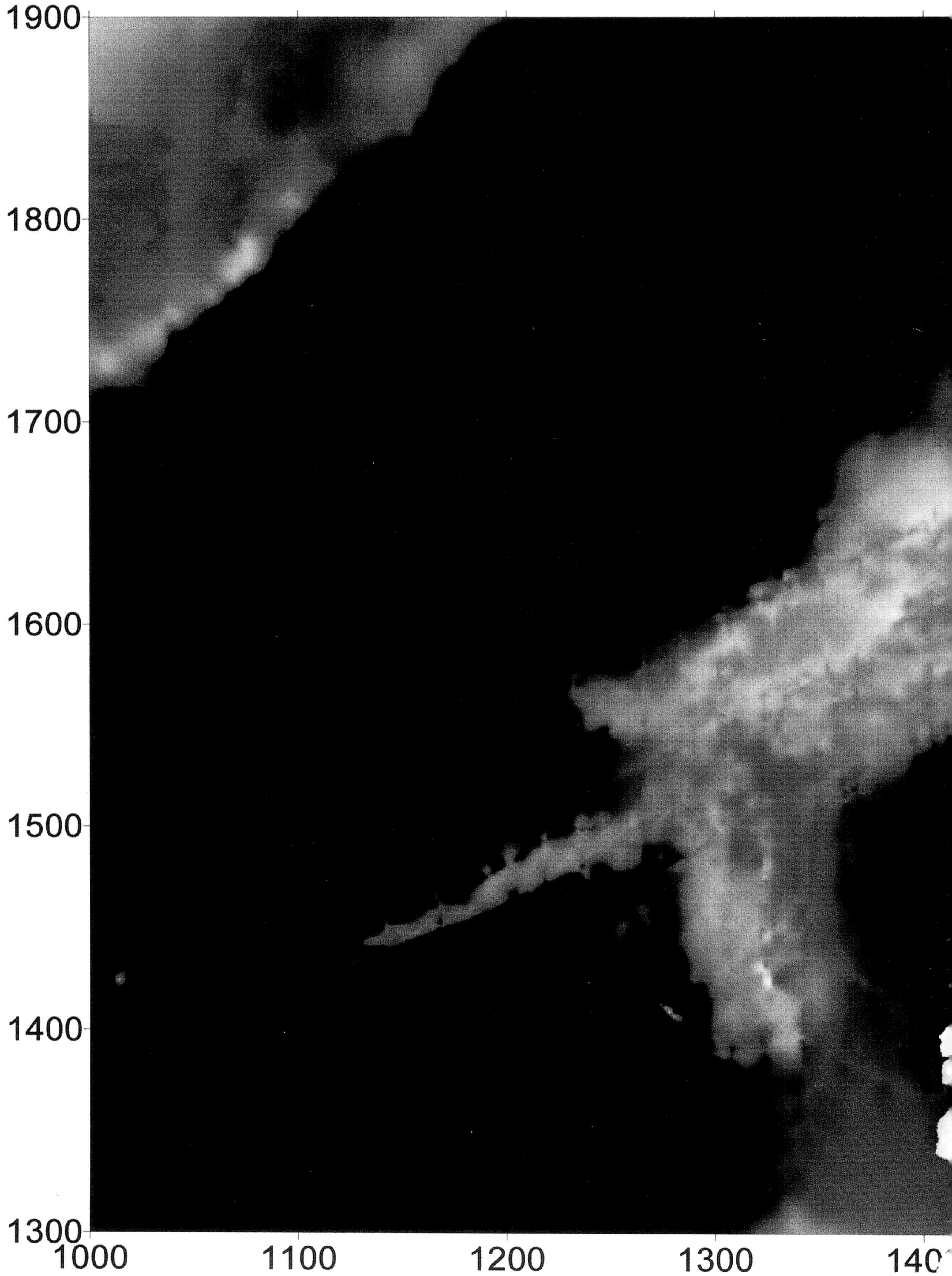
1900
1800
1700
1600
1500
1400
1300
1000
1100
1200
1300

The Island

Bathymetry 1997

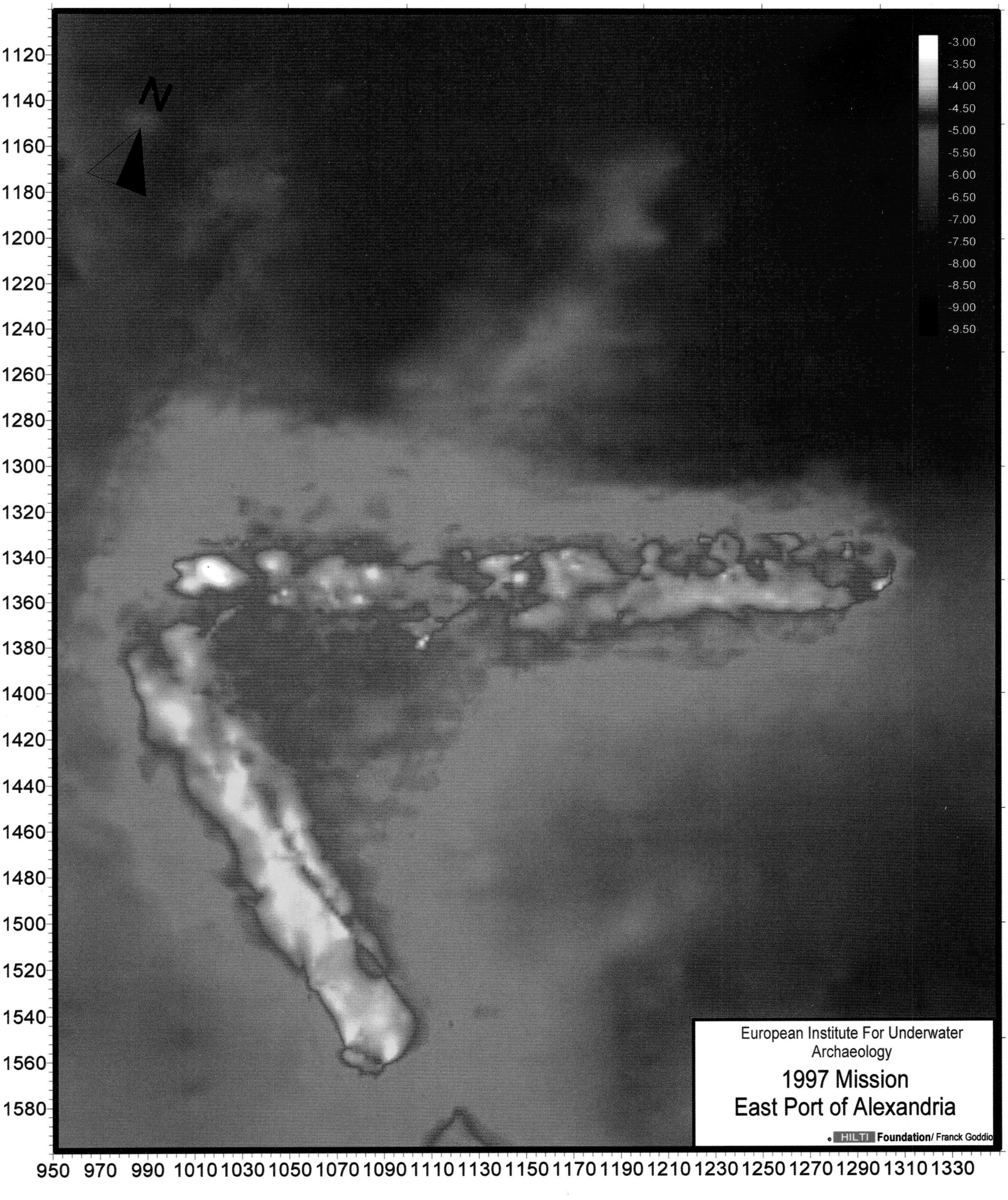

3. The seasons of 1996 and 1997

3.1. General data, conditions, techniques used and methodology

The east port of Alexandria is bordered on the east by Cape Silsileh, on the south by the coast and to the west by the Anfouchy peninsula. A chain of reefs join the tip of Cape Silsileh to the eastern point of the peninsula. The depth of the water falls away gently. On the side towards the shore, the water depths increase abruptly close to the coast.

The range of tides in the bay of Alexandria is moderate. The difference between the highest and lowest seas did not exceed 0.9 metres during the time of our observations.

The mean value of high water during our period of research was 0.385, while that of low water was 0.185.

The prevailing winds in summer are from the north-west. They are, however, often quite fresh.

In winter the wind blows mainly from the west and south west.

Winds are quite variable in autumn and spring.

Currents in the area are weak, between 0.1 and 0.7 knots and generally set towards the east.

Depths within the port range between 2 and 15 metres.

In spite of this shallowness, diving in the port is made very difficult due to the murkiness of the water.

3.2. Underwater techniques used

3.2.1 Positioning techniques

In order to offset somewhat the problem of the poor visibility due to pollution, which makes pinpointing every location particularly difficult across the area, a special underwater positioning system was developed by IEASM. Differential GPS (Global Positioning System) receptors

Photo 6: the DGPS location equipment under water

EAST PORT OF ALEXANDRIA

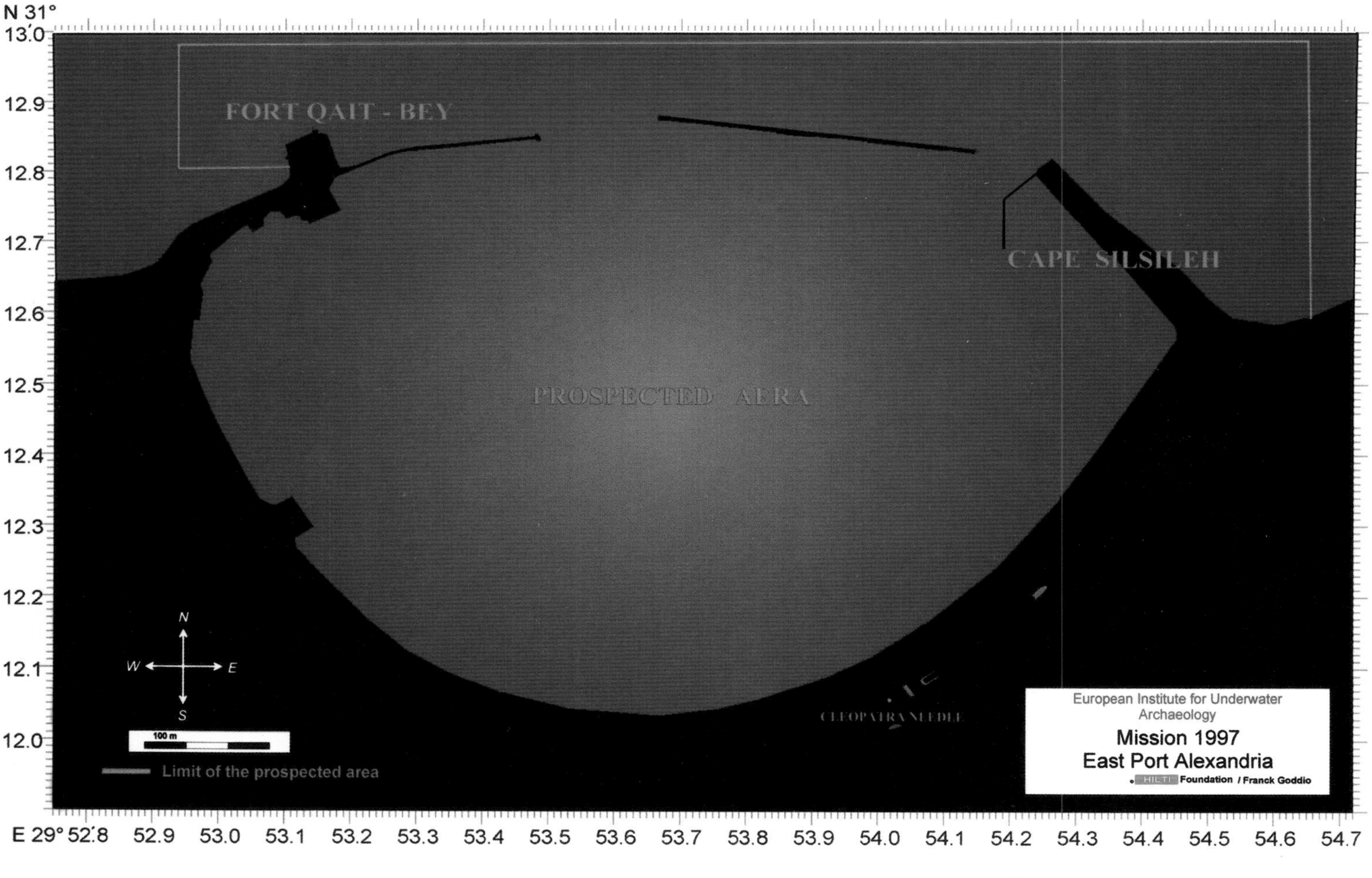

were therefore prepared in order to enable the fixing of geographical positions underwater. This was the first non-military use of the system for underwater archaeology.

Each device is attached to two floating antennae, one receiving the GPS satellite signals whilst the other receives the signal from a beacon ashore (located on the east tower of the fort of Qa'it-Bey) in order to obtain pinpoint accuracy. A diver-operator holds both antennae interdependently in the vertical at the positioning point by hauling on the cables whilst another operator inputs the data onto a keyboard of the differential GPPS underwater receiver.

The memory of this system has a capacity to hold 500 items of positioning data on each dive. It only requires the system receiver to be connected to a computer to create a database of contour points and the positions of artefacts.

The installation of this system made the task of submarine topography very effective over such surfaces and in such conditions. It would have been much slower if we had used more classical means of recording information.

3.2.2 Submarine epigraphy, the moulding process

In agreement with the Egyptian authorities the decision was taken not to lift any items from the water, with exceptions, to take mouldings of some small items, followed by a survey of the objects *in situ*.

To enable a precise study of the inscription, underwater impressions were made. The moulding itself was made from a flexible silicone developed by the Rhône-Poulenc company.

The product had two components which were mixed on the surface. It polymerises at an ambient temperature by the use of a catalyst. The addition of a thixotropant served to reduce the flow of the mixture thus allowing the

Photo 7: the fabric covering is passed to the divers

Photo 8: applying the fabric over the surface to take the moulding

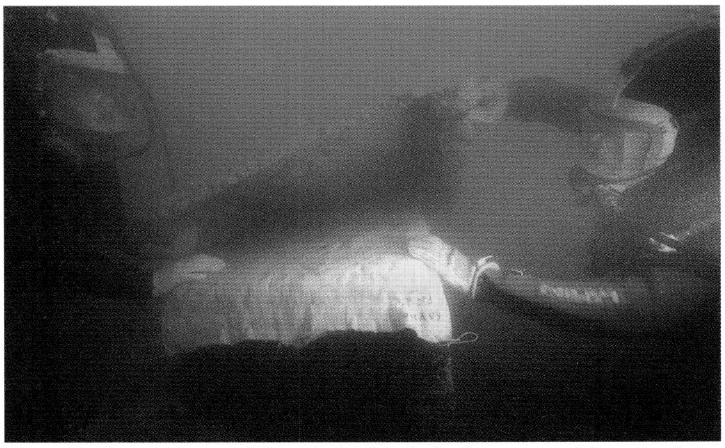

Photo 9: after being positioned the fabric is then covered by a lead sheet

Photo 10: removing the impression from the moulding

Photo 11: the moulded impression

moulding of curved objects. This mixture, with the air carefully expelled, is then stretched evenly on a cloth of Tergal on the ends of which buckle-type fasteners were fixed.

It was then handed to two divers who stretched out the cloth on the surface to be moulded. The latter had previously been carefully cleaned.

Lead weights were attached to the fixing buckles with snap hooks to hold the cloth. A lead sheet, already shaped to the item bearing the inscription is then put over the cloth in order to exert a constant pressure whilst the soft material polymerises.

It took some 16 hours at a water temperature of 25°C to complete a moulding.

The result is a flexible moulding, very strong and showing a remarkable faithfulness in reproducing details.

The mouldings were then photographed onto slides. The latter were projected and inverted to enable work on the Greek[4] and hieroglyphic[5] inscriptions to be carried out.

3.3 Methodology

Because of these surveys we were able to deduce that, in general, the submerged area and ancient lost structures were only covered by a thin layer of white sand and calcareous concretions. However, the inner areas of the ancient harbours, themselves also overwhelmed, retained their original silt, with moreover the scattering of a large number of various type of amphorae, both complete and broken. The reasons for this are probably the difference in levels between the submerged land and the seabed of the ancient harbours and the currents within the port.

Thus our task was made easier by the comparative ease with which it was possible to distinguish the limits of the land and the artefacts buried on the bottom of the ancient harbour areas.

This observation led us to adopt the following methodology: the noting of submerged artefacts and surfaces were made visually, without preliminary surveys, noting first the lowest visible level.

This approach kept for us in effect the possibility of indicating later those parts which stood out in antiquity after they had been recorded during excavation. These areas moreover appeared within the wide contours defined by traces of lower bases and foundations.

These first exhaustive and visual reports were subsequently completed by surveys which occasionally turned up sections covered in sand or silt which had escaped notice of the first surveys.

[4] Cf. E. Bernand, 'Epigraphic Documents', p. 143 *et seq*.
[5] Cf. J. Yoyotte, '*Pharaonica*', p. 223 *et seq*.

3.4 The 1996 Season

A team composed of 12 IEASM experts and 8 archaeologists from the Egyptian Supreme Council of Antiquities came together for a four-month season. A 30-metre support vessel, the *Oceanix*, served as the dive base.

Photo 12: the support vessel *Oceanex*

Two small additional vessels complemented the work. The team carried out 3550 dives, each lasting about 100 minutes between the months of June and November 1996.

The divers worked in water-tight suits with masks giving total face cover in order to minimise as far as possible the inherent danger from the water pollution.

In the 1996 season we were able to uncover and record areas and infrastructures of the ancient harbour buried in the eastern part of the East Port of Alexandria.

3.5 The 1997 Season

The 1997 season's main objective was to undertake archaeological excavations on the submerged island discovered during the 1996 season. A team came together comprising fourteen experts from IEASM and fourteen archaeologists from the Egyptian Supreme Council of Antiquities (Department of Underwater Archaeology). The same logistical support was put in place as for the 1996 season.

The undertaking lasted for the period between June and November. A total of 3,500 dives were carried out each lasting approximately 100 minutes. Numerous architectural remains (columns, blocks, lintels, capitals, parts of statues, etc.) were located on the submerged island. All these remains had become formless masses under a covering of calcareous concretions, sometimes 60 cm. thick, and had to be cleaned so as to identify them.

At the end of each archaeological survey or excavations, a new survey was made in the zone under consideration with magnetic detectors and side-scan sonars to give an electronic picture of the bottom.

Thanks to our systematic surveys and the special electronic equipment we were able to define exactly the contours of the submerged areas, the types of structures existing and the position of hundreds of archaeological artefacts strewn over the surface.

Once these items had been cleaned of their calcareous coating their position was plotted exactly. An inventory number was given to each artefact then its spot height, orientation and bearing recorded. The artefact was then photographed and drawn. The data was then recorded in our database.

A cartographic program automatically showed the artefact in question on the different maps.

It was thus possible to produce numerous drawings and plans at different scales. An exhaustive inventory in a database of the discovered artefacts was thus created with their actual positions, sizes, photos and drawings.

Photo 13: a diver cleaning an area of paving

Photo 14: paving after the removal of concretions

4. Survey and excavation maps, plans and other results in visual format

All the maps, plans and data from the surveys and excavations were plotted with absolute geographical co-ordinates (latitude and longitude), by the WGS.84 universal system, also used by our underwater differential system when establishing locations.

Thus these documents are presented as geographical or maritime charts. The error of the y-axis is 1/1000 of a minute of longitude (1.58 metres), and for the x-axis is 1/1000 of a minute of latitude (1.85 metres) (at the latitude of Alexandria one minute of longitude is equal to 1.584.99 metres and a minute of latitude is equal to 1.847.5 metres).

The method employed gave a high accuracy for the distances on the maps thus produced. It allowed us to create precise documents independent of any relative fix. The absolute nature of these positions gives us the fundamental advantage that these documents will not require any future updating as regards the positions shown, however much the topography might change hereafter.

To show the value of such a methodology, one only has to recall that at Saqqarah, for example, several *mastabas* were lost and took a long time to relocate, and having been removed by an unreliable marker, some plans

Photo 15: measuring an architectural feature

of sites today cannot be traced on the ground.[6] These tombs and monuments could immediately be found again if their descriptions and positions have been precisely plotted with latitude and longitude.

Indeed, certain so-called 'rescue digs', carried out on the ground before construction work covers them, have little interest for any later work which attempts to re-create the topography of the ancient city if the precise geographical position has not been established.

In effect, the topography of a modern site can be considerably modified over a period of time by works in the area and sightings, which seem clear when they are being recorded, can disappear completely in a short space of time.

It is worth noting that some research in survey archives, although complicated, can give interesting results, decreasing the chance that information about the site might be 'lost'.

Moreover, the importance for the orientation of certain monuments in ancient Egypt, notably temples, is well known. However, a great number of plans and records of monuments excavated in Egypt are aligned according to magnetic north, and not to true north which apparently is what interested the Egyptians. This type of recording by reference to magnetic north also carries with it the important problem than the direction of magnetic north varies over time (the phenomenon of magnetic variation).

The recording of all the contours of the area and submerged structures as well as archaeological artefacts were thus fixed precisely on the territorial globe in an absolute manner and not by reference to relative fixes.

In order to relate these plans to the actual town of Alexandria, the contours of the bay as well as the modern harbour structures and some particular points of interest were recorded according to the same procedure. These contours and points of interest were then recorded on our plans to reconcile exactly the remains discovered with the modern town (this task allowed us to correct certain errors apparent on the modern maps of the town, notably concerning the contour of the corniche running alongside the port. This point was a matter of great importance for our mapping).

We have also been able to plot the approximate geographical position of one of the famous obelisks known as 'Cleopatra's Needles', thanks to an old photograph taken before its removal to be taken to New York.

[6] For example the case of Kôm Gaief, excavated by Petrie: recreating the plan and the chronology of Naucratis posed great problems, see B. Muhs, *JARCE* 31, p. 99-113.

This site is of interest for the topography of the ancient town as these obelisks were erected at the entrance of the temple which Cleopatra VII had undertaken to build in honour of Julius Caesar, the temple being built after his death during the reign of Augustus under the name of the Kaisarion. The two obelisks were set up later in this position in 13 BC. Their position at the entrance of the Kaisarion is mentioned by Pliny.[7]

The plans show the topography of the surfaces and submerged harbour installations, as well as the positions of artefacts discovered, with a precision directly linked to the GPS differential system of ±1/10,000 of a minute (about 40 cm.)

The graphics of the surveys and excavations were achieved thanks to measurements made on the basis of an underwater grid whose extremities had previously been fixed in latitude and longitude. These measurements are accurate to a centimetre.

The geographic x and y co-ordinates were recorded on each plan and a scale added to facilitate their interpretation.

[7] Cf. '*Testimonia*', no. 49 bis, p. 112.

Photo 16: one of 'Cleopatra's Needles' being removed in 1879. This obelisk is today in Central Park, New York. The building in the background still stands.

Photo 17: one of 'Cleopatra's Needles' being removed.

On each plan, the area being worked was indicated by an inset showing its position within the port.

The plans were supported by photos and illustrations of noteworthy items.

The scales used in the documentation were as follows:

1/2500 general maps
1/500 maps and plans of particular zones
1/100 plans and results [rendus] of surveys and excavations
1/10 drawings of artefacts

During the 1996 and 1997 seasons, the overall picture took shape of the topography of the submerged royal quarter of ancient Alexandria, along with the positions of 1,300 visually identified artefacts which had been cleaned of their encrustations.

In addition, six excavation plans were built up which showed accurately the topography of several areas of great historical interest.

Photo 18: removing the deposits from an architectural feature

5. Topographical description of the submerged royal quarter

The survey, archaeological and topographical campaigns allowed for the first time the presentation of a complete panorama of the famous Magnus Portus, based on observations made *in situ*. The topography produced is very different from that which had been based on the interpretation of the texts.[8]

We observed that the submerged areas and the harbour substructures were at a maximum depth of 6.8 metres. By taking into account a likely minimum height of 2 metres above sea level for these structures in antiquity, it can be deduced that the various collapses/subsidences along with the rise in sea level might have resulted in a difference of perhaps up to 8 metres as regards the land and these structures in comparison with their original level.

It is also to be noted that where structures in the form of paved areas were laid out the surfaces were flat which suggests that, as elsewhere in Alexandria, the townspeople had set about levelling the original rocky terrain.[9]

In the harbour some ancient remains have been covered over, notably by the breakwaters of the 20th century and the military buildings on Cape Silsileh which actually closed the eastern harbour. These areas represent but a small part of the 'Magnus Portus'.

The site of the Magnus Portus as it was in ancient times is described in sequence from north to south.

To the topographical description is added a summary of the excavations and a description of the principal remains found by our investigations for each submerged area and harbour installations. These results, however, are only a beginning, as the importance of the area covered—more than 300 hectares—is considerable.

A reconciliation is then made between our actual observations and the ancient texts which describe these areas.

[8] Cf. 'Epilogue', after p. 254.

[9] It should be remembered that the development of the new town required from the 4th century the levelling of the former sandy relief as is noticed particularly at the Serapuem platform and the terraces where the Kaisarion stood (*BIFAO* 94, 1994, p. 447-448).

6. The Main Channel and the Reefs

6.1 Description of the outer reefs

The port itself is protected by two breakwaters, the one to the west was built in 1916 and that to the east some time after.

—to the north of the modern western breakwater is the 'Diamond' rock, which was a major feature above water in antiquity; it was an islet very close to the island of Pharos or an extension of it.

—at the eastern end of the same breakwater is a reef (R1), corresponding to the shoal known as Yarf al-Wasat; the absence of any erosion line seems to indicate that it was always under water.

At its eastern extremity the eastern breakwater rests on shoals (R2) where an erosion line indicating a former sea level has been recorded at a spot height of 6.8 metres. Thus, these were once reefs breaking the surface.

Towards its eastern end the eastern breakwater rests on shallows where an erosion line indicating an ancient sea level was identified at 6.8 metres. Thus, this points to ancient reefs just breaking the surface.

In different places there are remains, which do not appear to be part of the modern work, such as large blocks of very eroded limestone, which appear at the base of the breakwater. These items could have been re-used by modern builders. They might also indicate that the breakwater covers ancient workings.

To the north of the eastern breakwater a reef (R3) was found. This reef anciently must have been at sea level as no erosion line was noted.

To the south of the eastern breakwater appeared three vast reefs: R4, R5 and a large central reef.

The two reefs (R4, R5), which are the least extensive would not have broken the surface as there also no erosion line was observed.

6.2 The central reef

6.2.1 Description

The most important reef is that which is situated in the centre of 'Magnus Portus'. We were able, at certain places on this reef, to discover clearly visible traces of erosion left by the ancient sea level at a spot height of 6.7 metres.

Thus a part of this reef must have broken the surface.

There is no other trace of any revetment on the surface of the natural rock.

THE OUTLYING REEFS

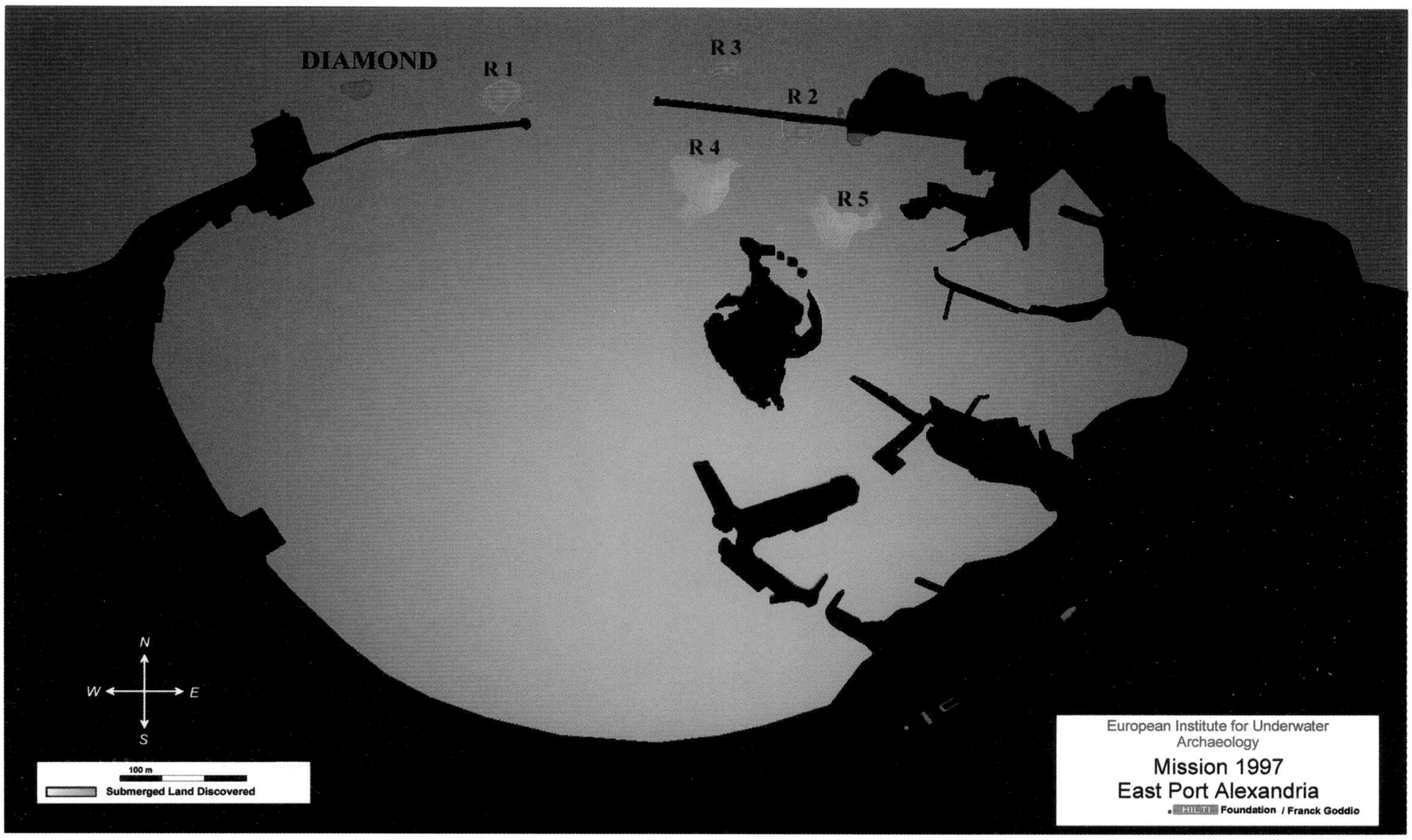

THE LARGE CENTRAL REEF

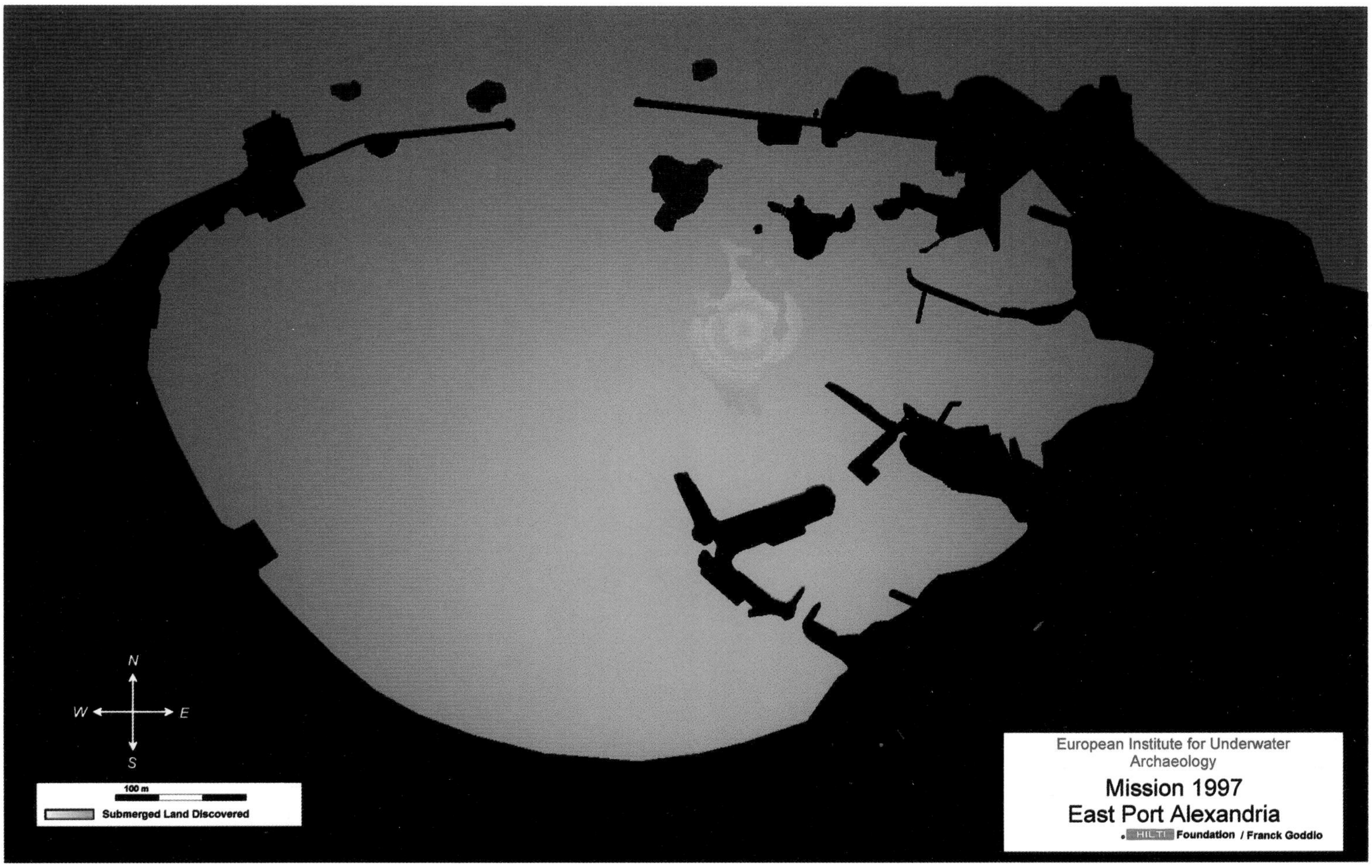

6.2.2 Remains discovered

On the central area – the highest – two rough, low walls came to light with ancient mortar joining small blocks of undressed limestone.

6.3 Comparison with ancient texts

The presence of reefs to the east of the entrance to the harbour is attested by Strabo[10] who was in Alexandria between 27 and 30 BC:

> … and thus makes the harbour narrow at the mouth; and in addition to the narrowness of the intervening passage there are also rocks, some under the water, and others projecting out of it, which at all hours roughen the waves that strike them from the open sea.
> … in the Great Harbour at the entrance, on the right hand, are the island and the tower Pharos, and on the other hand are the reefs and also the promontory Lochias, with a royal palace upon it …

The geographer adds more precisely:

> As for the Great Harbour, in addition to its being beautifully enclosed both by the embankment and by nature, it is not only so deep close to the shore that the largest ship can be moored at the steps …

Flavius Josephus[11] was aware of this and later mentioned:

> The port of Alexandria is difficult for ships to approach even in peace-time, the entrance being narrow and diverted by submerged rocks which preclude direct passage. On the left the channel is protected by artificial moles; on the right juts out the island called Pharos, supporting an enormous tower, emitting a light visible three hundred furlongs away to mariners making for port, to warn them to anchor at night at some distance off because of the difficulty of the navigation. Round this island immense walls have been reared by human hands; and the sea dashing against these and breaking around the piers opposite renders the passage rough and ingress through the strait perilous. The harbour inside is, however, perfectly safe and is thirty furlongs in length.

From these two direct witnesses about the facts, which all sailors should have been aware of, it emerges that the hidden reefs or those breaking the surface and usually visible lay at the east of the channel and that a large embankment had been built to the east to protect the harbour from the swell caused by northerly winds.

Our investigations show in effect that the great ancient sea wall had been covered by the modern breakwater which should to some extent follow the same outline; it protects the harbour from the swell and northerly winds.

An indirect witness, Pliny, writing after an unnamed source, notes that 'treacherous shoals' restrict access to the harbour of Alexandria[12] to three channels. The names from the Greek, which has kept these three channels, Steganus, Posideum and Taurus, seem to take their names from three notorious reefs.

Steganus, the Greek στεγανοσ, literally the 'Well-recovered'. *Taurus*, from the Greek ταυροσ is translated by the 'Bull'; indeed, the 'Bull's Horn' has been attested since Ptolemy II as the mark it was necessary to reach before doubling the Pharos.[13]

Posideum in Greek is a place frequented by the god of the sea, a toponym frequent on Hellenistic rivers. It is difficult for us to identify it with the Poseidon of Strabo, an area of the Magnus Portus, which we place on the Peniunsula.[14]

G Botti,[15] listed other Latin names which, he says, would have been those of 'the reef which make the channels': the *myrmex*, the *alveus steganus*, the *scopuli* (at least three).

The *alveus steganus* is taken from Pliny V, XXXIII, 128 (*Testimonia* no. 49). Scopulus, from the Greek σκοπελον, 'rocky outcrop, promontory', is the usual Latin term for 'rock', especially when speaking of reefs.

We have not been able to identify where Botti took the Alexandrian *myrmex* from. This Greek word, literally meaning 'ant' is known to have signified dangerous shoals on the coast of Thessaly and in the sea off Smyrna (known to Pliny V, XXXIII, 128: *myrmeces scopuli*). Even today in the Mediterranean and in Latin America there are reefs called 'ants'.

It seems rather that Botti confused his notes and until better informed preferred to keep the question of the Alexandrian *myrmex* out of the discussion of reefs and channels.

---

[10] *'Testimonia'*, no. 28, p. 94.

[11] *'Testimonia'*, no. 50, p. 113.

[12] *Ibid.*

[13] *'Testimonia'*, no. 6, p. 64.

[14] Below, § 10.3, p. 26.

[15] G Botti, 'La côte alexandrine dans l'antiquité', in *Bulletin de la Société Khédiviale de Géographie (BSGE),* IV series, no. 12 (1897), p. 58.

) ROYAL QUARTER

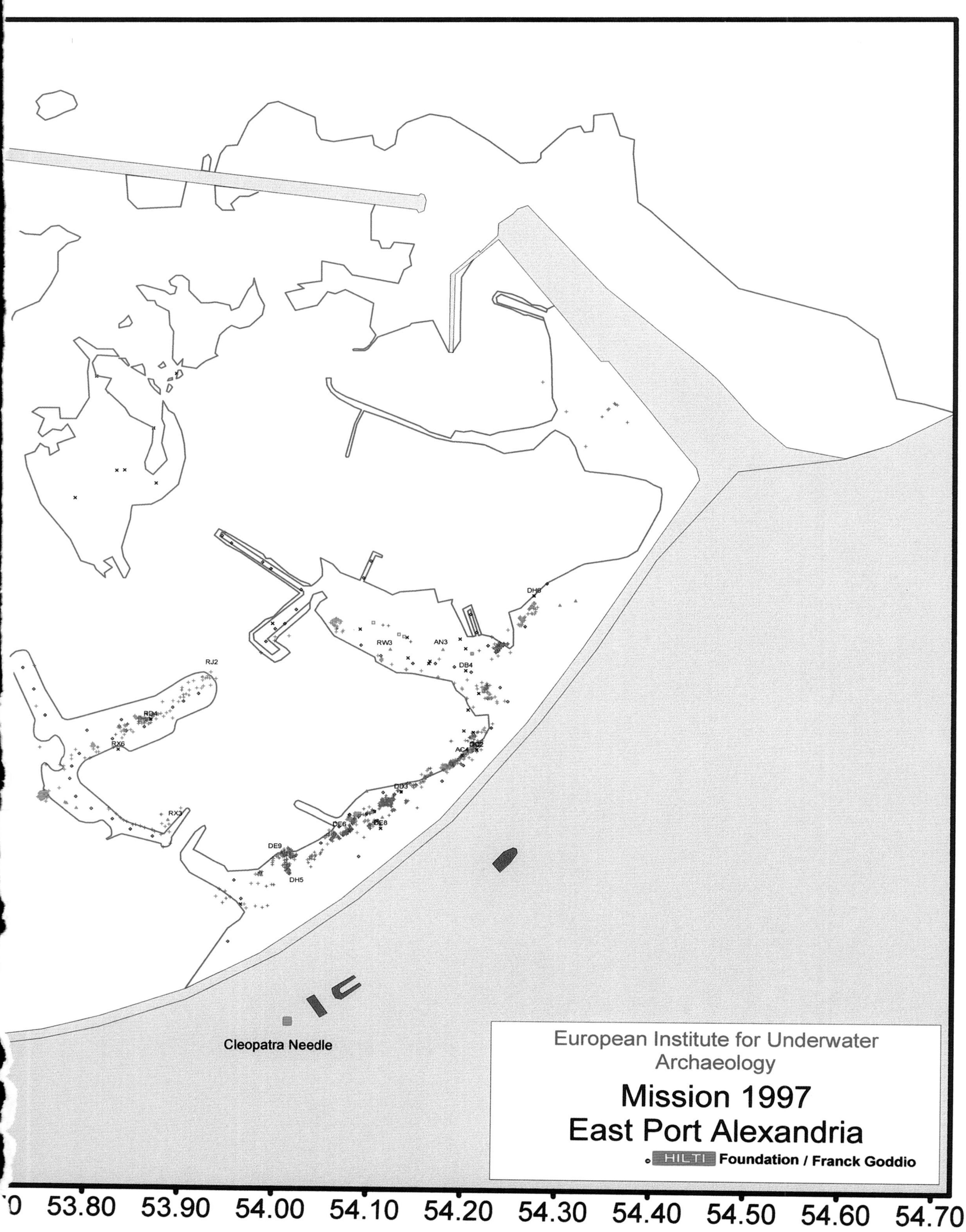
RJ2
RD4
RX6
RX3
DE9
DH5
DE6
DE8
DD3
AC4
DD2
DB4
AN3
RW3
DH6
Cleopatra Needle
European Institute for Underwater Archaeology
Mission 1997
East Port Alexandria
HILTI Foundation / Franck Goddio
'0
53.80
53.90
54.00
54.10
54.20
54.30
54.40
54.50
54.60
54.70

THE SUBMERGE

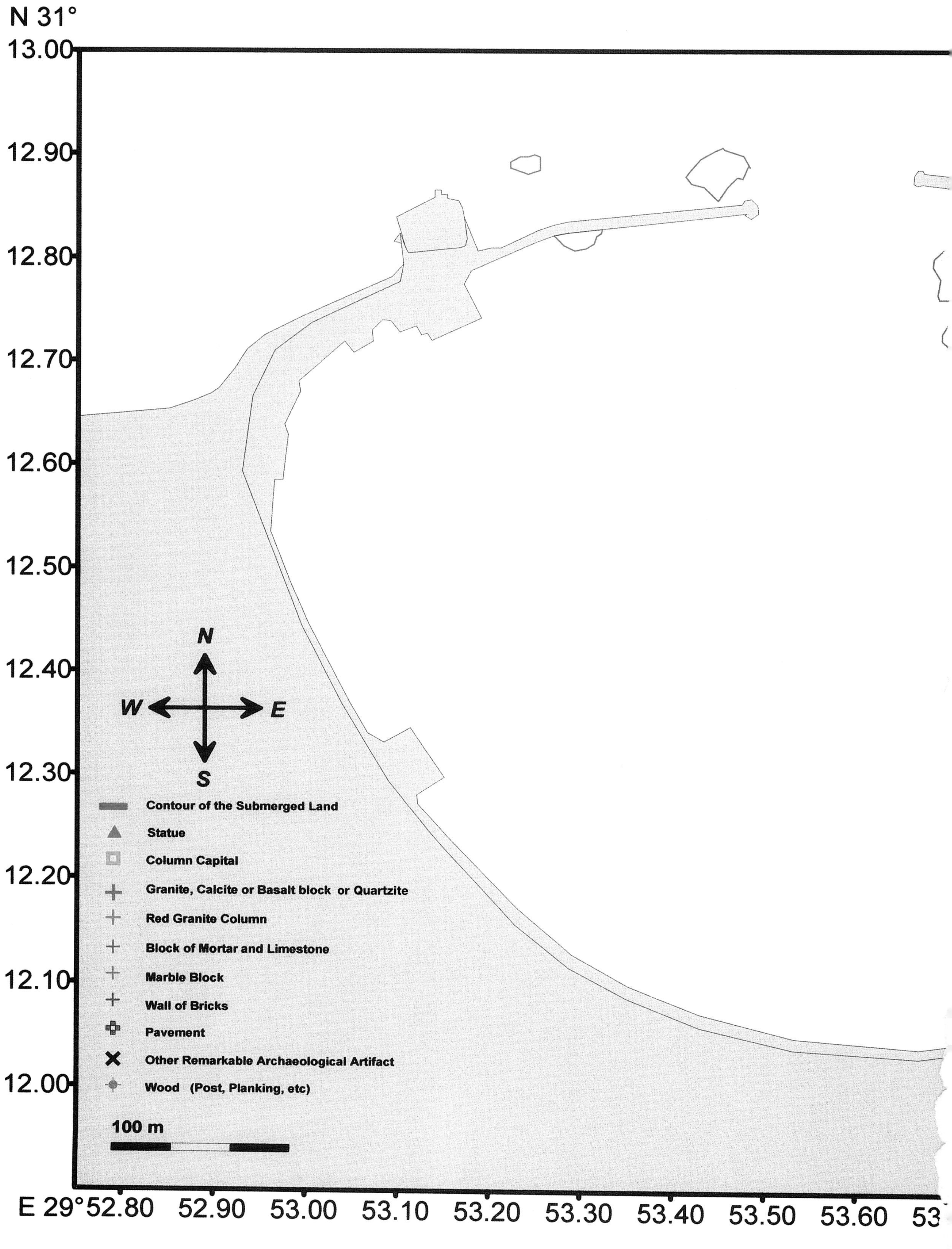

7. The main and secondary channels

7.1 Description

Between the reefs to the east and west was a channel at least 300 metres wide which corresponds to a marine ditch running north-south, perpendicular to the coast. It was by far the widest, deepest and safest channel affording entry to the 'Magnus Portus'.

It was situated exactly at the place of the actual channel to the harbour.

It is bordered:

—to the east by the two reefs R3 and R4.

The position of the reefs to the east seem to exclude the existence in antiquity of any secondary channel towards the east, unless the extreme end of the large ancient sea wall was less advanced than that of the modern breakwater and allowed entry between reefs R2 and R3.

—to the west by reef R1.

It is possible that other secondary channels were navigable between the reefs to the west, notably between R1 and the Diamond rock.

However, the presence of the modern eastern breakwater precludes the possibility today of verifying this.

7.2 Comparison with ancient texts

In 6-3 it was seen that Pliny named three channels. However, we do not know whether his source only mentioned access from the outside or whether it took into account the channels between the reefs and the interior of the harbour.

It is known that Poseidippos of Pella approached the 'Bull's Horn' and the Pharos.

According to Strabo and Josephus, a sailor arriving from the north had the Pharos on his right and the dangerous reef on his left, so those to the east, such as R1 and the Diamond, would not have presented any risk when making an approach.

> Moreover, on account of the narrowness of the passage there can be no entry for ships into the harbour without the consent of those who are in occupation of Pharos.[16]

This notice by Caesar shows that the position of the Pharos was such that the garrison he installed there could prevent enemy ships from entering the main harbour easily and, of course, allow the entry of large formations by the main channel.

[16] Cf. *'Testimonia'*, no. 19, p. 83.

THE MAIN CHANNEL

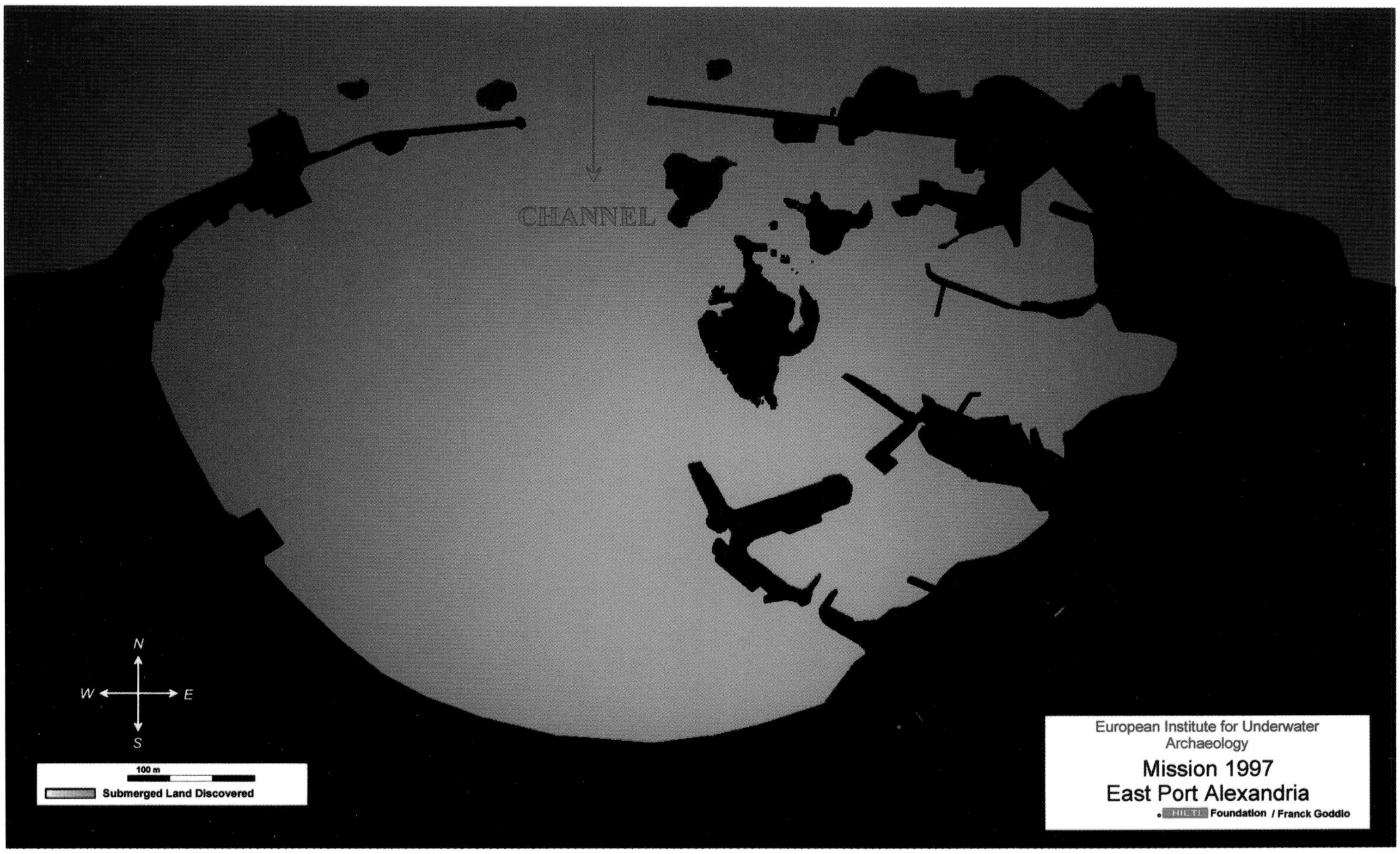

According to the later poem by Lucan,[17] chains barred the entrances during Caesar's time:

> But then Cleopatra, having bribed the guards to undo the chain across the harbour of Pharos, sailed in a small two-banked ship and entered the Macedonian palace without Caesar's knowledge ...

Research into the ancient channels raises of necessity the problem of the position of the Pharos which served to direct ships and keep them from reefs and shoals. If one retains the traditional position of the Pharos at the position of the Mamluk fort of Qa'it-Bey, for which there is no archaeological evidence at present, it is possible to believe that ships were guided by its light far to the west, towards the Diamond and reef R1 and not towards the safer, main channel.

Situated some 600 metres from this channel, the Pharos, even if higher than 100 metres, would not have been able to command this main entrance.

Recent underwater operations by the Centre des Etudes Alexandrines[18] seem very much to confirm that the soils lying to the east of the fort are an extension submerged through subsidence from the tip of the island. The chosen site of Qa'it-Bey was not in ancient times the eastern point of the island of the Pharos. As Strabo precisely says:

> And likewise the extremity of the isle is *a rock, which is washed all round by the sea* and has upon it a tower that is admirably constructed of white marble with many stories and bears the same name as the island.[19]

It would be useful to know exactly how far the island extended to the east, but the presence of the modern western breakwater prevents any verification. This structure has major foundations extending over more than 70 metres at the end which lines the main channel. Certain remains are, however, visible among the rocks and blocks of cement near the channel which indicate the existence of an ancient structure at this strategic point.

We would like to propose the hypothesis that the remains of the Pharos could be situated under the sea wall several hundred metres away from Qa'it-Bey; maps made before the construction of the western breakwater dating from the 15th, 17th, 18th and 19th centuries[20] moreover show shoals in this position. The map made by E. Napier in 1841 even mentions 'ruins under water' in two places now covered by the breakwater (cf. fig. 4 and 5).

However, an increase in topographical data from the western part of the main harbour could produce other hypotheses.

8. Ancient Cape Lochias

8.1 Description

The eastern part of the main harbour is defined by an important submerged extension of land which was part of the ancient Cape Lochias. This area is now covered in part by Cape Silsileh which is, besides, mainly made of modern backfill.

In ancient times Cape Lochias was appreciably wider and stretched over a distance of more than 450 metres to the west north-west of Cape Silsileh itself. Thus it formed an important natural protection for the ancient harbour.

The small modern sea wall, made of concrete blocks, which protects Cape Silsileh on its western side (D1), is perhaps built on ancient foundations, as indicated by certain remains which are still visible at its base (very eroded blocks of limestone).

At the western end of this cape the large Silsileh breakwater has been built which closes off the modern harbour. The base of this work rests to a large extent on the western point of the ancient, submerged Cape Lochias and probably covers the ancient great sea wall.

8.2 Remains discovered by surveys on Cape Lochias

The part of the cape near to the inner harbour (cf. § 9 description of the inner harbour) is covered by limestone paving which slopes away gently towards the basin to the south. It has still not been possible to determine whether this slope is due to landslip or if it is part of a particular development.

To the south west of the cape a concentration of remains choked with sand was located made up of column shafts and bases in red granite, and the foundations of walls made of dressed limestone, with areas covered with large limestone slabs, some 120 cms. by 60 cms.

8.3 Comparison with ancient texts

The name Lochias is attested by Strabo:[21]

---

[17] Cf. *'Testimonia'*, no. 30, p. 98.

[18] J. Y. Empereur, *Le Phare d'Alexandrie. La Merveille retrouvée*, Découverte Gallimard, Pris, 1998, maps p. 87.

[19] Cf. *'Testimonia'*, no. 28, p. 94.

[20] G. Jondet, *Mémoires présentés à la Société Sultanieh de Géographie*, tome II, *Atlas historique de la ville et des ports d'Alexandrie,* Le Caire, IFAO, 1921, especially pl. 1, X, XI, XII, XXXIV.

[21] Cf. *'Testimonia'*, no. 28, p. 94.

> ... for the shore of the mainland forms a bay, since it thrusts two promontories into the open sea, and between these is situated the island, which closes the bay, for it lies lengthwise parallel to the shore. Of the extremities of Pharos, the eastern one lies closer to the mainland and to the promontory opposite it (the promontory called Lochias), and thus makes the harbour narrow at the mouth.

The author again mentions this cape,[22] as we have already seen, in his description:

> ... in the Great Harbour at the entrance, on the right hand, are the island and the tower Pharos, and on the other hand are the reefs and also *the promontory Lochias*, with a royal palace upon it ...[23]

[22] *Ibid.*

[23] Adriani, *BSAA* 421 (1940-1945), p. 115-116, found the existence of an Isis called Lochias in an inscription of the Empire period at Beroia. On the other hand, the presence of this Isis Lochias at Tehneh in Middle Egypt rests on a misreading. Cf. E. Bernand, 'Inscriptions grecques et latines d'Akoris' (*BdeE* CIII, 1988), p. 3-4.

Photo 19: paving stones after cleaning

CAPE LOCHIAS

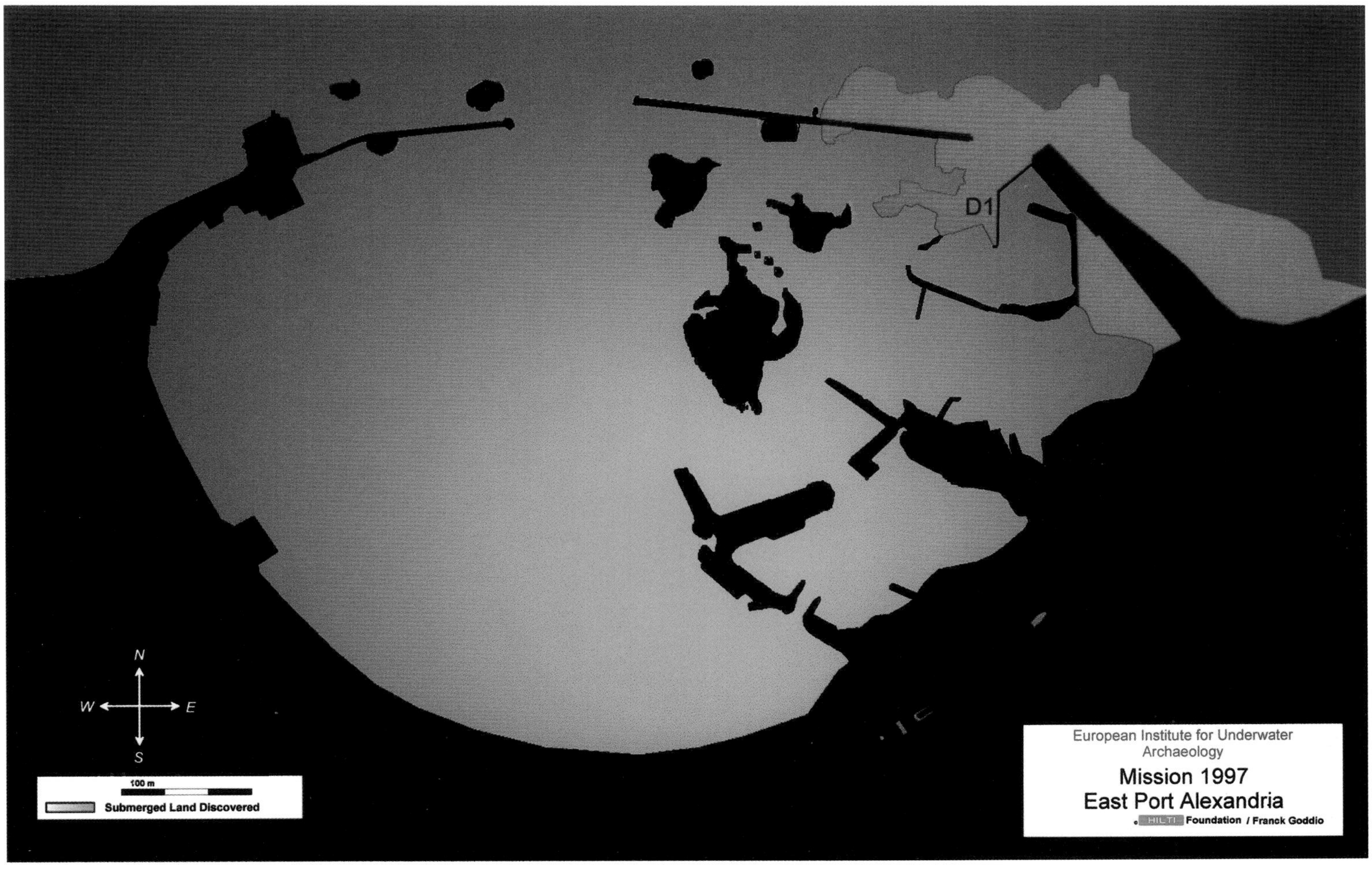

9. The inner harbour

9.1 Description

Within Cape Lochias was a well protected and much developed harbour, comprised of two basins.

This harbour is closed off on its south-west face by a large jetty (D2) 250 metres long, extending a rocky point by 180 metres.

The jetty is built of mortar and limestone. It is very well preserved in its north-west third, where it rises by more than three metres above the bottom of the harbour. It is about ten metres wide. Towards the centre, collapsed sections are visible.

The entrance to the harbour is situated to the north-west. This entrance is constrained by a small mole (D3), poorly preserved and made of mortar and limestone.

The interior of the harbour is divided into two basins by a mole (D4) constructed of limestone block of different sizes. This mole is 110 metres long and 20 metres wide. It is in a good state of preservation. Its direction is parallel to that of the main jetty. Its surface is flat; the blocks of limestone of which it is made have been laid flat on the top to form a sort of paving.

The bottom of the harbour is formed of sand and mud.

The whole forms a very secure harbour and seems inserted into Cape Lochias. The narrow entrance is well protected from the swell by the reefs to the north as well as by the return of the large jetty (D2) and by the small mole (D3). On the other hand, as this entrance required a vessel to sail along the large central reef, an easy entry was only available to oared vessels.

The surface of this harbour covered more than 7 hectares.

9.2 Remains discovered when surveying the inner harbour

Few remains were located on the sandy and mud bottom during visual surveys, apart from some fragments of amphorae spread about and some old stocks of anchors. The choking up with sand is important as it is likely that a large number of artefacts are covered by sediment.

9.3 Comparison with ancient texts

Strabo[24] mentions:

> Below these lies the harbour that was dug by the hand of man and is hidden from view, the private property of the kings ...

[24] Cf. *'Testimonia'*, no. 28, p.98.

THE INNER HARBOUR

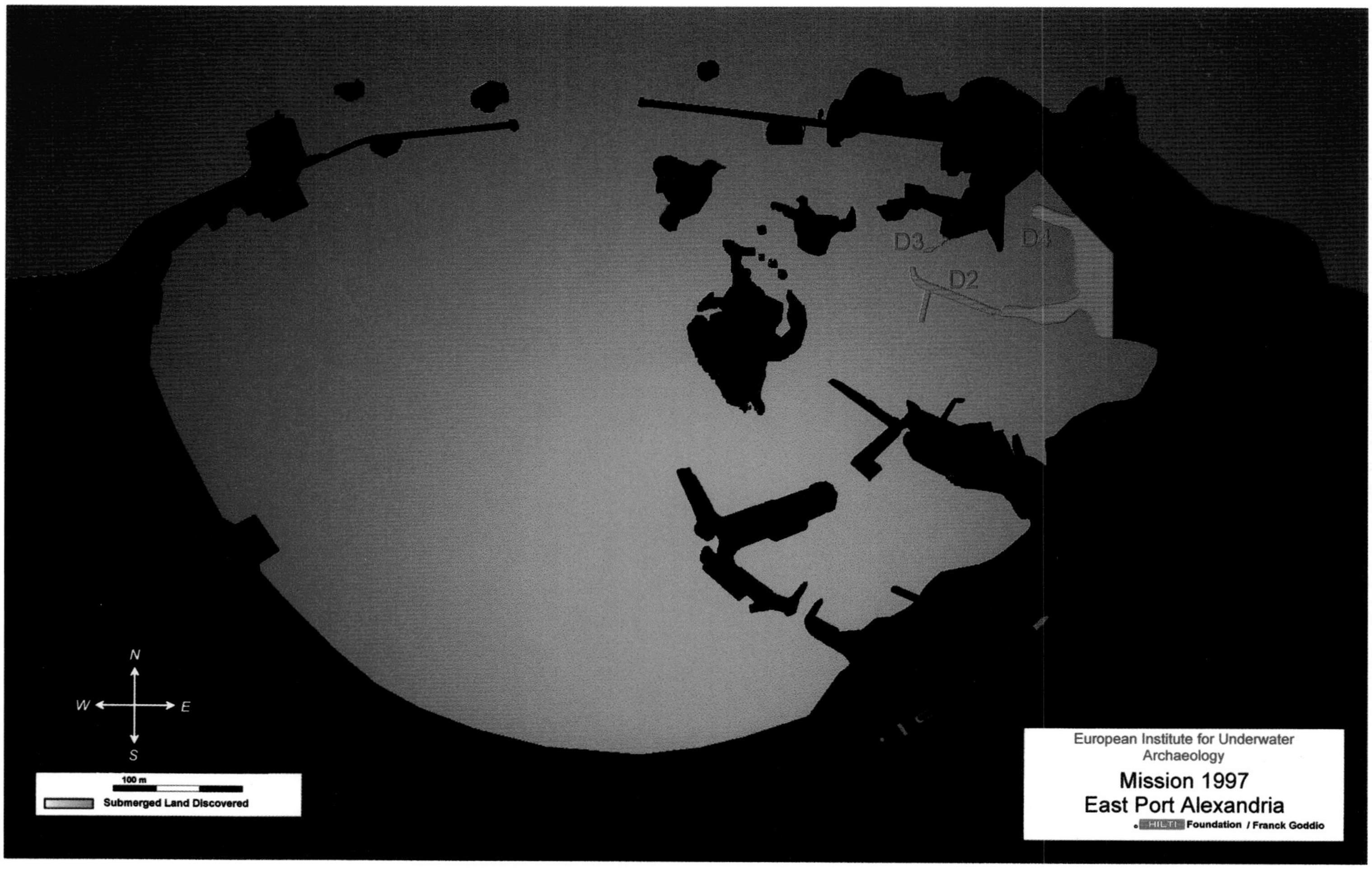

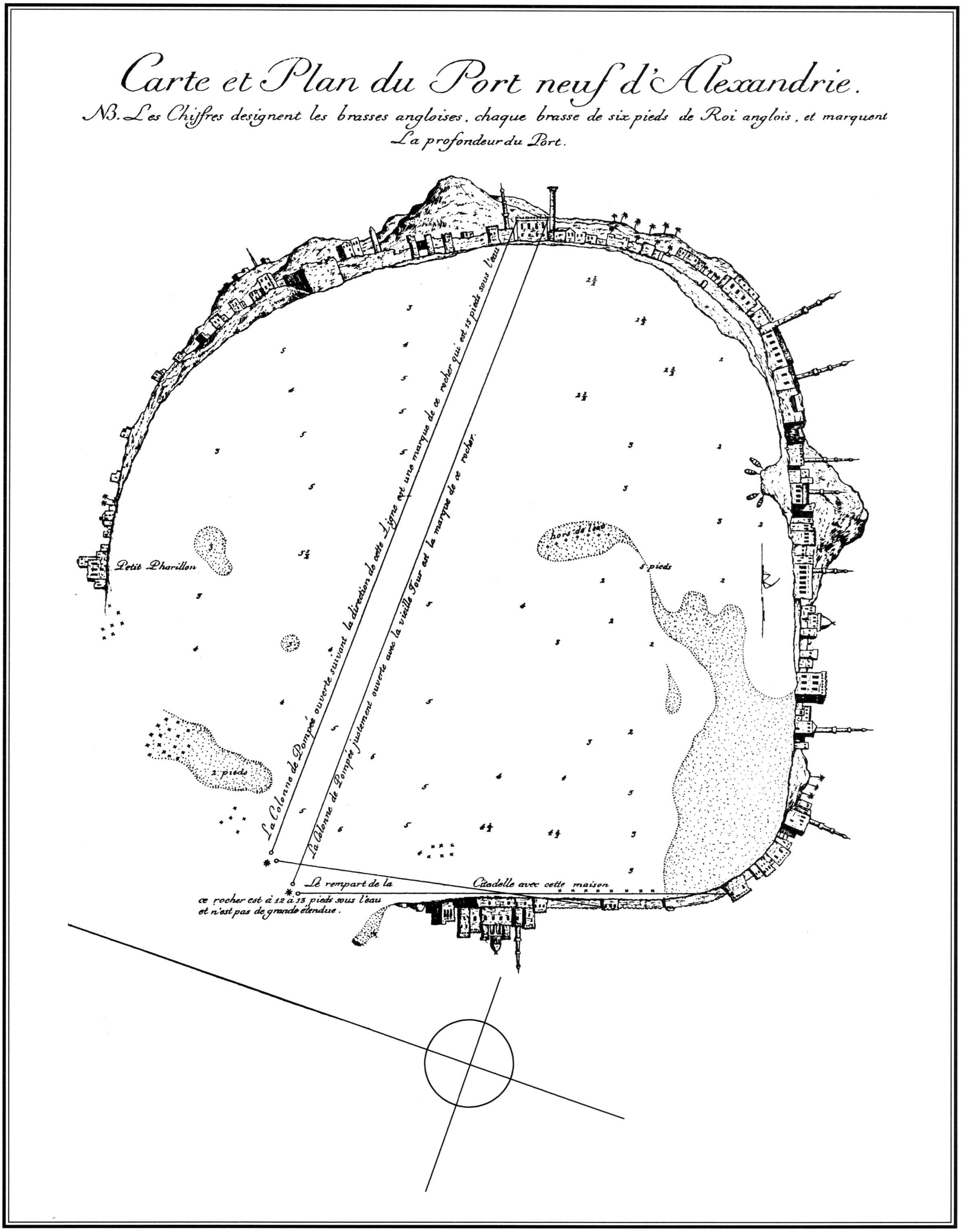

Fig 4: Plate XII: 1738. Map and plan of the New Harbour of Alexandria.
From *Travels in Egypt and Nubia*, by Frederick Lewis Norden FRS, Captain of the Danish Navy, translated from the original published by command of His Majesty the King of Denmark and enlarged by Dr Peter Templeman. London, Lockyear, Davis & Charles Reymers, Holborn, Printers of the Royal Society, 1757.

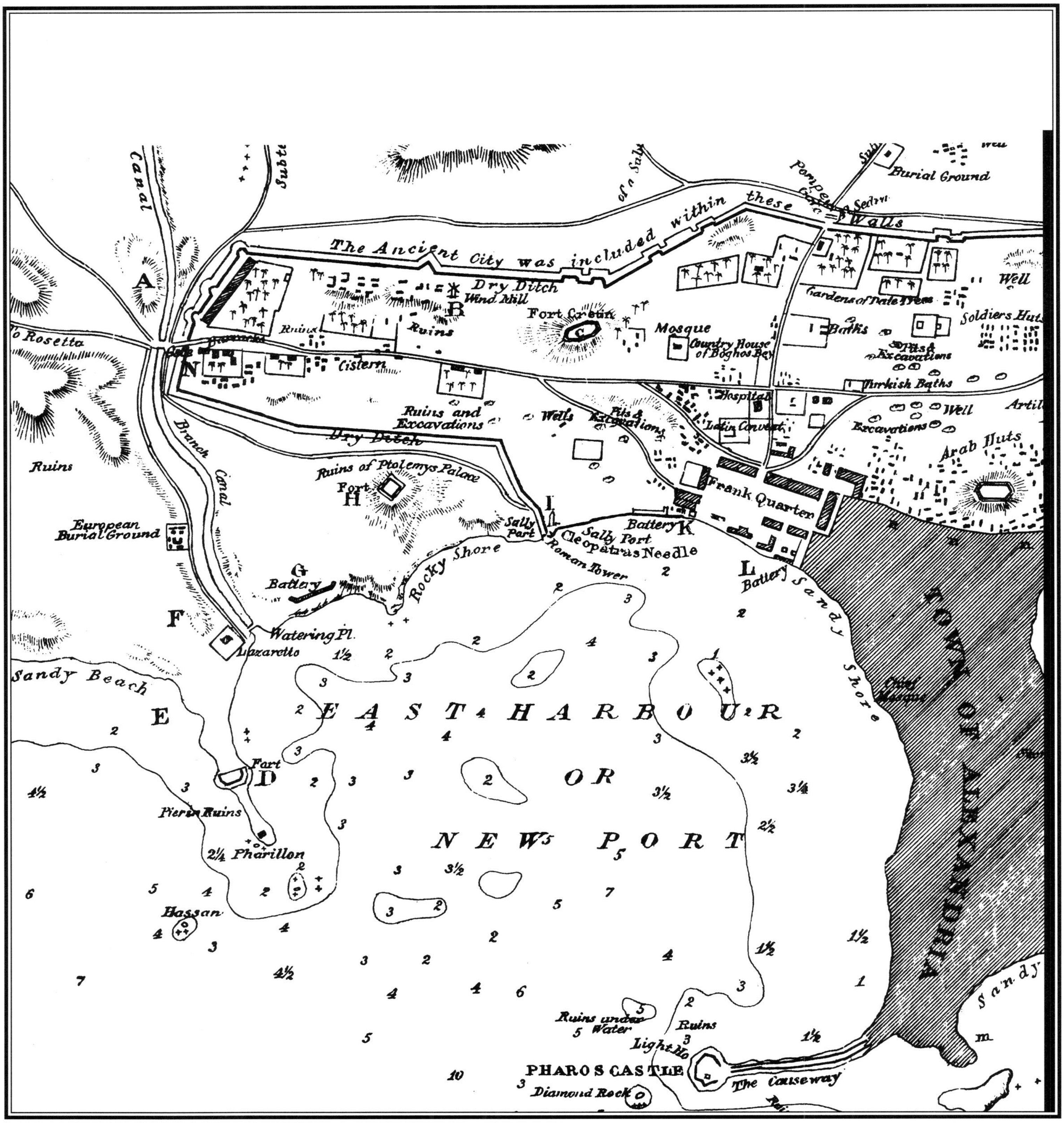

Fig 5: Plate XXXIII: 1841. Plan of Alexandria and its neighbourhood in 1841, by E. Napier, Lieutenant-Colonel 46th Regiment. Published by James Wyld, Geographer to the Queen and HRH Prince Albert, Charing Cross, East London, June 13th 1842.

Julius Caesar[25] refers to:

> In this region of the town [where Caesar was encamped] there was a small part of the palace to which he had been at first conducted for his personal residence, and a theatre was attached to the house which took the place of a citadel, and has approaches to the port and to the other docks.

The position of the harbour, such as it has been discovered, seems to correspond well with the location assigned to it by Strabo. Furthermore, the description given by Julius Caesar of the palace where he was entrenched near to the harbour accords well with the position of the inner harbour we have set out.

It is, however, probable, bearing in mind the small size of this harbour, that another military harbour should be linked to it. Caesar could in effect from his position set light to 72 ships[26] (50 quadriremes and quinquiremes as well as 22 vessels usually guarding the main harbour) moored in a harbour within his range. The inner harbour alone could not hold such a fleet (cf. § 11).

[25] Cf. *'Testimonia'*, no. 19, p. 83.
[26] Cf. *'Testimonia'*, no. 18, p. 82.

10. The Peninsula

10.1 Description

A peninsula 350 metres long and about 150 metres wide is located to the south-west of Cape Lochias. Its north east face was furnished with imposing quays which have suffered major damage due probably to landslides and subsidence.

They were built of mortar and limestone.

The south west edge of the peninsula is reinforced by limestone rocks.

Four harbour structures were built off this peninsula.

10.1.1 Description of the jetty to the south-east of the peninsula

Close to the base of the peninsula on the north east side is a small jetty (J1), 40 metres long, made of limestone blocks of various sizes. It is about 6 metres wide. Its surface is covered with limestone paving stones.

Plano-convex, circular ingots of ancient lead were discovered, some still stuck in the paving of the jetty, others having slid down the slope.

THE PENINSULA

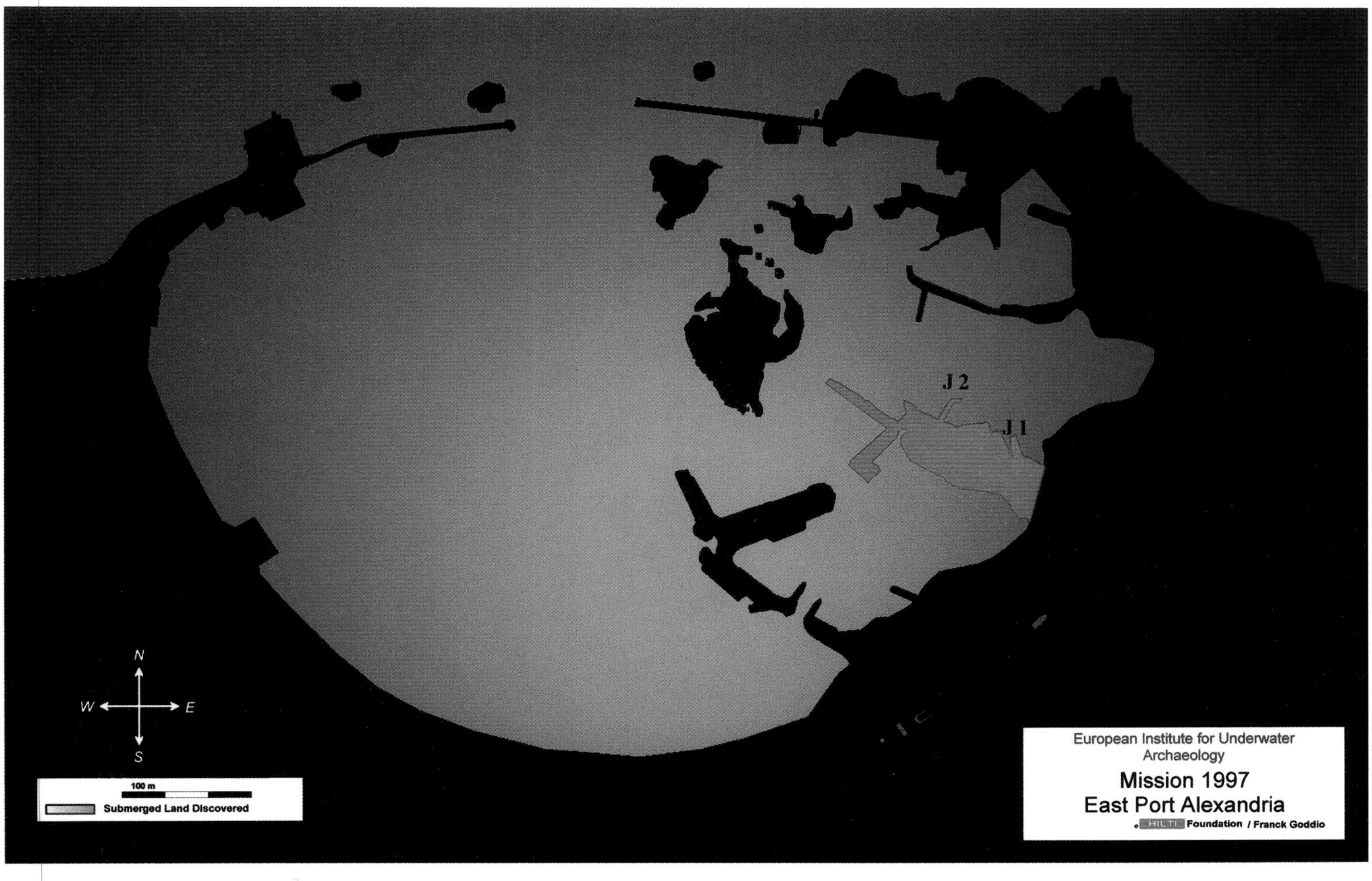

Photo 20: lead ingots *in situ* after cleaning

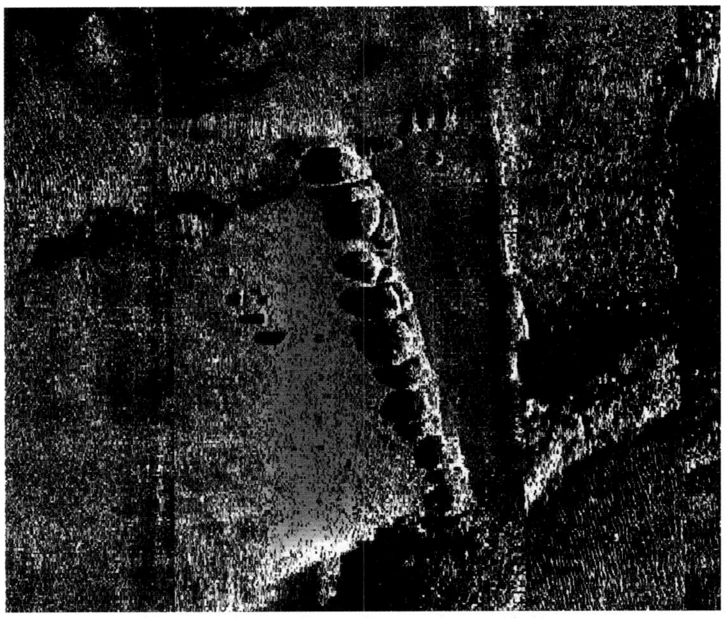

Fig 6: sonar side scan image from the north-west jetty

10.1.2 Description of the jetty to the north-west

Towards the north-west end, on the eastern side, is a jetty (J2) in a good state of preservation, made of mortar and limestone, running perpendicular to the quay. It is 50 metres long and 7 metres wide. At the end a 12 metre extension runs at a right angle towards the south-east. The limestones, some 10 x 10 cms in size, are set in horizontal courses in a lime mortar.

10.1.3 Description of the large breakwater

At the north-west end the peninsula is extended by an impressive breakwater. It is 180 metres long and about 18 metres wide. At its north-western end it is more than 3 metres above the bottom of the harbour.

THE BREAKWATER

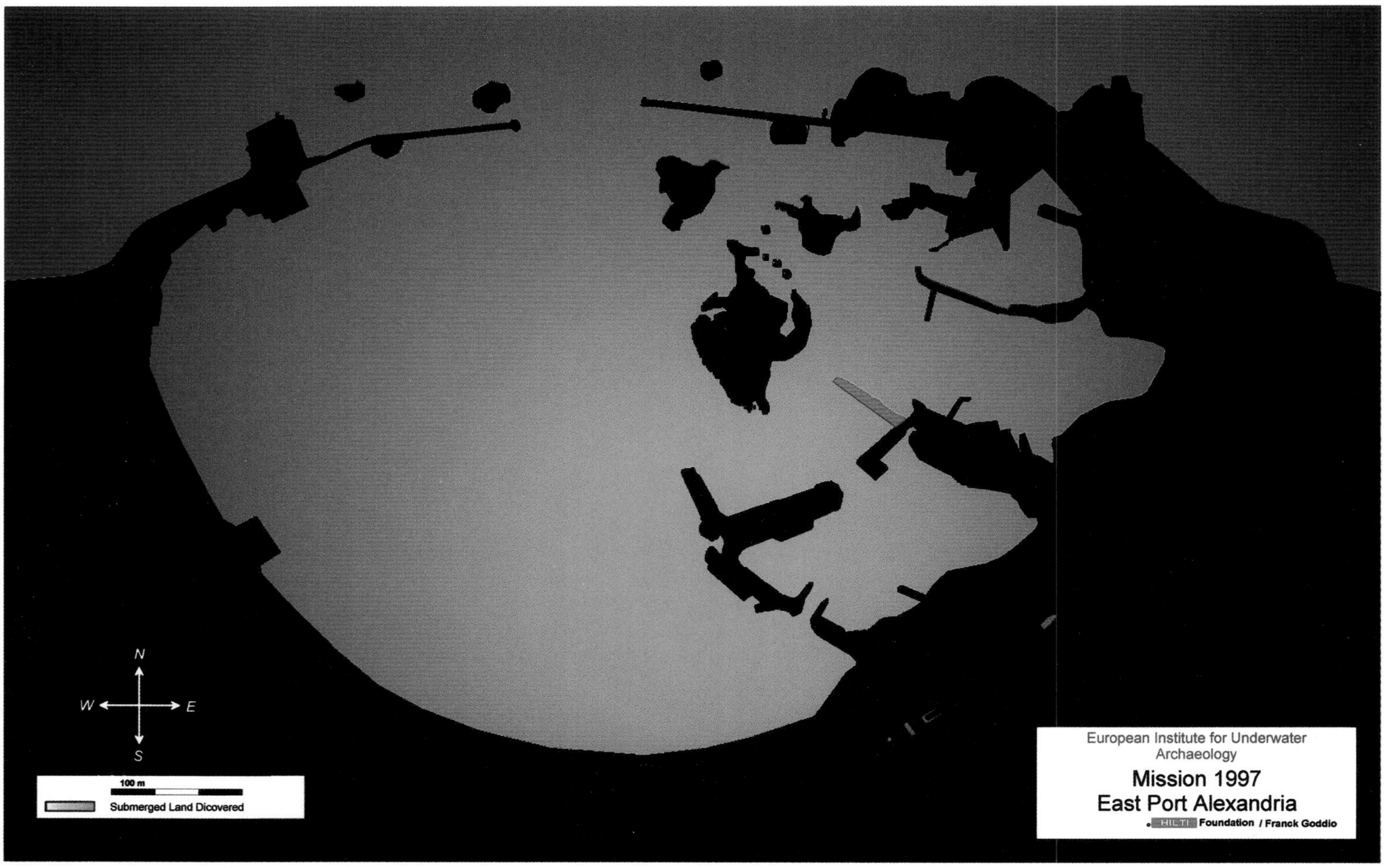

PROFILES OF THE MAIN PIER NORTH-WEST OF THE PENINSULA

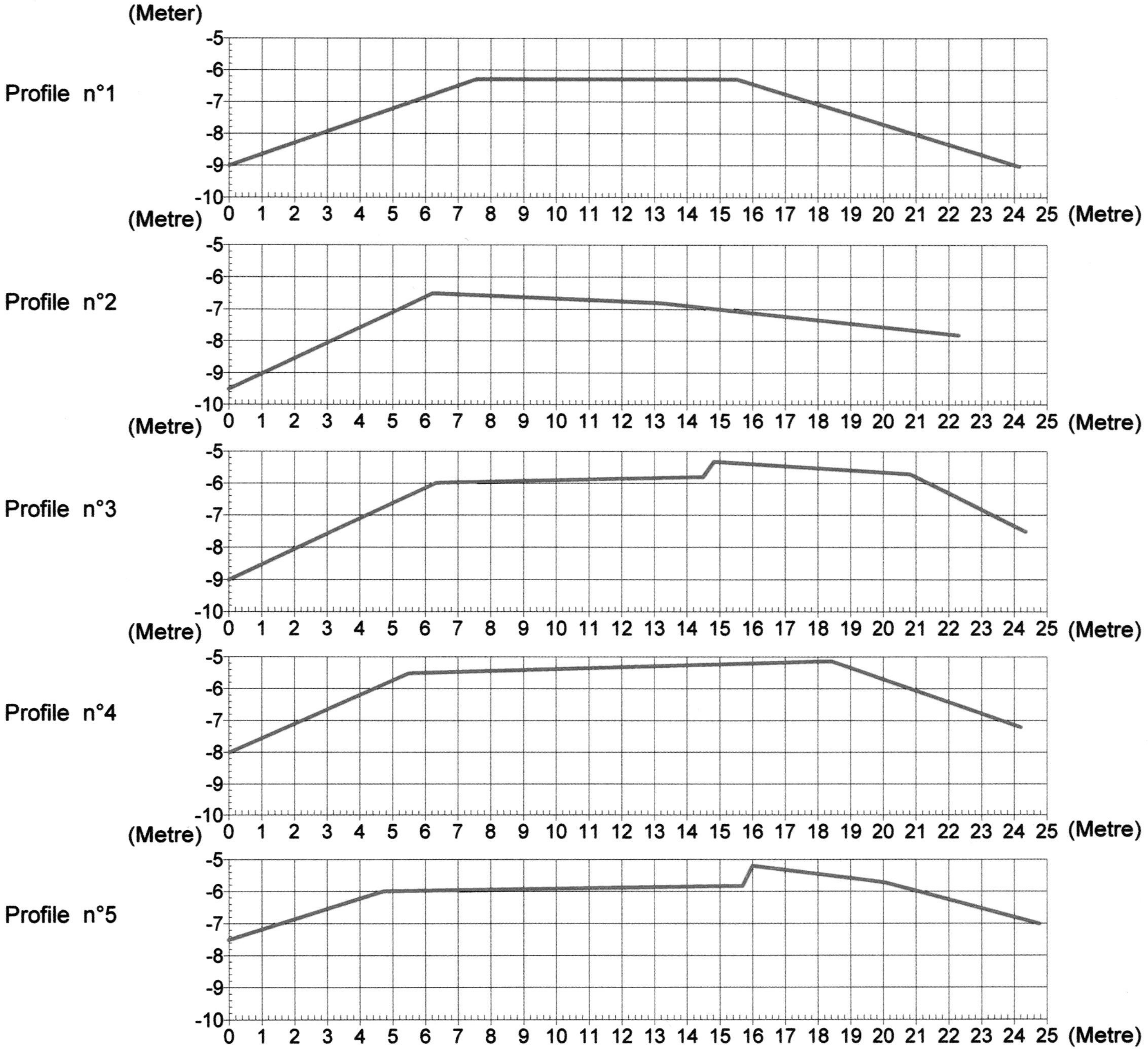

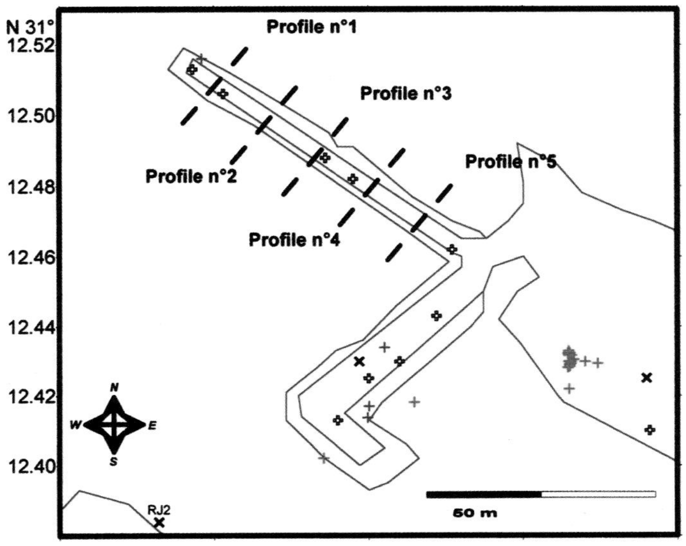

European Institute for Underwater Archaeology

Mission 1997

East Port Alexandria

HILTI Foundation / Franck Goddio

This important construction is made of limestone blocks of different sizes. On the surface the blocks are laid flat. Although this breakwater has been subject to subsidence in several places, it is in a reasonable state of preservation.

Its south-west face has a more pronounced slope than the north-east.

There is no construction at the end.

10.1.4 Description of the mole

From the same end of the peninsula a very important mole extends towards the south-west, making an angle of 70 degrees with the main breakwater. It is made of limestone blocks as well as blocks of lime mortar into which are set small limestones. The mole is 90 metres long and about 25 metres wide. The surface is covered with well-preserved limestone paving.

The mole ends in an esplanade 50 x 22 metres, made mainly of blocks of mortar and [small] limestones. The esplanade extends the mole towards the south east at an angle of 90 degrees. The blocks of mortar, some of which are more than three metres thick, are sometimes broken and upturned. The surface of the esplanade is also covered with limestone paving.

Limestone blocks of varying size are strewn about the esplanade and the area below. Red granite column shafts 90 cms. in diameter, related to items in marble and limestone, lie at the foot of this esplanade.

10.2 Remains discovered

A large number of archaeological remains were recovered from the peninsula during systematic surveys.

It has been possible to identify three main concentrations:

—towards the base of the peninsula, to the north, a large number of column shafts, bases and capitals of columns, all in red granite, blocks of granite and limestone were strewn over an area covered with limestone paving. The column shafts had diameters between 90 and 100 cms.

—at the base of the peninsula to the south is a vast area of limestone paving also covered with column shafts with diameters between 45 and 90 cms, capitals and column bases in red granite, items in marble, blocks of red granite and quartzite.

THE LARGE SOUTH-WEST MOLE

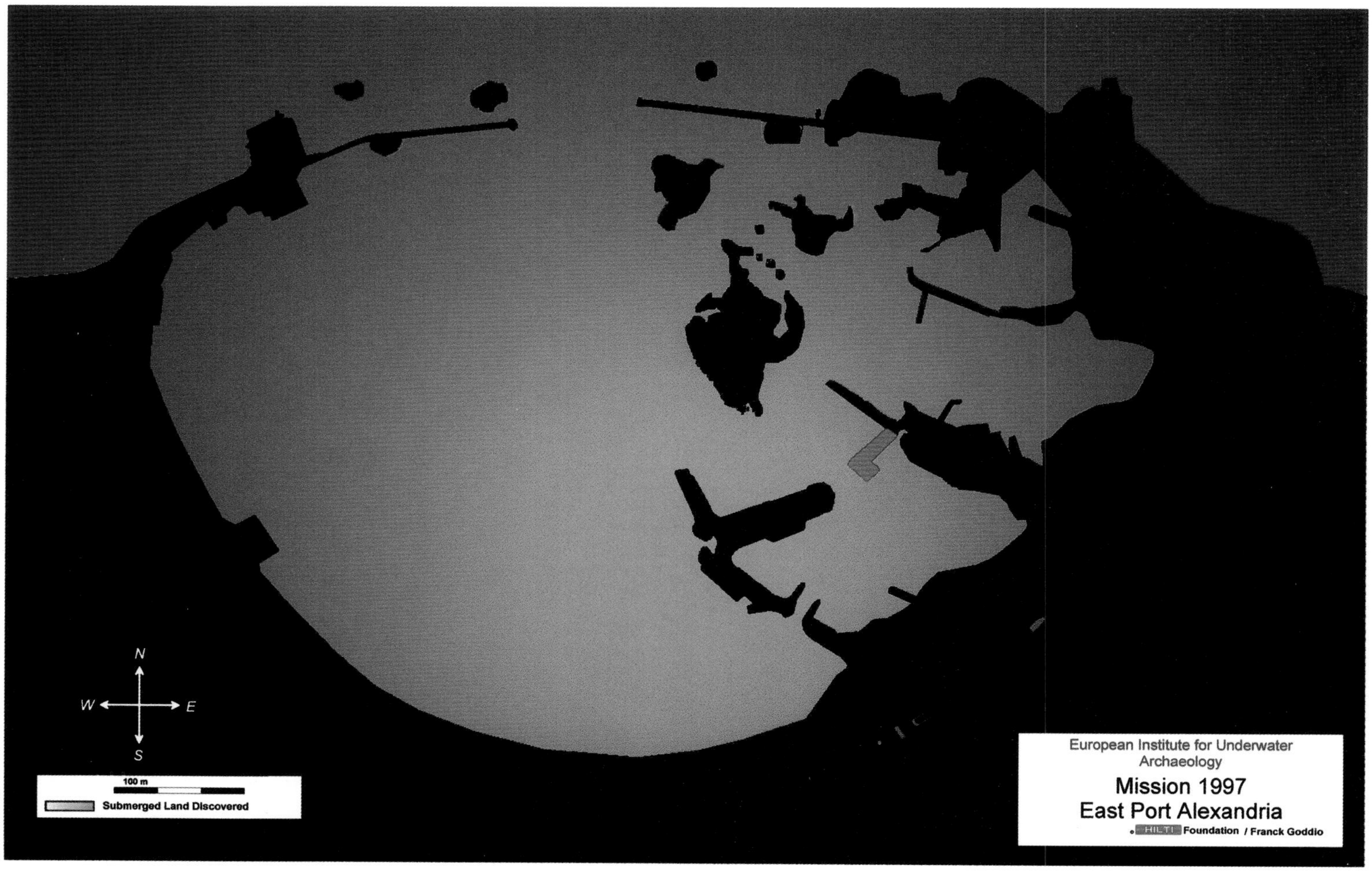

Photo 21: limestone paving

Photo 22: underwater photo of the block

—towards the end of the peninsula on the south-west side is an accumulation of red granite column shafts from 70 to 90 cms. in diameter, mostly covered in sand.

Remains are scattered over the whole of the peninsula and in several places paved areas can be seen.

Some remarkable items were revealed, such as:

—a block of grey granite with hieroglyphics on three faces (no. 747) [27]
—a quartzite sphinx (no. 900)[28]
—a head of a statue in white marble (no. 889)[29]
—fragments of sarcophagi
—red granite capitals of columns
—red granite column bases
—blocks of limestone basalt, red or grey granite
—fragments of lintels and cornices in red granite
—important blocks of mortar with small limestones
—parts of walls made of flat brick with mortar joints

Column shafts in red granite of various diameters (27 to 80 cms.) are scattered along the whole of the south-west face of the peninsula.

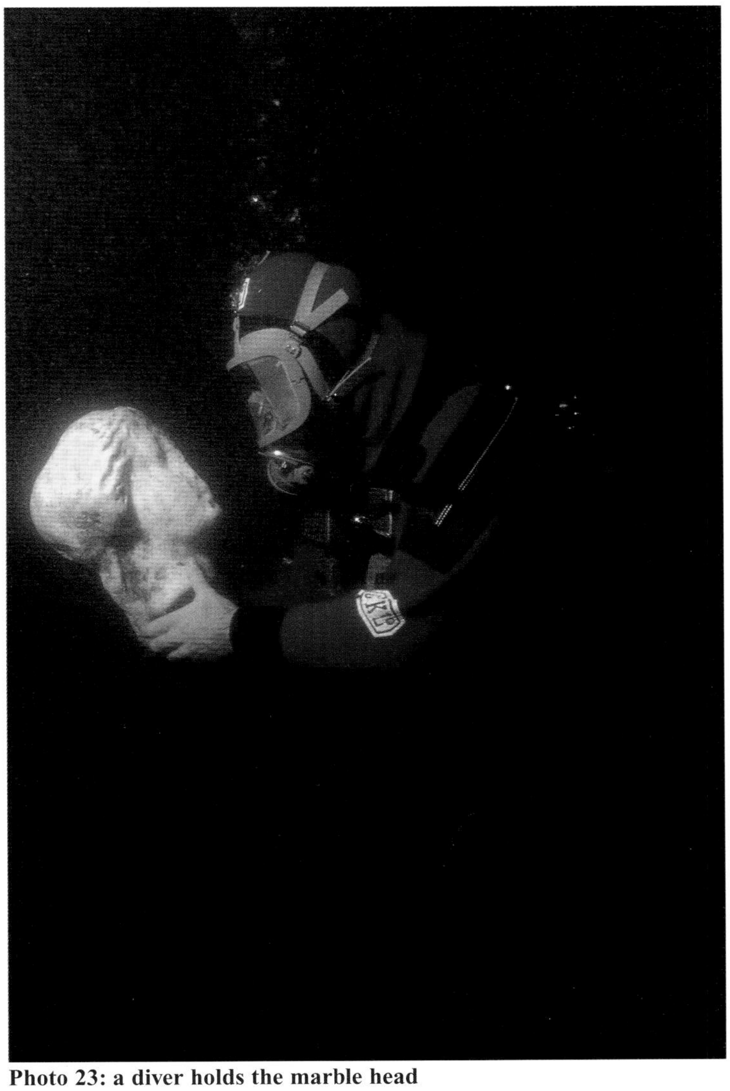

Photo 23: a diver holds the marble head

[27] Cf. J Yoyotte, '*Pharaonica*', p. 223.
[28] Cf. Z. Kiss, 'Sculptures', p. 174.
[29] Cf. Z. Kiss, 'Sculptures', p. 186.

Photo 24: section of a brick and mortar wall

Photo 25: sarcophagus fragment

10.3 Comparison with ancient texts

Strabo[30] mentions in his description of the 'Magnus Portus':

> Above the artificial harbour lies the theatre; then the Poseidium - an elbow, as it were, projecting from the Emporium, as it is called, and containing a temple of Poseidon. To this elbow of land Antony added a mole projecting still farther, into the middle of a harbour, and on the extremity of it built a royal lodge which he called Timonium. This was his last act, when, forsaken by his friends, he sailed away to Alexandria after his misfortune at Actium, having chosen to live the life of a Timon the rest of his days, which he intended to spend in solitude from all those friends.

The area that Strabo, by a sort of pleonasm, calls the Poseidion, apparently takes its name from the Poseidion, literally the temple of Poseidon which was built there. The definition as an 'elbow of land' agrees exactly with our peninsula.

However, the reference the geographer makes to the 'Emporium, as it is called' is obscured by a second reference he makes later on, namely when listing buildings towards the Heptastadion, to an Emporion placed to the west of the Kaisarion whose position is surely fixed by 'Cleopatra's Needles'.[31]

It is tempting to suppose, as has been done, that there were two places called *emporion*, that is a place for commerce: the vast market proper and its warehouses and arsenals towards the Heptastadion and another landing place for foodstuffs for the royal harbour, situated at the base of our peninsula and making an 'elbow' with the shore.

Thus it is on this peninsula that a temple of Poseidon should be sought. It has been seen that there are three main areas of remains on the peninsula. If this temple still existed, even in part, when the catastrophic events which caused the coastal subsidence took place, research should be urgently directed towards these concentrations to identify the temple.

Strabo[32] points out that a mole extend this 'elbow of land' and at its end was built the Timonion.

The peninsula had three jetties but there are no remains of their construction at the extremities. Moreover, the cramped situation at their extremities would not allow for the building of even a modest royal residence.

Only the large mole which projects towards the south-west and ends in a platform seems to correspond to the description of Strabo. The building remains which survive on this platform and below it reinforce this hypothesis.

11. The second main harbour

11.1 Description

Between the south-west jetty of the inner harbour (D2) and the peninsula a large harbour was built, 500 metres long and almost 300 metres wide, thus about 15 hectares. Its north-west entrance is protected from waves and the swell by the reefs.

The important breakwater at the end of the peninsula has the function of cutting off any swell coming in through the main channel of the 'Magnus Portus' and rebounding from the island (see § 12).

[30] Cf. *'Testimonia'*, no. 28, p. 94.

[31] See A. Adriani, *Repertorio d'Arte dell'Egitto greco-romano*, Ser. C, t. I-II, Bacno di Sicilia, 1966, p. 220 and 247-280.

[32] Cf. *'Testimonia'*, n° 28, p. 94.

Moreover, it very probably also serves to control the harbour by narrowing in a significant way the space between the peninsula and the large central reef.

The harbour installations comprised three jetties, two on the peninsula, already described, as well as a jetty (J3) about 80 metres long (as far as can be judged from the remains as this construction is in a poor state of preservation).

This last jetty is perpendicular to the main jetty of the inner harbour. It is made of blocks of limestone of various sizes. Its position within the harbour is defined by a line joining the ends of the breakwater and the jetty of the inner harbour. It prevents any remaining swell entering the harbour.

The bottom of this harbour is mud.

11.2 Remains discovered

Numerous amphorae, complete or broken of varying types and age are spread over the bottom.

Large concentrations of amphorae were noted in the following areas:

—at the foot of each side of the jetty running from the base of the peninsula.

—at the foot of the large breakwater along the whole of its northern side.

—along the whole of the north east face of the peninsula.

Several ancient stone anchor stocks were also found on the bottom of the harbour especially near to the small embankment at the foot of the peninsula.

11.3 Comparison with ancient texts

Strabo[33] unambiguously confirms that there are several harbours in the 'Magnus Portus':

> As for the Great Harbour, in addition to its being beautifully enclosed both by the embankment and by nature, it is not only so deep close to the shore that the largest ship can be moored at the steps, but also is cut up into several harbours.

This second harbour, adjoining the harbour of Cape Lochias, corresponds well with the description of the author. This harbour very probably sheltered part of the fleet that Caesar set fire to.[34]

[33] Cf. *'Testimonia'*, N° 28, p. 94.
[34] Cf §. 9-3.

THE SECOND HARBOUR

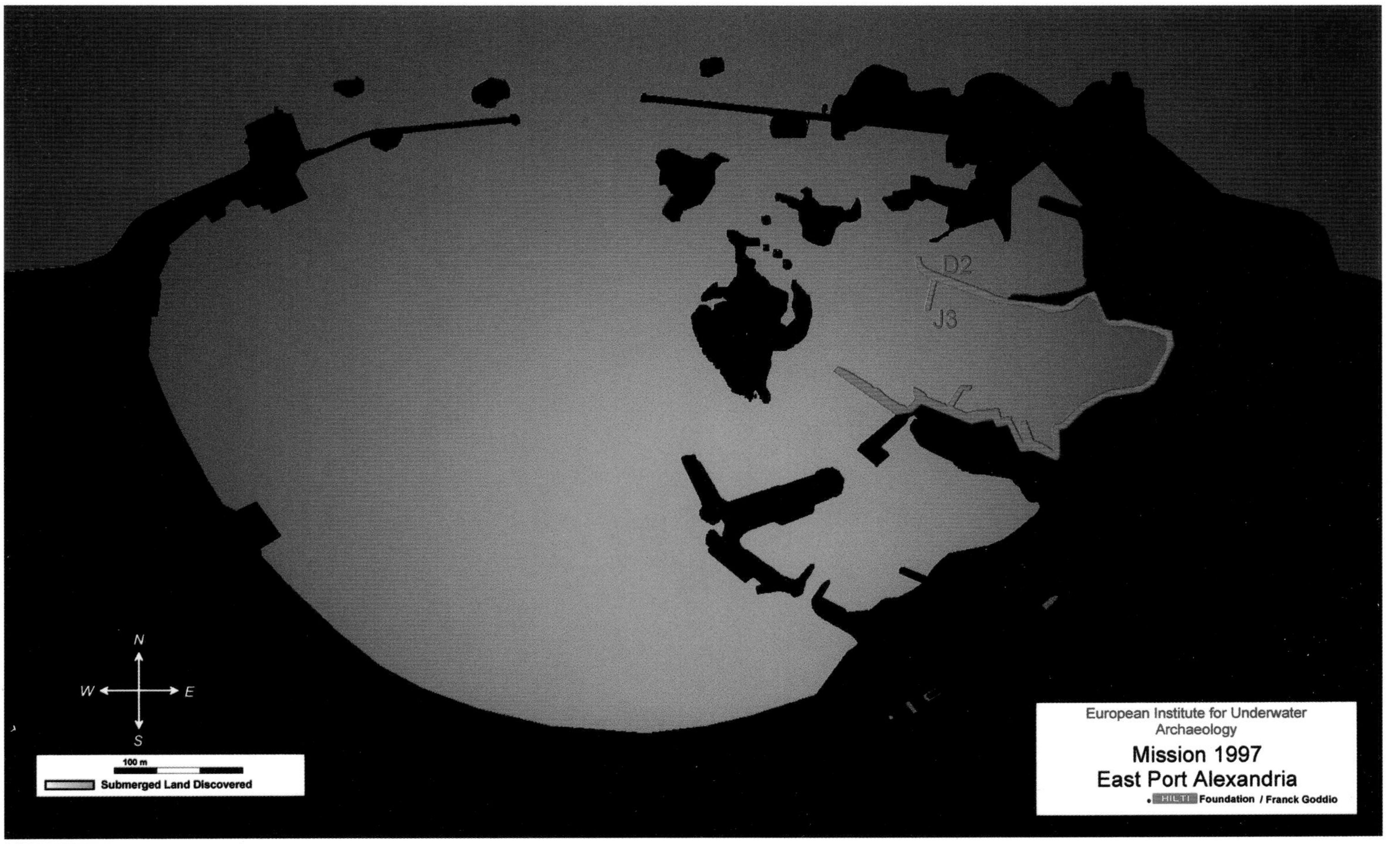

12. The Island

12.1 Description

At the south-east end of the peninsula lies an island some 350 metres long. Its widest point is 70 metres.

This island is formed of three branches.

The main branch (B1) is oriented south-west to north-east. It is in alignment with the mole and esplanade on the end of the peninsula. Also, this main branch is parallel to the ancient coastline.

On its north-west end the island is extended by a mole 340 metres long and 30 metres wide which forms the second branch (B2).

With the peninsula and the coast (cf. §13, description of the coast) the island forms a third large harbour.

At the centre of the island on its main branch is a wide esplanade which extends into the harbour.

The third branch of the island (B3) runs north-west to south-east. At its tip a jetty (J4), made of limestone blocks and rubble, projects to the north-east to create with the island a perfectly protected little harbour (H2).

The island commands the two entrances to the main harbour.

12.2 Remains discovered

The island has a great number of important archaeological remains.

An examination of the map shows that almost all of the red granite column shafts discovered on the island are aligned in a band 350 metres long and 45 metres wide and are associated with limestone and granite blocks as well as the seven pedestals of statues. Furthermore, this alignment extends from the other side of the channel of the harbour with the remains discovered around the platform adjacent to the mole.

The concentrations of remains are particularly dense on the central esplanade and at the south-west end of the island.

A visual survey carried out on the north-west mole seems to indicate that there is no material of an architectural nature on any of the paved surface. A few isolated blocks of mortar are to be seen on the periphery and at the end.

Excavations were carried out in different places on this island to determine its structure and to plot any constructions and other remains which covered it.

THE ANTIRHODOS ISLAND

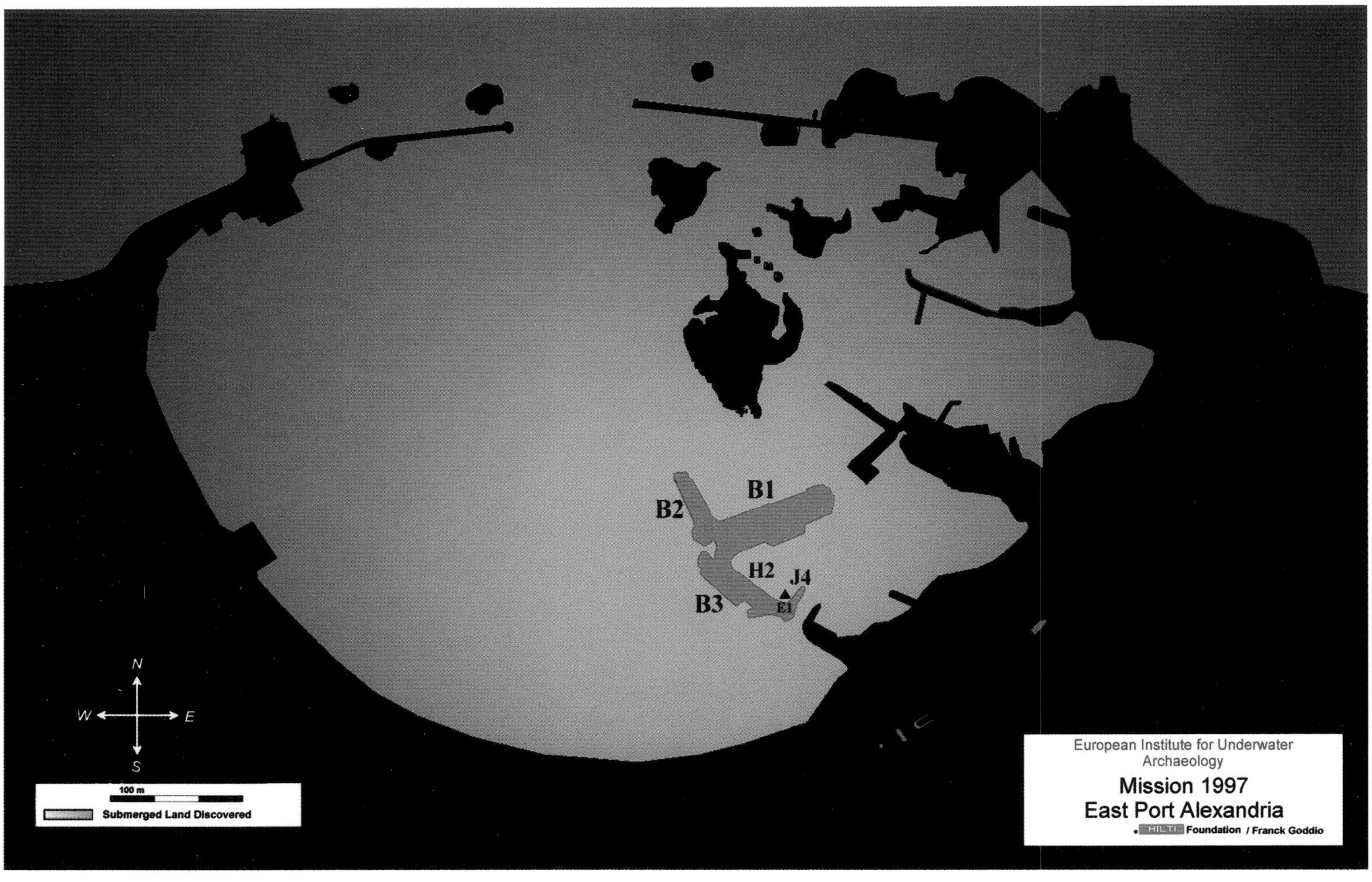

12.2.1 Excavations carried out on the island

12.2.1.1 Excavations at the eastern end

One excavation was carried out at the eastern end of the island.

At this point on the island a monolithic granite column with moulding lay by the channel on a sandy bottom. It was 5.2 m. long and 80 cm. wide (it was broken at one end). It was surrounded by ancient blocks of mortar of varying sizes.

The end facing the channel of the harbour is made of stone hardcore, mainly limestone which falls away in a gentle slope towards the channel of the harbour. Under about 60 cm. of rubble, wooden structures were discovered. These consisted of two rows of stakes or piles approximately parallel, running south-west to north-east, along the axis of the main branch of the island. The spacing of the two rows varied between 1.8 metres and 1.5 metres.

The first row was made of stakes with grooves. Planks had been slid into these grooves to form a palisade fixed in the ground. The spacing between the stakes when joined to the planks was about 40 to 50 cm. The ends of the stakes were sharpened. The stakes were stuck in the ground with mortar. The alignment of this sort of timber support disappears at the end of the slope of hardcore and at the

Photo 26: pile and timber base

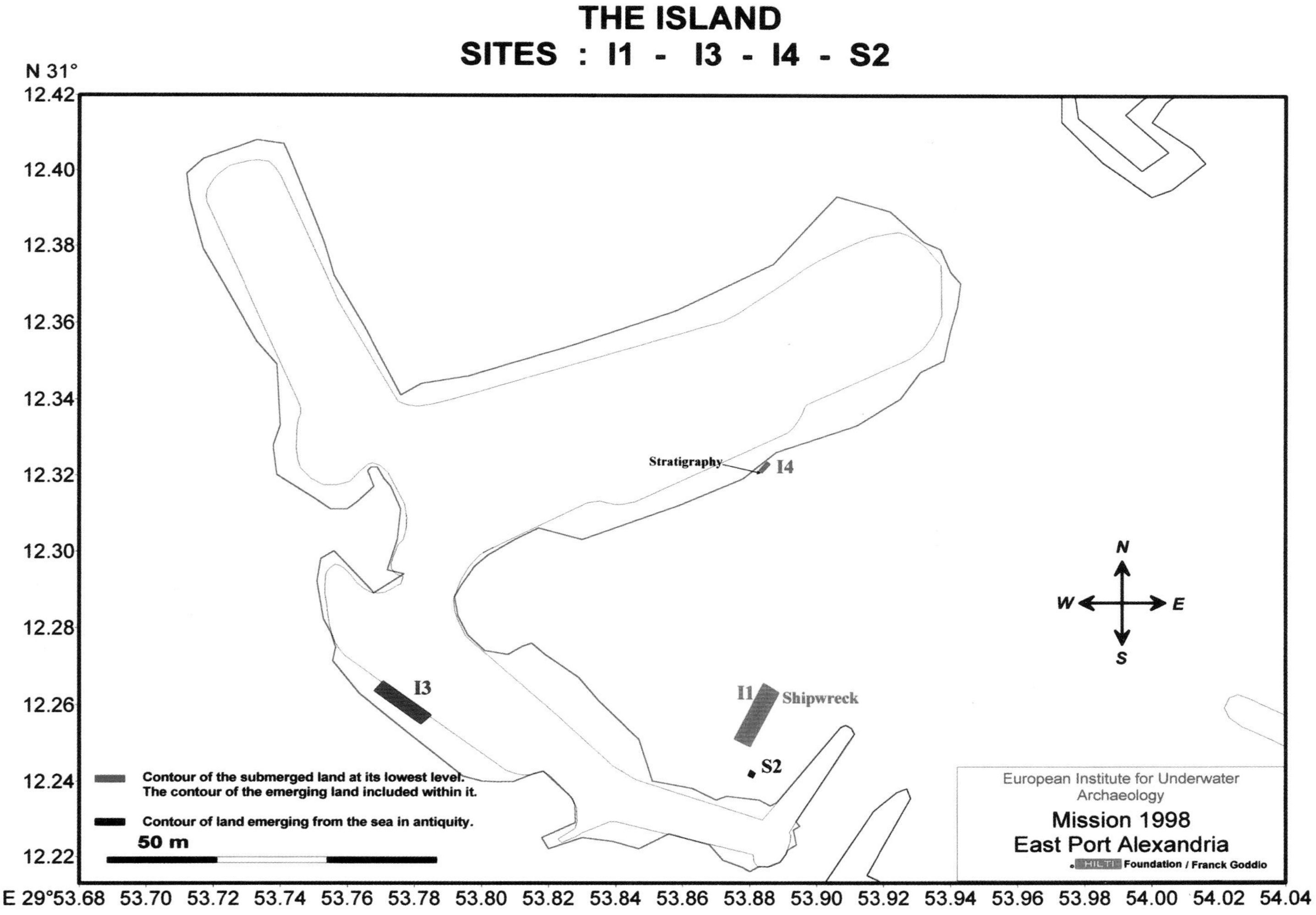

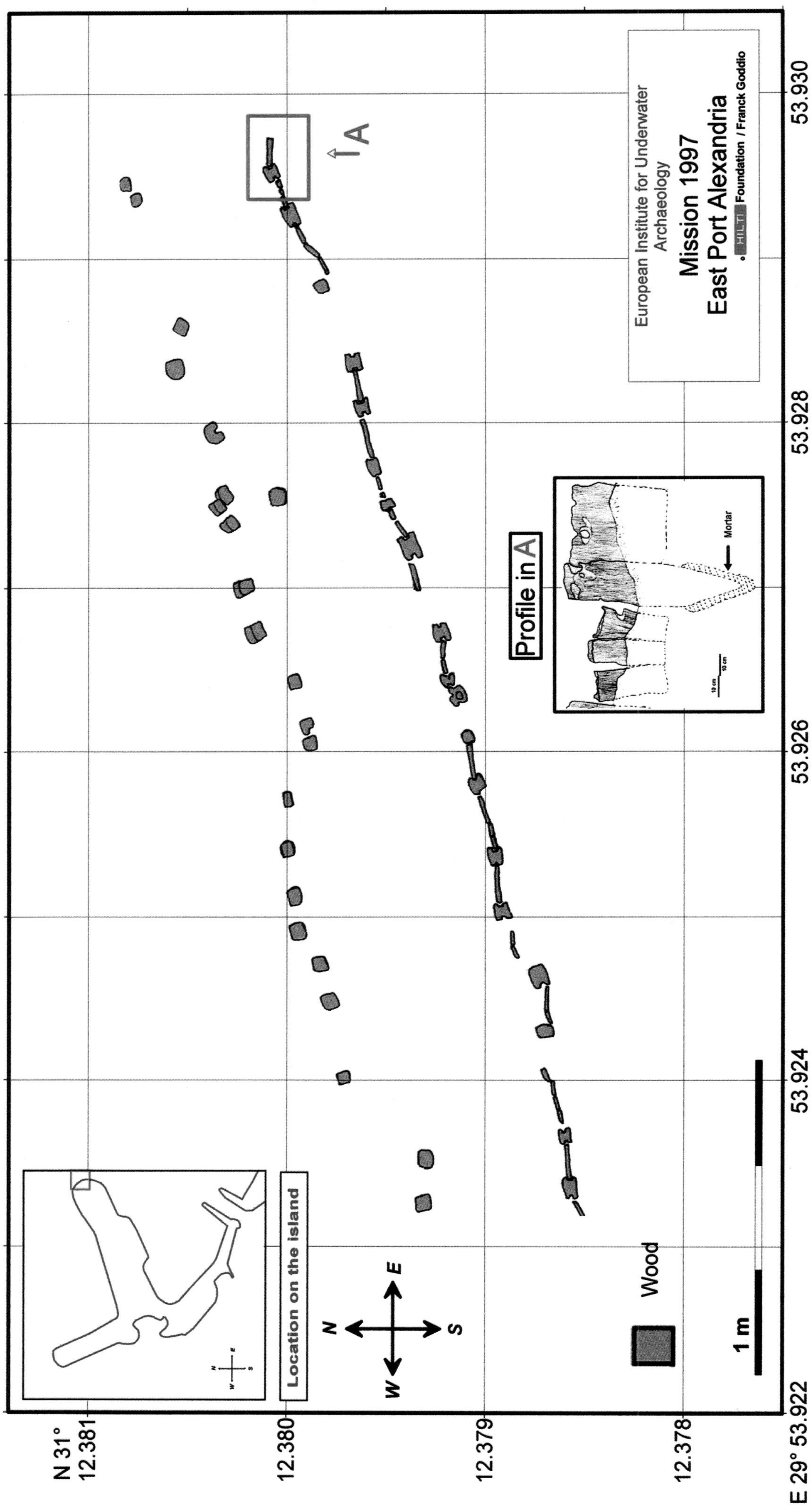

THE ISLAND
WOOD REMAINS ON THE NORTH-EAST TIP

sandy bottom of the channel. At the other end, towards the south-west, the line seems to continue under some important blocks of mortar that have slid down the slope.

The second row is made up of stakes without grooves which were not fixed with planks. This line of stakes also disappears towards the south-west under blocks of mortar. The stakes are ranged more tightly together than the other row. The spacing between them varies between 40 and 20 cms.

In section the stakes are about 14 x 14 cms. Some have a cross section of 18 x 14 cms.

An examination of the stakes showed that they are made from elm (*Ulmus* sp.) with 33 to 75 rings.

A dating analysis by Carbon 14 produced the following dating:

Calibrated C14 dating: 760 cal. BC – 360 BC (Stuiver and Becker calibration curve, 1986, radio carbon 28, 863-910) 'Archéolabs ref. ARC97/R1927C/2'
Probability of the calibrated date being:

—between 760 cal. BC and 520 cal. BC is from 28.2 percent.

—Between 520 cal. BC and 360 cal. BC is from 70.6 percent.

C14 conventional date: 410 BC (± 40 years).

The planks had an average thickness of 4 cms.

They were cut from pine (*Pinus* sp.) and have between 18 and 35 rings.

Calibrated C14 dating: 755 cal. BC – 255 cal. BC
Probability of the calibrated date being:

—between 755 cal. BC and 525 cal. BC is from 19.5 percent.

—between 525 cal. BC and 355 cal. BC is from 76.5 percent.

C14 conventional date: 395 BC (± 40 years).
'Archéolabs ref. ARC97/R1927C/2'

The hypothesis may be put forward that these structures were the base of a wooden jetty built at the end of the island.[35] In the upper stratum of this excavation, above a post, a fragment of white marble with some lettering was discovered (no. 1224).[36]

A column shaft in red granite with a Greek inscription in a frame was also found at the same eastern end of the island, close to a group of ancient blocks of mortar (C 347).[37]

[35] Cf. A. de Graauw, p. 55.
[36] Cf. E. Bernand, 'Epigraphic Documents', p. 147.
[37] *Ibid.* See F. Goddio, A. Bernand and E. Bernand, 'L'Epigraphie sous-marine dans le port orietal d'Alexandrie', *Zeitschrift für Papyrologie und Epigraphik* 121 (1998), p. 131-144.

12.2.1.2 Excavations in the centre

In the centre of the island is a vast esplanade which extends into a harbour. About 6,000 sq. m., this esplanade was cleaned of its limestone concretions. An important accumulation of remains appeared lying on an area completely paved with limestone. Column shafts of varying diameters (between 75 and 11 cm.) in red granite were uncovered, some of which ended in a moulding.; two bore hieroglyphic inscriptions[38] and had been re-dressed to be used again.

[38] Cf. J Yoyotte, '*Pharaonica*', p. 236.

Photo 27: a red granite block with a hieroglyphic inscription

Photo 28: another block found on the island

THE ISLAND

SHAFTS OF COLUMNS AND RED GRANITE BLOCKS ON THE CENTRAL PART

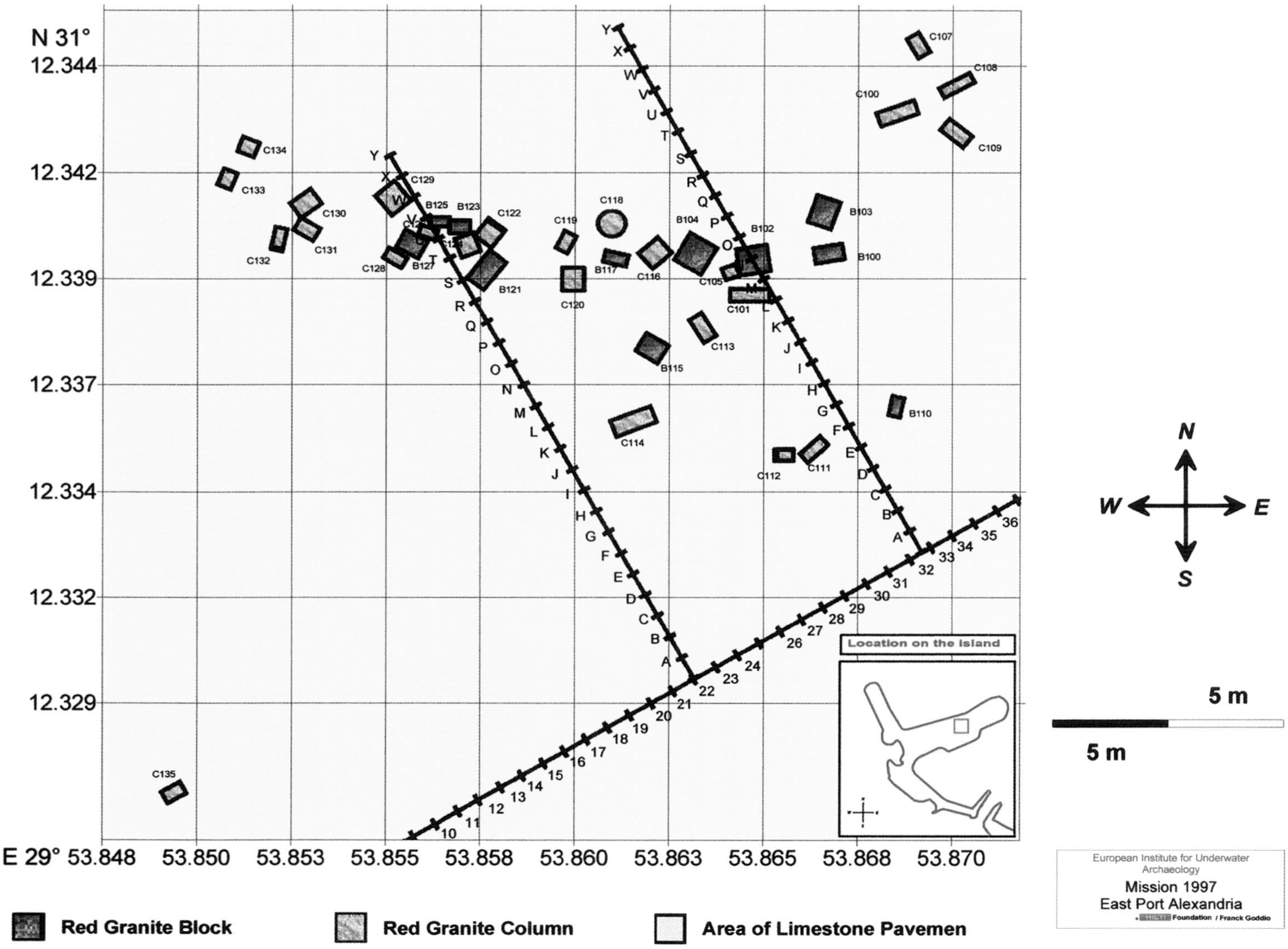

This esplanade is strewn with limestone and quartzite blocks of different sizes.

In other places, it was noted that the paving had been broken up or displaced by the fall or slippage of these items. Three column shafts with Greek inscriptions (C 116, C 118, C 129),[39] were found in this area. Two other shafts had a few fragments of a cartouche without any inscription (C 120, C 122) and another shaft with inscriptions was found at the far north-east limit of the esplanade (C 1174).[40] Shaft no. C 116 bore two grooves for re-use.

The columns with inscriptions, as well as various associated items, were found close to important blocks of mortar incorporating small limestones. From the evidence, some of these blocks had been broken or fallen following an earthquake or landslide. Others seem to be left in their original positions.

12.2.1.3 Excavation to the south-west of the central esplanade

An excavation was made around a block of mortar, apparently still in place in the south-east of the esplanade. It showed that this block was in fact made of alternating layers of mortar and flat limestones about 10 x 10 cm.

This excavation gave us interesting information about the planning of the island.[41]

The block had a horizontal surface, located at the same level as the surrounding paved area. It was about 15 m. long and 8 m. wide. Although broken into several pieces, the block had not been scattered. The colour of the mortar was grey green.

The last level, the surface, is made of stones which form a sort of limestone paving, with sections of wooden

[39] Cf. E. Bernand, 'Epigraphic Documents', p. 147 *et seq.*
[40] *Ibid.*

[41] A. de Graauw, 'A 20th Century Engineer's Viewpoint', p. 55.

Photo 29: limestone paving in the column area

Photo 30: a red granite base of a statue with a Greek inscription

Photo 31: a timber section seen on the surface of the block and with small limestone fragments

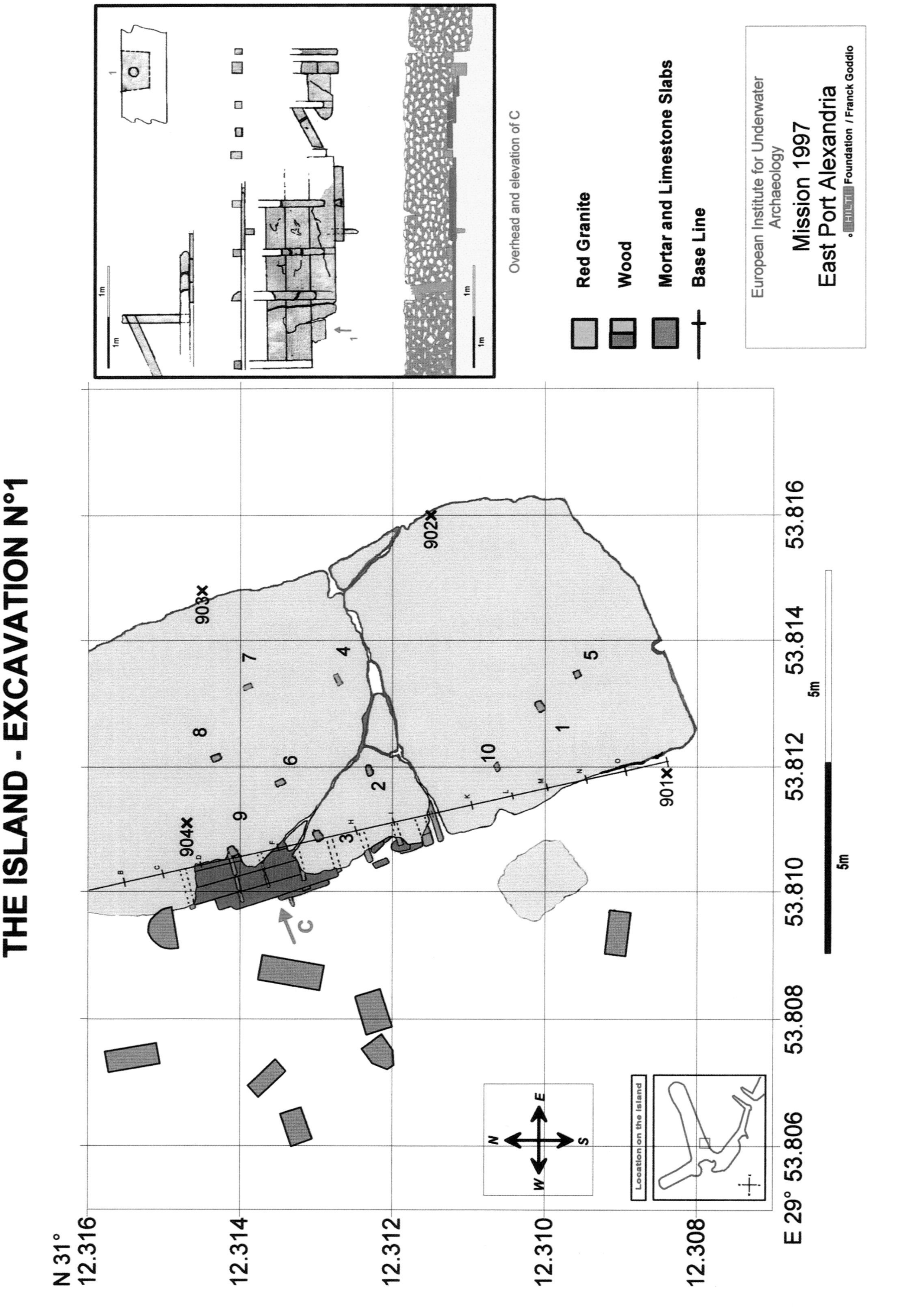

THE ISLAND - EXCAVATION N°1
N 31° 12.316
12.314
12.312
12.310
12.308
E 29° 53.806
53.808
53.810
53.812
53.814
53.816
901×
902×
903×
904×
C
5m
Location on the island
N
E
S
W
Overhead and elevation of C
1m
Red Granite
Wood
Mortar and Limestone Slabs
Base Line
European Institute for Underwater Archaeology
Mission 1997
East Port Alexandria
Foundation / Franck Goddio

beams about 10 x 12 cm. visible in several places.

Wooden framework shuttering in which to pour the mortar came to light under the block. It rested on the rocky bottom of the island. It is made of jointed planks 3 to 4 cms. thick, placed horizontally, fixed at the top by transversal beams, fixed together by dovetails. At times these beams are even placed on the natural rock, under the planks, in order to allow for the unevenness of the ground.

Vertical or sloping beams around the shuttering lend the whole more solidity. In spite of being broken it is these vertical beams which enabled the block to retain its cohesion. The sections of wood visible on the surface correspond in fact to the ends of the beams which go through the block. The state of conservation of the wood of the shuttering protected by the mortar or sediment is remarkable.

The lower layer of the mortar is attached to the wood of the shuttering.

It has been possible to see that the whole had been poured into shuttering as indicated by the vertical and smooth faces of the block where the marks from the planks are still sometimes visible. On the other hand, the wood of the shuttering in the vertical faces has disappeared; they may have been removed at the time after pouring or they were destroyed by rot through the action of marine worms and marine erosion.

The surface of the block is up to 40 cms. above the surrounding natural limestone where an overlay of river shingle stretches out. On this shingle is set a limestone paving. The thickness of the overlay and the paving is some 40 cms. Thus the paving is exactly at the same level as the surface of the block of mortar and small limestones. The same scheme seems to be applied over various parts of the island. The builders were thus able, in an efficient way and with economy of the means available, to level an important surface area of this island, whilst creating strong foundations which were capable of supporting the significant weight of any building.

Some blocks are only edged with paving on the side facing towards the inner side of the island; the face towards the harbour sometimes shows an occasionally important unevenness compared with the bottom. It is clear that these blocks are the remains of quays built along the same lines.

Analysis of the wood showed that the shuttering is made of pine (*Pinus* sp.). For the beams the wood has about 16 to 22 rings and 30 to 40 rings for the planks.

Dating by Carbon 14 was carried out in samples of wood from the shuttering which produced the following results:

Photo 32: wood from the shuttering under a mortar block

STRATIGRAPHY - I4

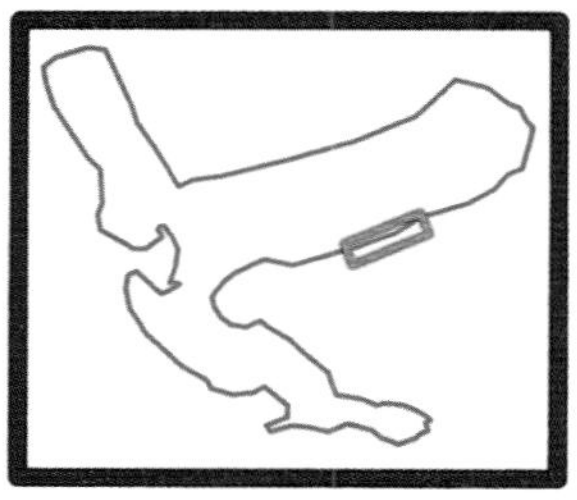

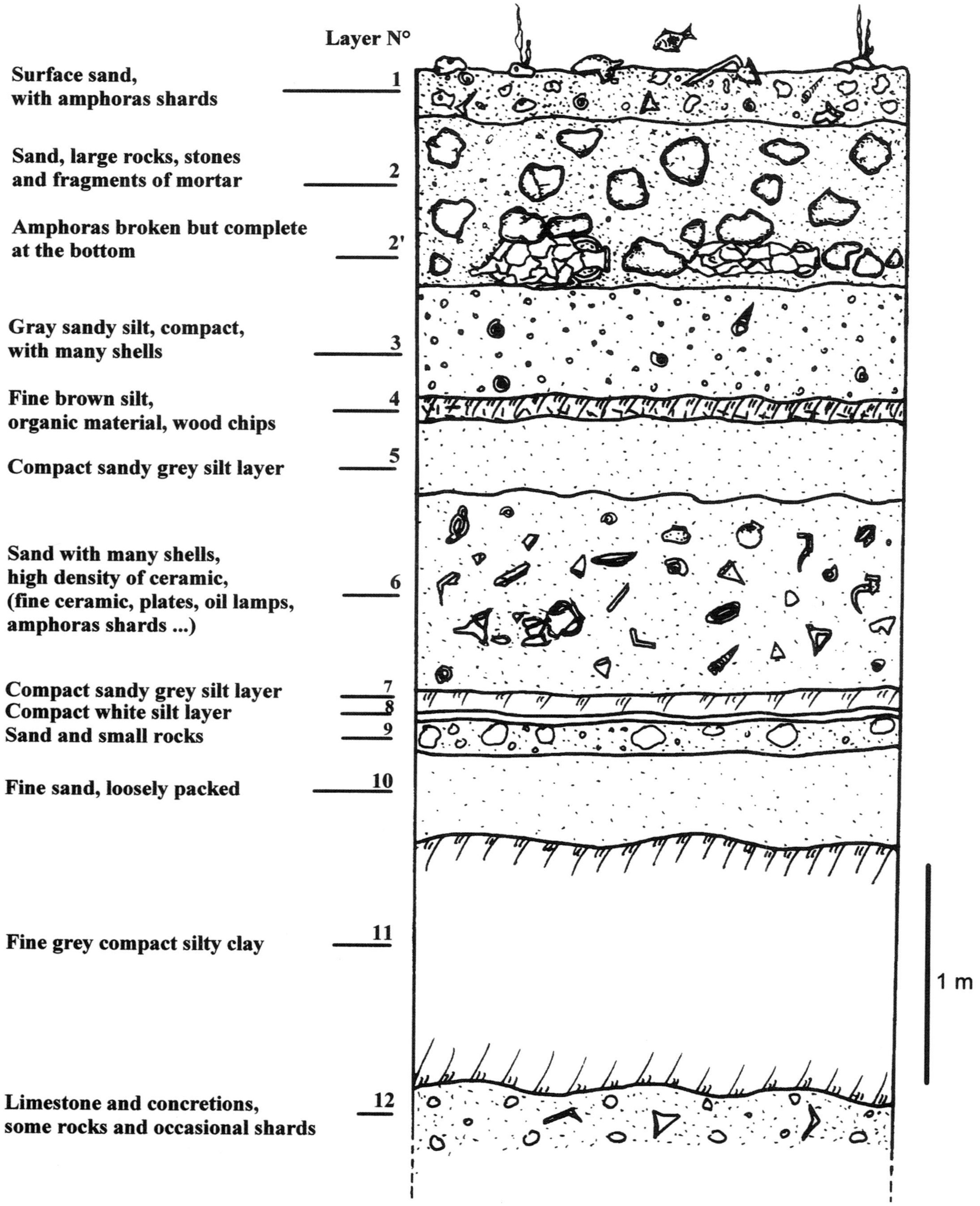
Layer N°
Surface sand, with amphoras shards 1
Sand, large rocks, stones and fragments of mortar 2
Amphoras broken but complete at the bottom 2'
Gray sandy silt, compact, with many shells 3
Fine brown silt, organic material, wood chips 4
Compact sandy grey silt layer 5
Sand with many shells, high density of ceramic, (fine ceramic, plates, oil lamps, amphoras shards ...) 6
Compact sandy grey silt layer 7
Compact white silt layer 8
Sand and small rocks 9
Fine sand, loosely packed 10
Fine grey compact silty clay 11
Limestone and concretions, some rocks and occasional shards 12
1 m

Calibrated Carbon 14 date: 390 cal. BC-130 cal. BC
The probability of the calibrated date being:
—between 390 cal. BC and 170 cal. BC is from 94.3 percent
—between 170 cal. BC and 130 BC is from 3.4 percent.
Conventional date: 250 BC ± 45 years.
Ref: Archéolabs 97/R1927C/1.

An analysis of the mortar was also carried out (ref. Archéolabs 97/R1927G).

It is a lime mortar with various elements (sand, gravel) and a binder of slaked lime or Ca(OH)2, transformed into carbonate.

The lime was made by heating limestone to between 900 and 1,000 degrees. This lime, known as quicklime, is slaked by water. When mixed with sand and water, it is transformed into carbonate in the presence of carbon dioxide gas in the air.

Microscopic examination showed that sand and gravel were often used which indicates they were brought from afar. It is thus deduced that they probably derive from alluvial deposits of a river draining sediments of various origins. Frequently, these elements were identified as grains of quartz and green coloured silica. The latter is probably responsible for giving the mortar its greenish appearance. Very fine sandstone, flakes of mica and pieces of oolithic limestone were also recovered in quantity.

The lime was most probably made close to the site, with relatively pure limestone, which was relatively pure and abundant in the neighbourhood as indicated by the fragments of oolithic limestone found in the mortar.

This lime mortar is of a good quality of production. After a long period in the open (perhaps six centuries) and a long period in the sea (probably sixteen centuries), it has only degraded a little and is still strong. The blending of the lime is comparatively well done and there are few poorly burnt limestone fragments.

On the south-west face of the block, lying on the paving, are three column shafts with Greek inscriptions in cartouches (C 308, C 309, C 310)[42] and three shafts of columns in red granite 100 cm. in diameter without any inscriptions.

12.2.1.4 Excavations in front of the central platform

An excavation (I4) was carried out in the small harbour in front of the central platform. This work allowed us to begin a stratigraphic study of this site. In effect this area had been filled in over the centuries by an important amount of sediment.

The excavation brought to light evidence for characteristic strata up to 4.5 m. in the sediment.

Ceramic material was uncovered in various levels which shows the different periods of occupation on this platform over the course of time.[43]

Carrying out archaeological excavations on such thicknesses creates technical difficulties under water. This excavation will be continued in further seasons.

12.2.1.5 Excavation of the north-west extremity

At the south-west end of the main branch is an important accumulation of about fifty column shafts. Their diameters, between 95 and 110 cm. make an impressive sight. The shafts are strewn over a sloping area from the limit of the island to one of the bottoms of the harbour. The harbour bottom at this point is sandy on the surface for 50 cm. Then mud (soundings made to 100 cm. in the mud below the layer of sand did not reach the natural rock). To the north-west of this zone, which corresponds to the mass of fallen rocks from the island, appears limestone pavement and important blocks of mortar. The total linear extent of these shafts is about 60 m.

[43] We thank Professor Grzegorz Majcherek of the Centre Polonais pour l'Archéologie du Caire for his expert examination of the ceramics from our excavations.

Photo 33: the important accumulation of columns at the south-west end

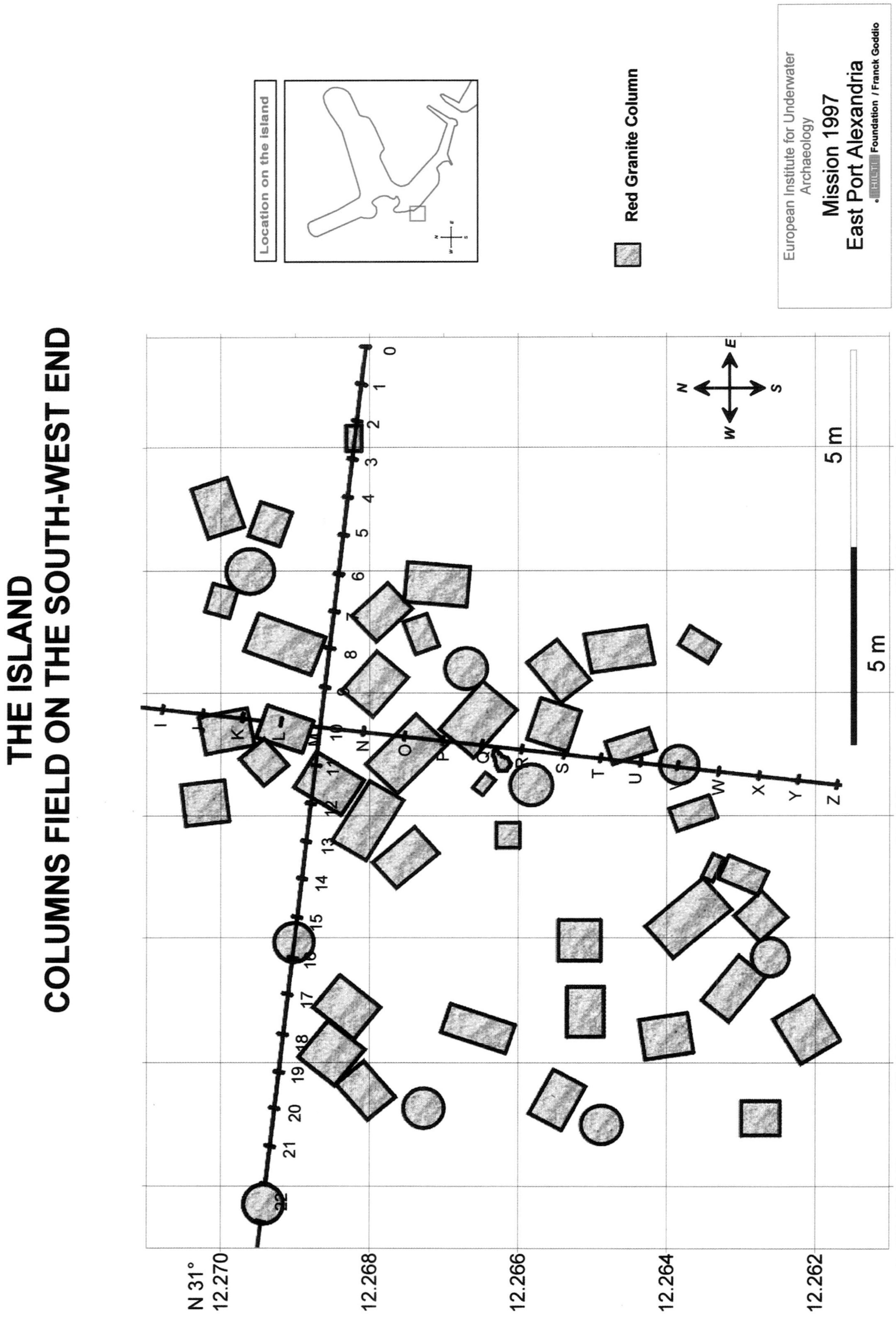
THE ISLAND
COLUMNS FIELD ON THE SOUTH-WEST END
Location on the island
Red Granite Column
European Institute for Underwater Archaeology
Mission 1997
East Port Alexandria
HILTI Foundation / Franck Goddio
5 m
5 m
N 31° 12.270
12.268
12.266
12.264
12.262
E 29° 53.750
53.752
53.754
53.756
53.758
53.760
53.762
N
S
E
W

It was noted that these column shafts were broken when they fell at this same place as is confirmed by the position and correspondence of the breaks on many of them. A systematic annotation of all the visible shafts was carried out after being cleaned of concretions.

12.2.1.6 Excavation (I3) of the south-west branch

Excavations were carried out on branch B3 of the island which heads towards the coastline.

The north-east face of this branch, which is to some degree strewn with debris, seems to be a gently curving long quay. This is particularly clear in one half where a group of mortar blocks and limestone are seen in good alignment still in their original positions. The inner facing is lined with paving.

At the end of the branch a small esplanade which has partly collapsed is very visible. It is from this espalanade that the jetty enclosing the harbour (H1) and defining the second channel (P2) is built out.
A column shaft of red granite 70 cm. in diameter was found at the end of the esplanade and the jetty.

The south-west face of the branch has collapsed along the whole of its length.

To the south-east of the great concentration of column shafts stretches a vast area covered with paving, or sometimes limestone flags, about 40 x 40 cm. And even 120 x 55 cm. In some places there are the remains of mortar.

This esplanade has collapsed towards the south-west in the direction of a sandy seabed of the harbour. This is confirmed by the composition of the debris. In effect it is formed from the same paving and flagstones as those that are still to be seen in place, mixed up with blocks of mortar and limestone as well as architectural items, much broken, of red and grey granite, basalt, quartzite and limestone blocks.

At the place where the esplanade is in a good condition there are very few remains to be found.

At the limit between the flagstones still in place and the collapsed material two sphinxes came to light, buried beneath about 30 cm. of paving and small fragments of blocks of granite and quartzite. There was a space of 3.5 m. between them and they both lay parallel, turned onto their right sides. Their left sides which were turned towards the surface were completely covered by a fine layer of very hard, calcareous algae deposits. The left sides were almost free of any concretions. Sphinx no. 1185[44] lay at an angle of 125° true north and sphinx no. 1198[45] at 127°.

They were in a remarkably well preserved condition.

Sphinx no. 1185, which was more to the north, is in grey granite. There was some damage on the right side on the cheek and at the base, which probably happened at the time of its fall.

Sphinx no. 1198 is diorite and the ends of its two front paws are broken. The rest of the sculpture is in a very good condition.

[44] Cf. Z. Kiss, 'Sculptures', p. 173.
[45] *Ibid.*, p. 169.

Photo 34: the field of columns

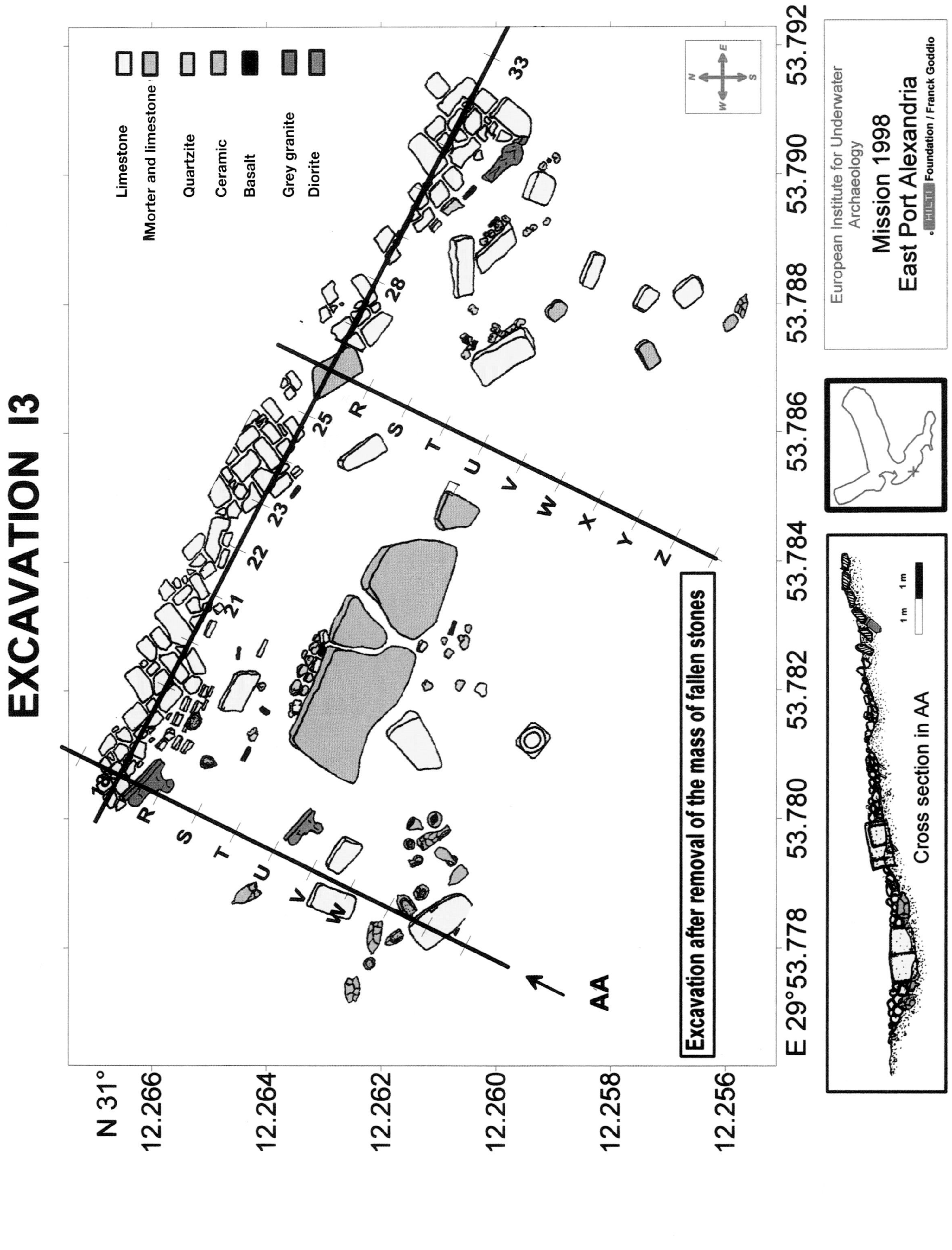
EXCAVATION I3
Limestone
Morter and limestone
Quartzite
Ceramic
Basalt
Grey granite
Diorite
Excavation after removal of the mass of fallen stones
AA
N 31°
12.266
12.264
12.262
12.260
12.258
12.256
E 29°53.778
53.780
53.782
53.784
53.786
53.788
53.790
53.792
European Institute for Underwater Archaeology
Mission 1998
East Port Alexandria
© HILTI Foundation / Franck Goddio
Cross section in AA
1 m
1 m

The state of the faces of the two sphinxes shows no hammer marks and this suggests that they were not wilfully destroyed. One may thus reasonably conclude that their fall was due to a natural cause.

On the axis of the two sphinxes, towards 125°, at a distance of 16 m. a statue (no. 1199)[46] made of grey granite was discovered. It too was situated at the end of the collapsed area and the conserved part of the paved platform. It lay with its face to the ground, partly covered by some paving stones. A calcareous crust had fixed the paving to the statue and completely hidden it. The statue was oriented with its head towards 130°. It was in a very good state of preservation.

The excavation also brought to light just under the collapsed material some ceramics[47] dating from the 1st century BC-2nd century AD crushed under the blocks. This gives us an indicator for the period after which an earthquake must have occurred to cause the collapse of this platform.

The remains of this branch of the island are covered with more irregular and smaller paving stones. A small landing stage made of mortar blocks and limestone, in a very bad condition, came to light on the inner third of the branch.

[46] Cf. F. Dunand, 'Priest ...', p. 189 *et seq*.

[47] Expert analysis by Professor Grzegorz Majcherek of the Centre Polonais pour l'Archéologie du Caire

12.2.1.7 Remains discovered in the little harbour (H1) of the island

A statue of white marble (no. 1204) was discovered during surveys in the small harbour.

Near to sea wall J4 in this harbour an important wreck (E1) of a ship was discovered, probably dating according to C14 analyses of wood samples from the 1st century BC-1st century AD. Remains of the wood which were well preserved in the mud have enabled a detailed study. This wreck will be the subject of a separate publication.

Excavations made in this small harbour, along the quays (S2) to the south and on the esplanade of the central branch (I4) have produced ceramic material whose dating, according to stratigraphy, is spread between the 3rd century BC to the 4th century AD.[48]

12.2.1.8 Some general remarks

We have been able to see that the blocks of mortar found in the centre of the island do not seem to indicate any remains of wood below them. This might indicate different building conditions.[49]

[48] *Ibid.*

[49] Cf. A. de Graauw, 'A 20th Century Engineer's Viewpoint', p. 55.

Photo 35: discovery of the grey granite statue no. 1199

Photo 36: small sphinx with diver

Photo 37: large sphinx with diver under water

The north face of the island, exposed to the swell of the open sea is protected for the whole of its length by important limestone blocks, sometimes dressed (110 x 50 x 50 cm. on average). Behind these blocks towards the inner part of the island, there are other limestone blocks, irregular and of smaller size.

The shores of the island facing harbour H2 have been fitted out with quays made of small limestones covered in a lime mortar.

One may note that, over the whole of the island, generally, the architectural remains are located to the south-west near the large blocks of mortar.

During excavations on the island eight column shafts bearing Greek inscriptions in cartouches, as well as two blocks in red granite with hieroglyphics, were discovered. The underwater moulding method gave satisfactory results f.. these items which were difficult to read under water.[50]

12.3 Comparison with ancient texts

This island is the only one in the whole area; all other land, except the reefs or harbour infrastructures now under water, are linked to the ancient shoreline.

This island can only correspond to the island of Antirhodos, as mentioned by Strabo[51] in his description:

> ... the private property of the kings, as also Antirhodos, an isle lying off the artificial harbour, which has both a royal palace and a small harbour.

Is it possible to determine the position of the royal palace seen by Strabo?

—the north-west branch does not have any remains of a foundation and is only a paved mole.

—the south–east branch presents on its north-east side a quay made of mortar and small pieces of limestone which is still quite visible. On the south-west is a small paved platform of limestone without any remains of foundations over two-thirds of its breadth. Further to the south-west remains of buildings cover it over a band about twenty metres wide at its maximum. It was here that the sphinxes no. 1185 and no. 1198 and statue no. 1199 were found on the edge of a mass of fallen rock. It thus seems very likely that the royal palace cited by Strabo was built in this cramped place.

—the main branch lends itself particularly well to an important building. The vast central esplanade, with its foundations dating to the 3rd-2nd centuries before our era, could easily accommodate a palace. The density of architectural remains in this place is certainly also revealing. These ruins are extended on each side of the platform by remains which are aligned for some 350 metres along the whole length of the branch.

The esplanade points to the small inner harbour and faces exactly the obelisks called 'Cleopatra's Needles, which marked the entrance to the Kaisarion.

The 'small harbour' referred to by Strabo indeed seems to have been the magnificent sheltered harbour formed between the two branches of the island and the jetty to the south-east. Its sides were covered by quays and the grand esplanade. Our work shows that this island was probably developed before the founding of Alexandria and that the great works were then carried out there towards the middle of the 3rd century BC. The importance of this island seems to have lasted beyond the end of the Ptolemies as shown by the presence of statue bases dating from the time of Commodus and Caracalla. This may be explained by its strategic position.

13. The ancient shoreline

13.1. Description

Before undertaking our topographical work, the hypothesis presented itself of the possibility of finding again the ancient shoreline. We knew that the sea had encroached on

Photo 38: the shoreline by the site of Cleopatra's Needle

[50] Cf. E. Bernand, 'Epigraphic Documents', p. 143, and J Yoyotte, '*Pharaonica*', p. 223 *et seq.*

[51] Cf. *'Testimonia'*, no. 28, p. 94.

Fig 7: colour drawing by Dejuine showing the obelisk

THE ANCIENT SEASHORE

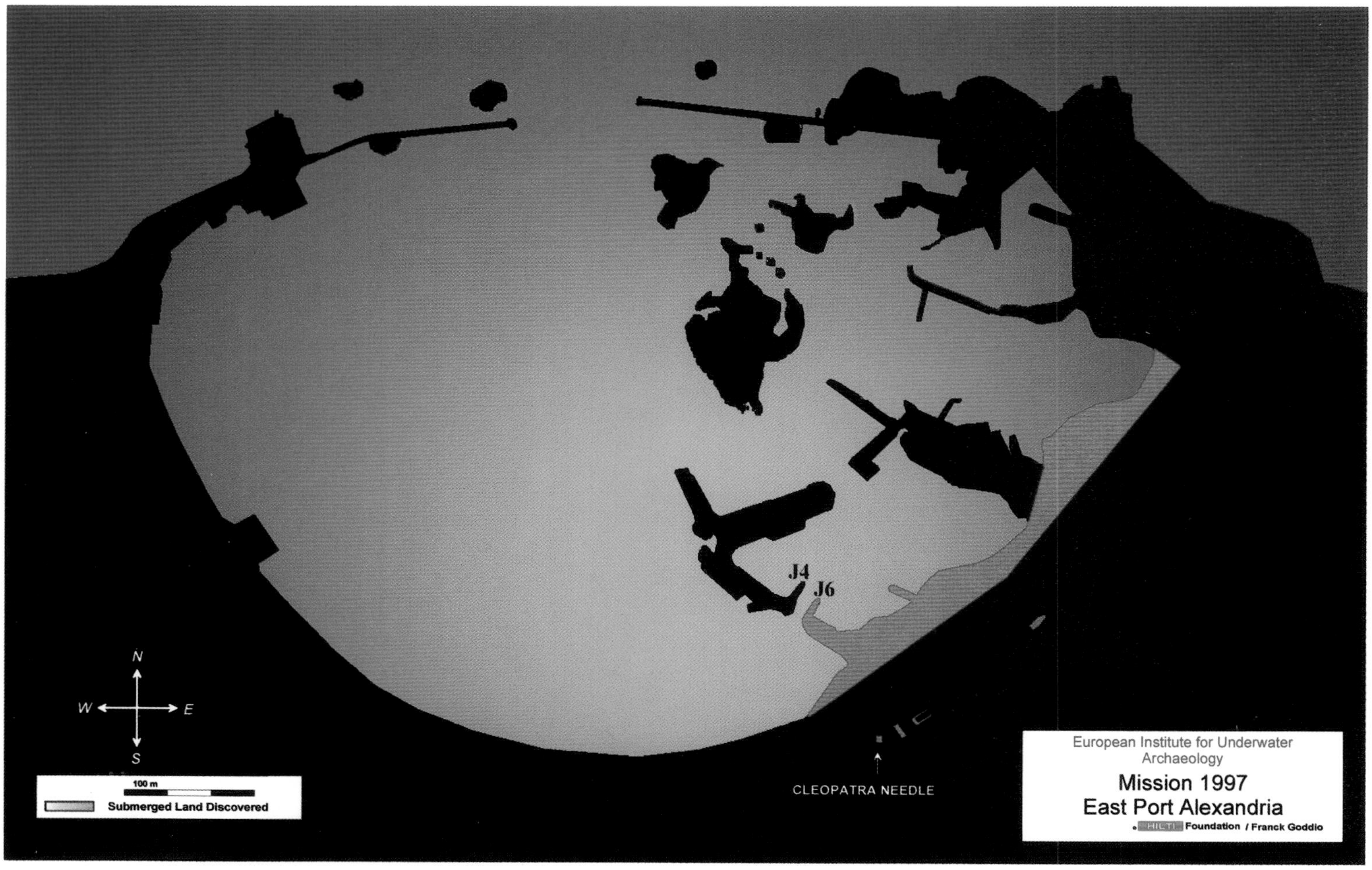

Photo 39: the coast with one of Cleopatra's Needles about 1860-1870

the land in the 4th-5th centuries. On the other hand, the embankments built at the end of the 19th century and at the beginning of the 20th century could have gained over the sea more than the advance the sea itself had made.

On the plan entitled 'The Ancient Coastline, we can measure the site of the obelisk shown in the photos above (cf. §4, p. 9) is situated about 120 metres from the actual shore[52] (the limit of the area shown in black). Thus these photos show that in about 1870 the seashore was only a few metres from this monument. The relative position of the shore and the obelisk had moreover also been shown by Dejuine between 1798-1801.

This shows that the ballast brought in when the work was carried out, after the obelisk was removed to build the 'Corniche', thus encroached onto the sea by a distance of 120 metres.

Fortunately this advance of the sea due to the development work of the 19th-20th centuries has not covered entirely the area submerged after the subsidence and collapse which occurred after the 4th-5th centuries of our era.

In fact the ancient coastline can be seen under the water joining Cape Lochias to the peninsula, then extending in the direction of the south-west as far as the middle of the Magnus Portus, where it in effect disappears under the modern earthworks of the Corniche.

This ancient coast is visible over all of the eastern part of the Magnus Portus.

At different places remains of quays and esplanades are visible. At the level of the island an important mole (J6) paved with limestone extends in the direction of the south-east branch of this island. Some slabs are 100 cm. long by 50 cm. wide.

The mole, which is parallel to the peninsula, is 130 m. long and 30 m. wide. It forms an elbow towards the north-east in front of the jetty of the island (J4).

[52] Cf. §4.

The coast is also parallel to the main branch of the island and to the large mole at the end of the peninsula.

13.2 Remains discovered

The ancient coast is strewn with numerous remains. Several hundred artefacts were cleared of their concretions for study and precise plotting.

Four important concentrations could be identified:

—at the north of the peninsula, where, on an area paved with limestone, were shafts of columns of red granite from 90 cm. in diameter and two remarkable items of statuary:

—a representation of a snake in the round in grey granite (no. 1182)[53]

—a small statue of an ibis in limestone (no. 1181)[54]

—in the south of the peninsula, where over a length of some 100m., there is an accumulation of column shafts (90 cm. in diameter), capitals and bases in red granite, sections of columns (from 50 cm. in diameter) and marble lintels, blocks of limestone as well as blocks of quartzite (especially no. 755). Three red granite beams bore hieroglyphic texts. (nos. 505, 771, 780).

An excavation was carried out over part of this area. It showed a coherent pattern of the deposit which seemed to indicate that the important remains uncovered came from a building which collapsed in place.

[53] Cf. Z. Kiss, 'The Sculptures', p. 181.
[54] *Ibid.*

Photo 40: the ibis with a diver under water

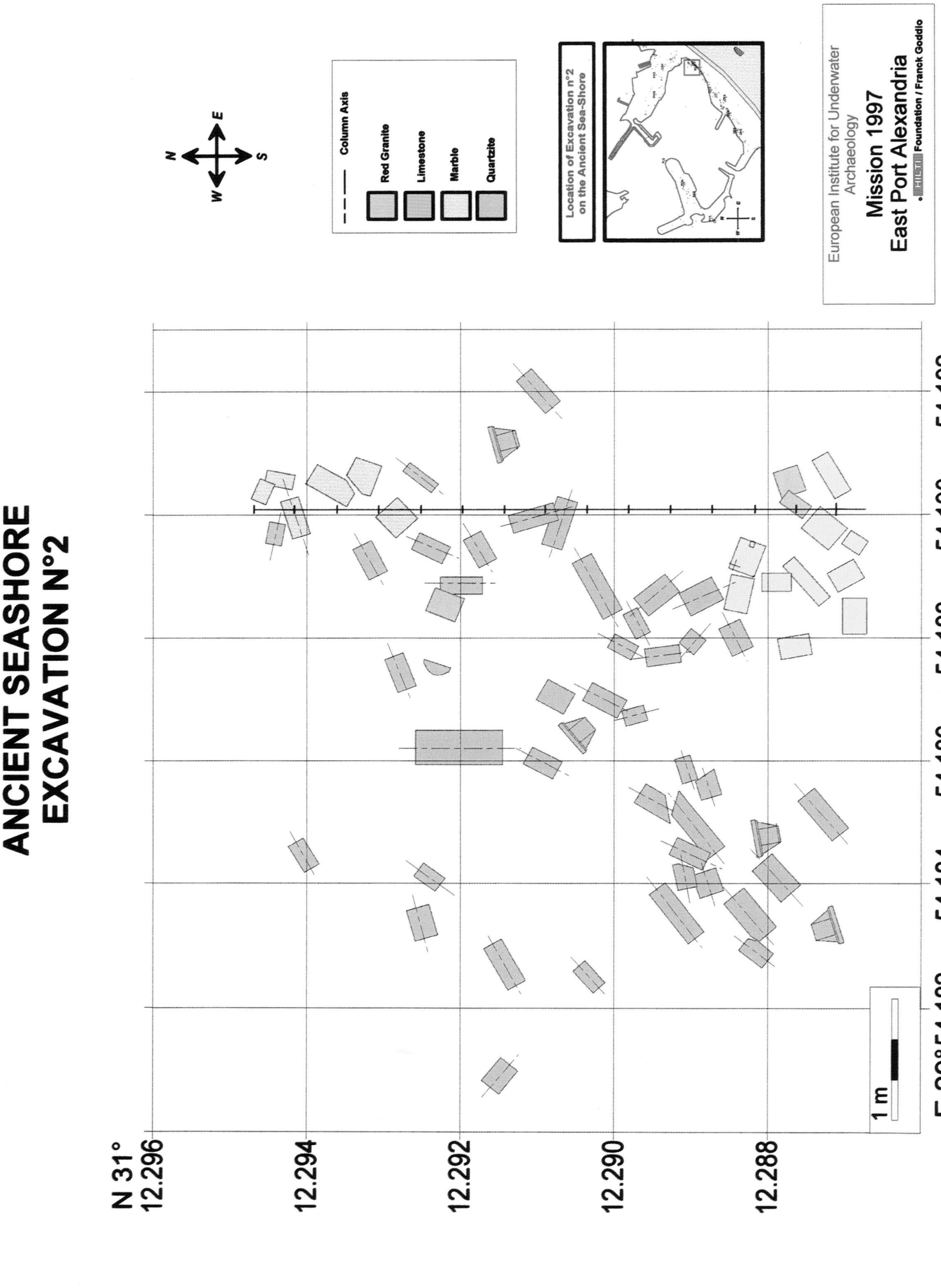

ANCIENT SEASHORE
EXCAVATION N°2
N
E
S
W
Column Axis
Red Granite
Limestone
Marble
Quartzite
Location of Excavation n°2 on the Ancient Sea-Shore
European Institute for Underwater Archaeology
Mission 1997
East Port Alexandria
HILTI Foundation / Franck Goddio
N 31° 12.296
12.294
12.292
12.290
12.288
E 29°54.182
54.184
54.186
54.188
54.190
54.192
1 m

—towards the central area between the peninsula and the big mole, in front of the jetty which stretched from the shore towards the north-west, there extended a vast area paved with limestone, where over 200 m. lay red granite shafts of columns (with diameters varying between 70 cm. and 90 cm.), blocks of red and grey granite and blocks of limestone, quartzite and basalt.

In this area some remarkable items have been revealed, such as:

—a basalt sphinx (no. 778)[55]
—grooved Doric type column shafts
—blocks of granite with hieroglyphics[56]
—the north of the large mole in an area paved with limestone are groups of column shafts in red granite, blocks of grey and red basalt granites, granite and basalt capitals, and items of statuary.

An excavation was carried out in this area which for this zone did not produce any coherence with regard to the position of the remains discovered. It may be that it was a site where quarrymen acted ruthlessly before the collapse of the coastline. It should be noted, however, that it was in this place that an important block of mortar was discovered, with small pieces of limestone, set in the paving and in which was embedded a red granite parallelepiped block which may indicate the presence of a vestige of the foundation of some building.

Some remarkable items came to light during this excavation, such as the human head adorned with a *nemes*[57] (no. 1015), a statue base with a fragment of a foot no. 781[58] and a head of a falcon,[59] no. 795.

[55] Cf. Zsolt, Kiss, 'The Sculptures, p. 174.
[56] Cf. J. Yoyotte, '*Pharaonica*', p. 223.
[57] Cf. Z. Kiss, 'The Sculptures, p. 175.
[58] Cf. J. Yoyotte, '*Pharaonica*', p. 232.
[59] Cf. J. Yoyotte, 'A Colossal Sphinx', p. 223.

Photo 42: red granite column and capital

Photo 43: red granite capital

Photo 41: the red granite column field

Photo 44: a fluted column shaft in red granite

ANCIENT SEASHORE
EXCAVATION N°1

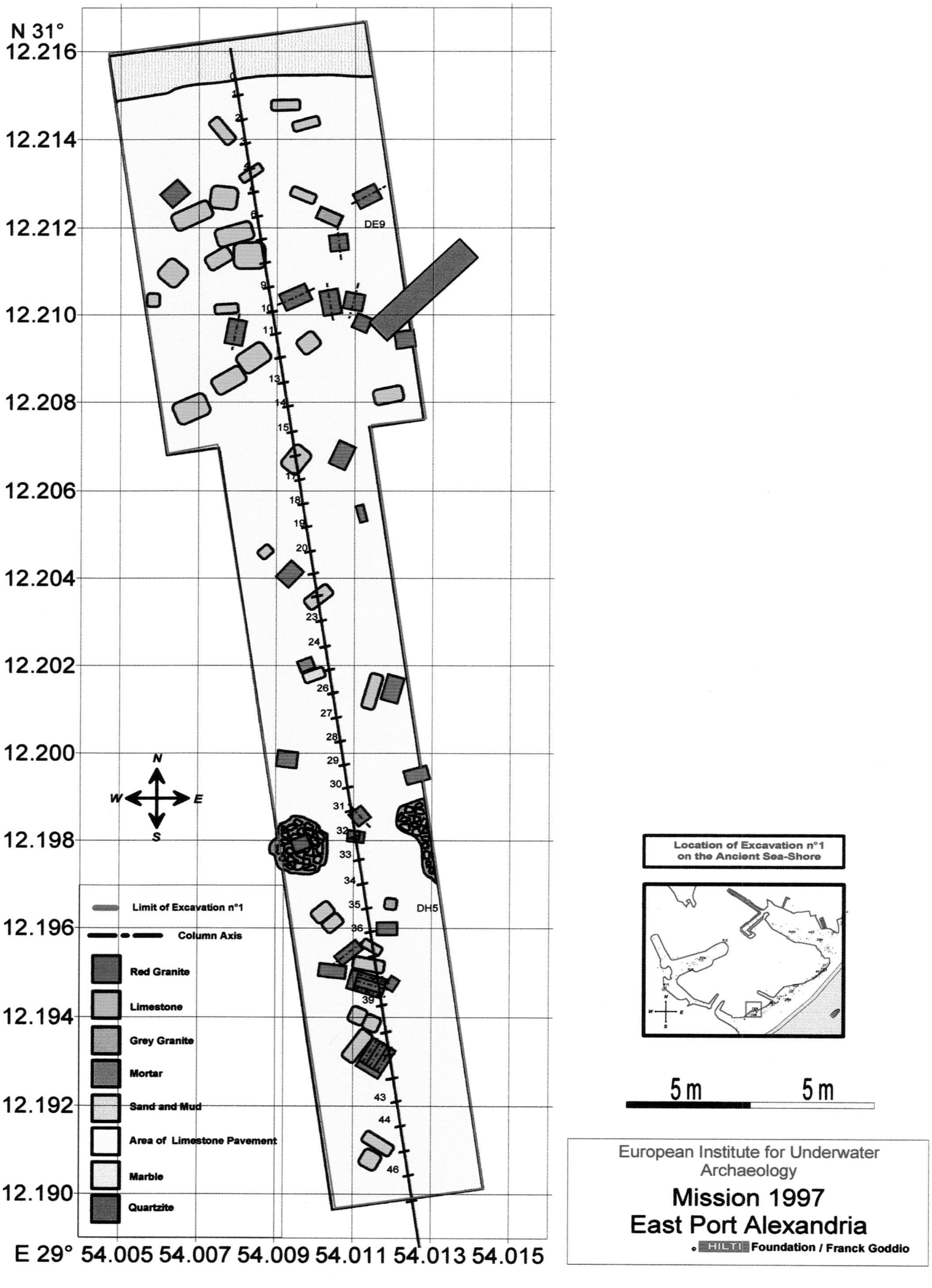
N 31°
12.216
12.214
12.212
12.210
12.208
12.206
12.204
12.202
12.200
12.198
12.196
12.194
12.192
12.190
E 29° 54.005 54.007 54.009 54.011 54.013 54.015
DE9
DH5
N
W
E
S
Limit of Excavation n°1
Column Axis
Red Granite
Limestone
Grey Granite
Mortar
Sand and Mud
Area of Limestone Pavement
Marble
Quartzite
Location of Excavation n°1 on the Ancient Sea-Shore
5 m
5 m
European Institute for Underwater Archaeology
Mission 1997
East Port Alexandria
HILTI Foundation / Franck Goddio

Along the whole length of the shoreline twenty precise excavations were carried out, each over an area of 9 sq. m., and all revealed the existence of paving or limestone paving stones. The two areas, now identified, which are covered with fine limestone flagstones, are each located at one end of the coastline: one near to Cape Lochias, the other at the base of the large mole.

13.3 Comparison with ancient texts

This part of the ancient coast provides a special interest as, thanks to the texts, we know that palaces were erected here.

Strabo[60] is quite precise and loquacious about their position:

> And the city contains most beautiful public precincts and also the royal palaces, which constitute one-fourth or even one-third of the whole circuit of the city; for just as each of the kings, from love of splendour, was wont to add some adornment to the public monuments, so also he would invest himself at his own expense with a residence, in addition to those already built, so that now, to quote the words of the poet "there is building upon building".[61] *All, however, are connected with one another and the harbour, even those that lie outside the harbour.*

> The author adds to this description:[62]

> … and on sailing into the harbour *one comes, on the left, to the inner royal palaces, which are continuous with those on Lochias and have groves and numerous lodges painted in various colours.*

The numerous remains uncovered during these excavations and soundings in the area bear witness to the density and importance of monuments erected along the shoreline to the east of the Magnus Portus.

Here the royal buildings (*basileia*) were located. As Prof. J. Yoyotte[63] has noted, these 'inner' *basileia*, standing on the shore at the base of Cape Lochias, joined the *basileion* of this cape to the vast quarter of *basileia* which during the Roman period was known as Brucheion.

[60] Cf. '*'Testimonia"*, no. 28, p. 94.
[61] Homer, *Odyssey*, XVII, 226.
[62] Cf. '*'Testimonia"*, no. 28, p. 94.
[63] Jean Yoyotte, Pascal Charvet, Stéphane Gompertz, *Strabon; le voyage en Egypte*, NiL éditons, Paris, 1997, p. 88.

Strabo[64] (as already shown) also gives us in succinct form the names of the remarkable buildings visible during his time in this area and mentions the position of the Emporion:

> Above the artificial harbour lies the theatre; *then the Poseidium—an elbow, as it were, projecting from the Emporium, as it is called*, and containing a temple of Poseidon. To this elbow of land Antony added a mole projecting still farther, into the middle of a harbour, and on the extremity of it built a royal lodge which he called Timonium. This was his last act, when, forsaken by his friends, he sailed away to Alexandria after his misfortune at Actium, having chosen to live the life of a Timon the rest of his days, which he intended to spend in solitude from all those friends. *Then one comes to the Caesarium and the Emporion and the warehouses*; and after these to the ship-houses, which extend as far as the Heptastadium. So much for the Great Harbour and its surroundings.

[64] Cf. '*Testimonia'*, no. 28, p. 94.

Photo 45: limestone paving

Photo 46: red granite block with hieroglyphs

Photo 48: releasing the grey granite statue

Photo 47: head of a statue with *nemes*

Photo 49: diver taking notes

14. The third large harbour

14.1 Description

This harbour, the most important in the whole of the Magnus Portus, is shaped like a parallelogram, about 500 m. by 320 m. and with an area of 16 hectares.

It is flanked by the peninsula with its large mole and esplanade, then by the island and finally by the shore and its mole to the south-west.

Its main channel (P1) is located on the north-east side, between the tip of the island and the esplanade adjacent to the mole on the peninsula. The channel is 80 m. wide.

It is protected from the swell by the large reef. It faces the prevailing winds. Thus this harbour presents easy access for vessels and small craft under sail.

A second channel (P2) has been created on the south-west side. This secondary channel is in fact about 40 m. wide, defined by the jetty (J4) running from the tip of the island and by the bend of the important mole (J6) joining the coast. This construction faces the south-west. The channel allows the passage of water into the harbour. Various soundings were made in this area in order to determine exactly the width of the channel and the nature of the bottom at this point.

Inside the harbour, a jetty (J5), 80 m. long and 15 m. wide and parallel to the peninsula forms with the mole (J6) to the south-west, a well-protected haven (H2). The jetty is built of limestone blocks.

Another small harbour (H1) is formed by the two main branches of the island and its jetty (J4); this small harbour is sheltered perfectly from the swell and the waves.

The whole of the bottom of the harbour is mud and muddy sand.

14.2 Remains discovered

A large number of amphorae, complete or broken, and fragments are strewn over the bottom of the harbour.

Some particularly important concentrations of these artefacts were noted in the following areas:

—in the small harbour of the island, on a mud bottom

—in the south-west channel, between the island and the mole running from the ancient coastline; the bottoms at these points are very muddy.

—all along the ancient coastline

—along the rocky areas of the south-west face of the peninsula.

THE THIRD HARBOUR

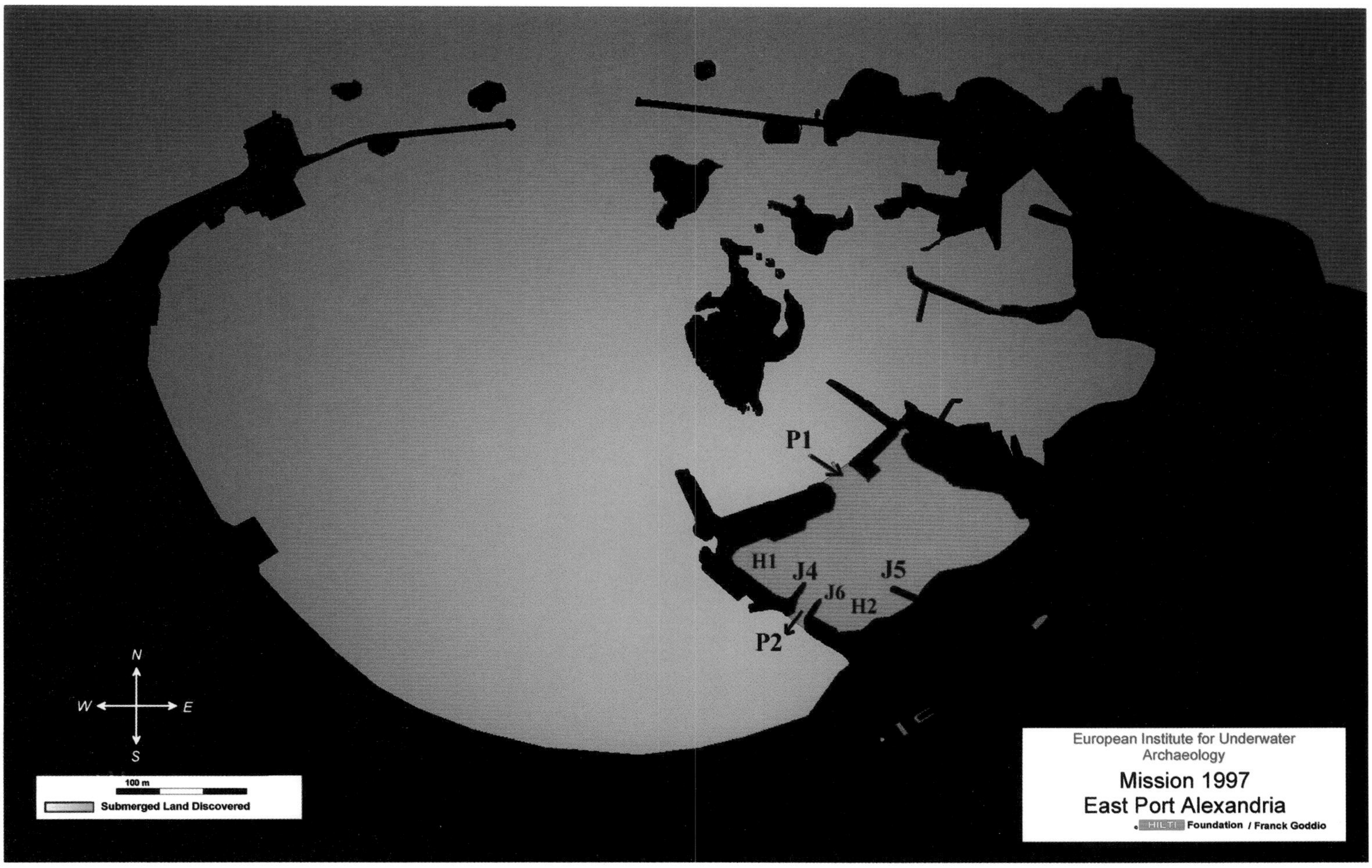

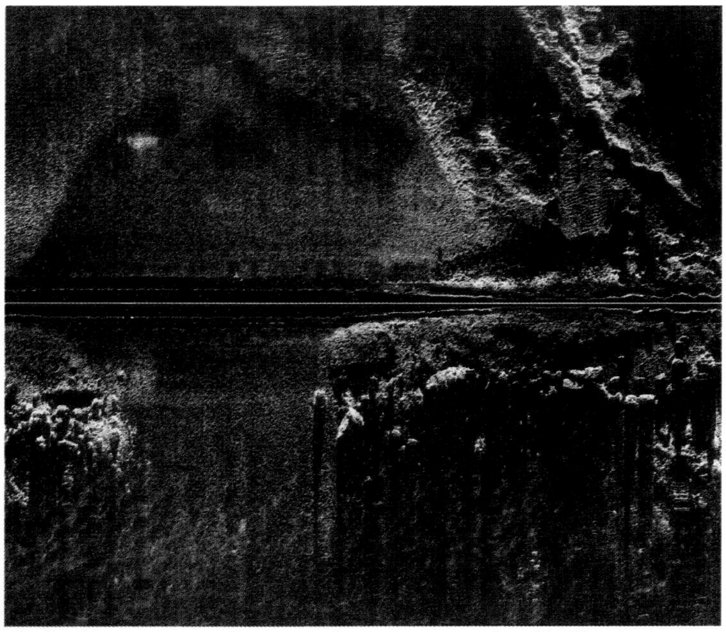

Fig 8: side scan sonar image at the entrance to the third harbour

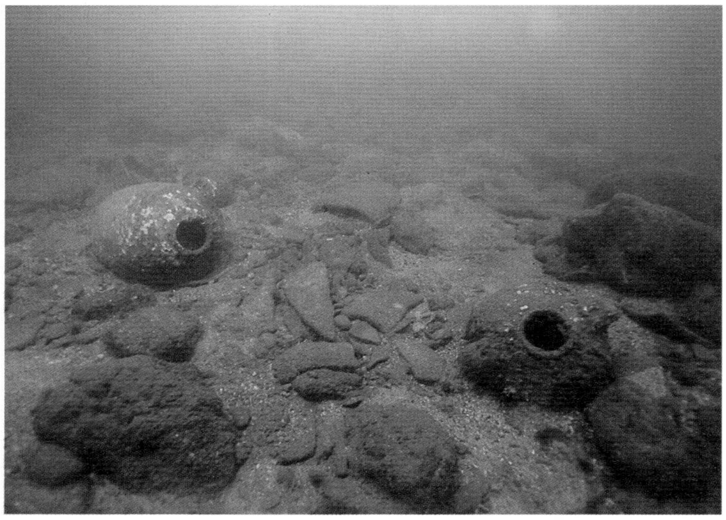

Photo 50: amphorae on the bottom of the harbour

Ancient wooden and lead anchor stocks were also found on the bottom of the harbour.

If one considers all the architectural remains lying around this harbour, one cannot but be struck by their number and position. In effect, one notes that this harbour was completely surrounded by monuments and colonnades. The sight of this harbour with its strictly geometrical layout, lined with important temples and palaces must have been striking.

14-3 Comparison with ancient texts

There exists an interesting notice of this harbour by Pliny.[65]

> There are two other obelisks at Alexandria in the precinct of the temple of Caesar near the harbour. These were cut by King Mesphres and measure 42 cubits.

This refers to the third harbour, as it has already been possible to locate these obelisks, the Cleopatra's Needles, on our map facing the mole, not far from the shore.

Philo of Alexandria,[66] describing the Kaisarion, mentions that this temple is situated : 'facing the harbours famed for their excellent moorage ...'

Moreover, Strabo[67] also mentions, as we have seen, that there were several harbours in the Magnus Portus. It must therefore refer, to among others, this magnificent harbour.

---

[65] Cf. *'Testimonia'*, no. 49, p. 112.
[66] Cf. *'Testimonia'*, no. 44, p. 109.
[67] Cf. *'Testimonia'*, no. 28, p. 94.

A 20TH CENTURY ENGINEER'S VIEWPOINT OF THE EASTERN HARBOUR OF ALEXANDRIA

Antoine de Graauw

a1. INTRODUCTION

The point of view of a specialist in harbour construction is based on the following considerations:[1]

Overall plan. The plan of a harbour depends on the conditions for navigation (winds, swell) and the types of ship which use it (sail, oar). The size of ships define the acceptable choppiness of the sea arising from the swell and the eventual necessity of building a defensive breakwater against storms. The number of ships which use the harbour defines the length of the quays and the surface area of the required basins.

Harbour structures. The draught of ships defines the depth at the quayside and thus the height and the structure of the latter. Materials locally available (wood, stone, mortar) as well as the construction methods define the specific structures for any place at any time.

2. OVERALL PLAN

Let us begin with what is of interest to all ships, the wind and swell (see the oceanographic conditions in the table, p. 57). It would be reasonable to assume that the conditions for wind and swell have varied little between ancient times and our own. Actual statistics show that the prevailing winds (and swell) in the open sea at Alexandria come from the sector west to north (more that 50 percent of the time as an annual average and 70 to 90 percent of the time in the summer months from June to September). A second important direction is that from north to east (20 to 30 percent of the time in the winter months from October to May). This last directional sector had a considerable importance for the harbour, as from it stems the choice for a double harbour.

The idea of constructing a double harbour is motivated by the presence of two main directions for wind and swell in the open sea. In this case, which is quite common, it is interesting to be able to move ships from one shelter to another to afford them better protection against rough water in all conditions. After the Heptstadion was built, the isle of Pharos became a peninsula which answered perfectly this criterion:

—to the west, the harbour of Eunostos would be built
—to the east would be built the Eastern Harbour.

And, with great nicety, the transfer of ships could be made without going out to sea by way of the channels cutting through the Heptstadion. Nevertheless it is to be noted that the western part of the roads of Alexandria must have begun progressively to fill with sand after the construction of the Heptastadion to end up with the familiar curved coastline that we know today in this part of the roads.

The first logical reaction would be to envisage the positioning of the harbour against the Heptastadion in the shelter of the Pharos island, in the place where today the fishermen shelter from the prevailing winds of the west to north sector. This purely technical argument does not seem to have prevailed as the three harbours discovered are situated quite the other way, under Cape Lochias (now Cape Silsileh) where the royal palace was. The eastern part of the roads of Alexandria is relatively more exposed to the swell of the open sea to the NW and this has necessitated the building of a protective sea wall to complete the natural protection offered by the reefs which broke the surface at that time.

Access to the harbours must thus have been gained by passing the reefs to the west and the south. This would allow entry with a following wind into the roads before furling sail and then to manoeuvre by oar towards the NE to regain entry to one of the three harbours (see p. 54).

Turning now to the types of vessel that used the harbour, although some commercial vessels of great size have been identified, fleets of warships are better known.

At the time when the Romans and Carthaginians faced each other with triremes and quinquiremes in the eastern Mediterranean (the battle of Aegates in 241 BC), the Macedonians and Alexandrians were building giant galleys the like of which had never been seen. These 'maxi' vessels seem to have existed for several centuries as Antony lined up a certain number of them to face the Romans at the battle of Actium (2 September 31 BC). The most productive without doubt had been Ptolemy II who on his death (in 246 BC) left a considerable war fleet:

- 2 '30' (i.e., 30 rowers a side)
- 1 '20'

[1] Mr de Graauw is a maritime harbour engineer, SOGREAH Ingénierie, Grenoble, France.

Figure 9 - **HARBOUR LAYOUT**

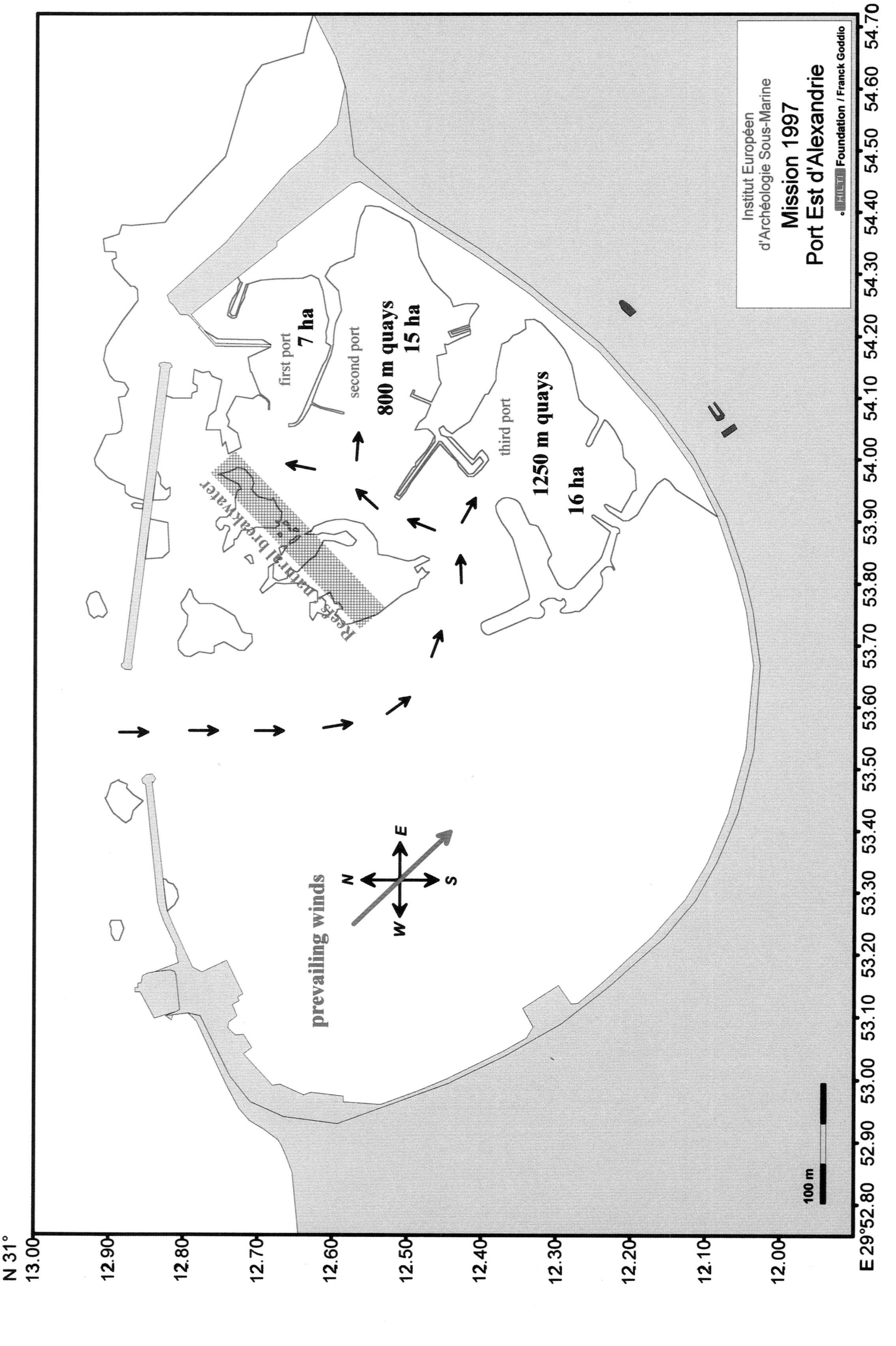
first port
7 ha
second port
800 m quays
15 ha
third port
1250 m quays
16 ha
Reefs, natural breakwater
prevailing winds
N
E
S
W
100 m
Institut Européen
d'Archéologie Sous-Marine
Mission 1997
Port Est d'Alexandrie
HILTI Foundation / Franck Goddio
N 31°
13.00
12.90
12.80
12.70
12.60
12.50
12.40
12.30
12.20
12.10
12.00
E 29°52.80
52.90
53.00
53.10
53.20
53.30
53.40
53.50
53.60
53.70
53.80
53.90
54.00
54.10
54.20
54.30
54.40
54.50
54.60
54.70

- 4 '13'
- '12'
- 14 '11'
- 67 '9' to '7'
- 22 '6' and '5' (quinquiremes)
- 4 '3' (triremes)
  150 (?) '2' (biremes)

That is a total of a dozen large vessels (from 50 x 10 m. to 70 x 20 m.), 80 medium sized ships (45 x 8.5 m.) and 175 small ships (from 20 x 2.5 m. to 35 x 5 m.), making about 265 ships.

This number is of the same order as those met with in other periods. The fleet of Pompey for his war against the pirates (in 67 to 66 BC) was made up of 200 quinquiremes and 30 triremes (Guillerm 1995, 82) and Antony's fleet for the battle of Actium had 220 ships (his biggest ship was a '10'). It is also known that at other times the Alexandrian fleet was much reduced. The fleet burnt by Caesar at the battle of Alexandria (in 48 BC) consisted of 50 triremes and quinquiremes, 22 other ships and 38 vessels beached in the arsenals (Bernand 1998, 311).

On the basis of the ideas outlined in our overall plan for the harbour, we have tried to fit into the harbours discovered space for all the ships in the fleet of Ptolemy II. The surface areas of the waters are approximately as follows:

- first harbour: about 7 hectares
- second harbour: about 15 hectares with close to 800 m. length of quays probable
- third harbour: about 16 hectares with close to 1,250 m. length of quays probable

It seems likely that it was possible to shelter easily the 10 large vessels mentioned above in the first harbour. The 80 medium sized vessels as well as the 25 small ones could be lined up side by side, stern to quay, in the second harbour. The remaining 150 small ships could be sheltered in the third harbour where the length of quay would allow up to 250 quinquiremes to be welcomed.

By way of comparison, one might also mention here the sizes of other major ports of antiquity (Guillerm 1995, 84, Redde 1986, Vitruvius 1986).

In the Piraeus at Athens there was:

Kantaros (commercial): 1,000 x 500 m. (50 hectares, 100 (?) covered berths
Zea (warships): circular, 300 m. in diameter (7 hectares), 196 covered berths
Mucnychia: 82 covered berths (about 5 hectares)

- Carthage:

Commercial harbour: 500 x 300 m. (15 hectares) in addition to the lake of Tunis
Cothon (warships): circular, 330 m. in diameter with a central islet (7 hectares of surface water), 220 covered berths.

- Rome:

Portus: Porto Claudio (about 60 to 80 hectares) and Porto Trajano (33 hectares)
Misenum (warships): base for Octavian's imperial fleet for the battle of Actium
Puteoli (commercial): situated next to Misenum in the Bay of Naples.

It can be concluded that the Portus Magnus was well within the average size for the largest harbours of the age.

3. HARBOUR STRUCTURES

It is an irony of civilisation that the harbours for the wars of antiquity are somewhat similar to sailing marinas as regards their size and by the dimensions of the vessels (actual luxury yachts range in size from 15 to 70 m. or more). The draughts of ancient galleys, however, was not so great, being in the order of 1 to 1.5 m. The biggest vessels (the '40' of Ptolemy IV or the *Isis*) must nevertheless have had a draught of as much as 4 m.

The two main types of harbour structures are sea walls for protection against the swell of the open sea and the quay.

Sea walls can be structures made of embankments on a rocky base or vertical structures in blocks. Because at Alexandria the remains of the sea walls on the open sea have not been investigated as they are probably under modern dykes, we will not linger on this matter.

The inner sea walls that protect each of the three harbours are built with an embankment on their outer face with, usually, a quay made of blocks of mortar on the inner face of the work.

The building of quays can be classified on the following basis according to the materials used (Prada, de la Pena 1995):

- with wood: platforms of wood on piles or pillars in stone blocks
- without mortar: blocks of dressed stone with a final fill between the facings
- with mortar, without *pouzzolane*; large blocks set dry in a wooden shuttering
- with mortar, with *pouzzolane*; large blocks set underwater in shuttering

The most ancient technique is that of dressed stone blocks. For work of a certain width, two separate facings were made using blocks of stone and then filled with rubble from quarries. The resulting surface was then

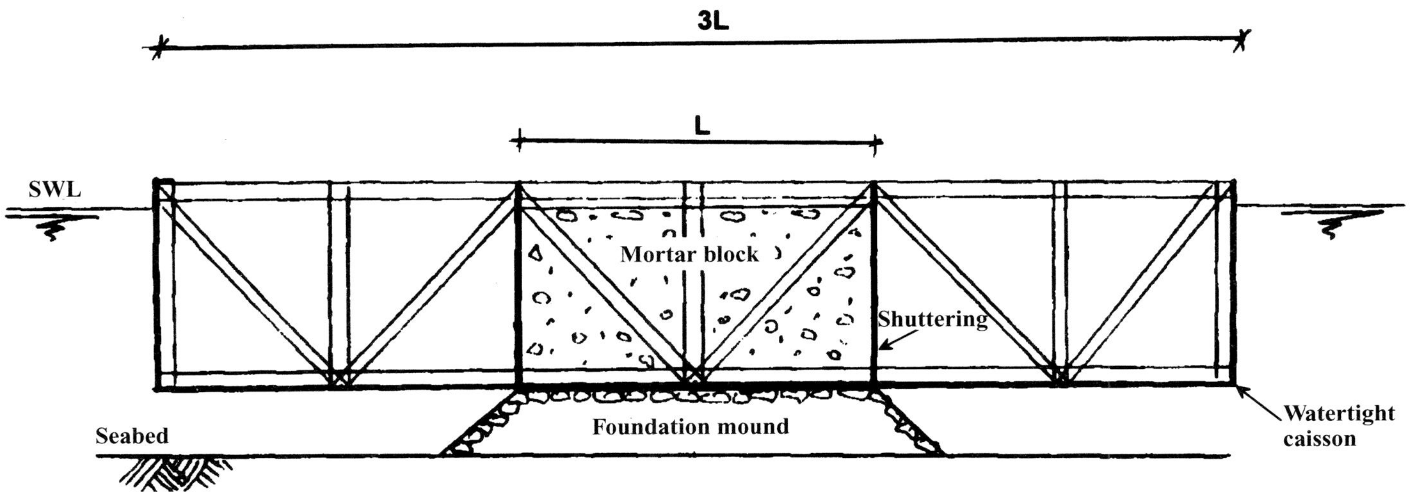

Figure 10 – FLOATING CAISSON

covered by flagstones. The weight of the blocks never exceeded a tonne so that they remained easily moveable by the means of leverage at the time. The blocks found at Tyre in the southern harbour weigh about 500 kg., blocks of 10 tonnes and more have been used in places exposed to a swell (Poidebard 1939).

Lime mortar was made of slaked lime, sand and water. It dries in air and cannot harden under water. From this fact the following outline has been imagined for its use in marine works. A wooden box shuttering is placed in the water where the quay is to be built. The shuttering is filled with sand until it is above water level. The block of lime mortar is then poured out of the water onto this mass of sand and can thus dry in the air. In order for the whole structure to sink down to its final position, it needs no more than to release the sand from the shuttering by opening the doors constructed in it (Prada, de la Pena 1995).

The introduction of *pouzzolane* by the Romans was, as explained by Vitruvius about 30 AD (Vitruvius 1998), a revolution for hydraulics. This silicio-aluminium material had a volcanic origin (Puteoli near Naples) and combines with lime in water and allows mortar made with this mixture to harden under water (Vitruvius 1998, II, ch. 6). The outline described above would thus be unnecessary and the mortar could be poured directly into the shuttering set on the sea bottom (Raban 1998, Vitruvius 1998, V, ch. 12). But this was not available to the Alexandrians at the time the eastern harbour was built.

The large blocks for the quay discovered in the third harbour of Alexandria (typically 5-8 m. wide, 10-15 m. long, 1-3 m. high) contain no *pouzzolane* and the dating of the wood indicates a period at which *pouzzolane* could not yet exist in Egypt (about 250 BC). The presence of wood *under the block* shows that the shuttering certainly formed part of a floating caisson (a technique also used at Caesarea under Herod [Raban 1998] and still used today).

We can therefore put forward the hypothesis that after having been floated upright to where the quay was to be built, the caisson was ballasted until it reached the sea bottom where a surface foundation had been prepared in advance. In order for the mortar to dry in the air, the caisson had to float sufficiently and be water-tight. The caisson thus was like a barge capable of carrying a block of mortar. To do this the caisson had to be about 2.5 to 3 times wider than the block of mortar (which has a density of about 2.5) so that in this case the draught of the caisson with its block is about equal to the height of the block to be set aground.

This explains the presence of beams and planks below the block, as well as the presence of vertical and inclined beams set in the mortar which gave the caisson its rigidity when it was afloat and set aground. This also explains the absence of vertical wooden sides as these must have been dismantled and recovered after the block of mortar was set on the bottom.

The double row of piles discovered at the eastern end of the Island of Antirhodos is more ancient than the large blocks mentioned above (about 400 BC). The presence of mortar at the bottom point of the piles of the south row shows that these rows of piles must have been built dry, that is to say that they were sunk below the level of the water after their construction.

One could further propose the following hypothesis that this double row of piles was the remains of an ancient wooden quay.

The southern row is made of piles with grooves into which planks were slid, thus forming a little curtain of timber shuttering in wood, capable of holding a hardcore composed of quarry rubbish. The northern row is made of simple piles which could have supported a decking in wood and be sunk in the bottom by as much as a metre (see figure 11).

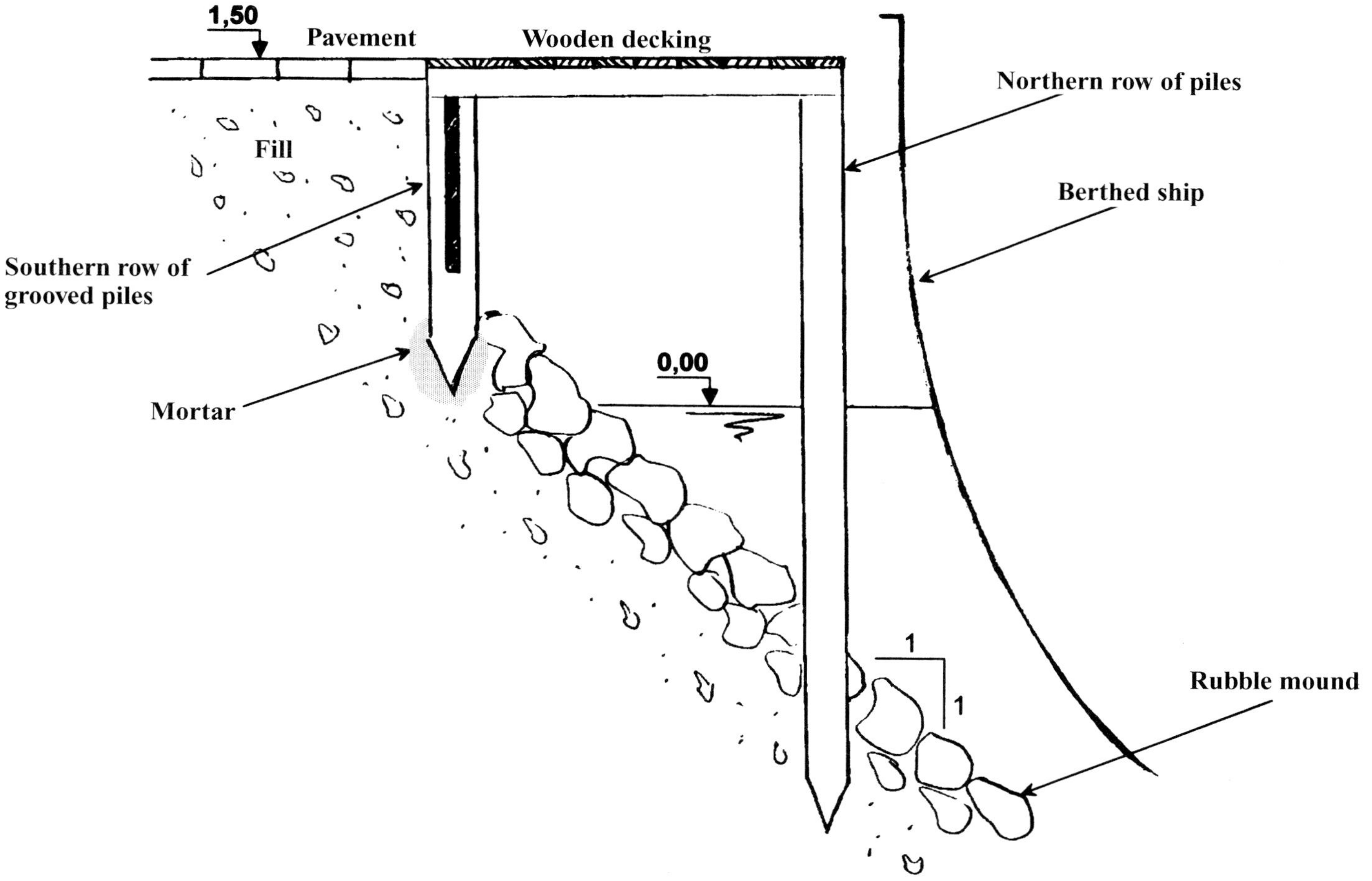

Figure 11 – ANCIENT QUAY

OCEANANIC CONDITIONS AT ALEXANDRIA

1. WINDS

The following statistics were provided by the meteorological station at Alexandria for the period 1973-1992 (expressed as a percentage of the time by direction as sectors)

The first four lines of the table give the frequency of winds in the four 90° sectors. The last two lines give figures for the 180° sectors which can be called 'east wind' for the sector N (E) S and 'west wind' for the sector S (W) N. The last column shows the annual average.

The following characteristics should be noted:

- for the annual average there are west winds for 2/3 of the time and east winds for 1/3 of the time for the annual average there are winds from the sector west
- to north (from the NW) for a little more than half the time
- summer winds (June to September) come from the NW sector most of the time; it is only in October, then during the winter until May that there are between 35 and 45 percent east winds.

These figures explain how sailing under sail from Rome to Alexandria was much easier than in the opposite direction. The voyage took between 2 and 3 weeks in one direction and twice as long in the other. Ships made an average of two voyages during the fine weather, from May to September, to avoid storms (Casson 1971, 270, 279).

month	1	2	3	4	5	6	7	8	9	10	11	12	year
N to E	19	20	29	30	30	17	5	7	16	30	30	20	21
E to S	15	17	15	15	11	5	2	2	5	12	13	16	11
S to W	35	26	15	9	6	6	5	4	5	10	21	35	15
W to N	31	37	41	46	53	72	88	87	74	48	36	29	53
N (E) S	34	37	44	45	41	22	7	9	21	42	43	36	32
S (W) N	66	63	56	55	59	78	93	91	79	58	57	64	68

2. SWELL

The statistics below were obtained from observations made during the period 1960-1980 in the eastern Mediterranean on board selected ships.

Sector	N285-N325	N325-N5	N5-N35	N35-N65	Calms	Total
H<0.1m	-	-	-	-	56	56
0.1>H>1m	10	6	2	2	-	20
H>1m	13	7	2	2	-	24
Total	23	13	4	4	56	100

The first four columns give the frequency of the appearance of swell in the open sea as a percentage of the time for the sectors of direction indicated. The fifth column gives the percentage of calms (and other sectors which do not affect Alexandria). The first line gives the calms. The second line the swells less than 1 m. and the third line swells greater than 1 m. (crest to trough).

The following characteristics are to be noted:

- on the coasts of Egypt and Libya the sea is calm for a little more than half the time.
- swells greater than 1 m. which create problems for sailing ships arise for a quarter of the time
- swells from the W-N sector (approx. 285° to 005°) account for 36 percent of the time and swells from the N-E sector (approx. 005° to 065° only represent 8 percent of the time.

3. SEA LEVEL

The following levels are given by the Egyptian authorities (reference is to the terrestrial datum point Robert Zero):

LLWL (Lowest Low Water Level)	-0.43 m.
CD (Chart Datum)	-0.34 m.
MLWL (Mean Low Water Level)	-0.05 m.
MSL (Mean Sea Level)	+0.08 m.
MHWL (Mean High Water Level)	+0.21 m.
HHWL (Highest High Water Level)	+0.74 m.

One notes that the lowest water levels are 9 cm. below Chart Datum and that the average level of the sea at Alexandria is 8 cm. above the Egyptian terrestrial datum point.

We would point out that over the last 2,500 years sea levels have changed. Without entering into an expert discussion on the matter, it is estimated that the rise in sea level during this period is about 1.5 m. (Franco 1996), i.e., about 6 cm. per century. It may be added that the actual rhythm of increase has risen more since it reached about 18 cm. a century for the last hundred years (1180-1980) (Flemming 1981) and is actually estimated at 30 to 110 cm. for the next century.

Variations in the average sea level seem to have taken place in the last two millennia. It is, however, very difficult to distinguish eustatic (relating to the sea) and tectonic (relating to the land) movements. The example of Crete is enlightening, as over the last 2,000 years the sea has sunk from 4 to 8 m. relative to the land at the western end of the island, whilst in the east it has risen from 1 to 4 m. during the same period (Flemming 1998).

At Alexandria it is agreed that sea level has risen from 1 to 1.5 m. and that the level of the land has sunk from 5 to 6 m. over the last 2,000 years.

We should also note that *tsunamis* have been reported on the coast of the Near East (tsunami is the Japanese word used by specialists to describe a tidal wave of seismic origin independent of local meteorology). The list in Douglas 1991 is doubtless not complete.

4. SEDIMENTOLOGY

The sediments found on the beaches and on the bottom of the sea in the roads of Alexandria are made of sand whose granular size (D50) varies between 0.2 and 0.5 mm. These sands certainly come from ancient Nile deposits. For some decades, the beaches of Alexandria have been generally eroded and measures to protect against this have been taken with varying degrees of success (replacing the beaches, works to provide protection through rocks). The erosion is due principally to the displacement of the sand on the beach towards the open sea which occurs during storms.

As well as the movement of sand towards the sea, there are also important movements along the coast, both towards the east and towards the west. Specialists estimate that the movement to both the east and the west are both to the order of 100,000 cu. m. per annum, which give a zero result. It is clear that if an obstruction was built perpendicular to the coast then the 100,000 cu. m. would be deposited on one side or other of the obstruction. This is what must have happened after the building of the Heptastadion when at least a part of this movement must have been dumped each year.

TESTIMONIA SELECTA DE PORTU MAGNO ET PALATIIS ALEXANDRIAE AD AEGYPTUM E SCRIPTORIBUS ANTIQUIS EXCERPTA [1]

André Bernand

[1] 'Selected Accounts on the Great Harbour and Palaces of Alexandria ad Egytptum according to ancient writers.'

7th century BC. Homer.

Homer, *The Odyssey*, IV, 354-360. Translation by A T Murray, revised by George E Dimock (The Loeb Classical Library, 1995).

Νῆσος ἔπειτά τίς ἐστι πολυκλύστῳ ἐνὶ πόντῳ
Αἰγύπτου προπάροιθε, Φάρον δέ ἑ κικλήσκουσι,
τόσσον ἄνευθ᾽ ὅσσόν τε πανημερίη γλαφυρὴ νηῦς
ἤνυσεν, ᾗ λιγὺς οὖρος ἐπιπνείῃσιν ὄπισθεν ·
ἐν δὲ λιμὴν εὔορμος, ὅθεν τ᾽ ἀπὸ νῆας εἴσας
ἐς πόντον βάλλουσιν, ἀφυσσάμενοι μέλαν ὕδωρ.
ἔνθά μ᾽ ἐείκοσιν ἦματ᾽ ἔχον θεοί· οὐδέ ποτ᾽ οὖροι
πνείοντες φαίνονθ᾽ ἁλιαέες, οἵ ῥά τε νηῶν
πομπῆες γίνονται ἐπ᾽εὐρέα νῶτα θαλάσσης.
καί νύ κεν ἤια πάντα κατέφθιτο καὶ μένος ἀνδρῶν,
εἰ μή τίς με θεῶν ὀλοφύρατο καί μ᾽ ἐλέησε,
Πρωτέος ἰφθίμου θυγάτηρ, ἁλίοιο Γέροντος,
Εἰδοθέη· τῇ γάρ ῥα μάλιστά γε θυμὸν ὄρινα·
ἥ μ᾽ οἴῳ ἔρροντι συνήντετο νόσφιν ἑταίρων·
αἰεὶ γὰρ περὶ νῆσον ἀλώμενοι ἰχθυάασκον
γναμπτοῖς᾽ ἀγκίστροισιν· ἔτειρε δὲ γαστέρα λιμός.

1.
Now there is an island in the surging sea in front of Egypt, and men call it Pharos, distant as far as a hollow ship runs in a whole day when the shrill wind blows behind her. There is a harbor there with good anchorage, from which men launch the shapely ships into the sea, when they have drawn supplies of black water. There for twenty days the gods kept me, nor ever did the winds that blow over the deep spring up, which speed men's ships over the broad back of the sea. And now would all my stores have been spent and the strength of my men, had not one of the gods taken pity on me and saved me: Eidothea, daughter of mighty Proteus, the old man of the sea; for her heart above all others had I moved. She met me as I wandered alone apart from my comrades, who continually roamed about the island fishing with bent hooks, for hunger pinched their bellies.

Reign of Ptolemaeus II Philadelphus (285-246 BC). Théocritus.

Theocritus, XV: *The Women at the Adonis Festival. Apud The Greek Bucolic Poets.* Translation by J M Edmonds (The Loeb Classical Library), vers 4-7; 44-55; 78-95.

Soldiers pour into the streets of Alexandria

2. vers 4-7: Γοργώ.
Ὦ τᾶς ἀλεμάτω ψυχᾶς. Μόλις ὔμμιν ἐσώθην,
Πραξινόα, πολλῶ μὲν ὄχλω, πολλῶν δὲ τεθρίππων·
παντᾷ κρηπῖδες, παντᾷ χλαμυδηφόροι ἄνδρες·
ἁ δ᾽ ὁδὸς ἄτρυτος· τὺ δ᾽ ἑκαστέρω αἰὲν ἀποικεῖς.

Congestion in Alexandria

3. Vers 44-55. Γοργώ

Ὦ θεοί, ὅσσος ὄχλος. Πῶς καὶ πόκα τοῦτο περᾶσαι
χρὴ τὸ κακόν; Μύρμακες ἀνάριθμοι καὶ ἄμετροι.
Πολλά τοι, ὦ Πτολεμαῖε, πεποίηται καλὰ ἔργα,
ἐξ ὧ ἐν ἀθανάτοις ὁ τεκών· οὐδεὶς κακοεργός
δαλεῖται τὸν ἰόντα παρέρπων Αἰγυπτισί,
οἷα πρὶν ἐξ ἀπάτας κεκροτημένοι ἄνδρες ἔπαισδον,
ἀλλάλοις ὁμαλοί, κακὰ παίγνια, πάντες ἐρινοί.
Ἁδίστα Γοργοῖ, τί γενοίμεθα ; Τοὶ πολεμισταί
ἵπποι τῶ βασιλῆος.῎Ανερ φίλε, μή με πατήσῃς.
Ὀρθὸς ἀνέστα ὁ πυρρός· ἴδ᾽ ὡς ἄγριος . Κυνοθαρσής
Εὐνόα, οὐ φευξῇ ; Διαχρησεῖται τὸν ἄγοντα.
Ὠνάθην μεγάλως, ὅτι μοι τὸ βρέφος μένει ἔνδοι.

At the Royal Palace

4. vers 78-95. Γοργώ

Πραξινόα, πόταγ᾽ ὧδε. Τὰ ποικίλα πρᾶτον ἄθρησον.
Λεπτὰ καὶ ὡς χαρίεντα· θεῶν τεχνάματα φασεῖς.

Πραξινόα

Πότνι᾽ Ἀθαναία, ποῖαί σφ᾽ ἐπόνασαν ἔριθοι,
ποῖοι ζῳογράφοι τἀκριβέα γράμματ᾽ ἔγραψαν;
Ὡς ἔτυμ᾽ ἑστάκαντι καὶ ὡς ἔτυμ᾽ ἐνδινεῦντι.
῎Εμψυχ᾽, οὐκ ἐνυφαντά. Σοφόν τοι χρῆμ᾽ ἄνθρωπος.
Αὐτὸς δ᾽ ὡς θαητὸς ἐπ᾽ ἀργυρέω κατάκειται
κλισμῷ [2], πρᾶτον ἴουλον ἀπὸ κροτάφων καταβάλλων,
ὁ τριφίλητος῎Αδωνις, ὃς κὴν Ἀχέροντι φιλεῖται.

῞Ετερος ξένος

Παύσασθ᾽ ὦ δύστανοι, ἀνάνυτα κωτίλλοισαι,
τρυγόνες· ἐκκναισεῦντι πλατειάσδοισαι ἅπαντα.

Πραξινόα

Μᾶ, πόθεν ὤνθρωπος ; Τί δὲ τίν, εἰ κωτίλαι εἰμές ;
Πασάμενος ἐπίτασσε. Συρακοσίαις ἐπιτάσσεις;
Ὡς εἰδῇς καὶ τοῦτο· Κορίνθιαι εἰμὲς ἄνωθεν,
ὡς καὶ Βελλεροφῶν . Πελοποννασιστὶ λαλεῦμες ·
δωρίσδεν δ᾽ ἔξεστι, δοκῶ, τοῖς Δωριέεσσι.
Μὴ φύη, Μελιτῶδες, ὃς ἁμῶν καρτερὸς εἴη,
πλὰν ἑνός. Οὐκ ἀλέγω. Μή μοι κενεὰν ἀπομάξῃς.

Eulogy to Ptolemy, master of the sea

5. Vers 77-105.

Μυρίαι ἄπειροί τε καὶ ἔθνεα μυρία φωτῶν
λήϊον ἀλδήσκουσιν ὀφελλόμενον Διὸς ὄμβρῳ ·
ἀλλ᾽ οὔτις τόσα φύει, ὅσα χθαμαλὰ Αἴγυπτος,
Νεῖλος ἀναβλύζων διερὰν ὅτε βώλακα θρύπτει.

[2] J M Edmonds (Loeb) adopts the correction of Kaibel, ἁρμοῖ, and translates accordingly.

Οὐδέ τις ἄστεα τόσσα βροτῶν ἔχει ἔργα δαέντων·
τρεῖς μὲν οἱ πολίων ἑκατοντάδες ἐνδέδμηνται,
τρεῖς δ΄ ἄρα χιλιάδες τρισσαῖς ἐπὶ μυριάδεσσι,
δοιαὶ δὲ τριάδες, μετὰ δέ σφισιν ἐννεάδες τρεῖς ·
τῶν πάντων Πτολεμαῖος ἀγήνωρ εἶς βασιλεύει.
Καὶ μὴν Φοινίκας ἀποτέμνεται ᾿Αρραβίας τε
καὶ Συρίας Λιβύας τε κελαινῶν τ΄ Αἰθιοπήων ·
Παμφύλοισί τε πᾶσι καὶ αἰχμηταῖς Κιλίκεσσι
σαμαίνει, Λυκίοις τε φιλοπτολέμοισί τε Καρσί,
καὶ νάσοις Κυκλάδεσσιν, ἐπεί οἱ νᾶες ἄρισται
πόντον ἐπιπλώοντι· θάλασσα δὲ πᾶσα καὶ αἶα
καὶ ποταμοὶ κελάδοντες ἀνάσσονται Πτολεμαίῳ .
Πολλοὶ δ΄ ἱππῆες, πολλοὶ δέ μιν ἀσπιδιῶται
χαλκῷ μαρμαίροντι σεσαγμένοι ἀμφαγέρονται.
Ὄλβῳ μὲν πάντας κε καταβρίθοι βασιλῆας·
τόσσον ἐπ΄ ἆμαρ ἕκαστον ἐς ἀφνεὸν ἔρχεται οἶκον
πάντοθε. Λαοὶ δ΄ ἔργα περιστέλλονται ἕκηλοι·
οὐ γάρ τις δηίων πολυκήτεα Νεῖλον ὑπερβὰς
πεζὸς ἐν ἀλλοτρίαισι βοὰν ἐστάσατο κώμαις,
οὐδέ τις αἰγιαλόνδε θοᾶς ἐξάλατο ναός
θωρηχθεὶς ἐπὶ βουσὶν ἀνάρσιος Αἰγυπτίῃσιν·
τοῖος ἀνὴρ πλατέεσσιν ἐνίδρυται πεδίοισι
ξανθοκόμας Πτολεμαῖος, ἐπιστάμενος δόρυ πάλλειν,
ᾧ ἐπίπαγχυ μέλει πατρώϊα πάντα φυλάσσειν
οἷ΄ ἀγαθῷ βασιλῆϊ, τὰ δὲ κτεατίζεται αὐτός.

....

5 bis. Vers 121-130.

Μοῦνος ὅδε προτέρων τε καὶ ὧν ἔτι θερμὰ κονία
στειβομένα καθύπερθε ποδῶν ἐκμάσσεται ἴχνη,
ματρὶ φίλᾳ καὶ πατρὶ θυώδεας εἵσατο ναούς·
ἐν δ΄αὐτοὺς χρυσῷ περικαλλέας ἠδ΄ ἐλέφαντι
ἵδρυται πάντεσσιν ἐπιχθονίοισιν ἀρωγούς.
Πόλλὰ δὲ πιανθέντα βοῶν ὅγε μηρία καίει
μησὶ περιπλομένοισιν ἐρευθομένων ἐπὶ βωμῶν,
αὐτός τ΄ ἰφθίμα τ΄ ἄλοχος, τᾶς οὔτις ἀρείων
νυμφίον ἐν μεγάροισι γυνὰ περιβάλλετ΄ ἀγοστῷ,
ἐκ θυμοῦ στέργοισα κασίγνητόν τε πόσιν τε.

2. Theocritus XV, 4-7. *Gorgo*

O what a silly I was to come! What with the crush and the horses, Praxonia, I've scarcely got alive. It's all big boots and people in uniform. And the street was never-ending, and you can't think how far your house is along it.

3. Theocritus XV, 44-55 *Gorgo* [3]

Heavens, what a crowd! How we're to get through this awful crush and how long it's going to take us, I can't imagine. Talk of an antheap!

---

[3] J M Edmonds places verses 44-45 in the mouth of Gorgo, but Ph-E Legrand attributes them to Praxinoa.

Praxinoa

I must say, you've done us many a good turn, my good Ptolemy, since your father went to heaven. We have no villains sneaking up to murder us in the streets nowadays in the good old Egyptian style. They don't play those awful games now-the thorough-paced rogues, every one of them the same, all queer!

Gorgo dearest! what shall we do? The Royal Horse! Don't run me down, my good man. That bay's rearing. Look, what temper! Stand back, Eunoa, you reckless girl! He'll be the death of that man.Thank goodness I left Baby at home!

4. Theocritus XV, 78-95. *Gorgo*

Praxinoa, do come here. Before you do anything else I insist upon your looking at the embroideries. How delicate they are! and in such good taste.They're really hardly human, are they?

Praxinoa

Huswife Athena! The weavers that made that material and the embroiderers who did that close detailed work are simply marvels. How realistically the things all stand and move about it! they're living! It is wonderful what people can do. And then the Holy Boy; how perfectly beautiful he looks lying on his silver couch; with the down of manhood just showing on his cheeks—(*religioso*) the thrice-beloved Adonis, beloved even down below!

Second Stranger

Oh dear, oh dear, ladies! do stop that eternal cooing. (*To the bystanders*). They'll weary me to death with their ah-ah-ah-ing.

Praxinoa

My word! where does that person come from? What business is it of yours if we do coo? Buy your slaves before you order them about, pray. You're giving your orders to Syracusans. If you must know, we're Corinthians by extraction, like Bellerophon himself. What we Peloponnesian. I suppose Dorians may speak Doric, mayn't they? Persephone! let's have no more masters than the one we've got. I shall do just as I like. Pray don't waste your breath.

5. Theocritus, XVII, 77-105.

Ten thousand are the lands and ten thousand the nations that make the crops to spring under aid of the rain of Zeus, but there's no country so fruitful as the low-country of Egypte when Nile comes gushing up to soak the soil and break it, nor no country, neither, possessed of so many cities of men learned in labour. The cities builded therein are three hundreds and three thousands ant three tens of thousands, threes twain and nines three, and in them the lord and master of all is proud Ptolemy. Aye, and of Phoenicia and Arabia he taketh to him a handle, and eke of Syria and Libya and of the swart Aethiop's country; and he giveth the word to all them of Pamphylia and all the warriors of Cilicia; and to the people of Lycia and warlike Caria and to the Cyclad Isles he giveth it; and this because he hath a noble navy sailing the main, so that all the sea, every land, and each of the sounding rivers doth acknowledge his dominion, and full many are the mighty warriorsa-horseback and full many the burnished brass-clad targeyeers afoot that rally for the battle around his standard.

For wealth, his would outweigh the wealth of all the princes of the earth together,- so much comes into his rich habitation both day by day and from every quarter. And as for his peoples, they occupy their business without let or hindrance, seeing that no foeman hath crossed afoot that river of monsters to set up a cry in alien townships, nor none leapt from swift ship upon that beach all mailed to make havoc of the Egyptian kine,-of such noble sort is the flaxen-haired prince that is throned in these level plains, a prince who not only hath cunning to wield the spear, but, as a good king should, makes it his chiefest care both to keep all that he hath of his father and to add somewhat for himself.

5. Theocritus XVII, 121-130.

And this man hath done that which none before hath done, be he of them of old, be he of those whose footmarks are yet warm in the dust they trod; he hath builded incense-fragrant temples to his mother and father dear, and hath set therein images of them in gold and ivory, very beautiful, to be the aid of all that live upon the earth. And many are the thighs of fatted oxen that as the months go round he consumes upon the reddening altars, he and that his fine noble spouse, who maketh him a better wife than ever clasped bridegroom under any roof, seeing that she loveth with her whole heart brother and husband in one.

3rd century BC. Poseidippos of Pella.

D L Page, *Greek Literary Papyri*, I, p. 444-447, no. 104 a: edition and translation of the epigram of Poseidippus.

6.

Ἑλλήνων σωτῆρα, Φάρου σκοπόν, ὦ ἄνα Πρωτεῦ,
Σώστρατος ἔστησεν Δεξιφάνο[υ]ς Κνίδιος.
οὐ γὰρ ἐν Αἰγύπτωι σκοπαὶ οὔρη σοι επὶ νήσων,
ἀλλὰ χαμαὶ χηλὴ ναύλοχος ἐκτέταται.
τοῦ χάριν εὐθεῖάν τε καὶ ὄρθιον αἰθέρα τέμνει
πύργος ὅ τ΄ ἀπλάτων φαίνετ΄ ἀπὸ σταδίων
ἤματι· παννύχιος δὲ θοῶς ἐν κύματι ναύτης
ὄψεται ἐκ κορυφῆς πῦρ μέγα καιόμενον,
καί κεν ἐπ΄ αὐτὸ δράμοι Ταύρου κέρας, οὐδ΄ ἂν ἁμάρτοι
σωτῆρος, Πρωτεῦ, Ζην[ὸ]ς [ὁ] τῆιδε πλέων.

6.

Lord Proteus: the saviour of Hellenes, this watchman of Pharos, was built by Sostratus, son of Dexiphanes, a Cnidian. In Egypt there are no mountain-peaks, as in the islands: but low lies the breakwater where ships may harbour. Therefore this tower, cleaving the sky straight and upright, shines in the daytime countless leagues away: and all night long the sailor who runs with the waves shall see a great light blazing from its summit. And he may run even to the Bull's Horn, and yet not miss the God of Safety, O Proteus, whosoever sails this way .

2nd-1st century BC (?). Pseudo-Callisthène.

Der Griechische Alexanderroman, 31-33: *Rezension Γ, Buch I, nach der Handschrift R herausgegeben,* by Ursula von Lauenstein, in *Beiträge zur Klassischen Philologie,* herausgegeben von Reinhold Merkelbach, Heft 4, p. 106-116 (Verlag Anton Hain, Meisenheim am Glan, 1962).

Alexander in the outer suburbs of Alexandria

7.

31. ἐκεῖθεν δὲ διοδεύσας ἦλθεν εἰς τὸ Ταφοσίριον. ἐπυνθάνετο παρὰ τῶ ἐγχωρίων διατί τὸ ὄνομα τοῦτο · οἱ δὲ ἔφησαν τάφον ᾽Οσίριος εἶναι τὸ ἱερόν · καὶ θύσας ἐκεῖ τὴν ἄφιξιν ἐποιεῖτο τῆς ὁδοιπορίας . καὶ παραγίνεται

ἐπὶ τοῦ ἐδάφους τοῦ νῦν. καὶ ὁρᾷ χώρημα μέγα, εἰς ἄπειρον ἐκτεῖνον δώδεκα κώμαις συνεχόμενον . ἀπὸ οὖν τῆς καλουμένης Πανδύσεως μέχρι τοῦ καλουμένου ʽΗρακλεωτικοῦ στόματος τὸ μῆκος τῆς πόλεως ʼΑλέξανδρος ἐχωρογράφησε, τὸ δὲ πλάτος ἀπὸ τοῦ Βενδηλέου μέχρι τῆς ʽΟρμουπόλεως · οὐ καλεῖται δὲ ʽΕρμούπολις ἀλλὰ ʽΟρμούπολις ὅτι πᾶς ὁ κατερχόμενος ἐκεῖ προσορμεῖ. μέχρι οὖν τοῦ τόπου ἐκείνου ἐχωρογράφησε τὴν πόλιν ʼΑλέξανδρος ὁ βασιλεύς, ὅθεν μέχρι τῆς δεῦρο ἡ ʼΑλεξανδρέων χώρα ἀναγράφεται.

Advice of the architects

συνεβούλευσε δὲ τῷ βασιλεῖ ʼΑλεξάνδρῳ Κλεομένης ὁ Ναυκρατίτης καὶ ὁ Νομοκράτης ʽΡόδιος μὴ τῷ μεγέθει τούτῳ κτίσαι πόλιν, οὐ γὰρ δυνήσῃ γεμίσαι αὐτὴν ὄχλων · ἐὰν δὲ καὶ γεμίσῃς οὐ δυνήσονται οἱ ὑπηρέται τὴν χρείαν αὐτῇ τῶν ἐπιτηδείων παρασχεῖν · πολεμήσουσιν ἑαυτοῖς οἱ ἐν τῇ πόλει κατοικοῦντες ὡς τοιαύτης ὑπερμεγέθους τυγχανούσης καὶ ἀπείρου · αἱ γὰρ μικραὶ πόλεις εὐσύμβουλοί εἰσιν καὶ πρὸς τὰ συμφέροντα τῇ πόλει συμβουλεύουσιν · ἐὰν δὲ οὕτως ὡς διεγράψω μεγίστην αὐτὴν κτίσῃς, οἱ κατοικοῦντες ἐν αὐτῇ διχοστατήσουσιν εἰς ἀλλήλους διαφερόμενοι ἀπείρου ὄχλου τυγχάνοντος. πεισθεὶς δὲ ʼΑλέξανδρος ἐπέτρεψεν τοῖς ἀρχιτέκτοσιν, οἷς βούλονται μέτροις τὴν πόλιν κτίζειν. οἱ δὲ κελευσθέντες ὑπὸ τοῦ βασιλέως ʼΑλεξάνδρου χωρογραφοῦσιν τὸ μῆκος τῆς πόλεως ἀπὸ τοῦ Δράκοντος τοῦ κατὰ τὴν Ταφοσιριακὴν ταινίαν μέχρι τοῦ ʼΑγαθοδαίμονος ποταμοῦ τοῦ κατὰ νότου, καὶ ἀπὸ τοῦ Βενδιδείου μέχρι τοῦ Εὐρόφου καὶ Μελανθίου τὸ πλάτος · καὶ κελεύει ʼΑλέξανδρος μεταβῆναι τοὺς κατοικοῦντας ἐν τοῖς τόποις τούτοις καὶ εἰς τὰς κώμας ἀπιέναι πρὸ τριάκοντα μιλίων τῆς πόλεως ἔξω, χωρήματα αὐτοῖς χαρισάμενος προσαγορεύσας αὐτοὺς ʼΑλεξανδρεῖς. ἦσαν δὲ ἀρχέποδες τῶν κωμῶν Εὐρύλιθος καὶ Μέλανθος ὅθεν καὶ ἡ ὀνομασία ἔμεινεν . σκέπταται δὴ ʼΑλέξανδρος καὶ ἑτέρους ἀρχιτέκτονας τῆς πόλεως, ἐν οἷς ἦν Νουμήνιος ὑδατικὸς λατόμος καὶ Κλεομένης μηχανικὸς Ναυκρατίτης καὶ Κάρτερος ʼΟλύνθιος · εἶχε δὲ ἀδελφὸν ὁ Νουμήνιος ὀνόματι ʽΥπόνομον· οὗτος συνεβουλεύσατο τῷ ʼΑλεξάνδρῳ τὴν πόλιν ἐκ θεμελίων κτίσαι ἐν αὐτῇ δὲ καὶ ὑδρηγοὺς πόρους καὶ ὀχετηγοὺς ἐπιρρέοντας εἰς τὴν θάλασσαν.

8.

32. κελεύει δὲ ʼΑλέξανδρος χωρογραφηθῆναι τὸ περίμετρον τῆς πόλεως πρὸς τὸ θεάσασθαι αὐτό. οἱ οὖν τεχνῖται ἄπλευρον πύρινον λαβόντες ἐχωρογράφησαν τὴν πόλιν · καταπτάντα δὲ ὄρνεα παντοδαπὰ κατεβοσκήθησαν τὰ ἄλευρα καὶ ἀπέπτησαν. συμφοραζόμενος δὲ ʼΑλέξανδρος περὶ τούτου, τί ἄρα δηλοῖ τὸ σημεῖον, μετεπέμψατο τοὺς σημειολύτας καὶ εἶπεν αὐτοῖς τὸ γεγονός. οἱ δὲ ἔφησαν ὅτι " ἡ πόλις ἣν ἐκέλευσας κτισθῆναι βασιλεῦ ὅλην τὴν οἰκουμένην θρέψει καὶ πανταχοῦ ἔσονται οἱ ἐν αὐτῇ γεννηθέντες ἄνθρωποι · τὰ γὰρ πετεινὰ πᾶσαν τὴν οἰκουμένην περικυκλοῦσιν. " ὁ δὲ ʼΑλέξανδρος ἐκέλευσε κτίζεσθαι τὴν πόλιν. θεμελιώσας δὲ τὸ πλεῖστον μέρος τῆς πόλεως ʼΑλέξανδρος καὶ χωρογραφήσας ἐπέγραψε γράμματα πέντε· α, β, γ, δ, ε · τὸ μὲν α ʼΑλέξανδρος, τὸ δὲ β βασιλεὺς, τὸ δὲ γ γένος, τὸ δὲ δ

Διός, τὸ δὲ ϵ ἔκτισεν πόλιν ἀμίμητον. ὑποζύγια δὲ καὶ ἡμίονοι εἰργάζοντο. ἱδρυμένου τοῦ πύλωνος τοῦ ἱεροῦ ἐξαίφνης δὲ πλὰξ μεγίστη ἐξέπεσεν ἀρχαιοτάτη πεπληρωμένη γραμμάτων · ἐξ ἧς καὶ ἐξέπεσεν ἀρχαιοτάτη πεπληρωμένη γραμμάτων ἐξ ἧς καὶ ἐξῆλθον ὄφεις πολλοὶ καὶ ἑρπύζοντες εἰσῆλθον εἰς τὰς ὁδοὺς τῶν ἤδη τεθεμελιωμένων οἰκιῶν - τὴν γὰρ πόλιν ἔτι παρὼν 'Αλέξανδρος καθίδρυσε Τῦβι ἤτοι ἰαννουαρίῳ νεομηνίᾳ, καὶ αὐτὸ τὸ ἱερόν - ὅθεν τούτους τοὺς ὄφεις σέβονται οἱ θυρωροὶ ὡς ἀγαθοὺς δαίμονας εἰσιόντας εἰς τὰς οἰκίας, οὔ εἰσιν ἰόβολα ζῷα· στεφανοῦσι δὲ καὶ τὰ κτήνη αὐτῶν, ἀνάπαυσιν αὐτοῖς παρεχόμενοι ὅθεν καὶ μέχρι τοῦ δεῦρο τὸν νόμον φυλάττουσιν 'Αλεξανδρεῖς < Τῦβι > πέμπτῃ καὶ εἰκάδι τὴν ἑορτὴν ἐκτελοῦντες .

Discovery of Alexandrian monuments

9.

33. Εὗρε δὲ 'Αλέξανδρος ἐν τοῖς ὑψηλοῖς λόφοις λεῖον ἱδρυμένον καὶ τοὺς 'Ηλίωνος στύλους καὶ τὸ ἡρῶον · ἐζήτει δὲ καὶ τὸ Σαραπεῖον κατὰ τὸν δοθέντα αὐτῷ χρησμὸν παρὰ τοῦ Ἄμμωνος εἰπόντος αὐτῷ. διὰ τοῦ χρησμοῦ οὕτως·

ὦ βασιλεῦ, σοι Φοῖβος μηλοκέρως ἀγορεύει
εἴ γε θέλεις αἰῶσιν ἀκηράτοισ<ιν> νεάζειν,
κτίζε πόλιν περίφημον ὑπὲρ Πρωτηίδα νῆσον
ἧς προκάθηται Αἰὼν Πλουτούνιος αὐτοῖς ἀνάσσων
πενταλόφοις κορυφαῖσιν ἀτέρμονα κόσμον ἑλίσσων.

ἐζήτει δὲ 'Αλέξανδρος τὸν θεὸν τὸν πάντα δεχόμενον, καὶ ἐποίησεν ἀπέναντι τοῦ ἡρώου βωμὸν μέγαν (ὃς νῦν καλεῖται βωμὸς 'Αλεξάνδρου πολυτελής) ἐν ᾧ θυσίαν ἐθέσπισεν καὶ προσευξάμενος εἶπεν· "ὅτι μὲν οὖν τυγχάνει θεὸς προνοούμενος ταύτης τῆς χθονὸς καὶ τὸν ἀτέρμονα κόσμον ἐπιδέρκει φανερὸν τοῦτο . αὐτὸς οὖν πρόδεξαί μου τὴν θυσίαν καὶ βοηθός μου γενοῦ εἰς τοὺς πολέμους." καὶ ταῦτα εἰπὼν ἐπέθηκε τὰ ἱερεῖα ἐπὶ τοῦ βωμοῦ · αἰφνίδιον δὲ μέγιστος ἀετὸς καταπτὰς ἥρπασε τὰ σπλάγχνα τοῦ θύματος καὶ διὰ τοῦ ἀέρος ἐφέρετο καὶ ἀφῆκεν αὐτὰ ἐν ἑτέρῳ βωμῷ . κατασκοπήσας δὲ 'Αλέξανδρος τὸν τόπον, παραγενόμενος ἐν τάχει εἶδε τὰ σπλάγχνα ἐπὶ τοῦ βωμοῦ κείμενα, τὸν δὲ βωμὸν ὑπὸ ἀρχαίων καθιδρυσθέντα, καὶ σηκὸν καὶ ξόανον ἔνδον προκαθεζόμενον καὶ τῇ δεξιᾷ χειρὶ κομίζοντα θηρίον πολύμορφον, τῇ δὲ εὐωνύμῳ σκῆπτρον κατέχον, καὶ παρειστήκει τῷ ξοάνῳ κόρη, ἄγαλμα μέγιστον. ἐπυνθάνετο δὲ 'Αλέξανδρος παρὰ τῶν ἐκεῖσε κατοικούντων, τίς ἄρα ὁ ἐντεῦθεν θεὸς τυγχάνει. οἱ δὲ ἔφησαν μὴ εἰδέναι, παρειληφέναι δὲ ὑπὸ τῶν προπατόρων αὐτῶν Διὸς καὶ Ἥρας ἱερὸν εἶναι, ἐν ᾧ καὶ τοὺς ὀβελίσκους ἐθεάσατο τοὺς μέχρι νῦν κειμένους ἐν τῷ Σαραπείῳ ἔξω τοῦ περιβόλου τοῦ νῦν κειμένου ἐν οἷς ἦν γράμματα ἱερογλυφικὰ περιέχοντα οὕτως · "τὸ μὲν γέρας αὐτῆς τῆς πόλεως · καλλίναος, ὑπερφέρουσα πλήθει ὄχλων πολλῶν, ἀέρων εὐκρασίαις ὑπερβάλλουσα. ἐγὼ δὲ προστάτης ταύτης γενήσομαι ὅπως μὴ τὰ χαλεπὰ τελείως ὑπομείνῃ, ἢ διὰ λοιμὸν ἢ σεισμὸν, ἀλλ' ὡς ὄνειρος διαδραμοῦντα τῇ πόλει. πολλοὶ δὲ βασιλεῖς ἥξουσιν εἰς αὐτὴν οὐ πολεμήσοντες ἀλλὰ προσκυνῆσαι φερόμενοι . σὺ δὲ ἀποθεωθεὶς προσκυνηθήσῃ νεκρὸς καὶ δῶρα λήψῃ ἐκ πολλῶν βασιλέων πάντοτε. οἰκήσεις δὲ αὐτὴν καὶ θανὼν καὶ μὴ θανών· τάφον γὰρ ἕξεις αὐτὴν ἣν κτίζεις πόλιν.

πείρασαι δὲ ’Αλέξανδρε τίς πέφυκα ; συντόμως ἐρῶ· δὶς ρ΄ καὶ α΄ ψῆφον συνθεὶς, εἶτα <ρ΄ καὶ α΄>καὶ τετρακὶς κ΄ καὶ ι΄, τὸ πρῶτον δὲ λαβὼν γράμμα ποίησον εἰς ἔσχατον. καὶ τότε νοήσεις τίς ἐφάνθη ." ταῦτα οὖν χρηματισθεὶς τὸν χρησμὸν ἐπέγνω Σάραπις εἶναι. καὶ τὰ μὲν τῆς διαταγῆς τῆς πόλεως οὕτως ἔχει καθὼς διέταξεν ὁ ’Αλέξανδρος · ἐκτίζετο δὲ ἡ πόλις ἡμέρᾳ τῇ ἡμέρᾳ κρατυνομένῃ .

7.

31 ... Then he came to Taphosirion. He asked the local people why it has that name, and they replied that the sanctuary was the grave of Osiris. After sacrificing there also, he approached the goal of his journey and reached the site of our present city. He saw a great open space, stretching into the infinite distance, and occupied by twelve villages.[4] Alexander marked out the plan of a city, stretching in length from the place called Pandysia as far as the Heracleotic mouth of the Nile, and in width from the sanctuary of Bendis to little Hormoupolis (it is called Hormoupolis, not Hermoupolis, because everyone who sails down the Nile puts in there). These were the dimensions of the city Alexander laid out, so that up to this day it is called 'the territory of the Alexandrians'.

Cleomenes of Naucratis and Nomocrates of Rhodes advised Alexander not to build such a large city. 'You will be unable to find the people to fill it,' they said. 'And if you do fill it, the ships will be unable to transport sufficient food to feed them. Those who live in the city will make war on one another, because the city is too big, endless. Small cities are harmonious in debate and take counsel together to their mutual advantage; but if you make this city as great as you have sketched it, those who live here will always be at odds with one another, because the population will be so huge.'

Alexander was persuaded, and ordered his architects to build a city on the scale they preferred. On receiving these orders, they marked out a city extending in length from the river Dracon opposite the promontory of Taphosirion as far as the river Agathodaimon, which is beyond Canobus, and in width from the sanctuary of Bendis as far as Europhoros and Melanthios. Then Alexander ordered all those who lived within 30 miles of the city to leave their villages and move to the city; he presented them with parcels of land and called them Alexandrians. The chief officials of those boroughs were Eurylichos and Melanthos, which is how those districts got their names.

Alexander took advice also from other builders, including Numenius the stone-mason, Cleomenes of Naucratis, the engineer, and Karteros of Olynthus. Numenius had a brother by the name of Hyponomos. He advised Alexander to built the city on stone foundations, and to construct water channels and drains running to the sea. So such canals are called Hyponomos after him, because of his advice.

8.

32. Then Alexander gave orders for the perimeter of the city to be marked out so that he could get an impression of it. The workmen marked out the limits with wheat flour, but the birds flew down, ate up the meal and flew away. Alexander was very disturbed at the possible meaning of this omen; he sent for interpreters and told them what had happened. Their reply was: 'The city you have ordered to be built, O king, will feed the whole inhabited world, and those who are born in it will reach all parts of the world; just as the birds fly over the whole earth'.

So he gave orders for building work to begin.

[4] Here Stoneman includes the translation of eight lines from A text which we omit.

When the foundations for most of the city had been laid and measured, Alexander inscribed five letters: A B G D E. A for 'Alexander '; B for *basileus,* 'king'; G for *genos*, 'descendant'; D for Dios, 'Zeus'; and E for *ektisen*, 'founded an incomparable city'. Beasts of burden and mules helped with the work. As the gate of the sanctuary was being put in place, a large and ancient tablet of stone, inscribed with many letters, fell out of it; and after it came a large number of snakes, which crept away into the doorways of the houses that had already been built. Nowadays the doors-keepers reverence these snakes as friendly spirits when they come into their houses—for they are not venomous—and they place garlands on their working animals and give them a rest day. Alexander was still in the city when it and the sanctuary were being built, in the month of Tybi, which is January. For this reason the Alexandrians still even now keep the custom of celebrating a festival on the twenty-fifth day of Tybi.

9

33. High in the hills Alexander discovered a cult image, and the Helonian columns and a hero-shrine. He searched for the Sarapeum according to the oracle that had been given to him by Ammon in the following words:

> 'O King, thus Phoebus of the ram's horns says to you:
> If you wish to bloom for ever in incorruptable youth,
> Found the city rich in fame opposite the isle of Proteus,
> Where Aion Ploutonios himself is enthroned as king,
> He who from his five-peaked mountains rolls round the
> endless world.'

So Alexander searched for the all-seeing one and built a great altar opposite the hero-shrine, which is now called the Grand Altar of Alexander, and made a sacrifice there. He prayed and said: 'That you are the god who watches over this land and looks across the endless world, is plain. Accept then this sacrifice of mine and be my helper against my enemies.' So saying, he placed the gifts on the altar. Suddenly a huge eagle swooped down and seized the entrails of the sacrifice, carried them off into the air, and then dropped them on another altar. Alexander noted the place where they landed, and went to it and saw the entrails lying on the altar, which was one built by the men of old. There was also a sacred precinct, and within it a seated cult-image holding in its right hand a three-headed beast and in its left a sceptre; beside the image stood a very large statue of a maiden. He inquired of those who lived there what god dwelt in this place. They told him that they did not know, but that they had heard from their forefathers that it was a sanctuary of Zeus and Hera.

Here also saw the obelisks that now lie in the Sarapeum, outside the present perimeter wall. On them were engraved hieroglyphic letters ...

'... Work out, now, Alexander, who I am: put together two hundred two hundred and one, then a hundred and one again, then eighty and ten; then take the first letter and put it at the end, and thus you shall know who I am who have appear to you.'

With this oracular pronouncement he disappeared. Alexander remembered the oracle and recognized the name of Sarapis.

The administration of the city remains just as Alexander drew it up, and the city, once founded, grew day by day in strength.[5]

[5] R Stoneman does not translate ten lines retained by Ursula Lauenstein and follows another tradition recounting the questions posed by Alexander to Serapis and the god's answers.

140 B C. Polybius (date of his stay in Alexandria).

The largest peristyle of the palace. The royal tomb.

Polybius, *The Histories*, XV, 25 a, 3-12. Translation by W R Paton (The Loeb Classical Library, vol. IV, 1925).

10.

XV, 25 a[6]. Μετὰ δ´ ἡμέρας τρεῖς ἢ τέτταρας ἐν τῷ μεγίστῳ περιστύλῳ τῆς αὐλῆς οἰκοδομήσαντες βῆμα συνεκάλεσαν τοὺς ὑπασπιστὰς καὶ τὴν θεραπείαν, ἅμα δὲ τούτοις τοὺς πεζῶν καὶ τοὺς ἱππέων ἡγεμόνας. ἀθροισθέντων δὲ τούτων ἀναβὰς ᾿Αγαθοκλῆς καὶ Σωσίβιος ἐπὶ τὸ βῆμα πρῶτον μὲν τὸν τοῦ βασιλέως καὶ τὸν τῆς βασιλίσσης θάνατον ἀνθωμολογήσαντο καὶ τὸ πένθος ἀνέφηναν τοῖς πολλοῖς κατὰ τὸ παρ´ αὐτοῖς ἔθος. μετὰ δὲ ταῦτα διάδημα τῷ παιδὶ περιθέντες ἀνέδειξαν βασιλέα, καὶ διαθήκην τινὰ παρανέγνωσαν πεπλασμένην, ἐν ᾗ γεγραμμένον ἦν ὅτι καταλείπει τοῦ παιδὸς ἐπιτρόπους ὁ βασιλεὺς ᾿Αγαθοκλέα καὶ Σωσίβιον · καὶ παρεκάλουν τοὺς ἡγεμόνας εὐνοεῖν καὶ διαφυλάττειν τῷ παιδὶ τὴν ἀρχήν · ἐπὶ δὲ τούτοις δύο κάλπιδας ἀργυρᾶς εἰσήνεγκαν, ὡς τῆς μὲν μιᾶς ἐχούσης τὰ τοῦ βασιλέως ὀστᾶ, τῆς δ ´ ἑτέρας τὰ τῆς ᾿Αρσινόης · εἶχε δ´ ἡ μὲν μία κατ´ ἀλήθειαν τὰ τοῦ βασιλέως, ἡ δ´ ἑτέρα πλήρης ἦν ἀρωμάτων . ταῦτα δὲ ποιήσαντες εὐθέως ἐπετέλουν τὴν ἐκφοράν . ἐν ᾧ καιρῷ πᾶσι τὰ κατὰ τὴν ᾿Αρσινόην συνέβη γενέσθαι δῆλα . τοῦ γὰρ θανάτου φωτισθέντος ὁ τρόπος ἐπεζητεῖτο τῆς ἀπωλείας · οὐκ οὔσης δὲ προφάσεως ἄλλης οὐδεμιᾶς, τῆς ἀληθινῆς φήμης προσπεπτωκυίας, ἀκμὴν δ´ ἀμφισβητουμένης, τὸ κατ´ ἀλήθειαν γεγονὸς ἐν ταῖς ἑκάστων γνώμαις ἐπεσφραγίσθη. διὸ καὶ συνέβη μεγάλην γενέσθαι τὴν σύγχυσιν τῶν ὄχλων. τοῦ μὲν γὰρ βασιλέως οὐθεὶς οὐθένα λόγον ἐποιεῖτο, περὶ δὲ τῆς ᾿Αρσινόης, ἀνανεούμενοι τινὲς μὲν τὴν ὀρφανίαν αὐτῆς, ἔνιοι δὲ τὴν ἐξ ἀρχῆς ἐν τῷ ζῆν ὕβριν, ἣν ὑπέμεινε, καὶ τὴν αἰκίαν, σὺν δὲ τούτοις τὸ περὶ τὴν τελευτὴν ἀτύχημα, εἰς τοσαύτην παράστασιν ἐνέπιπτον καὶ δυσθυμίαν ὥστε πλήρη γενέσθαι τὴν πόλιν στεναγμοῦ, δακρύων, οἰμωγῆς ἀκαταπαύστου . ταῦτα δ´ ἦν τοῖς ὀρθῶς λογιζομένοις οὐχ οὕτω τῆς πρὸς ᾿Αρσινόην εὐνοίας τεκμήρια, πολὺ δὲ μᾶλλον τοῦ πρὸς τοὺς περὶ τὸν ᾿Αγαθοκλέα μίσους · ὁ δὲ προειρημένος, ἐπειδὴ τὰς ὑδρίας εἰς τοὺς βασιλικοὺς οἴκους ἔθηκε, παραγγείλας ἀποθέσθαι τὰ φαιά, πρῶτον μὲν διμήνου τὰς δυνάμεις ὠψωνίασε, πεπεισμένος τὸ παρὰ τοῖς πολλοῖς μῖσος ἀμβλύνειν διὰ τῆς πρὸς τὸ λυσιτελὲς ὁρμῆς αὐτῶν, εἶτ´ ἐπεξώρκισε τὸν ὅρκον ὃν ἦσαν ὀμνύειν εἰθισμένοι κατὰ τὰς ἀναδείξεις τῶν βασιλέων.

[6] Concerning the events of 203 BC.

10.

After four or five days, erecting a tribune in the largest colonnade of the palace, they summoned a meeting of the bodyguard and household troops as well as of the officers of the infantry and cavalry. When all these had collected, Agathocles and Sosibius mounted the tribune, and in the first place acknowledged the death of the king and queen and enjoined the populace to go into mourning as was their usual practice. After this they crowned the boy and proclaimed him king, and then read a forgot will, in which it was written that the king appointed Agathocles and Sosibius guardians of his son. They begged the officers to remain well disposed and maintain the boy on his throne; and afterwards brought in two silver urns, the one said to contains the bones of the king and the other those of Arsinoë. As a fact, the one did contain the king's bones, but the other was full of spices. Hereupon they at once celebrated the funeral, and now the real circumstances of Arsinoë's fate became manifest to all. For on her death being made known, everyone began to inquire how she had perished. As there was no other cause assigned when the true report began to reach people's ears, though doubt still subsisted, the truth was impressed on the minds of all, and the people were much stirred in consequence. As for the king, no one cared, but concerning Arsinoë, when some recalled her orphanhood and others the insults and outrages inflicted on her during her whole life, and finally her unhappy death, the people fell into such a state of distraction and affliction that the town was full of groans, tears, and ceaseless lamentation, a testimony, in the opinion of those who judged correctly, not so much of affection for Arsinoë as of hatred of Agathocles. The latter, after depositing the urns in the royal vaults, ordered the public mourning to cease, and as a first step granted two month's pay to the troops, feeling sure of taking the edge off their hatred by appealing to the soldiers' spirit of avarice, and in the next place imposed on them the oath they were accustomed to take on the proclamation of a new king.

Revels in the palace of Alexandria

11.

20-26. Ὁ δ´ Ἀγαθοκλῆς, ἐπεὶ τοὺς ἐπιφανεστάτους τῶν ἀνδρῶν ἐκποδὼν ἐποίησε, καὶ τὸ πολὺ τῆς τοῦ πλήθους ὀργῆς παρακατέσχε τῇ τῶν ὀψωνίων ἀποδόσει, παρὰ πόδας εἰς τὴν ἐξ ἀρχῆς συνήθειαν ἐπανῆλθε. καὶ τὰς μὲν τῶν φίλων χώρας ἀνεπλήρωσε, παρεισαγαγὼν ἐκ τῆς διακονίας καὶ τῆς ἄλλης ὑπηρεσίας τοὺς εἰκαιοτάτους καὶ θρασυτάτους · αὐτὸς δὲ τὸ πολὺ τῆς ἡμέρας καὶ τῆς νυκτὸς ἐν μέθῃ διέτριβε καὶ ταῖς τῇ μέθῃ παρεπομέναις ἀκρασίαις, οὐ φειδόμεος οὔτ´ ἀκμαζούσης γυναικὸς οὔτε νύμφης οὔτε παρθένου, καὶ πὰντα ταῦτ´ ἔπραττε μετὰ τῆς ἐπαχθεστάτης φαντασίας . ὅθεν πολλῆς μὲν καὶ παντοδαπῆς γινομένης δυσαρεστήσεως, οὐδεμιᾶς δὲ θεραπείας οὐδὲ βοηθείας προσαγομένης, τὸ δ´ ἐναντίον ἀεὶ προσεπαγομένης ὕβρεως, ὑπερηφανίας, ῥᾳθυμίας, ἀνεθυμιᾶτο πάλιν ἐν τοῖς πολλοῖς τὸ προϋπάρχον μῖσος καὶ πὰντες ἀνενεοῦντο τὰ προγεγενημένα περὶ τὴν βασιλείαν ἀτυχήματα διὰ τοὺς ἀνθρώπους τούτους. τῷ δὲ μηδὲν ἔχειν πρόσωπον ἀξιόχρεων τὸ προστησόμενον, καὶ δι´ οὗ τὴν ὀργὴν εἰς τὸν Ἀγαθοκλέα καὶ τὴν Ἀγαθόκλειαν ἀπερείσονται, τὴν ἡσυχίαν ἦγον, ἔτι μίαν ἐλπίδα καραδοκοῦντες τὴν κατὰ τὸν Τληπόλεμον καὶ ταύτῃ προσανέχοντες.

XV, 31-33 ... Ο μὲν γὰρ Τληπόλεμος, ἐξιδιάζεσθαι σπεύδων τοὺς ἡγεμόνας καὶ ταξιάρχους καὶ τοὺς ἐπὶ τούτων τaττομένους, συνῆγε πότους ἐπιμελῶς, καὶ παρὰ τὰς συνουσίας τὰ μὲν ὑπὸ τῶν πρὸς χάριν λεγόντων αἰκαλλόμενος, τὰ δ´ ὑπὸ τῆς ἰδίας ὁρμῆς, ἅτε νέος ὢν καὶ παρὰ τὸν οἶνον γινομένης τῆς ὁμιλίας, ἐρρίπτει λόγους κατὰ τῆς συγγενείας τῆς τῶν περὶ τὸν 'Αγαθοκλέα, τὰς μὲν ἀρχὰς αἰνιγματώδεις, εἶτ᾽ ἀμφιβόλους, τὸ δὲ τελευταῖον ἐκφανεῖς καὶ τὴν πικροτάτην ἔχοντας λοιδορίαν. ἐπεχεῖτο γὰρ τοῦ θρανογράφου καὶ τῆς σαμβυκιστρίας καὶ τῆς κουρίδος, ἔτι δὲ τοῦ παιδαρίου τοῦ πάντα πεποιηκότος καὶ πεπονθότος παρὰ τοὺς πότους, ὅτ᾽ ἐῳνοχόει τῷ βασιλεῖ παῖς ὤν. ἐπὶ δὲ τούτοις ἀεὶ τῶν συμπαρόντων γελώντων καὶ συμβαλλομένων τι πρὸς τὸν χλευασμόν, ταχέως εἰς τοὺς περὶ τὸν'Αγαθοκλέα τὸ πρᾶγμα παρεγενήθη.

11.

XV, 20-26 ... Agathocles, as soon as he had removed all the most notable men and checked to a great extent by the advance of pay the disaffection among the troops, turned to his old course. He filled up the vacant places of the royal 'friends' by appointing from the body servants and other attendants those most remarkable for their effrontery and recklessness. He himself spent the greater part of the day and night in drinking and the debauchery which commonly accompanies it, sparing neither women in the flower of their age nor brides nor virgins, and all this he did with the most odious ostentation. So that as strong dislike against him was aroused on all sides, as no attempt was made to conciliate or help those aggrieved, but on the contrary there was a constant repetition of outrage, arrogance and neglect, the former hatred of the populace for him began to fume again, and all recalled the calamities that these men had brought on the kingdom. But since they have no leader of any weight, through whom to vent their anger on Agathocles and Agathoclea, they kept quiet, their only remaining hope, to which they eagerly clung, being in Tlepolemus ...

XV, 31-33 ... For Tlepolemus, as he was desirous of attaching to himself the commanders, taxiarchs, and inferiors officers, entertained them sedulously at banquets; and on these occasions, either flattered by those who wished to make themselves agreeable to him or on his own impulse, since he was young and they were talking over their wine, he would make remarks about the family of Agathocles, at first enigmatical, then of doubtful import, but finally quite outspoken and conveying the most venomous insults. For he used to toast the wall-dauber and the sackbut-girl and the lady-barber, and the young boy who was so complaisant at the drinking-bouts when he was cupbearer to the king in his childhood days. As his guests always laughed with him and contributed something of their own to his jests, the matter soon reached the ears of Agathocles.

The palace invaded by garrisons from the countryside

Polybius, *The Histories,* XV, 26. Translation by W R Paton (The Loeb Classical Library, 1925).

11 bis

XV, 26. Πρώτους δὲ συναθροίσας τοὺς Μακεδόνας, εἰς τούτους εἰσῆλθε[6] (Ἀγαθοκλῆς) μετὰ τοῦ βασιλέως καὶ τῆς 'Αγαθοκλείας. καὶ τὰς μὲν ἀρχὰς ὑπεκρίνετο τὸν οὐ δυνάμενον εἰπεῖν ἃ βούλεται διὰ τὸ πλῆθος τῶν ἐπιφερομένων δακρύων· ἐπεὶ δὲ πλεονάκις ἀπομάττων τῇ χλαμύδι κατεκράτησε τῆς ἐπιφορᾶς, βαστάσας τὸ παιδίον "Λάβετε" ἔφη "τοῦτον, ὃν ὁ πατὴρ ἀποθνήσκων εἰς μὲν τὰς ἀγκάλας ἔδωκε ταύτῃ " δείξας τὴν ἀδελφὴν" παρακατέθετο δ᾽ εἰς τὴν ὑμετέραν, ὦ ἄνδρες Μακεδόνες, πίστιν . ἡ μὲν οὖν [καὶ] ταύτης εὔνοια βραχεῖάν τινα ῥοπὴν ἔχει πρὸς τὴν τούτου σωτηρίαν, ἐν ὑμῖν δὲ κεῖται καὶ ταῖς ὑμετέραις χερσὶ τὰ τούτου νυνὶ πράγματα.

Τληπόλεμος γὰρ πάλαι μὲν ἦν δῆλος τοῖς ὀρθῶς σκοπουμένοις μειζόνων ἐφιέμενος ἢ καθ᾽ ἑαυτὸν πραγμάτων, νῦν δὲ καὶ τὴν ἡμέραν καὶ τὸν καιρὸν ὥρικεν, ἐν ᾗ μέλλει τὸ διάδημ᾽ ἀναλαμβάνειν ." καὶ περὶ τούτων οὐχ αὑτῷ πιστεύειν ἐκέλευεν, ἀλλὰ τοῖς εἰδόσι τὴν ἀλήθειαν καὶ παροῦσι νῦν ἐξ αὐτῶν τῶν πραγμάτων. καὶ τοῦτ᾽ εἰπὼν εἰσῆγε τὸν Κριτόλαον, ὃς ἔφη καὶ τοὺς βωμοὺς αὐτὸς ἑωρακέναι κατασκευαζομένους καὶ τὰ θύματα παρὰ τοῖς πλήθεσιν ἑτοιμαζόμενα πρὸς τὴν τοῦ διαδήματος ἀνάδειξιν. ὧν οἱ Μακεδόνες ἀκούοντες οὐχ οἷον ἠλέουν αὐτόν, ἀλλ᾽ ἁπλῶς οὐδὲν προσεῖχον τῶν λεγομένων, μυχθίζοντες < δὲ καὶ > διαψιθυρίζοντες ἐξελήρησαν οὕτως ὥστε μηδ᾽ αὐτον εἰδέναι [μήτε] πῶς τὸ παράπαν ἐκ τῆς ἐκκλησίας ἀπελύθη. παραπλήσια δὲ τούτοις ἐγίνετο καὶ περὶ τὰ λοιπὰ συστήματα κατὰ τοὺς ἐκκλησιασμούς . ἐν δὲ τῷ μεταξὺ πολὺς ἦν ὁ καταπλέων ἐκ τῶν ἄνω στρατοπέδων, καὶ παρεκάλουν οἱ μὲν συγγενεῖς, οἱ δὲ φίλους, βοηθεῖν τοῖς ὑποκειμένοις, καὶ μὴ περιιδεῖν σφᾶς ἀνέδην ὑφ᾽ οὕτως ἀναξίων ὑβριζομένους. μάλιστα δὲ παρώξυνε τοὺς πολλοὺς πρὸς τὴν κατὰ τῶν προεστώτων τιμωρίαν τὸ γινώσκειν ὅτι τὸ μέλλειν καθ᾽ αὑτῶν ἐστι διὰ τὸ πάντων τῶν παρακομιζομένων ἐπιτηδείων εἰς τὴν Ἀλεξάνδρειαν κρατεῖν τοὺς περὶ τὸν Τληπόλεμον.

11 bis

XV, 26. Agathocles in the first place summoned a meeting of the Macedonians and appeared together with Agathoclea and the young king. At first he pretended that he could not say what he wished owing to the abundance of the tears that choked him, but after wiping his eyes many times with his chlamys and subduing the outburst, he took the child in his arms and exclaimed, 'Take the child whom his father on his death-bed placed in the arms of this woman,' pointing to his sister, 'and confided to your faith, you soldiers of Macedon. Her affection indeed is of but little moment to ensure his safety, but his fate depends on you and your valour. For it has long been evident to those who judge correctly that Tlepolemus aspires to a position higher than it behoves him to covet, and now he has actually fixed the day and hour at which he will assume the diadem.' And as to this he told them not to rely on his own word but on that of those who knew the truth and had just come from the very scene of action. After speaking thus he brought forward Critolaus, who told them that he had himself seen the altars being erected and the victims being prepared in presence of the populace for the ceremony of proclaiming the coronation. When the Macedonians heard this, not only did they feel no pity for Agathocles but paid absolutely no attention to his words, and showed such levity by hooting and murmuring to each other that he did not know himself how he got away from the meeting. The same kind of thing took place at the meetings of the other regiments. Meanwhile numbers of men kept on arriving by boat from the garrisons in upper Egypt, and all begged their relatives or friends to help them at the present crisis and not allow them to be thus outrageously tyrannized over by such unworthy persons. The chief incentive to the soldiery to wreak their vengeance on those in power was their knowledge that any delay was prejudicial to themselves, as Tlepolemus controlled the entire supply of provisions reaching Alexandria.

Disturbances in the royal quarter and torture in the palace

Polybius, *The Histories*, XV, 27-28. Translation by W R Paton (The Loeb Classical Library, 1993).

12.

XV, 27. 'Εγένετο δέ τι καὶ ἐξ αὐτῶν <τῶν> περὶ τὸν'Αγαθοκλέα συνέργημα πρὸς τὸ τὴν ὀργὴν ἐπιτεῖναι τήν τε τῶν πολλῶν καὶ τὴν τοῦ Τληπολέμου · τὴν γὰρ Δανάην, ἥτις ἦν πενθερὰ τοῦ προειρημένου, λαβόντες ἐκ τοῦ τῆς Δήμητρος ἱεροῦ καὶ διὰ μέσου τῆς πόλεως ἑλκύσαντες ἀκατακάλυπτον εἰς φυλακὴν ἀπέθεντο, βουλόμενοι φανερὰν ποιεῖν τὴν πρὸς τὸν Τληπόλεμον διαφοράν. ἐφ' οἷς τὸ πλῆθος ἀγανακτοῦν οὐκέτι κατ' ἰδίαν οὐδὲ δι' ἀπορρήτων ἐποιεῖτο τοὺς λόγους, ἀλλ' οἱ μὲν τὰς νύκτας εἰς πάντα τόπον ἐπέγραφον, οἱ δὲ τὰς ἡμέρας συστρεφόμενοι κατὰ μέρη φανερῶς ἐξέφερον ἤδη τὸ μῖσος εἰς τοὺς προεστῶτας.

Οἱ δὲ περὶ τὸν 'Αγαθοκλέα βλέποντες τὰ συμβαίνοντα, καὶ μοχθηρὰς ἐλπίδας ἔχοντες περὶ αὐτῶν, τοτὲ μὲν ἐγίνοντο περὶ δρασμόν, οὐδενὸς δ' αὐτοῖς ἡτοιμασμένου πρὸς τοῦτο τὸ μέρος διὰ τὴν σφετέραν ἀβουλίαν ἀφίσταντο τῆς ἐπιβολῆς · τοτὲ δὲ συνωμότας κατέγραφον καὶ κοινωνοὺς τῆς τόλμης, ὡς αὐτίκα μάλα τῶν ἐχθρῶν τοὺς μὲν κατασφάξοντες, τοὺς δὲ συλληψόμενοι, μετὰ δὲ ταῦτα τυραννικὴν ἐξουσίαν περιποιησόμενοι. ταῦτα δ' αὐτῶν διανοουμένων προσέπεσε διαβολὴ κατά τινος Μοιραγένους, ἑνὸς τῶν σωματοφυλάκων, διότι μηνύοι πάντα τῷ Τληπολέμῳ καὶ συνεργοίη διὰ τὴν πρὸς 'Αδαῖον οἰκειότητα τὸν ἐπὶ τῆς Βουβαστοῦ τότε καθεσταμένον. ὁ δ' Ἀγαθοκλῆς εὐθέως συνέταξε Νικοστράτῳ τῷ πρὸς τοῖς γράμμασι τεταγμένῳ συλλαβόντι τὸν Μοιραγένη φιλοτίμως ἐξετάσαι, πᾶσαν προτιθέντα βάσανον. οὗτος μὲν οὖν παραχρῆμα συλληφθεὶς ὑπὸ τοῦ Νικοστράτου καὶ παραχθεὶς ἔις τινα μέρη τῆς αὐλῆς ἀποκεχωρηκότα, τὸ μὲν πρῶτον ἐξ ὀρθῆς ἀνεκρίνετο περὶ τῶν προσπεπτωκότων, πρὸς οὐδὲν δὲ τῶν λεγομένων ἀνθομολογούμενος ἐξεδύθη · καὶ τινὲς μὲν τὰ πρὸς τὰς βασάνους ὄργανα διεσκεύαζον, οἱ δὲ τὰς μάστιγας ἔχοντες μετὰ χεῖρας ἀπεδύοντο τὰς χλαμύδας . κατὰ δὲ τὸν καιρὸν τοῦτον προστρέχει τις τῶν ὑπηρετῶν πρὸς τὸν Νικόστρατον, καὶ ψιθυρίσας πρὸς τὴν ἀκοὴν ἅττα δήποτ' οὖν ἀπηλλάττετο μετὰ σπουδῆς. ὁ δὲ Νικόστρατος ἐκ ποδὸς ἐπηκολούθει τούτῳ, λέγων μὲν οὐδέν, τύπτων δὲ συνεχῶς τὸν μηρόν .

XV, 28. περὶ δὲ τὸν Μοιραγένην ἄφατον ἦν καὶ παράλογον τὸ συμβαῖνον. οἱ μὲν γὰρ μόνον οὐ διατεταμένοι τὰς μάστιγας παρέστασαν, οἱ δὲ πρὸ ποδῶν αὐτοῦ τὰ πρὸς ἀνάγκας ὄργανα διεσκεύαζον · τοῦ δὲ Νικοστράτου παραχωρήσαντος ἕστασαν ἀχανεῖς πάντες, ἐμβλέποντες ἀλλήλοις, προσδοκῶντες ἀεί ποτε τὸν προειρημένον ἀνακάμψειν. χρόνου δὲ γινομένου κατὰ βραχὺ διέρρεον οἱ παρεστῶτες, τέλος δ' ὁ Μοιραγένης ἀπελείφθη . καὶ μετὰ ταῦτα διελθὼν τὴν αὐλὴν ἀνελπίστως παρέπεσε γυμνὸς εἴς τινα σκηνὴν τῶν Μακεδόνων, σύνεγγυς κειμένην τῆς αὐλῆς . καταλαβὼν δὲ κατὰ τύχην ἀριστῶντας καὶ συνηθροισμένους, ἔλεγε τὰ περὶ αὐτὸν συμβεβηκότα καὶ τὸ παράλογον τῆς σωτηρίας . οἱ δὲ τὰ μὲν ἠπίστουν, τὰ δὲ πάλιν ὁρῶντες αὐτὸν γυμνὸν ἠναγκάζοντο πιστεύειν . ἐκ δὲ ταύτης τῆς περιπετείας ὅ τε Μοιραγένης μετὰ δακρύων ἐδεῖτο τῶν Μακεδόνων μὴ μόνον τῆς αὐτοῦ συνεπιλαβέσθαι σωτηρίας, ἀλλὰ καὶ τῆς τοῦ βασιλέως, καὶ μάλιστα τῆς σφῶν αὐτῶν · πρόδηλον γὰρ εἶναι πᾶσι τὸν ὄλεθρον, ἐὰν μὴ συνάψωνται τοῦ καιροῦ, καθ΄ ὅν ἀκμάζει τὸ τῶν πολλῶν μῖσος καὶ πᾶς ἕτοιμός ἐστι πρὸς τὴν κατ΄ ᾿Αγαθοκλέους τιμωρίαν. ἀκμάζειν δὲ νῦν μάλιστ΄ ἔφη καὶ προσδεῖσθαι τῶν καταρξομένων.

12.

XV, 27. There was also one thing done by Agathocles and his party which contributed to exasperate the populace and Tlepolemus. For they took Danaë, who was the latter's mother-in-law, from the temple of Demeter, and dragged her unveiled through the middle of the town and committed her to prison, with the express object of exhibiting their hostility to him. This so irritated the people that they no longer spoke of the matter in private and secretly, but while some expressed their detestation of those in power by scribbling it all over the town at night, others even began to meet openly in groups in the day-time for this purpose.

Agathocles, seeing what was happening and entertaining poor hopes of his own security, began to contemplate flight; but as owing to his own imprudence he had made no preparations for this purpose he desisted from the project, and his next step was to enrol conspirators ready to join in the venture, with a view to putting to death some of his enemies at once and arresting others, after which he could possess himself of tyrannical power. While he was engaged in this project an accusation was brought against a certain Moeragenes, one of the bodyguards, to the effect that he informed Tlepolemus of everything and worked for his cause owing to his relationship with Adaeus, then governor of Bubastus. Agathocles at once gave orders to Nicostratus, his secretary of state, to arrest Moeragenes and examine him diligently, menacing him with every kind of torture. Moeragenes was instantly arrested and conducted to a remote part of the palace, where he was at first questioned directly concerning these rumours, and on his denying every one of the charges was stripped. Some began to get the instruments of torture ready and others with the scourges in their hands were taking off their cloaks, when one of the servants ran up to Nicostratus and after whispering something into his ear made off in haste. Nicostratus immediately followed him without saying a word, but striking his thigh with his hand repeatedly.

28. It is difficult to describe the strange situation in which Moeragenes found himself. For some of the executioners stood there with their scourges almost raised to strike him and others were getting the instruments of torture ready before his eyes; but when Nicostratus departed all remained in mute astonishment, looking at each other, and each moment expecting Nicostratus to return; but after a little time had elapsed they gradually dispersed, and Moeragenes was left by himself. After that he was able, much to his surprise, to traverse the palace, and naked as he was rushed into a tent belonging to the Macedonian troops not far from the palace. Finding them by chance assembled there at breakfast he told his story and the extraordinary manner in which he had been delivered. They were disposed to discredit it, but afterwards seeing him naked they were compelled to believe him. Availing himself of this complete change of circumstances, Moeragenes begged the Macedonians with tears not only to help him to save himself, but to save the king also and chiefly themselves. He urged upon them that their destruction was inevitable if they did not avail themselves of the present opportunity, when the hatred of the populace was at its height and everyone was ready to take vengeance on Agathocles. This was just the time, he said, when the feeling was most thoroughly aroused and it only wanted someone to begin.

Scenes in the street near the palaces

Polybius, *The Histories*, XV, 29-30. Translation by W R Paton (The Loeb Classical Library).

13.

XV, 29. οἱ δὲ Μακεδόνες ἀκούσαντες τούτων παραξύνονται, καὶ πέρας ἐπείσθησαν τῷ Μοιραγένει, καὶ πρώτας μὲν εὐθέως ἐπῄεσαν τὰς τῶν Μακεδόνων σκηνάς, μετὰ δὲ ταῦτα τὰς τῶν ἄλλων στρατιωτῶν · εἰσὶ δ´ αὗται συνεχεῖς, πρὸς ἓν μέρος ἀπονενευκυῖαι τῆς πόλεως . οὔσης δὲ τῆς μὲν ὁρμῆς πάλαι προχείρου τῆς τῶν πολλῶν, προσδεομένης δὲ τοῦ προκαλεσομένου μόνον καὶ τολμήσοντος, ἅμα τῷ λαβεῖν ἀρχὴν τὸ πρᾶγμα ταχέως οἷον εἰ πῦρ ἐξέλαμψεν. οὐ γὰρ ἐγενήθησαν ὧραι τέτταρες καὶ πάντα τὰ γένη συμπεφωνήκει καὶ τ τρατιωτικὰ καὶ τὰ πολιτικὰ πρὸς τὴν ἐπίθεσιν. συνήργησε γὰρ μεγάλα καὶ ταὐτόματον ἐν τῷ καιρῷ τούτῳ πρὸς τὴν συντέλειαν. ὁ μὲν γὰρ ᾽Αγαθοκλῆς, ἀνενεχθείσης πρὸς αὐτὸν ἐπιστολῆς καὶ κατασκόπων ἐπαναχθέντων, καὶ τῆς μὲν ἐπιστολῆς γεγραμμένης πρὸς τὰς δυνάμεις παρὰ τοῦ Τληπολέμου καὶ δηλούσης ὅτι παρέσται ταχέως, τῶν δὲ κατασκόπων διασαφούντων ὅτι πάρεστιν, οὕτως ἐξέστη τῶν φρενῶν ὥστ´ ἀφέμενος τοῦ πράττειν τι καὶ διανοεῖσθαι περὶ τῶν προπεπτωκότων ἀπῆλθε κατὰ τὸν εἰθισμένον καιρὸν εἰς τὸν πότον, κἀκεῖ κατὰ τὴν εἰθισμένην ἀγωγὴν ἐπετέλει τὴν συνουσίαν . ἡ δ´ Οἰνάνθη περικακοῦσα παρῆν εἰς τὸ Θεσμοφορεῖον, ἀνεῳγμένου τοῦ νεὼ διά τινα θυσίαν ἐπέτειον. καὶ τὸ μὲν πρῶτον ἐλιπάρει γονυπετοῦσα καὶ μαγγανεύουσα πρὸς τὰς θεάς, μετὰ δὲ ταῦτα καθίσασα πρὸς τὸν βωμὸν εἶχε τὴν ἡσυχίαν . αἱ μὲν οὖν πολλαὶ τῶν γυναικῶν, ἡδέως ὁρῶσαι τὴν δυσθυμίαν καὶ περικάκησιν αὐτῆς, ἀπεσιώπων · αἱ δὲ τοῦ Πολυκράτους συγγενεῖς καί τινες ἕτεραι τῶν ἐνδόξων, ἀδήλου τῆς περιστάσεως αὐταῖς ἀκμὴν ὑπαρχούσης, προσελθοῦσαι παρεμυθοῦντο τὴν Οἰνάνθην. ἡ δ´ ἀναβοήσασα μεγάλῃ τῇ φωνῇ "μή μοι πρόσιτέ", φησι, "θηρία. καλῶς γὰς ὑμας γινώσκω, διότι καὶ φρονεῖθ´ ἡμῖν ἐναντία καὶ ταῖς θεαῖς εὔχεσθε τὰ δυσχερέστατα καθ´ ἡμῶν · οὐ μὴν ἀλλ´ ἔτι πέποιθα τῶν θεῶν βουλομένων γεύσειν ὑμᾶς τῶν ἰδίων τέκνων". καὶ ταῦτ´ εἰποῦσα ταῖς ῥαβδούχοις ἀνείργειν προσέταξε καὶ παίειν τὰς μὴ πειθαρχούσας. αἱ δ´ ἐπιλαβόμεναι τῆς προφάσεως ταύτης ἀπηλλάττοντο πᾶσαι, τοῖς θεοῖς ἀνίσχουσαι τὰς χεῖρας καὶ καταρώμεναι λαβεῖν αὐτὴν ἐκείνην πεῖραν τούτων, ἃ κατὰ τῶν πέλας ἐπανετείνετο πράξειν.

XV 30. Ἤδη δὲ κεκριμένου τοῦ καινοτομεῖν τοῖς ἀνδράσιν, ἐπιγενομένης καθ´ ἑκάστην οἰκίαν καὶ τῆς ἐκ τῶν γυναικῶν ὀργῆς διπλάσιον ἐξεκαύθη τὸ μῖσος · ἅμα δὲ τῷ μεταλαβεῖν τὸ τῆς νυκτὸς πᾶσα πλήρης ἦν ἡ πόλις θορύβου καὶ φώτων καὶ διαδρομῆς · οἱ μὲν γὰρ εἰς τὸ στάδιον ἠθροίζοντο μετὰ κραυγῆς, οἱ δὲ παρεκάλουν ἀλλήλους, οἱ δὲ κατεδύοντο διαδιδράσκοντες εἰς ἀνυπονοήτους οἰκίας καὶ τόπους · ἤδη δὲ τῶν περὶ τὴν αὐλὴν εὐρυχωριῶν καὶ τοῦ σταδίου καὶ τῆς πλατείας πλήρους ὑπαρχούσης ὄχλου παντοδαποῦ καὶ τῆς περὶ τὸ Διονυσιακὸν θέατρον προστασίας, πυθόμενος τὸ συμβαῖνον ᾽Αγαθοκλῆς ἐξηγέρθη μεθύων, ἄρτι καταλελυκὼς τὸν πότον, καὶ παραλαβὼν τοὺς συγγενεῖς πάντας πλὴν Φίλωνος ἧκε πρὸς τὸν βασιλέα. καὶ βραχέα πρὸς τοῦτον οἰκτισάμενος καὶ λαβόμενος αὐτοῦ τῆς χειρός, ἀνέβαινεν εἰς τὴν σύριγγα τὴν μεταξὺ τοῦ Μαιάνδρου καὶ τῆς παλαίστρας κειμένην καὶ φέρουσαν ἐπὶ τὴν τοῦ θεάτρου πάροδον . μετὰ δὲ ταῦτα, δύο θύρας ἀσφαλισάμενος τὰς πρώτας, εἰς τὴν τρίτην ἀνεχώρησε μετὰ δυεῖν ἢ τριῶν σωματοφυλάκων καὶ τοῦ βασιλέως καὶ τῆς αὑτοῦ συγγενείας . συνέβαινε δὲ τὰς θύρας εἶναι δικτυωτὰς διαφανεῖς, ἀποκλειομένας δὲ διττοῖς μοχλοῖς, κατὰ δὲ τὸν καιρὸν τοῦτον ἠθροισμένου τοῦ πλήθους ἐξ ἁπάσης τῆς πόλεως, ὥστε μὴ μόνον τοὺς ἐπιπέδους τόπους, ἀλλὰ καὶ τὰ βάθρα καὶ τὰ τέγη καταγέμειν ἀνθρώπων, ἐγίνετο βοὴ καὶ κραυγὴ σύμμικτος, ὡς ἂν γυναικῶν ὁμοῦ καὶ παίδων ἀνδράσιν ἀναμεμιγμένων · οὐ γὰρ ἔλαττω ποιεῖ τὰ παιδάρια τῶν ἀνδρῶν περὶ τὰς τοιαύτας ταραχὰς ἔν τε τῇ Καρχηδονίων πόλει καὶ κατὰ τὴν ᾽Αλεξάνδρειαν.

13.

XV 29. The Macedonians on hearing this were stimulated to action and finally took the advice of Moeragenes, first without delay visiting the Macedonians tents and then those of the other soldiers, which are all close together, and turned towards a single part of the city. As the people had long been disposed to revolt and required only some man of courage to appeal to them, once the movement began it spread like wildfire. Four hours had scarcely elapsed when men of all nationalities, both soldiers and civilians, had agreed to attack the government. Chance too co-operated much at this time to the accomplishment of their aim. For Agathocles, when a letter reached his hands, and some spies were brought before him, and when the letter proved to be one addressed by Tlepolemus to the troops announcing that he was on the point of coming, and the spies reported that he had actually arrived, so entirely lost his head that, neglecting to take any action or to consider the news he had received, he went to carouse at his usual hour and conducted himself at the banquet in his usual manner. Oenanthe, who was in great distress, betook herself to the Thesmophoreum, that temple being open for an annual sacrifice. She first of all fell on her knees and with many gestures prayed fervently to the goddesses, and afterwards seated herself by the altar and held her peace. Most of the women, pleased to see her so dejected and distressed, remained silent, but the relatives of Polycrates and some other noble ladies, who were not yet aware of the danger, came up to her to console her. 'Come not near me, you beasts', she cried aloud to them, 'I know well that you bear us ill-will and that you pray to the goddesses that the worst may befall us, but yet I trust that, if it be the will of heaven, I shall yet make you taste the flesh of your own children.' After saying this she bade her lictors drive them away from her and strike those who refused to leave. Availing themselves of this pretext all the ladies withdrew, holding up their hands to the goddesses and praying that she might be cursed with the fate that she threatened to bring on others.

30. The men had already decided on a revolution, but now that in each house the rage of the women was added to their own, the hatred of the usurper blazed twice as violent. When day again gave place to night, the whole town was full of disturbance and torches and movement. For some collected in the stadium shouting, some were encouraging each other, others running in different directions took refuge in houses and places not likely to be suspected. The open spaces round the palace, the stadium, and the great square were now filled by a mixed multitude, including all the crowd of supernumerary performers in the theatre of Dionysius, and Agathocles, when he heard what was occuring, aroused himself from his drunken slumber, having broken up the banquet a short time previously, and taking all his relatives except Philo went to the king. After lamenting his ill-fortune to the boy in a few words he took him by the hand and went up to the gallery between the Maeander and the palaestra leading to the entrance to the theatre. After this, having made fast the first two doors, he retired to the third with a few of the bodyguard, the king, and his own relatives. The doors were of open lattice-work and one could see through them, and they were each secured by two bolts. Meanwhile the populace were assembling from every part of the city, so that not only level spaces but the roofs and steps were full of people, and there was a confused hubbub and clamour, women and children being mixed

with the men. For in Carthage and also in Alexandria the children play no less a part in such tumults than the men.

The invasion of the palace by the Macedonians and the arrival of the king at the stadium

Polybius, *The Histories*, XV, 31-32. Translation by W R Paton (The Loeb Classical Library, 1970).

14.

XV 31. Ἤδη δὲ τῆς ἡμέρας ὑποφαινούσης ἦν μὲν ἄκριτος ἡ κραυγή, μάλιστα δ΄ ἐξ αὐτῆς ἐξέλαμψε τὸ καλεῖν τὸν βασιλέα. τὸ μὲν οὖν πρῶτον οἱ Μακεδόνες ἐξαναστάντες κατελάβοντο τὸν χρηματιστικὸν πυλῶνα τῶν βασιλείων· μετὰ δέ τινα χρόνον ἐπιγνόντες ποῦ τῆς αὐλῆς < ἦν > ὁ βασιλεύς, περιελθόντες τὰς μὲν πρώτας τῆς [πρώτης] σύριγγος ἐξέβαλον θύρας, ἐγγίσαντες δὲ τῆς δευτέρας ᾐτοῦντο τὸν παῖδα μετὰ κραυγῆς. οἱ δὲ περὶ τὸν 'Αγαθοκλέα, βλέποντες ἤδη τὰ καθ΄ αὑτούς, ἐδέοντο τῶν σωματοφυλάκων πρεσβεῦσαι περὶ αὐτῶν πρὸς τοὺς Μακεδόνας, δηλοῦντας ὅτι τῆς ἐπιτροπείας ἐκχωροῦσι καὶ τῆς ἄλλης ἐξουσίας καὶ τῶν τιμῶν, ἔτι δὲ τῶν χορηγίων ὧν ἔχουσι πάντων, αὐτὸ δὲ τὸ πνευμάτιον δέονται συγχωρηθῆναι σφίσι μετὰ τῆς ἀναγκαίας τροφῆς, ἵνα χωρήσαντες εἰς τὴν ἐξ ἀρχῆς διάθεσιν μηδὲ βουληθέντες ἔτι δύνωνται λυπεῖν μηδένα. τῶν μὲν οὖν ἄλλων σωματοφυλάκων οὐδεὶς ὑπήκουσεν, 'Αριστομένης δὲ μόνος ὑπέστη τὴν χρείαν ταύτην ὁ μετά τινα χρόνον ἐπὶ τῶν πραγμάτων γενόμενος. ὁ δ΄ ἀνὴρ οὗτος τὸ μὲν γένος ἦν 'Ακαρνάν, καθ΄ ὅσον δὲ προβαίνων κατὰ τὴν ἡλικίαν, γενόμενος κύριος τῶν ὅλων πραγμάτων, κάλλιστα καὶ σεμνότατα δοκεῖ προστῆναι τοῦ τε βασιλέως καὶ τῆς βασιλείας, κατὰ τοσοῦτον κεκολακευκέναι τὴν 'Αγαθοκλέους εὐκαιρίαν. πρῶτος μὲν γὰρ ὡς ἑαυτὸν ἐπὶ δεῖπνον καλέσας τὸν 'Αγαθοκλέα χρυσοῦν στέφανον ἀνέδωκε μόνῳ τῶν παρόντων, ὃ τοῖς βασιλεῦσιν αὐτοῖς ἔθος ἐστὶ μόνοις συγχωρεῖσθαι, πρῶτος δὲ τὴν εἰκόνα τοῦ προειρημένου φέρειν ἐτόλμησεν ἐν τῷ δακτυλίῳ· γενομένης δὲ θυγατρὸς αὐτῷ ταύτην 'Αγαθόκλειαν προσηγόρευσεν. ἀλλ΄ ἴσως ὑπὲρ μὲν τούτων ἐξαρκεῖ καὶ τὰ νῦν εἰρημένα · λαβὼν δὲ τὰς προειρημένας ἐντολὰς καὶ διά τινος ῥινοπύλης ἐξελθών, ἧκε πρὸς τοὺς Μακεδόνας. βραχέα δ΄αὐτοῦ διαλεχθέντος καὶ δηλώσαντος τὴν προαίρεσιν, ἐπεβάλοντο μὲν οἱ Μακεδόνες παραχρῆμα συγκεντῆσαι, ταχὺ δέ τινων ὑπερεχόντων αὐτοῦ τὰς χεῖρας καὶ παραιτησαμένων τοὺς πολλούς, ἐπανῆλθε λαβὼν ἐντολὴν ἢ τὸν βασιλέα πρὸς αὐτοὺς ἄγονθ΄ ἥκειν ἢ μηδ΄ αὐτὸν ἐξιέναι. τὸν μὲν οὖν 'Αριστομένην ταῦτ΄ εἰπόντες οἱ Μακεδόνες ἀπέπεμψαν, αὐτοὶ δὲ ταῖς δευτέραις θύραις ἐγγίσαντες ἐξέωσαν καὶ ταύτας. οἱ δὲ περὶ τὸν 'Αγαθοκλέα θεωροῦντες τὴν τῶν Μακεδόνων βίαν διά τε τῶν ἐνεργουμένων καὶ διὰ τῆς ἀποκρίσεως, τὸ μὲν πρῶτον ἐπεβάλοντο διὰ τῆς θύρας προτείναντες τὰς χεῖρας, ἡ δ΄ 'Αγαθόκλεια καὶ τοὺς μασθούς, οἷς ἔφη θρέψαι τὸν βασιλέα, δεῖσθαι τῶν Μακεδόνων, πᾶσαν προϊέμενοι φωνὴν πρὸς τὸ περιποιήσασθαι τὸ ζῆν αὐτὸ μόνον·

XV 32. ἐπεὶ δὲ πολλὰ κατολοφυρόμενοι τὴν αὑτῶν τύχην οὐδὲν ἤνυον, τέλος ἐξέπεμψαν τὸν παῖδα μετὰ τῶν σωματοφυλάκων. οἱ δὲ Μακεδόνες, παραλαβόντες τὸν βασιλέα καὶ ταχέως ἐφ΄ ἵππον ἀναβιβάσαντες, ἦγον εἰς τὸ στάδιον. ἅμα δὲ τῷ φανῆναι μεγάλης κραυγῆς καὶ κρότου γενηθέντος, ἐπιστήσαντες τὸν ἵππον καθεῖλον τὸν παῖδα καὶ προαγαγόντες ἐκάθισαν εἰς τὴν βασιλικὴν θέαν. περὶ δὲ τοὺς ὄχλους ἐγένετό τις ἅμα χαρὰ καὶ λύπη· τὰ μὲν γὰρ ἦσαν περιχαρεῖς ἐπὶ τῷ κεκομίσθαι τὸν παῖδα, τὰ δὲ πάλιν δυσηρέστουν τῷ μὴ συνειλῆφθαι τοὺς αἰτίους μηδὲ τυγχάνειν τῆς ἁρμοζούσης τιμωρίας. διὸ καὶ συνεχῶς ἐβόων, ἄγειν κελεύοντες καὶ παραδειγματίζειν τοὺς πάντων τῶν κακῶν αἰτίους. ἤδη δὲ τῆς ἡμέρας προβαινούσης, καὶ τοῦ πλήθους ἐπ᾽ οὐδένα δυναμένου πέρας ἀπερείσασθαι τὴν ὁρμήν, Σωσίβιος, ὃς ἦν μὲν υἱὸς Σωσιβίου τότε δὲ σωματοφυλαξ ὑπάρχων μάλιστα τὸν νοῦν προσεῖχε τῷ τε βασιλεῖ καὶ τοῖς πράγμασι, θεωρῶν τήν τε τοῦ πλήθους ὁρμὴν ἀμετάθετον οὖσαν καὶ τὸ παιδίον δυσχρηστούμενον διά τε τὴν τῶν παρεστώτων ἀσυνήθειαν καὶ διὰ τὴν περὶ τὸν ὄχλον ταραχήν, ἐπύθετο τοῦ βασιλέως εἰ παραδώσει τοῖς πολλοῖς τοὺς εἰς αὐτὸν ἢ τὴν μητέρα τι πεπλημμεληκότας. τοῦ δὲ κατανεύσαντος, τῶν μὲν σωματοφυλάκων τισὶν εἶπε δηλῶσαι τὴν τοῦ βασιλέως γνώμην, τὸ δὲ παιδίον ἀναστήσας ἀπῆγε πρὸς τὴν θεραπείαν εἰς τὴν ἰδίαν οἰκίαν, σύνεγγυς οὖσαν. τῶν δὲ διασαφούντων τὰ παρὰ τοῦ βασιλέως, κατερρήγνυτο πᾶς ὁ τόπος ὑπὸ τοῦ κρότου καὶ τῆς κραυγῆς · οἱ δὲ περὶ τὸν ᾿Αγαθοκλέα καὶ τὴν ᾿Αγαθόκλειαν ἐν τούτῳ τῷ καιρῷ διεχωρίσθησαν ἀλλήλων εἰς τὰς ἰδίας καταλύσεις. ταχὺ δὲ τῶν στρατιωτῶν τινες, οἱ μὲν ἐθελοντήν, οἱ δ᾽ ὑπὸ τοῦ πλήθους ἐξωθούμενοι, < παρ >ώρμησαν ἐπὶ τὸ ζητεῖν τοὺς προειρημένους.

14.

XV 31. When the day began to break it was difficult to distinguish the various cries, but that of 'Bring the king' predominated. At first the Macedonians got up and seized the gate of audience of the palace, but shortly after, when they discovered in what part of the building the king was, they went round and after taking the first door of the gallery off its hinges approached the second and clamoured loudly for the king. Agathocles was looking now to his own safety and begged the bodyguards to convey a message on his behalf to the Macedonians, stating that he abandoned the office of regent and all his powers and dignities as well as all his revenue, and begged simply for his poor life and a sufficient supply of food, so that retiring into his original obscurity he could not in future, even if he wished it, hurt anyone. None of the other bodyguards consented, but Aristomenes alone, who afterwards became minister, undertook this service. He was by birth an Acarnanian, and the adulation he had paid to Agathocles in the season of his prosperity was no less conspicuous than his admirable and scrupulous fidelity to the interests of the king and his kingdom when later in life he was at the head of affairs. For he was the first who having invited Agathocles to dinner presented to him alone among the guests a crown of gold, an honour which is customarily paid only to the king, and he was the first who ventured to wear a ring with Agathocles' portrait engraved on it, and when a daughter was born to him he actually called her Agathocleia. Perhaps regarding his character I have said enough; but now when he had received Agathocles' commission he went out by a wicket-gate to the Macedonians. After he had said a few words to them and explained the proposal, the Macedonians at once attempted to run him through, but when some few persons held their hands over him and begged them to spare him, he went back with orders either to return to them bringing the king or not to come at all. Aristomenes, then, was sent back by the Macedonians with this message, and they themselves came up to the second door and broke it in also. Agathocles and his people, seeing the violence of the Macedonians both by their actions and their determined demand, at first attempted to entreat the soldiers, leaving no word unspoken that might move them to spare their lives at least, Agathocles putting out his hands through the door and Agathocleia her breasts with which she said she had suckled the king.

32. When bitterly bewailing their evil fate they found all was useless, they sent out the boy with the bodyguard. The Macedonians then took the king and at once setting him on a horse conducted him to the stadium. His appearance was greeted with loud cheers and clapping of hands, and they now stopped the horse, took him off, and leading him forward placed him in the royal seat. The joy of the crowd was mingled with regret, for on the one hand they were delighted at having the boy in their hands, but on the other they were displeased that the guilty persons had not been arrested and punished as they deserved. So that they continued to shout, demanding that those who had caused all the evil should be taken into custody and made an example. The day had now advanced, and as the people after all could find no one on whom to vent their resentment, Sosibius, who was the son of Sosibius and at the present time, being a member of the bodyguard, particularly devoted his attention to the king and to affairs of state, seeing that there was no hope of appeasing the fury of the populace and that the boy was ill at ease, finding himself among strangers and amidst all the commotion of the mob, asked the king if he would give up to the people those who were in any way guilty of offenses to himself or his mother. When the boy nodded his head in assent Sosibius bade some of the bodyguard communicate the royal decision, and making the boy get up led him away to join his household at his own house which was quite near. When the king's consent was announced, there was a deafening outburst of cheering and applause all through the stadium. Meanwhile Agathocles and Agathoclea has separated and each retired to their own residence, and very soon a certain number of soldiers, some on their own initiative and others forced to go by the crowd, set off in search of both.

From the palace to the pillory

Polybius, *The Histories*, XV, 33. Translation by W R Paton (The Loeb Classical Library, 1925).

15.

XV 33. Τοῦ δὲ ποιεῖν αἷμα καὶ φόνους ἐγένετό τις ἐκ ταὐτομάτου καταρχὴ τοιαύτη. τῶν γὰρ ᾿Αγαθοκλέους ὑπηρετῶν καὶ κολάκων τις ὄνομα Φίλων ἐξῆλθε κραιπαλῶν εἰς τὸ στάδιον. οὗτος θεωρῶν τὴν ὁρμὴν τῶν ὄχλων εἶπε πρὸς τοὺς παρεστῶτας ὅτι πάλιν αὐτοῖς, καθάπερ καὶ πρῴην, ἐὰν ᾿Αγαθοκλῆς ἐξέλθῃ, μεταμελήσει. τῶν δ᾿ἀκουσάντων οἱ μὲν ἀπελοιδόρουν αὐτόν, οἱ δὲ προώθουν. ἐπιβαλομένου δ´ ἀμύνεσθαι ταχέως οἱ μὲν τὴν χλαμύδα περιέρρηξαν, οἱ δὲ τὰς λόγχας προσερείσαντες ἐξεκέντησαν . ἅμα δὲ τῷ τοῦτον εἰς τὸ μέσον ἑλκυσθῆναι μεθ´ ὕβρεως ἔτι σπαίροντα, καὶ γεύσασθαι τὰ πλήθη φόνου, πάντες ἐκαραδόκουν τὴν τῶν ἄλλων παρουσίαν. μετ´ οὐ πολὺ δὲ παρῆν ἀγόμενος πρῶτος ᾿Αγαθοκλῆς δέσμιος · ὃν εὐθέως εἰσιόντα προσδραμόντες τινὲς ἄφνω συνεκέντησαν, ἔργον ποιοῦντες οὐκ ἐχθρῶν, ἀλλ´ εὐνοούντων · αἴτιοι γὰρ ἐγένοντο τοῦ μὴ τυχεῖν αὐτὸν τῆς ἁρμοζούσης καταστροφῆς · μετὰ δὲ τοῦτον ἤχθη Νίκων, εἶτ´᾿Αγαθόκλεια γυμνὴ σὺν ταῖς ἀδελφαῖς, ἑξῆς δὲ τούτοις πάντες οἱ συγγενεῖς . ἐπὶ δὲ πᾶσιν ἐκ τοῦ Θεσμοφορείου τὴν Οἰνάνθην ἀποσπάσαντες ἧκον εἰς τὸ στάδιον, ἄγοντες γυμνὴν ἐφ´ἵππου. παραδοθὲντων δὲ πάντων ὁμοῦ τοῖς ὄχλοις, οἱ μὲν ἔδακνον, οἱ δ´ ἐκέντουν, οἱ δὲ τοὺς ὀφθαλμοὺς ἐξέκοπτον· ἀεὶ δὲ τοῦ πεσόντος τὰ μέλη διέσπων, ἕως ὅτου κατελώβησαν πάντας αὐτούς · δεινὴ γάρ τις ἡ περὶ τοὺς θυμοὺς ὠμότης γίνεται τῶν κατὰ τὴν Αἴγυπτον ἀνθρώπων . κατὰ δὲ τὸν καιρὸν τοῦτον σύντροφοι τῆς ᾿Αρσινόης γεγενημέναι τινὲς παιδίσκαι, πυθόμεναι παραγεγονέναι τὸν Φιλάμμωνα τριταῖον ἀπὸ Κυρήνης τὸν ἐπιστάντα τῷ φόνῳ τῆς βασιλίσσης, ὥρμησαν ἐπὶ τὴν οἰκίαν αὐτοῦ, καὶ βιασάμεναι τὸν μὲν Φιλάμμωνα τύπτουσαι τοῖς λίθοις καὶ τοῖς ξύλοις ἀπέκτειναν, τὸν δ΄ υἱὸν ἀπέπνιξαν, ἀντίπαιδα τὴν ἡλικίαν ὄντα, σὺν δὲ τούτοις τὴν γυναῖκα τοῦ Φιλάμμωνος γυμνὴν εἰς τὴν πλατεῖαν ἐξέλκουσαι διέφθειραν . Καὶ τὰ μὲν περὶ τὸν 'Αγαθοκλέα καὶ τὴν'Αγαθόκλειαν καὶ τοὺς τούτων συγγενεῖς τοιοῦτον ἔσχε τὸ τέλος.

15.

XV 33. The bloodshed and murders which followed were due to the following incident. Philo, one of Agathocles' attendants and parasites, came out into the stadium suffering from the effects of drink. When he observed the popular excitement, he said to those next him, that if Agathocles came out they would have cause to repent again as they had done some days before. Upon hearing this they began some of them to revile and others to hustle him, and when he attempted to defend himself some very soon tore off his cloak and others levelling their spears at him transpierced him. Then as soon as he was ignominiously dragged still breathing into the middle of the stadium and the people had tasted blood, they all eagerly awaited the arrival of the others. It was not long before Agathocles was led in in fetters, and as soon as he entered some people ran up and at once stabbed him, an act of benevolence rather than of enmity, for they thus saved him from suffering the fate he deserved. Next Nico was brought there and after him Agathoclea stripped naked with her sisters and then all her relatives. Last of all the dragged Oenanthe from the Thesmophorium and led her to the stadium naked on horse-back. All of them were delivered into the hands of the mob, and now some began to bite them with their teeth, some to stab them and others to dig out their eyes. Whenever one of them fell they tore the body limb from limb until they had thus mutilated them all. For terrible is the cruelty of the Egyptians when their anger is aroused. At the same time some young girls who had been Arsinoë's close companions, hearing that Philammon, who had directed the queen's murder, had arrived from Cyrene three days before, rushed to his house and forcing an entrance killed Philammon with clubs and stones; strangled his son who was no longer a child, and dragging out his wife naked into the square slew her. Such was the end of Agathocles, Agathoclea, and their kindred.

59 BC. Diodorus Siculus (date of his stay in Alexandria).

The development of Alexandria

Diodorus Siculus, *Library of History*, I, 50, 6-7. Translation by C H Oldfather (The Loeb Classical Library, 1933).

16.

I, 50, 6. Διόπερ ἀπὸ τούτων τῶν χρόνων ἤρξατο ταπεινοῦσθαι μὲν τὰ περὶ τὰς Θήβας, αὔξεσθαι δὲ τὰ περὶ τὴν Μέμφιν, ἕως'Αλεξάνδρου τοῦ Μακεδόνος · τούτου γὰρ ἐπὶ θαλάττῃ τὴν ἐπώνυμον αὐτῷ πόλιν οἰκίσαντος οἱ κατὰ τὸ ἑξῆς βασιλεύσαντες τῆς Αἰγύπτου πάντες ἐφιλοτιμήθησαν εἰς τὴν ταύτης αὔξησιν. 7. Οἱ μὲν γὰρ βασιλείοις μεγαλοπρεπέσιν, οἱ δὲ νεωρίοις καὶ λιμέσιν, οἱ δ΄ ἑτέροις ἀναθήμασι καὶ κατασκευάσμασιν ἀξιολόγοις ἐπὶ τοσοῦτον ἐκόσμησαν αὐτὴν ὥστε παρὰ τοῖς πλείστοις πρώτην ἢ δευτέραν ἀριθμεῖσθαι τῶν κατὰ τὴν οἰκουμένην πόλεων. 'Αλλὰ περὶ μὲν ταύτης τὰ κατὰ μέρος ἐν τοῖς ἰδίοις χρόνοις ἀναγράψομεν.

16.

... 6.6. And so happily did the founder of the city reckon upon the suitableness of the site that practically all subsequent kings left Thebes and established both their palaces and official residences here. Consequently from this time Thebes began to wane and Memphis to increase, until the time of Alexander the king; for after he had founded the city on the sea which bears his name, all the kings of Egypt after him concentrated their interest on the development of it. Some adorned it with magnificent palaces, some with docks and harbours, and others with further notable dedications and buildings, to such an extent that is generally reckoned the first or second city of the inhabited world. But a detailed description of this city we shall set forth in the appropriate period.

The construction of Alexandria

Diodorus Siculus, *Library of History*, XVII, 52, 1-7. Translation by C H Oldfather (The Loeb Classical Library, 1946).

17.

XVII, 52, 1. Κρίνας δ΄ ἐν ταύτῃ πόλιν μεγάλην κτίσαι προσέταξε τοῖς ἐπὶ τὴν ἐπιμέλειαν ταύτην καταλειπομένοις ἀνὰ μέσον τῆς τε λίμνης καὶ τῆς θαλάσσης οἰκίσαι τὴν πόλιν. 2. Διαμετρήσας δὲ τὸν τόπον καὶ ῥυμοτομήσας φιλοτέχνως τὴν πόλιν ἀφ΄ αὐτοῦ προσηγόρευσεν ᾿Αλεξάνδρειαν, εὐκαιρότατα μὲν κειμένην πλησίον τοῦ Φάρου λιμένος, εὐστοχίᾳ δὲ τῆς ῥυμοτομίας ποιήσας διαπνεῖσθαι τὴν πόλιν τοῖς ἐτησίοις ἀνέμοις καὶ τούτων πνεόντων μὲν διὰ τοῦ μεγίστου πελάγους, καταψυχόντων δὲ τὸν κατὰ τὴν πόλιν ἀέρα πολλὴν τοῖς κατοικοῦσιν εὐκρασίαν καὶ ὑγίειαν κατεσκεύασεν.

3. Καὶ τὸν μὲν περίβολον αὐτῆς ὑπεστήσατο τῷ τε μεγέθει διαφέροντα καὶ κατὰ τὴν ὀχυρότητα θαυμάσιον · ἀνὰ μέσον γὰρ ὢν μεγάλης λίμνης καὶ θαλάσσης δύο μόνον ἀπὸ τῆς γῆς ἔχει προσόδους στενὰς καὶ παντελῶς εὐφυλάκτους.

Τὸν δὲ τύπον ἀποτελῶν χλαμύδι παραπλήσιον ἔχει πλατεῖαν μέσην σχεδὸν τὴν πόλιν τέμνουσαν καὶ τῷ τε μεγέθει καὶ κάλλει θαυμαστήν · ἀπὸ γὰρ πύλης ἐπὶ πύλην διήκουσα τεσσαράκοντα μὲν σταδίων ἔχει τὸ μῆκος, πλέθρου δὲ τὸ πλάτος, οἰκιῶν δὲ καὶ ἱερῶν πολυτελέσι κατασκευαῖς πᾶσα κεκόσμηται. 4. Προσέταξεν δ΄ ὁ ᾿Αλέξανδρος καὶ βασίλεια κατασκευάσαι θαυμαστὰ κατὰ τὸ μέγεθος καὶ βάρος τῶν ἔργων. Οὐ μόνον δ΄ ὁ ᾿Αλέξανδρος, ἀλλὰ καὶ οἱ μετ΄ αὐτὸν βασιλεύσαντες Αἰγύπτου μέχρι τοῦ καθ΄ ἡμᾶς βίου σχεδὸν ἅπαντες πολυτελέσι κατασκευαῖς ηὔξησαν τὰ βασίλεια .

5. Καθόλου δ΄ ἡ πόλις τοσαύτην ἐπίδοσιν ἔλαβεν ἐν τοῖς ὕστερον χρόνοις ὥστε παρὰ πολλοῖς αὐτὴν πρώτην ἀριθμεῖσθαι τῶν κατὰ τὴν οἰκουμένην · καὶ γὰρ κάλλει καὶ μεγέθει καὶ προσόδων πλήθει καὶ τῶν πρὸς τρυφὴν ἀνηκόντων πολὺ διαφέρει τῶν ἄλλων. 6. Τὸ δὲ τῶν κατοικούντων αὐτὴν πλῆθος ὑπερβάλλει τοὺς ἐν ταῖς ἄλλαις πόλεσιν οἰκήτορας. Καθ΄ ὃν γὰρ ἡμεῖς παρεβάλομεν χρόνον εἰς Αἴγυπτον, ἔφασαν οἱ τὰς ἀναγραφὰς ἔχοντες τῶν κατοικούντων εἶναι τοὺς ἐν αὐτῇ διατρίβοντας ἐλευθέρους πλείους τῶν τριάκοντα μυριάδων, ἐκ δὲ τῶν προσόδων τῶν κατ΄ Αἴγυπτον λαμβάνειν τὸν βασιλέα πλείω τῶν ἑξακισχιλίων ταλάντων. 7. ῾Ο δ΄οὖν βασιλεὺς ᾿Αλέξανδρος ἐπιστήσας τινὰς τῶν φίλων ἐπὶ τὴν κατασκευὴν τῆς ᾿Αλεξανδρείας καὶ διοικήσας ἅπαντα τὰ κατὰ τὴν Αἴγυπτον ἐπανῆλθε μετὰ τῆς δυνάμεως εἰς τὴν Συρίαν.

17.

1. He decided to found a great city in Egypt, and gave orders to the men left behind with this mission to build the city between the marsh and the sea. 2. He laid out the site and traced the streets skilfully and ordered that the city should be called after him Alexandria. It was conveniently situated near the harbour of Pharos, and by selecting the right angle of the streets, Alexander made the city breathed with the etesian winds so that as these blow across a great expanse of sea, they cool the air of the town, and so he provided its inhabitants with a moderate climate and good health. 3. Alexander also laid out the walls so that they were at once exceedingly large and marvellously strong. Lying between a great marsh and the sea, it affords by land only two approaches, both narrow and very easily blocked.

In shape, it is similar to a chlamys, and it is approximately bisected by an avenue remarkable for its size and beauty. From gate to gate it runs a distance of forty furlongs; it is a plethron in width, and is bordered throughout its length with a rich facades of houses and temples. 4. Alexander gave orders to build a palace notable for its size and massiveness. And not only Alexander, but those who after him ruled Egypt down to our own time, with few exceptions have enlarged this with lavish additions. 5. The city in general has grown so much in later times that many reckon it to be the first city of the civilized world, and it is certainly far ahead of all the rest in elegance and extent and riches and luxury. 6. The number of its inhabitants surpasses that of those in other cities. At the time when we were in Egypt, those who kept the census returns of the population said that its free residents were more than three hundred thousand, and that the king received from the revenues of the country more than six thousands talents. 7. However that may be, King Alexander charged certain of his Friends with the construction of Alexandria, settled all the affairs of Egypt, and returned with his army to Syria.

48-47 BC. Caesar (date of the Alexandrian war).

Battle in the harbour of Alexandria

Caesar, *Civil Wars*, III, 111. Translation by A G Peskett (The Loeb Classical Library, 1996).

18.

His copiis fidens Achillas paucitatemque militum Caesaris despiciens occupabat Alexandriam praeter eam oppidi partem, quam Caesar cum militibus tenebat, primo impetu domum eius inrumpere conatus; sed Caesar dispositis per vias cohortibus impetum eius sustinuit. Eodemque tempore pugnatum est ad portum, ac longe maximam ea res adtulit dimicationem. Simul enim diductis copiis pluribus viis pugnabatur, et magna multitudine naves longas occupare hostes conabantur; quarum erant L auxilio missae ad Pompeium proelioque in Thessalia facto domum redierant, quadriremes omnes et quinqueremes aptae instructaeque omnibus rebus ad navigandum, praeter has XXII, quae praesidii causa Alexandriae esse consueverant, constratae omnes; quas si occupavissent, classe Caesari erepta portum ac mare totum in sua potestate haberent, commeatu auxiliisque Caesarem prohiberent. Itaque tanta est contentione actum, quanta agi debuit, cum illi celerem in ea re victoriam, hi salutem suam consistere viderent. Sed rem obtinuit Caesar omnesque eas naves et reliquas, quae erant in navalibus incendit, quod, tam late tueri parva manu non poterat, confestimque ad Pharum navibus milites exposuit.

18.

Achillas, trusting in these forces and despising the small number of Caesar's troops, was trying to occupy Alexandria, except that part of the town which Caesar held with his troops, though at the first assault he has endeavoured to burst into his house; but Caesar, placing cohorts about the streets, held his attack in check. And at the same time a battle was fought at the port, and this affair produced by far the most serious fighting. For at one and the same time battle was going on with scattered forces in several streets and the enemy were attempting in great numbers to seize the warships, of which fifty had been sent to the support of Pompeius and had returned home after the battle in Thessaly all of them quadriremes and quinqueremes fitted and equipped with everything necessary for navigation, and, besides these, twenty-two which had usually been on duty at Alexandria, all of them decked. And if they had seized these, by robbing Caesar of his fleet they would have the harbour and the whole seaboard in their control and would shut off Caesar from supplies and reinforcements. Consequently the struggle was fought with the intense eagerness that was bound to occur when the one side saw a speedy victory, the other their own safety, depending on the event. But Caesar gained his purpose. He burnt all those ships and the rest that were in the docks, because he could not protect so wide an extent with his small force, and at once he embarked his men and landed them on Pharos.

Entrance of the great harbour

Caesar, *De bello civili*, *The Civil Wars*, III, 112. Translation by A G Peskett (The Loeb Classical Library, 1914).

19.
Pharus est in insula turris magna altitudine, mirificis operibus exstructa; quae nomen ab insula cepit. Haec insula obiecta Alexandriae portum efficit; sed a superioribus regibus in longitudinem passuum DCCCC in mare iactis molibus angusto itinere et ponte[7] cum oppido coniungitur. In hac sunt insula domicilia Aegyptiorum et vicus oppidi magnitudine; quaeque ibique naves inprudentia aut tempestate paulum suo cursu decesserunt, has more praedonum diripere consueverunt. Eis autem invitis, a quibus Pharos tenetur, non potest esse propter angustias navibus introitus in portum. Hoc tum veritus Caesar, hostibus in pugna occupatis, militibus expositis Pharum prehendit atque ibi praesidium posuit. Quibus est rebus effectum, uti tuto frumentum auxiliaque navibus ad eum supportari possent. Dimisit enim circum omnes propinquas provincias atque inde auxilia evocavit. Reliquis oppidi partibus sic est pugnatum, ut aequo proelio discederetur et neutri pellerentur (id efficiebant angustiae loci), paucisque utrimque interfectis Caesar loca maxime necessaria complexus noctu praemuniit. In eo tractu oppidi pars erat regiae exigua, in quam ipse habitandi causa initio erat inductus, et theatrum coniunctum domui, quod arcis tenebat locum aditusque habebat ad portum et ad reliqua navalia. Has munitiones insequentibus auxit diebus, ut pro muro obiectas haberet neu dimicare invitus cogeretur.

19.
On the island there is a tower called Pharos, of great height, a work of wondereful construction, which took its name from the island. This island, lying over against Alexandria, makes a harbour, but it is connected with the town by a narrow roadway like a bridge, piers nine hundred feet in length having been thrown out seawards by former kings. On this island there are dwelling-houses of Egyptians and a settlement the size of a town, and any ships that went a little out of their course there through carelessness or rough weather they were in the habit of plundering like pirates. Moreover, on account of the narrowness of the passage there can be no entry for ships into the harbour without the consent of those who are in occupation of Pharos. Caesar, now fearing such difficulty, landed his troops when the enemy was occupied in fighting, and seized Pharos and placed a garrison on it. The result of these measures was that corn and reinforcements could be safely conveyed to him on shipboard. For he sent messengers to all the neighbouring provinces and summoned reinforcement from them. In the remaining parts of the town the result of the fighting was that they separated after an undecisive engagement and neither side was beaten, the reason of this being the narrowness of the space; and a few men having been slain on both side, Caesar drew a cordon round the most necessary positions and strengthened the defences by night. In this region of the town there was a small part of the palace

to which he had been at first conducted for his personal residence, and a theatre was attached to the house which took the place of a citadel, and has approaches to the port and to the other docks. These defences he increased on subsequent days so that they might take place of a wall as a barrier against the foe, and that he might not be obliged to fight against his will.

Preparations for the siege of Alexandria

Caesar (Hirtius), *De bello Alexandrin*, *Alexandrian War*, I. Translation by A G Way (The Loeb Classical Library, 1997).

20.

I. Bello Alexandrino conflato, Caesar Rhodo atque ex Syria Ciliciaque omnem classem arcessit; Creta sagittarios, equites ab rege Nabataeorum Malcho evocat; tormenta undique conquiri et frumentum mitti, auxilia adduci jubet. Interim munitiones cotidie operibus augentur atque omnes oppidi partes, quae minus esse firmae videntur, testudinibus ac musculis aptantur; ex aedificiis autem per foramina in proxima aedificia arietes inmittuntur, quantumque aut ruinis deicitur aut per vim recipitur loci, in tantum munitiones proferuntur. Nam incendio fere tuta est Alexandria, quod sine contignatione ac materia sunt aedificia et structuris ac fornicibus continentur tectaque sunt rudere aut pavimentis. Caesar maxime studebat ut, quam angustissimam partem oppidi palus a meridie interjecta efficiebat, hanc operibus vineisque agendis ab reliqua parte urbis excluderet, illud spectans primum ut, cum in duas partes esset urbs divisa, acies uno consilio atque imperio administraretur, deinde ut laborantibus succurri atque ex altera oppidi parte auxilium ferri posset, in primis vero ut aqua pabuloque abundaret, quarum alterius rei copiam exiguam, alterius nullam omnino facultatem habebat; quod utrumque large palus praebere poterat.

20.

I. When the Alexandrian war flared up, Caesar, summoned every fleet from Rhodes and Syria and Cilicia; from Crete he raised archers, and cavalry from Malchus, king of the Nabataeans, and ordered artillery to be procured, corn despatched, and auxiliary troops mustered from every quarter. Meanwhile the entrenchments were daily extended by additional works, and all those sectors of the town which appeared to be not so strong enough were provided with shelters and mantlets; battering-rams, moreover, were introduced from one building into the next through holes, and the entrenchments were extended to cover all the ground laid bare by demolitions or gained by force of arms. For Alexandria is well-nigh fire-proof, because its buildings contain no wooden joinery and are held together by an arched construction and are roofed with rough-cast or tiling. Caesar was particularly anxious that, by bringing to bear his siege-works and pent-houses, he should isolate from the rest of the city that narrowest part of the town which was most constricted by the barrier of marshland lying to the south; his object being first that, since his army was divided between two sectors of the city, it should be controlled by a single strategy and command; secondly, that if they got into difficulties in one sector of the town, assistance and support could be brought from the other sector. But above all his object was to secure himself abundance of water and fodder; of which, as regards the former, he had but a scanty supply, and, as regards the latter, no stocks whatever; and the marshland could afford him bountiful supplies of both.

Preparations by the Alexandrians

Caesar (Hirtius), *De bello Alexandrino*, *The Alexandrian War,* II. Translation by A G Way (The Loeb Classical Library, 1955).

21.

II. Neque vero Alexandrinis in gerendis negotiis cunctatio ulla aut mora inferebatur. Nam in omnes partes per quas fines Aegypti regnumque pertinet, legatos conquisitoresque, dilectus habendi causa, miserant magnumque numerum in oppidum telorum atque tormentorum convexerant et innumerabilem multitudinem adduxerant. Nec minus in urbe maximae armorum erant institutae officinae. Servos praetera puberes armaverant, quibus domini locupletiores victum cotidianum stipendiumque praebebant. Hac multitudine disposita, munitiones semotarumque partium tuebantur; veteranas cohortes vacuas in celeberrimis urbis locis habebant ut, quacumque regione pugnaretur, integris viribus ad auxilium ferendum opponi possent. Omnibus viis atque angiportis triplicem vallum obduxerant - erat autem quadrato exstructo saxo neque minus XL pedes altitudinis habebat - quaeque partes urbis inferiores erant, has altissimis turribus denorum tabulatorum munierant. Praeterea alias ambulatorias totidem tabulatorum confixerant subjectisque eas rotis, funibus jumentisque †objectis† derectis plateis in quacumque erat visum partem movebant.

21.
II. Not indeeed that this occasioned any hesitation or delay on the part of the Alexandrians in concerting their measures. They had in fact despatched emissaries and recruiting officers throughout the entire length and breadth of the territory and kingdom of Egypte for the purpose of holding a levy, and had conveyed into the town a large quantity of weapons and artillery and mustered a countless host. In the city too, no less, vast arms factories had been established. They had, moreover, armed the adult slaves, and these the wealthier owners furnished with their daily food and pay. This numerous force they deployed to guard the fortifications of outlying areas; while they kept their veteran cohorts unemployed in the most frequented quarters of the city so that, no matter in what district fighting occurred, they could be thrown in as fresh and lusty reinforcements. All the streets and alleys were walled off by a triple barricade, built of rectangular stone blocks and not less than forty feet high; while as for the lower quarters of the city, these were fortified with very lofty towers each ten stories high. Besides these there were other towers which they had contrived—mobile ones of the like number of stories; and these, being mounted on wheels with ropes and draught animals attached, they moved along the level streets to any area they saw fit.

Lack of water

Caesar (Hirtius), *De bello Alexandrino*, V, VIII, IX. Translation by A G Way (The Loeb Classical Library, 1997).

22.
V. Alexandria est fere tota suffossa specusque habet ad Nilum pertinentes, quibus aqua in privatas domos inducitur, quae paulatim spatio temporis liquescit ac subsidit. Hac uti domini aedificiorum atque eorum familiae consuerunt: nam quae flumine Nilo fertur, adeo est limosa ac turbida ut multos variosque morbos efficiat; sed ea plebes ac multitudo contenta est necessario, quod fons urbe tota nullus est. Hoc tamen flumen in ea parte erat urbis quae ab Alexandrinis tenebatur. Quo facto est admonitus Ganymedes posse nostros aqua intercludi; qui distributi munitionum tuendarum causa vicatim, ex privatis aedificiis specibus ac puteis extracta aqua utebantur... VIII. Caesar suorum timorem consolatione et ratione minuebat. Nam puteis fossis quam dulcem reperiri posse adfirmabat: omnia enim litora naturaliter aquae dulcis venas habere. Quodsi alia esset litoris Aegypti natura atque omnium reliquorum, tamen, quoniam mare libere tenerent, neque hostes classem haberent, prohiberi sese non posse quominus cotidie navibus aquam peterent, vel a sinistra parte a Paratonio, vel dextra ab insula, quae diversae navigationes numquam uno tempore adversis ventis praecluderentur ... IX. Hac oratione apud suos habita atque omnium mentibus excitatis, dat centurionibus negotium ut, reliquis operibus intermissis, ad fodiendos puteos animum conferant neve quam partem nocturni temporis intermittant. Quo suscepto negotio atque omnium animis ad laborem incitatis, magna una nocte vis aquae dulcis inventa est.

22.
V. Practically the whole of Alexandria is undermined with subterranean conduits running from the Nile, by which water is conducted into private houses; which water in course of time gradually settles down and becomes clear. This is what is normally used by the owners of mansions and their households; for what the Nile brings down is so muddy and turbid that it gives raise to many different diseases: yet the rank and file of the common sort are perforce content with the latter, inasmuch as there is not one natural spring in the whole city. The main stream in question, however, was in that quarter of the city which was held by the Alexandrians. This circumstance suggested to Ganymedes the possibility that the water supply could be cut off from our troops; who, posted as they were in various quarters of the town to guard our entrenchments, were using water drawn from conduits and cisterns in private buildings ... VIII. By encouragement and reasoning Caesar allayed his men's alarm, declaring that sweet water could be found in wells and trenches, inasmuch as all sea-shores naturally possesed veins of sweet water. But if the nature of the sea-shore of Egypt was different from all others, none the less, since they held unfettered command of the sea, while their enemies had no fleet, they could not be prevented from seeking water daily in their ships, either from Paratonium on their left, or the island on their right—voyages which being in opposite directions, would never be prevented by contrary winds at one and the same time ... Having harangued his men to this effect and put fresh heart into them all, he briefed his centurions as follows: they were to interrupt their other tasks and turn their attention to digging wells, continuing without any cessation all through the night. Whereupon, the business being once undertaken with unanimous enthusiasm for the task, in the course of that one night a great quantity of sweet water was discovered.

Activity in the naval shipyards

Caesar (Hirtius), *De bello Alexandrino*, XIII. Translation by A G Way (The Loeb Classical Library, 1997).

23.
XIII. Erant omnibus ostiis Nili custodiae exigendi portorii causa dispositae; naves veteres erant in occultis regiae navalibus, quibus multis annis ad navigandum non erant usi: has reficiebant, illas Alexandriam revocabant. Deerant remi: porticus, gymnasia, publica aedificia detegebant; asseres remorum usum obtinebant; aliud naturalis sollertia, aliud urbis copia subministrabat. Postremo non longam navigationem parabant, sed praesentis temporis necessitati serviebant et in ipso portu confligendum videbant. Itaque paucis diebus contra omnium opinionem quadriremes XXII, quinqueremes V confecerunt; ad has minores apertasque complures adjecerunt, et in portu periclitati remigio quid quaeque earum efficere posset idoneos milites imposuerunt seque ad confligendum omnibus rebus paraverunt.

23.
XIII. There were guardships posted at all the mouths of the Nile to levy customs dues, and in secret royal dockyards there were old ships which had not seen service afloat for many years. These last they proceeded to repair, while the guardships they recalled to Alexandria. There was a shortage of oars: the roofs of colonnades, gymnasia and public buildings were dismantled, and their beams made to serve as oars. In one case it was natural ingenuity that helped to bridge the gap, in another the city's resources. In fine it was no lengthy voyaging for which they were preparing; but perceiving that the conflict must take place in the harbour itself they obeyed the dictates of the moment. In a few days, therefore, they surprised everyone by completing 22 quadriremes and 5 quinqueremes, to which they added a considerable number of smaller, open craft; and then, after trying out in the harbour by rowing what each of them could do, they manned them with suitable troops and prepared themselves at all points for the conflict.

Dangers from shoals and the channel

Caesar (Hirtius), *De bello Alexandrino*, XV. Translation by A G Way, (The Loeb Classical Library, 1997).

24.
XV. Rhodiis navibus praeerat Euphranor, animi magnitudine ac virtute magis cum nostris hominibus quam cum Graecis comparandus. Hic ob notissimam scientiam atque animi magnitudinem delectus est ab Rhodiis qui imperium classis obtineret. Qui ubi Caesaris animum advertit: 'Videris mihi', inquit, 'Caesar, vereri, si haec vada primis navibus intraris, ne prius dimicare cogaris quam reliquam classem potueris explicare. Nobis rem committe: nos proelium sustinebimus - neque tuum judicium fallemus - dum reliqui subsequantur. Hos quidem diutius in nostro conspectu gloriari magno nobis et dedecori et dolori est.' Caesar illum adhortatus atque omnibus laudibus prosecutus dat signum pugnae. Progressis ultra vadum, IIII Rhodias naves circumsistunt Alexandrini atque in eas impetrum faciunt. Sustinent illi atque arte sollertiaque se explicant; ac tantum doctrina potuit ut in dispari numero nulla transversa hosti obiceretur, nullius remi detergerentur, sed semper venientibus adversae occurrerent. Interim sunt reliquae subsecutae. Tum necessario discessum ab arte est propter angustias loci, atque omne certamen in virtute constitit. Neque vero Alexandriae fuit quisquam aut nostrorum aut oppidanorum, qui aut in opere aut in pugna occupatum animum haberent, quin altissima tecta peteret atque ex omni prospectu locum spectaculo caperet precibusque et votis victoriam suis ab dis immortalibus exposceret.

24.
XV. The commander of the Rhodians squadron was Euphranor, a man who in point of personality and bravery deserved comparison with our people rather than with the Greeks. Thanks to the great fame which his professional skill and forceful personality enjoyed, the Rhodians chose him to command their fleet. When he perceived Caesar's hesitation, he said: 'It seems to me, Caesar, that you are afraid that, if you once sail into these shoals with your leading flotilla, you may be forced to fight before you can deploy the rest of your fleet. Leave it to us: we shall bear the brunt of the fighting—we won't let you down—until the others can come up with us. Certainly for these fellows to go on boasting yonder in our sight is a sore disgrace and mortification to us.' Caesar offered him encouragement and paid him every tribute of praise, and then gave the signal for battle. Four Rhodian ships advanced beyond the shoals to be at once surrounded and attacked by the Alexandrians. The Rhodians bore up and by skill and dexterity deployed their line; and of such powerful effect was their training that despite the odds not one of them exposed its broadside to the enemy, not one had its oars swept away, but they always met the oncoming foe head-on. Meanwhile the remaining ships came up with them. Then through lack of sea room skill had perforce to be sacrified and the whole struggle devolved on courage. And indeed there was not one man in Alexandria, either of our troops or of the townsfolk, whose attention was bespoken with either work or fighting, but he made for the loftiest roof-tops and from out of all the vantage points chose one from which to view that spectacle, and besought the immortal gods with prayers and vows to grant victory to his side.

The capture of Pharops and the Heptastadium by Caesar

Caesar (Hirtius), *De bello Alexandrino*, XVII, XVIII, XIX. Translation by A G Way (The Loeb Classical Library, 1997).

25.
XVII ... Caesar contendendum existimavit ut insulam molemque ad insulam pertinentem in suam redigeret potestatem. Perfectis enim magna ex parte munitionibus in oppido, et illa et

urbem uno tempore temptari posse confidebat. Quo capto consilio, cohortes X et levis armaturae electos quos idoneos ex equitibus Gallis arbitrabatur, in navigia minora scaphasque imponit et alteram insulae partem, distinendae manus causa, constratis navibus adgreditur, praemiisque magnis propositis qui primus insulam cepisset. Ac primo impetum nostrorum pariter sustinuerunt; uno enim tempore et ex tectis aedificiorum propugnabant et litora armati defendebant, quo propter asperitatem loci non facilis nostris aditus dabatur, et scaphis navibusque longis quinque mobiliter et scienter angustias loci tuebantur. Sed ubi primum locis cognitis vadisque pertemptatis, pauci nostri in litore constiterunt atque hos sunt alii subsecuti constanterque in eos qui in litore aequo institerant impetum fecerunt, omnes Pharitae terga verterunt. His pulsis +++ custodia portus relicta, naves ad litora et vicum adplicarunt seque ex navibus ad tuenda aedificia ejecerunt.

XVIII. Neque vero diutius ea munitione se continere potuerunt, etsi erat non dissimile atque Alexandreae genus aedificiorum, ut minora maioribus conferantur, turresque editae et conjunctae muri locum obtinebant, neque nostri aut scalis aut cratibus aut reliquis rebus parati venerant ad oppugnandum. Sed terror hominibus mentem consiliumque eripit et membra debilitat, ut tum accidit. Qui se in aequo loco ac plano pares esse confidebant, idem perterriti fuga suorum et caede paucorum, XXX pedum altitudine in aedificiis consistere ausi non sunt seque per molem in mare praecipitaverunt et DCCC passuum intervallum ad oppidum enataverunt. Multi tamen ex his capti interfectique sunt; sed numerus captivorum omnino fuit sex milium.

XIX. Caesar, praeda militibus concessa, aedificia diripi jussit castellumque ad pontem qui propior erat Pharo, communivit atque ibi praesidium posuit. Hunc fuga Pharitae reliquerant; fortiorem[7] illum proprioremque oppido Alexandrini tuebantur. Sed eum postero die simili ratione adgreditur, quod, his optentis duobus, omnem navigiorum excursum et repentina latrocinia sublatum iri videbat. Jamque eos qui praesidio eum locum tenebant, tormentis ex navibus sagittisque depulerat atque in oppidun redegerat et cohortium trium instar in terram exposuerat - non enim plures consistere angustiae loci patiebantur; reliquae copiae in navibus stationem obtinebant. Quo facto, imperat pontem adversus hostem praevallari, et qua exitus navibus erat, fornice exstructo quo pons sustinebatur, lapidibus oppleri atque obstrui. Quorum altero opere effecto, ut nulla omnino scapha egredi posset, altero instituto, omnes Alexandrinorum copiae ex oppido se ejecerunt et contra munitiones pontis latiore loco constiterunt, eodemque tempore quae consueverant navigia per pontes ad incendia onerariarum emittere, ad molem constituerunt. Pugnabatur a nobis, ex ponte, ex mole; ab illis ex area quae erat adversus pontem, et ex navibus contra molem.

25.

XVII ... Caesar thought that he ought at all costs to make an effort to gain control of the island and the mole extending to it. For as his entrenchments in the town were in the main completed, he was confident that a simultaneous attempt could be made against both island and city. Having formed this plan, he embarked in smaller craft and pinnaces ten cohorts, some picked light-armed troops and such of his Gallic cavalry as he deemed suitable; and, to distract the enemy garrison, he launched an attack with decked ships upon the other side of the island, offering large rewards to the first to capture it. At first the islanders held off our troops' attack, simultaneously fighting back from the roofs of buildings, and with equal success defending the beaches with armed parties—and there the roughness of the ground did not afford our troops an easy approach—and guarding the narrow waters with pinnaces and five warships displaying both speed and skill. But as soon as our men had become acquainted with the ground and tried out the shallows, a few got a footing on the beach, others followed in their wake, and a determined attack was launched upon those of the enemy who were drawn up against us on the level fore-shore; whereupon the men of Pharos all turned tail. Following their rout the enemy abandoned their defence of the harbour, brought their ships to the built-up area by the water-front, and hastily disembarked to defend the buildings.

[7] The manuscripts have *fortiorem* or *certiorem*. Vielhaber *artiorem*.

XVIII. They could not, however, hold on so very long with the defences these afforded, though the buildings were of a type not unlike those of Alexandria—to employ a flattering comparison—with a continuous line of lofty towers taking the place of a wall; and our troops had not come equipped with ladders or wicker screens or any other equipment for assault. But panic robs men of their sense and reason and palsies their limbs; and so it happened then. The very men who on level and unbroken ground were confident they were a match for us, none the less, utterly demoralised now by the flight of their fellows and the slaughter of a few, dit not venture to take up a position, on buildings thirty feet heigh, but at various points along the mole dived into the sea and swam the intervening 800 paces to the safety of the town. Many of these, notwithstanting, were captured or killed; indeed, the number of captives amounted all told to six thousand.

XIX. After granting his soldiers leave to plunder, Caesar ordered the buildings to be demolished. Near the bridge—the one closer to Pharos—he fortified a redoubt, and posted a garrison there. This bridge the inhabitants of Pharos had abandoned in their flight; while the other one, which was narrower and closer to the town, was guarded by the Alexandrians. However, on the next day he attacked it from a similar motive, because the possession of these two bridges seemed likely to do away with all the sallies and sudden forays of the enemies' ships. And by now he had dislodged the members of its garrison with artillery and arrows shot from his ships, had driven them back into the town, and put ashore approximately three cohors—the confined space would not afford a footing for more—while the rest of his forces remained at their posts aboard the ships. At this stage he ordered the bridge to be screened by a rampart on the side facing the enemy and the opening for the passage of ships—formed by an arch which supported the bridge—to be filled up and blocked with stones. The latter task being completed, so that not a single pinnace could come out, and the former one being under way, all the Alexandrians' forces burst out of the town and took post in a fairly open position over against our fortifications of the bridge; while at the same time they drew up near the mole the vessels which they had been in the habit of sending out under the bridges to set fire to our transports. And so the battle proceeded, with us fighting from the bridge and the mole, and with them from the area facing the bridge and from their ships opposite the mole.

Caesar swims across the harbour

Caesar (Hirtius), *De bello Alexandrino*, XXI. Translation by A G Way (The Loeb Classical Library, 1955).

26.
XXI. Caesar quoad potuit cohortando suos ad pontem ac munitiones continere, eodem in periculo versatus est; postquam universos cedere animadvertit, in suum navigium se recepit. Quo multitudo hominum insecuta cum inrumperet, neque administrandi neque repellendi a terra facultas daretur, fore quod accidit suspicatus, sese ex navigio ejecit atque ad eas quae longius constiterant naves adnatavit. Hinc suis laborantibus subsidio scaphas mittens nonnullos conservavit. Navigium quidem ejus multitudine depressum militum una cum hominibus interiit. Hoc proelio desiderati sunt ex numero legionariorum militum circiter CCCC et paulo <ultra> eum numerum classiarii et remiges. Alexandrini eo loco castellum magnis munitionibus multisque tormentis confirmarunt atque, egestis ex mari lapidibus, libere sunt usi postea ad mittenda navigia.

26.
XXI. So long as by words of encouragement Caesar was able to keep his men at the bridge and its emplacements, he too was involved in the same danger; but when he perceived that they were all retreating, he withdrew to his own vessel. As a large number of men followed him and kept forcing their way aboard it, and as no opportunity was afforded either of navigating it or easing it off shore, anticipating what actually happened he dived from the vessel and swam to those ships which were hove to farther off. From them he sent pinnaces to the help of his men who were in difficulties and saved not a few. His vessel was in fact capsized by the large number of

troops, and foundered with the men on board. In this battle the losses among the legionary troops amounted to approximately 400, with a slightly larger number of seamen and rowers. The Alexandrians reinforced the redoubt there with strong entrenchments and many pieces of artillery and removed the stones from the sea, subsequently making free use of the opening to despatch their vessels.

The surrender of Alexandrdia

Caesar (Hirtius), *De bello Alexandrino*, XXXII. Translation by A G Way (The Loeb Classical Library).

27.
XXXII. Re felicissime celerrimeque gesta, Caesar magna victoriae fiducia, proximo terrestri itinere Alexandriam cum equitibus contendit atque ea parte oppidi victor introiit quae praesidio hostium tenebatur. Neque eum consilium suum fefellit quin hostes, eo proelio audito, nihil jam de bello essent cogitaturi. Dignum adveniens fructum virtutis et animi magnitudinis tulit. Omnis enim multitudo oppidanorum, armis projectis munitionibusque suis relictis, veste ea sumpta qua supplices dominantes deprecari consuerunt, sacrisque omnibus prolatis quorum religione precari offensos iratosque animos regum erant soliti, advenienti Caesari occurrerunt seque ei dediderunt. Caesar in fidem receptos consolatus, per hostium munitiones in suam partem oppidi magna gratulatione venit suorum. Qui non tantum bellum ipsum ac dimicationem, sed etiam talem adventum ejus felicem fuisse laetebantur.

27.
XXXII. The signal victory, the outcome of a most speedy and successfull action, filled Caesar with such confidence that he hastened with his cavalry to Alexandria by the nearest overland route, and entered it triumphantly by that quarter of the town which was held by the enemy garrison. Nor was he mistaken in his own conclusion that, as soon as they heard of that battle, the enemy would cease to think any longer in terms of war. On his arrival he reaped the well-earned fruits of valour and magnanimity; for the entire population of townsfolk threw down their arms, abandoned their fortifications, assumed that garb in which suppliants are used to placate tyrants with earnest prayers, and brought forth all the sacred emblems by the sanctity of which they had been wont to conjure the embittered and wrathful hearts of their kings: even so did they hasten to meet Caesar on his arrival and surrendered themselves to him. Caesar took them formally under his protection and consoled them; then, passing through the enemy fortifications, he came to his own quarter of the town amid loud cheers of congratulation from his own troops, who rejoiced at the happy issue, not only of the war itself and the fighting, but also of his arrival under such circumstances.

26 to 20 BC. Strabo (date of his stay in Alexandria)

Strabo's visit to Alexandria

Strabo, *Geography*, 17, 1, 6-17, 1, 10 (Casaubon 791-795). Translation by G P Goold (The Loeb Classical Library, Strabo, VIII, London 1996).

28.
17, 1 §6 (C 791). Ἐπεὶ δὲ τὸ πλεῖστον τοῦ ἔργου τούτου καὶ τὸ κυριώτατον ἡ Ἀλεξάνδρειά ἐστι καὶ τὰ περὶ αὐτήν, ἐντεῦθεν ἀρκτέον. ἔστι τοίνυν ἡ ἀπὸ Πηλουσίου παραλία πρὸς τὴν ἑσπέραν πλέουσι μέχρι μὲν τοῦ Κανωβικοῦ

στόματος χιλίων που καὶ τριακοσίων σταδίων, ὃ δὴ καὶ βάσιν τοῦ Δέλτα ἔφαμεν· ἐντεῦθεν δ´ ἐπὶ **Φάρον** τὴν νῆσον ἄλλοι στάδιοι πεντήκοντα πρὸς τοῖς ἑκατόν. ἡ δὲ **Φάρος** νησίον ἐστὶ παράμηκες, προσεχέστατον τῇ ἠπείρῳ, λιμένα πρὸς αὐτὴν ποιοῦν ἀμφίστομον. ἠιὼν γάρ ἐστι κολπώδης, ἄκρας εἰς τὸ πέλαγος προσβεβλημένη δύο· τούτων δὲ μεταξὺ ἡ νῆσος ἵδρυται κλείουσα τὸν κόλπον, παραβέβληται γὰρ αὐτῷ κατὰ μῆκος. τῶν δ´ ἄκρων τῆς **Φάρου** τὸ μὲν ἑῷον μᾶλλόν ἐστι προσεχὲς τῇ ἠπείρῳ καὶ τῇ κατ´ αὐτὴν ἄκρᾳ (καλεῖται δ´ ἄκρα Λοχιάς), καὶ ποιεῖ τὸν λιμένα ἀρτίστομον· πρὸς δὲ τῇ στενότητι τοῦ μεταξὺ πόρου καὶ πέτραι εἰσίν, αἱ μὲν ὕφαλοι, αἱ δὲ καὶ ἐξέχουσαι, τραχύνουσαι πᾶσαν ὥραν τὸ προσπῖπτον ἐκ τοῦ πελάγους κλυδώνιον. ἔστι δὲ καὶ αὐτὸ τὸ τῆς νησῖδος ἄκρον πέτρα περίκλυστος, ἔχουσα πύργον θαυμαστῶς κατεσκευασμένον λευκοῦ λίθου πολυόροφον, ὁμώνυμον τῇ νήσῳ. τοῦτον δ´ ἀνέθηκε Σώστρατος Κνίδιος, φίλος τῶν βασιλέων, τῆς τῶν πλωϊζομένων σωτηρίας χάριν, ὥς φησιν ἡ ἐπιγραφή · ἀλιμένου γὰρ οὔσης καὶ ταπεινῆς τῆς ἑκατέρωθεν παραλίας, ἐχούσης δὲ καὶ χοιράδας καὶ βράχη τινά, ἔδει σημείου τινὸς ὑψηλοῦ καὶ λαμπροῦ τοῖς ἀπὸ τοῦ πελάγους προσπλέουσιν (C 792) ὥστ´ εὐστοχεῖν τῆς εἰσβολῆς τοῦ λιμένος. καὶ τὸ ἑσπέριον δὲ στόμα οὐκ εὐείσβολόν ἐστιν, οὐ μὴν τοσαύτης γε δεῖται προνοίας. ποιεῖ δὲ καὶ τοῦτο ἄλλον λιμένα τὸν τοῦ Εὐνόστου καλούμενον· πρόκειται δ´ οὗτος τοῦ ὀρυκτοῦ καὶ κλειστοῦ λιμένος · ὁ μὲν γὰρ ἐκ τοῦ λεχθέντος πύργου τῆς **Φάρου** τὸν εἴσπλουν ἔχων ὁ μέγας ἐστὶ λιμήν· οὗτοι δὲ συνεχεῖς ἐν βάθει ἐκείνῳ, τῷ ἑπτασταδίῳ καλουμένῳ χώματι διειργόμενοι ἀπ´ αὐτοῦ, παράκεινται. τὸ δὲ χῶμά ἐστιν ἀπὸ τῆς ἠπείρου γέφυρα ἐπὶ τὴν νῆσον κατὰ τὸ ἑσπέριον αὐτῆς μέρος ἐκτεταμένη, δύο διάπλους ἀπολείπουσα μόνον εἰς τὸν Εὐνόστου λιμένα, καὶ αὐτοὺς γεγεφυρωμένους · ἦν δ´ οὐ γέφυρα μόνον ἐπὶ τὴν νῆσον τὸ ἔργον τοῦτο, ἀλλὰ καὶ ὑδραγώγιον, ὅτε γε ᾠκεῖτο · νῦν δ´ ἠρήμωσεν αὐτὴν ὁ θεὸς Καῖσαρ ἐν τῷ πρὸς Ἀλεξανδρέας πολέμῳ, τεταγμένην μετὰ τῶν βασιλέων · ὀλίγοι δ´ οἰκοῦσι πρὸς τῷ πύργῳ ναυτικοὶ ἄνδρες. ὁ γοῦν μέγας λιμὴν πρὸς τῷ κεκλεῖσθαι καλῶς τῷ τε χώματι καὶ τῇ φύσει, ἀγχιβαθής τέ ἐστιν, ὥστε τὴν μεγίστην ναῦν ἐπὶ κλίμακος ὁρμεῖν, καὶ εἰς πλείους σχίζεται λιμένας . οἱ μὲν οὖν πρότεροι τῶν Αἰγυπτίων βασιλεῖς, ἀγαπῶντες οἷς εἶχον καὶ οὐ πάνυ ἐπεισάκτων δεόμενοι, διαβεβλημένοι πρὸς ἅπαντας τοὺς πλέοντας, καὶ μάλιστα τοὺς Ἕλληνας (πορθηταὶ γὰρ ἦσαν καὶ ἐπιθυμηταὶ τῆς ἀλλοτρίας κατὰ σπάνιν γῆς), ἐπέστησαν φυλακὴν τῷ τόπῳ τούτῳ, κελεύσαντες ἀπείργειν τοὺς προσιόντας · κατοικίαν δ´ αὐτοῖς ἔδοσαν τὴν προσαγορευομένην Ῥακῶτιν, ἣ νῦν μὲν τῆς Ἀλεξανδρέων πόλεώς ἐστι μέρος τὸ ὑπερκείμενον τῶν νεωρίων, τότε δὲ κώμη ὑπῆρχε · τὰ δὲ κύκλῳ τῆς κώμης βουκόλοις παρέδοσαν, δυναμένοις καὶ αὐτοῖς κωλύειν τοὺς ἔξωθεν ἐπιόντας. ἐπελθὼν δὲ Ἀλέξανδρος, ἰδὼν τὴν εὐκαιρίαν, ἔγνω τειχίζειν ἐπὶ τῷ λιμένι τὴν πόλιν· τῆς δ´ ὕστερον ἐπηκολουθηκυίας εὐδαιμονίας τῇ πόλει μνημονεύουσί τι σημεῖον κατὰ τὴν ὑπογραφὴν τοῦ κτίσματος συμβάν · τῶν γὰρ ἀρχιτεκτόνων γῇ λευκῇ διασημαινομένων τὴν τοῦ περιβόλου γραμμήν, ἐπιλιπούσης τῆς γῆς καὶ τοῦ βασιλέως ἐπιόντος, οἱ διοικηταὶ τῶν ἀλφίτων μέρος τῶν παρεσκευασμένων τοῖς ἐργάταις παρέσχον, δι´ ὧν καὶ αἱ ὁδοὶ κατετμήθησαν εἰς πλείους · τουτ´ οὖν οἰωνίσθαι λέγονται πρὸς ἀγαθοῦ γεγονός.

§7. Ἡ δ´εὐκαιρία πολύτροπος · ἀμφίκλυστόν τε γάρ ἐστι τὸ χωρίον δυσὶ πελάγεσι, τῷ μὲν ἀπὸ τῶν ἄρκτων τῷ Αἰγυπτίῳ λεγομένῳ, (C 793) τῷ δ´ ἀπὸ μεσημβρίας τῷ τῆς λίμνης τῆς Μαρείας, ἣ καὶ Μαρεῶτις λέγεται· πληροῖ δὲ ταύτην πολλαῖς διώρυξιν ὁ Νεῖλος, ἄνωθέν τε καὶ ἐκ πλαγίων, δι´ ὧν τὰ εἰσκομιζόμενα πολλῷ πλείω τῶν ἀπὸ θαλάττης ἐστίν, ὥσθ´ ὁ λιμὴν ὁ λιμναῖος ὑπῆρχε πλουσιώτερος τοῦ θαλαττίου · ταύτῃ δὲ καὶ τὰ ἐκκομιζόμενα ἐξ ᾿Αλεξανδρείας πλείω τῶν εἰσκομιζομένων ἐστί· γνοίη δ´ ἄν τις ἔν τε τῇ ᾿Αλεξανδρείᾳ καὶ τῇ Δικαιαρχίᾳ γενόμενος, ὁρῶν τὰς ὁλκάδας ἔν τε τῷ κατάπλῳ καὶ ἐν ταῖς ἀναγωγαῖς, ὅσον βαρύτεραί τε καὶ κουφότεραι δεῦρο κἀκεῖσε πλέοιεν. πρὸς δὲ τῷ πλούτῳ τῶν καταγομένων ἑκατέρωσε εἴς τε τὸν κατὰ θάλατταν λιμένα καὶ εἰς τὸν λιμναῖον, καὶ τὸ εὐάερον ἄξιον σημειώσεώς ἐστιν· ὃ καὶ αὐτὸ συμβαίνει διὰ τὸ ἀμφίκλυστον καὶ τὸ εὔκαιρον τῆς ἀναβάσεως τοῦ Νείλου. αἱ μὲν γὰρ ἄλλαι πόλεις αἱ ἐπὶ λιμνῶν ἱδρυμέναι βαρεῖς καὶ πνιγώδεις ἔχουσι τοὺς ἀέρας ἐν τοῖς καύμασι τοῦ θέρους · ἐπὶ γὰρ τοῖς χείλεσιν αἱ λίμναι τελματοῦνται διὰ τὴν ἐκ τῶν ἡλίων ἀναθυμίασιν· βορβορώδους οὖν ἀναφερομένης τοσαύτης ἰκμάδος, νοσώδης ὁ ἀὴρ ἕλκεται καὶ λοιμικῶν κατάρχει παθῶν. ἐν ᾿Αλεξανδρείᾳ δὲ τοῦ θέρους ἀρχομένου πληρούμενος ὁ Νεῖλος πληροῖ καὶ τὴν λίμνην καὶ οὐδὲν ἐᾷ τελματῶδες τὸ τὴν ἀναφορὰν ποιῆσον μοχθηράν · τότε δὲ καὶ οἱ ἐτησίαι πνέουσιν ἐκ τῶν βορείων και τοῦ τοσούτου πελάγους, ὥστε κάλλιστα τοῦ θέρους ᾿Αλεξανδρεῖς διάγουσιν.

§8. Ἔστι δὲ χλαμυδοειδὲς τὸ σχῆμα τοῦ ἐδάφους τῆς πόλεως · οὗ τὰ μὲν ἐπὶ μῆκος πλευρά ἐστι τὰ ἀμφίκλυστα, ὅσον τριάκοντα σταδίων ἔχοντα διάμετρον, τὰ δὲ ἐπὶ πλάτος οἱ ἰσθμοί, ἑπτὰ ἢ ὀκτὼ σταδίων ἑκάτερος, σφιγγόμενος τῇ μὲν ὑπὸ θαλάττης, τῇ δ´ ὑπὸ τῆς λίμνης. ἅπασα μὲν ὁδοῖς κατατέτμηται ἱππηλάτοις καὶ ἁρματηλάτοις, δυσὶ δὲ πλατυτάταις, ἐπὶ πλέον ἢ πλέθρον ἀναπεπταμέναις αἳ δὴ δίχα καὶ πρὸς ὀρθὰς τέμνουσιν ἀλλήλας. ἔχει δ´ ἡ πόλις τεμένη τε κοινὰ κάλλιστα καὶ τὰ βασίλεια, τέταρτον ἢ καὶ τρίτον τοῦ παντὸς περιβόλου μέρος · τῶν γὰρ βασιλέων ἕκαστος ὥσπερ τοῖς κοινοῖς ἀναθήμασι προσεφιλοκάλει τινὰ κόσμον, οὕτω καὶ οἴκησιν ἰδίᾳ περιεβάλλετο πρὸς ταῖς ὑπαρχούσαις, ὥστε νῦν τὸ τοῦ ποιητοῦ,

ἐξ ἑτέρων ἕτερ´ ἐστίν ·

ἅπαντα μέντοι συναφῆ καὶ ἀλλήλοις καὶ τῷ λιμένι, καὶ ὅσα ἔξω αὐτοῦ. Τῶν δὲ βασιλείων μέρος ἐστὶ καὶ τὸ Μουσεῖον, ἔχον περίπατον καὶ (C 794) ἐξέδραν καὶ οἶκον μέγαν, ἐν ᾧ τὸ συσσίτιον τῶν μετεχόντων τοῦ Μουσείου φιλολόγων ἀνδρῶν. ἔστι δὲ τῇ συνόδῳ ταύτῃ καὶ χρήματα κοινὰ καὶ ἱερεὺς ὁ ἐπὶ τῷ Μουσείῳ, τεταγμένος τότε μὲν ὑπὸ τῶν βασιλέων, νῦν δ´ ὑπὸ Καίσαρος. μέρος δὲ τῶν βασιλείων ἐστὶ καὶ τὸ καλούμενον Σῆμα, ὃ περίβολος ἦν, ἐν ᾧ αἱ τῶν βασιλέων ταφαὶ καὶ ἡ ᾿Αλεξάνδρου· ἔφθη γὰρ τὸ σῶμα ἀφελόμενος Περδίκκαν ὁ τοῦ Λάγου Πτολεμαῖος, κατακομίζοντα ἐκ τῆς Βαβυλῶνος καὶ ἐκτρεπόμενον ταύτῃ κατὰ πλεονεξίαν καὶ ἐξιδιασμὸν τῆς Αἰγύπτου· καὶ δὴ καὶ ἀπώλετο διαφθαρεὶς ὑπὸ τῶν στρατιωτῶν, ἐπελθόντος τοῦ Πτολεμαίου καὶ κατακλείσαντος αὐτὸν ἐν νήσῳ ἐρήμῃ . ἐκεῖνος μὲν οὖν ἀπέθανεν ἐμπεριπαρεὶς ταῖς σαρίσσαις, ἐπελθόντων ἐπ´ αὐτὸν τῶν στρατιωτῶν, σὺν αὐτῷ δὲ καὶ οἱ βασιλεῖς, ᾿Αριδαῖός τε καὶ τὰ παιδία τὰ ᾿Αλεξάνδρου, καὶ ἡ γυνὴ Ῥωξάνη ἀπῆραν εἰς Μακεδονίαν · τὸ δὲ σῶμα τοῦ ᾿Αλεξάνδρου κομίσας ὁ Πτολεμαῖος ἐκήδευσεν ἐν τῇ ᾿Αλεξανδρείᾳ, ὅπου νῦν ἔτι κεῖται· οὐ μὴν ἐν τῇ αὐτῇ πυέλῳ · ὑαλίνη γὰρ αὕτη, ἐκεῖνος δ´ἐν χρυσῇ κατέθηκεν· ἐσύλησε δ΄ αὐτὴν ὁ Κόκκης καὶ Παρείσακτος ἐπικληθεὶς Πτολεμαῖος, ἐκ τῆς Συρίας ἐπελθὼν καὶ ἐκπεσὼν εὐθύς, ὥστ΄ ἀνόνητα αὐτῳ τὰ σῦλα γενέσθαι.

§9. Ἔστι δ΄ ἐν τῷ μεγάλῳ λιμένι κατὰ μὲν τὸν εἴσπλουν ἐν δεξιᾷ ἡ νῆσος καὶ ὁ πύργος ὁ Φάρος, κατὰ δὲ τὴν ἑτέραν χεῖρα αἵ τε χοιράδες καὶ ἡ Λοχιὰς ἄκρα, ἔχουσα βασίλειον. εἰσπλεύσαντι δ΄ ἐν ἀριστερᾷ ἐστι συνεχῆ τοῖς ἐν τῇ Λοχιάδι τὰ ἐνδοτέρω βασίλεια, πολλὰς καὶ ποικίλας ἔχοντα διαίτας καὶ ἄλση · τούτοις δ΄ ὑπόκειται ὅ τε ὀρυκτὸς λιμὴν καὶ κρυπτός[8], ἴδιος τῶν βασιλέων, καὶ ἡ Ἀντίρροδος, νησίον προκείμενον τοῦ ὀρυκτοῦ λιμένος, βασίλειον ἅμα καὶ λιμένιον ἔχον · ἐκάλεσαν δ΄ οὕτως, ὡς ἂν τῇ Ῥόδῳ ἐνάμιλλον. ὑπέρκειται δὲ τούτου τὸ θέατρον · εἶτα τὸ Ποσείδιον, ἀγκών τις ἀπὸ τοῦ Ἐμπορίου καλουμένου προπεπτωκώς, ἔχων ἱερὸν Ποσειδῶνος · ᾧ προσθεὶς χῶμα Ἀντώνιος ἔτι μᾶλλον προνεῦον εἰς μέσον τὸν λιμένα ἐπὶ τῷ ἄκρῳ κατεσκεύασε δίαιταν βασιλικήν, ἣν Τιμώνιον προσηγόρευσε. τοῦτο δ΄ ἔπραξε τὸ τελευταῖον, ἡνίκα προλειφθεὶς ὑπὸ τῶν φίλων ἀπῆρεν εἰς Ἀλεξάνδρειαν μετὰ τὴν ἐν Ἀκτίῳ κακοπραγίαν, Τιμώνειον αὐτῷ κρίνας τὸν λοιπὸν βίον, ὃν διάξειν ἔμελλεν ἔρημος τῶν τοσούτων φίλων . εἶτα τὸ Καισάριον καὶ τὸ Ἐμπόριον καὶ αἱ ἀποστάσεις · καὶ μετὰ ταῦτα τὰ νεώρια μέχρι τοῦ ἑπτασταδίου. ταῦτα μὲν τὰ περὶ τὸν μέγαν λιμένα.

§10. Ἑξῆς δ΄ Εὐνόστου λιμὴν μετὰ τὸ ἑπταστάδιον · (C 795) καὶ ὑπὲρ τούτου ὁ ὀρυκτός, ὃν καὶ Κιβωτὸν καλοῦσιν, ἔχων καὶ αὐτὸς νεώρια. ἐνδοτέρω δὲ τούτου διῶρυξ πλωτὴ μέχρι τῆς λίμνης τεταμένη τῆς Μαρεώτιδος. ἔξω μὲν οὖν τῆς διώρυγος μικρὸν ἔτι λείπεται τῆς πόλεως· εἶθ΄ ἡ Νεκρόπολις τὸ προάστειον, ἐν ᾧ κῆποί τε πολλοὶ καὶ ταφαὶ καὶ καταγωγαὶ πρὸς τὰς ταριχείας τῶν νεκρῶν ἐπιτήδειαι. ἐντὸς δὲ τῆς διώρυγος τό τε Σαράπιον καὶ ἄλλα τεμένη ἀρχαῖα ἐκλελειμμένα πως διὰ τὴν τῶν νέων κατασκευὴν τῶν ἐν Νικοπόλει· καὶ γὰρ ἀμφιθέατρον καὶ στάδιον καὶ οἱ πεντετηρικοὶ ἀγῶνες ἐκεῖ συντελοῦνται· τὰ δὲ παλαιὰ ὠλιγώρηται. συλλήβδην δ΄εἰπεῖν ἡ πόλις μεστή ἐστιν ἀναθημάτων καὶ ἱερῶν· κάλλιστον δὲ τὸ γυμνάσιον, μείζους ἢ σταδιαίας ἔχον τὰς στοάς. ἐν μέσῳ δὲ τό τε δικαστήριον καὶ τὰ ἄλση. ἔστι δὲ καὶ Πάνειον, ὕψος τι χειροποίητον στροβιλοειδὲς ἐμφερὲς ὄχθῳ πετρώδει διὰ κοχλίου τὴν ἀνάβασιν ἔχον· ἀπὸ δὲ τῆς κορυφῆς ἔστιν ἀπιδεῖν ὅλην τὴν πόλιν ὑποκειμένην αὐτῷ πανταχόθεν. ἀπὸ δὲ τῆς Νεκροπόλεως ἡ ἐπὶ τὸ μῆκος πλατεῖα διατείνει παρὰ τὸ γυμνάσιον μέχρι τῆς πύλης τῆς Κανωβικῆς · εἶθ΄ Ἱππόδρομος καλούμενός ἐστι καὶ αἱ παρακείμεναι ἄλλαι μέχρι τῆς διώρυγος τῆς Κανωβικῆς. διὰ δὲ τοῦ Ἱπποδρόμου διελθόντι ἡ Νικόπολίς ἐστιν, ἔχουσα κατοικίαν ἐπὶ θαλάττῃ πόλεως οὐκ ἐλάττω· τριάκοντα δέ εἰσιν ἀπὸ τῆς Ἀλεξανδρείας στάδιοι. τοῦτον δὲ ἐτίμησεν ὁ Σεβαστὸς Καῖσαρ τὸν τόπον, ὅτι ἐνταῦθα ἐνίκα τῇ μάχῃ τοὺς ἐπεξιόντας ἐπ΄ αὐτὸν μετὰ Ἀντωνίου· καὶ λαβὼν ἐξ ἐφόδου τὴν πόλιν ἠνάγκασε τὸν μὲν Ἀντώνιον ἑαυτὸν διαχειρίσασθαι, τὴν δὲ Κλεοπάτραν ζῶσαν ἐλθεῖν εἰς τὴν ἐξουσίαν· μικρὸν δ΄ ὕστερον κἀκείνη ἑαυτὴν ἐν τῇ φρουρᾷ διεχειρίσατο λάθρα δήγματι ἀσπίδος ἢ φαρμάκῳ ἐπιχρίστῳ (λέγεται γὰρ ἀμφοτέρως), καὶ συνέβη καταλυθῆναι τὴν τῶν Λαγιδῶν ἀρχήν, πολλὰ συμμείνασαν ἔτη.

[8] The manuscripts have *kruptos* corrected to *kleistos* by Corais *et alii*.

28.

17, 1 §6 (C 791). Since Alexandria and its neighbourhood constitute the largest and most important part of this subject, I shall begin with them. The sea-coast then, from Pelusium, as one sails towards the west, as far as the Canobic mouth, is about one thousand three hundred stadia— the 'base' of the Delta, as I have called it; and thence to the island Pharos, one hundred and fifty stadia more. Pharos is an oblong isle, is very close to the mainland and forms with it a harbour with two mouths, for the shore of the mainland forms a bay, since it thrusts two promontories into the open sea, and between these is situated the island, which closes the bay, for it lies lengthwise parallel to the shore. Of the extremities of Faros, the eastern one lies closer to the mainland and to the promontory opposite it (the promontory called Lochias), and thus makes the harbour narrow at the mouth; and in addition to the narrowness of the intervening passage there are also rocks, some under the water, and others projecting out of it, which at all hours roughen the waves that strike them from the open sea. And likewise the extremity of the isle is a rock, which is washed all round by the sea and has upon it a tower that is admirably constructed of white marble with many stories and bears the same name as the island. This was an offering made by Sostratus of Cnidus, a friend of the kings, for the safety of mariners, as the inscriptions says: for since the coast was harbourless and low on either side, and also had reefs and shallows, those who were sailing from the open sea thither needed some lofty and conspicuous sign to enable them (C 792), to direct their course aright to the entrance of the harbour. And the western mouth is also not easy to enter, although it does not require so much caution as the other. And it likewise forms a second harbour, that of Eunostus ('harbour of the happy return'), as it is called, which lies in front of the closed harbour which was dug by the hand of man. For the harbour which affords the entrance on the side of the above-mentioned tower of Pharos is the Great Harbour, whereas these two lie continuous with that harbour in their innermost recess, being separated from it only by the embankment called the Heptastadium. The embankment forms a bridge extending from the mainland to the western portion of the island, and leaves open only two passages into the harbour of Eunostus, which are bridged over. However, this work formed not only a bridge to the island but also an aqueduct, at least when Pharos was inhabited. But in this present time it has been laid waste by the deified Caesar (Julius Caesar) in his war against the Alexandrians, since it had sided with the kings. A few seamen, however, live near the tower. As for the Great Harbour, in addition to its being beautifully enclosed both by the embankment and by nature, it is not only so deep close to the shore that the largest ship can be moored at the steps, but also is cut up into several harbours. Now the earlier kings of the Aegyptians, being content with what they had and not wanting foreign imports at all, and being prejudiced against all who sailed the seas, and particularly against the Greeks (for owing to scarcity of land of their own the Greeks were ravagers and coveters of that of others), set a guard over this region and ordered it to keep away any who should approach; and they gave them as a place of above the ship-houses, but was at that time a village; and they gave over the parts round about the village to herdsmen, who likewise were able to prevent the approach of outsiders. But when Alexander visited the place and saw the advantages of the site, he resolved to fortify the city on the harbour. Writers record, as a sign of the good fortune that has since attended the city, an incident which occurred at the time of tracing the lines of the foundation: When the architects were making the lines of the enclosure with chalk, the supply of chalk gave out; and when the king arrived, his stewards furnished a part of the barley-meal which had been prepared for the workmen, and by means of this the streets also, to a larger number than before, were laid out. This occurrence, then, they are said to have interpreted as a good omen.

§7. The advantages of the city's site are various; for, first, the place is washed by two seas, (C 793) on the north by the Aegyptian Sea, as it is called, and on the south by Lake Mareia, also called Mareotis. This is filled by many canals from the Nile, both from above and on the sides, and through these canals the imports are much larger than those from the sea, so that the harbour on the lake was in fact richer than that on the sea; and here the exports from Alexandria also are larger than the imports; and anyone might judge, if he were at either Alexandria or Dicaearchia (now Puteoli) and saw the merchant vessels both at their arrival and at their departure, how much heavier or lighter sailed thither or therefrom. And in addition to the great value of the things brought down from both directions, both into the harbour on the sea and into that of the lake, the salubrity of the air is also worthy of remark. And this likewise results from the fact that the land is washed by water on both sides and because of the timeliness of the Nile's risings; for the other cities that are situated on lakes have heavy and stifling air in the heats of summer, because the lakes then become marshy along their edges because of the evaporation caused by the sun's rays, and accordingly, when so much filth-laden moisture rises, the air inhaled is noisome and starts pestilential diseases, whereas at Alexandria, at the beginning of summer, the Nile, being full, fills the lake also, and leaves no marshy matter to corrupt the rising vapours. At that time, also, the Etesian winds blow from the north and from a vast sea, so that the Alexandrians pass their time most pleasantly in summer.

§8. The shape of the area of the city is like a chlamys; the long sides of it are those that are washed by the two waters, having a diameter of about thirty stadia, and the short sides are the isthmuses, each being seven or eight stadia wide and pinched in on one side by the sea and on the other by the lake. The city as a whole is intersected by streets practicable for horse-riding and chariot-driving, and by two that are very broad, extending to more than a plethrum in breadth, which cut one another into two sections and at right angles. And the city contains most beautiful public precincts and also the royal palaces, which constitute one-fourth or even one-third of the whole circuit of the city; for just as each of the kings, from love of splendour, was wont to add some adornment to the public monuments, so also he would invest himself at his own expense with a residence, in addition to those already built, so that now, to quote the words of the poet (*Odyssey* XVII, 266) 'there is building upon building.' All, however, are connected with one another and the harbour, even those that lie outside the harbour. The Museum is also a part of the royal palaces: it has a public walk, (C 794) an Exedra with seats, and a large house, in which is the common mess-hall of the men learning who share the Museum. This group of men not only hold property in common, but also have a priest in charge of the Museum, who formerly was appointed by the kings, but is now appointed by Caesar. The Sema[9] also, as it is called, is a part of the royal palaces. This was the enclosure which contained the burial-places of the kings and that of Alexander; for Ptolemy, the son of Lagus, forestalled Perdiccas by taking the body away from him when he was bringing it down from Babylon and was turning aside towards Aegypt, moved by greed and a desire to make that country his own. Furthermore, Perdiccas lost his life, having been slain by his soldiers at the time when Ptolemy attacked him and hemmed him up in a desert island. So Perdiccas was killed, having been transfixed by his soldiers' sarissae when they attacked him; but the kings who were with him, both Aridaeus and the children of Alexander, and also Rhoxanê, Alexander's wife, departed for Macedonia; and the body of Alexander was carried off by Ptolemy and given sepulture in Alexandria, where it still now lies—not, however, in the same sarcophagus as before, for the present one is made of glass, whereas the one wherein Ptolemy laid it was made of gold. The latter was plundered by the Ptolemy nicknamed 'Cocces' (Scarlet) and 'Pareisactus' (Usurper), who came over from Syria but was immediately expelled, so that his plunger proved unprofitable to him.

§9. In the Great Harbour at the entrance, on the right hand, are the island and the tower Pharos, and on the other hand are the reefs and also the promontory Lochias, with a royal palace upon it; and on sailing into the harbour one comes, on the left, to the inner royal palaces, which are continuous with those on Lochias and have groves and numerous lodges painted in various colours. Below these lies the harbour that was dug by the hand of man and is hidden from view, the private property of the kings, as also Antirhodos, an isle lying off the artificial harbour, which has both a royal palace and a small harbour, which has both a royal palace and a small harbour. They so called it as being a rival of Rhodes. Above the artificial harbour lies the theatre; then the Poseidium—an elbow, as it were, projecting from the Emporium, as it is called,

[9] The manuscripts have *Sôma* (the Body).

and containing a temple of Poseidon. To this elbow of land Antony added a mole projecting still farther, into the middle of a harbour, and on the extremity of it built a royal lodge which he called Timonium. This was his last act, when, forsaken by his friends, he sailed away to Alexandria after his misfortune at Actium, having chosen to live the life of a Timon the rest of his days, which he intended to spend in solitude from all those friends. Then one comes to the Caesarium and the Emporion and the warehouses; and after these to the ship-houses, which extend as far as the Heptastadium. So much for the Great Harbour and its surroundings.

§10. Next, after the Heptastadium one comes to the Harbour of Eunostus, and above this, to the artificial harbour, which is also called Cibotus; it too has ship-houses. Farther in there is a navigable canal, which extends to Lake Mareotis. Now outside the canal there is still left only a small part of the city; and then one comes to the suburb Necropolis, in which are many gardens and graves and halting places fitted up for the embalming of corpses, and, inside the canal, both to the Sarapium and the other sacred precincts of ancient times, which are now almost abandoned on account of the construction of the new buidings at Nicopolis; for instance, there are an amphitheatre and a stadium at Nicopolis, and the quinquennial games are celebrated there; but the ancient buildings have fallen into neglect. In short, the city is full of public and sacred structures; but the most beautiful is the Gymnasium, which has porticoes more than a stadium in length. And in the middle are both the court of justice and the groves. Here, too, is the Paneium, a 'height', as it were, which was made by the hand of man; it has the shape of a fir-cone, resembles a rocky hill, and is ascended by a spiral road; and from the summit one can see the whole of the city lying below on all sides. The broad street that runs lengthwise extends from Necropolis past the Gymnasium to the Canobic Gate; and then one comes to the Hippodrome, as it is called, and to the other (streets?) that lies parallel, extending as far as the Canobic canal. Having passed through the Hippodrome, one comes to Nicopolis, which has a settlement on the sea no smaller than a city. It is thirty stadia distant from Alexandria. Augustus Caesar honored this place because it was here that he conquered in battle those who came out against him with Antony; and when he had taken the city at the first onset, he forced Antony to put himself to death and Cleopatra to come into his power alive; but a little later she too put herself to death secretely, while in prison, by the bite of an aspic or (for two accounts are given) by applying a poisonous ointment; and the result was that the empire of the sons of Lagus, which had endured for many years, was dissolved.

39-65 AD. Lucan (dates of his life).

Caesar's entry into Alexandria; at the tomb of Alexander

Lucan, *The Civil War* X, 1-24. Translation by J D Duff (The Loeb Classical Library, 1928).

29.

Ut primum terras Pompei colla secutus
Attigit et diras calcavit Caesar harenas,
Pugnavit fortuna ducis fatumque nocentis
Aegypti, regnum Lagi Romana sub arma
Iret, an eriperet mundo Memphiticus ensis
Victoris victique caput.Tua profuit umbra,
Magne, tui socerum rapuere a sanguine manes,
Ne populus post te Nilum Romanus haberet.
Inde Paretoniam fertur securus in urbem

Pignore tam saevi sceleris sua signa secutam.
Sed fremitu vulgi fasces et jura querentis
Inferri Romana suis discordia sensit
Pectora et ancipites animos Magnumque perisse
Non sibi. Tunc vultu semper celante pavorem
Intrepidus superum sedes et templa vetusti
Numinis antiquas Macetum testantia vires
Circuit et nulla captus dulcedine rerum
Non auro cultuque deum, non moenibus urbis,
Effosum tumulis cupide descendit in antrum.
Illic Pellaei proles vesana Philippi,
Felix praedo, jacet terrarum vindice fato
Raptus; sacratis totum spargenda per orbem
Membra viri posuere adytis; fortuna pepercit
Manibus, et regni duravit ad ultima fatum.

29.

As soon as Caesar, following Pompey's head, reached land and trod those fatal sands, his fortune and the destiny of guilty Egypt contended whether the realm of Lagus should be conquered by Roman arms, or the Memphian sword should rid the world of the victor's head as well as of the loser's. The shade of Magnus did service; his ghost snatched his kinsman from the sword, that the Roman people might not, even after the death of Pompey, love the Nile. Thence free from care Caesar moved to the Egyptian capital, which was bound to his cause by the pledge of such a ruthless crime. But from the rage of the populace, who bore it ill that Romans and laws should invade their own, he learned that feeling was divided and allegiance wavering, and that not for his gain had Magnus fallen. Then undaunted, with looks that ever masked his fears, he visited the temples of the gods, and the ancient shrines of divinity which attest the former might of Macedonia. No thing of beauty attracted him, neither the gold and ornaments of the gods, nor the city walls; but in eager haste he went down into the vault hewn out for a tomb. There lies the mad son of Macedonian Philip, that fortunate free-booter, cut off by a death that avenged the world. The limbs that should have been scattered over the whole earth they laid in a hallowed shrine; Fortune spared his dead body, and the destiny of his reign endured to the last.

Caesar's entry into Alexandria: at Alexander's tomb.

Lucan, *The Civil War*, X, 53-60. Translation by J D Duff (The Loeb Classical Library, 1928).

30.

Jam Pelusiaco veniens a gurgite Nili
Rex puer inbellis populi sedaverat iras,
Obside quo pacis Pellaea tutus in aula
Caesar erat, cum se parva Cleopatra biremi
Corrupto custode Phari laxare catenas
Intulit Emathiis ignaro Caesare tectis,
Dedecus Aegypti, Latii feralis Erinys,
Romano non casta malo ...

30.
And now the boy-king came from the Pelusian mouth of the Nile, and allayed the discontent of his unwarlike people; and, with him as a hostage for peace, Caesar was safe in the Macedonian court. But then Cleopatra, having bribed the guards to undo the chain across the harbour of Pharos, sailed in a small two-banked ship and entered the Macedonian palace without Caesar's knowledge—Cleopatra, the shame of Egypt, the fatal Fury of Latium, whose unchastity cost Rome dear.

The splendour of the palace of Alexandria

Lucan, *The Civil War*, X, 107-127. Translation by J D Duff (The Loeb Classical Library, 1928).

31.

Pax ubi parta duci donisque ingentibus empta est,
Excepere epulae tantarum gaudia rerum,
Explicuitque suos magno Cleopatra tumultu
Nondum translatos Romana in saecula luxus.
Ipse locus templi, quod vix corruptior aetas
Extruat, instar erat; laqueataque tecta ferebant
Divitias, crassumque trabes absconderat aurum;
Nec summis crustata domus sectisque nitebat
Marmoribus, stabatque sibi non segnis achates
Purpureusque lapis, totaque effusus in aula
Calcabatur onyx, hebenus Mareotica vastos
Non operit postes, sed stat pro robore vili
Auxilium, non forma domus. Ebur atria vestit,
Et suffecta manu foribus testudinis Indae
terga sedent crebro maculas distincta zmaragdo.
Fulget gemma toris, et iaspide fulva supellex;
Strata micant, Tyrio quorum pars maxima fuco
Cocta diu virus non uno duxit aeno;
Pars auro plumata nitet, pars ignea cocco,
Ut mos est Pharii miscendi licia telis.
Tunc famulae numerus turbae populusque minister.

31.
When Caesar's favour was gained and bought by mighty gifts, so joyful an event was followed by a feast; great was the bustle, as Cleopatra displayed her magnificence—magnificience which Roman society had not yet adopted. The place itself was the size of a temple, such a temple as a corrupt age would hardly rear; the panels of the ceiling displayed wealth, and the rafters were hidden beneath a thick coating of gold. The walls shone with marble; nor were they merely overlaid with a thin surface of it; and agate stood there on its own account, no useless ornament, and porphyry. Alabaster was laid all over the hall to tread on; and the ebony of Meroe, no mere covering for the great doors, took the place of common wood—a support and no mere decoration of the dwelling. Ivory clothed the entrance hall; and Indian tortoise-shell, artificially coloured, was inlaid upon the doors, and its spots were adorned with many an emerald. Jewels glittered on the couches; the cups, tawny with jasper, loaded the tables, and the sofas were bright with coverlets of divers colours—most had long been steeped in Tyrian dye and took their hue from repeated soakings, while others were embroidered with bright gold, and others blazed with scarlet, as the Egyptian manner is of mingling leashes in the web. There was also a swarm of attendants, and a multitude to serve the banqueters, differing form one another in race or age.

The palace besieged

Lucan, *The Civil War,* X, 439-444; 486-519; 534-546. Translation by J D Duff (The Loeb Classical Library, 1928).

32.

Vers 439-444.
.... At Caesar moenibus urbis
Diffisus foribus clausae se protegit aulae,
Degeneres passus latebras; nec tota vacabat
Regia compresso: minima collegerat arma
Parte domus. Tangunt animos iraeque metusque,
Et timet incursus indignatur timere.
....

Vers 486-519.
Nec non et ratibus temptatur regia, qua se
Protulit in medios audaci margine fluctus
Luxuriosa domus. Sed adest defensor ubique
Caesar et hos aditus gladiis, hos ignibus arcet
Obsessusque gerit - tanta est constantia mentis-
Expugnantis opus. Piceo jubet unguine tinctas
Lampadas inmitti junctis in bella carinis;
Non piger ignis erat per stuppea vincula perque
Manantis cera tabulas, et tempore eodem
Transtraque nautarum summique arsere ceruchi.
Jam prope semustae merguntur in aequora classes,
Jamque hostes et tela natant. Nec puppibus ignis
Incubuit solis; sed quae vicina fuere
Tecta mari, longis rapuere vaporibus ignem,
Et cladem fovere noti, percussaque flamma
Turbine non alio motu per tecta cucurrit
Qam solet aetherio lampas decurrere sulco
Materiaque carens atque ardens aere solo.
Illa lues paulum clausa revocavit ab aula
Urbis in auxilium populos. Nec tempora cladis
Perdidit in somnos, sed caeca nocte carinis
Insiluit Caesar semper feliciter usus
Praecipiti cursu bellorum et tempore rapto:
Nunc claustrum pelagi cepit Pharon. Insula quondam
In medio stetit illa mari sub tempore vatis
Proteos, at nunc est Pellaeis proxima muris.
Illa duci geminos bellorum praestitit usus;
Abstulit excursus et fauces aequoris hosti
Caesar et auxiliis aditus ac libera ponti
Ostia permisit. Nec poenas inde Pothini
Distulit ulterius, sed non qua debuit ira,
Non cruce, non flammis rapuit, non dente ferarum:
Heu facinus! gladio cervix male caesa pependit;
Magni morte perit.
....

Vers 534-546.
Molis in exiguae spatio stipantibus armis,
Dum parat in vacuas Martem transferre carinas,

Dux Latius tota subitus formidine belli
Cingitur: hinc densae praetexunt litora classes,
Hinc tergo insultant pedites.Via nulla salutis,
Non fuga, non virtus, vix spes quoque mortis honestae;
Non acie fusa nec magnae stragis acervis
Vincendus tunc Caesar erat, sed sanguine nullo.
Captus sorte loci pendet, dubiusque timeret
Optaretne mori, respexit in agmine denso
Scaevam perpetuae meritum jam nomina famae
Ad campos, Epidamne, tuos, ubi solus apertis
Obsedit muris calcantem moenia Magnum».

32.

439-444. Caesar, on his part, distrusted the city walls and defended himself by closing the gates of the palace, thus submitting to an unworthy hiding-place. Hemmed in as he was, the whole palace was not at his disposal: he had gathered his forces in one corner of it. His pride was touched by rage and fear—fear of attack, and wrath at his own fear …

486-519. They assailed the palace also by means of ships, at the point where the splendid pile projected with bold frontage right over the water. But Caesar was present everywhere in defence, driving back some attacks with the sword and others with fire; and such was his courage, that while besieged he did the work of besieger. He ordered brands steeped in resin to be hurled at the sails of the crowded ships; and the fire coursed swiftly along the ropes of tow and the decks running with wax, till the rowers' benches and the towering yards blazed up to together. Soon the ships, almost half-consumed, sank beneath the surface, and soon the assailants and their weapons were swamped. Nor did the fire fall upon the vessels only: the houses near the sea caught fire from the spreading heat, and the winds fanned the conflagration, till the flames, smitten by the eddying gale, rushed over the roofs as fast as the meteors that often trace a furrow through the sky, though they have nothing solid to feed on and burn by means of air alone. This calamity for a time called off the crowd from the close-barred palace to rescue the city. Caesar did not waste in slumber the time granted by the fire, but sprang on board ship in the darkness of night. He had ever made successful use of haste in warfare, and now with all speed he seized Pharos, which gives access to the sea. Once, in the time of the seer Proteus, it was an island out at sea, but now it stands close to the walls of Alexandria. To Caesar it was doubly useful in his warfare. For, when he has prevented the enemy from sailing out to the sea by the narrow passage and saw the harbour open for reinforcements, he postponed no longer the punishment of death which Pothinus had so richly earned. But Caesar's wrath did not destroy him by fitting means—the gallows, or the stake, or the teeth of wild beasts: he died the death of Magnus ...

534-546. Round him stood his soldiers in the narrow space of the mole; and he was preparing to embark his men on the empty ships, when he was suddenly surrounded by all the fearfulness of war: on the other, the infantry assaulted his rear. There was no path of safety either in flight or in valour; he could scarcely hope even for an honourable death. To conquer Caesar then, no rout of an army and no heaps of dead were needed, nor any bloodshed at all. Made helpless by the nature of his position, he stood perplexed; and even as he doubted whether to fear death or pray for it, he saw Scaeva in the serried ranks, that Scaeva who had already won immortal glory on the plains of Epidamnus; for there, when the walls were breached and Magnus trod the ramparts underfoot, Scaeva single-handed beleaguered Magnus.

Circa 13-50 AD. Philo.

The shores of the Mareotic lake: the climate of Alexandria

Philo, *On the Contemplative Life or Suppliants (de Vita Contemplativa),* §21-24. Translation by F H Colson (The Loeb Classical Library, 1941).

33.
§21. Πολλαχοῦ μὲν οὖν τῆς οἰκουμένης ἐστὶ τὸ γένος - ἔδει γὰρ ἀγαθοῦ τελείου μετασχεῖν καὶ τὴν Ἑλλάδα καὶ τὴν βάρβαρον-, πλεονάξει δὲ ἐν Αἰγύπτῳ καθ΄ ἕκαστον τῶν ἐπικαλουμένων νόμων καὶ μάλιστα περὶ τὴν Ἀλεξάνδρειαν. §22. οἱ δὲ πανταχόθεν ἄριστοι καθάπερ εἰς πατρίδα [θεραπευτῶν] ἀποικίαν στέλλονται πρός τι χωρίον ἐπιτηδειότατον, ὅπερ ἐστὶν ὑπὲρ λίμνης Μαρείας κείμενον ἐπὶ γεωλόφου χθαμαλωτέρου, σφόδρα εὐκαίρως, ἀσφαλείας τε ἕνεκα καὶ ἀέρος εὐκρασίας. §23. τὴν μὲν οὖν ἀσφάλειαν αἱ ἐν κύκλῳ παρέχουσιν ἐπαύλεις τε καὶ κῶμαι, τὴν δὲ περὶ τὸν ἀέρα εὐκρασίαν αἱ ἔκ τε τῆς λίμνης ἀνεστομωμένης εἰς τὴν θάλατταν καὶ τοῦ πελάγους ἐγγὺς ὄντος ἀναδιδόμεναι συνεχεῖς αὖραι, λεπταὶ μὲν αἱ ἐκ τοῦ πελάγους, παχεῖαι δὲ αἱ ἀπὸ τῆς λίμνης, ὧν ἡ μῖξις ὑγιεινοτάτην κατάστασιν ἀπεργάζεται. §24. αἱ δὲ οἰκίαι τῶν συνεληλυθότων σφόδρα μὲν εὐτελεῖς εἰσι, πρὸς δύο τὰ ἀναγκαιότατα σκέπην παρέχουσαι, πρός τε τὸν ἀφ΄ ἡλίου φλογμὸν καὶ τὸν ἀπ΄ ἀέρος κρυμόν · οὔτε δὲ ἐγγύς, ὥσπερ αἱ ἐν τοῖς ἄστεσιν, ὀχληρὸν γὰρ καὶ δυσάρεστον τοῖς ἐρημίαν ἐζηλωκόσι καὶ μεταδιώκουσιν αἱ γειτνιάσεις οὔτε πόρρω, δι΄ ἣν ἀσπάζονται κοινωνίαν καὶ ἵνα, εἰ λῃστῶν γένοιτο ἔφοδος, ἀλλήλοις ἐπιβοηθῶσιν.

33.
§21. This kind exists in many places in the inhabited world, for perfect goodness must needs be shared both by Greeks and the world outside Greece, but it abounds in Egypt in each of the nomes as they are called and especially round Alexandria. §22. But the best of these votaries journey from every side to settle in a certain very suitable place which they regard as their fatherland. This place is situated above the Mareotic Lake on a somewhat low-lying hill very happily placed both because of its security and the pleasantly tempered air. §23.The safety is secured by the farm buildings and villages round about and the pleasantness of the air by the continuous breezes which arise both from the lake which debouches into the sea and from the open sea hard by. For the sea breezes are light, the lake breezes close and the two combining together produce a most healthy condition of climate. §24. The houses of the society thus collected are exceedingly simple, providing protecting against two of the most pressing dangers, the fiery heat of the sun and the icy cold of the air. They are neither near together as in towns, since living at close quarters is troublesome and displeasing to people who are seeking to satisfy their desire for solitude, nor yet at a great distance because of the sense of fellowship which they cherish, and to render help to each other if robbers attack them.

The voyage of King Agrippa of Pouzzoles to Alexandria

Philo, *In Flaccum*, §25-29. Translation by F H Colson, (The Loeb Classical Library, 1941).

34
§25. Προσεπέρρωσε δ΄ αὐτοῦ τὴν ἐκ μαθήσεως τὸ πλέον ἢ φύσεως ἐπιτετηδευμένην ἀπόνοιαν καὶ συντυχία τις τοιαύτη. Γάιος Καῖσαρ Ἀγρίππᾳ τῷ Ἡρῴδου βασιλέως υἱωνῷ δίδωσι βασιλείαν τῆς παππῴας λήξεως τρίτην μοῖραν, ἣν Φίλιππος τετράρχης θεῖος ὢν αὐτῷ πρὸς πατρὸς ἐκαρποῦτο.

§26. μέλλοντι δ΄ ἀπαίρειν συνεβούλευσεν ὁ Γάιος τόν μὲν ἀπὸ Βρεντεσίου μέχρι Συρίας πλοῦν μακρὸν ὄντα καὶ καματηρὸν παραιτήσασθα, χρῆσθαι δ΄ ἐπιτόμῳ τοὺς ἐτησίας ἀναμείναντι τῷ διὰ τῆς 'Αλεξανδρείας · ταῖς τε γὰρ ἐκεῖθεν ὁλκάδας ταχυναυτεῖν ἔφασκε καὶ ἐμπειροτάτους εἶναι κυβερνήτας, οἳ καθάπερ ἀθλητὰς ἵππους ἡνιοχοῦσιν ἀπλανῆ παρέχοντες τὸν ἐπ΄ εὐθείας δρόμον. ὁ δὲ πειθαρχεῖ ὡς δεσπότῃ τε ἅμα καί τὰ δοκοῦντα συμφέρειν παραγγέλλοντι. §27. καταβὰς δ΄ εἰς Δικαιάρχειαν καὶ ναῦς ὑφόρμους 'Αλεξανδρίδας ἰδὼν εὐτρεπεῖς πρὸς ἀναγωγήν, ἐπιβὰς μετὰ τῶν ἰδίων, εὐπλοίᾳ χρησάμενος, ὀλίγαις ὕστερον ἡμέραις ἀνεπιφάτως καὶ ἀφωράτως κατάγεται, κελεύσας τοῖς κυβερνήταις - περὶ γὰρ δείλην ὥραν ὁ Φάρος ἀναφαίνεται- τὰ μὲν ἱστία συνάγειν, ἔξω δὲ περὶ αὐτὸν μὴ μακρὰν ἀφισταμένους θαλαττεύειν ἄχρι τοῦ βαθεῖαν ἑσπέραν ἐπιγενέσθαι καὶ νυκτὸς τοῖς λιμέσι προσσχεῖν, ἵν΄ ἀποβὰς ἤδη τετραμμένων [ἁπάντων] πρὸς ὕπνον, μηδενὸς ὁρῶντος, ἀφίκηται πρὸς τὸν ξενοδόχον. § 28. ὁ μὲν δὴ μετὰ τοσαύτης αἰδοῦς ἐπεδήμησε βουλόμενος εἴ πως οἷόν τε ἦν, ἅπαντας τοὺς ἐν τῇ πόλει λαθὼν ὑπεξελθεῖν· οὐ γὰρ κατὰ θέαν ἀφῖκτο τῆς 'Αλεξανδρείας ἐπιδεδημηκὼς αὐτῇ πρότερον, ἡνίκα τὸν ἐπὶ 'Ρώμης πλοῦν ἐστέλλετο πρὸς Τιβέριον, ἀλλ΄ ὁδῷ χρησόμενος ἐπιτόμῳ τῆς οἴκαδε ἀφίξεως . §29 . οἱ δ΄ ὑπὸ φθόνου ῥηγνύμενοι - βάσκανον γὰρ φύσει τὸ Αἰγυπτιακόν- καὶ τὰς ἑτέρων εὐτυχίας ἰδίας ὑπελάμβανον εἶναι κακοπραγίας καὶ ἅμα διὰ τὴν παλαιὰν καὶ τρόπον τινὰ [φύσει] γεγενημένην πρὸς 'Ιουδαίους ἀπέχθειαν ἤσχαλλον ἐπὶ τῷ γεγενῆσθαί τινα βασιλέα 'Ιουδαῖον οὐχ ἧττον, ἢ εἰ αὐτός τις ἕκαστος βασιλείαν προγονικὴν ἀφῄρητο.

34.

§25. The infatuation due to instruction from others rather than to his own nature, which thus was shown in his conduct, was further strengthened by the following incident. Gaius Caesar gave to Agrippa, the grandson of King Herod, the kingship over that third part of his grandfather's territory, the revenues of which were taken by Philip the tetrarch Agrippa's paternal uncle. §26. When he was about to set out thither, Gaius advise him not to undertake the voyage from Brundisium to Syria which as long and wearisome but wait for the etesian winds and take the short route through Alexandria. He told him that thence there were swift-sailing merchant vessels and highly skilled pilots who manage them as a charioteer manages race-horses and provide a straightforward passage along the direct route. Agrippa did as he was told, partly out of the deference to his lord and master, and also because the course he enjoined seemed to be advisable. §27. He went down to Dicaearchia (=Puteoli), and seeing there some ships of Alexandria lying at anchor and ready to sail he embarked with his retinue, and after a good voyage came to land a few days later without being expected or his purposes detected. He had ordered the pilots when they sighted Pharos in the late afternoon to furl the sails and lie outside round about it and not far off until the evening had well set in, and then by night to put in at the harbour, so that he might disembark when every one had settled down to sleep and rearch the house of his host without anyone seeing him. §28. His reason for making his visit in such an unassuming way was that he wished if possible to slip out of the city quietly and unobserved by the whole population. For he had not come to see Alexandria as he had stayed there before on his voyage to Rome to join Tiberius, and he only wanted to get a short route for his journey home. §29. But jealousy is part of the Egyptian nature, and the citizens were bursting with envy and considered that any good luck to others was misfortune to themselves, and in their ancient, and we might say innate hostility to the Jews, they resented a Jew having been made a king just as much as if each of them had thereby been deprived of an ancestral throne.

The Gymnasium of Alexandria

Philon, *In Flaccum*, §33-34. Translation by F H Colson (The Loeb Classical Library, 1941).

35.
§33. Τῷ γὰρ ἀργοῦντι καὶ σχολάζοντι τῆς πόλεως ὄχλῳ - πλῆθος δ΄ ἐστὶν ἐπιτετηδευκὸς γλωσσαλγίαν καὶ ἐνευκαιροῦν διαβολαῖς καὶ βλασφημίαις - ἐπιτρέπει κακηγορεῖν τὸν βασιλέα εἴτε ἀρξάμενος δι΄ ἑαυτοῦ τῶν λοιδοριῶν εἴτε πτοτρεψάμενος καὶ ἐναγαγὼν αὐτὸς διὰ τῶν ὑπηρετεῖν τὰ τοιαῦτα εἰωθότων. §34. οἱ δ΄ ἀφορμῆς λαβόμενοι διημέρευον ἐν τῷ γυμνασίῳ χλευάζοντες τὸν βασιλέα καὶ σκώμματα συνείροντες · πῇ δὲ καὶ ποιηταῖς μίμων καὶ γελοίων διδασκάλοις χρώμενοι τὴν ἐν τοῖς αἰσχροῖς εὐφυΐαν ἐπεδείκνυντο, βραδεῖς μὲν ὄντες τὰ καλὰ παιδεύεσθαι, τὰ δ΄ ἐναντία μανθάνειν ὀξύτατοι καὶ προχειρότατοι.

35.
§33. For the lazy and unoccuppied mob in the city, a multitude well practised in idle talk, who devote their leisure to slandering and evil speaking, was permitted by him to vilify the king, whether the abuse was actually begun by himself or caused by his incitement and provocation addressed to those who were his regular ministers in such matters. §34. Thus started on their course they spent their days in the gymnasium jeering at the king and bringing out a succession of gibes against him. In fact they took the authors of farces and jests for their instructors and thereby showed their natural ability in things of shame, slow to be schooled in anything good but exceedingly quick and ready in learning the opposite.

Imperial effigies in the synagogues

Philon, *In Flaccum*, §41-43. Translation by F H Colson (The Loeb Classical Library, 1967).

36.
§41.῞Οπερ συναισθόμενος ὁ ὄχλος - οὐχ ὁ καθεστὼς καὶ δημοτικός, ἀλλ΄ ὁ πάντα θορύβου καὶ ταραχῆς εἰωθὼς ἀναπιμπλάναι διὰ φιλοπραγμοσύνην καὶ ζῆλον ἀβιώτου βίου καὶ τὴν ἐξ ἔθους ἀργίαν καὶ σχολήν, πρᾶγμα ἐπίβουλον - συρρυέντες εἰς τὸ θέατρον ἐξ ἑωθινοῦ Φλάκκον ἤδη τιμῶν ἀθλίων ἐωνημένοι, ἃς ὁ δοξομανὴς καὶ παλίμπρατος ἐλάμβανεν οὐ καθ΄ αὑτοῦ μόνον ἀλλὰ καὶ τῆς κοινῆς ἀσφαλείας, ἀνεβόησαν ἀφ΄ ἑνὸς συνθήματος εἰκόνας ἐν ταῖς προσευχαῖς ἀνατιθέναι, καινότατον καὶ μηδέπω πραχθὲν εἰσηγούμενοι παρανόμημα. §42. καὶ τοῦτ΄ εἰδότες - ὀξύτατοι γὰρ τὴν μοχθηρίαν εἰσί - κατασοφίζονται τὸ Καίσαρος ὄνομα προκάλυμμα ποιησάμενοι, ᾧ προσάπτειν τι τῶν ἐπαιτίων οὐ θεμιτόν. §43. τί οὖν τῆς χώρας ἐπίτροπος ; ἐπιστάμενος, ὅτι καὶ ἡ πόλις οἰκήτορας ἔχει διττούς, ἡμᾶς τε καὶ τούτους, καὶ πᾶσα Αἴγυπτος, καὶ ὅτι οὐκ ἀποδέουσι μυριάδων ἑκατὸν οἱ τὴν᾿Αλεξάνδρειαν καὶ τὴν χώραν ᾿Ιουδαῖοι κατοικοῦντες ἀπὸ τοῦ πρὸς Λιβύην καταβαθμοῦ μέχρι τῶν ὁρίων Αἰθιοπίας, καὶ ὡς ἡ πεῖρα κατὰ πάντων ἐστὶ καὶ ὡς οὐ λυσιτελὲς ἔθη πάτρια κινεῖν, ἀμελήσας ἁπάντων ἐπιτρέπει ποιήσασθαι τὴν ἀνάθεσιν, μυρία καὶ πάντα προνοητικὰ δυνάμενος ἢ ὡς ἄρχων κελεύειν ἢ συμβουλεύειν ὡς φίλος.

36.
§41. When the crowd perceived this, not the peaceful, public-spirited crowd, but the crowd which regularly fills everything with confusion and turmoil, which by its love of meddling, its eager pursuit of the worthless life, its habitul laziness and idling, is a thing that means mischief, they streamed into the theatre at early dawn, and having Flaccus purchased by the miserable price which he crazy for fame and everеady to be sold took to the destruction not only of himself but of the public safety, called out with one accord for installing images in the meeting-houses. §42. What they proposed was a breach of the law entirely novel and unprecedented and knowing this, quick-witted as they are for villainy, they cunningly glozed it by using the name of Caesar as a screen, that name with which no guilty action can lawfully be associated. §43. What then did the governor of the country do? He knew that both Alexandria and the whole of Egypt had two kinds of inhabitants, us and them, and that there were no less than a million Jews resident in Alexandria and the country from the slope into Libya to the boundaries of Ethiopia; also that this was an attack against them all, and that ancestral customs cannot be disturbed without harm, yet he disregarded all these facts and permitted the installation of the images though there were a host of considerations all tending to caution which he might have set before them either as orders from a ruler or advice from a friend.

The beaches of Alexandria, rubbish dumps and cemeteries—refuges of the Jews

Philo, *In Flaccum*, §55-57. Translation by F H Colson (The Loeb Classical Library, 1941).

37.
§55. Οἱ δὲ λαβόντες ἄδειαν τί πράττουσι ; πέντε μοῖραι τῆς πόλεως εἴσιν, ἐπώνυμοι τῶν πρώτων στοιχείων τῆς ἐγγραμμάτου φωνῆς · τούτων δύο ’Ιουδαϊκαὶ λέγονται διὰ τὸ πλείστους’Ιουδαίους ἐν ταύταις κατοικεῖν · οἰκοῦσι δὲ καὶ ἐν ταῖς ἄλλαις οὐκ ὀλίγοι σποράδες . τί οὖν ἐποίησαν ; ἐκ τῶν τεσσάρων γραμμάτων ἐξῴκισαν τοὺς’Ιουδαίους καὶ συνήλασαν εἰς ἑνὸς μοῖραν βραχυτάτην. §56. οἱ δὲ ἐξεχέοντο διὰ τὸ πλῆθος εἰς αἰγιαλοὺς καὶ κοπρίας καὶ μνήματα πάντων στερόμενοι τῶν ἰδίων. ἐκεῖνοι δὲ τὰς οἰκίας ἐρήμους καταδραμόντες ἐφ´ ἁρπαγὴν ἐτράποντο καὶ ὡς ἐκ πολέμου λείαν διενέμοντο, μηδενὸς δὲ κωλύοντος καὶ τὰ ἐργαστήρια τῶν ’Ιουδαίων συγκεκλεισμένα διὰ τὸ ἐπὶ Δρουσίλλῃ πένθος ἀναρρήξαντες ὅσα εὗρον - πολλὰ δὲ καὶ ταῦτ´ ἦν - ἐξεφόρησαν καὶ διὰ μέσης ἀγορᾶς ἐκόμιζον ὡς οἰκείοις τοῖς ἀλλοτρίοις καταχρώμενοι. §57. τῆς δ´ ἁρπαγῆς ἡ ἀπραξία κακὸν ἦν βαρύτερον, τὰς μὲν ἐνθήκας ἀπολωλεκότων τῶν ποριστῶν, μηδενὸς δὲ ἐωμένου, μὴ γεώργου, μὴ ναυκλήρου, μὴ ἐμπόρου, μὴ τεχνίτου, τὰ συνήθη πραγματεύεσθαι, ὡς διχόθεν κατεσκευάσθαι πενίαν, ἔκ τε τῆς ἁρπαγῆς, ἐξουσίων μιᾷ ἡμέρᾳ γενομένων καὶ περισεσυλημένων τὰ ἴδια, κἀκ τοῦ μὴ δεδυνῆσθαι πορίζειν ἐκ τῶν συνήθων ἐπιτηδευμάτων.

37.
§55. Having secured this immunity what did they do? The city has five quarters named after the first letters of the alphabet, two of these are called Jewish because most of the Jews inhabit them, though in the rest also there are not a few Jews scattered about. So then what did they do? From the four letters they ejected the Jews and drove them to herd in a very small part of one. §56. The Jews were so numerous that they poured out over beaches, dunghills and tombs, robbed of all their belongings. Their enemies overran the houses now left empty and turned to pillaging them, distributing the contents like spoils of war, and as no one prevented them they broke open the workshops of the Jews which had been closed as a sign of mourning for Drusilla, carried out all

the articles they found, which were very numerous, and bore them through the middle of the market-place, dealing with other people's property as freely as if it was their own. §57. A still more grievous evil than the pillaring was the unemployment produced. The tradespeople had lost their stocks, and no one, husbandman, shipman, merchant, artisan, was allowed to practice his usual business. Thus poverty was established in two ways; first, the pillaging, by which in the course of a single day they had become penniless, completely stripped of what they had, and secondly, their inability to make a living from their regular employments.

Scenes of horror in the theatre of Alexandria

Philo, *In Flaccum*, §73-75. Translation by F H Colson (The Loeb Classical Library, 1941).

38.

§73. Πάντα δὲ διορύξας καὶ τοιχωρυχήσας ὁ Φλάκκος καὶ μηδὲν μέρος τῶν Ἰουδαϊκῶν ἀμέτοχον ἐπιβουλῆς τῆς ἀνωτάτω καταλιπὼν ἐπενόησεν ἔκτοπόν τινα καὶ παρηλλαγμένην ἐπίθεσιν, ὁ μεγαλουργός, ὁ καινῶν ἀδικημάτων εὑρετής. §74. τῆς γὰρ ἡμετέρας γερουσίας, ἣν ὁ σωτὴρ καὶ εὐεργέτης Σεβαστὸς ἐπιμελησομένην τῶν Ἰουδαϊκῶν εἵλετο μετὰ τὴν τοῦ γενάρχου τελευτὴν διὰ τῶν πρὸς Μᾶγιον Μάξιμον ἐντολῶν μέλλοντα πάλιν [ἀπ´] Ἀλεξανδρείας καὶ τῆς χώρας ἐπιτροπεύειν, ὀκτὼ καὶ τριάκοντα συλλαβὼν τοὺς εὑρεθέντας ἐν ταῖς οἰκίαις εὐθὺς μὲν δῆσαι κελεύει, καὶ στείλας καλὴν πομπὴν διὰ μέσης ἀγορᾶς πρεσβύτας δεσμίους ἐξηγκωνισμένους, τοὺς μὲν ἱμάσι, τοὺς δὲ σιδηραῖς ἁλύσεσιν, εἰς τὸ θέατρον εἰσάγει - θέαν οἰκτίστην καὶ ἀλλοτριωτάτην τῷ καιρῷ - §75. καὶ στάντας ἀντικρὺ ἐχθρῶν καθεζομένων πρὸς ἐπίδειξιν αἰσχύνης προστάττει πάντας περιδυθέντας αἰκισθῆναι μάστιξιν αἷς ἔθος τοὺς κακούργων πονηροτάτους προπηλακίζεσθαι, ὡς ἐκ τῶν πληγῶν τοὺς μὲν φοράδην ἐκκομισθέντας αὐτίκα τελευτῆσαι, τοὺς δὲ νοσήσαντας ἐπὶ πλεῖστον χρόνον εἰς ἀπόγνωσιν σωρηρίας ἐλθεῖν.

§73. Having broken into everything like a burglar and left no side of Jewish life untouched by a hostility carried to the highest pitch, Flaccus devised another monstrous and unparalleled line of attack worthy of this perpetrator of enormities and inventor of novel iniquities. §74. Our Senate had been appointed to take charge of Jewish affairs by our saviour and benefactor Augustus, after the death of the ethnarch, orders to that effect having been given to Magius Maximus when he was about to take office for the second time as Governor of Alexandria and the country. Of this Senate the members who were found in their houses, thirty-eight in number, were arrested by Flaccus, who having ordered them to be straithway put in bonds marshalled a fine procession through the middle of the market of these elderly men trussed and pinioned, some thongs and others with iron chains, and then taken into the theatre, a spectacle most pitiable and incongruous with the occasion. §75. Then as they stood with their enemies seated in front to signalize their disgrace he ordered them all to be stripped and lacerated with scourges which are commonly used for the degradation of the vilest malefactors, so that in consequence of the flogging some had to be carried out on stretchers and died at once, while others lay sick for a long time despairing of recovery.

Harbours on the river and the streets across leading to the royal palaces

Philo, *In Flaccum* §92. Translation by F H Colson (The Loeb Classical Library, 1941).

39.
§92. Καίτοι γ΄ οὐ πρὸ πολλοῦ τῶν κατὰ τὴν χώραν Αἰγυπτίων ὁπλολογηθέντων ὑπὸ Βάσσου τινός, ᾧ προσέταξεν ὁ Φλάκκος τουτὶ τὸ ἔργον, [ἀλλ΄] ἦν τότε ἰδεῖν στόλον μέν πολὺν νεῶν καταπεπλευκότα καὶ ἐνορμοῦντα τοῖς τοῦ ποταμοῦ λιμέσι, γέμοντα παντοίων ὅπλων, ἀχθοφόρα δ΄ ὑποζύγια παμπληθῆ συνδεδεμένων δοράτων φορμηδὸν ἀφ΄ ἑκατέρας πλευρᾶς εἰς τὸ ἰσόρροπον, τὰς δὲ ἀπὸ τοῦ στρατοπέδου πάσας σχεδὸν ἁρμαμάξας μεστὰς πανοπλιῶν, αἳ στοιχηδὸν ὑπὸ μίαν ὄψιν καὶ τὴν αὐτὴν σύνταξιν ἐν κόσμῳ προῄεσαν· τὸ δὲ μεταξὺ τῶν λιμένων καὶ τῆς ἐν τοῖς βασιλείοις ὁπλοθήκης, εἰς ἣν ἔδει κατατεθῆναι τὰ ὅπλα, δέκα σταδίων που διάστημα σύμπαν ἔχον.

39.
§92. And yet not long before, when the Egyptians in the country district had their weapons collected by one Bassus, on whom Flaccus had laid this task, there was a great array of ships to be seen which had sailed to the bank and moored in the harbours of the river brimful of all manner weapons, also a great number of beasts of burden with spears tied in bundles hung on each side to balance equally. Also there was a procession of waggons sent from the camp, nearly all full of outfits of armour, moving regularly one after the other so as to form a single ordered line, all visible at once, and the space between the harbours and the armoury in the palace where the arms had to be deposited was, taken altogether, about ten stades long.

The clandestine disembarkment of the centurion Bassus at the harbour of Alexandria

Philo, *In Flaccum*, §109-111. Translation by F H Colson (The Loeb Classical Library, 1941).

40.
§109 ... Πέμπεται μὲν γὰρ ἀπὸ τῆς 'Ιταλίας Βάσσος ἑκατοντάρχης ὑπὸ Γαΐου χειροτονηθεὶς μετὰ τῆς τάξεως τῶν στρατιωτῶν, ἧς ἀφηγεῖτο. §110. σκάφους δ΄ ἐπιβὰς τῶν μάλιστα ταχυναυτούντων ὀλίγαις ἡμέραις πρὸς τοῖς λιμέσι γίνεται τῆς 'Αλεξανδρείας κατὰ τὴν Φάρον νῆσον περὶ δείλην ἑσπέραν καὶ κελεύει τῷ κυβερνήτῃ μέχρις ἡλίου καταδύσεως ἔξω θαλαττεύειν, τεχνάζων τὸ ἀνεπίφαντον ἕνεκα τοῦ μὴ προαισθόμενον Φλάκκον καὶ βουλευσάμενόν τι νεώτερον ἄπρακτον αὐτῷ τὴν ὑπηρεσίαν ἐργάσασθαι. §111. γενομένης δ΄ ἑσπέρας, ἡ μὲν ναῦς προσέσχεν, ὁ δὲ Βάσσος μετὰ τῶν ἰδίων ἀποβὰς προῄει, μήτε γνωρίζων τινὰ μήτε γνωριζόμενος ὑπό του, στρατιώτην δέ τινα τῶν ἐν τοῖς τετραδίοις φυλάκων καθ΄ ὁδὸν εὑρὼν κελεύει δεικνύναι τὴν οἰκίαν τοῦ στρατάρχου · τούτῳ γὰρ ἐβούλετο τὸ ἀπόρρητον ἀνενεγκεῖν, ἵνα, κἂν δέῃ πολυχειρίας, ἔχῃ τὸν συναγωνιούμενον.

40.
§109. ... A centurion named Bassus was sent from Italy by Gaius's appointement with the company of soldiers which he commanded. §110. Having embarked on one the swiftest sailing ships, he arrived in a few days at the harbours of Alexandria, off the island of Pharos, in the late afternoon and bade the pilot wait at sea outside till sunset, his scheme being to avoid observation, so that Flaccus might not get knowledge of it before-hand and by planning some

act of violence, make his mission unsuccessful. §111. When it was evening the ship was brought to land and Bassus disembarking with his men went forward without recognizing or being recognized by anyone. And finding on the way a soldier belonging to the quaternions acting as sentries, he ordered him to show him the house of the military commander. For he wished to communicate his secret instructions to him, so that if a strong force was required he might have someone to support him in the contest.

Refugees in the cemeteries and on the beaches

Philo, *On the Embassy to Gaius*, §127. Translation by F H Colson (The Loeb Classical Library, 1962).

41.
§127. μηκέτι οὖν ὑπομένειν τὴν δυσχωρίαν οἷοί τε ὄντες ἐξεχέοντο εἰς ἐρημίας καὶ αἰγιαλοὺς καὶ μνήματα, γλιχόμενοι σπάσαι καθαροῦ καὶ ἀβλαβοῦς ἀέρος. εἰ δέ τινες ἢ προσκαταλήφθησαν ἐν τοῖς ἄλλοις μέρεσι τῆς πόλεως ἢ ἀγνοίᾳ τῶν κατασκηψάντων κακῶν ἀγρόθεν παρεγένοντο, πολυτρόπων ἀπέλαυον συμφορῶν ἢ καταλευόμενοι ἢ κεράμῳ τιτρωσκόμενοι ἢ πρίνου κλάδοις καὶ δρυὸς τὰ καιριώτατα μέρη τοῦ σώματος καὶ μάλιστα κεφαλὴν ἄχρι θανάτου καταγνύμενοι.

41.
§127. So the Jews, unable to endure any longer the painful want of space, poured out into deserted spots and beaches and tombs, eager to get a breath of pure and innocuous air. And if any were caught in the other parts of the city before they could escape or if they came up from the country in ignorance of the disasters which had fallen upon us they experienced manifold misfortunes, being stoned or wounded by tiles or branches of ilex or oak in the most vital parts of the body and particularly in the head, the fracture of which proved fatal.

Ambushes in the harbours on the Nile

Philo, *On the Embassy to Gaius*, §129. Translation by F H Colson (The Loeb Classical Library, 1962).

42.
§129. ἕτερος δὲ λόχος ἦν ἐφεδρεύων τοῖς τοῦ ποταμοῦ λιμέσι πρὸς ἁρπαγὴν τῶν καταγομένων Ἰουδαίων καὶ ὧν κατ᾽ ἐμπορίαν ἐκόμιζον · ἐπεισβαίνοντες γὰρ ταῖς ναυσὶ τὸν φόρτον ἐν ὄψεσι τῶν κυρίων ἐξεφόρουν καὶ αὐτοὺς ἐξαγκωνίζοντες ἐνεπίμπρασαν, ὕλῃ χρώμενοι πηδαλίοις, οἴαξι, κοντοῖς καὶ ταῖς ἐπὶ τῶν καταστρωμάτων σανίσι.

42.
§129. There was another company who lay in waiting at the harbours of the river to rob the Jews who put in there and seize the goods which they were bringing for trade. They boarded the vessels and carried out the cargo before the eyes of the owners, whom they pinioned and burnt, using for fuel rudders, tillers, poles and the planks on the deck.

Imperial statues in the synagogues of Alexandria

Philo, *The Embassy to Gaius*, §134-135. Translation by F H Colson (The Loeb Classical Library, 1962).

43.

§134. βουλόμενοι δὲ καινοτέραις κολακείαις ὑπελθόντες αὐτὸν ἀνυπευθύνοις χρῆσθαι κατὰ τὸ παντελὲς ταῖς εἰς ἡμᾶς ἐπηρείαις τί ποιοῦσι ; προσευχὰς ὅσας μὴ ἐδυνήθησαν ἐμρήσεσι καὶ κατασκαφαῖς ἀφανίσαι διὰ τὸ πολλοὺς καὶ ἀθρόους πλησίον οἰκεῖν 'Ιουδαίους ἕτερον τρόπον ἐλυμήναντο μετὰ τῆς τῶν νόμων καὶ ἐθῶν ἀνατροπῆς · εἰκόνας γὰρ ἐν ἁπάσαις μὲν ἱδρύοντο Γαΐου, ἐν δὲ τῇ μεγίστῃ καὶ περισημοτάτῃ καὶ ἀνδριάντα χαλκοῦν ἐποχούμενον τεθρίππῳ. §135. καὶ τοσοῦτον ἦν τὸ τάχος καὶ τὸ σύντονον τῆς σπουδῆς, ὥστε οὐκ ἔχοντες ἐν ἑτοίμῳ καινὸν τέθριππον ἐκ τοῦ γυμνασίου παλαιότατον [ἐκόμιζον] ἰοῦ γέμον, ἠκρωτηριασμένον ὦτα καὶ οὐρὰς καὶ βάσεις καὶ ἕτερα οὐκ ὀλίγα, ὡς δὲ φασί τινες καὶ ὑπὲρ γυναικὸς ἀνατεθὲν τῆς ἀρχαίας Κλεοπάτρας, ἥτις ἦν προμάμμη τῆς τελευταίας.

43.

§134. And as they wished to ingratiate themselves with him by further novelties in flattering and so secure complete immunity for their maltreatment of us, what do you suppose they did? The meeting-houses which they could not raze or burn out of existence, because so many Jews live massed together in the neighbourhood, they outraged in another way, thereby overthrowing our laws and customs. For they set up images of Gaius in them all and in the largest and most notable a bronze statue of a man mounted on a chariot and four. §135. And so speedy and impetuous were they in their eagerness, that not having a new chariot of the kind at hand they fetched a very old one out of the gymnasium, a mass of rust with the ears, tails, feet and many other parts mutilated, and as some say dedicated to the honour of a woman, the original Cleopatra, great-grand-mother of the last queen of that name.

Description of the Sebasteum (temple of Augustus) in Alexandria

Philo, *The Embassy to Gaiu*, §150-151. Translation by F H Colson, (The Loeb Classical Library, 1972).

44.

§150. καὶ μαρτυροῦσι ναοί, προπύλαια, προτεμενίσματα, στοαί, ὡς ὅσαι τῶν πόλεων, ἢ νέα ἢ παλαιά, ἔργα φέρουσι μεγαλοπρεπῆ, τῷ κάλλει καὶ μεγέθει τῶν Καισαρείων παρευημερεῖσθαι, καὶ μάλιστα κατὰ τὴν ἡμετέραν 'Αλεξάνδρειαν . §151. οὐδὲν γὰρ τοιοῦτόν ἐστι τέμενος, οἷον τὸ λεγόμενον Σεβαστεῖον, ἐπιβατηρίου Καίσαρος νεώς, < ὃς > ἀντικρὺ τῶν εὐορμοτάτων λιμένων μετέωρος ἵδρυται μέγιστος καὶ ἐπιφανέστατος καὶ οἷος οὐχ ἑτέρωθι κατάπλεως ἀναθημάτων, [ἐν] γραφαῖς καὶ ἀνδριάσι καὶ ἀργύρῳ καὶ χρυσῷ περιβεβλημένος ἐν κύκλῳ, τέμενος εὐρύτατον στοαῖς, βιβλιοθήκαις, ἀνδρῶσιν, ἄλσεσι, προπυλαίοις, εὐρυχωρίαις, ὑπαίθροις, ἅπασι τοῖς εἰς πολυτελέστατον κόσμον ἠσκημένον, ἐλπὶς καὶ ἀναγομένοις καὶ καταπλέουσι σωτήριος.

44.
§150. These are so well attested by temples, gateways, vestibules, porticoes, that every city which contains magnificent works new and old is surpassed in these by the beauty and magnitude of those appropriated to Caesar and particularly in our own Alexandria. §151. For there is elsewhere no precinct like that which is called the Sebasteum, a temple to Caesar on shipboard, situated on an eminence facing the harbours famed for their excellent moorage, huge and conspicuous, fitted on a scale not found elsewhere with dedicated offerings, around it a girdle of pictures and statues in silver and gold, forming a precinct of vast breadth, embellished with porticoes, libraries, chambers, groves, gateways and wide open courts and everything which lavish expenditure could produce to beautify it—the whole a hope of safety to the voyager either going into or out of the harbour.

The voyage to Egypt via Asia Minor and Syria

Philo, *The Embassy to Gaius*, §250-253. Translation by F H Colson (The Loeb Classical Library, 1962).

45.
§250. Διεγνώκει μὲν γάρ, ὡς λόγος, πλεῖν εἰς ʼΑλεξάνδρειαν τὴν πρὸς Αἰγύπτῳ, πελάγει δὲ οὐκ ἀξιώσει τοσοῦτος ἡγεμὼν διά τε τοὺς κινδύνους καὶ διὰ τὸ πλῆθος τοῦ παραπέμποντος στόλου καὶ ἅμα διὰ τὴν ἐπιμέλειαν τοῦ σώματος, ἃ δὴ πάντα γίνεται ῥαδίως τὸν δι΄ ʼΑσίας καὶ Συρίας κύκλον περαιουμένῳ . §251. δυνήσεται γὰρ καθ΄ ἑκάστην ἡμέραν καὶ πλεῖν καὶ ἀποβαίνειν, καὶ μάλιστα τὰς πλείστας ναῦς ἐπαγόμενος μακράς, ἀλλ΄ οὐχ ὁλκάδας, αἷς ὁ παρὰ γῆν πλοῦς ἀνυσιμώτερος, ὡς ταῖς φορτίσι διὰ πελάγους ἐστίν. § 252. ἀναγκαῖον οὖν καὶ χιλὸν κτήνεσι καὶ τροφὰς ἀφθόνους ἐν ἁπάσαις ταῖς Συριακαῖς πόλεσιν εὐτρεπίσθαι, καὶ μάλιστα ταῖς παράλοις. ἀφίξεται γὰρ παμπληθὴς ὄχλος καὶ δία γῆς καὶ διὰ θαλάττης, οὐ μόνον ἀπ΄ αὐτῆς ʽΡώμης καὶ ʼΙταλίας ἀναστάς, ἀλλὰ καὶ ἀπὸ τῶν ἑξῆς ἄχρι Συρίας ἐπικρατειῶν ἐπηκολουθηκώς, ὁ μὲν τῶν ἐν τέλει, ὁ δὲ στρατιωτικός, ἱππέων, πεζῶν, τῶν ἐν ταῖς ναυσίν, ὁ δὲ οἰκετικὸς οὐκ ἀποδέων τοῦ στρατιωτικοῦ. §253. δεῖ δὲ χορηγιῶν οὐ πρὸς τὰ ἀναγκαῖα συμμεμετρημένων αὐτὸ μόνον, ἀλλὰ καὶ πρὸς περιττὴν δαψίλειαν, ἣν ἐπιζητεῖ Γάιος. τούτοις ἐὰν ἐντύχῃ τοῖς γράμμασιν, ἴσως πρὸς τῷ μὴ δυσχερᾶναι καὶ τῆς προνοίας ἡμᾶς ἀποδέξεται ὡς ποιησαμένους τὴν ὑπέρθεσιν, οὐ χάριτι τῇ τῶνʼΙουδαίων, ἀλλ΄ ἕνεκα τῆς τῶν καρπῶν συγκομιδῆς.

45.
§250. For Gaius had determined, they were told, to sail to Alexandria by Egypt, but so great a potentate would not think it right to go by the open sea because of the dangers and the numbers of ships required for a convoy, and also the need of providing for his bodily comfort, all which ends are easily obtained by taking the circuitous route along Asia and Syria. §251. For he would be able every day to combine the voyage with landing, particularly as most of the vessels which he would take would be no merchant ships but warships for which coasting is more feasible, just as an open sea voyage is for cargo boats. §252. It would be necessary therefore to have fodder for the beasts and a vast stock of food got ready in all the cities of Syria, particularly on the coast. For a huge crowd would come both by sea and by land, drawn not only from Rome itself and Italy, but also from the successive provinces right up to Syria, a crowd composed partly of persons of hight rank, partly of soldiers, infantry and cavalry and marines, while the multitude

of servants would be not less than the military. §253. Supplies were needed calculated not merely for absolute necessities but for the excessive expenditure which Gaius demanded. If he reads this letter, thought Petronius, he will probably not merely refrain from anger but approve our forethought, recognising that the postponement which we have made is not due to favouritism to the Jews but in order to insure the carrying of the harvest.

Caius's love for Alexandria and where he wanted to put up his statue

Philo, *The Embassy to Gaius*, §337-338. Translation by F H Colson (The Loeb Classical Library, 1962).

46.
§337 ... προστάττει γὰρ ἕτερον ἀνδριάντα δημιουργεῖσθαι κολοσσιαῖον χαλκοῦν ἐπίχρυσον ἐν ῾Ρώμῃ, μηκέτι τὸν ἐν Σιδῶνι κινῶν, ἵνα μὴ τῇ κινήσει διαταράξῃ τὸ πλῆθος, ἀλλ´ ἠρεμοῦντος καὶ τῆς ὑπονοίας ἀπηλλαγμένου κατὰ πολλὴν ἡσυχίαν ἀφανῶς ἐν ταῖς ναυσὶ κομισθέντα λαθὼν τοὺς πολλοὺς ἐξαίφνης ἱδρύσηται. §338. τοῦτο δὲ πράξειν ἔμελλεν ἐν παράπλῳ κατὰ τὴν εἰς Αἴγυπτον ἀποδημίαν . ἄλεκτος γάρ τις αὐτὸν ἔρως κατεῖχε τῆς ᾽Αλεξανδρείας, εἰς ἣν ἐπόθει σπουδῇ πάσῃ παραγενέσθαι καὶ ἀφικόμενος πλεῖστον χρόνον ἐνδιαιτηθῆναι, νομίζων τὴν ἐκθέωσιν, ἣν ὠνειροπόλει, μίαν ταύτην πόλιν καὶ γεγεννηκέναι καὶ συναυξήσειν, καὶ ταῖς ἄλλαις παράδειγμα γεγενῆσθαι τοῦ σεβασμοῦ, μεγίστην τε οὖσαν καὶ ἐν καλῷ τῆς οἰκουμένης · τὰ γὰρ τῶν μεγάλων εἴτε ἀνδρῶν εἴτε πόλεων τοὺς καταδεεστέρους ἄνδρας τε καὶ δήμους ζηλοῦν ἐπιχειρεῖν.

46.
§337 ... He ordered another bronze statue of colossal size coated with gold to be constructed in Rome. The one in Sidon he forbore from moving, for he did not wish to perturb the multitude by moving it, but intended when they were tranquil and freed from suspicion to have the other conveyed very quietly and secretly on shipboard and suddenly erected unobserved by the mass of the population. §338. This he intended to do while coasting along on his voyage to Egypt. For he was possessed by an extraordinary and passionate love for Alexandria. His heart was entirely set upon visiting it and on his arrival staying there for a very considerable time. For he thought this city was unique in that it had both given birth to and would foster the idea of godship which occupied his dreams, and that its vast size and the world-wide value of its admirable situation had made it a pattern to other cities of the worship due to him, since it is true both of individual men and of whole populations that the inferior try to emulate the qualities of the great men and cities respectively.

Imperial effigies in the synagogues of Alexandria

Philo, *On the Embassy to Gaius*, §346. Text and translation by P H Colson (The Loeb Classical Library, 1962).

47.
§346. Τοσαύτη μὲν οὖν τις ἡ περὶ τὸ ἦθος ἦν ἀνωμαλία πρὸς ἅπαντας, διαφερόντως δὲ πρὸς τὸ ᾽Ιουδαίων γένος, ᾧ χαλεπῶς ἀπεχθανομένος τὰς μὲν ἐν ταῖς ἄλλαις πόλεσι προσευχὰς ἀπὸ τῶν κατ´ ᾽Αλεξάνδρειαν ἀρξάμενος σφετερίζεται, καταπλήσας εἰκόνων καὶ ἀνδριάντων τῆς ἰδίας μορφῆς - ὁ γὰρ

ἑτέρων ἀνατιθέντων ἐφεὶς αὐτὸς ἱδρύετο δυνάμει -, τὸν δὲ ἐν τῇ ἱεροπόλει νεών, ὃς λοιπὸς ἦν ἄψαυστος ἀσυλίας ἠξιωμένος τῆς πάσης, μεθηρμόζετο καὶ μετεσχημάτιζεν εἰς οἰκεῖον ἱερόν, ἵνα Διὸς'Επιφανοῦς Νέου χρηματίζῃ Γαου.

47.
§346. This great inconstancy of conduct affected all, but particularly the Jewish race. Having conceived a violent enmity to them he took possession of the synagogues in the other cities after beginning with those of Alexandria, by filling them with images and statues of himself in bodily form. For by permitting others to instal them he virtually did it himself. The temple in the Holy City, which alone was left untouched being judged to have all rights of sanctuary, he was proceeding to convert and transmogrify into a temple of his own to bear the name of Gaius 'the new Zeus made manifest'.

23-79 AD. Pliny.

The site of Rhacotes

Pliny, *Natural History*, V, XI, 62-63. Translation by H Rackham (The Loeb Classical Library, 1942).

48.
V, XI, 62. Sed jure laudetur in littore Aegyptii maris Alexandria a Magno Alexandro condita in Africae parte ab ostio Canopico XXII millia passuum juxta Mareotim lacum, qui locus antea Rhacotes nominabatur. Metatus est eam Dinochares architectus pluribus modis memorabili ingenio, XV m.p. laxitate insessa ad effigiem Macedonicae chlamydis orbe gyrato laciniosam, dextra laevaque anguloso procursu, iam tum tamen quinta situs parte regiae dicata. 63 Mareotis lacus a meridiana urbis parte Euripo e Canopico ostio mittitur ex mediterraneo commercia, insulas quoque plures amplexus, XXX m. passuum traiectu, CCL ambitu, ut tradit Claudius Caesar. Alii schoenos in longitudine patere XL faciunt, schoenumque stadia XXX, ita fieri longtudinis CL m.p., tantundem et latitudinis.

48.
62. But justice requires that praise shall be bestowed on Alexandria, built by Alexander the Great on the coast of the Egyptian Sea on the side of Africa, 12 miles from the Canopic mouth and adjoining Lake Mariout; the site was previously named Rhacotes. It was laid out by the architect Dinochares, who is famous for his talent in a variety of ways; it covered an area spreading 15 miles in the shape of a Macedonian soldier's cape, with indentations in its circumference and projecting corners on the right and left side; while at the same time a fifth of the site was devoted to the King's palace. 63 Lake Mariout, which lies on the south side of the city, carries traffic from the interior by means of a canal from the Canopic mouth of the Nile; also it includes a considerable number of islands, being 30 miles across and 250 miles in circumference, according to Claudius Caesar. Others make it 40 *schoeni* long and reckon the *schoenus* at 30 furlongs, which makes the length 150 miles, and they give the same figure for the breadth.

The channels of the great harbour

Pliny, *Natural History*, V, XXXIV, 128. Translation by H Rackham (The Loeb Classical Library, 1942).

49.
Insularum ante Asiam prima est in Canopico ostio Nili, a Canopo Menelai gubernatore, ut ferunt, dicta. Altera iuncta ponte Alexandriae, colonia Caesaris dictatoris, Pharus, quondam diei navigatione distans ab Aegypto, nunc a turri nocturnis ignibus cursum navium regens; namque fallacibus vadis Alexandria tribus omnino aditur alveis maris, Stegano, Posideo, Tauro.

49.

Of the islands off the coast of Asia the first is at the Canopic mouth of the Nile, and takes its name, it is said, from Menelaus's helmsman Canopus. The second, called Pharos, joined by a bridge to Alexandria, was settled by the Dictator Caesar; it was formerly a day's sail from Egypt, but now it carries a lighthouse to direct the course of vessels at night; for owing to the treached shoals Alexandria can be reached by only three channels of the sea, those of Steganus, Posideum and Taurus.

The obelisks near the harbour

Pliny, *Natural History* X, XXXVI-XXXVII. Translated by D E Eichholz (Loeb Classical Library 1971).

49 bis.

Hic fuit in Arsinoeo positus a rege supra dicto, munus amoris in conjuge eademque sorore Arsinoe. Inde cum navalibus incommodum Maximus quidem praefectus transtulit in forum ... Et alii duo sunt Alexandriae ad portum in Caesaris templo, quos excidit Mesphres rex quadragenum binum cubitorum.

49 bis.

The obelisk was once in the Arsinoeum, having been placed there by the king to whom we previously referred as a tribute to his affection for his wife and sister Arsinoe. From there, because it was in the way of the dockyards, it was moved to the market-place by a certain Maximus, a governor of Egypt. There are two other obelisks at Alexandria in the precinct of the temple of Caesar near the harbour. These were cut by King Mesphres and measure 42 cubits.

41-54 AD. Reign of Claudius: Curtius Quintus.

Curtius Quintus, *History of Alexander*, IV, 8, 1-2 and 8, 4-5; X, 10, 20. Translation by John C Rolfe (The Loeb Classical Library, 1946).

50.

IV, 8, 1-2. Alexander ab Hammone rediens ut Mareotin paludem haud procul insula Pharo sitam uenit. Contemplatus loci naturam, primum in ipsa insula statuerat urbem nouam condere; inde, ut adparuit magnae sedis insulam haud capacem esse, elegit urbi locum, ubi nunc est Alexandria, appellationem trahens ex nomine auctoris. Conplexus quidquid soli est inter paludem ac mare, octoginta stadiorum muris ambitum destinat et, qui exaedificandae urbi praeessent relictis, Memphin petit...

IV, 8, 4-5. Itaque Aegypto praefecit Aeschylum Rhodium et Peucesten Macedonem, quattuor milibus militum in praesidium regionis eius datis, claustra Nili fluminis Polemonem tueri iubet; XXX ad hoc triremes datae. Africae deinde, quae Aegypto iuncta est, praepositus Apollonius, vectigalibus eiusdem Africae Aegyptique Cleomenes. Ex finitimis urbibus commigrare Alexandriam iussis, novam urbem magna multitudine impleuit. Fama est, cum rex orbem futuri muri polenta, ut Macedonum mos est, destinasset, avium greges advolasse, et polenta esse pastas; cumque id omen pro tristi a plerisque esset acceptum, respondisse vates, magnam illam urbem advenarum frequentiam culturam, multisque eam terris alimenta praebituram...

X, 10, 20. Ceterum corpus eius (*id est* Alexandri) a Ptolomaeo, cui Aegytus cesserat, Memphim et inde paucis post annis Alexandream translatum est, omnisque memoriae ac nomini honos habetur.

50.

IV, 8, 1-2. Alexander, as he returned from Ammon, came to the Mareotic Lake, situated not far from the island of Pharos. Contemplating the nature of the place, he had decided at first to build a city on the island itself; then, as it was apparent that the island was not large enough for a great settlement, he chose for the city the present site of Alexandria, which derives its name from that of its founder. Embracing all the ground between the Lake and the sea, he planned a circuit of eighty stadia for the walls, and having left men to take charge of building the city, he went to Memphis.

IV, 8, 4-5. ... Therefore he put Aeschylus the Rhodian and Peucestes the Macedonian in charge of Egypt, giving them 4000 soldiers for the defence of that region, and ordered Polemon to defend the mouths of the Nile; for this purpose thirty triremes were given. Then Apollonius was put in command of the part of Africa which is adjacent to Egypt, and Cleomenes was made collector of the tributes of that part of Africa and of Egypt. Having ordered inhabitants of the neighbouring cities to move to Alexandria, he filled the new city with a great population. It is reported that when the king has marked out the circuit of the new city with peely barley, as is the custom of the Macedonians, flocks of birds flew to the spot and ate the barley; and when that was regarded by many as a bad omen, the seers predicted that a great number of new-comers would dwell in that city, and that it would furnish sustenance to many lands.

X, 10, 20. But Ptolemy, under whose control Egypt had come, transported the king's body to Memphis and from there a few years later to Alexandria where every honour was paid to his memory and his name.

37-95 AD. Flavius Josephus.

Josephus, *The Jewish War* III, IV, 612-615. Translated by H S T J Thackeray (Loeb Classical Library 1957).

50 bis.

§612. Δυσπρόσιτος δὲ λιμὴν ναυσὶ καὶ κατ´ εἰρήνην ’Αλεξανδρείας · στενός τε γὰρ εἴσπλους καὶ πέτραις ὑφάλοις τὸν ἐπ´ εὐθὺ καμπτόμενος δρόμον. §613. Καὶ τὸ μὲν ἀριστερὸν αὐτοῦ μέρος πέφρακται χειροκμήτοις σκέλεσιν, ἐν δεξιᾷ δὲ ἡ προσαγορευομένη Φάρος νῆσος πρόκειται, πύργον ἀνέχουσα μέγιστον ἐκπυρσεύοντα τοῖς καταπλέουσιν ἐπὶ σταδίους τριακοσίους, ὡς ἐν νυκτὶ πόρρωθεν ὁρμίζοιντο πρὸς τὴν δυσχέρειαν τοῦ κατάπλου. §614. Περὶ ταύτην τὴν νῆσον καταβέβληται χειροποίητα τείχη μέγιστα, προσαρασσόμενον δὲ τούτοις τὸ πέλαγος καὶ τοῖς ἄντικρυς ἔρκεσεν ἀμφηγνυμένον ἐκτραχύνει τὸν πόρον καὶ σφαλερὰν διὰ στενοῦ τὴν εἴσοδον ἀπεργάζεται. §615 Ὁ μέντοι γε λιμὴν ἀσφαλέστατος ἔνδον καὶ τριάκοντα σταδίων τὸ μέγεθος εἰς ὃν τά τε λείποντα τῇ χώρᾳ πρὸς εὐδαιμονίαν κατάγεται καὶ τὰ περισσεύοντα τῶν ἐπιχωρίων ἀγαθῶν εἰς πᾶσαν χωρίζεται τὴν οἰκουμένην .

50 bis.

The port of Alexandria is difficult for ships to approach even in peace-time, the entrance being narrow and diverted by submerged rocks which preclude direct passage. On the left the channel is protected by artificial moles; on the right juts out the island called Pharos, supporting an enormous tower, emitting a light visible three hundred furlongs away to mariners making for port, to warn them to anchor at night at some distance off because of the difficulty of the navigation. Round this island immense walls have been reared by human hands; and the sea dashing against these and breaking around the piers opposite renders the passage rough and ingress through the strait perilous. The harbour inside is, however, perfectly safe and is thirty furlongs in length.

Circa 46-circa 120 AD. Plutarch.

The layout of the city

Plutarch, *Lives*, *Alexander*, 26, 3-11. Translation by B Perrin (The Loeb Classical Library, 1919).

51.
26.3 Εἰ δ', ὅπερ Ἀλεξανδρεῖς λέγουσιν Ἡρακλείδῃ πιστεύοντες, ἀληθές ἐστιν, οὔκουν ἀργὸς οὐδ' ἀσύμβολος αὐτῷ συστρατεύειν ἔοικεν Ὅμηρος. 4 Λέγουσι γὰρ ὅτι τῆς Αἰγύπτου κρατήσας ἐβούλετο πόλιν μεγάλην καὶ πολυάνθρωπον Ἑλληνίδα συνοικίσας ἐπώνυμον ἑαυτοῦ καταλιπεῖν, καί τινα τόπον γνώμῃ τῶν ἀρχιτεκτόνων ὅσον οὐδέπω διεμετρεῖτο καὶ περιέβαλλεν. 5 Εἶτα νύκτωρ κοιμώμενος ὄψιν εἶδε θαυμαστήν· ἀνὴρ πολιὸς εὖ μάλα τὴν κόμην καὶ γεραρὸς τὸ εἶδος ἔδοξεν αὐτῷ παραστὰς λέγειν τὰ ἔπη τάδε·

Νῆσος ἔπειτά τις ἔστι πολυκλύστῳ ἐνὶ πόντῳ,
Αἰγύπτου προπάροιθε· Φάρον δέ ἑ κικλήσκουσιν.

Εὐθὺς οὖν ἐξαναστὰς ἐβάδιζεν ἐπὶ τὴν Φάρον, ἣ τότε μὲν ἔτι νῆσος ἦν τοῦ Κανωβικοῦ μικρὸν ἀνωτέρω στόματος, νῦν δὲ διὰ χώματος ἀνῆπται πρὸς τὴν ἤπειρον. 7 Ὡς οὖν εἶδε τόπον εὐφυΐᾳ διαφέροντα (ταινία γάρ ἐστιν ἰσθμῷ πλάτος ἔχοντι σύμμετρον ἐπιεικῶς διείργουσα λίμνην τε πολλὴν καὶ θάλασσαν ἐν λιμένι μεγάλῳ τελευτῶσαν), εἰπὼν ὡς Ὅμηρος ἦν ἄρα τά τ' ἄλλα θαυμαστὸς καὶ σοφώτατος ἀρχιτέκτων, ἐκέλευσε διαγράψαι τὸ σχῆμα τῆς πόλεως τῷ τόπῳ συναρμόττοντας. 8 Καὶ γῆ μὲν οὐ παρῆν λευκή, τῶν δ' ἀλφίτων λαμβάνοντες ἐν πεδίῳ μελαγγείῳ κυκλοτερῆ κόλπον ἦγον, οὗ τὴν ἐντὸς περιφέρειαν εὐθεῖαι βάσεις ὥσπερ ἀπὸ κρασπέδων εἰς σχῆμα χλαμύδος ὑπελάμβανον ἐξ ἴσου συνάγουσαι τὸ μέγεθος. 9 ἡσθέντος δὲ τῇ διαθέσει τοῦ βασιλέως, αἰφνιδιον ὄρνιθες ἀπὸ τοῦ ποταμοῦ καὶ τῆς λίμνης πλήθει τ' ἄπειροι καὶ κατὰ γένος παντοδαποὶ καὶ μέγεθος ἐπὶ τὸν τόπον καταίροντες νέφεσιν ἐοικότες οὐδὲ μικρὸν ὑπέλιπον τῶν ἀλφίτων, ὥστε καὶ τὸν Ἀλέξανδρον διαταραχθῆναι πρὸς τὸν οἰωνόν. 10 Οὐ μὴν ἀλλὰ τῶν μάντεων θαρρεῖν παραινούντων (πολυαρκεστάτην γὰρ οἰκίζεσθαι πόλιν ὑπ' αὐτοῦ καὶ παντοδαπῶν ἀνθρώπων ἐσομένην τροφόν), ἔργου κελεύσας ἔχεσθαι τοὺς ἐπιμελητάς, 11 αὐτὸς ὥρμησεν εἰς Ἄμμωνος ὁδὸν μακράν...

51.
26.3. ... And if what the Alexandrians tell us on the authority of Heracleides is true, then it would seem that Homer was no idle or unprofitable companion for him in his expedition. They say, namely, that after his conquest of Egypt he wished to found a large and populous Greek city which should bear his name, and by the advice of his architects was on the point of measuring off and enclosing a certain site for it. 4. Then, in the night, as he lay asleep, he saw a wonderful vision. A man with very hoary locks and a venerable aspect appeared to stand by his side and recite these verses:

'Now, there is an island in the much-dashing sea,
In front of Egypt; Pharos is what men call it.'

Accordingly, he rose up at once and went to Pharos, which at that time was still an island, a little above the Canobic mouth of the Nile, but now it has been joined to the mainland by a causeway. 5. And when he saw a site of surpassing natural advantages (for it is a strip of land like enough to a broad isthmus, extending between a great lagoon and a stretch of sea which terminates in a large harbour), he said he saw now that Homer was not only admirable in other ways, but also a very wise architect, and ordered the plan of the city to be drawn in conformity with this site.

6. There was no chalk at hand, so they took barley- meal and marked out with it on the dark soil a rounded area, to whose inner are straight lines extended so as to produce the figure of a chlamys, or military cloak, the lines beginning from the skirts (as one may say), and narrowing the breadth of the area uniformly. The king was delighted with the design; but suddenly birds from the river and the lagoon, infinite in number and of every sort and size, settled down upon the place like clouds and devoured every particle of the barley-meal, so that even Alexander was greatly disturbed at the omen. 7. However, the seers exhorted him to be of good cheer, since the city here founded by him would have most abundant and helpful resources and be a nursing mother for men of every nation, and so he ordered those in charge of the work to proceed with it, while he himself set out for the temple of Ammon.

The project for a tomb for Hephaestion

Plutarch, *Lives, Alexander*, 72, 5-8. Translation by B Perrin (The Loeb Classical Library, 1919).

52.

72.5 Τύμβον δὲ καὶ ταφὴν αὐτοῦ καὶ τὸν περὶ ταῦτα κόσμον ἀπὸ μυρίων ταλάντων ἐπιτελέσαι διανοούμενος, ὑπερβαλέσθαι δὲ τῷ φιλοτέχνῳ καὶ περιττῷ τῆς κατασκευῆς τὴν δαπάνην, ἐπόθησε μάλιστα τῶν τεχνιτῶν Στασικράτην (Δεινοκράτην;), μεγαλουργίαν τινὰ καὶ τόλμαν καὶ κόμπον ἐν ταῖς καινοτομίαις ἐπαγγελλόμενον. 6 Οὗτος γὰρ αὐτῷ πρότερον ἐντυχὼν ἔφη τῶν ὀρῶν μάλιστα τὸν Θρᾴκιον Ἄθων διατύπωσιν ἀνδρείκελον δέχεσθαι καὶ διαμόρφωσιν· 7 ἂν οὖν κελεύῃ, μονιμώτατον ἀγαλμάτων αὐτῷ καὶ περιφανέστατον ἐξεργάσεσθαι τὸν Ἄθων, τῇ μὲν ἀριστερᾷ χειρὶ περιλαμβάνοντα μυρίανδρον πόλιν οἰκουμένην, τῇ δὲ δεξιᾷ σπένδοντα ποταμοῦ ῥεῦμα δαψιλὲς εἰς τὴν θάλασσαν ἀπορρέοντος. 8 ταῦτα μὲν οὖν παρῃτήσατο, πολλῷ δ΄ ἀτοπώτερα καὶ δαπανηρότερα τούτων σοφιζόμενος τότε καὶ συμμηχανώμενος τοῖς τεχνίταις διέτριβεν.

52.

72.5 …Upon a tomb and obsequies for his friend, and upon their embellishments, he purposed to expend ten thousand talents, and wished that the ingenuity and novelty of the construction should surpass the expense. He therefore longed for Stasicrates above all other artists, because in his innovations there was always promise of great magnificence, boldness, and ostentation. This man, indeed, had said to him at a former interview that of all mountains the Thracian Athos could most readily be given the form and shape of a man; if, therefore, Alexander should so order, he would make out of Mount Athos a most enduring and most conspicuous statue of the king, which in its left hand should hold a city of ten thousand inhabitants, and with its right should pour forth a river running with generous current into the sea. This project, it is true, Alexander had declined; but now he was busy devising and contriving with his artists projects far more strange and expensive than this.

The arrival of Cleopatra before Caesar in the palace

Plutarch, *Lives*, *Caesar*, 49, 1-3. Translation by B Perrin (The Loeb Classical Library, 1919).

53.

49.1 Κἀκείνη παραλαβοῦσα τῶν φίλων ᾿Απολλόδωρον τὸν Σικελιώτην μόνον, εἰς ἀκάτιον μικρὸν ἐμβᾶσα, τοῖς μὲν βασιλείοις προσέσχεν ἤδη συσκοτάζοντος · 2 ἀπόρου δὲ τοῦ λαθεῖν ὄντος ἄλλως, ἡ μὲν εἰς στρωματόδεσμον ἐνδῦσα προτείνει μακρὰν ἑαυτήν, ὁ δ 'Απολλόδωρος ἱμάντι συνδήσας τὸν στρωματόδεσμον εἰσκομίζει διὰ θυρῶν πρὸς τὸν Καίσαρα. 3 Καὶ τούτῳ τε πρώτῳ λέγεται τῷ τεχνήματι τῆς Κλεοπάτρας ἁλῶναι, λαμυρᾶς φανείσης, καὶ τῆς ἄλλης ὁμιλίας καὶ χάριτος ἥττων γενόμενος, διαλλάξαι πρὸς τὸν ἀδελφὸν ὡς συμβασιλεύσουσαν.

53.
49.1. So Cleopatra, taking only Apollodorus the Sicilian from among her friends, embarked in a little skiff and landed at the palace when it was already getting dark; and as it was impossible to escape notice otherwise, she stretched herself at full length inside a bed-sack, while Apollodorus tied the bed-sack up with a cord and carried it indoors to Caesar. 2. It was by this device of Cleopatra's, it is said, that Caesar was first captived, for she showed herself to be a bold coquette, and succumbing to the charm of further intercourse with her, he reconcilied her to her brother on the basis of a joint share with him in the royal power.

Ceasar in danger in the Grand Harbour

Plutarch, *Lives*, *Caesar*, 49, 6-10. Translation by B Perrin (The Loeb Classical Library, 1919).

54.
49.6 Εν ᾧ πρῶτον μὲν ἐκινδύνευσεν ὕδατος ἀποκλεισθείς · αἱ γὰρ διώρυχες ἀπῳκοδομήθησαν ὑπὸ τῶν πολεμίων · δεύτερον δὲ περικοπτόμενος τὸν στόλον, ἠναγκάσθη διὰ πυρὸς ἀπώσασθαι τὸν κίνδυνον, ὃ καὶ τὴν μεγάλην βιβλιοθήκην ἐκ τῶν νεωρίων ἐπινεμόμενον διέφθειρε · 7 τρίτον δὲ περὶ τῇ Φάρῳ μάχης συνεστώσης, κατεπήδησε μὲν ἀπὸ τοὺ χώματος εἰς ἀκάτιον καὶ παρεβοήθει τοῖς ἀγωνιζομένοις, ἐπιπλεόντων δὲ πολλαχόθεν αὐτῷ τῶν Αἰγυπτίων, ῥίψας ἑαυτὸν εἰς τὴν θάλασσαν ἀπενήξατο μόλις καὶ χαλεπῶς. 8 ὅτε καὶ λέγεται βιβλίδια κρατῶν πολλὰ μὴ προέσθαι βαλλόμενος καὶ βαπτιζόμενος, ἀλλ´ ἀνέχων ὑπὲρ τῆς θαλάσσης τὰ βιβλίδια τῇ ἑτέρᾳ χειρὶ νήχεσθαι· τὸ δ´ ἀκάτιον εὐθὺς ἐβυθίσθη . 9 Τέλος δέ, τοῦ βασιλέως πρὸς τοὺς πολεμίους ἀποχωρήσαντος, ἐπελθὼν καὶ συνάψας μάχην ἐνίκησε, πολλῶν πεσόντων αὐτοῦ τε τοῦ βασίλεως ἀφανοῦς γενομένου. 10 Καταλιπὼν δὲ τὴν Κλεοπάτραν βασιλεύουσαν Αἰγύπτου καὶ μικρὸν ὕστερον ἐξ αὐτοῦ τεκοῦσαν υἱόν, ὃν 'Αλεξανδρεῖς Καισαρίωνα προσηγόρευον, ὥρμησεν ἐπὶ Συρίας.

54.
49.6 In this war, to begin with, Caesar encountered the peril of being shut off from water, since the canals were dammed up by the enemy; in the second place, when the enemy tried to cut off his fleet, he was forced to repel the danger by using fire, and this spread from the dockyards and destroyed the great library; and thirdly, when a battle arose at Pharos, he sprang from the mole into a small boat and tried to go to the aid of his men in their struggle, but the Egyptians sailed up against him: from every side, so that he threw himself into the sea and with great difficulty escaped by swimming. At this time, too, it is said that he was holding many papers in his hand and would not let them go, though missiles were flying at him and he was immersed in the sea, but held them above water with one hand and swam with the other; his little boat had been sunk at the outset. But finally, after the king had gone away to the enemy, he marched against him and conquered him in a battle where many fell and the king himself disappeared. Then, leaving Cleopatra on the throne of Egypt (a little later she had a son by him whom the Alexandrians called Caesarion), he set out for Syria.

Royal fishing party in the harbour at Alexandria

Plutarch, *Lives*, *Antony*, 29, 1-7. Translation by B Perrin (The Loeb Classical Library, 1920).

55.

29.1 Ἡ δὲ Κλεοπάτρα τὴν κολακείαν οὐχ, ὥσπερ ὁ Πλάτων φησί, τετραχῆ, πολλαχῆ δὲ διελοῦσα, καὶ σπουδῆς ἁπτομένῳ καὶ παιδιᾶς ἀεί τινα καινὴν ἡδονὴν ἐπιφέρουσα καὶ χάριν, [ῇ] διεπαιδαγώγει τὸν Ἀντώνιον οὔτε νυκτὸς οὔθ᾽ ἡμέρας ἀνιεῖσα. 2 Καὶ γὰρ συνεκύβευε καὶ συνέπινε καὶ συνεθήρευε καὶ γυμναζόμενον ἐν ὅπλοις ἐθεᾶτο, καὶ νύκτωρ προσισταμένῳ θύραις καὶ θυρίσι δημοτῶν καὶ σκώπτοντι τοὺς ἔνδον συνεπλανᾶτο καὶ συνήλυε, θεραπαινιδίου στολὴν λαμβάνουσα. 3 Καὶ γὰρ ἐκεῖνος οὕτως ἐπειρᾶτο σκευάζειν ἑαυτόν. Ὅθεν ἀεὶ σκωμμάτων, πολλάκις δὲ καὶ πληγῶν ἀπολαύσας ἐπανήρχετο· τοῖς δὲ πλείστοις ἦν δι᾽ ὑπονοίας. 4 Οὐ ᾽μὴν ἀλλὰ προσέχαιρον αὐτοῦ τῇ βωμολοχίᾳ καὶ συνέπαιζον οὐκ ἀρρύθμως οὐδ᾽ ἀμούσως οἱ Ἀλεξανδρεῖς, ἀγαπῶντες καὶ λέγοντες ὡς τῷ τραγικῷ πρὸς τοὺς Ῥωμαίους χρῆται προσώπῳ, τῷ δὲ κωμικῷ πρὸς αὐτούς. 5 Τὰ μὲν οὖν πολλὰ τῶν τόθ᾽ ὑπ᾽ αὐτοῦ παιζομένων διηγεῖσθαι πολὺς ἂν εἴη φλύαρος · ἐπεὶ δ᾽ ἁλιεύων ποτὲ καὶ δυσαγρῶν ἤχθετο παρούσης τῆς Κλεοπάτρας, ἐκέλευσε τοὺς ἁλιεῖς ὑπονηξαμένους κρύφα τῷ ἀγκίστρῳ περικαθάπτειν ἰχθῦς τῶν προεαλωκότων, καὶ δὶς ἢ τρὶς ἀνασπάσας οὐκ ἔλαθε τὴν Αἰγυπτίαν. 6 Προσποιουμένη δὲ θαυμάζειν τοῖς φίλοις διηγεῖτο, καὶ παρεκάλει τῇ ὑστεραίᾳ γενέσθαι θεατάς. ἐμβάντων δὲ πολλῶν εἰς τὰς ἁλιάδας καὶ τοῦ Ἀντωνίου τὴν ὁρμιὰν καθέντος, ἐκέλευσέ τινα τῶν αὐτῆς ὑποφθάσαντα καὶ προσνηξάμενον τῷ ἀγκίστρῳ περιπεῖραι Ποντικὸν τάριχος. 7 ὡς δ᾽ ἔχειν πεισθεὶς ὁ Ἀντώνιος ἀνεῖλκε, γέλωτος, οἷον εἰκός, γενομένου, «Παράδος ἡμῖν ἔφη, τὸν κάλαμον, αὐτόκρατορ, τοῖς Φαρίταις καὶ Κανωβίταις βασιλεῦσιν · ἡ δὲ σὴ θήρα πόλεις εἰσὶ καὶ βασιλεῖαι καὶ ἤπειροι».

55.

29.1 But Cleopatra, distributing her flattery, not into the four forms of which Plato speaks, but into many, and ever contributing some fresh delight and charm to Antony's hours of seriousness or mirth, kept him in constant tutelage, and released him neither night nor day. She played at dice with him, drank with him, hunted with him, and watched him as he exercised himself in arms; and when by night he would station himself at the doors or windows of the common folk and scoff at those within, she would go with him on his round of made follies, wearing the garb of a serving maiden. 2 For Antony also would try to array himself like a servant. Therefore he always reaped a harvest of abuse, and often of blows, before coming back home; though most people suspected who he was. However, the Alexandrians took delight in his coarse wit, and joined in his amusements in their graceful and cultivated way; they liked him, and said that he used the tragic mask with the Romans, but the comic mask with them. 3 Now, to recount the greater part of his boyish pranks would be great nonsense. One instance will suffice. He was fishing once, and had bad luck, and was vexed at it because Cleopatra was there to see. He therefore ordered his fishermen to dive down and secretely fasten to his hook some fish that had been previously caught, and pulled up two or three of them. But the Egyptians saw through the trick, and pretending to admire her lover's skill, told her friends about it, and invited them to be spectators of it on the following day. 4 So great numbers of them got into the fishing boats, and when Antony had let down his line, she ordered one of own attendants to get the start of him by swimming to his hook and fastening on it a salted Pontic herring. Antony thought he had caught something, and pulled it up, whereupon there was great laughter, as was natural, and Cleopatra said: 'Imperator, hand over thy fishing-rod to the fishermen of Pharos and Canopus; thy sport is the hunting of cities, realms, and continents.'

Vaults, tomb and treasure near the Temple of Isis

Plutarch, *Lives*, *Antony,* 74, 1-6. Translation by B Perrin (The Loeb Classical Library, 1920).

56.

74.1 Ἔσχεν οὖν ἀναβολὴν ὁ πόλεμος τότε· τοῦ δὲ χειμῶνος παρελθόντος αὖθις ἐπῄει διὰ Συρίας, οἱ δὲ στρατηγοὶ διὰ Λιβύης. Ἁλόντος δὲ Πηλουσίου, λόγος ἦν ἐνδοῦναι Σέλευκον οὐκ ἀκούσης τῆς Κλεοπάτρας . 2 Ἡ δ᾽ ἐκείνου μὲν γυναῖκα καὶ παῖδας Ἀντωνίῳ κτεῖναι παρεῖχεν, αὐτὴ δὲ θήκας ἔχουσα καὶ μνήματα κατεσκευασμένα περιττῶς εἴς τε κάλλος καὶ ὕψος, ἃ προσῳκοδόμησε τῷ ναῷ τῆς Ἴσιδος, ἐνταῦθα τῶν βασιλικῶν συνεφόρει τὰ πλείστης ἄξια σπουδῆς, χρυσόν, ἄργυρον, σμάραγδον, μαργαρίτην, ἔβενον, ἐλέφαντα, κινάμωμον, ἐπὶ πᾶσι δὲ δᾷδα πολλὴν καὶ στυππεῖον, 3 ὥστε δείσαντα περὶ τῶν χρημάτων Καίσαρα, μὴ τραπομένη πρὸς ἀπόγνωσιν ἡ γυνὴ διαφθείρῃ καὶ καταφλέξῃ τὸν πλοῦτον, ἀεί τινας ἐλπίδας αὐτῇ φιλανθρώπους προσπέμπειν ἅμα τῷ στρατῷ πορευόμενον ἐπὶ τὴν πόλιν. 4 Ἱδρυθέντος δ᾽ αὐτοῦ περὶ τὸν ἱππόδρομον, Ἀντώνιος ἐπεξελθὼν ἠγωνίσατο λαμπρῶς καὶ τροπὴν τῶν Καίσαρος ἱππέων ἐποίησε, καὶ κατεδίωξεν ἄχρι τοῦ στρατοπέδου. 5 Μεγαλυνόμενος δὲ τῇ νίκῃ παρῆλθεν εἰς τὰ βασίλεια, καὶ τὴν Κλεοπάτραν κατεφίλησεν ἐν τοῖς ὅπλοις, καὶ τὸν ἠγωνισμένον προθυμότατα τῶν στρατιωτῶν συνέστησεν. 6 Ἡ δ᾽ ἀριστεῖον αὐτῷ θώρακα χρυσοῦν καὶ κράνος ἔδωκεν . Ἐκεῖνος μὲν οὖν ὁ ἄνθρωπος λαβὼν ταῦτα διὰ νυκτὸς ηὐτομόλησεν ὡς Καίσαρα.

56.

74.1 Accordingly, the war was suspended for the time being; but when the winter was over, Caesar again marched against his enemy through Syria, and his generals through Libya. When Pelusium was taken there was a rumor that Seleucus had given it up, and not without the consent of Cleopatra; but Cleopatra allowed Antony to put to death the wife and children of Seleucus, and she herself, now that she had a tomb and monument built surpassingly lofty and beautiful, which she had erected near the temple of Isis, 2 collected there the most valuable of the royal treasures, gold, silver, emeralds, pearls, ebony, ivory, and cinnamon; and besides all this she put there great quantities of torch-wood and tow, so that Caesar was anxious about the treasure, and fearing lest the woman might become desperate and burn up and destroy this wealth, kept sending on to her vague hopes of kindly treatment from him, at the same time that he advanced with his army against the city. 3 But when Caesar had taken up position near the hippodrome, Antony sallied forth against him and fought brilliantly and routed his cavalry, and pursued them as far as their camp. Then, exalted by his victory, he went into the palace, kissed Cleopatra, all armed as he was, and presented to her the one of his soldiers who had fought most spiritedly. 6 Cleopatra gave the man as a reward of valour a golden breastplate and a helmet. The man took them, of course, and in the night deserted to Caesar.

The fleet of Augustus enters the Grand Harbour. Suicide of Antony.

Plutarch, *Lives*, *Antony*, 76, 1-11. Translation by B Perrin (The Loeb Classical Library, 1920).

57.

76.1 Ἅμα δ᾽ ἡμέρᾳ τὸν πεζὸν αὐτὸς ἐπὶ τῶν πρὸ τῆς πόλεως λόφων ἱδρύσας, ἐθεᾶτο τὰς ναῦς ἀνηγμένας καὶ ταῖς τῶν πολεμίων προσφερομένας · καὶ περιμένων ἔργον τι παρ᾽ ἐκείνων ἰδεῖν ἡσύχαζεν. 2 Οἱ δ᾽ ὡς ἐγγὺς ἐγένοντο, ταῖς κώπαις ἠσπάσαντο τοὺς Καίσαρος, ἐκείνων τ᾽ ἀντασπασαμένων μετεβάλοντο, καὶ πάσαις ἅμα ταῖς ναυσὶν ὁ στόλος εἷς γενόμενος ἐπέπλει πρὸς τὴν πόλιν ἀντίπρῳρος . 3 Τοῦτ᾽ Ἀντώνιος ἰδὼν ἀπελείφθη μὲν εὐθὺς ὑπὸ τῶν ἱππέων μεταβαλομένων, ἡττηθεὶς δὲ τοῖς πεζοῖς ἀνεχώρησεν εἰς τὴν πόλιν, ὑπὸ Κλεοπάτρας προσδεδόσθαι βοῶν οἷς δι᾽ ἐκείνην ἐπολέμησεν. 4 Ἡ δὲ τὴν ὀργὴν αὐτοῦ φοβηθεῖσα καὶ τὴν ἀπόνοιαν, εἰς τὸν τάφον κατέφυγε καὶ τοὺς καταρράκτας ἀφῆκε κλείθροις καὶ μοχλοῖς καρτεροὺς ὄντας · πρὸς δ᾽ Ἀντώνιον ἔπεμψε τοὺς ἀπαγγελοῦντας ὅτι τέθνηκε. 5 Πιστεύσας δ᾽ ἐκεῖνος καὶ εἰπὼν πρὸς αὐτόν, «Τί ἔτι μέλλεις, Ἀντώνιε; τὴν μόνην ἡ τύχη καὶ λοιπὴν ἀφῄρηκε τοῦ φιλοψυχεῖν πρόφασιν», εἰσῆλθεν εἰς τὸ δωμάτιον, 6 καὶ τὸν θώρακα παραλύων καὶ διαστέλλων, «Ὦ Κλεοπάτρα, εἶπεν, οὐκ ἄχθομαι σου στερούμενος, αὐτίκα γὰρ εἰς ταὐτὸν ἀφίξομαι, ἀλλ᾽ ὅτι γυναικὸς ὁ τηλικοῦτος αὐτοκράτωρ εὐψυχίᾳ πεφώραμαι λειπόμενος». 7 Ἦν δέ τις οἰκέτης αὐτοῦ πιστὸς Ἔρως ὄνομα. Τοῦτον ἐκ πολλοῦ παρακεκληκώς, εἰ δεήσειεν, ἀνελεῖν αὐτόν, ἀπῄτει τὴν ὑπόσχεσιν. 8 Ὁ δὲ σπασάμενος τὸ ξίφος ἀνέσχε μὲν ὡς παίσων ἐκεῖνον, ἀποστρέψαντος δὲ τὸ πρόσωπον ἑαυτὸν ἀπέκτεινε. 9 Πεσόντος δ᾽ αὐτοῦ πρὸς τοὺς πόδας, ὁ Ἀντώνιος «Εὖ γε, εἶπεν, ὦ Ἔρως, ὅτι μὴ δυνηθεὶς αὐτὸς ἐμὲ ποιεῖν ὃ δεῖ διδάσκεις» καὶ παίσας διὰ τῆς κοιλίας ἑαυτὸν ἀφῆκεν εἰς τὸ κλινίδιον. 10 Ἦν δ᾽ οὐκ εὐθυθάνατος ἡ πληγή . Διὸ καὶ τῆς φορᾶς τοῦ αἵματος, ἐπεὶ κατεκλίθη παυσαμένης, ἀναλαβὼν ἐδεῖτο τῶν παρόντων ἐπισφάττειν αὐτόν. 11 Οἱ δ᾽ ἔφευγον ἐκ τοῦ δωματίου βοῶντος καὶ σφαδάζοντος, ἄχρι οὗ παρὰ Κλεοπάτρας ἧκε Διομήδης ὁ γραμματεύς, κομίζειν αὐτὸν ὡς ἐκείνην εἰς τὸν τάφον κελευσθείς.

57.

76.1 At daybreak, Antony in person posted his infantry on the hills in front of the city, and watched his ships as they put out and attacked those of the enemy; and as he expected to see something great accomplished by them, he remained quiet. But the crews of his ships, as soon as they were near, saluted Caesar's crews with their oars, and on their returning the salute changed sides, and so all the ships, now united into one fleet, sailed up towards the city prows on. 2 No sooner had Antony seen this than he was deserted by his cavalry, which went over to the enemy, and after being defeated with his infantry he retired into the city, crying out that he had been betrayed by Cleopatra to those with whom he waged war for her sake. But she, fearing his anger and his madness, fled for refuge into her tomb and let fall the drop-doors, which were made strong with bolts and bars; then she sent messengers to tell Antony that she was dead. 3 Antony believed the message, and saying to himself, 'Why dost thou longer delay, Antony? Fortune has taken away thy sole remaining excuse for clinging to life', he went into his chamber. Here, as he unfastened his breast-plate and laid it aside, he said: 'O Cléopatra, I am not grieved to be bereft of thee, for I shall straightway join thee; but I am grieved that such an imperator as I has been found to be inferior to a woman in courage.'

4 Now Antony had a trusty slave named Eros. Him Antony had long before engaged, in case of need, to kill him, and now demanded the fulfilment of his promise. So Eros drew his sword and held it up as though he would smite his master, but then turned his face away and slew himself. And as he fell at his master's feet Antony said: 'Well done, Eros! though thou waste not able to do it myself, thou teachest me what I must do'; and running himself through the belly he dropped upon the couch. 5 But the wound did not bring a speedy death. Therefore, as the blood ceased flowing after he had lain down, he came to himself and besought the bystanders to give him the finishing stroke. But they fled from the chamber, and he lay writhing and crying out, until Diomedes the secretary came from Cleopatra with orders to bring him to her in the tomb.

The Mausoleum

Plutarch, *Lives*, *Antony*, 77, 1-4; 78, 4; 79, 1- 4. Translation by B Perrin (The Loeb Classical Library, 1920).

58.

77,1 Γνοὺς οὖν ὅτι ζῇ, προθύμως ἐκέλευσεν ἄρασθαι τοῖς ὑπηρέταις τὸ σῶμα, καὶ διὰ χειρῶν προσεκομίσθη ταῖς θύραις τοῦ οἰκήματος. 2 Ἡ δὲ Κλεοπάτρα τὰς μὲν θύρας οὐκ ἀνέῳξεν, ἐκ δὲ θυρίδων τινῶν φανεῖσα σειρὰς καὶ καλώδια καθίει. Καὶ τούτοις ἐναψάντων τὸν Ἀντώνιον ἀνεῖλκεν αὐτὴ καὶ δύο γυναῖκες, ἃς μόνας ἐδέξατο μεθ´ αὐτῆς εἰς τὸν τάφον. 3 Οὐδὲν ἐκείνου λέγουσιν οἰκτρότερον γενέσθαι οἱ παραγενόμενοι θέαμα. Πεφυρμένος γὰρ αἵματι καὶ δυσθανατῶν εἵλκετο, τὰς χεῖρας ὀρέγων εἰς ἐκείνην καὶ παραιωρούμενος. 4 Οὐ γὰρ ἦν γυναιξὶ ῥᾴδιον τὸ ἔργον, ἀλλὰ μόλις ἡ Κλεοπάτρα ταῖν χεροῖν ἐμπεφυκυῖα καὶ κατατεινομένη τῷ προσώπῳ τὸν δεσμὸν ἀνελάμβανεν, ἐπικελευομένων τῶν κάτωθεν αὐτῇ καὶ συναγωνιώντων. 5 Δεξαμένη δ´ αὐτὸν οὕτως καὶ κατακλίνασα περιερρήξατό τε τοὺς πέπλους ἐπ´ αὐτῷ, καὶ τὰ στέρνα τυπτομένη καὶ σπαράττουσα ταῖς χερσί, καὶ τῷ προσώπῳ τοῦ αἵματος ἀναματτομένη, δεσπότην ἐκάλει καὶ ἄνδρα καὶ αὐτοκράτορα· καὶ μικροῦ δεῖν ἐπιλέληστο τῶν αὐτῆς κακῶν οἴκτῳ τῶν ἐκείνου. 6 Καταπαύσας δὲ τὸν θρῆνον αὐτῆς Ἀντώνιος ᾔτησε πιεῖν οἶνον, εἴτε διψῶν, 7 εἴτε συντομώτερον ἐλπίζων ἀπολυθήσεσθαι. 8 Πιὼν δὲ παρῄνεσεν αὐτῇ τὰ μὲν ἑαυτῆς, ἂν ᾖ μὴ μετ´ αἰσχύνης, σωτήρια τίθεσθαι, μαλίστα τῶν Καίσαρος ἑταίρων Προκληΐῳ πιστεύουσαν, αὐτὸν δὲ μὴ θρηνεῖν ἐπὶ ταῖς ὑστάταις μεταβολαῖς, ἀλλὰ μακαρίζειν ὧν ἔτυχε καλῶν, ἐπιφανέστατος ἀνθρώπων γενόμενος καὶ πλεῖστον ἰσχύσας, καὶ νῦν οὐκ ἀγεννῶς Ῥωμαῖος ὑπὸ Ῥωμαίου κρατηθείς.

78,5. Εἰς μὲν οὖν χεῖρας τῷ Προκληΐῳ συνελθεῖν οὐκ ἠθέλησεν· ἐγίνοντο δὲ λόγοι [ἐν] τῷ οἰκήματι προσελθόντος ἔξωθεν αὐτοῦ κατὰ θύρας ἐπιπέδους, ἀποκεκλειμένας μὲν ὀχυρῶς, φωνῇ δὲ διέξοδον ἐχούσας. 6 Καὶ διελέχθησαν ἡ μὲν αἰτουμένη τοῖς παισὶ τὴν βασιλείαν, ὁ δὲ θαρρεῖν καὶ πάντα πιστεύειν Καίσαρι κελεύων.

79,1 Ὡς δὲ κατιδὼν τὸν τόπον ἀπήγγειλε Καίσαρι, Γάλλος μὲν ἐπέμφθη πάλιν ἐντευξόμενος αὐτῇ· καὶ πρὸς τὰς θύρας ἐλθὼν ἐπίτηδες ἐμήκυνε τὸν λόγον. 2 Ἐν τούτῳ δὲ Προκλήϊος κλίμακος προστεθείσης διὰ τῆς θυρίδος εἰσῆλθεν ᾗ τὸν Ἀντώνιον αἱ γυναῖκες ἐδέξαντο. Καὶ πρὸς τὰς θύρας αὐτὰς εὐθὺς αἷς ἡ Κλεοπάτρα παρειστήκει προσέχουσα τῷ Γάλλῳ, κατέβαινεν ὑπηρέτας ἔχων δύο μεθ´ αὐτοῦ. 3 Τῶν δὲ συγκαθειργμένων τῇ Κλεοπάτρᾳ γυναικῶν τῆς ἑτὲρας ἀνακραγούσης «Τάλαινα Κλεοπάτρα, ζωγρεῖ», μεταστραφεῖσα καὶ θεασαμένη τὸν Προκλήϊον ὥρμησε μὲν αὑτὴν πατάξαὶ · παρεζωσμένη γὰρ ἐτύγχανέ τι τῶν ληστρικῶν ξιφιδίων· 4 προσδραμὼν δὲ ταχὺ καὶ περισχὼν αὐτὴν ταῖς χερσὶν ἀμφοτέραις ὁ Προκλήϊος «Αδικεῖς, εἶπεν, ὦ Κλεοπάτρα, καὶ σεαυτὴν καὶ Καίσαρα, μεγάλην ἀφαιρουμένη χρηστότητος ἐπίδειξιν αὐτοῦ, καὶ διαβάλλουσα τὸν πρᾳότατον ἡγεμόνων ὡς ἄπιστον καὶ ἀδιάλλακτον». 5 Ἅμα δὲ καὶ τὸ ξίφος αὐτῆς παρείλετο καὶ τὴν ἐσθῆτα, μὴ κρύπτοι τι φάρμακον ἐξέσεισεν. 6 Ἐπέμφθη δὲ καὶ παρὰ Καίσαρος τῶν ἀπελευθέρων Ἐπαφρόδιτος, ᾧ προσετέτακτο ζῶσαν αὐτὴν φυλάττειν ἰσχυρῶς ἐπιμελόμενον, τἆλλα < δὲ > πρὸς τὸ ῥᾷστον ἐνδιδόναι καὶ ἥδιστον.

58.

77, 1 Having learned, then, that Cleopatra was alive, Antony eagerly ordered his servants to raise him up, and he was carried in their arms to the doors of her tomb. Cleopatra, however, would not open the doors, but showed herself at a window, from which she let down ropes and cords. To these Antony was fastened, and she drew him up herself, with the aid of the two women whom alone she had admitted with her into the tomb. 2 Never, as those who were present tell us, was there a more piteous sight. Smeared with blood and struggling with death he was drawn up, stretching out his hands to her even as he dangled in the air. For the task was not an easy one for women, and scarcely could Cleopatra, with clinging hands and strained face, pull up the rope, while those below called out encouragement to her and shared her agony. 3 And when she had thus got him in, and laid him down, she rent her garments over him, beat and tore her breast with her hands, wiped off some of his blood upon her face, and called him master, husband, and imperator; indeed, she almost forgot her own ills in her pity for his. But Antony stopped her lamentations and asked for a drink of wine, either because he was thirsty, or in the hope of a speedier release. 4 When he had drunk, he advised her to consult her own safety, if she could do it without disgrace, and among all the companions of Caesar to put most confidence in Proculeius, and not to lament him for his last reverses, but to count him happy for the good things that had been his, since he had become most illustrious of men, had won greatest power, and now had been not ignobly conquered, a Roman by a Roman …

78, 4 Into the hands of Proculeius, however, Cleopatra would not put herself; but she conferred with him after he had come close to the tomb and stationed himself outside at a door which was on a level with the ground. The door was strongly fastened with bolts and bars, but allowed a passage for the voice. So they conversed, Cleopatra asking that her children might have her kingdom, and Proculeius bidding her be of good cheer and trust Caesar in everything.

79, 1-3 After Proculeius had surveyed the place, he brought back word to Caesar, and Gallus was sent to have another interview with the queen; and coming up to the door he purposely prolonged the conversation. Meanwhile Proculeius applied a ladder and went in through the window by which the women had taken Antony inside. Then he went down at once to the very door at which Cleopatra was standing and listening to Gallus, and he had two servants with him. 2 One of the women imprisoned with Cleopatra cried out, 'Wretched Cleopatra, thou art taken alive', whereupon the queen turned about, saw Proculeius, and tried to stab herself; for she had at her girdle a dagger such as robbers wear. But Proculeius ran swiftly to her, threw both his arms about her, and said:'O Cleopatra, thou art wronging both thyself and Caesar, by trying to rob him of an opportunity to show great kindness, and by fixing upon the gentlest of commanders the stigma of faithlessness and implacability.' At the same time he took away her weapon, and shook out her clothing, to see whether she was concealing any poison. And there was also sent from Caesar one of his freedmen, Epaphroditus, with injunction to keep the queen alive by the strictest vigilance, but otherwise to make any concession that would promote her ease and pleasure.

Circa 75-circa 160. Suetonius.

Ceasar swims across the Grand Harbour

Suetonius, *The Lives of the Caesars*, I, *Divus Iulius*, LXIV. Translation by J C Rolfe (The Loeb Classical Library, 1951).

59.
LXIV. Alexandriae circa oppugnationem pontis, eruptione hostium subita conpulsus in scapham, pluribus eodem praecipitantibus cum desiluisset in mare, nando per ducentos passus evasit ad proximam nauem, elata laeua, ne libelli quos tenebat madefierent, paludamentum mordicus trahens, ne spolio poteretur hostis.

59.
LXIV. At Alexandria, while assaulting a bridge, he was forced by a sudden sally of the enemy to take to a small skiff; when many others threw themselves into the same boat, he plunged into the sea, and after swimming for two hundred paces, got away to the nearest ship, holding up his left hand all the way, so as not to wet some papers which he was carrying, and dragging his cloak after him with his teeth, to keep the enemy from getting it as a trophy.

Augustus' arrival in Alexandria. Works carried out in the City.

Suetonius, *The Lives of the Caesars*, II, *Divus Augustus,* XVII-XVIII. Translation by J C Rolfe (The Loeb Classical Library, 1998).

60.
XVII ... nec amplius quam septem et vigenti dies, donec ad desideria militum *omnia* ordinarentur, Brundisii commoratus, Asiae Syriaeque circuitu Aegyptum petit obsessaque Alexandrea, quo Antonius cum Cleopatra confugerat, brevi potitus est. Et Antonium quidem seras condiciones pacis temptantem ad mortem adegit viditque mortuum. Cleopatrae, quam servatam triumpho magno opere cupiebat etiam psyllos admovit, qui venenum ac virus exugerent, quod perisse morsu aspidis putabatur. Ambobus communem sepulturae honorem tribuit ac tumulum ab ipsis incohatum perfici iussit. Antonium iuuenem, maiorem de duobus Fulvia genitis, simulacro Divi Iuli, ad quod post multas et irritas preces confugerat, abreptum interemit. Item Caesarionem, quem ex Caesare patre Cleopatra concepisse praedicabat, retractum e fuga supplicio adfecit. Reliquos Antonii reginaeque communes liberos non secus ac necessitudine iunctos sibi et conservavit et mox pro condicione cuiusque sustinuit ac fouit.

XVIII. Per idem tempus conditorium et corpus Magni Alexandri, cum prolatum e penetrali subiecisset oculis, corona aurea imposita ac floribus aspersis veneratus est consultusque, num et Ptolemaeum inspicere vellet, 'regem se voluisse' ait 'videre, non mortuos'. Aegyptum in provinciae formam redactam ut feraciorem habilioremque annonae urbicae redderet, fossas omnis, in quas Nilus exaestuat, oblimatas longa vetustate militari opere detersit. Quoque Actiacae victoriae memoria celebratior et in posterum esset, urbem Nicopolim apud Actium condidit ludosque illic quinquennales constituit et ampliato vetere Apollinis templo locum castrorum, quibus fuerat usus, exornatum navalibus spoliis Neptuno ac Marti consecravit.

60.
XVII. He delayed at Brindisium only twenty-seven days—just long enough to satisfy all the demands of the soldiers—and then went to Egypt by a roundabout way through Asia and Syria, laid siege to Alexandria, where Antony had taken refuge with Cleopatra, and soon took the city. Although Antony tried to make terms at the eleventh hour, Augustus forced him to commit suicide, and viewed his corpse. He greatly desired to save Cleopatra alive for his triumph, and

even had Psylli brought to her, to suck the poison from her wound, since it was thought that she died from the bite of an asp. He allowed them both the honour of burial, and in the same tomb, giving orders that the mausoleum which they had begun should be finished. The young Antony, the elder of Fulvia's two sons, he dragged from the image of the Deified Julius, to which he had fled after many vain entreaties, and slew him. Caesarion, too, whom Cleopatra fathered on Caesar, he overtook in his flight, brought back, and put to death. But he spared the rest of the offspring of Antony and Cleopatra, and afterwards maintained and reared them according to their several positions, as carefully as if they were his own kin.

XVIII. About this time he had the sarcophagus and body of Alexander the Great brought forth from its shrine, and after gazing on it, showed his respect by placing upon it a golden crown and strewing it with flowers; and being then asked whether he wished to see the tomb of the Ptolemies as well, he replied, 'My wish was to see a king, not corpses.' He reduced Egypt to the form of a province, and then to make it more fruitful and better adapted to supply the city with grain, he set his soldiers at work cleaning out all the canals into which the Nile overflows, which in the course of many years had become choked with mud. To extend the fame of his victory at Actium and perpetuate its memory, he founded a city called Nicopolis near Actium, and provided for the celebration of games there every five years; enlarged the ancient temple of Apollo; and after adorning the site of the camp which he had occupied with naval trophies, consecrated it to Neptune and Mars.

Circa 105-circa 180 AD. Arrian.

Foundation of Alexandria

Arrian, *History of Alexander*, III, 1-2. Translation by P A Brunt (The Loeb Classical Library, 1976).

61.

III, 1, 1'Αλέξανδρος δὲ ἐπ' Αἰγύπτου, ἵναπερ τὸ πρῶτον ὡρμήθη, ἐστέλλετο, καὶ ἑβδόμῃ ἡμέρᾳ ἀπὸ τῆς Γάζης ἐλαύνων ἧκεν εἰς Πηλούσιον τῆς Αἰγύπτου. ὁ δὲ ναυτικὸς στρατὸς παρέπλει αὐτῷ ἐκ Φοινίκης ὡς ἐπ' Αἴγυπτον · καὶ καταλαμβάνει τὰς ναῦς ἐν Πηλουσίῳ ὁρμούσας, 2 Μαζάκης δὲ ὁ Πέρσης, ὃς ἦν σατράπης Αἰγύπτου ἐκ Δαρείου καθεστηκώς, τήν τε ἐν 'Ισσῷ μάχην ὅπως συνέβη πεπυσμένος καὶ Δαρεῖον ὅτι αἰσχρᾷ φυγῇ ἔφυγεν, καὶ Φοινίκην τε καὶ Συρίαν καὶ τῆς'Αραβίας τὰ πολλὰ ὑπὸ'Αλεξάνδρου ἐχόμενα, αὐτῷ τε οὐκ οὔσης δυνάμεως Περσικῆς, ἐδέχετο ταῖς τε πόλεσι φιλίως καὶ τῇ χώρᾳ 'Αλέξανδρον. 3 ὁ δὲ εἰς μὲν Πηλούσιον φυλακὴν εἰσήγαγε, τοὺς δὲ ἐπὶ τῶν νεῶν ἀναπλεῖν κατὰ τὸν ποταμὸν κελεύσας ἔστε ἐπὶ Μέμφιν πόλιν αὐτὸς ἐφ' 'Ηλιουπόλεως ᾔει, ἐν δεξιᾷ ἔχων τὸν ποταμὸν τὸν Νεῖλον, καὶ ὅσα καθ' ὁδὸν χωρία ἐνδιδόντων τῶν ἐνοικούντων κατασχὼν διὰ τῆς ἐρήμου ἀφίκετο ἐς 'Ηλιούπολιν· ἐκεῖθεν δὲ διαβὰς τὸν πόρον ἧκεν ἐς Μέμφιν · 4 καὶ θύει ἐκεῖ τοῖς τε ἄλλοις θεοῖς καὶ τῷ ῎Απιδι καὶ ἀγῶνα ἐποίησε γυμνικόν τε καὶ μουσικόν · ἧκον δὲ αὐτῷ οἱ ἀμφὶ ταῦτα τεχνῖται ἐκ τῆς 'Ελλάδος οἱ δοκιμώτατοι. ἐκ δὲ Μέμφιος κατέπλει κατὰ τὸν ποταμὸν ὡς ἐπὶ θάλασσαν τούς τε ὑπασπιστὰς ἐπὶ τῶν νεῶν λαβὼν καὶ τοὺς τοξότας καὶ τοὺς 'Αγριᾶνας καὶ τῶν ἱππέων τὴν βασιλικὴν ἴλην τὴν τῶν ἑταίρων. 5 ἐλθὼν δὲ ἐς Κάνωβον καὶ κατὰ τὴν λίμνην τὴν Μαρίαν περιπλεύσας ἀποβαίνει, ὅπου νῦν 'Αλεξάνδρεια πόλις ᾤκισται, 'Αλεξάνδρου ἐπώνυμος. καὶ ἔδοξεν αὐτῷ ὁ χῶρος κάλλιστος κτίσαι ἐν αὐτῷ πόλιν καὶ γενέσθαι ἂν εὐδαίμονα τὴν πόλιν. πόθος οὖν λαμβάνει αὐτὸν τοῦ ἔργου, καὶ αὐτὸς τὰ σημεῖα τῇ πόλει ἔθηκεν, ἵνα τε ἀγορὰν ἐν αὐτῇ δείμασθαι ἔδει καὶ ἱερὰ ὅσα καὶ θεῶν ὥντινων, τῶν μὲν Ἑλληνικων, Ἴσιδος δὲ Αἰγυπτίας, καὶ τὸ τεῖχος ᾗ περιβεβλῆσθαι. καὶ ἐπὶ τούτοις ἐθύετο, καὶ τὰ ἱερὰ καλὰ ἐφαίνετο.

III, 2, 1. Λέγεται δέ τις καὶ τοιόσδε λόγος, οὐκ ἄπιστος ἔμοιγε· ἐθέλειν μὲν Ἀλέξανδρον καταλείπειν αὐτὸν τὰ σημεῖα τοῦ τειχισμοῦ τοῖς τέκτοσιν, οὐκ εἶναι δὲ ὅτῳ τὴν γῆν ἐπιγράψουσιν· τῶν δὴ τεκτόνων τινὰ ἐπιφρασθέντα, ὅσα ἐν τεύχεσιν ἄλφιτα οἱ στρατιῶται ἐκόμιζον ξυναγαγόντα ἐπιβάλλειν τῇ γῇ, ἵναπερ ὁ βασιλεὺς ὑφηγεῖτο, καὶ τὸν κύκλον οὕτω περιγραφῆναι τοῦ περιτειχισμοῦ, ὅντινα τῇ πόλει ἐποίει. 2 τοῦτο δὲ ἐπιλεξαμένους τοὺς μάντεις καὶ μάλιστα δὴ Ἀρίστανδρον τὸν Τελμισσέα, ὅς δὴ πολλὰ μὲν καὶ ἄλλα ἀληθεῦσαι ἐλέγετο Ἀλεξάνδρῳ, φάναι εὐδαίμονα ἔσεσθαι τὴν πόλιν τά τε ἄλλα καὶ τῶν ἐκ γῆς καρπῶν εἵνεκα.

61.

III, 1, 1 Alexander now set out for Egypt, his original goal, and marching from Gaza arrived after six days at Pelusium in Egypt. His fleet coasted along with him from Phoenicia towards Egypt; and he found them already at anchor at Pelusium. 2 Mazaces the Persian, who had been appointed satrap of Egypt by Darius, on learning how the battle of Issus had gone, of the shameful flight of Darius, and that Phoenicia, Syria, and the greater part of Arabia were in Alexander's hands, and being without any Persian force, received Alexander in a friendly way into the cities and the country. 3 Alexander put a garrison into Pelusium, told the officers of his fleet to sail up the river as far as Memphis and went in person towards Heliopolis, with the river Nile on his right; he took over all the districts on his route through the surrender of the inhabitants, and traversed the desert to reach Heliopolis. 4 Thence he crossed the river and went to Memphis, where he sacrificed to the gods, especially Apis, and held athletic and musical games; the most famous performers in both athletics and music came to him there from Greece. From Memphis he sailed downstream towards the sea, taking on board the hypaspists, archers and Agrianians, and from the cavalry the royal squadron of the Companions. 5 When he had reached Canobus and sailed round Lake Mareotis, he went ashore where the city of Alexandria, named after him, is now situated. It struck him that the position was admirable for founding a city there and that it would prosper. A longing for the work therefore seized him; he himself marked out where the city's market-place was to be built, how many temples there were to be and the gods, some Greek, and Isis the Egyptian, for whom they were to be erected, and where the wall was to be built round it. With this in view he offered sacrifice, and the sacrifice proved favourable.

III, 2, 2 A story of the following sort is told, and personally I do not disbelieve it; Alexander desired to leave the builders outlines of the fortification, but had no means of marking the ground. One of the builders, however, had the happy thought of collecting the meal which the soldiers carried in vessels, and of dropping it on the ground wherever the king indicated. In this way was the circle of the surrounding wall which he proposed to make for the city marked out. 2 The soothsayers, and especially Aristander the Telmissian, who was reported to have made many other correct prophecies to Alexander, reflecting upon this, said that the city would be prosperous, but particularly in the fruits of the earth.

Temples dedicated to Hephaestion

Arrianus, *Anabasis of Alexander,* VII, 14, 8-10; VII, 23, 6-8. Translation by P A Brunt (The Loeb Classical Library, 1939).

62

VII, 14, 8. Ἐκεῖνα δὲ πρὸς πάντων ξυμφωνούμενα, ἐς τρίτην ἀπὸ τοῦ θανάτου τοῦ Ἡφαιστίωνος ἡμέραν μήτε σίτου γεύσασθαι Ἀλέξανδρον μήτε τινὰ θεραπεῖαν ἄλλην θεραπεῦσαι τὸ σῶμα, ἀλλὰ κεῖσθαι γὰρ ἢ ὀδυρόμενον ἢ πενθικῶς σιγῶντα · καὶ πυρὰν κελεῦσαι αὐτῷ ἑτοιμάζεσθαι ἐν Βαβυλῶνι ἀπὸ ταλάντων μυρίων, οἱ δὲ καὶ πλειόνων ἀνέγραψαν · 9 καὶ ὅτι πένθος ποιεῖσθαι περιηγγέλη κατὰ πᾶσαν τὴν χώραν τὴν βάρβαρον· καὶ ὅτι πολλοὶ τῶν ἑταίρων τῶν 'Αλεξάνδρου ἐς θεραπείαν τὴν ἐκείνου σφᾶς τε αὐτοὺς καὶ τὰ ὅπλα 'Ηφαιστίωνι ἀνέθεσαν ἀποθανόντι· πρῶτον δὲ Εὐμενῆ ἄρξαι τοῦ σοφίσματος, ὅντινα ὀλίγῳ πρόσθεν ἔφαμεν ὅτι διηνέχθη πρὸς 'Ηφαιστίωνα· καὶ τοῦτο δὲ δρᾶσαι, τῷ 'Αλεξάνδρῳ ὡς μὴ ἐφήδεσθαι δοκοίη τελευτήσαντι 'Ηφαισιστίωνι. 10 οὔκουν οὐδὲ ἄλλον τινὰ ἔταξεν ἀντὶ 'Ηφαιστίωνος χιλίαρχον ἐπὶ τῇ ἵππῳ τῇ ἑταιρικῇ 'Αλέξανδρος, ὡς μὴ ἀπόλοιτο τὸ ὄνομα τοῦ 'Ηφαιστίωνος ἐκ τῆς τάξεως, ἀλλὰ 'Ηφαιστίωνός τε ἡ χιλιαρχία ἐκαλεῖτο καὶ τὸ σημεῖον αὐτῆς ἡγεῖτο <τὸ > ἐξ 'Ηφαιστίωνος πεποιημένον. ἀγῶνά τε ἐπενόει ποιῆσαι γυμνικόν τε καὶ μουσικὸν πλήθει τε τῶν ἀγωνιζομένων καὶ τῇ εἰς αὐτὸν χορηγίᾳ πολύ τι τῶν ἄλλων τῶν πρόσθεν ἀριδηλότερον· τρισχιλίους γὰρ ἀγωνιστὰς τοὺς σύμπαντας παρεσκεύασε. καὶ οὗτοι ὀλίγον ὕστερον ἐπ' 'Αλεξάνδρου τῷ τάφῳ λέγουσιν ὅτι ἠγονίσαντο.

VII, 23, 6. 'Ηκον δὲ καὶ παρὰ "Αμμωνος οἱ θεωροὶ οὕστινας ἐστάλκει ἐρησομένους ὅπως θέμις αὐτῷ τιμᾶν 'Ηφαιστίωνα· οἱ δὲ ὡς ἥρωϊ ἔφησαν ὅτι θύειν θέμις ὁ "Αμμων λέγει. ὁ δὲ ἔχαιρέ τε τῇ μαντείᾳ καὶ τὸ ἀπὸ τοῦδε ὡς ἥρωα ἐγέραιρε . καὶ Κλεομένει, ἀνδρὶ κακῷ καὶ πολλὰ ἀδικήματα ἀδικήσαντι ἐν Αἰγύπτῳ, ἐπιστέλλει ἐπιστολήν. καὶ ταύτην τῆς μὲν ἐς 'Ηφαιστίωνα καὶ ἀποθανόντα φιλίας ἕνεκα καὶ μνήμης οὐ μέμφομαι ἔγωγε, ἄλλων δὲ πολλῶν ἕνεκα μέμφομαι. 7 ἔλεγε γὰρ ἡ ἐπιστολὴ κατασκευασθῆναι 'Ηφαιστίωνι ἡρῷον ἐν 'Αλεξανδρείᾳ τῇ Αἰγυπτίᾳ, ἔν τε τῇ πόλει αὐτῇ καὶ ἐν τῇ νήσῳ τῇ Φάρῳ, ἵνα ὁ πύργος ἐστὶν ὁ ἐν τῇ νήσῳ, μεγέθει τε μέγιστον καὶ πολυτελείᾳ ἐκπρεπέστατον, καὶ ὅπως ἐπικρατήσῃ ἐπικαλεῖσθαι ἀπὸ 'Ηφαιστίωνος, καὶ τοῖς συμβολαίοις καθ' ὅσα οἱ ἔμποροι ἀλλήλοις ξυμβάλλουσιν ἐγγράφεσθαι τὸ ὄνομα 'Ηφαιστίωνος. 8 ταῦτα μὲν οὐκ ἔχω μέμψασθαι, πλήν γε δὴ ὅτι οὐκ ἐπὶ μεγάλοις μεγάλως διεσπουδάζετο. ἐκεῖνα δὲ καὶ πάνυ μέμφομαι. ἢν γὰρ καταλάβω ἐγώ, ἔλεγε τὰ γράμματα, τὰ ἱερὰ τὰ ἐν Αἰγύπτῳ καλῶς κατεσκευασμένα καὶ τὰ ἡρῷα τὰ 'Ηφαιστίωνος, εἴ τέ τι πρότερον ἡμάρτηκας, ἀφήσω σε τούτου, καὶ τὸ λοιπόν, ὁπηλίκον ἂν ἁμάρτῃς, οὐδὲν πείσῃ ἐξ ἐμοῦ ἄχαρι. τοῦτο ἀνδρὶ ἄρχοντι πολλῆς μὲν χώρας, πολλῶν δὲ ἀνθρώπων ἐκ βασιλέως μεγάλου ἐπεσταλμένον, ἄλλως τε καὶ κακῷ ἀνδρί, οὐκ ἔχω ἐπαινέσαι.

62.

VII, I4, 8 The following, however, harmonizes in all accounts, that for two days after Hephaestion's death Alexander tasted no food and took no care of his body, but lay either moaning or in a sorrowful silence, that he ordered a pyre to be made ready for him in Babylon at a cost of ten thousand Talents (by some accounts, even more) and commanded mourning throughout the whole barbarian country; 9 and that many of Alexander's 'Companions' in respect for him dedicated themselves and their arms to the dead Hephaestion; and that the first to initiate this expedient was Eumenes, of whose quarrel with Hephaestion we spoke a little earlier, and that he did this to prevent Alexander thinking that he rejoiced at Hephaestion's death. 10 At any rate Alexander never appointed anyone in place of Hephaestion as chiliarch over the Companions' cavalry, so that the name of Hephaestion might never be lost to the unit; the chiliarchy was still called Hephaestion's, and the standard went before it which had been made by his order. Alexander also planned athletic and musical games far more splendid than any before in the number of competitions and the cost of production; he provided three thousand performers in all. Those were the men, it is said, who competed a little at Alexander's burial.

VII, 23, 6-8 The sacred envoys from Ammon also arrived, whom Alexander had sent to enquire what honour it was lawful to pay Hephaestion; they reported that Ammon said that it was lawful to sacrifice to him as a hero. Alexander was pleased with the oracle and henceforward gave him heroic honours. Cleomenes, a rascal who had been guilty of many wrongful acts in Egypt, was sent a letter which I personally censure, not for its affectionate recollection of Hephaestion, even in death, but for many other reasons; 7 it said that a hero's shrine was to built in Egyptian Alexandria, not just in the city itself but actually on the isle of Pharos, where the tower stands on the island; it was to be unparalleled in dimensions and sumptuous splendour, and he was to insist that it be called after Hephaestion, and that his name should be written into the contracts by which traders do business with each other. 8 All this I cannot censure, except in so far as he was showing such great care over matters of no great importance. But what follows I do censure strongly. The letter ran: 'If I find these temples set in good order in Egypt, and these shrines of Hephaestion, whatever wrong you have hitherto done, I pardon it; and for the future, of whatever nature your fault may be, you shall receive no harm at my hands.' I cannot approve this mandate from a great king to a man who was ruling a large and populous area, all the more as the man was wicked.

2nd century AD. Appian.

Caesar and the Alexandria war

Appian, *Roman History, The Civil Wars,* II, 89-90. Translation by Horace White (The Loeb Classical Library, vol. III (1995), p. 390-395).

63.

II, XIII, 89. Διασωθεὶς δ´ οὕτω παραδόξως ὁ Καῖσαρ καὶ τὸν Ἑλλήσποντον περαιωθεὶς Ἴωσι μὲν καὶ Αἰολεῦσι καὶ ὅσα ἄλλα ἔθνη τὴν μεγάλην χερρόνησον οἰκοῦσι (καὶ καλοῦσιν αὐτὰ ἑνὶ ὀνόματι Ἀσίαν τὴν κάτω), συνεγίγνωσκε πρεσβευομένοις ἐς αὐτὸν καὶ παρακαλοῦσι, πυθόμενος δὲ Πομπήιον ἐπ´ Αἰγύπτου φέρεσθαι διέπλευσεν ἐς Ῥόδον. καὶ οὐδ´ ἐνταῦθα τὸν στρατὸν αὑτοῦ κατὰ μέρη προσιόντα περιμείνας ἐς τὰς Κασσίου καὶ Ῥοδίων τριήρεις ἐνέβη σὺν τοῖς παροῦσιν · οὐδενί τε ἐκφήνας, ὅπῃ τὸν πλοῦν ποιήσεται, περὶ ἑσπέραν ἀνήγετο, ἐπαγγείλας τοῖς λοιποῖς κυβερνήταις πρὸς τὸν λαμπτῆρα τῆς ἑαυτοῦ νεὼς καὶ μεθ´ ἡμέραν πρὸς τὸ σημεῖον εὐθύνειν · τῷ δ´ αὑτοῦ κυβερνήτῃ, πολὺ τῆς γῆς ἀποσχών, προσέταξεν ἐς Ἀλεξάνδρειαν φέρεσθαι. καὶ ὁ μὲν τρισὶν ἡμέραις πελάγιος ἀμφὶ τὴν Ἀλεξάνδρειαν ἦν · ἐσδέχονται δ´ αὐτὸν οἱ τοῦ βασιλέως ἐπιτροπεύοντες, ἔτι τοὺ βασιλέως ἀμφὶ τὸ Κάσσιον ὄντος. καὶ πρῶτα μὲν ἀπραγμοσύνην τινὰ διὰ τὴν ὀλιγότητα τῶν συνόντων ὑπεκρίνετο φιλοφρόνως τε τοὺς ἐντυγχάνοντας ἐξεδέχετο καὶ τὴν πόλιν περιιὼν τοῦ κάλλους ἐθαύμαζε καὶ τῶν φιλοσόφων μετὰ τοῦ πλήθους ἑστὼς ἠκροᾶτο · ὅθεν αὐτῷ χάρις τε καὶ δόξα ἀγαθὴ ὡς ἀπράγμονι παρὰ τοῖς Ἀλεξανδρεῦσιν ἐφύετο.

II, XIII, 90. Ἐπεὶ δ´ ὁ στρατὸς αὐτῷ κατέπλευσε, Ποθεινὸν μὲν καὶ Ἀχιλλᾶν ἐκόλασε θανάτῳ τῆς ἐς τὸν Πομπήιον παρανομίας, Θεόδοτον δὲ διαδράντα Κάσσιος ὕστερον ἐκρέμασεν, εὑρὼν ἐν Ἀσίᾳ . θορυβούντων δ´ ἐπὶ τῷδε τῶν 'Αλεξανδρέων καὶ τῆς στρατιᾶς τῆς βασιλικῆς ἐπ' αὐτὸν ἰούσης, ἀγῶνες αὐτῷ ποικίλοι περὶ τὸ βασίλειον ἐγένοντο καὶ ἐν τοῖς παρ' αὐτὸ αἰγιαλοῖς, ἔνθα καὶ φεύγων ἐς τὴν θάλατταν ἐξήλατο καὶ ἐς πολὺ ἐν τῷ βυθῷ διενήξατο · καὶ τὴν χλαμύδα αὐτοῦ λαβόντες οἱ 'Αλεξανδρεῖς περὶ τρόπαιον ἐκρέμασαν . τελευταῖον δ' ἀνὰ τὸν Νεῖλον αὐτῷ γίνεται πρὸς τὸν βασιλέα ἀγών, ᾧ δὴ καὶ μάλιστα ἐκράτει . καὶ ἐς ταῦτα διετρίφθησαν αὐτῷ μῆνες ἐννέα, μέχρι Κλεοπάτραν ἀντὶ τοῦ ἀδελφοῦ βασιλεύειν ἀπέφηνεν Αἰγύπτου . καὶ τὸν Νεῖλον ἐπὶ τετρακοσίων νεῶν, τὴν χώραν θεώμενος, περιέπλει μετὰ τῆς Κλεοπάτρας, καὶ τἆλλα ἡδόμενος αὐτῇ. ἀλλὰ τάδε μὲν ἕκαστα ὅπως ἐγένετο, ἀκριβέστερον ἡ περὶ Αἰγύπτου συγγραφὴ διέξεισι · τὴν δὲ κεφαλὴν τοῦ Πομπηίου προσφερομένην οὐχ ὑπέστη, ἀλλὰ προσέταξε ταφῆναι, καί τι αὐτῇ τέμενος βραχὺ πρὸ τῆς πόλεως περιτεθὲν Νεμέσεως τέμενος ἐκαλεῖτο · ὅπερ ἐπ' ἐμοῦ κατὰ 'Ρωμαίων αὐτοκράτορα Τραϊανόν, ἐξολλύντα τὸ ἐν Αἰγύπτῳ 'Ιουδαίων γένος, ὑπὸ τῶν 'Ιουδαίων ἐς τὰς τοῦ πολέμου χρείας κατηρείφθη.

63.

II, XIII, 89. Being thus unexpectedly saved, Caesar passed the Hellespont and granted pardon to the Ionians, the Aeolians, and the other peoples who inhabit the great peninsula called by the common name of Lower Asia, and who sent ambassadors to him to ask it. Learning that Pompey was making for Egypt he sailed for Rhodes. He did not wait even there for his army, which was coming forward by detachments, but embarked with those he had on the triremes of Cassius and the Rhodians. Letting nobody know whither he intended to go he set sail toward evening, telling the other pilots to steer by the torch of his own ship by night and by his signal in the daytime; his own pilot, after they had proceeded a long way from the land, he ordered to steer for Alexandria. After a three day's sail he arrived there, and was received by the king's guardians, the king himself being still at Casium. At first, on account of the smallness of his forces, he pretended to take his ease, receiving visitors in a friendly way, traversing the city, admiring its beauty, and listening to the lectures of the philosophers while he stood among the crowd. Thus he gained the good-will and esteem of the Alexandrians as one who had no designs against them.

90. When his soldiers arrived by sea he punished Pothinus and Achillas with death for their crime against Pompey. (Theodotus escaped and was afterward crucified by Cassius, who found him wandering in Asia.) The Alexandrians thereupon rose in tumult, and the king's army marched against Caesar and various battles took place around the palace and on the neighbouring shores. In one of these Caesar escaped by leaping into the sea and swimming a long distance in deep water. The Alexandrians captured his cloak and hung it up as a trophy. He fought the last battle against the king on the banks of the Nile, in which he won a decisive victory. He consumed nine months in this strife, at the end of which he established Cleopatra on the throne of Egypt in place of her brother. He ascended the Nile with 400 ships, exploring the country in company with Cleopatra and generally enjoying himself with her. The details, however, of these events are related more particularly in my Egyptian history. Caesar could not bear to look at the head of Pompey when it was brought to him, but ordered that it be buried, and set apart for it a small plot of ground near the city which was dedicated to Nemesis, but in my time, while the Roman emperor Trajan was exterminating the Jewish race in Egypt, it was devastated by them in the exigencies of the war.

155-235 AD. Dio Cassius.

Arrival of Octavian's fleet in the Easern Harbour and Antony's suicude in the mausoleum

Dio Cassius, *Roman History*, 51, 10, 1-9 and 11,1; 51, 18, 1. Translation by Earnest Cary, on the basis of the version of Herbert Baldwin Foster (The Loeb Classical Library, 1994).

64.

51, 10, 1 Ὁ δ᾽ οὖν Ἀντώνιος ἐκ τοῦ Παραιτονίου πρὸς τὴν περὶ τοῦ Πελουσίου πύστιν ἐπανελθὼν προαπήντησε πρὸ τῆς Ἀλεξανδρείας τῷ Καίσαρι, καὶ αὐτὸν κεκμηκότα ἐκ τῆς πορείας ὑπολαβὼν τοῖς ἱππεῦσιν ἐνίκησεν. 2 ἀναθαρσήσας τε ἔκ τε τούτου καὶ ὅτι βιβλία ἐς τὸ στρατόπεδον αὐτοῦ τοξεύμασιν ἐσέπεμψε πεντακοσίας σφίσι καὶ χιλίας δραχμὰς ὑπισχνούμενος, συνέβαλε καὶ τῷ πεζῷ καὶ ἡττήθη · 3 ὁ γὰρ Καῖσαρ αὐτὸς τὰ βιβλία ἐθελοντὴς τοῖς στρατιώταις ἀνέγνω, τόν τε Ἀντώνιον διαβάλλων καὶ ἐκείνους ἔς τε τὴν τῆς προδοσίας αἰσχύνην καὶ ἐς τὴν ὑπὲρ ἑαυτοῦ προθυμίαν ἀντικαθιστάς, ὥστε καὶ διὰ τοῦτο αὐτοὺς τῇ τε τῆς πείρας ἀγανακτήσει καὶ τῇ τοῦ μὴ ἐθελοκακεῖν δόξαι ἐνδείξει σπουδάσαι. 4 καὶ ὁ μὲν ἐπειδὴ παρὰ δόξαν ἡλαττώθη, πρός τε τὸ ναυτικὸν ἀπέκλινε, καὶ παρεσκευάζετο ὡς καὶ ναυμαχήσων ἢ πάντως γε ἐς τὴν Ἰβηρίαν πλευσούμενος · 5 ἰδοῦσα δὲ τοῦθ᾽ ἡ Κλεοπάτρα τάς τε ναῦς αὐτομολῆσαι ἐποίησε, 5 καὶ αὐτὴ ἐς τὸ ἡρίον ἐξαίφνης ἐσεπήδησε, λόγῳ μὲν ὡς τὸν Καίσαρα φοβουμένη καὶ προδιαφθεῖραι τρόπον τινὰ ἑαυτὴν βουλομένη, ἔργῳ δὲ καὶ τὸν Ἀντώνιον ἐκεῖσε ἐσελθεῖν προκαλουμένη· ὑπετόπει μὲν γὰρ προδίδοσθαι, οὐ μέντοι καὶ ἐπίστευεν ὑπὸ τοῦ ἔρωτος, ἀλλὰ καὶ μᾶλλον ὡς εἰπεῖν ἐκείνην ἢ ἑαυτὸν ἠλέει. 6 Ὅπερ που ἡ Κλεοπάτρα ἀκριβῶς εἰδυῖα ἤλπισεν ὅτι, ἂν πύθηται αὐτὴν τετελευτηκυῖαν, οὐκ ἐπιβιώσεται ἀλλὰ παραχρῆμα ἀποθανεῖται. Καὶ διὰ τοῦτο ἔς τε τὸ μνημεῖον σύν τε εὐνούχῳ τινὶ καὶ σὺν θεραπαίναις δύο ἐσέδραμε, καὶ ἐκεῖθεν ἀγγελίαν αὐτῷ ὡς καὶ ἀπολωλυῖα ἔπεμψε. 7 Καὶ ὅς ἀκούσας τοῦτο οὐκ ἐμέλλησεν, ἀλλ᾽ ἐπαποθανεῖν αὐτῇ ἐπεθύμησε. Καὶ τὸ μὲν πρῶτον τῶν παρόντων τινὸς ἐδεήθη ἵνα αὐτὸν ἀποκτείνῃ· ἐπεὶ δὲ ἐκεῖνος σπασαμένος τὸ ξίφος ἑαυτὸν κατειργάσατο, ζηλῶσαί τε αὐτὸν ἠθέλησε καὶ ἑαυτὸν ἔτρωσεν, καὶ ἔπεσέ τε ἐπὶ στόμα καὶ δόξαν τοῖς παροῦσιν ὡς καὶ τεθνηκὼς παρέσχε. 8 Θορύβου τε ἐπὶ τούτῳ γενομένου ᾔσθετό τε ἡ Κλεοπάτρα καὶ ὑπερέκυψεν ὑπὲρ τοῦ μνημείου· αἱ μὲν γὰρ θύραι αὐτοῦ συγκλεισθεῖσαι ἅπαξ οὐκέτ᾽ ἀνοιχθῆναι ἐκ μηχανήματός τινος ἐδύναντο, τὰ δ᾽ ἄνω πρὸς τῇ ὀροφῇ οὐδέπω παντελῶς ἐξείργαστο. 9 Ἐντεῦθεν οὖν ὑπερκύψασαν αὐτὴν ἰδόντες τινὲς ἀνεβόησαν ὥστε καὶ τὸν Ἀντώνιον ἐσακοῦσαι· καὶ ὅς μαθὼν ὅτι περίεστιν, ἐξανέστη μὲν ὡς καὶ ζῆσαι δυνάμενος, προχυθέντος δ᾽ αὐτῷ πολλοῦ αἵματος ἀπέγνω τε τὴν σωτηρίαν, καὶ ἱκέτευσε τοὺς παρόντας ὅπως πρός τε τὸ μνῆμα αὐτὸν κομίσωσι καὶ διὰ τῶν σχοινίων τῶν πρὸς τὴν ἀνολκὴν τῶν λίθων κρεμαμένων ἀνιμήσωσι.

51, 11, 1 Καὶ ὁ μὲν ἐνταῦθα οὕτω καὶ ἐν τοῖς τῆς Κλεοπάτρας κόλποις ἐναπέθανεν, ἐκείνη δὲ ἐθάρσησε μέν πως τὸν Καίσαρα, καὶ εὐθὺς αὐτῷ τὸ γεγονὸς ἐδήλωσεν, οὐ μὴν καὶ πάνυ ἐπίστευε μηδὲν κακὸν πείσεσθαι. Κατεῖχεν οὖν ἑαυτὴν ἔνδον, ἵν᾽ εἰ καὶ διὰ μηδὲν ἄλλο σωθείη, τῷ γε φόβῳ τῶν χρημάτων καὶ τὴν ἄδειαν καὶ τὴν βασιλείαν ἐκπρίηται.

51, 18, 1 Ὁ δ᾽ οὖν Καῖσαρ ὡς τά τε προειρημένα ἔπραξε, καὶ πόλιν καὶ ἐκεῖ ἐν τῷ τῆς μάχης χωρίῳ συνῴκισε, καὶ τὸ ὄνομα καὶ τὸν ἀγῶνα αὐτῇ ὁμοίως τῇ προτέρᾳ δούς τάς τε διώρυχας τὰς μὲν ἐξεκάθηρε τὰς δὲ ἐκ καινῆς διώρυξε, καὶ τἆλλα τὰ προσήκοντα προσδιῴκησεν, ἔς τε τὴν Ἀσίαν τὸ ἔθνος διὰ τῆς Συρίας ἦλθε, κἀνταῦθα παρεχείμασε, τά τε τῶν ὑπηκόων ὡς ἕκαστα καὶ τὰ τῶν Πάρθων ἅμα καθιστάμενος.

64.

51, 10, 1-9. At the news concerning Pelusium Antony returned from Paraetonium and went to meet Caesar in front of Alexandria, and attacking him with his cavalry, while the other was wearied from his march, he won the day. 2 Encouraged by this success, and because he had shot arrows into Caesar's camp carrying leaflets which promised the men six thousand sesterces, he joined battle with his infantry and was defeated. 3 For Caesar of his own accord personally read the leaflets to his soldiers, at the same time reviling Antony and trying to turn them to a feeling of shame for the suggested treachery and of enthusiasm for himself; the result was that they were fired by zeal through this very incident, both by reason of their indignation at the attempt made upon their loyalty and by way of demonstrating that they were not subject to the suspicion of being base traitors. 4 After his unexpected setback, Antony took refuge in his fleet, and was preparing to give battle on the sea or at any rate to sail to Spain. But Cleopatra upon perceiving this, caused the ships to desert, 5 and she herself rushed suddenly into the mausoleum, pretending that she feared Caesar and desired by some means or other to forestall him by taking her own life, but really as an invitation to Antony to enter there also. He had a suspicion, to be sure, that he was being betrayed, yet in his infatuation he could not believe it, but actually pitied her more, one mighy say, than himself. 6 Cleopatra, doubtless, was fully aware of this and hoped that if he should be informed that she was dead, he would not wish to survive her, but would die at once. Accordingly she hastened into the tomb with a eunuch and two maidservants, and from there sent a message to him from which he should infer that she was dead. 7 And he, when he heard it, did not delay, but was seized by a desire to follow her in death. He first asked one of the bystanders to slay him: but when the man drew his sword and slew himself, Antony wished to imitate his courage and so gave himself a wound and fell upon his face, causing the bystanders to believe that he was dead. 8 At this an outcry was raised, and Cleopatra, hearing it, peered out over the top of the tomb. By a certain contrivance its doors, once closed, could not to be opened again, but the upper part of it next to the roof was not yet fully complited. 9 Now when some of them saw her peering out at this point, they raised a shout so that even Antony heard. So he, learning that she survived, stood up, as he had still the power to live; but, as he had lost much blood, he despaired of his life and besought the bystanders to carry him to the monument and to hoist him up by the ropes that were hanging there to lift the stone blocks.

11, 1. So Antony died there in Cleopatra's bosom; and she now felt a certain confidence in Caesar and immediatly informed him of what had taken place; still, she was not altogether convinced that she would suffer no harm. She accordingly kept herself within the building, in order that, even if there should be no other motive for her preservation, she might at least purchase pardon and her kingdom through his fear for the money.

51, 18, 1. After accomplishing the things just related Caesar founded a city there on the very site of the battle and gave to it the same name and the same games as to the city he had founded previously. He also cleared out some of the canals and dug others over again, besides attending to other important matters. Then he went through Syria into the province of Asia and passed the winter there settling the various affairs of the subject nations as well as those of the Parthians.

Circa 175-250 AD. Herodian.

Importance of Alexandria.

Herodian, *History of the Empire* IV, 3, 7; VII, 6, 61. Translation C R Whittaker (The Loeb Classical Library 1969).

65.

IV, 3, 7. τῇ τε βασιλείᾳ τῇ αὐτοῦ αὐτάρκη ἔσεσθαι ὑποδοχὴν ὁ Γέτας ἔλεγεν ἢ τὴν ᾽Αντιόχειαν ἢ τὴν ᾽Αλεξάνδρειαν, οὐ πολύ τι τῆς ῾Ρώμης [ὡς ᾤετο] μεγέθει ἀποδεούσας.

VII, 6, 1. ὁ δὲ Γορδιανὸς ἐνδιατρίψας τῇ Θύστρῳ, ἔνθα ταῦτα ἐπράχθη, ἡμερῶν τινῶν, ἤδη φέρων βασιλέως ὄνομα καὶ σχῆμα, ἀπάρας τε τῆς Θύστρου ἐς τὴν Καρχηδόνα ἠπείχθη, ἣν ᾔδει μεγίστην τε οὖσαν καὶ πολυάνθρωπον, ἵν᾽ ὥσπερ ἐν ῾Ρώμῃ πάντα πράττοι· ἡ γὰρ πόλις ἐκείνη καὶ δυνάμει χρημάτων καὶ πλήθει τῶν κατοικούντων καὶ μεγέθει μόνης ῾Ρώμης ἀπολείπεται, φιλονεικοῦσα πρὸς τὴν ἐν Αἰγύπτῳ ᾽Αλεξάνδρου πόλιν περὶ δευτερείων.

65.

IV, 3, 7. Geta declared that either Antioch or Alexandria, which were not much smaller than Rome [in his opinion], would be a suitable capital for his empire.

VII, 6, 1. For a few days Gordian remained at Thysdrus where the events had taken place, by this time with the title and style of emperor. Then he left Thysdrus and marched to Carthage, the largest and most heavily populated city (as Gordian knew), so that he could act exactly as if he were in Rome. The city is the next after Rome in wealth, population and size, though there is rivalry for second place between it and Alexandria in Egypt.

Caracalla's massacre in Alexandria

Herodian, *History of the Empire*, IV, 8, 6-9; IV, 9, 1-8. Translation by C R Whittaker (The Loeb Classical Library, 1969).

66.

IV, 8, 6 ἀπάρας δὲ τῆς ᾽Ιλίου διά τε τῆς ἄλλης ᾽Ασίας καὶ Βιθυνίας τῶν τε λοιπῶν ἐθνῶν, κἀκεῖσε διοικήσας τὰ πρακτέα, ἐς τὴν ᾽Αντιόχειαν ἀφίκετο . ἐκεῖ τε ὑποδεχθεὶς πολυτελῶς καὶ διατρίψας χρόνου τινὸς ἐπὶ τὴν ᾽Αλεξάνδρειαν ἐστέλλετο, πρόφασιν μὲν ποιούμενος ποθεῖν τὴν ἐπ᾽ ᾽Αλεξάνδρῳ κτισθεῖσαν πόλιν, καὶ τῷ θεῷ χρήσασθαι ὃν ἐκεῖνοι σέβουσιν ἐξαιρέτως · 7 δύο γὰρ ταῦτα ὑπερβαλλόντως προσεποιεῖτο, τήν τε τοῦ θεοῦ θρησκείαν καὶ τὴν τοῦ ἥρωος μνήμην. ἑκατόμβας τε οὖν κελεύει παρασκευασθῆναι ἐναγισμούς τε παντοδαπούς. ὡς δὲ διηγγέλη τῷ τῶν ᾽Αλεξανδρέων πλήθει, φύσει μὲν ὄντι τὰς γνώμας κουφοτάτῳ καὶ ἐπὶ τοῖς βραχυτάτοις ῥᾷστα κινουμένῳ, τότε δ᾽ ἐξεπτόηντο τὴν τοῦ βασιλέως σπουδήν τε καὶ εὔνοιαν πυνθανόμενοι. 8 ὑποδοχὴ δὴ παρεσκευάζετο οἵαν μηδενὶ πώποτε βασιλεῖ γενέσθαι φασί· πάσης τε γὰρ μούσης ὄργανα πανταχοῦ διαικείμενα ποικίλον ἦχον εἰργάζετο, ἀρωμάτων τε παντοδαπῶν καὶ θυμιαμάτων ἀτμίδες εὐωδίαν παρεῖχον ταῖς εἰσόδοις, δᾳδουχίαις τε καὶ ἀνθέων βολαῖς ἐτίμων τὸν βασιλέα. 9 ὡς δὲ εἰσήλασεν ἐς τὴν πόλιν σὺν παντὶ τῷ στρατῷ, πρῶτον μὲν ἐς τὸν νεὼν ἀνελθὼν πολλὰς ἑκατόμβας κατέθυσε λιβάνῳ τε τοὺς βωμοὺς ἐσώρευσεν, ἐκεῖθεν δ᾽ ἐλθὼν ἐς τὸ ᾽Αλεξάνδρου μνῆμα, τὴν τε χλαμύδα ἣν ἔφερεν ἀλουργῆ, δακτυλίους τε οὓς εἶχε λίθων τιμίων, ζωστῆράς τε καὶ εἴ τι πολυτελὲς ἔφερε, περιελθὼν ἑαυτοῦ ἐπέθηκε τῇ ἐκείνου σορῷ . IV, 9, 1 ἃ δὴ ὁρῶν ὁ δῆμος ὑπερέχαιρε, παννυχίζων τε καὶ ἑορτάζων, οὐκ εἰδὼς τὴν τοῦ βασιλέως λανθάνουσαν γνώμην· ταῦτα γὰρ πάντα ἐκεῖνος ὑπεκρίνατο βουλόμενος τὸ πλῆθος αὐτῶν διαφθεῖραι. ἡ δ΄ αἰτία τοῦ λανθάνοντος μίσους τοιάδε τις ἦν . 2 ἀπηγγέλλετο αὐτῷ διατρίβοντι ἐπὶ τῆς Ῥώμης ἔτι, καὶ τοῦ ἀδελφοῦ περιόντος καὶ μετὰ τὸν ἐκείνου φόνον, ὅτι ἄρα εἶεν πολλὰ ἐς αὐτὸν ἀποσκώψαντες. πεφύκασι δέ πως εἶναι φιλοσκώμμονες καὶ λέγειν εὐστόχους ὑπογραφὰς ἢ παιδιάς, ἀπορριπτοῦντες ἐς τοὺς ὑπερέχοντας πολλὰ χαρίεντα μὲν αὐτοῖς δοκοῦντα, λυπηρὰ δὲ τοῖς σκωφθεῖσι · τῶν γὰρ τοιούτων κνίζει μάλιστα ὅσα ἐλέγχει τῶν ἁμαρτημάτων τὴν ἀλήθειαν. 3 πολλὰ τοίνυν ἐκείνων αὐτὸν σκωψάντων ἔς τε τὴν τοῦ ἀδελφοῦ ἀναίρεσιν, καὶ τὴν πρεσβῦτιν Ἰοκάστην καλούντων, ἐκεῖνον δὲ χλευαζόντων ὅτι δὴ μικρὸς ὢν Ἀλέξανδρον καὶ Ἀχιλλέα γενναιοτάτους καὶ μεγίστους ἥρωας ἐμιμεῖτο, τοιαῦτά τινα παίζειν αὐτῶν δοκούντων, ὀλέθρια καὶ ἐπίβουλα κατ΄ αὐτῶν σκέψασθαι τὸν Ἀντωνῖνον ἠνάγκασαν, φύσει ὄντα ὀργίλον καὶ φονικόν.

4 συμπανηγυρίσας τοίνυν αὐτοῖς καὶ συνεορτάσας, ὡς εἶδε πᾶσαν τὴν πόλιν πλήθους μεγίστου πεπληρωμένην τῶν ἀπὸ πάσης περὶ αὐτὴν χώρας ἐκεῖ συνελθόντων, διὰ προγράμματος πᾶσαν τὴν νεολαίαν ἔς τι πεδίον κελεύει συνελθεῖν, φήσας ἐς τὴν Ἀλεξάνδρου τιμὴν φάλαγγα βούλεσθαι συστήσασθαι, ὥσπερ Μακεδονικὴν καὶ Σπαρτιᾶτιν, οὕτω καὶ τοῦ ἥρωος ἐπωνύμους. 5 κελεύει δὴ στιχηδὸν τοὺς νεανίας πάντας διαστῆναι, ὡς ἂν ἐπελθὼν ἕκαστον ἴδῃ πῶς τε ἡλικίας ἔχοι καὶ μεγέθους σώματος καὶ εὐεξίας ἐς στρατείαν ἐπιτηδείου. ταύταις αὐτοῦ ταῖς ὑποσχέσεσι πιστεύσαντες οἱ νεανίαι πάντες, ἐοικότα τε ἐλπίσαντες διὰ τὴν προϋπάρξασαν παρ΄ αὐτοῦ ἐς τὴν πόλιν τιμήν, συνῆλθον ἅμα γονεῦσί τε καὶ ἀδελφοῖς συνηδομένοις αὐτῶν ταῖς ἐλπίσιν. 6 ὁ δ΄ Ἀντωνῖνος διεστῶτας αὐτοὺς ἐπιών, ἑκάστου ἐφαπτόμενος καὶ ἄλλου ἄλλο λέγων ἐγκώμιον παρῄει, ἔστε αὐτοὺς οὔτε τι ὁρῶντας οὔτε προσδοκῶντας τὸ στρατιωτικὸν πᾶν ἐκυκλώσατο. ὡς δὲ ἐτεκμήρατο ἤδη αὐτοὺς εἶναι ἐντὸς τῶν ὅπλων περιειλημμένους καὶ ὥσπερ ἐν δικτύοις σεσαγηνευμένους, ἐπελθὼν πάντας αὐτὸς μὲν ὑπεξέρχεται μεθ΄ ἧς εἶχε φρουρᾶς περὶ ἑαυτόν, ὑφ΄ ἑνὶ δὲ σημείῳ προσπεσόντες πανταχόθεν οἱ στρατιῶται τὴν ἐν μέσῳ πᾶσαν νεολαίαν, καὶ εἴ τινες ἄλλως παρῆσαν, παντὶ τρόπῳ φόνων ἀναιροῦσιν, ὡπλισμένοι τε ἀόπλους καὶ πανταχόθεν περιειληφότες. 7 τῶν δὲ στρατιωτῶν οἱ μὲν ἐφόνευον οἱ δ΄ ἔξωθεν ὤρυττον ὀρύγματα μέγιστα ἕλκοντές τε τοὺς πίπτοντας ἐνέβαλλον, πληρουῦτες σωμάτων · καὶ τὴν γῆν ἐπιχέοντες μέγιστον ἤγειραν ταχέως πολυάνδριον. πολλοί τε καὶ ἡμιθνῆτες εἱλκύσθησαν, ἔτι τε ἄτρωτοι συνώσθησαν . 8 ἀλλὰ μὴν καὶ τῶν στρατιωτῶν οὐκ ὀλίγοι προσαπώλοντο· ὅσοι γὰρ ἔτι ἐμπνέοντες καὶ δυνάμεως μετρίως ἔχοντες συνωθοῦντο, περιπλεκόμενοι συγκαθεῖλκον αὐτούς. τοσοῦτος δὲ ἐγένετο φόνος ὡς ῥείθροις αἵματος διὰ τοῦ πεδίου τάς τε ἐκβολὰς τοῦ Νείλου μεγίστας οὔσας τόν τε περὶ τὴν πόλιν αἰγιαλὸν πάντα φοινιχθῆναι. τοιαῦτα δὴ ἐργασάμενος τὴν πόλιν, ἀπάρας ἐς Ἀντιόχειαν ἀφίκετο.

66.

IV. 8, 6. After leaving Ilium, Antoninus travelled through the rest of Asia and Bithynia and the other provinces, making what administrative decisions were necessary, until he came to Antioch. Here he was given an elaborate welcome and spent a certain amount of time there before setting off for Alexandria. The excuse he made for going there was that he longed to see the city founded in honour of Alexander and to sacrifice to the god whom the people there hold in special veneration. 7 There were two particular reasons, he alleged, one to worship the god and the other to honour the memory of the hero. So he gave orders for large public sacrifices of cattle and all kinds of offerings to the dead to be made ready. The people of Alexandria are by nature extremely frivolous and easily roused for very trivial reasons. On this occasion, when the news came, they were greatly excited to hear of the emperor's enthusiastic goodwill towards them. 8 So they made ready to give him such a reception as, they say, had never been given to an emperor before. All kinds of musical instruments were set up everywhere and produced a variety of sounds. Clouds of perfume and incense of all sorts presented a sweet odour at the city gates. The emperor was regaled with torch processions in his honour and showered with flowers. 9 As soon as Antoninus entered the city with his whole army he went up to the temple, where he made a large number of sacrifices and laid quantities of incense on the altars. Then he went to the tomb of Alexander where he took off and laid upon the grave the purple cloak he was wearing and the rings of precious stones and his belts and anything else of value he was carrying.

9, 1 When the people saw this they were extremely pleased and spent the whole night in celebrations without realizing the secret intention of the emperor. All this show was a pretence by him as part of a plan to massacre a large number of them. 2 The reason for his concealed antagonism was that he kept receiving reports while he was living in Rome during his brother's lifetime, and also after his assassination, that the Alexandrians had actually been making great fun of him. To a certain extent it was a natural feature of the people to indulge in lampoons and repetition of many pungent caricatures and jokes belittling the authorities, since they are considered very witty by the Alexandrians, even if libellous to the victims. The witticisms that really irritate are those which expose the truth of one's shortcomings. 3 Many of their lampoons against Antoninus referred to the destruction of his brother and to his old mother, calling her Jocasta, and jeering at him for imitating Alexander and Achilles who were very strong, tall men, while he himself was only a small man. Though the Alexandrians considered this kind of insult light-hearted comedy, Antoninus had a murderous, hot temper and was driven to work out plans for the destruction of the people.

4 So he celebrated the occasion with them and took part in their festivities, but when he saw that the entire city was crammed with a vast number of people as the result of an influx from the entire surrounding district, he issued an edict that all the young men should assemble on an open piece of ground, saying that he intended to enrol a phalanx in honour of Alexander which would be called after the hero, just as he had given a name to the Macedonian and the Spartan phalanx. 5 The young men were told to muster in ranks so that the emperor could examine each man and decide how far his age, size and condition were up to standard for the army. All the youth believed Antoninus' promises and credited the probability of what he said because he had already honoured the city. They arrived with their parents and brothers, who were equally pleased at the prospects for their relations. 6 Antoninus inspected the ranks as they stood there and passed from man to man, saying a different word of encouragement to each man as he came to him, while the entire army encircled them without being noticed or rousing suspicion. After he had gone up and down all the ranks, he judged they were by this time surrounded by arms like animals trapped in a net. So he actually left the field with his personal bodyguard, while from every side the soldiers at a single signal fell upon all the encircled young men and any who were there for other reasons. They wiped them out with every kind of slaughter, armed soldiers against defenceless men who were totally surrounded. 7 Some of the troops did the killing, while the rest outside the ring dug huge pits, to which they dragged the fallen and threw them in until they were filled with bodies. Earth was thrown on top of them and a vast communal burial mound quickly raised. Lots of people were half alive when they were dragged away, and unwounded men were forced into the grave along with the rest. 8 Still worse, several soldiers lost their lives, because, when those who were still alive and fairly vigorous were being pushed into the pits, they pulled the soldiers in with them by hanging on to them. So great was the slaughter that the mouths of the Nile (a vast area) and the whole seashore around Alexandria

grew red from the streams of blood which flowed through the plain. So much for what Antoninus did to Alexandria, after which he left for Antioch.

3rd century AD (211-217: Reign of Caracalla = Imperator Caesar Marcus Aurelius Severus Antoninus Pius Augustus). *Historia Augusta.*

Scriptores Historiae Augustae, Antoninus Caracalla, IX, VI, 2-3. Translation by D Magie (The Loeb Classical Library, volume II, 1924).

67.
VI, 2-3. Inde Alexandriam petit, in gymnasium populum convocavit eumque obiurgavit; legi etiam validos ad militiam praecepit. 3 Eos autem quos legerat, occidit exemplo Ptolomaei Euergetis, qui octavus hoc nomine appellatus est. Dato praeterea signo militibus, ut hospites suos occiderent, magnam caedem Alexandreae fecit.

67.
VI, 2 Then he betook himself to Alexandria, and here he called the people together into the Gymnasium and heaped abuse on them; he gave orders, moreover, that those who were physically qualified should be enrolled for military service. 3 But those whom he enrolled he put to death, following the example of Ptolemy Euergetes, the eighth of those who bore the name Ptolemy. In addition to this he issued an order to his soldiers to slay their hosts and thus caused great slaughter at Alexandria.

3rd century AD (?). Achilles Tatius.

General view of Alexandria

Achilles Tatius. *The adventures of Leuccippe and Clitophon,* Book V, 1-2. Translation by S Gaselee (The Loeb Classical Library, 1969).

68.
V, 1. Τριῶν δὲ πλεύσαντες ἡμερῶν εἰς Ἀλεξάνδρειαν ἤλθομεν. ἀνιόντι δέ μοι κατὰ τὰς Ἡλίου καλουμένας πύλας, συνηντᾶτο εὐθὺς τῆς πόλεως ἀστράπτον τὸ κάλλος, καί μου τοὺς ὀφθαλμοὺς ἐγέμισεν ἡδονῆς. στάθμη μὲν κιόνων ὄρθιος ἑκατέρωθεν ἐκ τῶν Ἡλίου πυλῶν εἰς τὰς Σελήνης πύλας. οὗτοι γὰρ τῆς πόλεως οἱ πυλωροί. ἐν μέσῳ δὴ τῶν κιόνων τὸ πεδίον· ὁδὸς δὲ διὰ τοῦ πεδίου πολλὴ καὶ ἔνδημος ἀποδημία. ὀλίγους δὲ τῆς πόλεως σταδίους προελθών, ἦλθον εἰς τὸν ἐπώνυμον Ἀλεξάνδρου τόπον. εἶδον δὲ ἐντεῦθεν ἄλλην πόλιν καὶ σχιζόμενον ταύτῃ τὸ κάλλος · ὅσος γὰρ κιόνων ὄρχατος εἰς τὴ̀ν εὐθυωρίαν, τοσοῦτος ἕτερος εἰς τὰ ἐγκάρσια . ἐγὼ δὲ μερίζων τοὺς ὀφθαλμοὺς εἰς πάσας τὰς ἀγυιάς, θεατὴς ἀκόρεστος ἤμην καὶ τὸ κάλλος ὅλως οὐκ ἐξήρακουν ἰδεῖν. τὰ μὲν ἔβλεπον, τὰ δὲ ἔμελλον, τὰ δὲ ἠπειγόμην ἰδεῖν, τὰ δὲ οὐκ ἤθελον παρελθεῖν · ἐκράτει τὴν θέαν τὰ ὁρώμενα, εἷλκε τὰ προδοκώμενα. περιάγων οὖν ἐμαυτὸν εἰς πάσας τὰς ἀγυιὰς καὶ πρὸς τὴν ὄψιν δυσερωτιῶν, εἶπον καμών· " Ὀφθαλμοί, νενικήμεθα". Εἶδον δὲ δύο καινὰ καὶ παράλογα, μεγέθους πρὸς κάλλος ἅμιλλαν καὶ δήμου πρὸς πόλιν φιλονεικίαν

καὶ ἀμφότερα νικῶντα · ἡ μὲν γὰρ ἠπείρου μείζων ἦν, ὁ δὲ πλείων ἔθνους. καὶ εἰ μὲν εἰς τὴν πόλιν ἐπεῖδον, ἠπίστουν εἰ πληρώσει τις δῆμος αὐτὴν ἀνδρῶν, εἰ δὲ εἰς τὸν δῆμον ἐθεασάμην, ἐθαύμαζον, εἰ χωρήσει τις αὐτὸν πόλις. τοιαύτη τις ἦν ἰσότητος τρυτάνη.

2. Ἦν δέ πως κατὰ δαίμονα ἱερομηνία τοῦ μεγάλου θεοῦ, ὅν Δία μὲν Ἕλληνες, Σέραπιν δὲ καλοῦσιν Αἰγύπτιοι· ἦν δὲ καὶ πυρὸς δᾳδουχία . καὶ τοῦτο μέγιστον ἐθεασάμήν · ἑσπέρα μὲν γὰρ ἦν καὶ ὁ ἥλιος κατεδύετο καὶ νὺξ ἦν οὐδαμοῦ, ἀλλ᾽ ἄλλος ἀνέτελλεν ἥλιος κατακερματίζων · τότε γὰρ εἶδον πόλιν ἐρίζουσαν περὶ κάλλους οὐρανῷ . ἐθεασάμην δὲ καὶ τὸν Μειλίχιον Δία, καὶ τὸν Διὸς Οὐρανίου νεών. προσευξάμενοι δὴ τῷ μεγάλῳ θεῷ καὶ ἱκετεύσαντες στῆσαι ἡμῖν ποτὲ τὰ δεινά, εἰς τὴν καταγωγὴν ἤλθομεν, ἣν ἔτυχεν ὁ Μενέλαος ἡμῖν μεμισθωμένος. οὐκ ἐῴκει δὲ ἄρα ὁ θεὸς ἐπινεύειν ταῖς ἡμετέραις εὐχαῖς, ἀλλ᾽ ἔμενεν ἡμᾶς καὶ ἄλλο τῆς Τύχης γυμνάσιον.

68.

V, 1. After a voyage lasting for three days, we arrived at Alexandria. I entered it by the Sun Gate, as it is called, and was instantly struck by the splendid beauty of the city, which filled my eyes with delight. From the Sun Gate to the Moon Gate- these are the guardian divinities of the entrances- led a straight double row of columns, about the middle of which lies the open part of the town, and in it so many streets that walking in them you would fancy yourself abroad while still at home. Going a few hundred yards further, I came to the quarter called after Alexander, where a saw a second town; the splendour of this was cut into squares, for there was a row of columns intersected by another as long at right angles. I tried to cast my eyes down every street, but my gaze was still unsatisfied, and I could not grasp all the beauty of the spot at once; some parts I saw, some I was on the point of seeing, some I earnestly desired to see, some I could not pass by; that which I actually saw kept my gaze fixed, while that which I expected to see would drag it on the next. I explorated therefore every street, and at last, my vision unsatisfied, exclamed in weariness, 'Ah, my eyes, we are beaten.' Two things struck me as especially strange and extraordinary—it was impossible to decide which was the greatest, the size of the place or its beauty, the city itself or its inhabitants; for the former was larger than a continent, the latter outnumbered a whole nation. Looking at the city, I doubted whether any race of men could ever fill it; looking at the inhabitants, I wondered whether any city could ever be found large enough to hold them all. The balance seemed exactly even.

§2. It so fortuned that it was at that time the sacred festival of the great god whom the Greeks call Zeus, the Egyptians Serapis, and there was a procession of torches. It was the greatest spectacle I ever beheld, for it was late evening and the sun had gone down; but there was no sign of night—it was as though another sun had arisen, but distributed into small parts in every direction; I thought that on that occasion the city vied with the sky for beauty. I also visited the Gracious Zeus and his temple in his aspect as god of Heaven; and then praying to the great god and humbly imploring him that our troubles might be at last at an end, we came back to the lodgings which Menelaus hard hired for us. But the god, it seems, was not prepared to assent to our prayers, but still another of the trials and exercises of Fate was in store for us.

Pirates invade from the Eastern Harbour to the Isle of Pharos

Achilles Tatius, *The Adventures of Leucippe and Clitophon*, V, 6-7. Translation by S Gaselee (The Loeb Classical Library, 1969).

69.

V, 6. Τότε μὲν οὖν οὕτως ἐξεφύγομεν τὴν ἐπιβουλήν· ἐκερδήσαμεν δὲ οὐδὲν ἤ μίαν ἡμέραν. Τῇ γὰρ ὑστεραίᾳ παρῆν ἕωθεν ὁ Χαιρέας · καὶ ἡμεῖς αἰδεσθέντες ἀντιλέγειν οὐκ εἴχομεν. ἐπιβάντες οὖν σκάφος, ἤλθομεν εἰς τὴν Φάρον · ὁ δὲ Μενέλαος ἔμεινεν αὐτοῦ, φήσας οὐχ ὑγιῶς ἔχειν. πρῶτον μὲν οὖν ἡμᾶς ὁ Χαιρέας ἐπὶ τὸν πύργον ἄγει καὶ δείκνυσι τὴν κατασκευὴν κάτωθεν θαυμασίαν τινὰ καὶ παράλογον. ὄρος ἦν ἐν μέσῃ τῇ θαλάσσῃ κείμενον, ψαῦον αὐτῶν τῶν νεφῶν. ὑπέρρει δὲ ὕδωρ κάτωθεν αὐτοῦ τοῦ ποιήματος· τὸ δὲ ἐπὶ θαλάσσης ειστήκει κρεμάμενον · ἐς δὲ τὴν τοῦ ὄρους ἀκρόπολιν ὁ τῶν νεῶν κυβερνήτης ἀνέτελλεν ἄλλος ἥλιος. μετὰ δὲ ταῦτα ἡγεῖτο ἡμῖν ἐπὶ τὴν οἰκίαν· ἦν δὲ ἐπ΄ ἐσχάτων τῇ νήσῳ κειμένη ἐπ΄ αὐτῇ τῇ θαλάσσῃ .

7. Ἑσπέρας οὖν γενομένης, ὑπεξέρχεται μὲν ὁ Χαιρέας, πρόφασιν ποιησάμενος τὴν γαστέρα. Μετὰ μικρὸν δὲ βοή τις ἐξαίφνης περὶ τὰς θύρας ἦν, καὶ εὐθὺς εἰστρέχουσιν ἄνθρωποι μεγάλοι καὶ πολλοί, μαχαῖρας ἐσπασμένοι, καὶ ἐπὶ τὴν κόρην πάντες ὥρμησαν. ἐγὼ δὲ ὡς εἶδον φερομένην μοι τὴν φιλτάτην, οὐκ ἐνεγκὼν ἵεμαι διὰ τῶν ξιφῶν· καί με παίει τις κατὰ τοῦ μηροῦ μαχαίρᾳ καὶ ὤκλασα · ἐγὼ μὲν δὴ καταπεσὼν ἐρρεόμην αἵματι· οἱ δὲ ἐνθέμενοι τῷ σκάθει τὴν κόρην ἔφευγον. θορύβου δὲ καὶ βοῆς οἷα ἐπὶ λῃσταῖς γενομένης, ὁ στρατηγὸς τῆς νήσου παρῆν. ἦν δέ μοι γνώριμος ἐκ τοῦ στρατοπέδου γενόμενος. δεικνύω δὴ τὸ τραῦμα καὶ δέομαι διῶξαι τοὺς λῃστάς. ὥρμει δὲ πολλὰ πλοῖα ἐν τῇ πόλει· τούτων ἐνὶ ἐπιβὰς ὁ στρατηγός, ἐδίωκεν ἅμα τῇ παρούσῃ φρουρᾷ, κἀγὼ δὲ συνανέβην φοράδην κομισθείς.

69.

V, 6. For the moment then we had by this incident escaped the plot laid against us; but we only gained one day. On the morrow came Chaereas at dawn; for very shame we could make no further excuses and got aboard a boat to go to Pharos; Menelaus stayed behind, saying that he was not well. Chaereas first took us to the light-house and shewed us the most remarkable and extraordinary structure upon which it rested; it was like a mountain, almost reaching the clouds, in the middle of the sea. Below the building flowed the waters; it seemed to be as it were suspended above their surface, while at the top of the mountain rose a second sun to be a guide for ships. After this he took us to his house, which was on the shore at the extremity of the island.

7. As soon as evening was come, Chaereas went out, alleging as a pretence the demands of nature. Not long after there was a sudden tumult at the door, and in rushed a large number of tall men, their swords drawn, all directing themselves upon the maiden. Seeing my dearest being taken from me, I could not bear it, and rushed into the fray; one of them wounded me with his sword in the thigh, and I sank to the ground. While I was such falling, streaming with blood, they put her aboard a boat and made off. Such was the noise and tumult caused by the pirates that the commander of the island came up, who happened to be an acquaintance of mine because he had been in our former camp. I shewed him my wound and implored him to pursue the pirates. There were plenty of ships anchored there about the town; the commander entered one of them and went in chase, his bodyguard with him, while I followed them, carried aboard in a litter.

Circa 330-400 AD. Ammianus Marcellinus.

Ammianus Marcellinus, XXII, 16, 7-13. Translation by John C Rolfe (The Loeb Classical Library, 1986).

70.

XXII. 16. 7. Alexandria enim vertex omnium est civitatum, quam multa nobilitant et magnifica, conditoris altissimi et architecti sollertia Dinocratis, qui cum ampla «moenia fundaret et pulchra, paenuria calcis ad» momentum parum repertae, omnes ambitus liniales farina respersit, quod civitatem post haec alimentorum uberi copia circumfluere fortuito monstravit. 8 Inibi aurae salubriter spirant, et aer est tranquillus et clemens atque, ut periculum docuit, per varias collectum aetates, nullo paene die incolentes hanc civitatem solem serenum non vident. 9 Hoc litus cum fallacibus et insidiosis accessibus affligeret antehac navigantes discriminibus plurimis, excogitavit in portu Cleopatra turrim excelsam, quae Pharos a loco ipso cognominatur, praelucendi navibus nocturna suggerens ministeria, cum quondam ex Parthenio pelago venientes vel Libyco, per pandas oras et patulas, montium nullas speculas vel collium signa cernentes, harenarum inlisae glutinosae mollitiae frangerentur. 10 Haec eadem regina heptastadium sicut vix credenda celeritate, ita magnitudine mira construxit, ob causam notam et necessariam. Insula Pharos, ubi Protea cum phocarum gregibus diversatum, Homerus (*Odyss.* IV, 400 ff.) fabulatur inflatius, a civitatis litore mille passibus disparata, Rhodiorum erat obnoxia vectigali. 11 Quod cum in die quidam nimium quantum petituri venissent, femina callida semper in fraudes, sollemnium specie feriarum isdem publicanis secum ad suburbana perductis, opus iusserat inrequietis laboribus consummari, et septem diebus totidem stadia, molibus iactis in mari solo propinquante, terrae sunt vindicata; equorumque «cum» vehiculo ingressa erat Rhodios, insularum non continentis portorium flagitantes.

12 His accedunt altis sufflata fastigiis templa, inter quae eminet Serapeum, quod licet minuatur exilitate verborum, atriis tamen columnatis amplissimis, et spirantibus signorum figmentis, et reliqua operum multitudine ita est exornatum, ut post Capitolium, quo se venerabilis Roma in aeternum adtollit, nihil orbis terrarum ambitiosius cernat. 13 In quo duo bibliothecae fuerunt inaestimabiles: et loquitur monumentorum veterum concinens fides septinginta voluminum milia, Ptolomaeis regibus vigiliis intentis conposita, bello Alexandrino, dum diripitur civitas, sub dictatore Caesare conflagrasse.

70.

XXII, 16, 7 But the crown of all cities is Alexandria, which is made famous by many splendid things, through the wisdom of its mighty founder and by the cleverness of the architect Dinocrates. The latter, when laying out its extensive and beautiful walls, for lack of lime, of which too little could not at the time be found, sprinkled the whole line of its circuit with flour, which chanced to be a sign that later the city would abound with a plentiful store of food. 8 There healthful breezes blow, the air is calm and mild, and as the accumulated experience of many ages has shown, there is almost no day on which the dwellers in that city do not see a cloudless sun.

9 Since this coast in former times, because of its treacherous and perilous approaches, involved seafarers in many dangers, Cleopatra devised a lofty tower in the harbour, which from its situation is called the Pharos and furnishes the means of showing lights to ships by night; whereas before that, as they came from the Parthenian or the Libyan sea past flat and low shores, seeing no landmarks of mountains or signs of hills, they were dashed upon the soft, tenacious sandbanks and wrecked. 10 This same queen built the Heptastadium, remarkable alike for its great size and for the incredible speed with which it was constructed, for a well-known and sufficient reason. The island of Pharos, where Proteus, as Homer relates in lofty language, lived with his herd of seals, lay a mile from the shore of the city, and was subject to tribute by the Rhodians. 11 When they had come one day to collect this tax, which was excessive, the queen, who was ever skilled in deception, under pretence of a solemn festival, took the tax-collectors

with her to the suburbs, and gave orders that the work should be completed by unremitting toil. In seven days, by building dams in the sea near the shore, the same number of stadia were won for the land; then the queen rode to the spot in a carriage drawn by horses, and laughed at the Rhodians, since it was on islands and not on the mainland that they imposed duty.

12 There are besides in the city temples rising with lofty roofs, conspicuous among them the Serapeum, although no description can do it justice yet is so adorned with extensive columned halls, with almost breathing statues, and a great number of other works of art, that next to the Capitolium, with which revered Rome elevates herself to eternity, the whole world beholds nothing more magnificent. 13 In this were invaluable libraries, and the unanimous testimony of ancient records declares that 700,000 books, brought together by the unremitting energy of the Ptolemaïc kings, were burned in the Alexandrine war, when the city was sacked under the dictator Caesar.

The obelisk of Constantinople

363 AD. Julian.

Julian, *The Works of the Emperor Julian*, III, *Letters*, 48. Translation by Wilmer Cave Wright (Loeb Classical Library, 1923).

71.

Αλεξανδρεῦσιν.- 'Οβελὸν εἶναι παρ΄ ὑμῖν ἀκούω λίθινον εἰς ὕψος ἱκανὸν ἐπηρμένον, ἐπὶ τῆς ἠιόνος ὥσπερ ἄλλο τι τῶν ἀτιμοτάτων ἐρριμμένον.'Επὶ τοῦτον ἐναυπηγήσατο σκάφος ὁ μακαρίτης Κωνστάντιος, ὡς μετάξων αὐτὸν εἰς τὴν ἐμὴν πατρίδα Κωνσταντίνου πόλιν · ἐπεὶ δὲ ἐκείνῳ συνέβη θεῶν ἐθελόντων ἐνθένδε ἐκεῖσε πορευθῆναι τὴν εἱμαρμένην πορείαν, ἡ πόλις ἀπαιτεῖ παρ΄ ἐμοῦ τὸ ἀνάθημα, πατρὶς οὖσά μου καὶ προσήκουσα πλέον ἤπερ ἐκείνῳ · ὁ μὲν γὰρ αὐτὴν ὡς ἀδελφήν, ἐγὼ δὲ ὡς μητέρα φιλῶ · καὶ γὰρ ἐγενόμην παρ΄αὐτῇ καὶ ἐτράφην ἐκεῖσε, καὶ οὐ δύναμαι περὶ αὐτὴν ἀγνώμων εἶναι. Τί οὖν ; ἐπειδὴ καὶ ὑμᾶς οὐδὲν ἔλαττον τῆς πατρίδος φιλῶ, δίδωμι καὶ παρ΄ ὑμῖν ἀναστῆναι τὴν χαλκῆν εἰκόνα . πεποίηται δὲ ἔναγχος ἀνδριὰς τῷ μεγέθει κολοσσικός, ὅν ἀναστήσαντες ἕξετε «ἀντὶ» ἀναθήματος λιθίνου χαλκοῦν, ἀνδρός, οὗ φατε ποθεῖν, εἰκόνα καὶ μορφὴν ἀντὶ τριγώνου[10] λίθου χαράγματα ἔχοντος Αἰγύπτια. Καὶ τὸ λεγόμενον δὲ ὥς τινές εἰσιν οἱ θεραπεύοντες καὶ προσκαθεύδοντες αὐτοῦ τῇ κορυφῇ, πάνυ με πείθει χρῆναι τῆς δεισιδαιμονίας ἕνεκα ταύτης ἀπάγειν αὐτόν · οἱ γὰρ θεώμενοι τοὺς καθεύδοντας ἐκεῖ, πολλοῦ μὲν ῥύπου, πολλῆς δὲ ἀσελγείας περὶ τὸν τόπον ὡς ἔτυχεν οὔσης, οὔτε πιστεύουσιν αὐτὸν θεῖον εἶναι, καὶ διὰ τὴν τῶν προσεχόντων αὐτῳ δεισιδαιμονίαν ἀπιστότεροι περὶ τοὺς θεοὺς καθίστανται. Δι΄αὐτὸ δὴ οὖν τοῦτο καὶ μᾶλλον ὑμῖν προσήκει συνεπιλαβέσθαι καὶ πέμψαι τῇ ἐμῇ πατρίδι,τῇ ξενοδοχούσῃ καλῶς ὑμᾶς, ὅτε εἰς τὸν Πούτον εἰσπλεῖτε, «και» ὥσπερ εἰς τὰς τροφάς, καὶ εἰς τὸν ἐκτὸς κόσμον συμβάλλεσθαι. Πάντως οὐκ ἄχαρι καὶ παρ΄αὐτοῖς ἑστάναι τι τῶν ὑμετέρων, εἰς ὅ προσπλέοντες τῇ πόλει μετ΄ εὐφροσύνης ἀποβλέψετε .

[10] τριγώνου Hertlein, MSS; τετραγώνου La Bléterie, 'as the obelisk is four-sided' (Wright).

71.

I am informed that there is in your neighbourhood a granite obelisk[11] which, when it stood erect, reached a considerable height, but has been thrown down and lies on the beach as though it were something entirely worthless. For this obelisk Constantius of blessed memory had a freight-boat built, because he intended to convey it to my native place, Constantinople. But since by the will of heaven he has departed from this life to the next on that journey to which we are fated, the city claims the monument from me because it is the place of my birth and more closely connected with me that with the late Emperor. For though he loved the place as a sister I love it as my mother. And I was in fact born there and brought up in the place, and I cannot ignore its claims. Well then since I love you also, no less than my native city, I grant to you also permission to set up the bronze statue in your city. A statue has lately been made of colossal size. If you set this up you will have, instead of a stone monument, a bronze statue of a man whom you say you love and long for, and a human shape instead of a quadrangular block of granite with Egyptian characters on it. Moreover, the news has reached me that there are certain persons who worship there and sleep[12] at its very apex, and that convinces me beyond doubt that on account of these superstitious practices I should take it away. For me who see those persons sleeping there and so much filthy rubbish and careless and licentious behaviour in that place, not only do they believe that it[13] is sacred, but by the influence of the superstition of those who dwell there come to have less faith in the gods. Therefore, for this very reason, it is the more proper for you to assist in this business and to send it to my native city, which always receives you hospitably when you sail into the Pontus, and to contribute to its external adornment, even as you contribute to its sustenance. It cannot fail to give you pleasure to have something that has belonged to you standing in the city, and as you sail towards that city, you will delight in gazing at it.

[11] This granite monolith, which stands in the At Meidan (the Hippodrome) in Constantinople, was originally erected by Thothmes III (about 1515 BC), probably at Heliopolis. The Alexandrians obeyed Julian's orders, but the boat containing the obelisk was driven by a storm to Athens, where it remained until the Emperor Theodosius (379-395 AD) conveyed it to Constantinople. There, as an inscription base records, it took 32 days to erect; see *Palatine Anthology* 9, 682 (note of Wright).

[12] Possibly there was a martyr's grave near, at which Christians worshipped; more probably, Christian or Jewish ascetics who flourished at Alexandria and were called *therapeuts*, 'worshippers', has settled near the obelisk. Sozomen, 6. 29, says that about 2,000 ascetic monks lived in the neighbourhood of Alexandria. See also Sozomen, 1. 12 (Wright).

[13] I.e., the obelisk, which was originally dedicated to the sun (Wright).

Chronological list of authors cited

7th century BC. Homer.
Odyssey, IV, 354-360.

285-246 BC. (Reign of Ptolemaeus II Philadelphus). Theocritus.
Idylles, XV, 4-7; 44-55; 78-95. XVII, 77-105;121-130.

3rd century BC. Poseidippos of Pella.
Epigram.

2nd-1st century BC. Pseudo-Callisthenes.
Alexander Romance, 31, 32, 33.

140 BC. Polybius.
The Histories, XV, III, 25a; XV, III, 26, 27-28, 29-30, 31-32, 33.

59 BC. Diodorus Siculus (date of his stay in Alexandria).
Library of History, I, L, 6-7.

48- 47 BC. Caesar.
Civil Wars, III,111; 112.
Alexandrian War, I, II, V, VIII, IX, XIII, XV, XVII, XVIII, XIX,XXI, XXXII.

26-20 BC. Strabo (date of his travel in Egypt).
Geography, 17, 1, 6-17, 1, 10 (Casaubon, 791-795).

39- 65 AD. Lucan.
The Civil War (Pharsalia): X, 1-24; 53-60; 107-127; 439-444; 486-519; 534-546.

13-50 AD. Philo.
On the Contemplative Life: §21-24.
In Flaccum, §25-29, §33-34, §41-43,§55-57, §73-75, §92, §109-111.
On the Embassy to Gaius, §127, §129, §134-135, §150-151, §250-253, §337-338, §346.

27-79 AD. Pliny.
Natural History, V, XL, 62-63.

41-54 AD. Curtius Quintus
History of Alexander, IV, 8, 2; 8,5; X, 10, 20.

Circa 46-circa 120 AD. Plutarch.
Lives, *Alexander*, 26, 3-11; 72, 5-8.
Lives, Caesar, 49, 1-3; 49, 6-10.
Lives, Antony, 29, 1-7; 74, 1-6; 76, 1-11; 77, 1-4; 78, 4; 79, 1-4.

Circa 75-circa 160 AD. Suetonius.
The Lives of Caesars, I, LVIV; I, XVII-XVII.

Circa 105-circa 180 A.D. Arrian.
History of Alexander, III, 1-2; VII, 14, 8-10; VII, 23, 6-8.

2nd century AD. Appian.
Roman History, *The Civil Wars*, II, 89-90.

155-235 AD. Dio Cassius.
Roman History, 51, 10, 1-9 and 11, 1; 51, 18, 1.

175-250 AD. Herodian.
History of the Empire, IV, 3, 7; VII, 6, 1; IV, 8, 6-9; IV, 9,1-8.

3rd century AD. *Historia Augusta.*
Caracalla: IX, VI, 2-3.

3rd century AD (?). Achilles Tatios.
Leucippe and Clitophon, V, 1-2; V, 6-7.

330-400 AD. Ammianus Marcellinus.
XXII, 16, 7-13.

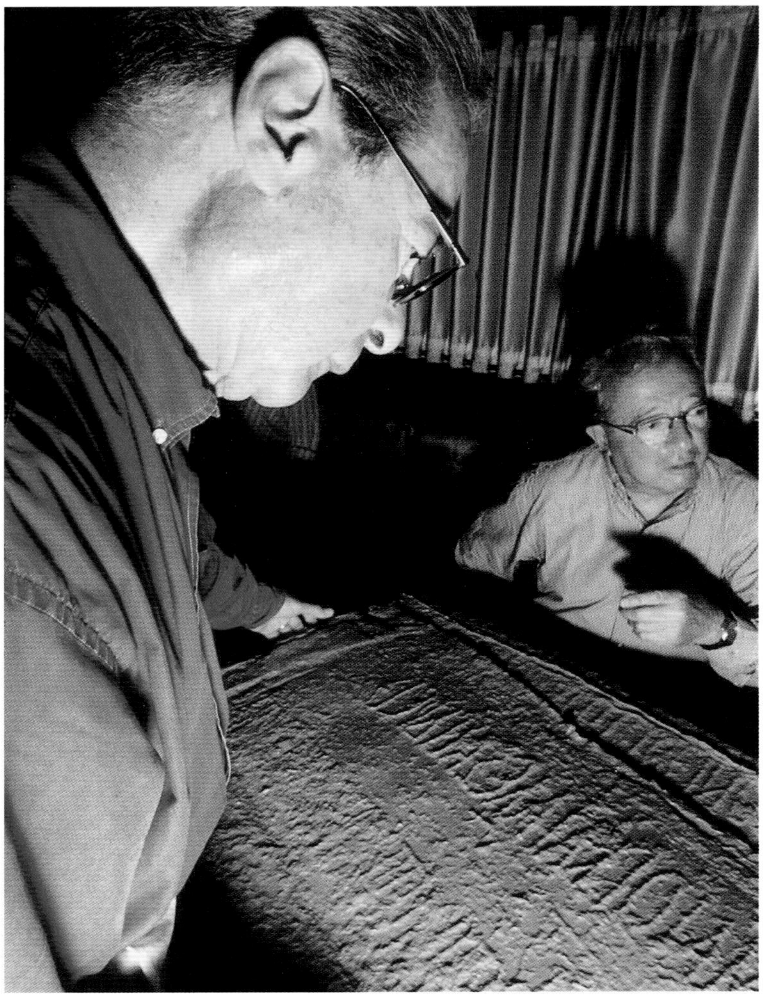

Photo 51: André and Etienne Bernand

Photo 52: applying a moulding *in situ*

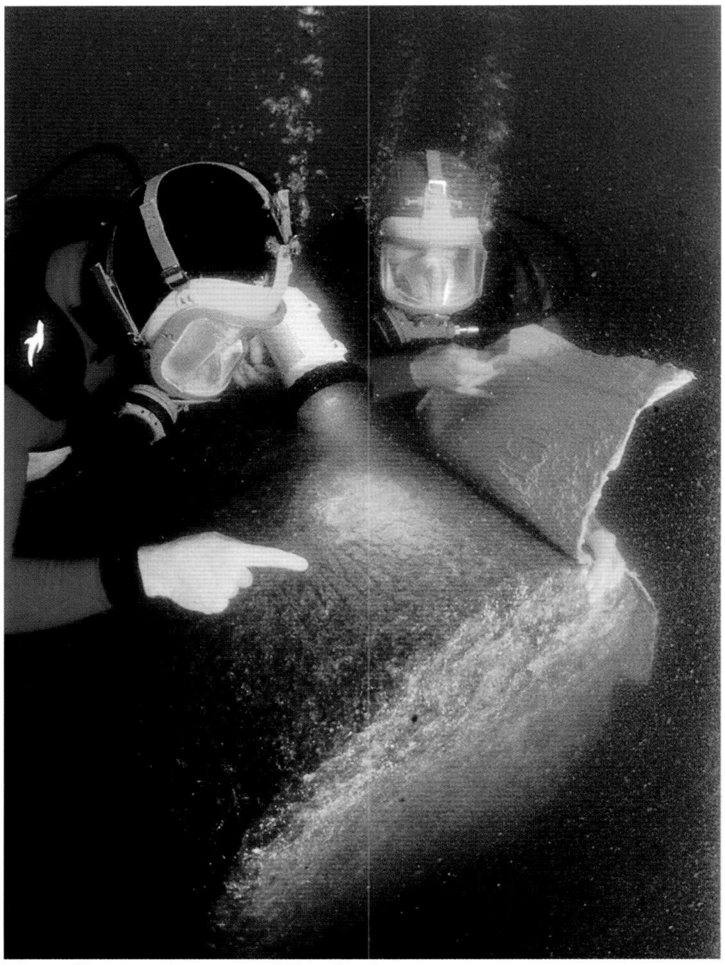

Photo 53: removing a moulding *in situ*

EPIGRAPHICAL DOCUMENTS AND CARACALLA IN EGYPT

Etienne Bernand

GREEK AND LATIN INSCRIPTIONS IN ALEXANDRIA

In order to correctly appreciate the importance of the epigraphical discoveries made by the European Institute of Underwater Archaeology (IEASM) in the Eastern Harbour of Alexandria, it is preferable to put them briefly into perspective within the Greek as well as Latin inscriptions of Alexandria as a whole.

Mémoires de Sable, Memories in the Sand, is the well-chosen title of the French translation by P. Chuvin (Paris, Armand Colin, 1988) of Naphtali Lewis' excellent book *Life in Egypt Under Roman Rule* (Oxford, Clarendon Press, 1983). This 'memory' is made up of thousands of papyri found in the dry sands, particularly in Fayum, and what they preserved of Egypt's past. This inestimable source is practically non-existent for Alexandria and the Nile delta, where a humid and muddy soil fostered decomposition of this 'paper' made from a lovely marsh plant, named *cyperus papyrus* by Linneus. This emphasises the importance of epigraphic documentation found in Alexandria. It constitutes the parlance of the stones, *saxa loquuntur,* as the Dutch scientist J. J. Hondius wrote in his very useful bibliography of Greek inscriptions (Leyden, 1938).

The giant of science Theodor Mommsen (1817-1903), Nobel prize-winner for literature in 1902, and creator of the monumental *Corpus Inscriptorium Latinarium*, quite rightly foresaw that 'the 20th century shall be that of papyrology, as the 19th was that of epigraphy.' Before the great upsurge of papyrography—a word coined in England in 1898 after a number of important discoveries were made by British researchers in the nineties—epigraphy started off with inscriptions found in Egypt, and was developed in France by Jean-Antoine Letronne (1787-1848), whom Johannes Franz (who continued work on the publication of the illustrious A. Boeckh's *Corpus Inscriptorium Graecarium*) described as *vir immortalis*. Letronne had tenure of the Chair of History and Morals at the Collège de France. He followed François Champollion, on the latter's death on March 4, 1832, to tenure of the Chair of Oriental Archaeology, and became director of the Collège de France from 1840 on. He noted in his introduction to volume I (1842) of his *Recueil des Inscriptions Grecques et Latines d'Egypte* (p. 1) that 'the history of Greek and Roman domination in Egypt is one of the most amazing, and unfortunately also one of the most unknown parts of ancient history.' At his early death at 62, he had finished only part of his ambitious project to 'know the outcome of the permanent combat between the Greek [and Roman] civilisation and that other culture which goes back to the very cradle of humanity,' working with imprints and copies obtained from others, without ever having set foot on Egyptian soil. His collection's subtitle points out the method of studying these inscriptions 'in their relation to political history, internal government, and civil and religious institutions in the country, from Alexander's conquest up to that of the Arabs (in AD 641).

Already in volume I (Introd. p. XXX), Letronne regrets that 'in the area of Canopus and Alexandria, where most of the Greek inscriptions could have been expected, hardly a dozen were found ...', and their origins still uncertain. Yet he set the accent precisely on 'the necessary link' between nascent papyrology and the inscriptions (p. XXXV) and the importance of the least of them: 'I consider all these items, even the most insignificant in appearance, as so many historical documents, some of which are completely isolated, and others linked to known facts which they explain and complete' (p. XXXIX).

We know what followed. Letronne's unfinished work was not continued for a long time and it was only in the times of L. Robert (*Op. Min. Sel.*, vol. 3, p. 1674), Letronne's distant successor in tenure of the Chair of Greek Antiques and Epigraphy at the Collège de France in 1939, that the corpus of Egyptian inscriptions was taken up again, a hundred years after Letronne, adding what had been achieved in the meantime.

For a major part of the last forty years of work on this corpus, Alexandrian inscriptions remained separate from it, for various reasons which are contained in the *Minutes of the International Centenary Colloquium* held during the Epigraphic Year (Paris, PUF 1990, 283-301). Essentially, Alexandrine epigraphy was collected in Evaristo Brecchia's *Iscrizioni greche e latine,* published in 1911 within the framework of the General Catalogue of Egyptian Antiques of the Alexandrian Museum, despite some insufficiencies. P. M. Fraser's fundamental three-volume work *Ptolemaic Alexandria* (I: *text*, II: notes, III: *Index*; Oxford, Clarendon Press, 1972)—which should be re-issued—contained, thanks to notes and comments, a veritable corpus *in ovo* of the inscriptions of Ptolemaic Alexandria.

ISLAND OF ANTIRHODOS
VESTIGES SHOWING GREEK INSCRIPTIONS

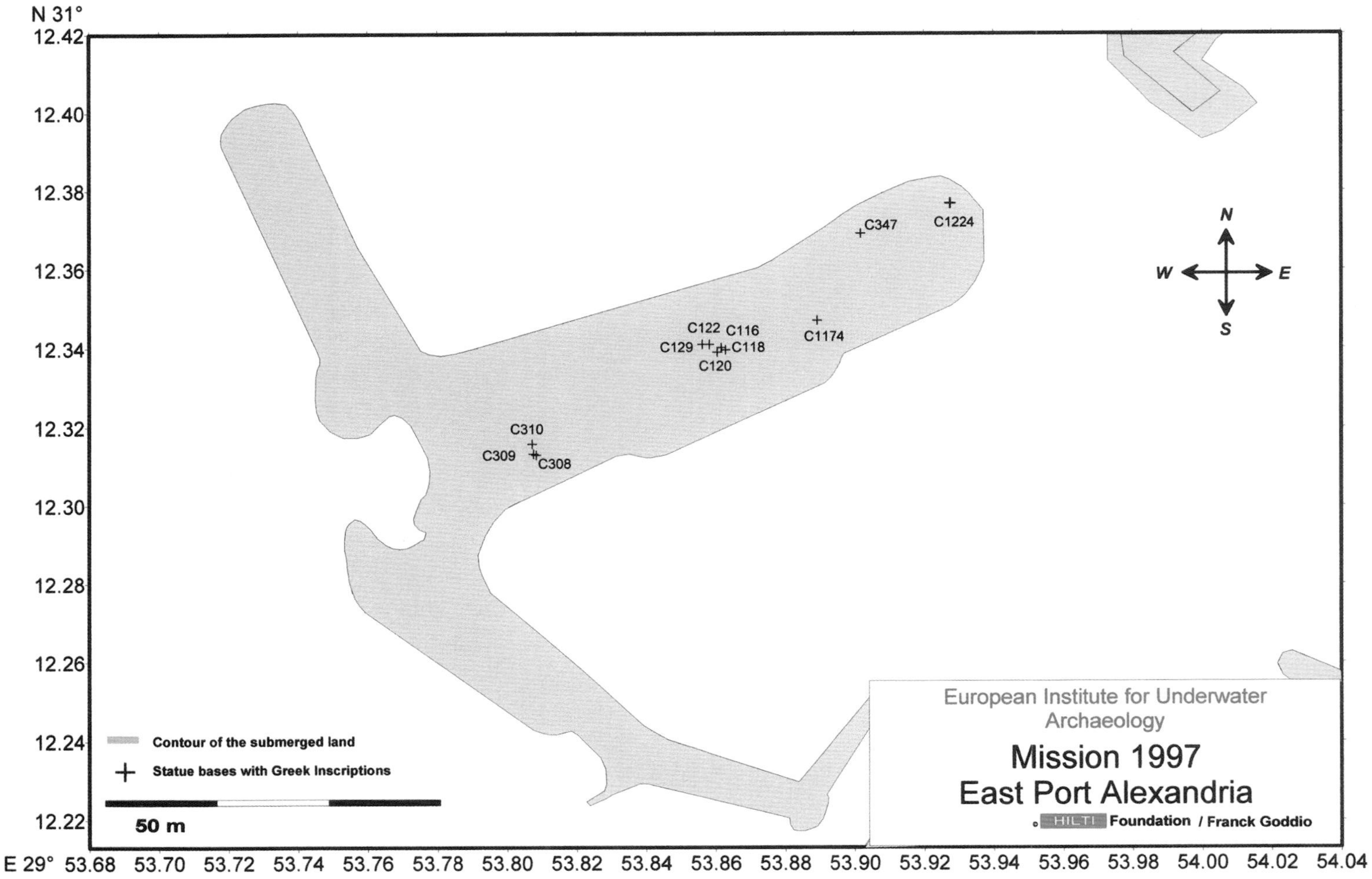

No	North Latitude	East Longitude	Length (cm)	Azimuth (degrees)	Diameter (cm)	Inscription	Width of panel (cm)	Depth under water (m)*
C116	31°12',3470	29°53',8629	137	360	105	X	107	-4,4
C118	31°12',3402	29°53',8617	100	360	105	X	100	-4, 3
C120	31°12',3390	29°53',8605	100	360	105	empty	100	-4,4
C122	31°12',3410	29°53',8582	100	39	105	empty	100	-4,2
C129	31°12',3410	29°53',8561	110	140	105	X	98	-4,3
C308	31°12',3130	29°53',8084	160	10	105	X	110	-4,8
C309	31°12',3133	29°53',8076	85	330	105	X	95	-4,7
C310	31°12',3158	29°53',8072	155	170	105	X	95	-4,8
C347	31°12',3691	29°53',9018	120	10	105	X	90	-5,4
C1174	31°12',3470	29°53',8892	135	225	105	X	113	-4,5
N1224	31°12',3771	29°53',9278	20x20	_	_	X	no panel	-5,7

* the depths in metres were measured at low tides (point Zero at Zero level of lowest tide)

But all these texts, which had often been studied separately, needed to be collected into one volume, rendering them more easily accessible, and adding up-to-date comments. This I have now completed, and the corpus is ready for printing. For the Roman period, the *Recueil des inscriptions grecques et latines (non funéraires) d'Alexandrie impériale (century I-III AD)* was handsomely published by F. Kayser (IFAO, 1994) and represents an incomparable working tool. This was not yet published when Barbara Tkaczow, in her *Topography of Ancient Alexandria* (Warsaw, 1993), established a list of inscriptions of the Roman period (*Catalogue of Objects,* nos. 205-238), and of Ptolemaic inscriptions (nos. 34-49) which need to be completed.

Whether for the Ptolemaic or the imperial period, any elaboration on the corpus of Greek inscriptions in Alexandria requires particular attention to their precise origins. A sizeable number of epigraphic texts are, in fact, presented by earlier writers as stemming from Alexandria because they found their way into the Graeco-Roman Museum, or because they came out of private collections of residents in Alexandria, or even merely from acquisitions made there. This, however, is insufficient proof of Alexandrine origin. It is therefore preferable to exclude from the Alexandrine corpus such inscriptions as are attributed to the city by conjecture, particularly those which show a question mark about their origins in Brecchia's catalogue.

One example will suffice: Neurotsos suggests in his *Ancient Alexandria*, p. 59, that there was a temple dedicated to Isis Lochias, 'who presides over deliveries', at the tip of Cape Lochias (Silsileh Point) and that 'inscriptions attest to this' (*sic*). However, he cites no epigraphic text, for excellent reason, because there is no known dedication from Alexandria or anywhere else, concerning an Isis Lochias, neither from Ptolemaic nor from imperial times.

Neurotsos' claim is based on an interpretation from Letronne (*Recueil* I, 1842, p. 377-380, no. XXVIII) of an inscription from Akôris, i.e., Tehna el Djebel, in Central Egypt (now in E. Bernand, *Inscr. gr. et lat. d'Akôris* [IFAO, 1988], p. 1-4, no. 1). There, Letronne had thought he detected an Isis Lochias, but which was, in fact, an Isis Mochias, the epithet being attributable to a place, as attested by the existence of the topographical attribute *Mochites* in the Hermopolite nome. In the *addenda* to his *Recueil*, Vol. II (1848), p. 536, Letronne had corrected this interpretation, having perfectly understood that the Isis from Akôris bore a toponymic epithet.

Neurotsos' error spread, however: Alexandre-Max de Zogheb, *Etudes sur l'ancienne Alexandrie* (Paris, 1910), p. 192-193, states that an Isis Lochias temple stood on the site of the same name, and adds it to his map 'as said in the inscriptions' (*sic*) and this item became generally accepted (F. Dunand, *Le culte d'Isis* [Brill, 1973], p. 111, no. 1).

A. Adriani (*Repertorio, Serie C* [1964], *Glossario*, p. 226, *s. v.* Lochias, and p. 251, no. 7) related to this an inscription of imperial times in Beroia in Macedonia (J. M. R. Cormack, *ABSA* 41 [1940-45], p. 105-106; *SEG* XII, no. 316; see also F. Dunand, *op. cit.* vol. II, p. 190 and vol. III, p. 214), which mentions an Isis Lochias, but of course without any indication that any Isis of that name existed in Alexandria (P. M. Fraser, *Ptolemaic Alexandria,* Vol. II, [1972], p. 33, note 81; *BGU* XVI, 1995, p. 2663). The affirmation that the name of Cape Lochias for Silsileh Point might have its origin in an Isis Lochias temple is not sustained by any epigraphic document, and thus remains pure hypothesis. J. Yoyotte (*Strabon, Le voyage en Egypte,* Paris, 1977, p. 88, no. 104), remains cautious and merely cites Adriani's connection with the Beroia inscription.

A dedication to Isis from imperial days had been found on a small limestone column near Cape Lochias, according to E. Brecchia, who indicates '*Mazarita, non lungi da Capo Lochias*' as its origin in *ASAE* 7, 1906, p. 146, and '*forte Silsileh, presso Capo Lochias*' in his *Iscrizioni* (1911), no. 129 (see also B. Tkaczow, *op. cit.*, p. 271, *Cat. of Obj., no.* 230). But the Isis epithet, read erroneously by Brecchia, is surely *myrionymos*, 'of ten thousand names', which is well documented throughout Egypt during the imperial period, as F. Kayser, *loc. cit., no.* 60 and plate XXXII, recognised.

The corpus of Alexandrine epitaphs of Ptolemaic and Roman times still remains to be compiled. It would certainly contribute a documentary basis to the study of the Alexandrian population, particularly under an onomastic approach. I have only compiled the metric epitaphs, the most 'speaking' ones, so far, in *Metric Inscriptions of Graeco-Roman Egypt* (Annales Littéraires de l'Université de Besançon, Vol. 98, Diffusion Les Belles Lettres, 1969), a great part of which are used in *Alexandrie la Grande* (Hachette, 1998).

At the end of this short outline of epigraphic documentation from Alexandria, one is astonished, as Letronne already was, by the relatively small number of inscriptions of indisputably Alexandrian origin which were so far discovered: this capital site has so far rendered 79 non-funerary inscriptions (of which 11 are insignificant fragments) spanning the entire period from the foundation of Alexandria in 331 BC to the Roman conquest in 30 BC, and a further 128 non-funerary inscriptions of imperial times between the 1st and 3rd century AD. In this context, the discovery of eight new inscriptions, and the possibility of finding additional ones through the methodical and thorough exploration carried out by the IEASM acquires the utmost importance.

THE IEASM'S EPIGRAPHIC DISCOVERIES

The IEASM's divers found all eight inscriptions in 1997 on the central esplanade of the main section of Antirhodos Island, where Franck Goddio established their precise

Photo 54: Berlin Medallion (Staatliche Museen, 31329). The Emperor Septimus Severus, his wife Julia Domna, and their sons, Caracalla and Geta, the latter's face erased.

Photo 55: Caracalla; marble, height 28 cm. Palazzo dei Conservatori, Via dei Fori Imperiali, Rome.

positions and contours (see chart, p. 144) with the help of a newly developed technology. Three of these (C116, C118, C129) were found in the central area, close to the two shafts containing fragments of panels without inscription. The segment containing C1174 was found at the north-eastern tip of the esplanade. Three inscriptions (C308, C309, C310) were lying on the south-western pavement, next to three shafts of red granite, 100 cm. in diameter, bare of inscriptions. Another one (C347) was discovered at the eastern tip of the island, together with a fragment of white marble (N1224) containing only a few letters that cannot be restored. Franck Goddio's chart positions these items with the utmost precision, and his table indicates dimensions of the columns with inscriptions, as well as the depths at which they were found.

With the exception of the marble fragment (20 by 20 cm), all inscriptions are engraved on panels on the shafts of red granite columns, the longest (C308) measuring 160 cm, the shortest (C309) 85 cm; the others have lengths between these two, usually above one meter. Their diameter is uniformly of 105 cm. The lettering is tight, narrow, and stretched to 8-12 cm. height, characteristic for the early 3rd century AD. One single text (C116) is dated from the reign of Commodus. All others belong in the reign of Caracalla, which, officially and fictitiously, lasted 25 years.

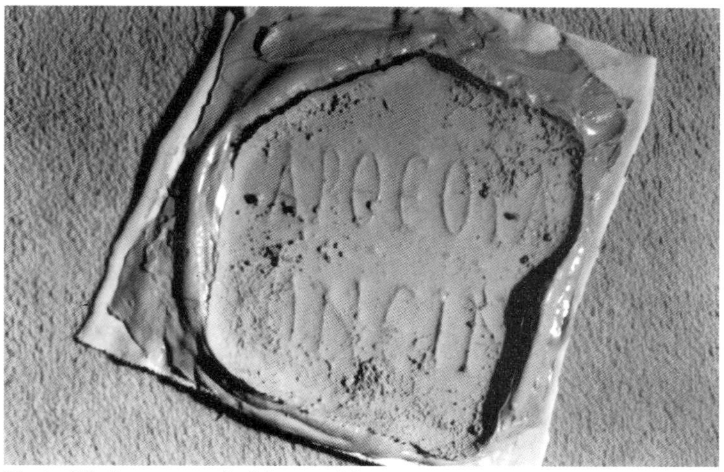

Photo 56: fragment of white marble

(year I: early April-28 August, 193; year 25: 29 August, 216-8 April, 217). As in the case of Commodus, the official count includes the reign of his father Septimus Severus (193-211). We know that at the latter's death (4 February, 211), Caracalla shared power for one year with his brother Geta, who was assassinated in the arms of his mother Julia Domna in February 212. Caracalla's own reign lasted only from that date to his own assassination on April 8, 217.

No 1: Column C116 carries the oldest inscription, which goes back to the reign of Commodus (180-193). It is engraved in a panel, the upper part of which has disappeared. Length of the shaft is 137 cm, the diameter 105 cm; the letters are 9-10 cm. high, line space 10 cm. The first line has been completely effaced by hammering; the third one contains only the day and month in the centre of the line.

[Μ. Αὐρήλιον Κόμμοδον 'Αντωνῖνον Σεβαστὸν]
ἐπὶ Κοΐντῳ Τινηΐῳ Δημητρίῳ, ἐπάρχῳ Αἰγύπτου,
Τῦβι ϛʹ.

Photo 57: moulding C116

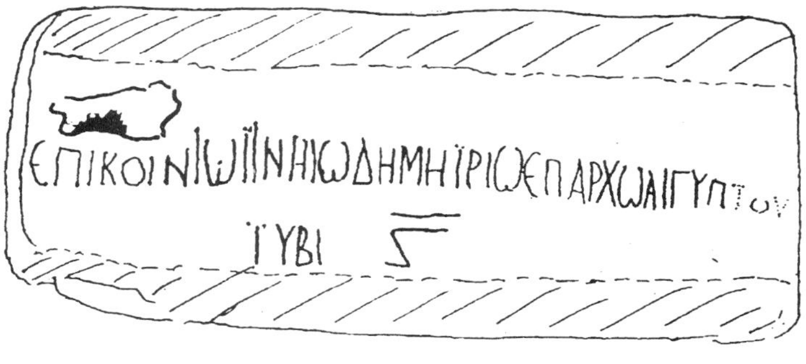

M(arcus) Aurelius Commodus Antoninus Augustus, under Quintus Tinaeus Demetrius, prefect of Egypt, the 6th Tubi (1-2 January).

The inscription can be dated precisely because of the mention of the prefect of Egypt, Quintus Tinaeus Demetrius, whom we know from papyrus documents to have filled this office in 189-190.[1] It is the first source

[1] A. Stein, *Präfekte* (1950), 103-104; O. Renmuth, *A Working List of the Prefects of Egypt*, 1967, 102-104; P. Bureth in *ANRW*, 11, 10, I (1988), 489, as well as G. Bastianini, *ibid.*, Add. 1973-1985, p. 511.

indicating the prefect's *praenomen* spelt entirely, however, instead of a mere abbreviation.

The column probably supported a statue of emperor Commodus, no doubt with a capital like those in the Graeco-Roman Museum in Alexandria. The emperor's name, under *damnatio memoriae,* is hammered flat according to well-known custom, later to be rehabilitated (E. Van t'Dack, *CdE* LXV, 1990, 301). The title of emperor Commodus, *M. Aurelius Commodus Antoninus,* regularly appearing in the Greek texts of Egypt (Kayser, no. 10), attests to a date between 180 and 190.

The prefect's official title was *praefectus Alexandreae et Aegypti*, or shorter *praefectus Aegypti (eparchos Aigyptou* in Greek). He was chosen by the emperor from among his knights, and was his trusted representative in the province. His was in the top echelon in the hierarchy of *equites,* just below the praetorian prefect which was the highest charge, and certain Egyptian prefects subsequently acceded to it. He remained in place at the emperor's will, usually for the duration of one or two years, but rarely for five, six, or seven. He was in charge of the government of the province in the emperor's name. He fulfilled his legislative tasks by promulgating edicts, and pronounced justice throughout the country by holding regular civil and criminal courts at fixed dates (*conventus, dialogismos*) in Alexandria, Pelusis, and Memphis. During such sessions, he received complaints from the population and examined the accounts and activities of the local administrators.[2] The prefect also controlled the Roman legions stationed in Egypt.[3] This office of high trust must have been particularly difficult to hold during the last years of Commodus' reign, in the sulphurous atmosphere of the day, constantly fed and maintained by the emperor's mental disorders.

No 2: (C129). This fragment shows the end of an inscription of which the entire first part has disappeared, leaving only a single word. It was engraved on a panel of 98 cm. width, the inscription is 54 cm. wide, the letters 10 cm. high. The lettering indicates the beginning of the 3rd century. It says:

....
...Λυκοπολείτης...
...*de Lykopolis*...

The two initial letters are hard to read, justifying some hesitation between NI and ΛΥ, i.e., between Nikopoleites and Lykopoleites. But apart from the fact that there is no Nikopoleites in Egypt, a photograph of the impression clearly points toward Lykopolis.

Photo 58: moulding C129

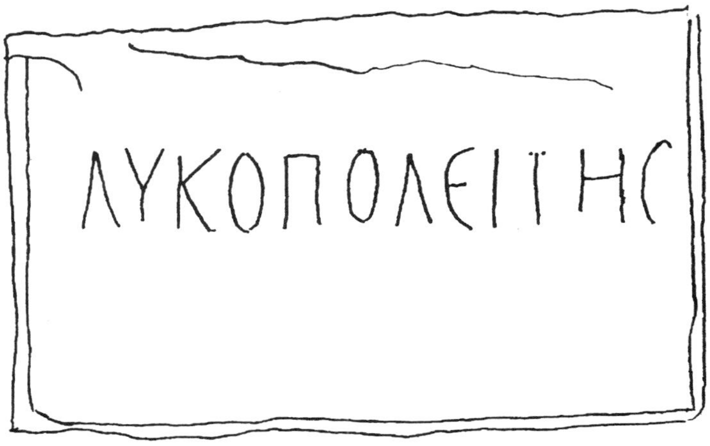

Does it refer to the Lykopolis of the Busiris region in the Delta, or the town of the same name on the borderline between Middle and Upper Egypt, i.e., Asiut? The Greeks called this 'Wolf City' because of its principal local divinity Wepwawet, the black jackal-headed god mostly appearing in a funereal context, like Anubis. According to a generally accepted tradition, Asuit is said to have been the home of the famous neoplatonic philosopher Plotinus (born in 205 AD), who in his youth followed the teachings of the *rhetors* of Alexandria. This latter hypothesis about the origin is no less plausible than the first one, according to Jean Yoyotte. Lycopolitans did sojourn in Alexandria, e.g. a young man of sixteen from Lykopolis, known by a metric inscription, who 'lost his life on the island of Pharos', where he may well have been studying.[4]

All the other inscriptions discovered by the IEASM concern the reign of Caracalla.

Three among these contain merely that emperor's titles, without any indication as to the person (or persons) who dedicated them. It must be assumed that this was a foregone conclusion for anyone who read the inscription, therefore it could only have been the local community, i. e., the city.[5]

[2] Fundamental study by Wilcken, *Archiv. f. Pap.* 4, 1908, 366-422, completed by 6 (1920), 373-376, 423; see also M. Sartre, *L'Orient Romain* (Seuil, 1991), 416-418; J. Mélèze-Modrzcjewski, ap. *Rome et l'Intégration de l'Empire,* I, 2 (PUF, 199), 452-455.

[3] H. Devijver, 'L'Egypte et l'histoire de l'armée romaine', in *Actes de Bologne,* 1989, 38-41.

[4] E. Bernand, *Inscriptions metriques de l'Egypte Gréco-romaine,* 1969, no. 73, and *IG de l'Egypte et de Nubie au Musée du Louvre*, CNRS, 1992, no. 93.

[5] On the ellipsis of the subject in the epigraphy of lintels during imperial times, see E. Bernand, *Hommage à L. Lerat,* Besançon, 1984, 83-84; inversely, for mention of the *polis* in imperial Alexandrian dedications, see F. Kayser, nos. 12, 14, 29, 30, 31, 42, 117.

No 3: (C308). The inscription is engraved on a panel of 110 cm. width. Dimensions of the inscription: 56 cm. high, 110 cm. large, height of the letters 8 cm, line space 3 cm.

Photo 59: C308, lines 1-5.

Photo 60: C308, lines 5-8.

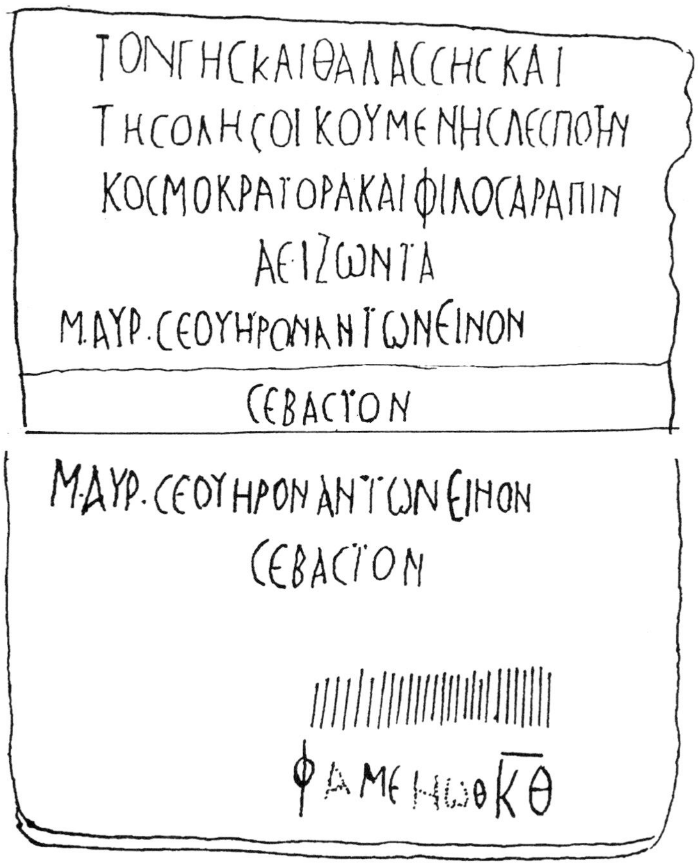

C308

Τὸν γῆς καὶ θαλάσσης καὶ
τῆς ὅλης οἰκουμένης δεσπότην,
κοσμοκράτορα καὶ φιλοσάραπιν
ἀεὶ ζῶντα
M. Αὐρ. Σεουῆρον 'Αντωνεῖνον
Σεβαστόν.
vacat
....
φαμεὼθ κθ΄.

(In honour of) the master of Earth, Sea and all the inhabited world, sovereign of the universe, adorer of Sarapis, living eternally, M(arcus) Aur(elius) Severus Antoninus Augustus ... the 25 Phamenoth (=25 March).

No 4: (C309). The inscription is engraved on a panel 95 cm. wide. Dimensions of the inscription: height 75 cm, width 90 cm, height of letters 10-12 cm, line space 4 cm.

Photo 61: C309

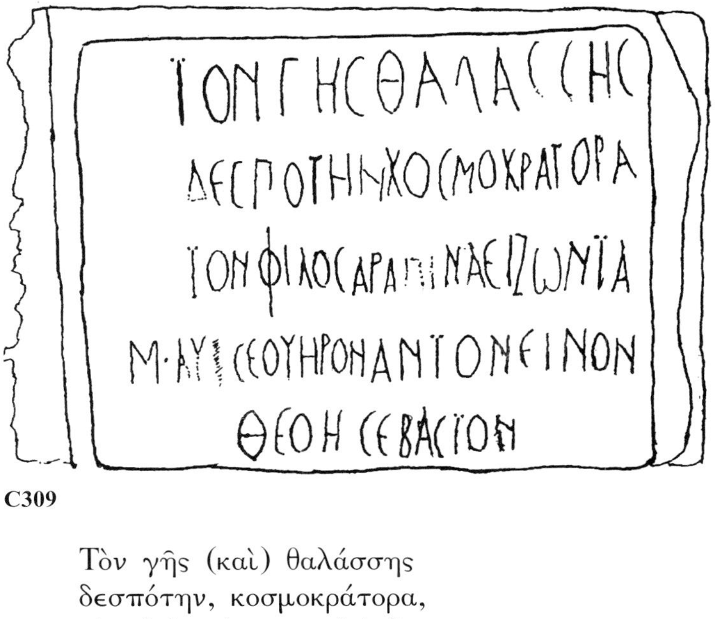

C309

Τὸν γῆς (καὶ) θαλάσσης
δεσπότην, κοσμοκράτορα,
τὸν φιλοσάραπιν, ἀεὶ ζῶντα
M. Αὐρ. Σεουῆρον 'Αντωνεῖνον
θεὸν Σεβαστόν.

(In honour of) the master of Earth and Sea, sovereign of the universe, adorer of Sarapis, eternally living, M(arcus) Aur(elius) Severus Antoninus, god Augustus.

No 5: (C118). The inscription in a panel of 100 cm. contains the same text as the one on column 309. Its measurements and disposition are precisely the same as the preceding inscription. The linking prefix (1.1) is omitted in both cases, as is the disposition in *ekthesis* of the *praenomen* (M) (on line 4), which is intact, as well as the *nomen*.

The three other dedications concerning Caracalla mention the dedicants, designated as 'Romans and Alexandrians'.

No 6: (C310). The panel is 95 cm. large; the inscription contains seven lines. Line 5 has been hammered flat over a length of about fifteen letters in the second part. Line 6 is much erased but readable with a slide projector. Height of the first four lines: 56 cm; height of the three last lines: 40 cm. Width: 84 to 86 cm, height of the letters 10 cm; line space 3 cm. Lacking space in the epigraphic field, the engraver was forced to squeeze up the lettering of line 4, and to use abbreviations.

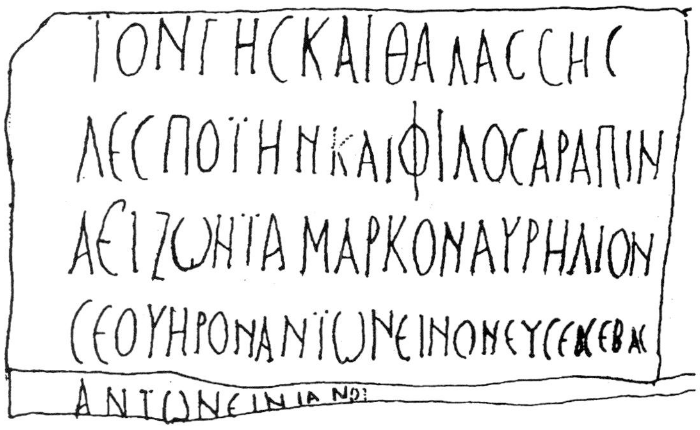

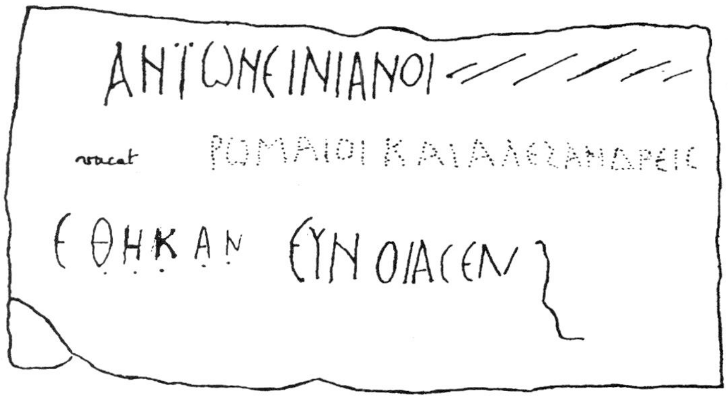

C310

Photo 62: C310, lines 1-4.

Photo 63: C310, lines 5-7.

Τὸν γῆς καὶ θαλάσσης
δεσπότην καὶ φιλοσάραπιν
ἀεὶ ζῶντα, Μᾶρκον Αὐρήλιον
Σεουῆρον Ἀντωνεῖνον Εὐσεβ(ῆν) Σεβασ(τὸν)
Ἀντωνειν̣ιανοὶ ......
    Ῥ[ω]μαῖοι καὶ Ἀλεξανδρεῖς
ἔθη̣κ̣αν vac. εὐνοίας ἕν[εκεν]

(In honour of) the master of Earth and Sea, adorer of Sarapis, eternally living, M(arcus) Aur(elius) Severus Antoninus, Pious Augustus, the Antoninians ... Romans and Alexandrians, have dedicated (the statue), because of his devotion.

No 7: (C1174). Panel width 113 cm; inscription height 86 cm, width 110 cm, letter height 11 cm, line space 4-5 cm. The second half of line 4 has been hammered flat over some 20 letters. A leaf separates the two words on line 5. After the indication of the year, which itself has disappeared, the emperor's designation has been destroyed. On line 7, there only remains the *mu* of the *praenomen* and the first three letters of the *nomen*.

Photo 64: C1174

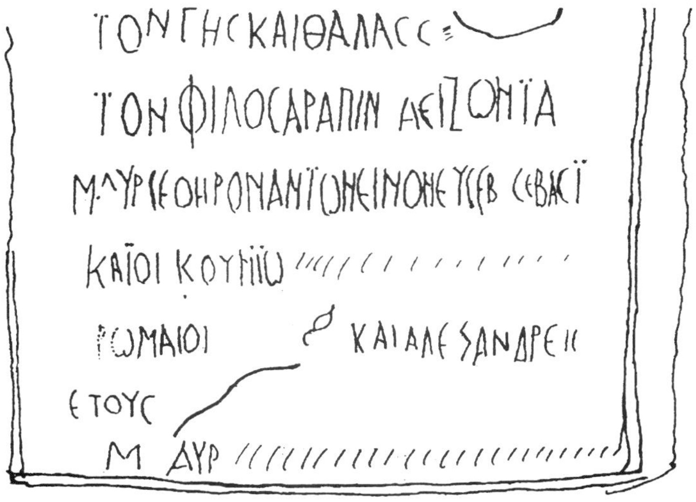

C1174, lines 1-7

Τὸν γῆς καὶ θαλάσσ[ης δεσπότην]
τὸν φιλοσάραπιν ἀεὶ ζῶντα
Μ.Αὐρ.Σεουῆρον 'Αντωνεῖνον
Εὐσεβ(ῆν) Σεβαστ(όν)
κατοικούντω[ν..................]
'Ρωμαῖοι *feuille* καὶ 'Αλεξανδρεῖς
ἔτους. [Αὐτοκράτορος Καίσαρος]
Μ. Αὐρ[ηλίου 'Αντωνίνου].

(In honour of) the master of Earth and Sea, adorer of Sarapis, eternally living, M(arcus) Aur(elius) Severus Antoninus, Pious, Augustus, among the residents of ... Romans and Alexandrians, in the year (?) of the emperor Caesar M(arcus) Aurelius Antoninus.

No 8: (C347). Panel width 90 cm. The shaft is broken in the upper part, with only one line left which contains identification of the dedicants and the line which first indicates the year, followed by the emperor's name, which has been destroyed. But the shortened *praenomen* can be read, as well as the initial *alpha* of the emperor's *nomen*.

Photo 65: C347

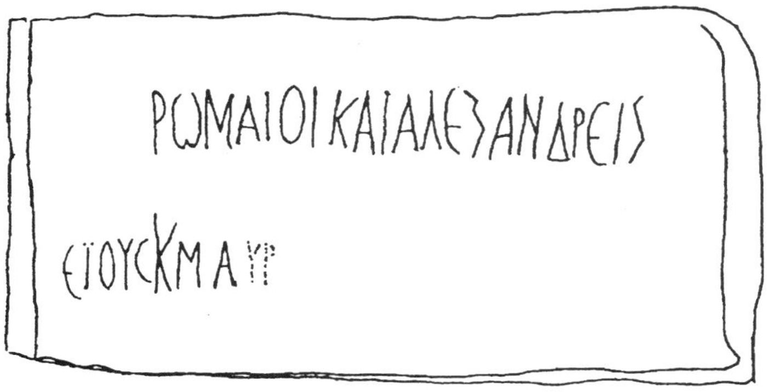

'Ρωμαῖοι καὶ 'Αλεξανδρεῖς
ἔτους κ´ Μ. Α[ὐρ. Σεουήρου 'Αντωνίνου]

The Romans and Alexandrians, in the year 20 of M(arcus) Aur(elius) Severus Antoninus (213 AD)

Nb: transcription and translation by A. and E. Bernand; facsimiles by André Bernand.

COMMENTARY: The emperor's title and the dedicants' designation in these texts are of the utmost interest.

THE EMPEROR'S TITLES: The late R. Bloch (*L'épigraphie latine*, 1952, p. 50), stated that 'a precise study on the history of imperial denominations and titles would be very precious ... because these titles, despite their stable and almost hieratic character, underwent modifications which often depended on the deepest thoughts and politics of the successive emperors.' In other words, the way the emperors composed their titles reflect in a certain way the image that their bearers wished to cast upon their subjects. In the present case, it allows us to perceive Caracalla's personality.

The obligatory and traditional theme of universal Roman domination[6] is expressed with particular insistence in his titulature, first by using the formula ὁ γῆς καὶ θαλάσσης δεσπότης *'master of Earth and Sea'* (nos. 3 and 7), which is very frequent in Caracalla's titles, especially after promulgation of the *Constitutio Antoniana* of 212.[7] The title had already been awarded to Trajan in an honorific inscription in Tyas on the northern shore of the Black Sea, dated 117 or 118 (*SEG* XXXIII, 1983, 619). It appears in Egypt after 161.[8]

The same idea is then taken up again and amplified by the mention (no. 3) of the *oikumenè (orbis terrarum)*, the 'inhabited, i.e. 'civilised' earth. The title of 'saviour of the inhabited earth' reappears frequently in Caracalla's titles,[9] as he aspired to universal kingship in imitation of Alexander, his chosen model. Marcus Aurelius, whose name Caracalla bore, had already received the title of σωτὴρ καὶ εὐεργέτης τῆς ὅλης οἰκουμένης[10]. One single Alexandrian dedication to Caracalla (Kayser, no. 13) adds ὅλης before οἰκουμένης.

The new dedication (no. 3) now provides a second example.

Lastly, the title of *kosmokratôr* (nos. 3 and 5) 'sovereign of the universe', further emphasises the previous designations and attracts attention. It is rarely claimed by emperors, but Marcus Aurelius and Lucius Verus are both called οἱ θειότατοι κοσμοκράτορες Σεβαστοί in a bilingual dedication (in Greek and Nabataean) found in Rawwafa (north-western Saudi Arabia), dated from 116-169.[11] In Caracalla's case,[12] and in conjunction with *philosarapis*, the epithet takes on a particular meaning, underlining the emperor's devotion to Serapis as the god of health, who from 212[13] on is represented each year on the reverse side of his coins: the emperor adopts the god's own epithet,[14] especially in an inscription in the Mithraeum in the Baths of Caracalla in Rome: 'Unique (is) Zeus Sarapis Helios, invincible master of the world.'[15]

Until now, only one single dedication to Caracalla which included the title of *philosarapis* (Kayser, no. 14) was known in Alexandria. The dedications found in the Eastern Harbour provide five more examples. R. Turcan (*ANWR* II, 16, 2 [1978], 1059) uses the word in the passive sense, as 'beloved by Sarapis',[16] and interprets it as a local and particular use of the notion implied in the superlative *theophilestatos,* which qualifies all emperors in the phrasing of the 3rd century AD. The papyrus found in Touna el Djebel (the necropolis of Hermopolis Magna) by Sami Gabra, and published by P. Benoit and J. Schwartz (*Etudes de Pap.* 7, 1948, 17-33)[17] seems to indicate—if the reading (Col. I, line 3) is correct— that it is Serapis who loves the emperor. G. Wagner[18] also takes the word in the passive sense, 'dear to Serapis' in the context of an inscription in Douch (*SEG* XXXVIII, 1988, 1806), unless this is an anthroponym specific to the Great Oasis. But the epithet may well be taken in the active sense of 'he who loves Sarapis' (*Dict. LSJ*), i.e., 'the adorer of Sarapis' (F. Kayser, no. 14).

There are a number of testimonials as to Caracalla's devotion to Serapis.[19] The most spectacular manifestation is the emperor's colossal temple dedicated to that god[20] on the Quirinal in Rome itself.

The five new dedications (nos. 3 to 7) use a so far unknown expression to describe the traditional notion of the emperor's eternity,[21] which may also be expressed by the adjective *aiônios (perpetuus)*, which is rarely present in Caracalla's titles (Mastino p. 78), but which reappears in titles in native idioms of a certain number of emperors.[22]

---

[6] Claude Nicolet, *L'Inventaire du Monde*, 1988, p. 43 ff. and p. 234, no. 8.

[7] A. Mastino, *Le titolature di Caracalla e Geta attraverso le Iserzioni,* Bologna, 1981, p. 72-73.

[8] K.A. Worp and D. Hagedorn, 'Von "kurios' zu 'despotes"; Eine Bemerkung zur Kaiser-Titulatur im 3/4 Jhdt', in *ZPE 39,* 1980, 166-167.

[9] A. Mastino, *op. cit.*, p. 72 and 132 ff.

[10] *IGRR* I, 1096; *SB* I, 176; Brecchia, *Iscrizioni*, no. 76 (Khôm Khanziri, Pachnemunis); bibliography in A. Bernand, *Delta* (1070), p. 910, no. 2. See also *SEG* II, 870; *SB* 6674 (Kômel-Wahal), in the Alexandria Museum, inv. 21121.

[11] Published by J. T. Milik, *Bull. Inst. Arch. Univ. London* 10, (1972), 54-57; studied by G. Bowersock, *Hommage à Claire Préaux,* 1975, 513-522 (*Bull. épigr. REG* 1976, 739).

[12] Abd el Mohsen el-Khachab, 'O Karakallos Kosmokratôr', *JEA* 47 (1961), 119-133.

[13] R. Turcan, 'Le culte impérial au IIIe siècle', *ANRW* II, 16, 2 (1978), 1059; *idem*, *Les cultes orientaux dans le monde romain,* 1989, 94.

[14] A. Mastino, *Le titolature di Caracalla* (1981), p. 63, no. 262 (bibliography).

[15] L. Moretti, *IGUR* I, (1968), no. 194; L. Vidman, *Sylloge* (1969) no. 389. On *Sarapis kosmokratôr* and *Isis kosmokratèira* see P. Hombert, *Ant. Class. XIV,* 1945, 319-329.

[16] R. Turcan, *Les cultes orientaux,* 1989, p. 94, also translated as 'beloved by Serapis'.

[17] H. A. Musurillo, *Acts of the Pagan Martyr,* Oxford, 1954, XVIII: *Acta Heracliti;* idem, *Acta Alexandrinorum,* Teubner, 1961, 61-64, XVIII.

[18] G. Wagner, *Les oasis d'Egypte,* 1987, p. 55-56.

[19] W. Hornbustel, *Sarapis*, 1973, index 427, *s.v.* Caracalla.

[20] M. Malaise, *Inventaire préliminaire*, p. 180 ff, (Roma, 334-336); temple dedication in L. Vidman, *Sylloge*, no. 374.

[21] On the formulae relating to the emperors' eternity see H. U. Instinsky, *Hermes*, 77, (1942), 325, 329, 339-344.

[22] J-Cl. Grenier, *Les titulatures des empereurs romains dans les documents en langue egyptienne,* Brussels, 1989, p. 99.

Photo 66: Caracalla as pharaoh. Whitish limestone. Height 1.42 m. Origin: Mendes. Cairo Museum, no. 702

According to R. Turcan (*ANRW* II, 16, 2, 1043 and no. 759), 'it is in the times of the Severus emperors that the doctrine of the eternity of the Roman emperors takes root, with dynastic considerations in mind.'

The name of the emperor appears in various forms in four inscriptions:

M. Αὐρ. Σεουῆρος Ἀντωνεῖνος Σεβαστός (no. 3)
M. Αὐρ. Σεουῆρος Ἀντωνεῖνος θεὸς Σεβαστός (nos 4-5)
Μᾶρκος Αὐρήλιος Σεουῆρος Ἀντωνεῖνος Εὐσεβ(ής) Σεβαστ(ός) (no.6),
the *praenomen* and *nomen* not being abbreviated,
M. Αὐρ. Σεουῆρος Ἀντωνεῖνος Εὐσεβ(ής) Σεβαστ(ός) (no. 7).

In two inscriptions (no. 7, lines 6-7 and no. 8), the name of the emperor must be reconstructed from the *praenomen* and those letters of the *nomen* which remain on the stone, although the name of Caracalla has been hammered out, which is rare (Mastino, *op. cit.* p. 78 and no. 402). The fact implies *damnatio memoriae* of the emperor's name, no doubt following the bloody repression of the disorders which took place in Alexandria during Caracalla's visit between November-December 215 and March-April 216.

The year is mentioned on two inscriptions. In one of them (no. 7), the figure has disappeared, in the other one it subsists, indicating the year 20 of the reign (to count from Septimus Severus), i.e., the year 213. This is the only text that is dated with precision (no. 8).

As the eldest son of Septimus Severus—who was the first emperor of North African origin—and of his second wife Julia Domna, a Syrian princess, Caracalla was born in Lyon in 188 and initially bore the name of his maternal grandfather Julius Bassianus, who was Grand Priest of Baal at Amisus in what is today northern Turkey. In 195, Septimus Severus used a fictitious adoption to declare himself the son of Marcus Aurelius and brother to Commodus, and made his son change his name on that occasion. Proclaimed Caesar in 196, the young son then changed his name to Marcus Aurelius, *Marcus Aurelius Antoninus*, thus confirming the (fictitious) hereditary character of imperial power.[23]

On 28 June, 198, the date of his *dies imperii* (P. Herz, *ZPE* 31 [1978], 286), he received the title of *Augustus* (*Sebastos* in Greek), which the emperors used as *cognomen*. His younger brother, born on March 27, 189, called P. Septimus Geta, bore his paternal grandfather's *cognomen*. He was named Caesar in 198, and Augustus in 209. From 209 to 211, the empire was thus headed by three Augusti, the third being soon eliminated: his elder brother assassinated him on 26 December, 211 or, according to tradition, on 27 February, 212, and struck his images with *damnatio memoriae.*[24]

After his father's death (4 February, 211), Caracalla, surnamed after a military overcoat, added the surname of *Severus* to his official denomination (P. Kneissl, *Die Siegestitulatur der römischen Kaiser [Hypomnemata 23]*, Göttingen, 1969, 158-159).

Inscriptions nos. 6 and 7 are the only ones to add *Eusebios* to Caracalla's titles, abridged due to lack of space; usually, this precedes *Sebastos*, whereas the formula *Sebastos Eusebios* is official under Antoninus Pius. E. van t'Dack (*CdE* 65, 1990, 298-301), following P. J. Siipesteijn, uses this instance to attribute an inscription in Akoris (*IGL d'Akôris* [1988], no. 13) to Commodus and not to Caracalla.

The inscription no. 4, on the shaft of column C309, exactly reproduced on shaft C118 (no. 5) presents a variation which appears to be unique in Caracalla's titulature in Egypt, θεὸν Σεβαστόν, after the emperor's names.

In his relations to his subjects, the emperor does not, of course, normally appear as a 'god'. It is they who call him thus, rather, as a way of expressing their veneration towards him who holds supreme power. As Paul Veyne (*Le pain et le cirque,* 1976, p. 562-3) writes, 'in the Graeco-Roman world, adoration of the sovereign is more often an initiative coming from the subjects, or rather from the autonomous townships, and not due to a decree issued by the ruler himself. The emperor does not demand adoration, as the saying goes a little loosely, he lets them adore him ...' In the summary of his course at the Collège de France (*Ann. du CdF,* 1993-94, p. 803), the same scholar commented on the question of 'what is a Roman emperor?' that 'the emperor was a god by metaphor', and notes particularly that private letters (Mitteis-Wilcken, *Papyruskunde* I, 1, p. 117) never mention an emperor's divinity and that there does not exist a single *ex voto* dedicated to him (A. D. Nock, *Essays*, II, p.833).

Some emperors were called 'god' in their own lifetime. Augustus, for example, was thus addressed by his priests at Ancyra (*OGI,* 533), where he is described as *theos Sebastos*, as well as 'god and son of god' in the dedicatory inscription in the temple of Soknopaios at Dimeh (*IG Fayoum* I, no. 73). Likewise for Tiberius at Odessos (*IGRR* I, 659), as well as Caracalla on an altar in Bithynia (*IGRR* III, 1). According to R. Turcan (*ANWR* II, 16, 2 [1978], 1053-4), this mode of address to living Augusti 'is one of the isolated affirmations proceeding from local initiatives or private organisations.' In Egypt,

[23] J. LeGall & M. LeGlay, *L'empire Romain*, I (2nd ed. 1992), p. 548-549; M. LeGlay, J-L. Voisin, Y. LeBohec, *Histoire Romaine* (PUF, 1991), p. 385.

[24] M. Christol, *L'Empire romain du IIIe siècle* (1997), p. 37 and 65, no. 4; Chris Searre, *Atlas de la Rome antique,* Autrement (1995), p. 89.

[25] H. G. Pflaum, *Les sodales Antoniniani de l'époque de Marc-Aurèle,* 1966, particularly p. 1-3 and 87; *id., Mélanges Piganiol.* I (1966), p. 277-278.

this divinisation of the living emperor results from the fact that the emperors, like the Ptolemaic kings before them, took the place of the pharaoh, guarantor of the world's equilibrium and general prosperity. As Jean Yoyotte says of Augustus (*Strabon*, 1997, p. 39), 'the ancient Egyptian religion had for all eternity assigned the Prince to guarantee the *pax deorum*.'

Upon his death, the emperor became *divus* (divine), which is not the same as *deus*. But the Greeks translated *divus* with *theos* instead of the adjective *theios* in their inscriptions. G. W. Bowersock's explanation is that Greek only has those two words (*theos* and *theios*) where there are three in Latin (*deus, divus, divinus*). Still, says M. Sartre (*Orient Romain,* p. 116-117) on taking up the subject, 'in *theios*, the Greeks have the equivalent to *divus*. If they did not use it, they did so on purpose, because for them, the emperor was *theos* and not merely *theios*.'

P. Veyne says that 'the ancient god was not some gigantic being, whose infinity set him well above the world he had created, ... the word 'god' does not designate one and the same essence throughout the centuries' (p. 803). A god is identified through his efficiency, his power to do. Maurice Sartre insists precisely on this concept which links the notion of the divine to that of power in the eyes of the masses, who do not concern themselves with theological problems. He invokes quite rightly 'these maxims of commonplace appearance, which may reflect deeply rooted and widespread conceptions as they can be found in Artemidorus Daldianus' *Interpretation of Dreams*. Thus, it is said, 'everything that has power is divine' (II, 36, trad. A. J. Festugière, Paris, 1975, p.149; the same principle is cited by Artemidorus in II, 69 with more precise comments): it is to underline in luminous fashion the link between power and the divine. 'Even more explicitly,' adds M. Sartre, 'a maxim written on a papyrus of the 2nd century establishes this relationship between the divine and the imperial power: 'What is a god? He who exercises power. What is a king? An *isothéos*' (references p. 117, Note 3).

The two identical inscriptions (nos. 4 and 5) were without doubt conceived by a single author, and executed by the same workman, and the shafts come from the same workshop. Were these columns erected in such a way as to form counterparts in some architectural *ensemble*?

THE DEDICANTS

One inscription (no. 6) indicates as dedicants the members of a college bearing the name of an Antoninus, the *Antoniniani*, adding more precisely 'Roman and Alexandrian'. These latter also appear in the inscription of no. 7, where they seem to be part of the inhabitants of some precise location, to judge from the partitive genitive κατοικούντων (as compared to the unusual genitive in inscription Kayser, no. 65). The same 'Roman and Alexandrian' dedicants appear separately in the mutilated inscription of no. 8.

Sodales Antoniniani are known from the passages in the *Historia Augusta*, which gives this name to a brotherhood destined to celebrate the cult of the deified princes after the death of L. Verus, M. Aurelius, and Caracalla.[25] In order to avoid any confusion among the emperors, the nomenclature distinguished the priests of the divine Marcus Aurelius and above all those of the cult of the divine Caracalla by addition of a further epithet, such as *Marcianus* for Marcus Aurelius, and *Aurelianus* for Caracalla. It must be these *sodales Antoniniani*, because the dedication is done in honour of Caracalla in his lifetime, whose *eunoia*, i.e., whose 'devotion', to his subjects is celebrated in inscription no. 6 (see no. 7).

We are reduced to conjecture about these *Antoniniani*, seemingly unknown everywhere else. Are they the members of some association faithful to the imperial cult? Or a body of auxiliary troops? The epithet *Antoniniani* is used for different groups, especially in Caracalla's days (Y. Le Bohec, *L'armée romaine,* 1989, 216-7). But it is usually post-positioned, which is not the case here, where the word stands at the beginning of the line. The designation of these *Antoniniani* figured perhaps on the effaced line 5, thus encouraging the search in the direction of an emperor subjected to *damnatio memoriae*, as were both Commodus and Geta.

Whatever may be the case, these *Antoniniani* are described as 'Romans and Alexandrians'. They could be two ethnically different groups occasionally mentioned in papyrus documents.[26] But it is more likely that this *Antoniniani* brotherhood formed a homogenous group. One may thus more easily think of Romans of Alexandria, similar to the tissue manufacturers from Tarsus in Cilicia, who had grouped together in Alexandria (Kayser, no. 99). The citizenship of these 'Romans of Alexandria' may have come by right of the citizenship granted by the Antoninian Constitution of 212. The expression 'Romans and Alexandrians' is documented in texts from the 3rd century and describes a category privileged among the free people who enjoyed *civitas* (D. Hagedorn, *BASP*, 16, 1979, p. 54). Roman immigrants are known to have lived in Alexandria and to have participated in the Roman higher and middle civil administration (M. Sartre, p. 425).

CARACALLA IN ALEXANDRIA ACCORDING TO THE INSCRIPTIONS.

Before the IEASM made its epigraphic discoveries, Caracalla's presence in Alexandria was documented by a small number of inscriptions throughout the city.

[25] H. G. Pflaum, *Les sodales Antoniniani de l'époque de Marc-Aurèle,* 1966, particularly p. 1-3 and 87; *id., Mélanges Piganiol.* I (1966), p. 277-278.

[26] Diana Delin, *Alexandrian Citizenship during the Roman Principate*, Scholars Press, Atlanta, 1991, p. 34.

1. One single text, engraved on a stone which is lost, is the dedication of a statue (Kayser, no. 13) erected by a Marcus Aurelius Melas, in the year 21 of Caracalla's reign, on the 11th Hathyr, which corresponds to 8 November, 212. The inscription is known due to two early travellers. Charles-Marie de la Condamine (1701-1774), member of the French Academy of Sciences and the Académie Française, had seen the stone in Alexandria around 1730, during a voyage of study with the squadron of the French corsair Duguay-Trouin. The second one is the famous traveller Richard Pococke (1704-1765), who copied the stone in Alexandria in 1737, noticing in the process that the stone had been reused and recut to make a trough.

(some 30 letters) Μᾶρκον
[Αὐρήλι]ον Σεουῆ[ρο]ν Ἀντωνῖνον Εὐτυχῆ Εὐσεβῆ
Σεβαστὸν
τὸν σωτῆρα τῆς ὅλης οἰκουμένης,
Μ(ᾶρκος) Αὐρήλιος Μέλας καὶ ὡς χρηματίζω,
(vac.) ἔτους κα´, Ἀθὺρ ιβ´.

(Statue of....) Marcus Aurelius Severus Antoninus, Happy, Pious, Augustus, saviour of the entire Earth (erected by me), Marcus Aurelius Melas, etc., in the year 21, on the 11 Hathyr.

2. Caracalla is mentioned together with Septimus Severus, in a mutilated inscription (Kayser, no. 11), engraved in the fragment of a white marble column, found in Alexandria in 1894 (B. Tkaczow, *Topography of Ancient Alexandria, Cat. of Objects* (1993), no. 229. The inscription dates from the reign of both Septimus Severus and Caracalla (198-211).

....
... τῶν κυρίω[ν
Αὐτοκρατόρων
[Σεο]υήρου καὶ Ἀντων[ίνου] ...
.........ο.........

...of our sovereigns, the emperors Severus and Antoninus ...

3. Caracalla is associated to his mother Julia Domna and to Septimus Severus, deified in an honorific inscription (Kayser, no. 14), engraved on a white marble plaque which is broken into several fragments, dated on 15 Phamenoth of the year 24 of his reign (11 March, 216) The monument is set up by the 'town' through the offices of two dignitaries.

Τὸν κοσμοκράτορα Μ(ᾶρκον) Αὐρ(ήλιον) Σεουῆρον
(vac.) Ἀντωνῖνον (vac.)
Παρθικὸν μέγιστον, Βρεταννικὸν μέγιστον,
Γερμανικὸν μέγιστον, Εὐτυχῆ Εὐσεβῆ Σεβαστὸν,
(vac.) τὸν Φιλοσάραπιν καὶ (vac.)
Ἰουλίαν Δόμναν Σεβαστὴν μητέρα τῶν ἀη[ττήτων]
στρατοπέδων καὶ θεὸν Σεου[ῆρον]
(vac.) ἡ πόλις (vac.)
[διὰ *(ca. 15)*-]ωνος καὶ ὡς χρηματίζω, ἐνάρχου
[*(ca. 25)*]Αὐρηλίου Κόμωνος
[*(ca. 15)* καὶ ὡς χρη]ματίζει, ἀρχιερατεύσαντος
[*(ca. 25)* ἔ]τους κδ Φαμενῶθ ιε.

In honour of ...) the master of the universe, Marcus Aurelius Severus Antoninus, Very Great Victor over the Parthians, Very Great Victor over the Bretons, Very Great Victor over the Germans, Happy, Pious, Augustus, Adorer of Sarapis, Julia Domna Augusta, mother of invincible armies, and the God Severus, the city (has built this monument), (through the offices of me, N.......)ôn etc. (and) of Aurelius Comôn (...) etc., former high priest (...), in the year 24, the 15 Phamenoth.

The date attracts attention because it fixes the event about a year before Caracalla's assassination (8 April, 217), and about a year after the emperor's visit to Alexandria in 215, and the massacres which continued into the early days of 216 (*P. Flor.*, 382). The dedication thus appears as a kind of rehabilitation of Caracalla on the part of dignitaries who had been former high priests.

4. Caracalla is present, in *paralypsis*, as it were, on an inscription engraved on a small marble plaque (Kayser, no. 12), no doubt originally inserted into a block which served as basis for a statue of Julia Domna, erected on 27 Phamenoth of year 19 of Caracalla (23 March, 211), by the city of Alexandria, through the offices of one Didymos, son of Sarapion, high priest in charge of the sovereign Augusti.

['Ι]ουλίαν Δόμναν Σεβαστὴν
μητέρα Σεβαστ(ῶν) καὶ
ἀνικήτων στρατοπέδων
ἡ πόλις (vac.) (*hedera*)
διὰ Διδύμου Σαραπιώνος
τοῦ ἐνάρχου ἀρχιερέως τῶν
κυρίων Σεβαστῶν (vac.) (*hedera*)
γενομένου βασιλικοῦ γρ(αμματέως)
νομοῦ Ἑρμοπολίτου
ἔτους ιθ Φαμενὼθ κζ.

(Statue of) Julia Domna, mother of the August(i) and the invincible armies, (erected by) the city, through the offices of Didymos, son of Sarapiôn, high priest in charge of the sovereign Augusti, former basilicogrammatus of the Hermopolite nome, in the year 19, the 27 Phamenoth.

A year after Geta's *damnatio memoriae* following his assassination on 26 February, 212, the 'mother of the Augusti' has become the 'mother of Augustus', thanks to a correction making a singular out of a plural.

Two Latin inscriptions refer to Caracalla.

5. One is engraved on three fragments of a marble plaque (Kayser, no. 107), two of which were found by G. Botti in 1893, near the 'Roman Tower' (Ramleh Station), and a third one in 1890 by L. Avicrino (B. Tkaczow, *op. cit., Objects*, no. 229). The emperor's titles fix the date as between 213 and 217.

I. [Imp(eratori) Caesari]
M(arco) Aur(elio) S [evero Antonino Pio]
Aug(usto) Felici Parth[ico Maximo]
4. Britannico Maxim[o Germanico]
(vac.) Maximo

(To the emperor Caesar) Marcus Aurelius Severus (Antoninus Pius), Augustus, Happy. (Very Great) Victor over the Parthians, Very Great Victor over the Bretons, Very Great (Victor over the Germans) ...

6. The second Latin inscription (Kayser, no. 108) is engraved into the base of a white marble statue of the Spirit of the Century, for the health of Caracalla, and dates, to judge from the imperial titles, from 211 to 217. The emperor bears the very frequently documented title of *dominus noster.*

Pro salute d(omini) nostri
Antonini genium (centuriae)
Aurel(ius) Aeternalis posuit.

For the health of Our Lord Antoninus, Aurelius Aeternalis has consecrated (this statue of the) Genius of the century.

In total, only six Alexandrian texts relating to Caracalla were so far known. The discoveries of the IEASM have doubled that number.

It should also be pointed out, for reference, that some inscriptions (Kayser, nos. 53, 106 bis, and 112) of which there remain only fragments, are of dubious attribution, and may concern either Caracalla or Septimus Severus.

CARACALLA IN ALEXANDRIA ACCORDING TO THE SOURCES

THE IMPERIAL VISITS TO EGYPT

Few emperors visited Egypt (M. Sartre, *L'orient romain,* 415, no. 4). Augustus never returned there once the province was conquered. Among the Julio-Claudians, only Nero ever thought of going to Egypt, but turned away from the project after some ill omens (Suetonius, *Nero*, 19, I). Among the Flavians, Vespasian, proclaimed emperor in Alexandria, remained there during the winter of 69-70, and visited the Serapis temple[27] before his solemn entry into Rome (*adventus*) in the autumn of 70. The first emperor to stay in Egypt for a long time was Hadrian, no doubt from the summer of 130 until March or even the end of the summer of 131. In November 130, he sailed up the Nile to Thebes, where, accompanied by the empress Sabine and a suite of high administrators, officers, and scholars, he went to 'hear' the colossus of Memnon on the left bank. This was the broken statue of the pharaoh Amenophis III, set up together with another colossus in front of his funerary temple, which has now disappeared. At sunrise, due to some warming of the stones, the statue emitted a sound which was attributed to a legendary hero Memnon, son of Aurora and a king of Egypt, and killed by Achilles under the walls of Troy. His 'song' was believed to be in greeting to his mother as soon as she appeared. An inscription from the empress herself, as well as four epigrams composed by Julia Balbilla, a poetess from an illustrious family, commemorate the event (*Le Colosse de Memnon,* nos. 28-32). During the same trip, the emperor's favourite Antinoüs drowned in the Nile, and the emperor founded the Greek city of Antinoopolis to develop a cult which was to be promoted throughout the empire.

Among the Antonines, only Marcus Aurelius sojourned in Alexandria. He spent the winter of of 175/176 there, forgiving the inhabitants for coming out in favour of the usurper Avidius Cassius. According the the *Historia Augusta* (*Life of Marcus Aurelius* XXVI, 3), 'he behaved in Egypt both like a simple citizen and a philosopher in all studious places, temples, and other places. And although the inhabitants of Alexandria had pronounced very clearly in favour of Cassius, he pardoned them one and all ...' (see P. Grimal, *Marc Aurèle,* Fayard, 1991, p. 221-225.)

Only Septimus Severus, like Hadrian, made an extended stay in Egypt, accompanied by Julia Domna and Caracalla, in the winter of 199-200. *P. Columbia* 123, concerning judiciary decisions made by the emperors Septimus Severus and Caracalla, as well as some other texts, allows a precise dating of his stay in Alexandria from December 199 to April 200 (M. Christol, *L'empire Romain du IIIe s.* [1977], 24 and 63, no. 5). The *Historia Augusta* (Sev. 17, 4) echoes the emperor's pleasure about this trip, which took him to the border of Nubia, to Premis (Ibrim), where a monument from Septimus Severus still survives (J. Lesquier, *Armée romaine d'Egypte*, 1918, 31 and 466): 'Severus never ceased, afterwards, to recall the pleasure which this voyage had procured in him, where he had become acquainted with the Serapis cult, had contemplated antique monuments, and seen new animals and places. He had paid a detailed visit to Memphis, the statue of Memnon, the pyramids, and the labyrinth.

[27] Ph. Derchain, *CdE* 1953, 216-279; Ph. Derchain and J. Hibaux, *Latomus*, 1953, 32-52.

The label of a mummy related to the burial of an old man from Panopolis bears an allusion to the passage of 'the pharaohs' (M. Chauveau, *Revue d'Egyptologie* 37 [1986], p. 37-42).

During this voyage, the emperor granted the Alexandrians the right to have their own municipal senate (*boulè*), a right which Augustus had refused (Dion, LI, 17, 2). This reform was subsequently extended to other Greek townships in Egypt, and to the capitals of the nomes.

To Septimus Severus was also attributed the restoration of the broken colossus of Memnon, which caused a compacting of the stones and the end of the phenomenon. But as the colossus was still 'singing' at sunrise in 205 (*I. Colosse de Memnon*, nos. 60-61), the responsibility for this repair is disputed. G. W. Bowersock (*BASP* 21 [1984], 21-32) thought of attributing it to Queen Zenobia of Palmyra, who reigned in Egypt in the years 270-272, but J. Bingen (*Bull. épigr.,* 1988, 982) criticised this viewpoint, and A. Lukaszewicz (*Aegyptiaca Antoniniana*, Warszaw, 1993) considered Caracalla. The quartzite blocks which were used in the restoration were extracted from a quarry on the left bank near Aswan, where one can read the signature of a 'smith of Memnon', and of an architect (J. L. Fournet, *BIFAO* 96, p. 144-146).

Caracalla did not come to a city and country which were new to him when he undertook what was, in fact, his second, and very unfortunate trip to Alexandria in the fall of 215.

He was preceded by an abominable reputation, to judge from his biographers who paint him thoroughly black. We must therefore try to perceive more clearly this ambiguous and disquieting personality, whose faults explain at least in part the bloody repression in which he indulged, and which has disconcerted historians.

CARACALLA ACCORDING TO HIS BIOGRAPHERS

There are three essential sources concerning Caracalla's life.

1) The *Romaika,* a Roman History written in Greek by Dion Cassius (*ca.* 165-235), where books LXXVII to LXXXIX relate Caracalla's life in chronological order. These last books of his work are known to us only from a shortened version by John Xiphilinus, a Byzantine monk and lawyer of the 11th century. Contemporary to the Severus dynasty, a senator in 180, praetor in 194 or 195, consul in 205 and again in 229, Dion Cassius came from a rich family of senators from Asia Minor, witnessed the great events of his time, and occupied important functions, such as proconsul of Africa, and then legate in Dalmatia and Upper Pannonia. Towards the end of his life, he returned to his native Nicaea in Bithynia, and continued his history, dying at an advanced age.

2) *Herodian* (*ca.* 175-245), whose life is little known, is no doubt also from a family in Asia Minor. He declares himself to have 'exercised imperial and public office' (1, 2, 5), probably of a rather junior nature, and spent several years in Rome. At the end of his life, he composed a *History of the Roman Emperors*, often called the *History of Marcus Aurelius' Successors*. His information, collected from various sources which are difficult to define, complete those from Dion Cassius—whom he imitates, incidentally. The life of Caracalla fills books III, 10, 1 to IV, 13, 8 and describes episodes which are significant for the better understanding of the emperor's character.

3) The *Historia Augusta*, a collection of thirty biographies of emperors from Hadrian to Carinus (283-285), with a gap between 244 and 260, was no doubt written by one single author who disguised his work under different signatures, at the end of the 4th century. It contains a Life of Septimus Severus, and of Caracalla, focusing on that emperor's personal rule from his father's death on 4 February, 211, until his own on 1 April, 217, at the age of 29, after a reign of six years; there is also a brief Life of Geta. Based on the information from Dion Cassius and Herodian, they also used Latin sources difficult to identify; these lives appear less as historical evidence than as a literary and polemical work which is sometimes capricious and to be used with some caution.

All these ancient authors uniformly paint Caracalla in the most sombre colours.

Dion Cassius points out his mixed blood (78, 6, Ia), noting that in him were accumulated the defaults of three 'races' without any of their qualities: the fickleness, cowardice, and carelessness of the Gauls, the rudeness and cruelty of the Africans, the shiftiness of the Syrians, which latter he is supposed to have inherited through both his paternal and maternal ancestry.

More objectively, Herodian (I, 6) ranks him among the rulers who have come into power too young, and lacking maturity, like Commodus, Geta, and Severus Alexander, as opposed to experienced emperors like Marcus Aurelius or Septimus Severus: 'The older of the holders (of empire), thanks to their experience, knew better how to control themselves as well as their subjects. The young ones, on the other hand, due to their rather indolent lifestyle, provoked an avalanche of upheavals. Therefore, this difference in age and authority has naturally engendered a different behaviour.' Septimus Severus was, in fact, fifty years old when he acceded to the throne in April 193, and Commodus a mere 18 when he became emperor at the death of Marcus Aurelius in March 180. Caracalla and Geta were almost 23 and 21, respectively, at the death of Septimus Severus in 211.

Aged five when his father became emperor, the *Historia Augusta* (I, 3-5) describes Caracalla in his childhood and youth as a charming and sensitive being: 'He was a charming child, amiable to his parents, considerate to friends, well accepted by the people, well received by the Senate, all of which allowed him to attract general sympathy. He displayed neither laziness in his studies, nor was he sparing in kindness, nor holding back in generosity, nor insensitive to clemency, at least as long as he was under parental authority. Thus, on seeing convicts handed over to wild beasts, he wept and turned away his gaze, which brought him more than mere affection from the people.'

These nice dispositions did not prevail. It is not easy to perceive the reasons.

No doubt he did suffer from his physique. He was small and ugly, to judge from his portraits. Th. Mommsen sees him as his father's caricature (*Hist. rom.*, Fr. transl. Nicolet, 2, 1972). Dion Cassius gives him the nickname of *Tarautas,* from a gladiator small in size and vile in appearance, reckless and bloodthirsty (79, 9, 3). Herodian also points out his small size and wonders at his capacity for painful efforts (IV, 7, 6-7): 'In the travels in which he participated with (the soldiers), he marched mostly on foot, rarely on a chariot or horse, and himself carried his arms. At times, he was even seen to take on his shoulders the long army ensigns with their numerous golden embellishments, and to carry them, which was tough even for the most seasoned soldiers. For these reasons, and other similar ones, the troops loved him as a good soldier and marvelled at his valour. And one could truly admire a man of such small size who displayed such endurance in hard and unpleasant tasks like these.'

This will to surpass himself pushed him into the most violent physical exercise. According to Dion Cassius (78, 10, 1) he supposedly massacred with his own hands a hundred boars in a single day, and participated in the chariot races in the blue tunic (see Herodian IV, 7, 2). He beat records riding on horseback, and swimming (78, 11, 3). He was much more avid to acquire physical prowess than to complete his intellectual knowledge, although he lacked neither judgement nor quality of expression (78, 11, 3-4).

This exaltation of physical prowess explains his taste for the most violent forms of spectacle, the massacre of animals in the arena, and the gladiators' combats (78, 6, 2). He loved to see blood flow, Dion Cassius says.

No wonder then that he was particularly at his ease among the soldiers. He shared their frugal life (78, 13, 1), and according to Herodian (IV, 7, 4-6), 'always behaved like a simple soldier when among them. Was there a trench to dig, a bridge to throw up, a pit to fill in? He was the first to shovel. In anything requiring manual work or physical strength, he was always the first to begin. His meals were sparse, and sometimes he even used wooden recipients for his food. He made his bread ready to eat, grinding in his hands just enough flour for one, kneaded a cake, cooked it on embers, and promptly ate it. He renounced every luxury and only used what the simplest and poorest soldiers could easily obtain. When they called him companion, rather than emperor, he feigned to be pleased.'

In his speech to the Praetorians in February 212, after Geta's murder, he declared that 'his most cherished wish was to live among them, or else to die with them, for he did not fear death, and a man should die in war and nowhere else' (Dion 78, 3, 2). He distributed incessant largesse among the soldiers throughout his reign and often repeated that 'nobody should own any money except him, whose wish was to distribute it' (78, 10, 4). In this, he followed the last advice which Septimus Severus is said to have given his sons in the hour of his death: 'maintain harmony, enrich the soldiers, and do not worry about the rest' (Dion 77, 15, 2).

The ancient authors wondered about the character of this strange person, who had received a good education from his preceptor L. Fabius Cilo, one of Septimus Severus' great generals, and from the Syrian sophist Antipater of Hierapolis, as well as *ab epistulis* from his father—and who then suddenly transmuted into a trooper despite the influence of his mother Julia Domna, who was surrounded by a court of *literati*, including the physician Galienus, poets (Oppian), scholars (Diogenes Laerces, Elianus, Philostratos who wrote a Life of Apollonius of Tyana at her request), and legal minds like Ulpian and Papinian.

Dion Cassius, who dislikes Caracalla, points out his capricious character (78, 5, 2: ἔμπληκτος γὰρ φύσει πρὸς πάντα τὰ πράγματα) which led him to put forward or disgrace the members of his circle without apparent reason. The same author insists on his impulsiveness and the changing nature of his decisions, which he attributes to the shifty cunning inherited from his mother of Syrian descent (78, 10, 2). He also denounces his obstinacy, and his refusal to listen to the least advice (78, 11, 5). He does not hesitate to see him as mentally and physically unhinged, and a drug addict (78, 15, 3: ἐνόσει μὲν γὰρ καὶ τῷ σώματι τὰ μὲν ἐμφανέσι τὰ δὲ καὶ ἀρρήτοις ἀρρωστήμασι, ἐνόσει δὲ καὶ τῇ ψυχῇ πικροῖς τισὶ φαντάσμασι...), and even as sexually impotent (78, 16, 1-2).

Herodian is no less severe with Caracalla when he compares him to Geta (IV, 3, 2-4) who 'presented an image of moderation, showed himself level-headed and soft towards those who approached him, who had more thoughtful occupations, preferred the company of men of culture, and had a passion for wrestling and physical exercise proper for free men. His honesty and the goodwill he displayed towards his friends brought him into excellent reputation and made most people willing to befriend him. Antoninus, on the other hand, always acted with harshness and in sudden fits, hastily fled such occupations as were just enumerated for his brother, and pretended to have a great love for military life and warlike activities. In his actions, he was always guided by irascibility.

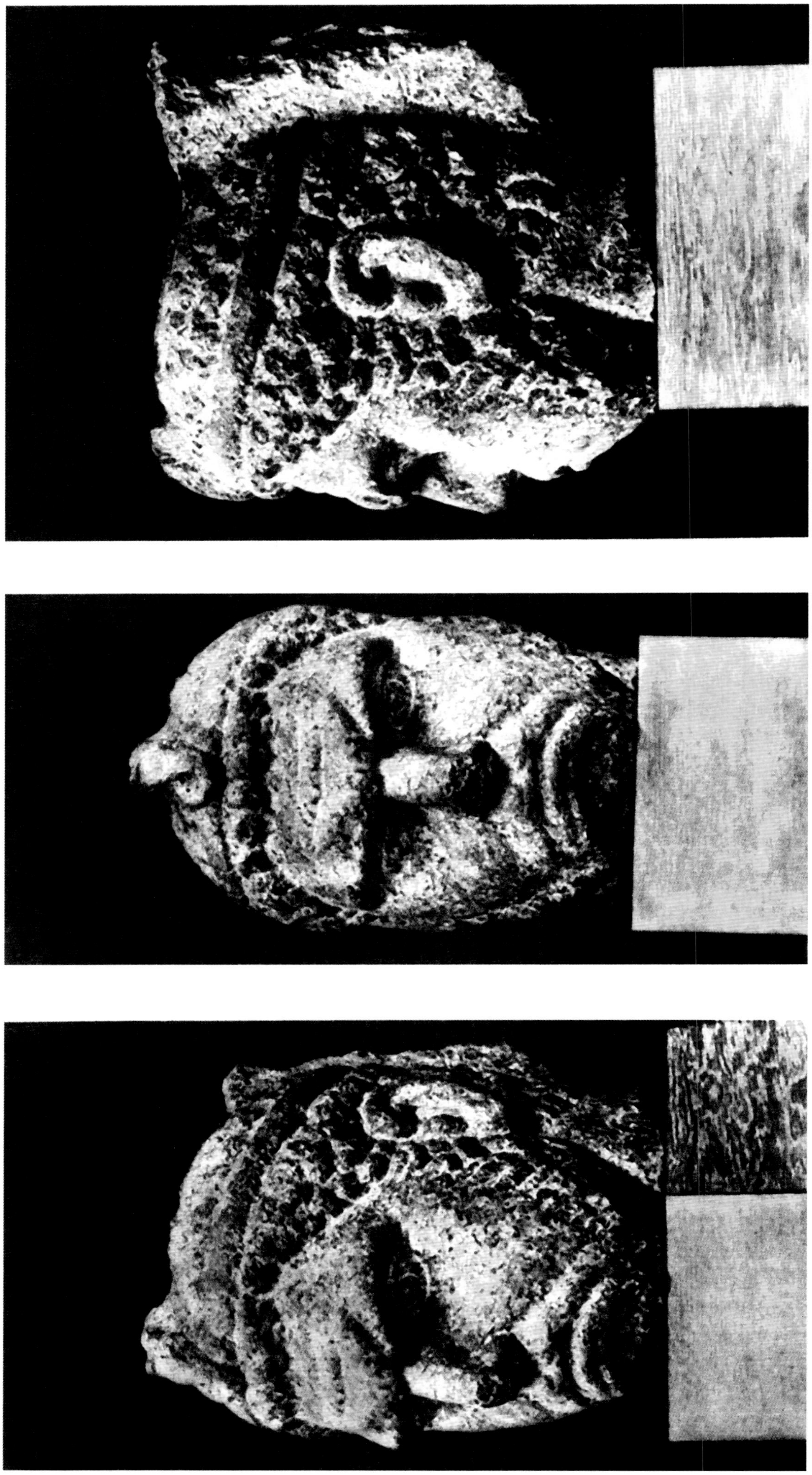

Photo 67: Colossal head of Caracalla. Red granite, found on the stairs of the Isis temple in Koptos. University of Philadelphia Museum (CE 976).

He preferred menace to persuasion and relied more on cruelty than on sympathy to acquire friends.'

Like other emperors who were sons of emperors, such as Nero, Domitian, and Commodus, Caracalla illustrated the point noted by P. Veyne, that the role of emperor is hard on mental sanity. 'The Roman emperor is a person who is one of his kind, alone in the world; he has no examples from other kings who might be his cousins, because the Roman empire was considered as the only state which existed in the world' (Mommsen, *Staatsrecht* II, 2, p. 751, 769, 781; and *ibid.*, III, 1, p. 826). This 'megalomania' in imperial heirs is at the same time 'over-compensation of doubts about themselves'.

Caracalla experienced the greatest honours at a very young age. In 196, at the age of eight, he was appointed Caesar and given the name of Marcus Aurelius. Two years later, at Ctesiphon next to his father, whom he followed during the second Parthian war, he was made Augustus, at the age of ten, on 28 January, 198. In 199, he received from the Senate the title of 'Very Great Victor over the Parthians' at the age of 11. Shortly afterwards, he became *Pius* in 200, and *pater patriae* at the age of 17 in 205. In 208, during the expedition to Upper Brittany, he directed military operations while Septimus Severus was gravely ill, and was awarded the title of 'Very Great Victor over the Bretons' in 210. Before his father's death in 211, at 23, he had been consul three times in 202, 205, and 208.

So many honours could only exhilarate a young man with a tendency for excess, and comfort him in his dreams of grandeur and his thirst for the ultimate power. He felt above all the need to eliminate all those who might become dangerous rivals.

At the age of 14, in 205, he had had married Plautilla, as young as himself, and daughter of the powerful prefect of the Praetorian Guard Plautianus (Dion 77, 1, 1) Seven years later, Plautianus was massacred on Septimus Severus' orders. Plautilla and her brother were exiled to the island of Lipari, and then killed in 211, as soon as Septimus Severus had disappeared. Caracalla never remarried, but lived with his mother, which fed rumours of incest, wrongly sustained by the *Historia Augusta*.

In February 212, it became Geta's turn. Promised to become co-emperor, Geta was assassinated under pretext of some conspiracy against his brother, in an ambush organised at the house of Julia Domna, who wished to reconcile the two brothers (Dion 78, 2, 1-3; Herodian IV, 4, 3-4; *Hist. Aug.*, Car. II, 4). A general massacre of Geta's followers ensued, which Dion evaluates as high as 20,000 victims. Geta's memory was condemned, his name disappeared from the inscriptions and even from the papyri, his portraits and statues were effaced or smashed, and the coins in his effigy were melted down (Dion 78, 12, 6).

This was the beginning of Caracalla's and Julia Domna's joint rule. Dion Cassius suggests some kind of shared power (78, 18, 2-3), the empress-mother directing internal affairs and her son, wishing to become a conqueror of a prestige equalling that of Alexander the Great, taking care of the defence of the frontiers.

Dion Cassius qualifies him as *philalexandrotatos* (78, 9, 1) and relates numerous anecdotes concerning this 'alexandromania' (78, 7-8), as does Herodian (IV, 8,1-5).[28] He notes especially that Caracalla 'even wrote to the senate that Alexander's soul had entered into the body of the Augustus, in order to find there a new and longer existence, the first one having been of such short duration' (Dion 78, 7, 2).

From 213 to his death, the emperor's life was merely a succession of military expeditions: to Upper Germania against the Alamans in 213; into the Orient in the spring of 214, and across Asia Minor where he appeared as the 'new Achilles' after having visited the hero's tomb in Ilion. In April 215, he reached Antioch, and went from there to Alexandria in the fall of 215, according to a commonly agreed dating. His stay there was a disaster.

The reason for Caracalla's megalomania was believed to stem from a nervous disorder which led him to increased use of miraculous cures and pilgrimages to healer gods (Dion 78, 15, 6): from the sanctuary of Apollo Grannus in Baden-Baden he rushed to the Apollo of Claros, then to Asklepios in Pergamum, as witnessed by his coins, and finally in 215 to the great Serapis of Alexandria.[29]

Such was the warlord, at once brutal and fragile, who pretended to be 'the most pious of men' (Dion 78, 16, 1), who basked in the attribute of 'Great' (*Megas, Magnus)*, which is documented from 213 on by epigraphic as well as papyrological sources, and who decided to follow the example of Septimus Severus and visit Alexandria.[30]

CARACALLA IN ALEXANDRIA

There were manifold reasons to motivate this voyage, especially the desire to visit Alenxander's tomb, and the Serapeum because of the emperor's particular devotion to Sarapis. These avowed motivations are reflected by Herodian (IV, 8, 6-7), who maintains that they masked the intention to massacre the population: 'He spent some time (in Antioch), after which he moved towards Alexandria, pretending that he wished to see the city founded in honour of Alexander and to consult the god who was venerated

[28] Chr. Badel and Agnès Bérenger, *L'empire romain du IIIème siècle, textes et documents,* Sedes 1998, 18-21, texts, a commentary, and a useful bibliography; M. Christol, *L'empire romain du IIIème siècle, Histoire politique*, 192-235, Errance, 1997, 40-41: Alexander's imitator.

[29] J. LeGall and M. LeGlay, *L'empire romain, I. Le Haut-Empire*, 2nd ed. 1992, 588

[30] A. Lukaszewicz, 'Alexandrie sous les Sévères et l'historiographie', *Egitto e Storia Anticha*, Actes de Bologne (1989), 491-496.

there more than anywhere else. These, he pretended, were the two foremost reasons: the cult of the god and the memory of the hero. He therefore ordered the preparation of hecatombs and expiatory sacrifices of all kinds.'

Herodian is the only one to describe the enthusiasm of the Alexandrine population, perhaps to enhance the contrast with the subsequent massacres (IV, 8, 8-9): 'They prepared a reception for him like no ruler had had before, so it is said: musical instruments of many kinds were dispersed in all places, producing various melodies; the most diverse aromatic essences and incense perfumed the entrances to the city; torches were brandished and flowers strewn in the emperor's honour. When Antoninus had entered the city with all his troops, he began by walking up to the temple, carried out numerous sacrifices and covered the altar with incense. From there, he went to Alexander's tomb. He took off the purple surcoat he wore, his belts and all objects of value on his person, and deposited them on the coffin.' Herodian gives no indication as to the site of the tomb which, according to this, was still in existence at the beginning of the 3rd century, with Caracalla as its very last visitor.[31]

The same biographer adds (IV, 9, 1) that 'seeing this, the population was at the height of joy and celebrated incessantly day and night, ignoring the emperor's hidden intentions. For him, this was, in fact, mere comedy, for he intended to massacre the population of the city.'

In this, Herodian joins Dion Cassius, who does not mention the general rejoicing but merely states that 'from his arrival, and despite the love he professed for Alexander, Caracalla massacred almost the entire population of Alexandria' (78, 22, 1).

The *Historia Augusta* relates events in a sober manner (*Car.* VI, 2-3): '(From Antioch) Caracalla rejoined Alexandria, where he summoned the people to the gymnasium to remonstrate with them, and decided that all valid men were to be enlisted; he then had them put to death in the manner of Ptolemy (VIII Phiscon) Evergetes (II) (who had ordered a massacre in Alexandria in 125 BC). He further ordered the soldiers to massacre those who had offered them hospitality: in this way, he provoked a horrible killing in Alexandria.'

Outside this short description of events in the *Historia Augusta*, the recitals of Dion Cassius and Herodian, sensibly divergent,[32] provide the bulk of the information concerning the tragedy which unrolled in Alexandria during Caracalla's visit.

None of the sources provide any date, nor the duration of the emperor's stay. But it is certain to have taken place between November 215, the date on which the papyrus of Oxyrhinchos (LI, 3602-3605) states that Pelusis in the delta expected his visit, and 27 May, 216, following an inscription in the temple of Dmeir, which proves that the emperor was in Syria at that date, presiding over a trial in Antioch.[33] The events reported by Dion Cassius and Herodian must therefore have taken place, continuously or in a disrupted manner, over some five or six months.

It is important to relate the tales of both biographers.

1) Dion Cassius, 77 (78) 22, 1-3-23, 1-4 (E. Gros and V. Boissée, *Hist. romaine de Dion Cassius*, vol. X, Paris, F. Didot 1870): '22 ... Having been informed that (the Alexandrian population) criticised and reproached him with various crimes, foremost among them his brother's murder, he left for Alexandria, hiding his wrath, and pretending to wish to stay among them. But as he approached the city, and after having kindly received and even invited to dine the leading citizens who had come out to meet him, and had brought certain objects of their mysterious cult with them, he put them to death; he then bade his entire army take up their weapons, rushed into the city after having ordered the inhabitants to stay at home, and having beforehand occupied every street and every roof. In order to hide the details of these calamities which had fallen on the unfortunate city one after another, the massacre took such proportions that he did not dare to reveal the number of victims, but wrote to the Senate (τῇ βουλῇ) that it mattered little how many had perished, and of what quality, because they had all merited the same sort. Their belongings were partly pilfered and partly destroyed. 23. Several foreigners τῶν ξένων πολλοί perished together with the inhabitants, as well as a certain number of Antoninus' own followers who were not recognised in time—as the city was huge and the killing continued day and night, nobody could distinguish anyone, even with the best goodwill; people died at random, at chance encounters, and the bodies were immediately thrown into deep ditches to hide the extent of the horror. This is what befell the inhabitants (ἐπιχώριοι); as to the foreigners (ξένοι), they were all chased away except for the merchants, whose possessions were pillaged the same, that goes without saying in view of the fact that even some temples (ἱερά) were despoiled. Antoninus personally presided over and supervised most of the executions; there were others which he ordered from the temple of Serapis, for he stayed within its compound even during the days and nights when he made the blood run.

While he had the throats of the Alexandrian population cut from within the holy compound, he wrote to the Senate (τῇ γερουσίᾳ) that he had stayed pure during

[31] G. Grimm, 'Le tombeau d'Alexandre le Grand', in *La Gloire d'Alexandrie* (Catalogue of the Exhibition at the Petit Palais), 1998, p. 92.

[32] F. Kolb, *Literarische Beziehungen zwischen Cassius Dio, Herodian und der Historia Augusta*, Bonn,1972, p. 97-111.

[33] P. Roussel and F. de Visscher, 'Les inscriptions du temple de Dmeir', *Syria* 23 (1942-3), 173-194 and L. Wenger, *Mél. Grégoire* 3—*Ann. de l'Inst. de philol. et d'hist. orient.* 11 (1951), 468-504.

these days of sacrificing animals in the honour of god, as well as humans in his own honour.

But what good reporting these horrors in view of the fact that he dedicated to god the sword with which he had killed his own brother? Then, he cancelled all the Alexandrians' games and banquets (τάς τε θέας καὶ τὰ συσσίτια), and decreed that the city be divided into two parts, with fortresses to be built, so that the inhabitants could no longer communicate without fear among themselves.

This was the treatment inflicted on unfortunate Alexandria by the Ausonian monster, a name which had been given him by some oracle at the end of its answer—an oracle which pleased him, it is said, because he relished being called a monster, but which did not keep him from putting several people to death because they had related this oracle to others.'

2) Herodian, IV. 9: 'This is the cause of this latent hate (of the Alexandrians). 2. At the time when he stayed in Rome, during Geta's lifetime as well as after his death, he had received reports saying that the Alexandrians often mocked him. These people are naturally prone to jesting, joking, and caricature. They cover the powerful with manifold comments which are mere jesting in their own eyes, but afflict their victims with their mockery, and among these jests, the most vexing are those which denounce real faults. 3. Yet the Alexandrians had often picked on Antoninus, especially on the occasion of his brother's murder, calling his already aged mother Jocasta, and making fun of him because, so they mocked, the little man tried to imitate heroes like Alexander and Achilles, the greatest examples of strength and valour. Such talk, which was just so much joking for them, led the naturally irascible and bloodthirsty Antoninus into hatching dangerous and pernicious schemes against the Alexandrian citizens. 4. After assisting at their solemn assemblies and their feasts, and having noticed that the entire city was filled with a considerable crowd come in from the surrounding countryside, the emperor issued an edict requesting the young people to gather on an esplanade: he stated that he wished to create a phalanx in Alexander's honour, which like the Macedonian and Spartan ones of old would carry the ensign of the hero and be given his name. 5. So he ordered all the young people to stand in successive lines so that he could learn their age, height, and their possible natural aptitudes for entering the army upon inspection. Trusting his promises, which they judged logical in view of the marks of esteem which he had so far shown the city, the entire young population rendered themselves to the indicated place, accompanied by their parents and brothers who shared in their hopes. 6. Antoninus came to review them, and passed from one to the next as they stood separate from each other, incessantly extending new and different praise. So he reviewed them until the point where, unbeknownst to them and to their utter surprise, the entire army surrounded them. When he felt that the young people were completely surrounded by his troops like fish in a seine, he withdrew discreetly at the end of this general inspection, together with the guardsmen he had with him. One signal was enough for the soldiers to fall from all sides on the youngsters—entirely crowded together inside the circle they had formed—as well as on the other people who had come there for other reasons, and proceeded to massacre them in all possible ways: armed as they were, they fell on unarmed people whom they surrounded on all sides. 7. But while part of the army went on with the massacre, other soldiers were digging huge pits towards which they subsequently dragged the bodies and threw them in, filling them up with corpses. Then they threw earth over all and quickly built a huge burial mound. Many were pulled to the pit still half alive, other were thrown in without even a single wound. 8. A sizeable number of soldiers found their end in this way, too, as all those in the pit who were still breathing and had some strength left in them clung to the soldiers and took them along in their fall. The carnage was such that the rivers flowing across the esplanade reddened the mouth of the Nile, vast as it was, and the entire coastline around Alexandria and its surrounding countryside. Then, once he had inflicted this treatment to the city, Antoninus went away to Antioch.'

For Dion Cassius as for Herodian, the massacres committed by Caracalla in Alexandria were premeditated, and are presented as a vengeance which the emperor took on a mocking, troublesome population whose sarcasms he had found insupportable. Like Herodian, Dion points out that it had been Geta's murder, above all, with which they reproached him. The latter adds that they called Julia Domna 'Jocasta', the mother of brothers in enmity with each other enemy who in addition had had incestuous relations with her son, as an unfounded slander accused Caracalla, and that they represented him as Alexander's and Achilles' little monkey. For the ancient authors, the massacres were due to a sudden fit of rage or of bloodthirsty madness in an emperor well known for his irascibility, and who disconcerted modern historians.'[34]

Dion Cassius's and Herodian's tales do not agree. The former (77 [78], 22, 2) mentions a massacre of dignitaries come out in procession to meet the emperor, carrying sacred objects in the manner of a Dionysiac offering, when he arrived on the outskirts of the city, most likely in some place situated near Canopus. Caracalla is said to have feigned to receive them with favour, offering them a banquet, and then to have put them to death.

This episode, which has been deemed improbable, is not reported by Herodian, who focuses his recital on the massacre of the youths, briefly mentioned in the *Historia Augusta*, but which Dion Cassius does not mention.

[34] For F. Millar, *A Study of Dion Cassius,* Oxford, 1964, 156, 'the real course of events and the causes of the Alexandrian massacre carried out late in 215 remain a mystery.' According to D. Roques, *Herodian,* 1990, 256, no. 6, 'neither the real reasons for this massacre, nor its chronological or geographical sequence of events are in any way clear.'

However, the three sources agree on the general massacre of the population.

Fresh information on these tragic events has come from a papyrus, which unfortunately is heavily damaged, and which was found at Touna el Djebel, the necropolis of Hermupolis Magna.[35]

This papyrus has preserved a part of the minutes of an audience on March 16, 215, presided over by Caracalla, which implicates Aurelius Septimus Heraclitus, known to have been prefect of Egypt at the time, and who was subsequently executed by Caracalla's orders.[36] This shredded papyrus tells a different tale of the events during Caracalla's visit.

It specifically mentions the *eikones*, the imperial images (col. I, 6 to 18), which are said to have been damaged in the course of some rioting, and the foundries of statues directed by *ergolaboi*, contractors under the control of the prefect. What statues were concerned? Those which Caracalla multiplied in honour of Alexander (Dion Cassius 78, 7, 1; Herodian IV, 8, 1), or statues of the emperor himself which must have stood throughout Alexandria in great number? (J. Gagé, *Basiléia* [1968] 281). It so happens that the *Excerptum Vaticanum* of Dion Cassius's history mentions precisely the massacre of a great number of *ergolaboi* of Alexandria,[37] as indicated by the scribes of the papyrus. These (*op. cit.*, 23-24) attribute to the contractors the responsibility for damage to the statues during the riot which, according to Schwarz, had been provoked surreptitiously by the richer classes, irritated at being paid in depreciated coin. The prefect thus paid with his life for being unable to suppress these riots.

For the writers of the papyrus (*op. cit.*, 30-31), the trial took place after a riot which is not mentioned by the ancient authors, fomented by the 'contractors', and aimed at the prefect 'accomplice, at least by his weakness, with the foremost category of rioters.' According to Schwarz, 'the hearing must be part of the first series of repressive measures, the one on arrival.'

It may therefore be assumed that the massacre of dignitaries which Dion Cassius is alone mentioning, presenting it at the beginning of his recital to underline the emperor's duplicity, was, in fact, part of this policy of repression against the wealthy classes.

The massacre of the youths is then said to have followed, in order to suppress further hotbeds of trouble. This is the episode reported in detail by Herodian, who uses it to illustrate Caracalla's crafty and cruel character, who pretends to intend to create a Macedonian phalanx (IV, 8, 2-3), then proceeds to inspect the young recruits himself, and delivers them into an ambush where they are exterminated by the soldiery during a general and massive killing.

Dion Cassius places the massacre of the population directly after that of the dignitaries at the very arrival of Caracalla. Each biographer clearly isolates one distinctive episode in a long series of events into which he does not delve in detail. The idea cannot be excluded that this massacre was provoked by rioting among the Alexandrian population, accused in the Hermupolis Magna papyrus of πρεσβεῦσαι καὶ στασιᾶσαι, i.e. of manifesting their opposition to official power by delegations or by revolt (A. Lukaszewicz, *loc. cit.*, 494). The massacre certainly went on for several days. According to Dion Cassius, Caracalla presided over the executions himself or ordered them from the Serapeum where he locked himself up during 'nights and days'. The emperor's cynicism becomes manifest in the letter which, according to Dion Cassius, was probably sent to the city council of Alexandria (the *boulè*), telling them that the number and quality of the victims were of small matter, since they all merited to die.

Dion Cassius, more precise than Herodian, distinguished the fate reserved for the city's inhabitants (the *epichôrioi*) from that of the foreigners (the *xénoi*), who, according to him, 'were all driven off with the exception of the merchants, whose property was plundered.'

The orders from the emperor concerning them are preserved in the Papyrus Giessen 40, II (E. Hunt, *Select Papyri* 2, 1956, no. 215) disclose whom they concern: 'All Egyptians in Alexandria, and particularly the rural people who have taken refuge there and who are easy to single out, must absolutely be expulsed by any means, except, however, the pig traders, the boatmen, and those who bring in the reeds for heating the baths. Chase away all the others, they bring trouble to the city by their number and their poverty. I am informed that during the Serapis festival and certain other celebrations—and on other days, too—the Egyptians have custom to bring steers and other animals for sacrifice. This must not be prevented. Those who must be prevented are the ones who flee from their land to avoid labouring the earth, and not those who come to Alexandria with the wish to see this illustrious city, or who descend there to lead a more refined life, or for occasional business. *[Infra]* ... among the linen weavers, it is easy to discern the true Egyptians by their manner of speaking which will reveal that they assume the aspect and clothing of others. Their lifestyle, moreover, their manners which are so far from an urban behaviour, reveal that they

[35] P. Benoit & J. Schwartz, 'Caracalla et les troubles d'Alexandrie en 215 ap. J.C., dans *Etudes de Papyrologie* VII (IFAO 1958), p. 17-33, taken up again by H.A. Musurillo, *The Acts of the Pagan Martyrs Acta, Alexandrinorum* (Teubner, 1961), p. 61-64, XVIII: *Acta Heracliti.*

[36] A. Stein, Präfekte (1950), 117-120; O.W. Reinmuth, *A Working List of the Prefects of Egypt* (1967), p. 111

[37] *Patr. Petr. Exc. Vat.* 149, p. 231, Mai p. 215, 1-4 Dind. (in a note in Boissevain's edition of Dion Cassius 77, 22, 3).

are nothing but Egyptian ruffians' (N. Lewis, *Life in Egypt Under Roman Rule*, Clarendon Press, Oxford, 1983, p. 196).

It would be an oversimplification to explain the bloody events in Alexandria by a mere bloodthirsty whim on the emperor's part (see J. Lesquier, *Armée romaine d'Egypte*, 1918, 31). A number of other reasons may have motivated the bloody repression. No doubt the emperor's animosity toward this traditionally troublesome population which dared to mock him and his mother may have pushed him into the violence to which he was naturally inclined anyway. Too often, the people of Alexandria have been depicted as troublemakers.[38] Undeniably, however, there was deep unrest among the population. For a long time, there existed a serious 'bone of contention between Rome and Alexandria'[39] documented by the *Acts of The Pagan Martyrs (Acta Alexandrinorum)*, published by H. Musurillo (Oxford, Clarendon Press, 1954). These supposed minutes of the defenders of Hellenism before the imperial tribunal, from Augustus to Commodus—and perhaps Caracalla—really do express violent animosity towards the Roman authorities. Possibly, the wealthy, like the *ergolaboi,* were indeed in a state of undercurrent rebellion against the emperor. Few Egyptian dignitaries participated in political activity. We know of only two senators of Egyptian origin created by Caracalla, P. Aelius Coiranus, father and son.[40] Caracalla's prodigalities towards his soldiers, the devaluation of the currency in 215, perhaps the extension of right of citizenship to all free subjects of the empire through the *Constitution Antoniniana* of 212, were so many subjects for contention.

On the basis of the literary, papyrological and epigraphical documentation, K. Buraselis *(ZPE* 108 [1955], 168-188) has shown which elements of the population were likely to worry the imperial authorities, who strove to eliminate them: peasants—we would say, without fixed residence—who were refugees in Alexandria, traders' guilds suspected of conspiring, cultural associations like the *syssitoi* of the Museum. Repressive measures taken by Caracalla after the massacres, as enumerated by Dion Cassius, are characteristic of the emperor's will to break any opposition on the part of the population by preventing meetings: suppression of all shows and community banquets, construction of a wall cutting though the middle of the city, and of forts to isolate and monitor the population. This cordoning-off of the city suppressed any possible agitation that might cut off the supplies for the army which Caracalla made ready to lead against the Parthians.

[38] *Contra* W. D.Barry, in *BSA Alex.* 45 (1993), 19-34

[39] J. Mélèze-Modrzejewski in *Rome et l'intégration de l'Empire* (dir. Cl. Lepelley) vol. 2, 1988, 473 ff.

[40] J. Reynolds, 'Senators Originating In The Provinces of Egypt And of Crete and Cyrene', *Tituli* 5 (1982), 680, cited by M. Sartre, *L'Orient Romain*, 426.

A. Lukaszewicz (*loc. cit.* 495-6) bases himself on the dedication in honour of Caracalla, undertaken by the city through the offices of the two dignitaries, one of whom is a high priest in office, and the other possibly his predecessor, dated 11 March, 216 (Kayser, no. 14, *supra*) to suggest that the date of inscription 'may be interpreted as the *terminus post quem* of the massacres,' admitting that such a dedication to the city's tormentor would be unthinkable after the butchery which had just taken place. Still, it is an official text, perhaps of a propagandist nature, destined to gain credit to the thesis that Caracalla's draconian purge had been salutary—in which case the events of Alexandria could indeed have preceded the inscription.

The date of Caracalla's departure from Alexandria can only be conjecture. For the Polish scholar, 'it is not very likely that Caracalla had any intention of leaving Alexandria before April, the month of dynastic celebrations and above all those of the city. It is even possible that these celebrations became the occasion for events which degenerated into the general extermination of the population. It is, in fact, very likely that Caracalla left the city, as Herodian says, immediately after the massacre, and it seems possible that his departure fell into the month of April.'

However that may be, about a year after his catastrophic visit to Alexandria, the emperor was assassinated on 8 April, 217, during his campaign against the Parthians, between Edessa (Urfa) and Carrhae in Mesopotamia (in the principality of Osroena), by Julius Martialis, an officer in the Praetorian Guard, under an order from the praetorian prefect Opellius Macrinus whom the army proclaimed emperor.

ARCHAEOLOGICAL SEARCH FOR CARACALLA

1. Some effort was made to find traces of Caracalla's massacre in the field. G. Botti describes in dramatic terms the view which opened up to him on discovery of a burial chamber at Kom al-Hadîd (the iron hill?), near the 'stadium' which he positioned between the Serapeum and Kom al Choqafa.[41]

The burial chamber was found in the area called 'Antoninian necropolis' (B. Tkaczow, *Topographie,* 1993, fig. 15c and Site no. 14): 'The view which opened up to my eyes,' Botti declares, 'as I penetrated into the chamber for the first time was utterly terrifying. Under the blocks and rubble, skeletons of men and horse were lying about all over the floor, and I could not walk without disturbing them.' The Italian scientist put forward the idea that these must have been the young people who fell victim to the killing mentioned in Herodian. One would like to find some proof.

[41] *Von Steglin Expedition* I, *Text* (1908), Chpt. XXI, p. 365, reproduced *in toto* in *Alexandrie la Grande* (1998), p. 165-166.

Photo 68: Caracalla's Head, found in Tanis. Grey granite. Height 30 cm. Graeco-Roman Museum storerooms, Alexandria (no. 3233).

The neighbouring burial chamber of the three-floor funeral complex of Kom al-Choqafa (B. Tkaczow, *op. cit.* Site no. 12), which contains a group of tombs lightened by a square shaft, was given the name, albeit traditional, of 'Hall of Caracalla' by G. Botti, due to the accumulation of bones of both men and horses, supposed victims of the massacre in question.[42]

For E. Brecchia (*Alexandria. ad Aegyptum*, 1914, p. 144) 'one cannot exclude the hypothesis, but it could well not correspond to reality.' This 'very doubtful' conjecture, according to E. M. Forster (*Alexandria* ...) has been criticised by Alan Rowe (*BSA Alex.*, 35 [1942], 31-32) who imagined a burial site for race horses, buried with their masters, which did not convince A. Andriani (*Repertorio C,* 1966, p. 179), but seduced J-Y. Empereur in the above brochure. G. Botti's hypothesis does not appear unlikely to A. Bernand (*Alex. la Grande,* 1998, p. 202-204). While further proof is lacking, the question remains open.

2. As regards knowledge of Caracalla, we are on more solid ground with the *statuaire*, thanks to research by Z. Kiss (*Etudes sur le portrait impérial romain en Egypte,* Warszaw 1984) and his predecessors.
Among the portraits recognised to be Caracalla's, several demand our attention:

—the head discovered in Rome, now in the Palazzo del Conservatorio, in a beautiful style, where the frowning eyebrows, hard gaze and disdainful mouth express contempt[43]

— the statue found in Mendes, now in the Cairo Museum (CG no. 702). The emperor is represented standing, in pharaonic costume. The face is idealised and the expression of brutality softened[44]

— the colossal head of red granite found in the Isis temple in Koptos, now in the Philadelphia University Museum (CE 976), with a particularly pronounced expression of brutality[45]

— and finally the head found in Tanis, now in the storerooms of the Graeco-Roman Museum in Alexandria (no. 3233), which is almost a caricature in its bestiality[46]

It must be admitted that, looking at the portraits, the personality is fearsome.

We know that these 'images' (*eikones* in Greek) of themselves which the emperors multiplied, were the object of particular attention. A Greek inscription found in Alexandria on 13 October, 1993 during rescue diggings on the site of the former 'Billiard' palace in 59, Safia Zaghloul Street, mentioned an imperial procurator (*epitropos*), member of an association (τὸ συσσίτιον) dedicated to the 'images of the emperor and Faustina Pharia, protectress of the fleet (σωσίστολος), "new Augusta"', meaning the Younger Faustina, wife of Marcus Aurelius[47] (*SEG* XLIV 1994 [1997], no. 1442; A. and E. Bernand, *ZPE* 122, 1998, p. 97-101, pl. VIII). On the problem of Caracalla and the *syssitiae*, see lastly A. Favuzzi, 'Ancora su Caracalla e i syssitia degli Alessandrini',*ZPE* 121, (1998), p. 251-6.

3. Numismatics, finally, offer some elements of information on Caracalla.
The coins show a succession of Caracalla's effigies from the age of eight until his end at twenty-nine. Philip V. Hill[48] distinguished the different stages in the emperor's representation on the coins, from the first period (196-198), where he appears under childish traits, then juvenile (198-204), then going through an intermediary stage (204-209) where the traits of the adult become more pronounced, developing a beard, and ending finally in the last period (209-217) where the face becomes fuller, the beard denser, the air menacing and hard.

This disquieting emperor, who died young after a turbulent life in which he mainly appeared as a warlord, has found few historians to defend him. O. Th. Schulz[49] tried to rehabilitate him, but 'as skilful as the plea may be, it does not generate conviction.'[50] His name remains tied to the *Constitutio Augustiniana* which attracted many studies and which, according to Dion Cassius (78, 9, 5), appeared less as a financial measure to guarantee new revenue for the empire than as a kind of 'decolonisation venture' destined to reinforce unity in the empire.[51] The ruins of the gigantic Roman *thermes* bearing his name stand witness to the dreams of greatness of this uncommon emperor.[52]

[42] Photos in J-Y. Empereur, *A Short Guide to the Catacombs of Kom al Choquafa* (Sarapis, Alexandria 1995), p. 18-19 and 20, Fig. 23 and 25d; idem *La tombe de Caracalla (sic!)* in *Alexandria redécouverte* (1998), p. 170-173.

[43] Beautiful photograph in *L'Egypte Romaine, l'autre Egypte* (Exhib. cat. Musée de l'Archéologie Méditerranéenne, Marseille 1997), p. 53 no. 25.

[44] P. Graindor, *Bustes et statues-portraits d'Egypte romaine* (Cairo 1937), p. 144-5, no. 79, pl. LXX; H. De Meulenaere & P. Mac Kay, *Mendes II* (1976), p. 201, no. 82, with photograph; H. Cuvigny in *Alexandrie entre deux mondes* (Edisud 1987), p. 33; Z. Kiss, *op. cit.*, p. 81 and Fig. 205-206.

[45] P. Graindor, p. 145-6, no. 80 and pl. LXXI; Z. Kiss, p. 82, Fig. 209.

[46] *Götter, Pharaonen* (P. von Zabern, Mainz, n.d.), no. 172; Z. Kiss, p. 81 and fig. 207-8. The portrait is also indicated in the *Catalogue* (1900), p. 216, no. 179, by G. Botti.

[47] The stone was deposited at Kom al Choqafa, behind the Tigranus tomb.

[48] 'The Coin Portraiture of Severus and his Family from the Mint of Rome', *Numism. Chron.* XIX (1979), p. 41 and pl. 7.

[49] O. Th. Schulz, *Der römische Kaiser Caracalla: Genie, Wahnsinn oder Verbrechen,* Leipzig, 1909.

[50] Maurice Besnier, *Hist. rom.* vol. IV, I (1937), p. 57.

[51] P. Petit, *Histoire générale de l'empire romain, 2. La crise de l'Empire,* Seuil, 1974, p. 71.

[52] Chris Searre, *Chronicle of the Roman Emperors,* London, Thames and Hudson, 1995, repr. 1997, p.140-141.

STATUARY

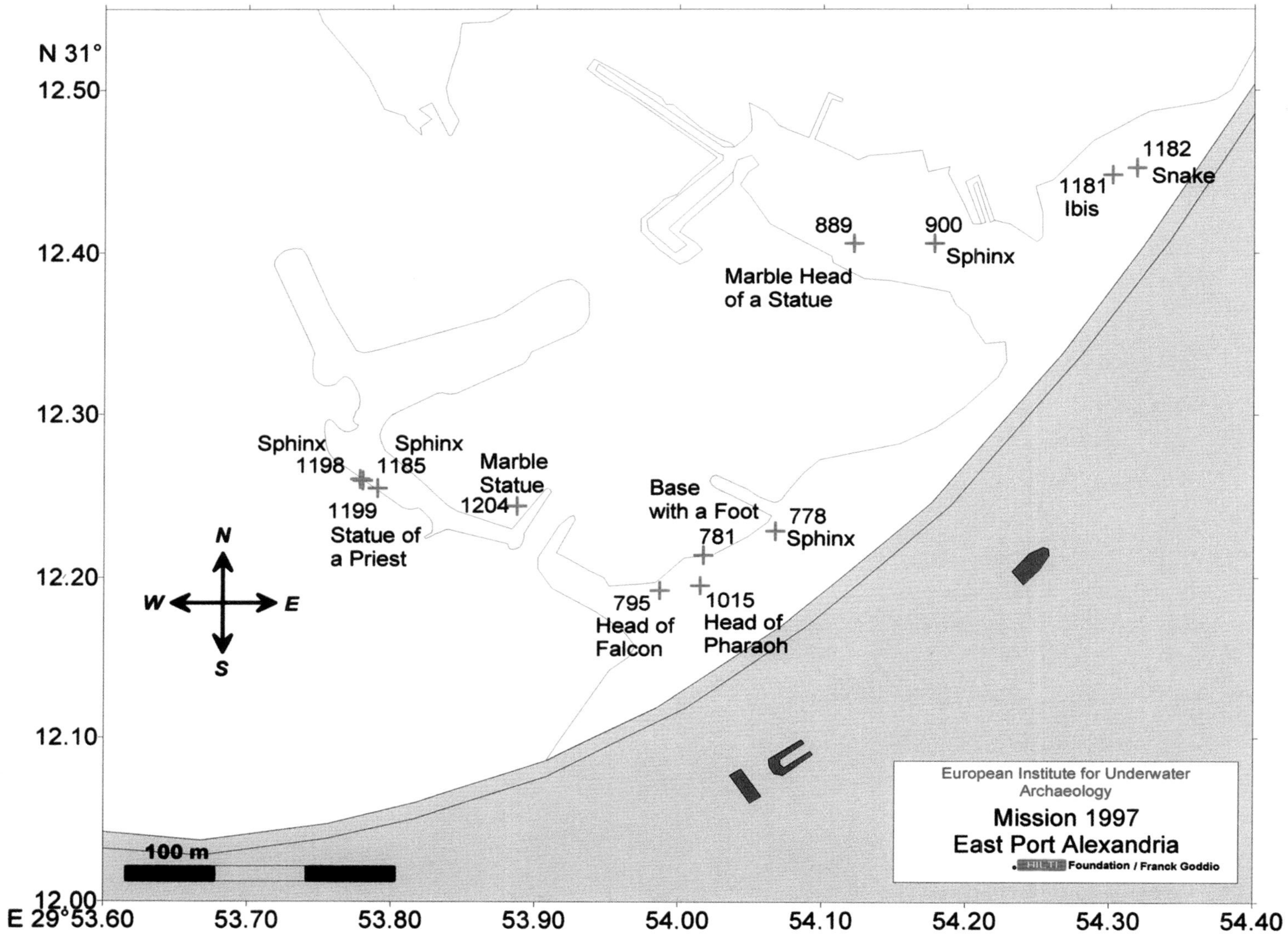
N 31°
12.50
12.40
12.30
12.20
12.10
12.00
E 29°53.60
53.70
53.80
53.90
54.00
54.10
54.20
54.30
54.40
1182
Snake
1181
Ibis
889
900
Sphinx
Marble Head
of a Statue
Sphinx
1198
Sphinx
1185
Marble
Statue
1204
1199
Statue of
a Priest
Base
with a Foot
781
778
Sphinx
795
Head of
Falcon
1015
Head of
Pharaoh
N
W
E
S
100 m
European Institute for Underwater
Archaeology
Mission 1997
East Port Alexandria
Foundation / Franck Goddio

THE SCULPTURES

Zsolt Kiss

One of the most spectacular aspects of underwater research in Alexandria's Eastern Harbour must certainly be to perceive the outlines of some sculptures in this opaque and often blurred universe. Initial underwater survey naturally first focuses on the biggest elements, such as the 12 fragments of sculptures which are listed here. There must certainly be other and smaller pieces buried in the sands in the same area, which could possibly be brought to light by a very detailed and meticulous excavation. The 12 fragments found during the campaigns of 1996 and 1997, and left or re-stored *in situ*, were found in four different sites (see map, p. 168): four paved banks, covered with damaged architectural rubble, and looking much like abandoned demolition workings. None of them were found in anything like their original position, or even near their original site. Thus, they are unfortunately not to be considered as *in situ*, standing or even collapsed where they stood, whereas the pavement found intact had not moved, and the columns which had crumbled but were grouped together are no doubt lying near their original location.

Despite this disparity, there is the remarkable find of four sphinxes (representing one third of the total harvest of sculptures!).

Discovered together with the sphinx no. 1185[1] on the south-eastern branch of the island, the sphinx no. 1198 (photos 69, 70) is of diorite, 1.40 m. long and 0.75 m. high. There is a fracture in the left front paw, and an oblique one on the right rear paw. The entire surface is corroded through the long exposure to salt water, as well as the friction from sand and other particles swept by the currents.

The animal is put on a narrow pedestal with eroded corners, which gives it an oval appearance. The rear of the sculpture is vertically in line with the pedestal. The sphinx is in its traditional position, the front paws bent and resting forward, the rear paws are drawn under the body. The tail rests along the pedestal along the sphinx's left haunch and then rises and bends inward, always following the line of the haunch. The flanks are powerful, resting on the base, and the belly is contracted. The most interesting element is the human head of the sphinx, because in the great majority of cases, it represents some ruler,[2] so that the face is that of the king whose name is engraved on the pedestal or the chest of the animal—which is unfortunately not the case with our specimen.

The head is covered with the royal *nemes* with two parts falling down upon the chest, and the long cylindrical plait descending along the animal's spine. A flat overlying band lines the *nemes* in front, hiding the hair. The large well-sculptured ears stick out, resting on the lateral parts of the *nemes*. The face is oval, the jowls are full and softly shaped. The pointed chin is cracked on the right side, as is the tip of the long and thin nose. The lips are thick and very carefully sculpted; the corners of the mouth are sagging. The eyes are big, and bordered by two rolls of eyelids. Above the forehead, on the front of the *nemes*, traces of the broken-off royal *uraeus* are still to be seen.

Despite this rather characteristic face, the sculptural work is immaculate and of very good quality. Noticeably, the animal is hardly clear from the pedestal: chest and rear are separated from it only by a groove. The chest is somewhat summarily, the flanks very carefully sculpted: the ribs are finely traced under the skin. The junction of shoulders and forepaws is marked by two deep arched lines. The tail is well sculpted at its root, although it then has little profile along the left haunch. The depiction of the eyes is very flat in contrast to the much better rendered jowls.

The pharaonic *spolia* found in Alexandria, but coming originally from the interior of pharaonic Egypt, were of high quality, which justified their transportation. As regards our sculpture, if the rendering of face and body of the sphinx is well done, the work on the queue, the pedestal, and above all the eyes of the pharaoh are much less so, which leads us to look to a local Alexandrian production.

This is the moment to ask the question: who is the ruler? The *nemes* entirely covers the hair, contrary to the portraits of Ptolemy VI, Ptolemy XII (?) or the first Roman emperors (see below). A face might match the coiffure. A purely pharaonic face was not really something totally new,

[1] See above, F. Goddio, p. 39, § 12.2.1.6.

[2] Chr. Coche-Zivie, *Sphinx*, LÄV, Wiesbaden 1977, col. 1144.

Photo 69: sphinx no. 1198, diorite, *in situ*, right side

Photo 70: sphinx no. 1198, diorite, *in situ*, left side

Photo 71: sphinx no. 1185, grey granite, front (after cleaning)

Photo 72: sphinx no. 1185, left profile (after cleaning)

Photo 73: sphinx no. 1185, forward part, facing (after cleaning)

Photo 74: sphinx no. 1185, right profile (after cleaning)

Photo 75: sphinx no. 1185, *in situ*

if one thinks, for example, of the famous head of Ptolemy VIII Physkon in Brussels,[3] or the one in the Louvre.[4]

An excellent parallel in style is provided by the sphinx heads from Madinat Madi (*in situ*[5] or at Milan[6]). In that case, a string of hair emerges from under the *nemes*, but we find again the heavy lower part of the face and the big eyes. Prudently, H. Kyrieleis and R. R. R. Smith interpret them merely as the images of a late Ptolemy. The same prudence must be observed in the identification of our sphinx. It would be tempting to put it parallel to the next sphinx presented here. The dimensions are very similar, but the faces are not the same.

The second sphinx, no. 1185 (photos 71-75), of grey granite, was found close to the preceding one, but in a disrupted context (which does not exclude an intentional layout together with the preceding sphinx). The dimensions are really very similar: 1.50 m. length and 0.70 m. height. It is practically intact, but the surface is strongly corroded from long exposure in salt water. The extremely flat pedestal immediately attracts attention, with its edges closely following the contours of the sculpture, as if the corners had been clipped off, or as if the original block had imposed such 'economy'. This unaesthetic economy of the pedestal suggests that the entire object might possibly have been inserted into a more amply developed support. The idea of an excessive 'economy' of form, imposed by the pedestal, is enhanced by the statue's proportions. The animal's forehead and chest are extremely narrow, in inharmonious discrepancy to the prominent hindquarters.

The sphinx's pose is traditional: the powerful forepaws, with well-marked toes and claws, are stretched out, the rear ones crouched under the belly. The chest is long, the belly very hollow. The tail is bulbous at the root, then eroded until it reappears alongside the animal's right haunch.

Although very much eroded, the head is entire, covered by the *nemes* with the two flaps falling down on each side of the chest, and a thick plait resting along the back. On the front of the *nemes*, the royal *uraeus* is clearly visible, neck upright, but the head has disappeared. The ruler's head is lengthy, the chin pointed. The rather flat ears do not rest on the two sides of the *nemes*. The nose is long and thin, the eyes big and bordered by two rolls of eyelids. Contrary to the preceding sphinx, however, there seems to be hair protruding under the ribbon, and despite the erosion of the stone's surface, one seems to distinguish a row of locks falling down over the forehead (?).

The lengthy face is characteristic for two styles of royal effigies, intermingling pharaonic canon with the physiognomic portrait and Hellenistic coiffure. The cartouche of Ptolemy VI allows us to positively identify a head found in Aegina as an effigy of that king in the same mixed style, today in the National Museum in Athens.[7] A granite head in the same style, in the Graeco-Roman Museum of Alexandria, presents the same physiognomic characteristics.[8] Apart from the same lengthy face as on our sphinx, the same soft thick locks protruding from under the *nemes* on the forehead can be discerned.

But these two works are of a quality entirely different from that of our sphinx. The style of this one is much closer to the style of those found in Madinat Madi, mentioned above, which also present a long face with big eyes.

The sphinxes of Madinat Madi (and by analogy our sphinx no. 1198) can be attributed to a late Ptolemy. A colossal granite head in the Graeco-Roman Museum in Alexandria represents a king with a *nemes* devoid of the royal *uraeus*, and surmounted by a *hemhem* crown.[9] Because of the soft and disorderly locks protruding from under the *nemes*, the effigy was initially attributed wrongly to Ptolemy VI,[10] but the face of this colossus does not correspond in any way to the characteristic traits of Philometor.

We have already suggested that the mixed style in the effigies of the Alexandrian sovereigns cannot be affirmed before Ptolemy VI (or maybe Ptolemy V).[11] If we

3 B. V. Bothmer, *Egyptian Sculpture of the Late Period, 700 BC to AD 100,* Brooklyn Museum 1960, p. 177; H. Kyrieleis, *Bildnisse der Ptolemäer*, Berlin 1975, p. 64, G 2, pls. 52-53; R. R. R. Smith, *Hellenistic Royal Portraits*, Oxford 1988, pp. 93-94, 170, no. 73; R. S. Bianchi in *Cleopatra's Egypt, Age of the Ptolemies*, Brooklyn Museum 1988, pp. 148-149, no. 53.

4 Bothmer, *op. cit.*, pp. 90-91, no. 73, pl. 69, recognising Nekhtnebef I., followed by R. S. Bianchi in *Cleopatra's Egypt, op. cit.* p. 143, no. 48, and K. Myśliwiec, *Royal Portraiture of the Dynasties XXI-XXX*, Mainz 1988, p. 71; attribution to Ptolemy VIII is accepted by K. Parlasca, 'Probleme der späten Ptolemäerbildnisse', *Das ptolemäische Ägypten*, Mainz 1978, p. 26.

5 Kyrieleis, *op. cit.*, pp. 77 and 177, H 16 and H 17, pl. 67, 5.

6 Smith, *op. cit.*, pp. 87, 97, and 171, no. 82, pl. 50, 6-7.

7 G. M. A. Richter, *Portraits of the Greeks*, London 1965, III, p. 266, figs 1839-1840; Kyrieleis, *op. cit.*, pp. 59-60, 174, F 1, pl. 47; Smith, *op. cit.*, pp. 87, 93, 170, no. 71, pl. 46, 2; *The World of Egypt in the Nat'l Arch. Museum*, Athens 1995, p. 165, LVII.

8 Richter, *op. cit.*, p. 266, Figs 1842-1843; Kyrieleis, *op. cit.*, pp. 60, 174, F 2, pl. 48; Smith, *op. cit.*, pp. 87, 93-94, 171, no. 72, pl. 46, 3-4; only C. Aldred in *L'Egypte du Crépuscule,* Paris 1980, p. 295, fig. 328, attributes the portrait to Ptolemy V.

9 The *hemhem* crest, which appeared in the New Empire as the attribute of the sun god, frequently crowns the hair of Ptolemaic kings and young gods of the Horus type. It appears to have been the sign of power in war, see *Rev. Arch.*1986, I, p. 44-47 and *BIFAO* 88 (1988), p. 170-178.

10 Bothmer, pp. 131-132. Recently C. Brouwier, 'Deux fragments d'une statue colossale de reine ptolémaïque à Mariemont', *ChrE* LXIV, 1989, pp. 25-43 (particularly pp. 40-43) does not pronounce a positive identification of the monument, but regarding the queen's statue which forms a pair with it, she tends to Cleopatra II or III, which amounts to recognising Ptolemy VI in the Alexandrian head.

11 Z. Kiss, 'Notes sur le portrait impérial romain en Egypte', *MDAIK* 31, 1975, pp. 293-295. Other authors have recently proposed to put the apparition of pharaos with locks under the *nemes* much earlier. The colossal head from Qa'it-Bey, inv. 1001, might well represent Ptolemy II, as J. P. Corteggiani says in *La Gloire*, p. 103, no. 64; as regards the colossal head from Canopis in the Graeco-Roman Museum, inv. 3364, see Queyrel (*ibid.*, p.209, no. 155) maintains the attribution to Ptolemy IV.

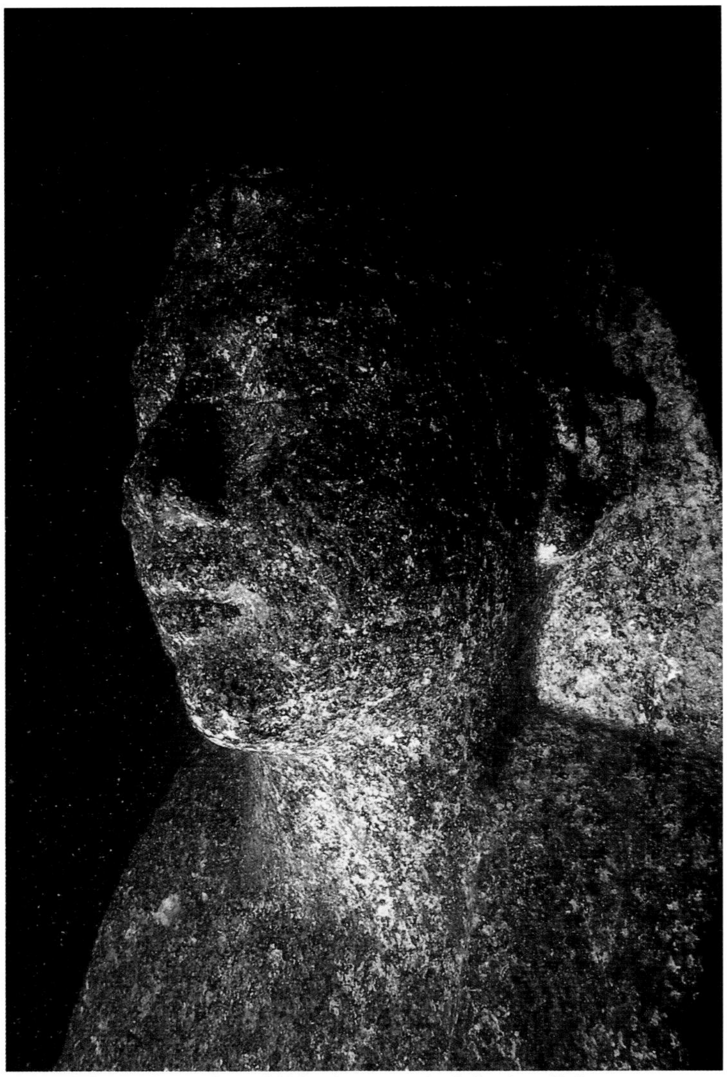

Photo 76: the face of no. 1185, photographed during diving

reject the Philometor version, we must look among his successors. Most scientists have limited themselves to the term 'late Ptolemy'.[12] We are of the opinion, however, that this new style of hairdressing with the particularly plastic and disorderly locks can be found on the coins of Ptolemy XII Auletes Neos Dionysos[13] (father of the great Cleopatra VII), which is why we have attributed the colossal effigy in the Museum of Alexandria to that ruler.[14]

Yet it is difficult to perceive an obvious resemblance between the regular face on the colossus and the elongated one of our sphinx, although in both cases, the eyes are big and globulous. For reasons of style, we therefore decidedly opt in favour of Ptolemy XII rather than Ptolemy VI.

Note that these two sphinxes were found close to one another (and to the statue of the priest, no. 1199, to be discussed below). Does there exist a link between sphinx no. 1185, which we interpret to be a portrait of Ptolemy XII, and the other sphinx no. 1198, which we have merely identified as a 'late Ptolemy'? There are the already mentioned similar features, to which we must add the specific appearance of their pedestals. The modelling of the animal's body is different between the two, however, and the modelling of the face is more plastic in sphinx no. 1198, more linear in no. 1185. Even taking into account the erosion of the stone and the poor quality of the work in both cases, they do not show the same face. And lastly, if the two formed, in fact, a pair, why would the hair be hidden under the ribbon of the *nemes* in one case, and, in the other, the characteristic locks would protrude from beneath it? A secondary grouping of two objects brought in from other sites could, however, be envisaged.

The underwater research of 1996-97 has brought to light two further sphinxes in two sites well away from the island where their brethren were found: no. 778 among the rubble of the ancient shoreline,[15] and no. 900 on the Peninsula bordering the small harbour to the east.[16] It was noticed on an exploratory dive, lying on one side on a limestone pavement, near a collection of column shafts of pink granite. The sphinx of basalt no. 778 (photo 77), with 1.90 m. length and 1.10 m. height, is bigger than the preceding ones. It is considerably damaged, so that face and animal body are only distinguished with difficulty. The face as well as the forepaws have disappeared. The left side of the monument is completely effaced. On the right side, the chest and the hollow belly can still be distinguished. The animal lies on an oval pedestal, the right haunch deeply modelled. The tail is rounded off toward the rear, and lies alongside the contours of the haunch. This small part of the surface which is still relatively well preserved, allows to assert that initially, the sculpture was of good quality.

The head is in a very poor state (photo 76), yet it is possible to recognise that it was covered with a *nemes*, of which the right flap can be seen. In the strongly damaged face, one can perceive the deep right orbit (originally, the eye was probably inlaid).

Under such circumstances, there is, of course, no way to date this sphinx, nor to identify the depicted ruler. As regards its function, the dimensions exclude that it could have been part of the same arrangement as the preceding ones. This also goes for the fourth sphinx, no. 900 (photo 78), which also differs in the material, which is quartzite. It measures 1.60 m. in length, 0.70 m. in width, and 0.80 m. in height. The head has disappeared as well as the forward part of the pedestal and the forepaws. The entire surface of the remaining sculpture is severely effaced, but the lengthy form of the animal can be recognised. The chest and the contracted belly are set well

[12] Kyrieleis, *op. cit.*, pp. 74, 175, H 13, pl. 67; Smith, *op. cit.*, pp. 97, 171, no. 81, pl. 50, 4-5; R. S. Bianchi in *Cleopatra's Egypt, op. cit.*, p. 181.
[13] N. Svoronos, Athens 1908, pl. XI, 7-27; H. Overbeck in *Cleopatra's Egypt, op. cit.*, p. 163, no. 61m.
[14] Z. Kiss, 'Notes, *op. cit.*, p. 296, pl. 88; *idem., Etudes sur le portrait impérial romain en Egypte,* Warsaw 1984, pp. 22-23, fig. 3.

[15] See above, F. Goddio, p. 45, §13.2.
[16] *Idem.*, p. 24, §10.2.

apart from the mass of stone. The pit of the forepaw as well as the hollow in the belly are cut deeply.

Clearly, this disparate assembly of four sphinxes cannot have stood in a single context, such as one of the avenues so frequent in front of pharaonic temples. Only the first two, found together, could eventually be paired, although they were sculpted separately and probably do not represent the same sovereign.

The use of sphinxes in architectural ensembles is well known throughout the Ptolemaic and Roman periods in Alexandria. In Egypt, their essentially religious content would imply their presence in a religious compound. There is no direct example inside Alexandria, but in the necropolis of Anfouchy of the final period of the Ptolemies, we find a chapel flanked by sphinxes,[17] and in a less directly religious context, such sphinxes decorate the more ancient necropolis of Mustapha Pasha.[18] Sphinxes brought from Egypt were also part of the decoration of the Iseum Campense in Rome,[19] using very obviously the Ptolemaic sanctuaries of Egypt as a model (and the most accessible source being, of course, Alexandria ...). We are led to believe, therefore, that finding these sphinxes in three different sites on the banks of the East Harbour implies religious installations in the neighbourhood. Especially the two sphinxes nos. 1198 and 1185 on the island could well have been part of the same religious edifice, which could also have contained the statue of the priest no. 1199.

A particularly interesting find was made on the ancient coastline.[20] On the bottom of the sea, partly buried, lay a great sculpture of grey granite. The visible part was covered with white concretions. Once it was laid bare, it turned out to be a head covered by a *nemes*, no. 1015 (photos 79-81), bigger than life-size: height 80 cm. from the base of the neck to the top of the skull, and 65 cm. wide at the height of the shoulders—which implies that the entire figure standing must have reached a height of some 5 metres!

There only remained the head with its headgear, the neck, and the tip of the shoulders. The surface of the stone is slightly eroded, the nose is broken off, and at the extension of this fracture, the lips are smashed. The face is oval, with smooth jowls. With its sagging corners, the mouth is deeply hollowed out, and the lips, better preserved on the right corner, are softly sculpted. The chin is round, the ears very large, deeply but schematically sculpted. The huge almond eyes are full, the eyelids in two rolls, the lower one well sculpted. The forehead is very short, and crowned by a fringe of hair peeking out from under the *nemes.*

The fringe is short, regular, and rounded. The locks are marked by long curved incisions, and form a 'fork' above the outward corner of the left eye, and a 'dovetail' on the right side of the forehead. On the temples, the hair is sculpted a little more deeply. The *nemes* is flattened above the top of the head, the ribbon above the forehead is very thin, and the royal *uraeus* seems absent, although a slight bulge at the centre suggests some broken-off ornament. Above each ear, a cylindrical hole of over 1 cm. in diameter is drilled into the head, at each end of the ribbon. These holes may have served to fix a metallic band (gold?) surrounding the forehead, evoking a diadem. The two flaps with sharp lateral edges fall just behind the ears and cover the shoulders, which are round, but little developed. The extremely short neck hardly emerges from the base of the two flaps of the *nemes.*

The dimensions plainly indicate that this must be a royal effigy, despite the absent *uraeus*. The face itself is rather conventional, but we note its regularity, and a

[17] A. Andriani, 'Nécropoles de l'Ile de Pharos', *Annuaire du Musée Gréco-Romain* III, 1940-1950, pp. 98-105, pl. XXVI, 1; F. Daumas in *L'Egypte du Crépuscule, op. cit.,* p. 28, fig. 13.

[18] A. Andriani, 'La nécropoles de Moustapha Pasha', *Ann. du Musée Gréco-Romain* 1933/34-1934/35, pp. 109-112, pl. XXVII; R.S. Bianchi, 'The Pharaonic Art of Ptolemaic Egypt', in '*Cleopatra's Egypt, op. cit.,* p. 79, fig. 46.

Photo 77: sphinx no. 778, basalt, *in situ*

Photo 78: sphinx no. 900, basalt, *in situ*

[19] K. Lembke,*Das Iseum Campense in Rom,* Heidelberg 1994, pp. 225-227, Nrs 15-17.

[20] See above, F. Goddio, p. 45, §13.2.

Photo 79: head of a royal colossus, no. 1015, grey granite, *in situ*

Photo 80: frontal view of Head no. 1015

tendency to softness. As already said, the hair appearing under the *nemes* leads us to the Ptolemies, beginning with Ptolemy V or Ptolemy VI. In our case, the regular and rather schematic fringe is far removed from the soft and disorderly locks of the portraits of these two kings. Such an arrangement is close to certain portraits which conform to the pharaonic convention in which we have endeavoured to recognise the Roman emperors of the Julio-Claudian dynasty.

Resemblance to the so-called 'Alexander' colossus of Karnak, now in the Cairo Museum[21], is remarkable. It has been attributed to Ptolemy V by Kyrieleis,[22] to Ptolemy X by K. Parlasca,[23] whereas M. Strocka proposed Augustus[24] based on the headdress, and myself (for historical more than iconographic reasons) Tiberius.[25] Even closer to our head in the treatment of face and headdress, is a granite head in the National Museum in Athens, in which we recognised Augustus because of his characteristic arrangement of the fringe of hair,[26] whereas H. Kyrieleis prudently proposed one of the last Ptolemies.[27]

Depiction of the hair on forehead and temples is also close to the granite head in the Cairo Museum, in which B.V. Bothmer and G. Grimm as well as H. Jucker saw Mark Antony, due to the missing *uraeus*.[28] We hold the same argument valid for Octavian.[29] We also note the absence of the *uraeus* on a head in the John Soane's Museum in London, which shows an identical presentation of the fringe of hair underneath the *nemes*. We had some doubts about its authenticity,[30] but K. Massner recently acknowledged it, without any reservations, as an image of the emperor Claudius.[31] A particular softness characterises a statue in the Louvre, in which we see an effigy of Nero.[32] Still, the fringe is especially bulging, and the streaks in the fringe are arranged longer and more freely.

Photo 81: head no. 1015, left profile (note the hole above the ear)

In conclusion, we believe this head can be attributed to Augustus. It is perfectly plausible that a colossal effigy was sculpted in Alexandria for the new ruler, renewing thus the Ptolemies' tradition of effigies, addressed to the mixed population of the city. It must be remembered that Augustus never posed as the victor of the Ptolemies, but as the continuator of their administration, religion, ideology, and their art. This attribution would also explain the absence of the *uraeus* as a sign of moderation in adopting pharaonic insignia impregnated with divine symbolism. And the presence of such a colossus facing the sea dominating the royal harbour is very understandable.

Another piece of exceptional size was found in the debris along the coastline: the granite head of a falcon, no. 795 (photo 82). It its current state, it is 70 cm. high, 43 cm. wide, and 70 cm. deep. It therefore must have belonged to a statue of similar size to the preceding one.

It is broken at the level of the neck, but the surface is in good condition, apart from the white concretions. The squat head on the massive neck seems slightly lifted, the beak is broken and shows a horizontal rift. The huge eyes are bulging and surmounted by round and protruding eyebrows. Above this can be noticed the bulge of the wig which covered the animal's head, and which fell down on both sides in sizeable, rounded flaps streaked with vertical grooves. The right-hand flap is broken at the level of the neck, the left one descends a little further. On the bird's temple a big human ear can be seen to overflow into the wig. The wig made of big streaks, which frames the head, is the coiffure which characterised all divinities in the

[21] G. Grimm, D. Johannes, *Kunst der Ptolemäer und Römerzeit im Ägyptischen Museum Kairo,* Mainz 1975, pp. 18-19, no. 13, pls. 14-15.
[22] Kyrieleis, *op. cit.*, pp. 57-58, 173, E 1, pl. 45, 2-4.
[23] Parlasca, *op. cit.*, pp. 26-28, figs 41-43.
[24] V.M. Strocka, 'Augustus als Pharaoh, Eikones', *Festschrift H. Jucker,* Bern 1980, pp. 177-180, pl. 60.
[25] Kiss, *Etudes, op. cit.*, pp. 42-43, figs. 67-68.
[26] *Ibid.*, pp. 45-46, figs. 38-39.
[27] Kyrieleis, *op. cit.*, pp. 75, 176-177, H 11, pl. 66, 1-2
[28] Bothmer, *op. cit.*,p. 177; Grimm-Johannes, *op. cit.*, p. 19, no. 14, pls 16-19; Grimm in *Götter-Pharaonen,* Mainz 1979, no. 130; H. Jucker, 'Römische Herrscherbildnisse aus Ägypten', *ANRW* II, 12, 2, Berlin 1981, pp. 676-677, fig. 8, a-c; F. Queyrel, *La Gloire* 1998, p. 285, no. 229.
[29] Kiss, *Etudes, op. cit.*, pp. 31-32, figs. 25-26;
[30] *Ibid.*, p. 46, fig. 78.
[31] C. C. Vermeule, *Roman Imperial Art in Greece and Asia Minor,* Cambridge (Mass.) 1968, p. 388, no. 13; K. Massner, 'Ägyptisierende Bildnisse des Kaisers Claudius', *Ant.K* 29, 1986, pp. 63-67, pl. 10,1.
[32] Kiss, 'Quelques portraits impériaux romains d'Egypte', *Etudes et Travaux* XVII, 1995, pp. 57-58, figs, 6-7.

Photo 82: gigantic granite falcon head, no. 795, *in situ*, (see below, p. 195 *et seq.*)

traditional Egyptian iconography, whether their ordinary image was purely anthropomorphous, or whether they were given an animal's head set upon a human body. This is therefore some divine being of which the falcon is the hypostasis. Several important deities were falcon gods, and were represented hieracocephalous: Re-Horakhte, one of the three forms of the sun; Horus, prototype of the pharaoh who was adored under various names and attributes in different cities; Mentu the warrior; Sopdet the master of Asia; etc. ...[33] The fragment obviously does not allow to decide offhand which one is represented in this huge granite effigy. The only thing certain is that it is not merely zoomorphous, because images presenting a god in the form of the bird never do so with the headgear.

Additional graphic information revealed in a dive by Franck Goddio allowed our colleague Jean Yoyotte to formulate a theory on the nature, period, and identity of this unusual colossus: a great hieracocephalous sphinx, a 'hieracosphinx' representing an original divinity.[34] Details indicate that this statue of great quality cannot be dated earlier than the 7th or 6th century BC, and we cannot determine whether it has been sculpted for Alexandria by good native stonecutters, or whether it was done in the times of an earlier dynasty, and brought in from elsewhere.

Finding such an ostensibly divine statue among the debris which occupies the southern shore of the royal harbour is worthy of particular attention. This statue was brutally broken, without any trace of recutting as an architectural block.

We have already interpreted the discovery of sphinxes as an indication of the presence of Egyptian religious buildings on the island, in the royal quarter, and on Lochias. An idol such as this could only have been set up in a sanctuary of noble proportions, dedicated to an Egyptian ritual.[35] Whether finding this colossal Horus head in the neighbourhood of the colossal king's head no. 1015 is pure coincidence, or whether the two monumental effigies were originally part of the same complex, cannot be determined.

Another proof of the presence of pharaonic statues on the southern coastline is the fragment of a pedestal in grey granite, with part of one foot of a huge statue, no. 781 (p. 232). The entire rectangular plinth and the forward part of the left foot, i. e., the toes and the beginning of the solid part of the foot, are preserved, measuring 35 by 29 cm. The toes are separated by deep grooves, the big toe is slightly separate from the others. They are uniformly sculpted so that their tip is slightly lifted from the support. The big toe is separated from the basis on its entire outer side, the bulge of the pad is rounded. There is, however, no trace of modelling neither of the phalanx, nor of the toenails. Execution is of the best pharaonic tradition and excellent quality.

The positioning of the foot close to the rim of the basis could indicate that the person was depicted marching, putting the left foot forward. On the basis of this minuscule remnant of a statue, there is no way to determine either the origin or the date of execution. More eloquent indices can be gleaned from its hieroglyphic inscriptions, however, which are interpreted by Jean Yoyotte.[36]

Another exceptional item is a statue of grey granite representing a priest carrying an effigy of Osiris of Canopus, no. 1199, which was found on the south-eastern branch of the island, not far from sphinxes 1185 and 1198. In its current status, broken off at the level of the knees, it is 1.50 m. high. The entire surface is considerably corroded, and covered with white spots. The person is standing, closely wrapped in an ample cloak. The statue holds close to the left side of its chest an effigy of Osiris in the form of a jar topped by the god's head. The face of the god is discernible only by traces of nose and mouth, big eyes, and the postiche beard. The person holds the jar in both hands, which are covered by his cloak. Both arms are bent at the elbows. The folds of the cloak spread out fan-like from the bottom of the jar towards the arms. The folds are flat, whereas the more rounded and prominent folds fall down from the same point to the legs.

[33] H. Altenmüller, *Falke*, LÄ II, Wiesbaden 1977, col. 95.
[34] See above, F. Goddio, p. 45, §13.2.

[35] If the sphinxes could also possibly have served to decorate some lay buildings, this is totally excluded in the case of such a Horus statue.
[36] See below, 'The Egyptian inscriptions', p. 230.

Photo 83: priest carrying Osiris-Canopis, no. 1199, granite, *in situ*

Photo 84: the great coiled serpent Agathodaïmon, no. 1182, grey granite, *in situ*

The face of the person, slightly turned towards the god, is oval, the chin pointed, with a long nose and huge, deep-set eyes. The forehead appears as if crossed by a wrinkle, and the skull is shaved. This piece is studied in detail by F. Dunand, so we shall limit our comments to some general observations.[37] Identification is simple: the object held by the person is undoubtedly a representation of Osiris-Canopus.[38] It is well supported in the texts that in the 'isiac' ritual, during processions a priest carried the 'sacred jar'.[39] This pattern is encountered frequently in terracotta statuettes.[40] The same spirit is no doubt expressed in the statue of a priest holding the image of Harpocrates or of the god himself, carrying his own effigy.[41] A perfect illustration of the ritual of the priest carrying an image of Osiris-Canopus in hands hidden in the folds of his clothes can be seen on the reliefs on the columns of the Iseum Campense in Rome.[42]

Contrary to the tradition in pharaonic sculpture, the folds of the garment do not obey some geometrical convention but fall according to the real tensions in the fabric as it is pulled up by the priest's gesture. If the folds going from the forearm to the shoulder are large and flat as they are in well-known representations from the Ptolemaic period,[43] the folds falling down from the forearm, on the other hand, follow an entirely Hellenistic trend. The priest's headdress also differs from the pharaonic customs. In principle, all priests were expected to have their skull shaved, in Egypt as well as in the temples dedicated to Egyptian gods throughout the rest of the Graeco-Roman world. On the photograph, on the other hand, one clearly perceives a groove crossing the person's forehead from one ear to the other. At first sight, this might be interpreted as a fringe, which is, however, not compatible with the obligatory shaved skull. Could it be a deep wrinkle?

The discovery of this object on the island demonstrates once again the presence of cult buildings within the complex of royal palaces. As already pointed out above, the discovery of this statue in the neighbourhood of the two sphinxes nos. 1198 and 1185 may indicate that they all belonged, in fact, to the same building.

An enigmatic piece of grey granite, no. 1182 (photo 84), which was found on the central part of the coastline, towards the base of the Peninsula, appears to be a fragment of a representation of a coiled serpent. It is 30 cm. high and 25 cm. large. Four rings of increasing diameter can be distinguished. The second such ring from below is bigger and partly overlays the third one. The lower ring is interrupted by a deep dent, probably an accidental degradation. A cavity is drilled into the centre of the stone, without piercing the block or the sculpture.

Although this is only a fragment, it is easy to recognise the circles of a coiled serpent with a smashed head. There is not a single instance of such a serpent among the statuary of pharaonic origin. In addition, in two dimensional images, the serpent is more often lying flat, or rampant with just the head reared up, or winding, or else coiled into a figure 8.

In the religion of Graeco-Roman Egypt, a snake-god was also venerated: Agathodaïmon. This Greek term, which signifies 'the Good Spirit', corresponds to the Egyptian *Shaï*, 'Destiny', a god taking the form of a snake in the pharaonic imagery.[44] Each person at home, each town in the land in its temple, venerated his or their guardian spirit, protector of their happiness. The Agathodaïmon of Alexandria herself, guarantor of the prosperity of the metropolis and her inhabitants, had its own well-known temple in Graeco-Roman times.

The images of Agathodaïmon appear frequently in the Hellenistic iconography of the period. The god can be seen on reliefs, in sinuous coils around a jar, as in the Graeco-Roman Museum in Alexandria,[45] or another one in Berlin.[46] On another bas-relief in the Museum of Alexandria,[47] it coils around the altar. The best explanation for the cavity in the middle of this sculpture would be the insertion of some other piece, but it does not seem likely to be a jar or an altar. The most likely solution could be provided by the numerous images on Alexandrian coins of the 2nd and 3rd century AD,[48] representing Agathodaïmon coiling around a less voluminous object: poppy flowers, a club (an attribute of Hercules), a palm, or more frequently still, a *caduceus* (an attribute of Hermes). In the present case, we would opt for one of the two latter elements. Unfortunately, the absence of the serpent's upper part will not allow us to decide definitely in favour of identification

[37] See below, F. Dunand, 'Priest Bearing …', p. 189 *et seq.*

[38] J. Leclant, 'Osiris Kanopos', *LIMC* VIII, Zürich 1995, pp. 116-131.

[39] F. Dunand, *Religion populaire en Egypte romaine,* Leyden 1979, pp. 88-89.

[40] J. Fisher, *Griechisch-römische Terrakotten aus Ägypten*, Tübingen 1994, p. 209, Nrs. 382-383, pl. 36.

[41] E. Brecchia, *Terrecotte greche e greco-egizie del Museo di Alessandria* 2, Bergamo 1934, pl. XXI, 85; Dunand, *Religion populaire, op. cit.*, pp.260-263, Nrs. 332-338, pls. CVIII-CXI; Dunand, Musée du Louvre, *Terres cuites gréco-romaines d'Egypte,* Paris 1990, pp. 101-102, Nrs. 229-231, pls. 20-21; E. Bayer-Niemeiner, 'Bildwerke der Sammlung Kaufmann I' *Griechisch-römische Terrakotten,* Melsungen 1988, pp. 96-97, Nrs. 105-112, pls. 20-21; Fisher, *op. cit.*, p. 275, no. 610, pl. 63.

[42] K. Lembke, *op. cit.*, pp. 186-188, Nrs. 4-5, pls. 6-7; Rouillet, *op. cit.*, p. 58, Nrs 17-19, pl. XXX.

[43] B.H. Stricker, 'Graeco-egyptian private scyptur' *Oudheidkundige Mededelingen* XL, 1959, pp. 1-16, pls. I-VII; R.S. Bianchi, 'The Striding Draped Male Figure of Ptolemaïc Egypt', in *Das ptolemäische Ägypten, op. cit.*, pp. 95-102, pls. 52-69.

[44] F. Dunand, 'Agathodaïmon', *LIMC* I, Zürich 1982, pp. 180-182 (commentary); J. Quaegebeur, 'Du dieu égyptien Shaï dans la religion et l'onomastique', *OLA* 2, Leuwen 1975, p. 110-111 and 170-176.

[45] F. Dunand, *ibid.*, pp. 278-279, no. 15, pl. 205.

[46] *Ibid.*, p. 279, no. 16.

[47] *Ibid.*, p. 279, no. 17.

[48] *Ibid.*, p. 179-180, no. 35.

Photo 85: a small statue of an ibis: Thot-Hermes, no. 1181, limestone, *in situ*

Photo 86: the ibis in the Louvre E. 17375

with the god Agathodaïmon. If this were the case, and in view of the dimensions, we would here have the first specimen of an effigy in statue of this protective divinity which is so important in Alexandrian rituals.

There is another object which could well provide food for further thought, however. In the Cairo Museum, there is a sculpture in black granite, representing a coiled snake, its head reared; it was set upon the lid of a collection receptacle for offerings in the Asklepios temple of Ptolemaïs.[49] The object is dated into the 2nd century AD. It is interesting to note that one ring of the animal's body covers the following one, just as in our fragment. Here, we have a function of guardian of the serpent. In the case of our fragment, it is possible that the animal was destined for such a purpose, but it is certainly not a lid, and the cavity in the middle is too small for it to represent a collection box for offerings. Agathodaïmon remains the most likely choice for what was probably a cult statue in a temple.

Another animal representation has been found in the same area as the snake: the white limestone statue of a bird, no. 1181. Unfortunately, the head has disappeared (photo 85). The rectangular pedestal measures 55 cm. by 21 cm, and the body itself 45 cm. in length and 28 cm. in height, which makes it a rather sizeable sculpture. The long feet are folded, the entire forward part is resting on the pedestal. The feet are round and slim, well separate from the stone. Three long fingers spread well apart are fine, rounded at their tips, and display short claws. The fourth finger, which is shorter, is pulled backwards, towards the lateral rim of the pedestal. The two outside fingers of the left claw have disappeared. The animal's thighs point obliquely forward and are bulging where they join the body.

The right side of that body and the pedestal are blackened from the long stay under water. The bird looks as if it were sitting on the block. Its body is full, very large, and of oval shape. The forward part is larger, standing obliquely, lengthening the thighs. It is well detached from the stone, as is the rear part. The tail shrinks but remains round, and reaches the rearward rim of the pedestal. The body is smooth, neither wings nor feathers are profiled. The onset of the neck rearing up remains visible above the chest.

The form of the body and above all the long, slim feet with their fingers spread, and the short claws, allow us to identify without hesitation an ibis. The onset of the slim neck, too, points toward this species. Its image was widely spread all over Egypt, as the sacred bird of Thot[50] and remained so during the entire Graeco-Roman period, when that god was identified with Hermes. Still, any three-dimensional representation of the god's animal hypostasis presented problems. The ibis could be depicted walking on its long legs, the head with its fine curved beak lifted up high, in wood or bronze. As an example, we shall merely cite a bronze figurine in the Hermitage Museum in St Petersburg,[51] dated from the lower period, or what is almost a statue (41 cm. high!!) in bronze, incrusted with jasper and gold ornaments, in the Pelizäus Museum in Hildesheim,[52] dated from the end of the late period. Technical and static reasons did not allow to cut such a statue standing on such frail supports as the thin legs, and in addition the sculpting of the long, fine, curved beak would have presented insurmountable problems for a sculptor working with stone. The problem of the legs was easily solved if one stuck to the model—rather frequent in traditional iconography—which consisted in representing Thot's bird sitting in repose rather than strutting about on its long legs.[53] This is valid for a great number of bronze votives dedicated by private persons during the Saït and Persian periods,[54] as well as for numerous wooden figurines fixed on the lids of boxes which served as coffins for mummified ibises, such as were found in great numbers in the necropolis of Hermopolis (Tunah el-Djebel).[55] Still, the stump of the neck indicates that the head stretched up high. The pose of our statue thus finds a far better analogy in a great and beautiful Hermopolitan ibis, Louvre E 17375, which is 47 cm. long and 35.5 cm. high (photo 86).[56] The body is sculpted in stucco-covered

[49] Grimm-Johannes, *op. cit.*, p. 23, no. 36, pls. 70-71.
[50] A.P. Zivie, *Ibis*, LA III, Wiesbaden 1980, cols. 115-120.
[51] N. Landa, I. Lapis, *Egyptian Antiquities in the Hermitage*, Leningrad 1974, fig. 123.
[52] A. Eggebrecht, in: *Pelizäus Museum Hildesheim. Die ägyptische Sammlung*, Mainz 1993, p. 88, fig. 85.
[53] A good example is on the naos of Hermopolis-Baqlieh (dynasty XXVI), Cairo CG 7008, Roeder, *Naos*, (CGC), 1914, p. 35, § 173b, pl. 9.
[54] Roeder, Ägyptische Bronzefiguren ... Berlin (1956), p. 402-403, § 541-542.
[55] One example among dozens: M. Page-Gasser in *Egypte-Moments d'Eternité; Art egyptien dans les collections privées de Suisse*, Mainz 1997, no. 169.
[56] J. Vandier, 'Une statue d'ibis', dans *RDE* 12 (1950), p. 33-35 and pl. IV.

Photo 87: ibis no. 1181, right side, *in situ*.

Photo 88: torso of the god Hermes, no. 1204, white marble

wood, and painted. The feet, bent low and inserted into the wooden pedestal with the help of tenons, are made of bronze. The neck which, together with the head, is a single piece of bronze, is stuck into the body in the same manner. As regards the dimensions, the body executed without any detail of plumage and in the profile the resemblance between this work and our Alexandrian example is striking. The technical solution for the head and neck must be taken into consideration for our sculpture: a bronze piece could well have been adapted to the stump of the neck cut in the stone.

A work of average quality, cut from limestone, this image of Thot-Hermes is no doubt the work of a local craftsman of Hellenistic times, but comes from the imagery of Egypt proper. We believe that the god's effigy must have belonged in a religious building near the banks of the Eastern Harbour. Judging from its form and size, this small object cannot have been brought there as building material, which strengthens the idea that the classical sphinx 778, the formidable hieracosphinx 781, another idol, the snake, and the royal colossus 1015 must mark the site of some ruined sanctuary.

Linked without any doubt to the god Hermes is a torso of white marble, no. 1204 (photo 88) which was collected from the bottom of a slope covered with fallen rocks on the southern branch of the island. It currently measures 1.7 m, but it is broken at the level of the shoulders, the left leg is fractured at the height of the calf, and the right one in the middle of the thigh; both arms have also vanished. The entire sculpture must have measured some 2.0 m, hardly above human size. The person is standing, wears only a cloak (*hima-tion*) fastened on the right shoulder. The torso is naked, the chest muscles are rather soft and the right side of the chest is slightly more bulging towards the armpit, where the arm, probably extended outward, is broken off. The stomach is round, and the muscles of the hip are protruding. The pubic hair forms a triangle of curly hair, the penis and the testicles are carefully pronounced. The rounded right thigh is linked to the left one at its rear by part of the stone which has not been cut away. The left leg, better preserved, is set forward, the knee slightly bent. The thigh is well sculpted, the knee is angular. A sizeable muscular bulge follows the inside of the knee and the forward inside rim of the calf, reflecting strong tension in the leg.

The cloak fastened on the right shoulder falls obliquely to the left hip, forming folds which bulge toward the edge. The left shoulder is covered with two flat folds. The thicker folds on the rim fall down over the forearm, which has disappeared leaving only a round hole in a rough-hewn cavity, which is, in fact, the point where the forearm, made of a separate piece of marble, was joined to the body with a tenon. Further down, the cloak falls in folds of varied length to the calf. These folds are particularly soft and well executed.

Images of a young man wearing merely a cloak fastened on the shoulder were a particularly current theme for the god Hermes. We see him with his cloak thrown over the left forearm and falling down to the calves in the Hermes Ludivisi in the Museo Nazionale in Rome,[57] or in the Hermes Ludovisi in the National Museum in Athens.[58] The god is represented with his cloak fastened on the right shoulder crossing the chest on a statue in the Boboli Garden in Florence,[59] and in the Paul Getty Museum in Malibu.[60] Generally, the god holds a *caduceus* in his outstretched left hand. This convention in the tradition of Polycleites is attributed to late Hellenism, although M. Bieber interprets the *himation* as a Roman addition.[61] She further states that in that period Roman art adapted the image of Diomedes created by Cresilas[62] to Hermes. This image is indeed very close to that of Hermes, but the chest is crossed by the shoulder strap of the sword which the hero holds in his left hand, as Hermes does the *caduceus*. The motive is well illustrated by the statues in the Museo Nazionale in Naples[63] or the Glyptothek in Munich.[64]

Still, it is much more plausible to recognise a Hermes in our statue, especially as, apart from the simple image of the god himself, this could well be a case of royal propaganda. Among the gods to which the Ptolemies were assimilated, Hermes holds front rank. Ptolemy III has been recognised in a bronze figurine representing Hermes as a wrestler.[65] But there is also an Egyptian element represented in the form of the head decorated by lotus petals, and an even more characteristic theme, the pharaonic 'ring of youth' can be found on Ptolemy V as Hermes the Wrestler on two bronze groups with the same motive.[66] And finally, there is a group of similar composition in the British Museum in London,[67] representing Hermes the Wrestler, crowned by the *nemes*. In that case, Hermes seems to be assimilated to an even later Ptolemy.

In three more figurines, the standing athlete Hermes, crowned by lotus petals, is an effigy of Ptolemy III.[68]

---

[57] B. Palma in *Museo Nazionale Romano*, La sculpture I, 5 Rome 1983, pp. 177-180, no. 75; C. Maderna, *Jupiter Diomedes und Merkur als Vorbilder für römische Bidnisstatuen,* Heidelberg 1988, pp. 91-92, pl. 26, 1.

[58] Maderna, *op. cit.*, pp. 86-88, pl. 27, 1.

[59] G. Siebert, 'Hermes' *LIMC* V, Zürich 1990, p. 321, no. 396.

[60] *Ibid.*, p. 364, no. 918a, pl. 282.

[61] M. Bieber, 'Ancient Copies', *Contribution to the History of Greek and Roman Art,* New York University Press, 1977, p. 41.

[62] A. Furtwängler, *Masterpieces of Greek Sculpture,* Chicago 1964, pp. 146-156.

[63] Maderna, *op. cit.*, pp. 56-57, pl. 18, 1.

[64] *Ibid.*, pp. 56-57, pl. 19, 1.

[65] Istanbul: Kyrieleis, *op. cit.*, pp. 36-37, 170, C 14, pl. 19, 3-4; Stuttgart: S. Lehmann, 'Ptolemaios III Evergetes—Hermes Enagonios als Pentathlos Pancratias' in *Griechische und römische Statuetten und Grossbronzen,* Wien 1988, pp. 290-301.

[66] Athens: Kyrieleis, *op. cit.*, pp. 54-55, 173, E6, pl. 43, 1, and 3-4. Baltimore: *ibid.*, pp. 54-55, 173, E 7, pl. 43, 2 and 5.

[67] H. Kyrieleis, *Ant.PI* XII, 1973, p. 134, no. 4, Figs. 16-18.

[68] Bonn: Kyrieleis, *Bildnisse,* pp. 36-37, 170, C 15, pl. 26, 6-8 and 27, 1-4; D. Svenson, *Darstellungen hellenistischer Könige mit Götterattributen,* Frankfurt 1995, p. 249. no. 184, pl. 28; Ionnina: Svenson, *op. cit.*, pp. 248-249, no. 183, pl. 29; 'Bronze Fouquet': Svenson, *op. cit.*, p. 249, no. 185, pl. 28.

These items are particularly close to our marble statue. The cloak is fastened on the right shoulder and crosses the chest, the left leg is bent and the forearm stretched out in the same manner. But we know of no statue of a Ptolemy as Hermes. For Roman emperors, however, this is an entirely different matter. Augustus already had himself represented as Hermes,[69] likewise the grandsons Caius and Lucius Caesar.[70] But the 'warrior' version was much more successful, i.e., the theme adopted from Diomedes, in which mode we know of statues of Augustus,[71] Trajan,[72] and particularly Hadrian.[73]

It is difficult to analyse the style of our statue, because the surface is roughened by the long stay under water. The execution of the folds of the cloak and of the muscles of the left leg, however, indicate great subtlety and expertise. The particularly soft rendering of the chest characterises Hellenistic sculpture, rather than the stiffer and more elaborate Roman execution, which would incline us to the Hellenistic period.

It only remains to examine whether this is a representation of the god Hermes or of a Ptolemy assimilated to the god. As already mentioned, the bronze figurines in the image of Ptolemy III follow the same pattern. It would be tempting to see here an execution as a large statue of what was subsequently reproduced in the form of small effigies of Ptolemy III as Hermes.

The presence of a Hermes statue in this area makes sense, and even more of a statue of Ptolemy III in the neighbourhood of the royal palaces, but lacking the head, there is no definite confirmation.

A last sculpture, no. 889 (photos 89-92), of more than human size again, is a woman's head in white marble. This lovely piece of Greek art was found during a prospecting dive on the Peninsula.[74] It is 35 cm. high. The surface is considerably roughened, and a number of details are no longer recognisable. It is broken in an oblique plane at the base of a rather long neck. The mouth with deeply grooved corners, the nose, and the eyes are largely effaced, and the coiffure is difficult to reconstitute. The hair is parted in the middle, the two thick parts descending in soft waves obliquely to the nape. Above these, the hair on top of the head is flattened but just as undulating, although because of the level of deterioration it is difficult to follow the way it is shaped. Two thick lateral ribbons cover half of the ears, and then meet behind, covering the beginnings of big, long locks, rolled up or braided, which fall down the neck into the nape.

This arrangement of her hair is particularly characteristic: it can be observed on coins in the effigy of Augusta Minor, mother of Germanicus and Claudius.[75] However, even if the photographs leave no doubt about the hair arrangement on top of the head, the element descending into the nape can be interpreted in different ways: a ponytail, several 'brushes' or braids, but always tied together at the occiput.

Some sculptures were identified on the basis of the effigies on coins, like, e.g. the specimens in the Ny

[69] K. de Kersauson, Musée du Louvre, *Catalogue des portraits romains* I, Paris 1986, pp. 46-47, no. 18 (Marcellus); Maderna, *op. cit.*, pp. 223-225, H 1, pl. 26. 2.

[70] Corinth: Maderna, *op. cit.*, pp. 236-248, H 17 and H 18, pl. 30.2-3; Thasos: Maderna, *op. cit.*, pp. 238-240, H 19.

[71] Vatican: Maderna, *op. cit.*, pp. 199-200, D 4, pl. 18.3.

[72] Copenhague: V. Poulson, *Les portraits romains* II, Copenhagen 1974, p. 63, no. 34, pl. LV; F. Johansen, Ny Carlsberg Glyptotek, *Catalogue of Roman Portraits* II, Copenhagen 1995, pp. 92-95, no. 33; Maderna, *op. cit.*, pp. 200-201, D 5, pl. 20.1.

[73] Vaison-la-Romaine: Maderna, *op. cit.*, pp. 201-202, D 7, pl. 20.2; Antalya: J. Inan, E. Alföldi-Rosenbaum, *Römische und frühbyzantinische Poträtplastik aus der Türkei, Neue Funde*, Mainz 1979, p. 95, no. 45, pl. 38.1; Maderna, *op. cit.*, p. 203, D 9; Sousse: Maderna, *op. cit.*, pp. 203-204, D 10, pl. 20. 3.

[74] See above, F. Goddio, p. 24, §10.2.

[75] W. Trillmich, 'Zur Formgeschichte von Bildnis-Typen', *JdL* 86, 1971, pp. 196-203, figs. 7-12; *idem.*, 'Familienpropaganda der Kaiser Caligula und Claudius, Agrippina Maior und Antonia Augusta auf Münzen', Berlin 1978, pp. 17-24, 63-77, pls. 17-20.

Photo 89: head of a woman: Antonia Minos (?), no. 889, white marble, *in situ*.

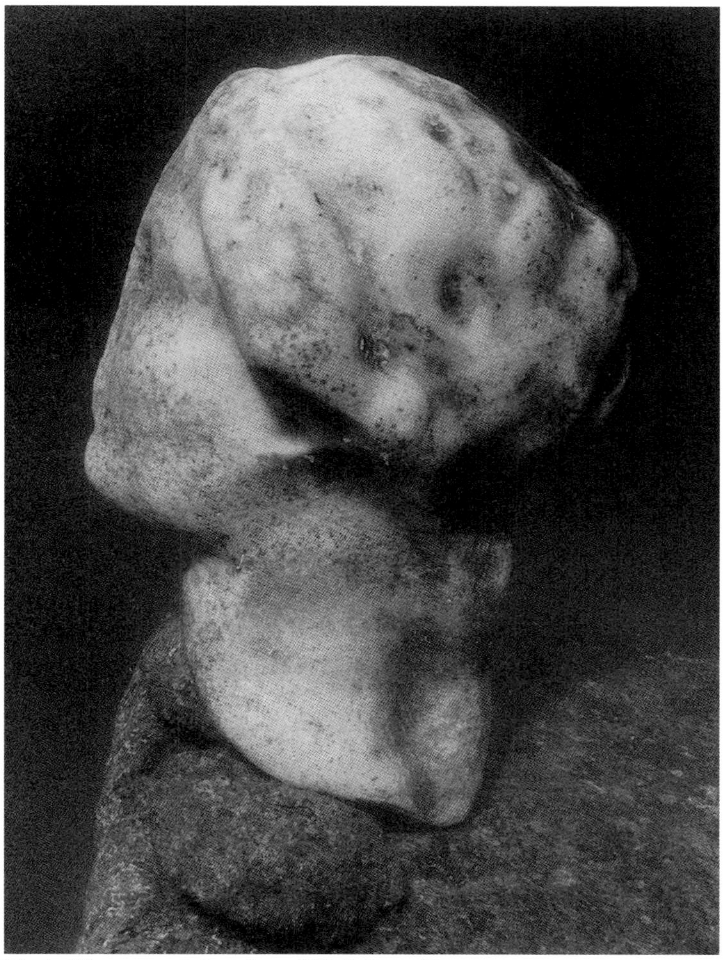

Photo 90: woman's head no. 889, left profile.

Carlsberg Glyptotek in Copenhagen,[76] in Rome,[77] or Erbach Castle,[78] on which, however, there are no lateral ribbons, and the hair at the back forms an undivided thick mass. On one head in the Louvre,[79] the mass at the back of the head is carefully separated into strains; on another one in the Vicenza Museum,[80] one clearly perceives the tresses. The same hair arrangement has led to the attribution—with some caution—to Augusta Minor whose portraits are in the Archaeological Museum in Venice[81] or in the Museo Nazionale[82] in Rome. All these effigies present an oval face (sometimes squat) with a pointed chin.

This fashion was widely imitated in private portraits, and we know of numerous examples of female images wearing the same or very similar headdress, e.g., in the Vatican Museum,[83] another in the Museo Capitolino[84] or else in the Museum of Antiquities in Leyden.[85] Another portrait from the Museo Capitolino[86] shows a large ponytail bordered by rolled-up locks (which may resemble our sculpture). In order to illustrate the popularity of this fashion even outside the metropolis, a head in Ephesus[87] may be mentioned, which shows tresses closely tied in the rear to form a ponytail.

The size of our sculpture might point in the direction of an official portrait of Antonia Minor, who was honoured throughout the empire in the time of Tiberius, her brother-in-law, until the days of Claudius.

As we said in the beginning, nothing allows us to

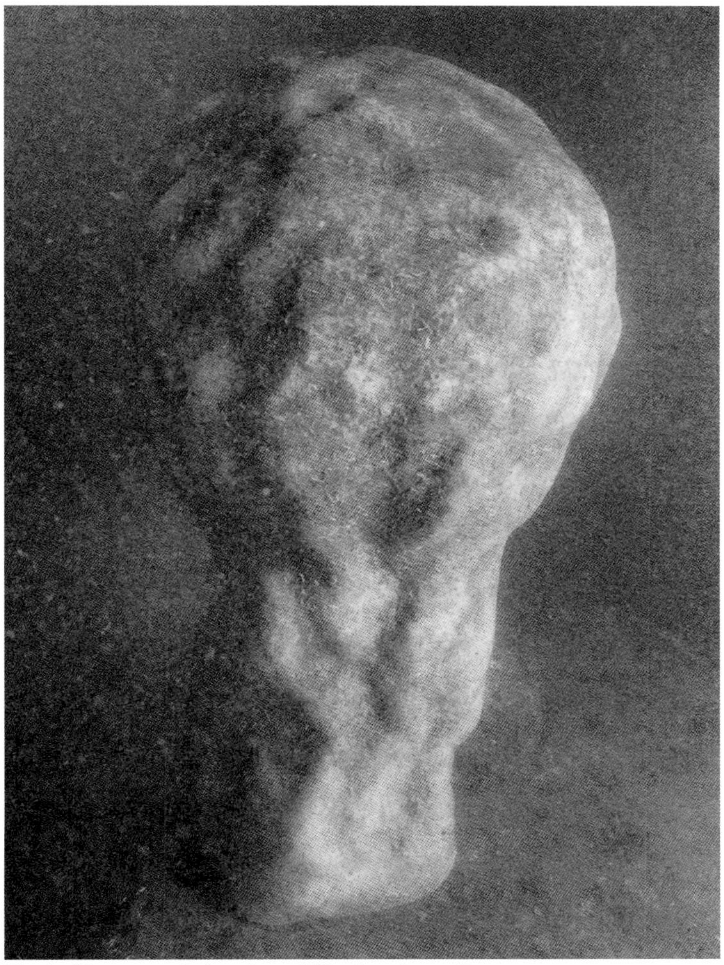

Photo 91: woman's head no. 889, view from the rear.

[76] V. Poulsen, *Les portraits romains* I, Copenhagen 1973, pp. 77-70, no. 42, pls. LXX-LXXI; F. Johansen, *op. cit.,* I, Copenhagen 1994, pp. 110-111, no. 43; Trillmich, *op. cit.,* p. 202-204, figs. 13-17; K. Polaschek, *Studien zur Ikonographie der Antonia Minor,* Rome 1973, pp. 42-43.

[77] Trillmich, *op. cit.,* p. 206-208, figs. 18-21; Polaschek, *op. cit.,* pp. 19-20, pls. 4.1. and 6.1.

[78] K. Fittschen, *Katalog der antiken Skulpturen im Schloss Erbach,* Berlin 1977, pp. 58-61, no. 18, pl. 20, pp. 61-62, no. 19, pl. 21; Polaschek, *op. cit.,* pp. 20-22, pls. 2.2, 3.1, 4. 2, and 6. 2.

[79] Kersauson, *op. cit.,* pp. 170-171, no. 79, pp. 172-173, no. 80 (ponytail of 4 tresses); Polaschek, *op. cit.,* pp. 29-30, pls. 7. 2, 12. 1, 13. 1, and 15. 1.

[80] Polaschek, *op. cit.,* pp. 46-54, pls. 22. 1, and 23. 1.

[81] G. Traversari, Museo Archeologico di Venezia, I, ritratti, Rome 1968, pp. 42-43, no. 22, pl. 25.

[82] V. Piciotti Giormetti, in: Museo Nazionale Romano. La scultura I.1, Rome 1979, pp. 338-340, no. 202.

[83] W. Amelung, *Die Skulpturen des Vatikanischen Museums* I, Berlin 1903, pp. 755-756, no. 653A; *Bildkatalog der Skulpturen des Vatikanischen Museums* I, Museo Chiaramonti, Berlin 1995, I, pls. 144-145; III., p. 18; Polaschek, 'Studien zu einem Frauenkopf im Landesmuseum Trier und zur weibliche Haartracht der julisch-claudischen Zeit' *TrZ* 35, 1972, p. 167, Figs. 8, 12.

[84] K. Fittschen, P. Zanker, *Katalog der römischen Porträts in den Capitolinischen Museen und den anderen kommunalen Samm-lungen der Stadt Rom,* III, Mainz 1983, p.45, no. 54, pls. 68-69; Polaschek, 'Studien ...', *op. cit.,* p. 166, fig. 8, 13.

[85] F.L. Bastet, H. Brunsting, *Catalogus van het klassieke beeld-houwerk in het Rijksmuseum van Oudheden Leiden,* Zutphen 1982, p. 259, no. 497, pl. 146; Polaschek, 'Studien...' *op. cit.,* pp. 164-166, fig. 8. 6.

[86] Fittschen-Zanker, *op. cit.,* pp. 445-446, no. 55, pls. 70-71; Pola-schek, 'Studien ... *op. cit.,* pp. 166, fig. 8. 7.

[87] Inan, Alföldi-Rosenbaum, *op. cit.,* pp. 170-171, no. 124, pl. 103; Polaschek, 'Studien ...', *op. cit.,* p. 165, fig. 8, 12.

bring together twelve sculptures into a single coherent entity, excepting their considerable size (which is an incidental link ...). It is possible, however, to assert that they are all of religious character (sphinx, falcon head, priest holding a sacred jar, snake, ibis), some having possibly also a political connotation (head of Augustus, torso of Hermes-Ptolemy (?), head of Antonia Minor). This corresponds perfectly to what could have been expected in the environment of the royal palaces and the area of the *basileia.*

Photo 92: woman' head, no. 889, at time of discovery.

PRIEST BEARING AN 'OSIRIS-CANOPUS' IN HIS VEILED HANDS

Françoise Dunand

This lovely sculpture cut out of a dark granitoid stone (no. 1199) was found on the south-western banks of the island, in the immediate neighbourhood of the paved area and the masses of fallen rocks, and near the two sphinxes of Ptolemaic times. The lower part is missing from the ankles down, a cylindrical mortise in the centre of the fracture was obviously destined to receive a tenon, and there is a trace of no doubt antique restoration following upon an ancient fracture. The height of the complete statue must have been of some 1.7 m, i.e., of life size.[1]

The man is standing, dressed in a cloak which closely envelopes the upper part of his body including the arms, over a long pleated tunic.

When looked at from behind, from the left, or the right sides, the skull appears carefully shaven. From texts as well as from figurative representations, it is well known that in Egypt and in the temples of Egyptian sensibility throughout the Greek and Roman world, the state of priesthood required a shaven skull, moustache, and beard. Identifying the man as a priest is thus an obvious matter. Looking at the face, however, one notices a groove deeply engraved in the forehead from one temple to the other, without reaching any further, which excludes a ribbon. Either a deep wrinkle may come to mind, a sign of an expression corresponding to the gravity of his office, rather than the 'sign of age' with which Egyptian sculptors of more recent times equipped their dignitaries and priests. The face in its entity certainly looks like that of a young man.

The young man carries a jar with a round belly in both hands, which are hidden under the folds of his cloak. The jar is held resting against his left cheek, and is covered by a human head. Forward on the jar's belly, a relief ornament in the form of a crown is visible; the male head on the lid wears the beard and the *nemes*, from under which appears the hair cut in fringes, which allows to identify the object as what is generally termed an 'Osiris-Canopus'. An ancient Greek legend concerning the voyages of Menelaos relates that his pilot named Canobos or Canopos died from the sting of a serpent, was buried at the mouth of the western branch of the Nile, and left his name to a nearby town which was called Pe-gouti in Egyptian. A Christian historian of the 4th century, Rufinus (*Historia Ecclesiastica* II, XXVI) relates that the local god of Canopus, in fact the Osiris of the town of Pe-gouti, had a jar covered by a human head for an idol. From this, the antique dealers of the 18th century extended the term of 'Canope' generally to jars with lids in the form of human heads, and in which the embalmers put the entrails of the deceased—in inappropriate designation, but which Egyptologists maintained for reasons of convenience. We are thus in the presence of a young priest bearing a divine image, no doubt during some procession, or in any case during some ritual ceremony.

The motive is well-known, paradoxically, however, more widely outside Egypt than within, where this statue discovered in Alexandria appears extremely rare. Some Egyptian parallels are known, particularly among the existing moulded terracottas[2] from Alexandrian necropoli, as well as among the bronzes.[3] But the pieces most closely resembling the statue found in Alexandria—whose dimensions are exceptional—are two rather sizeable statues of diorite (1.36 m. and 1.38 m. preserved height) found in Benevent and coming no doubt from the Isis temple built in that South Italian town by the emperor Domitian.[4] Dated probably from the times of Hadrian, they represent a priest upright, walking, dressed in a long cloak with fringes on its rims; the hands dissimulated under the cloak hold the round-bellied jar against his chest and shoulder. The jar is decorated with a disc surrounded by *uraei*. The head of the priest and that of Canopus have both disappeared. This motive seems to have been used frequently for the decoration of Egyptian or 'egyptianising' monuments in Italy, particularly in Rome on the reliefs of the Iseum of the Field of Mars, where three

[1] See a first description above, Z. Kiss, p. 178.

[2] See E. Brecchia, *Terracotte figurate greche e greco-egizie,* II, 1, no. 280, who indicates two more figurines of the same type and origin in the Alexandria collection (necropolis of Ibrahimieh); J. Vogt, *Terrakotten,* Exp. E. von Sieglin II, 2, pl. I, 3; J. G. Griffiths, *Apuleios of Madauros, The Isis Book,* Leyden 1975, p. 229, indicates a very comparable terracotta to the one published by Vogt in the collection of the Egyptological Department of Uppsala University.

[3] A small bronze from the former Fouquet collection, originating in Hermonthis, which is now in the Louvre, shows a priest with veiled hands, holding an object against his chest which has meanwhile disappeared; see also P. Perdrizet, *Bronzes grecs d'Egypte de la collection Fouquet*, Paris 1911, pl. XXII, reproduced in *La Gloire d'Alexandrie* (1988 exhibition catalogue), Paris 1988, no. 55. If the vanished object really is an Osiris-Canopus, the item should probably be dated in the imperial rather than the Hellenistic period, see *infra*.

[4] Benevent is part of ancient Samnium, but lies close to Campagna, which has adopted the Egyptian cult early. The two statues, preserved in the Museum of the Samnium, Inv. 1926 and 1922, are reproduced by R. A. Wild, *Water in the cultic worship of Isis and Sarapis,* EPRO 87, Leyden 1981, pl. XXV; see also the catalogue of the Milan exhibition *Iside, il mito, il mistero, la magia,* Milan 1997, nos. V. 193 and V. 194.

Photo 93: priest bearing Osiris-Canopus, no. 1199, granite, front view

Photo 94: same in profile

columns are decorated with priests: on each one, three priests carry an Osiris-Canopus in their veiled hands[5]. The motive is also contained on a bas-relief preserved in Klein-Glienicke (Potsdam), probably of Italian origin, showing an 'isiac procession'.[6] In addition, the motive of the priest carrying a cult jar, which can be different from the canopic one, appears on quite a number of monuments, from frescoes from Herculanum—now in the Naples Museum[7] which shows a priest presenting to the faithful a round-bellied jar in what is manifestly a liturgical context—up to the silver beakers found in Pompei,[8] and touching also on the famous bas-relief of the Vatican Museum,[9] where the priest with his head and both hands veiled, carries in procession a jar with a long beak and an anse decorated with an *uraeus* well-known in Egyptian contexts.[10]

Apuleius,[11] same as Plutarch[12] and Clemens of Alexandria,[13] attest to the ritual use of a jar, possibly of varying nature, in Egyptian processions; this use is also documented by the statue from Alexandria. But the object which the priest is carrying is not only a ritual object: it is the image of the divinity itself. The link between the 'canopic jars' which were destined to contain the

Photo 95: no. 1199, rear view

[5] On these reliefs, see A. Roullet, *The Egyptian and Egyptianizing Monuments of Imperial Rome,* EPRO 20, Leyden 1972, pl. XXVI-XXXIV, figs. 39-47; M. Malaise, *Inventaire préliminaire des documents égyptiens découverts en Italie,* EPRO 21, Leyden 1972, Nrs. 352, 363, 368; R.A. Wild, *Wate ...,* pl. XVIII. Two of these canopi have Osiris' head, the third one has two heads, one of a man and the other of a jackal.

[6] Reproduced by M. P. Nilsson, *Geschichte der griechischen Religion,* II, Munich 1950, pl. 11.1; see also M. Malaise, *Inventaire...* Nrs 442a, pl. 26; R.A. Wild, *Water ...,* pl XXXVI. The priest carrying Osiris-canopus has no veiled hands, however.

[7] Naples Museum, Inv. 8919; see V. Tran Tam Tinh, *Le culte d'Isis à Pompei,* Paris 1964, pl. XXIII; *idem, Le culte des divinités orientales à Herculanum,* EPRO 17, Leyden 1971; R. A. Wild, *Water ...,* pl. XIV.

[8] Naples Museum, Inv. 6045 and 6044, reproduced in *Iside, il mito ...,* Nr. V.52 and V.53.

[9] Reproduced in F.R. Cumont, *Les religions orientales dans le paganisme romain,* 4th edition, Paris 1929, pl. VIII.1; see also M. Malaise, *Inventaire ...,* frontispiece; R. A. Wild, *Water ...,* pl. XIII.

[10] This jar is also found on a fresco from Stabies, between the hand of priestesses, R. A. Wild, *Water ...,* pl. XI, but its origin is manifestly Egyptian; two specimens figure more particularly in the decoration of the painted tunic of Saqqarah, where they are placed on the table of offerings, and are part of a scene representing the union of Isis and Osiris-Sarapis in the form of a great snake wearing the *atef* crown, P. Perdrizet, 'La tunique liturgique historiée de Saqqarah', *Monuments Piot* XXXIV, 1934, p. 97-128, pl. VII-VIII; see also about this jar F. Dunand, 'Les représentations de l'Agathodémon, à propos de quelques bas-reliefs du Musée d'Alexandrie', *BIFAO,* LXVII, 1969, p. 35-36 and Fig. 9; R. A. Wild, *Water ...,* p. 103-113 and Fig. 23. This jar seems to correspond to to the very precise description which Apuleius gives (*Metamorphoses,* XI, 11) of the *urnula faberrime cavata* which is carried by a priest in the isiac procession of Cenchraeus, and which is supposed to be 'the effigy of the supreme divinity'.

[11] see note *supra*

[12] *De Iside et Osiride* (translation and comments by J. G. Griffiths, Univ. of Wales Press 1970), 36: at the head of the procession walks a priest bearing a 'water jar', *hydreion*, in honour of Osiris, because 'everything humid is an emanation' from that god.

[13] *Stromates,* VI, 4: in the processions, after the 'specialists' comes the prophet, 'holding the scared jar to his chest'.

Photo 96: no. 1199, detail: the face of the God Canopus

Photo 97: no. 1199, detail: the shaved head

Photo 98: no. 1199, detail: the fracture at the ankles

Photo 99: no. 1199, detail: the face and the God Canopus

mummified entrails of the defunct, and the 'Osiris-Canopus' has been suggested—which would mean that these latter could have been considered as containing the water of the Nile flood, assimilated to the 'humours' emanating from the body of Osiris,[14] in fact, the reliefs in the Osirian chapel in Dendera represent a procession of the gods of the nomes, carrying vases of the 'canopic' type which contain pieces of the body of Osiris.[15] The fact remains, however, that the images preserved of Osiris-Canopus, whether they are in terracotta, clay, limestone, or bronze, were never destined to contain anything. It would appear that they were used, not as recipients—even for sacred water—but as representations of one of the aspects of the god: 'Osiris-in-the-jar'. Several of these images, of rather large size, in fact, were discovered in temples of Hellenistic style, where they manifestly played the role of cult statues; this is the case, for example, of the one from the small Roman Sarapeion in Luxor, as well as the two items found in the small temple of Ras el-Sodah, near Alexandria, where they were placed between the statue of Isis and those of Hermanubis and Harpocrates, on a ledge

[14] On that hypothesis, see. J. F. Kettel, 'Canopes, rdw-w d'Osiris et Osiris-Canope', dans *Hommages à J. Leclant*, III, Cairo, IFAO 1994, p.315-330.

[15] See H. Beinlich, '*Die Osirisreliquien': zum Motiv der Körperzergliederung in der altägyptischen Religion,* Wiesbaden, 1984.

of masonry at the rear of the sanctuary[16]. In addition, the *canopi* with Osiris' head on the coins of Hadrian's reign are represented inside the temples, or in a portable naos looking like a stretcher, which clearly indicated that they are cult images[17].

During the second half of the 1st century AD, the motive of Osiris-Canopus appears for the first time on Alexandrian coins, still rare under Galba, Otho, and Vitellius, it became much more widespread from the year 4 of Vespasian in AD 73, and from then all through the 2nd century; the last series of this type is dated from the year 15 of Gallienus (AD 267). As early as in Augustus' time, it would appear that a series of 14 *canopi* whose heads correspond to the 14 gods of the college who reconstruct the Eye of Horus, i.e. the moon, are represented on a curious monument from Akhmim, below some reliefs evoking Greek gods like Ares, Poseidon, Zeus and Hades (?) by their emblems—evident proof of the co-existence of cultures in late Egypt[18]. It would seem that most representations of Osiris-Canopis, inside or outside Egypt, date from imperial times, and it can be admitted with R. Bianchi[19] that it was at that time that a 'canopic' theology developed, as well as a codification of the images; their complex decoration evokes water as the source of life—the water which, according to the funereal inscriptions in Greek language coming out of Egypt and Italy, at the same period, Osiris is supposed to dispense to the defunct for their regeneration.[20]

The Alexandrian statue thus finds its place in an iconographic evolution and in a theological context which are specific for the imperial period in its initial phase. But its exceptional aesthetic quality puts a versoecial accent on the sacrality of the divine image, the image which a priest cannot touch with his bare hands—for fear of sullying it, or because its contact could be dangerous? What is expressed in the veiled hands, is perhaps 'the religious fear of forbidden contact'.[21] But the serene attitude of the young priest and his almost tender gesture holding against his cheek the image which he carries, translates the love of his god as well as well as the wish, so often expressed in Egyptian texts, to remain forever in his presence.[22]

[16] On the Sarapeion in Luxor, see J. F. Leclant, *Orientalia* 20, 1951, p. 455-456, Fig. 4-5, pl. XLVII; J. C. Golvin *et al.*, 'Le petit Sarapieion romain de Louqsor', *BIFAO* 81, 1981, p. 115-148. On the one in Ras el-Sodah and the Osiris-canopi, see A. Andriani, *Annuaire du Musée Gréco-Romain [1935-1939]*, 1940, p. 136-138, pl. LII and LIII.2.

[17] See *Iside, il mito* ..., IV, 101-103 (the canopi in a temple); S. Handler, 'Architecture on the roman coins of Alexandria', *AJA* 75, 1971, p. 57-74, pl. XI, 10-12 (canopi on a stretcher). On these motives, see J. Winand, 'Divinités-canopes sur les monnaies impériales d'Alexandrie', *Hommages à J. Leclant*, III, p. 493-503.

[18] O. Gueraud, 'Le monument d'Agrios au Musée du Caire', *ASAE* 39, 1939, p. 279-303, pl. XL-XLIII. The author of the poems, Agrios, presents himself, according to Gueraud, as 'the faithful subject, good soldier, and pious servant of the gods'.

[19] R. S. Bianchi in *Cleopatra's Egypt. Age of the Ptolemies* (catalogue of the Brooklyn exhibition, 1988-1989), The Brooklyn Museum, 1988, no. 136, p. 248-249. L. Török, *Hellenistic and Roman Terracottas from Egypt* (Rome 1995), proposes a dating at the end of the Ptolemaic for an Osiris-Canopus which he publishes, pl. LVIII, no. 109; it must be agreed, however, that most known images do not reach back further than the first century AD. R. A. Wild, *Water* ..., (p. 114-115) thinks that the appearance of the motive on the coins of the 1st century suppose a prior development in the iconography, although he admits to the 'total absence' of Hellensitic documentation.

[20] R. A. Wild, *Water* ..., p. 123-126.

[21] According to J. Vernant, 'Le Pur et l'Impur', in *Mythe et société en Grèce ancienne*' Paris, 1974, p. 132

[22] Additional bibliography:
W. Weber, Zwei Formen des Osiris, in *Drei Untersuchungen zur ägyptisch-griechischen Religion*, Heidelberg 1911.
Fr. von Bissing, 'Das heilige Bild von Canopus', *BSAA* 24, 1929, p..38-59, and 25, 1930, p. 97 ff.
E. Panofsky, 'Canopus Deus. The Iconography of a Non-Existent God', *Gazette des Beaux Arts*, 57, 1961, p. 193-216.
A. Fouquet, 'Quelques représentations d'Osiris canope au Musée du Louvre', *BIFAO*, 73, 1973, p. 61-69.

A COLOSSAL SPHINX WITH FALCON'S HEAD

Jean Yoyotte

A falcon's head (no. 795), the remains of a granite sculpture measuring from the throat to the top of the skull 70 cm, at first sight would suggest in its original form a truly alarming divine effigy[1] (photo 100, 101). With the hair in the form of a wig appropriate to the gods, it was a type of Horus; if one imagined it standing like the Ramesside Horus in the Vienna Museum,[2] one would be in the presence of a statue measuring almost four and a half metres high, almost as big as the royal colossus whose head was found in the same sector.[3] Yet, with the exception of Amenhotep II who increased the large effigies of the state gods and the multiform Sekhmet, and to a lesser extent his imitator, Ramesses II, it is known that the pharaohs left behind comparatively few statues showing, seated or standing, gods and goddesses and none so colossal.

Human ears have been put on the sides of the temples, gently spilling onto the wig as if the mask of an animal had been substituted by the completely anthropomorphic mask of the gods. The ears are a valuable indicator of the date. We know that none of the representations of falcon-headed divinities in the round, be they in stone, wood or metal, were endowed with human ears. On the other hand, from the XXVIth dynasty on, they are found placed on the side of wigs on an appreciable number of votive statuettes in bronze featuring Horus or other falcon-type gods.[4] This addition, which is moreover met on statuettes of other divinities with a human body bearing an animal head framed with a great wig, is, one might believe, characteristic of those images which some consecrated as those of gods 'who listened to the prayers' of people.[5] One may deduce that head no. 795 could not have been created before the 7th century BC. Too little of the work, whose polish and modelling was of quality, remains to be able to establish whether it was made before or after the accession of the Graeco-Macedonian rulers. The surprising dimensions which the head implies do not contradict in themselves an attribution to later periods. Under the native dynasties, then under the Ptolemies, effigies of kings, and even of certain major dignitaries, were sculpted in hard stone, full length and in super-human size.[6] Nevertheless a divine colossus, of whatever period it might be, is an embarrassing exception.

Observations made whilst diving by Mr F. Goddio and the sketch (figure 12) which he made allow us to resolve the difficulty. The mass of curls of the wig, instead of falling vertically at the back of the neck, incline to the horizontal, as if they had just come to rest on the back of a body in a stretched out position; the curve of the shoulder seems to confirm this, as if the front limbs were resting flat in front. These observations lead to two possible reconstructions.

Head no. 795 belonged to a large falcon-headed sphinx.

In order to show the king as the warrior god Montou,[7] to portray the solar god[8] or Nubian Horus on guard at the door of the holy place and protecting the king,[9] the New Empire invented a type of sphinx which sat on the neck of a prone lion the head of a falcon, wearing the divine wig (figures 13, 14). This type, quite rarely attested in the round, was little known in three dimensional iconography before the 4th century BC.[10] The Alexandrian monument would have been a large sphinx representing Re or Horus. It is be noted that its size approached that of certain classic, royal sphinxes that date from the XXXth dynasty or the time of the first Ptolemies.[11]

The head is the remains of a god shown in the form of a 'hawk-headed crocodile-sphinx'.

[1] See the description of this piece in Z. Kiss, above, p. 178.
[2] *Sammlung, Ägyptischer Kunst*, Münche, 2te Auflage, 1976, p. 40-41, no. 22.
[3] Z. Kiss, above, p. 175.
[4] G. Roeder, *Ägyptischer Bronzefiguren* ..., Berlin, 1956, p. 75-79.
[5] Concerning the origins and late developments of the devotion to 'the ears that listen', J. Quaegebeur and G. Wagner, *BIFAO* 73 (1973), p. 41-60. Fr. Kayser, 'Oreilles et couronnes. À propos des cultes de Canope', *BIFAO* 91 (1991), p. 207-217, pl. 61, 62.

[6] In particular the colossal statue of Amenhotep son of Hapou, CG 1199, about 3 m. high, made in granite to suggest devotion to the famous minister of Amenhotep III who had become a saint.
[7] Cf. the representation of statues consecrated for Amenhotep at Karnak at the tomb of Qenamoun, Vandier, *Manuel* III, p. 377, fig. 16.5. Here fig. 13 (after Prisse 'Avennes, *Histoire de l'Art égyptien*, Paris, 1878, pl. 352).
[8] British Museum, 11, 13, from the great temple of Abu Simbel, PM VII, p. 103.
[9] Second court of the temple of Wadi el-Seboua, PM VII, p. 53-54 and 57 (VII-X).
[10] Representation of idols from Saft on the naos of Nekhnebef, Cario CG 70021, XXXth dynasty; E. Neville, 'The Shrine of Saft el Henneh'. EEF 5, London 1887, pl. 4, 2nd reg., pl. 5, 3rd reg.
[11] For example the pair of sphinxes (length 3.9 and 4.1 m.) found on the south slope of the Serapeum and exposed on site; head, Graeco-Roman Museum. Reg. 23048 (Tkaczow, *Topography*, p. 242, obj. 152 photo).

Photo 100: the colossal head of the hawk-headed sphinx, no. 795, granite, *in situ*.

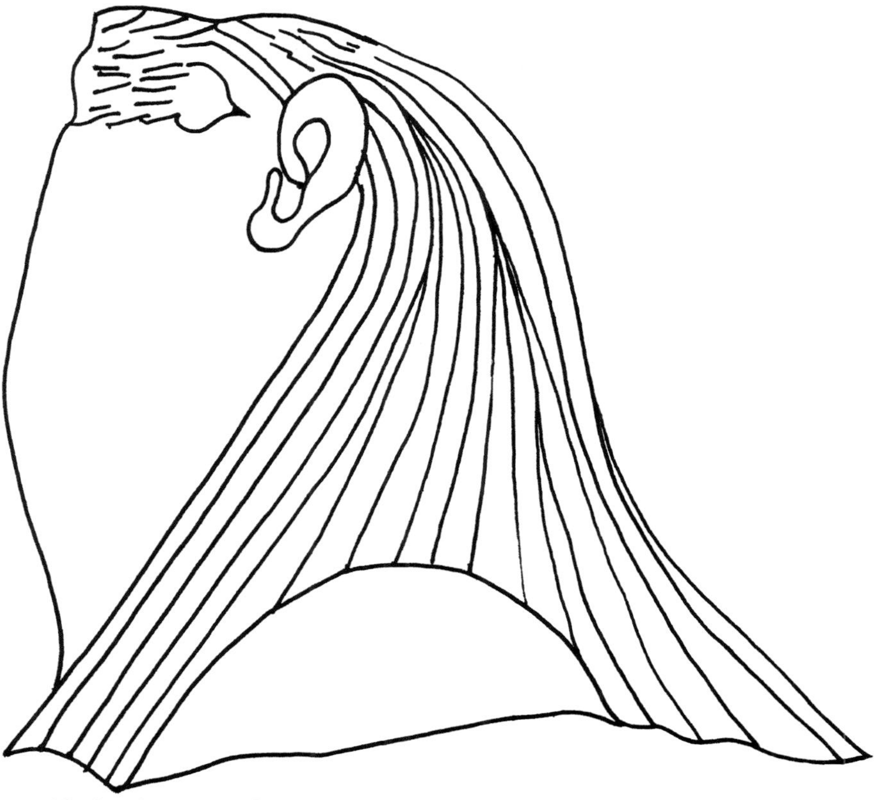

Figure 12: sketch made under water.

Figure 14: Horus-Hekenou in the form of a hawk-headed sphinx, after the naos of Saft (reign of Nekhtnebef)

Figure 13: Amenhotep II as a hawk-headed sphinx, after the tomb of Qenamoun

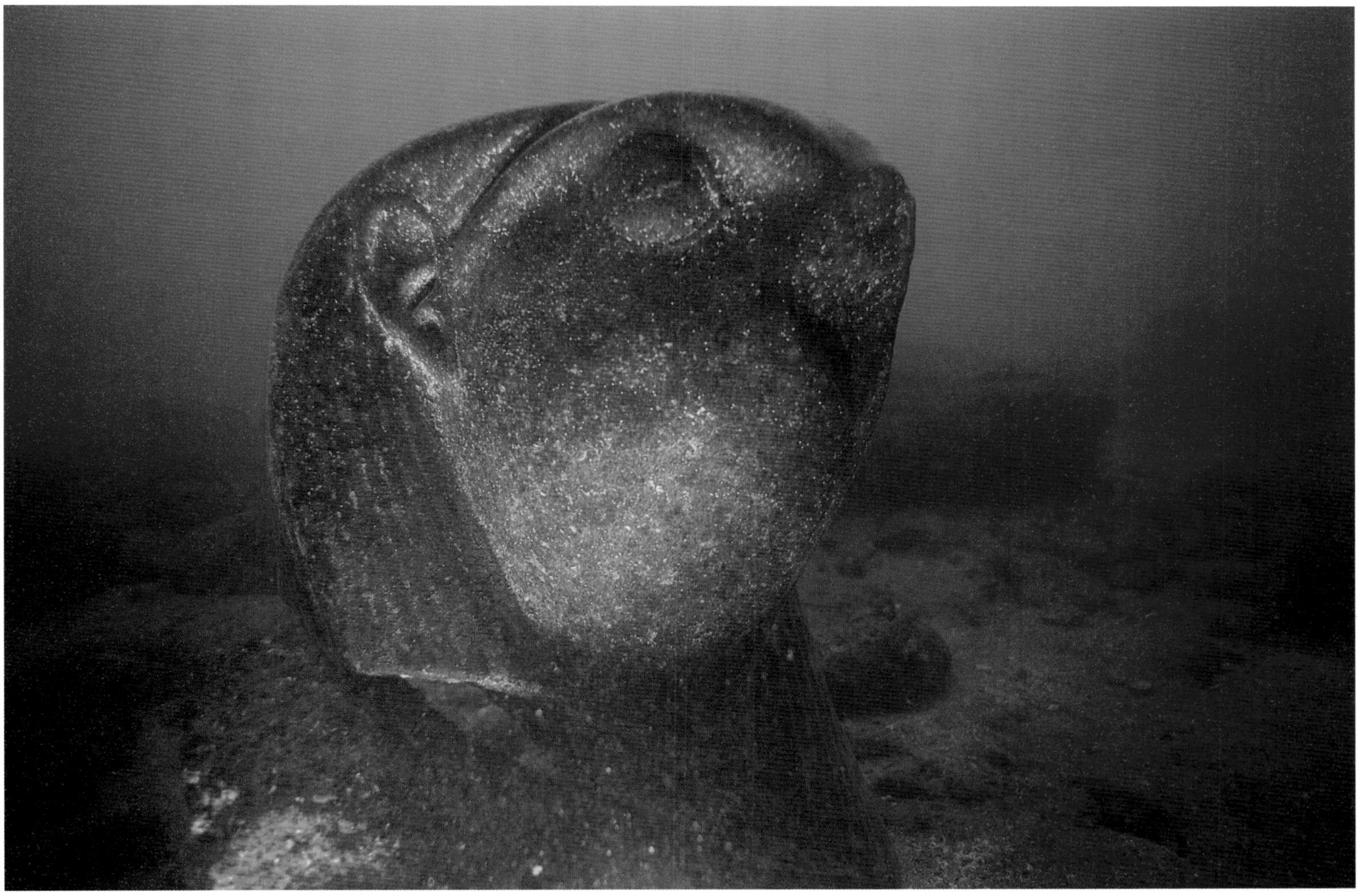

Photo 101: the colossal head of the hawk-headed sphinx, no. 795, face on, *in situ*

Figure 15: the Horus of Sohag, after a 'magical' statue

Figure 16: the Horus of Sohag, after the Borgia torso

Amongst the monumental divine statues at the Theban temple of Amenhotep II (1391-1353 BC), there is an alabaster figure (5.33 at the base on 1.05 m.) whose front part is a lion and the back part a crocodile.[12] Lacking any inscription, the name of this mixed entity is unknown and, as the head has disappeared, it is not possible to say whether it was of a man, falcon or another animal. This sculpture in any case anticipates an iconographic type well attested later and of which the oldest examples date from the 5th century.[13]

Different designs feature a divinity in the form of a composite beast whose protome is a lion, the back part from a crocodile and the head a hawk, often set on a high base in the form of a temple (figures 15, 16).[14] This imagery has some variants: thus the type of crested crown varies; sometime a dog's head ends in a lizard's tail, but the composition of this sort of 'pantheos', that is to say the whole composition of the various attributes of the divinity, is typical. It serves to dress up a certain Horus 'who holds the bonds' (?) *(ímy-šnw.t)*, an ancient local god of the Sohag region who, since the Old Empire, is known as a redoubtable magician who cures ills and destroys enemies and wrong-doers. He is met, for example, among the theories of armed divinities on statues and small stelae, stone objects inscribed with curative formulae which important people in the 4th-3rd centuries place at the disposition of sick people.[15] The same image combines an anonymous solar entity which was invoked at Memphis and in the Meroitic region during the period of Roman domination (1st-5th centuries AD).[16] Here the forelegs extend into human hands to present the palm which symbolises eternity. Figurines[17] and amulets[18] were made from this baroque idol. It belongs to those divinities modelled in relief with votive steatite *patera*.[19] It was to assume a place among the cosmic powers on Greaeco-Roman 'gnostic' talismans.[20] Horus, the magician of Sahag, was currently invoked in incantations recited for the protection of the cosmos and the state and as the guardian of human beings in the Ptolemaic period. From all the evidence, an idol endowing the omnipresent saviour god with the power of the celestial hawk, the terrestrial lion and the crocodile of the waters, and which was supposed to ensure eternity, enjoyed a singular popularity in late Egypt. Also, it would not be unreasonable to imagine that in the Ptolemaic or Roman period, a gigantic example of this idol has been brought from elsewhere, indeed sculpted from new, to defend the pharaoh and the well-being of Alexandrians.[21] Borrowed from the iconography of other Horuses, the addition of the ears shows the god as attentive to their prayers.[22]

Only the discovery of other fragments would enable us to decide whether this sphinx was simply hieracocephalic or a composite triple sphinx. In any case, 796 is undeniably the remains of a near classic sphinx.

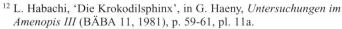

[12] L. Habachi, 'Die Krokodilsphinx', in G. Haeny, *Untersuchungen im Amenopis III* (BÄBA 11, 1981), p. 59-61, pl. 11a.

[13] 'Représentations des idoles dans la cella à Hibis, règne d'un Darius', reprduced by L. V. Žabkar (cited below n. 16), p. 151, fig. 3.

[14] Fig. 16, after a photograph of the Borgia torso, Maples, Museo Nazionale, inv. 1065. See Lanzone, *Dizionario di Mitologia egizia II*, p. 580, pl. CCXVI, fig. 3.

[15] Borgia torso (above n. 14); Lanzome, *op. cit.*, p. 578, pl. CCXVI, fig. 1; p. 581, pl. CCXVII, fig.2; British Museum 36250, W. Budge, *The Mummy*, 2nd ed., London, 1925, pl. XXXIII; Metternich stele, W. Gotenischeff, *Die Metternichstele*, pl. V, reg. XXXVI; VI, re. XXXVI, etc.

[16] L. V. Žabkar, 'A Hieracocephalus Deity from Naqa, Qustul and Philoé', in *ZÄS* 102 (1975), p. 143-153.

[17] A small limestone statuette found in a temple at Faranis, 1st century AD. A. E. R. Baok, *Karanis, The Temples. Seasons 1924-1931*, Univ,. of Michigan, 1930, p. 9-10, pl. V, fig. 10.

[18] Strasbourg amulets. Musée Rohan S452; Cairo, cf., P. Perdrizet, *Mon Pot* XXXIV (1934), p. 107, etc.

[19] P. Perdrizet, *op. cit.*, p. 106-108, fig. 5; A. Wiedemann, *PSBA* 36 (1914), p. 117-119, pl. VIII.

[20] Bronze pendant, Petrie, Amulets, London, 1914, pl. XLIX, cf. p. 30-31; *intaglio*, Perdrizet, *op. cit.*, p. 106, fig. 4.

[21] Notices of the lying hieracocephalic sphinx are most rare in the Graeco-Roman period (one case, CG 33248, Edgar, *Sculptor's Studies*, CGC, p. 62, pl. XXIX). Manifestations of the 'pantheos' and Horus *ímy-šnw.t* on the other hand are very common.

[22] Drawn images of the crocodilo-sphinx most often show on the head of the hawk a *pschent*, a *hemhem* or a solar disk. This is not to exclude that such a crown had been put at the beginning on our colossal sphinx.

PHARAONICA

Jean Yoyotte

I. REFLECTIONS CONCERNING ALEXANDRIA'S PHARAONICA

Note: *As the fruit of preliminary research to understand the presence of Egyptian monuments in the Greek and Roman city of Alexandria, and to try to explain this presence in terms of cultural interaction between the old pharaonic and the young Hellenistic world, this text was intended as a practical analysis of a vast range of questions, for the IEASM team on the one hand, and for the general public interested in the history of Alexandria on the other. We must beware of hasty and simplistic explanations of what is seen and found on site, and keep the questions and their answers within the general framework of research in ancient history. Thus, professionals will pardon our lengthy discussions on 'the status of questions' with which they are perfectly familiar, and the lay reader will have to bear with our detailed and complex discussions, interspersed with references which we shall keep as sparse as possible.*

The term *aegytiaca* is presently used very generally in inquiries and descriptions covering objects found outside Egypt and Sudan. Any product of authentic Egyptian art is thus defined, as well as imitations stemming from workshops in Phoenicia, Cyprus, or Rhodes. The term equally includes more or less 'orientalising' objects and, further, those monuments in a Greek style, as well as Greek inscriptions testifying to the expansion of Egyptian cults and divinities throughout the Hellenistic world and the Roman empire, and even the Greek inscriptions which the Ptolemies bequeathed to the cities and islands of Hellas which they had annexed to their Egyptian kingdom.

As regards the 'capital' of this kingdom, I prefer to use the term *pharaonica*, which is meant to describe monuments which by their kind, style, and hieroglyphic decoration, stand out on this pinnacle of Hellenistic art and culture in the time of pharaohs, who are, however, of Graeco-Macedonian origin. It goes without saying that in Alexandria, Greek inscriptions cannot be called *aegyptiaca,* and neither can effigies of Isis, if their posture and clothing are Greek, i.e. *hellenica*. And, above all, Alexandrian monuments of native tradition and manufacture, i.e., of 'pharaonic' style, are not exclusively antique *aegyptiaca* imported into the city founded by Alexander; some were made in the native style at the time of the Ptolemies, and even that of the Caesars. The term *pharaonica* conveniently covers both categories, in contrast to the *hellenica* of this exquisitely Greek City.

Supreme commander of the Hellene confederation, Alexander had, naturally, founded a Greek city. Greek architects had built a city in the Greek style. With the Macedonian kings, the city is the seat of the central government of Egypt and of its totally Hellenistic outside dependencies: Greek is spoken in town and court, in offices and among the inhabitants, whether of the various *demes* or township residents, and even among foreign minorities, including the Jews. As throughout the Roman Orient, people continue to govern, speak, trade, and write in that language, and the first Christian church, too, is Greek. With the Macedonian kings, Alexandria on the border of Egypt (*ad Aegyptum*), becomes one of the pivots of Hellenistic culture. Welcoming wise men, thinkers and writers from all over Hellas, the Museum participates in the creation of Greek science, and in the Library are stored and studied, as far as anyone can say, exclusively Greek texts. Alexandrian city planning, houses, objects, mosaics, and pottery are Hellenistic, as are the way of life and the names of places and inhabitants. The hierarchy of the court is built on the Greek model, and the priests of the deified sovereigns are Greeks. Temples are built to Zeus, Poseidon, and other Olympians, and in Graeco-Roman iconography such images clearly dominate, Dionysiac associations prosper ...

Alexandria quickly adopted as its patron the Memphite god Osiris-Apis, enthroned on its acropolis under the name of Serapis (or Sarapis). Greeks, as well as the Carian mercenaries residing in Egypt, had venerated him since the times of the pharaohs of Saïs. Also venerated in several sanctuaries in the city was the popular goddess Isis, the enchantress who resuscitates the dead and protects people. However, these indigenous deities were covered with Greek drapery by Alexandrian artists, so that Sarapis' effigies resembled those of Zeus, Hades and Asclepios. Gradually, a specific Isis cult developed, Greek in form and language, which gained theological pre-eminence unknown previously to the Egyptians, spreading with its initiatory rites throughout the Hellenistic Mediterranean and well into the Roman West.

There is no need to elaborate further. Alexandria was and always remained a completely Greek city, outside and apart from the heart of ancient Egypt. In its texts and its remains, it belongs to the Hellenists; Egyptology, concerned with the history of the *chôra*—the native hinterland—and with the study of native texts, is concerned very little by it. Yet ...

From the 18th century on, and including Napoleon's Expedition to Egypt, visiting travellers noted, and sometimes carried away with them, one vestige or another of ancient Alexandria, as they lay scattered about the smaller Ottoman town, or on the bare land on both sides of the old Arab wall dating from the Tulunid period: re-used or crumpled columns and their sections, capitals and other parts of buildings, statues and their pedestals, texts on stone, etc. Amazingly, some hieroglyphic inscriptions could be found among these mostly Greek or Graeco-Roman vestiges. In the following centuries, many more items of all kinds were found by house- or land-owners, the township's civil servants, and later, during the city's rehabilitation and development in the times of the viceroys and the monarchy, by the curators of the Graeco-Roman Museum. In addition to such chance findings on the surface or during superficial digging, the successive directors of the Graeco-Roman Museum had added to the collection of antique stones by more systematic excavations, undertaken since 1891 in various locations. Such work brought better descriptions of the sites, but was generally carried out hastily, and lacked taphonomic and stratigraphic precision. Still, the Graeco-Roman Museum acquired an appreciable amount of *pharaonica* of more or less definite origin.

The inventory of *pharaonica,* as that of *hellenica*, is not an easy undertaking. For long periods of time, the discoverers had only indicated sites approximately, referring to districts, neighbourhoods, properties, or sites in the urban infrastructure, and were brief if not outright silent about the archaeological context *in situ*. Descriptions of items themselves are vague and often erroneous, particularly as regards the simple petrographic identification of rocks. Cases are known, furthermore, where items found in Alexandria ought to be excluded from both the inventory and the set of problems, like the five statues bearing Ramesside names, found in Tanis in 1825, abandoned by J-J. Rifaud on the quayside, and subsequently dispersed throughout the old town.[1] Likewise the naos D. 29 in the Louvre, which was brought in 1822 from Kôm el-Ahmar in Menûfiyah for Drovetti, and which had to be fished 'out of the sea in Alexandria Harbour' following an accident during its transfer aboard the ship taking it to Europe.[2] And the same applies to the several small sphinxes from the Saqqarah Sarapeum, which Harris and Mariette saw in various Alexandrian collectors' houses in 1847 and 1850.[3]

The inventory of Egyptian remains in Alexandria has recently been considerably increased, both in number and in quality, following the extensive survey of the underwater topography which the IEASM has carried out in the eastern part of the Eastern Harbour, and even more through the extensive rescue diggings from the nearest of the various vast piles of huge antique stones which lie submerged at the foot of Fort Qa'it-Bey. The number of remains of Greek and Graeco-Roman origin vastly exceeds those of pharaonic style, as is the case in those parts of Alexandria which remained dry land. Nevertheless, modern man's fascination with the most ancient Egyptian past, and the all-pervading egyptomania which is its corollary, have caused the vestiges of Egyptian culture to overshadow the remnants of classical civilisation predominant in Alexandria: both the press and the audiovisual media—once they had emphasised the Macedonian Cleopatra and the Ptolemaeic lighthouse—quickly and more frequently mentioned colossi, sphinxes, obelisks hewn out of Aswan granite, papyrus-style columns and hieroglyphs, Sethos and Ramses, rather than the ionic, doric, and corinthian style Roman columns, of the Lagide dynasty or the Caesars. The stars of photographic representation were, here and there, sphinxes located by divers under water. Alexandria equal to Karnak! This presentation naturally evoked in the public's mind a distorted image of the reality of Alexandria, and transferred Alexandrian archaeology there from the realm of classical studies to that of Egyptology. One even went so far as to salute the discovered hieroglyphs as proof of the prosperity of the port of Alexandria in pharaonic days. The discoverers themselves, incidentally, were seduced by these exotic monuments, far less in number, but more familiar and more spectacular, with the result that to this day, scientists have learnt more about the inventory and details of underwater *egyptiaca* than *hellenica*. Admittedly, the ancient Egyptians' sacral art, and its splendid use of hieroglyphic writing, contribute much to this dazzling view: on the walls of the great and solid temples, as on the statues of kings and commoners, texts are engraved in profusion, whereas on Greek architecture and sculpture, the use of writing is soberly reduced to small surfaces which are generally more exposed to damage. At an estimate, some eighty Egyptian inscriptions, more or less well published, have been found in Alexandria—a

[1] This relates to Cairo CG 384 (= Tkaczow, *Topography*, Obj. # 134), Cairo CG 620A (Obj. # 620 and 135), of the group formerly of the Graeco-Roman Museum, reg. no. 346, now in Cairo (Obj. Nr 120B and 124), further to the statue Graeco-Roman Museum, reg. no. 620 (Obj. no. 120 and 126), the upper part of which is exhibited in the Serapeum and the lower part kept in the Museum (J. Y., *Egyp. Inscrips.*, p. 228, n. 21); and finally to Copenhagen, Nat. Mus. inv. no. 345.

[2] According to one of Drovetti's letters (transmitted by Sylvie Guichard). The exact origin of the naos is known from a drawing with notes by Pascal Coste 1822, Marseille City Library, Ms 1307.

[3] J. Malek in *CdE* LVIII no. 115-116 (1983), p. 65-72. It is a moot point whether some pharaonic monuments said to come from Alexandria were not in reality pieces which had come from elsewhere, but had at some point been part of the collections of consuls or foreign residents.

temporary figure, of course—whereas the epigraphic corpus of Greek or Latin non-funereal texts or fragments of texts amounts only to about two hundred items. The proportion changes drastically, however, when considering just the remnants of statues and architectural elements. As an example, the submerged land around Qa'it-Bey contains 882 Graeco-Roman 'smooth-shafted' columns against a mere half dozen papyriform ones.[4] Almost without exception, all antique Graeco-Roman and pharaonic stones collected before the most recent decades have been found in or near buildings of Arab-Islamic times, or were buried under recent accumulations, which themselves have been interfered with. These are, in fact, errant stones, moved and even scattered far away from their presumed original sites. Their context *in situ* is of Ottoman times and places them within the history of mediaeval or even modern urban space, but rarely allows their attribution topographically to the monuments to which they originally belonged. The excellent last-minute excavations carried out by the Centre d'Etudes Alexandrines and the Greek Museum (1991-98) have sometimes reached down as far as the Ptolemaic level, finding profane buildings here and there, but unluckily they could not discover the foundations of temples, and have rarely produced notable *pharaonica*. The harvest of Egyptian-style elements (15 items out of 110) among the sculptural debris discovered between 1960 and 1982 in the Roman and Byzantine sector of Kôm el-Dikka by various teams from the Centre of Mediterranean Archaeology of the Polish Academy of Sciences, and the Polish Centre of Mediterranean Archaeology of Warsaw University requires much reflection.[5] They constitute a haphazard collection of large debris and small splinters of divine, royal, and common figures, found scattered over the thermal baths, cisterns, houses, and streets. Analysis of these samples, which stem from the haphazard passage of successive limeburners, marble cutters, quarriers and building workers, allows us to visualise more clearly the disastrous state of the sites from which *pharaonica* were extracted in former times, to better understand the extent of irrecuperable loss of documentation, and to conclude with Zsolt Kiss that 'the correlation between sculptural vestiges and urban topography [is] purely accidental.'

The underwater sites currently explored present the considerable advantage that, even if their vestiges are not found in their original location, they are nevertheless witnesses which, since being covered by water, have not been disturbed by subsequent building, demolition, and rebuilding, let alone relocation, of monuments in urban Alexandria. Invited by Franck Goddio firstly to take stock of his discoveries, and then to translate and comment on the hieroglyphic inscriptions which he had found, there was no way for me to evade these preliminary reflections on the Alexandrian *pharaonica*, if I wanted to define properly my own area of research and at the same time help IEASM and its archaeologists define, exploit, and interpret this material and the disconcerting—to say the least—data of its location. Once the general amazement was overcome, once the Egyptologists were satisfied to dispose of new documents concerning their dynasties and their temples in Heliopolis, the Egyptian monuments found in the Royal Quarter—like those taken out of the waters around Qa'it-Bey, and, incidentally, those found here and there on land across Alexandria in earlier times—raised more questions rather than provide quick answers.

A study of the maps plotted by the IEASM, and of the photos taken by its divers, still left us a long way from recognising the patterns of palaces or temples. Instead, we found what looked like a collection of empty lots, stacked with more or less dense concentrations of dismembered buildings, or else like abandoned demolition sites, in which a few sculptures and inscription-bearing blocks dating from pharaohs prior to Alexander had been mislaid. There were few limestone blocks compared to an abundance of those of hard rock. These submerged Alexandrian 'royal quarters', protected from the invasions of the modern city, looked in fact much like the sites of the great stone temples of Lower Egypt, themselves likewise spared mediaeval or latter-day invasions. My thinking is therefore largely based on my knowledge of the temples of Tanis (Sân el-Hagar), a historical township resembling in various ways the royal and religious monuments of Alexandria. Obelisks, great statues, sphinxes and other sizeable stone objects had been taken away from Pi-Ramses, the prestigious residence which Ramses II had created in 1280, and brought to this town (founded around 1100 BC) under dynasties XXI and XXII. The blocks constituting the temple walls at Pi-Ramses were used to build those in Tanis, and some of them were recycled several times for different uses. By the end of the pagan period, the limestone had been consumed by the limeburners, and the hard stones cut up by the manufacturers of grindstones, mortar, troughs and other building material. Despite the disastrous configuration of this abandoned quarry, surviving inscriptions and texts led to the 'discovery' over time of Ramses the Great's temples and residences in Sân el-Hagar—until an objective evaluation of this chaotic heap of stones, and examination of the material state of the blocks, together with various ceramic or petrological indications, allowed the reconstruction of the various stages of the building and subsequent destruction of Tanis.

In order to evaluate the new *pharaonica* discovered by the IEASM, it seemed useful to define more generally the archaeological context from which *pharaonica* have so

[4] J-Y. Empereur, *Le Phare,* p. 87-88.

[5] Z. Kiss, *Sculptures des fouilles polonaises à Kôm el-Dikka (1960-1982).* (Coll. *Alexandria IV),* Warszaw, PWN, 1988 ed.

far originated. As already stated, this was not an easy task. In view of existing inventories and publications, even the survey of the items themselves was only partially possible. Since 1991, Paolo Gallo has compiled a catalogue of the corpus of Egyptian-style remains found in the Alexandrian area, from the huge slabs bearing hieroglyphic texts down to the smallest debris without the any trace of inscription,[6] and reached a total of some 600 items.[7] The present essay is based on a hundred noteworthy items—dateable and mostly bearing inscriptions—because they provide information of real use.[8] We hope that the major part of the questions and answers discussed here shall not, in time, be found to vary overmuch from the statistics gleaned from the definitive listing.

This *exposé* aims, at the same time, at maintaining methodical doubt, directing detailed investigation, and also at submitting to historians a general hypothesis which may be surprising, as it goes against a number of commonplace ideas about relations between the Egyptian and Greek worlds, which supposedly excluded each other. From the study of *pharaonica*, one is encouraged to suppose that specific temples, the typical works of art, the proper ritual practices, and the traditional conceptions of the Egyptians were far from marginal in Greek Alexandria, even at the time of the very first Ptolemies.[9]

In view of our *pharaonica,* two essential questions must be put to the archaeologists studying Alexandrian sites on the one hand, and to the historians of the Greek and Roman period of Egypt on the other:

Could the location of the findings and their material appearance tell us something about the topography of the monuments, and the history of Alexandria?

And what, above all, does this omnipresence of objects of the 'barbaric' art of a colonised people mean in the Greek conquerors' metropolis? In other words, what were they, archaeologists and historians, able to learn about the relations between two cultural traditions? With what intentions did the Greek City's builders bring parts of temples and the statues of the Egyptians from the interior? '*To know*', as Letronne put it, '*the outcome of the permanent combat between the Greek civilisation with that other culture which goes back to the very cradle of humanity …*' And to confirm whether it really was a combat, or rather a kind of symbiosis, without any radical conflict, between the culture of the Hellenes and the immemorial past of the Egyptian culture, still very much alive at the time.

In the matter of religious architecture, of sacral art, and of ritual, the traditions of the two cultures were, indeed, very different. The Egyptian temple is closed, the Greek one is open, etc. Concepts of designing, fitting out and the presentation of images are radically different and exerted little, if any, mutual influence. The Greeks did indeed accept as gods—and even as their own gods, at the price of *interpretatio graeca*—the local divinities. The result over time is some borrowing of iconography: an image of Khonsou, Heracles in Greece, carries a bludgeon, but in an image of purely Egyptian graphism; a Harpocrates modelled in the Greek style is covered by the *pschent* or the *hemhem*, etc. Yet, such purely iconographic exchanges cannot allow any concept of mixed art. The Greek taste in representing the gods for the private use of the population carries the day up to Roman times. Inside the great temples, however, Egyptian tradition and taste remain alive to the very end of paganism, even if some additions in the Greek forms of the cult can be found inside the sacred areas. This is the situation concerning official art, architecture and ritual in the Valley (but which should not forget a certain hellenisation of native priestly elites on the one hand, nor the devotion which inhabitants of Greek culture and status bring to the gods of their village).

We are accustomed to visualise Hellenistic Alexandria as a city of purely Greek environment, where temples looked the same as in Athens or Ephesus, where the dominant part of the population displayed Greek habits and tastes, with no time for the exotic works and practices proper to the indigenous population of the *chôra*—or even the rejection of them. The presence of people of Egyptian extraction in the city is well known, but still the commonplace idea is that '*there should not exist any indication of truly organised indigenous cult following the Egyptian tradition in Alexandria.*[10] How, then, can we explain the *pharaonica* of Alexandria? What was their role, visible or hidden, in the beliefs, practices and existing monuments in the city?

Among the products of traditional pharaonic sacerdotal art found throughout Alexandria, we notice that many are dated to dynasties prior to the foundation of the city, and were brought there from the temples of the *chôra*. The initial site of many monuments, obelisks, statues, bas-reliefs and architectural elements can indeed be determined from the names of sites and local divinities figuring in their hieroglyphic inscriptions. Some rare cases

6 See *BIFAO* 93 (1993), p. 488.

7 See Gallo, *Ostraca* (1997), note 18 *in fine*, p. XXIV.

8 The list compiled by PM IV (1934), p. 2-6 et add. p. 270 was rather complete for the time; withdraw from it *Descr. Ant.* V., pls. 47 (6-8) and 60 (1-4). The inventories of Barbara Tkazkow, *Topography* (1993) offer a practical topology of sites, but contain a number of confusions and imprecisions, but use the *Register* of the Graeco-Roman Museum. The *Comptes rendus des foui-les et travaux,* published annually by Jean Leclant in *Or* provide precious additions. On some *pharaonica* falsely supposed to be Alexandrine, see above, notes 1-3.

9 J-Y. Empereur, in *Libération* of Sept. 28, 1995, p. 32, transmits well the amazement at such an innovative conclusion, which he then courageously makes his own: *'Antique Alexandria was a blend of purely Hellenistic monuments—which was known—and of pharaonic buildings, which is much more surprising.'*

10 D. Valbelle and G. Husson, *L'État et les institutions en Egypte des premiers Pharaons aux Empereurs romains* (Coll. U. Histoire ancienne Paris, Armand Colin, 1992, p. 217).

may be noted where monuments have been taken out of the temples of Memphis,[11] and some other rare instances from Saïs.[12] It has been established for at least a century, however, that the major part of the Alexandrian *pharaonica* of pre-Ptolemaic days, and whose origin can be determined, was initially to be found in Heliopolis, the very ancient centre of the sun cult, situated just north of Cairo. They consist of movable objects such as obelisks, statues of kings, sphinxes, as well as monolithic elements, parts of monumental buildings, such as architraves, lintels, uprights, transoms, or wall columns. Only names characteristic of the town and the holy places of Heliopolis can been read there. Divinities represented or named, those of whom pharaoh is 'beloved', are Re, the sun god, under the different names and images which theology had conferred on the creator[13] star, and the group of powers (or 'Souls') which are of the highest importance in Heliopolitan mythology.[14] The sculptures and blocks are in granite or granitoïd Aswan stone, some others come from the greywacke of Wadi Hammâmât. A high percentage of quartzite from Djebel Ahmar, the 'Red Mountain' close to Heliopolis, is also notable. The collection of Alexandrian relics presents a sizeable list of pharaohs who have contributed to the beauty of the House of Re throughout the ages: Sesostris III (dyn. XII), Thutmose III (dyn. XVIII), Seti I and Ramses II (dyn. XIX), the Psammetichuses, Apries, and Amasis (dyn. XXVI), Nekhtnebef, and Nekhtharhebe (dyn. XXX). Materials used, divinities invoked and founder kings constitute much the same selection as the one made up by the rare remaining vestiges which have been found, either *in situ* or re-utilised, in the Arabo-Islamic city of Cairo, stemming from the same grand and famous buildings in the Sun City, which today, too, is almost entirely submerged by the growth of a modern metropolis.[15]

According to the present state of the inventory, the greatest group of objects coming obviously from Heliopolis has been collected in the neighbourhood of the Serapeum. An appreciable number has recently been pulled out of the vast and enigmatic collection of stones submerged along the quayside. Several have been found in ill-determined contexts in the city centre, and some other rare ones in the eastern quarters. Everywhere, these *pharaonica* are lost in the tangle of Greek remains. Contrary to what might be concluded after a superficial reading of the map, Heliopolis has very obviously not served for centuries as a quarry for the building and ornamentation of all buildings in all parts of Alexandria. Much rather we should conclude that some massive transfers of stone were initiated by the authorities, then distributed to be used in some monuments, and that these monuments are grouped in Alexandria in just a few temples following Egyptian rites or at least with some pharaonic decoration.

One observation appears obvious: among the pharaonic vestiges of all kinds whose origin is certain, the percentage of items taken from Heliopolis is overwhelming; this percentage has again been increased by the recent discoveries under water. Unless the still ongoing evaluation of the entire corpus radically changes matters, it looks very much as if the vast temples of the sun complex had at one time constituted the main—if not the only—reserve from which to draw obelisks, statues, sphinxes, and was likewise the main reserve of prefabricated architectural elements for building and fitting out Alexandrian temples in the ancient style.

This in turn begs the question why, and under what circumstances, was that venerable holy place chosen to provide Alexandria with Egyptian stones and artefacts. And whether the removal was one vast operation, or spread out over a longer period? And at what date between the original creation of the Greek city and the end of paganism did this removal take place ...?

Two prompt answers to these questions have recently become public:

1. Concerning the blocks and sculptures taken out of the water east of Qa'it-Bey, J-P. Corteggiani and J-Y. Empereur, following Honor Frost, suppose that a submerged deposit of antique stone at the foot of the Mamluk fort is the result of the collapse of the lighthouse which Sostrates of Knidos had built under Ptolemy I and Ptolemy II, around 297-283 BC.[16]

[11] Thus the bundled columns from the temple of Thutmosis IV, see below, p. 214.

[12] Like the statue of the chief medical officer Horkheb (H. S. Bakry, in *Orins Antis* 9, p. 333-341, and a capital in the name of king Apries (J. Y. *Inscr. ég.*, p. 242, note 40)

[13] The Sun receives the name of Re-Harakhti, of Khepri, and of Atum. The first name designates the star in zenith, Khepri is the god who manifested himself to create the world, and is also the regenerated sun which reappears in the morning. Atum is the same god, inert before the creation, and the sun which in the evening goes to rest on the inferior world. Each name has its own iconography. J. Y., *Inscr. ég.*, p. 228.

[14] Apart from the 'Souls (*eg. bai*) of Heliopolis', we meet 'the college or *ennead* (*eg. pesedjet*) of the lords of Heliopolis', or 'All the gods, lords of Heliopolis', as well as those of Kher-Aha, an important religious centre dependent on the Sun City.

[15] About the site of Matarîyeh, *PM* IV (1934), p. 59-65; about the Cairo fragments, *ibid.*, p. 69-73.

[16] This very major conclusion and its ramifications concerning the origins of *pharaonica* have been published from September 1995 in a great number of interviews to the general printed press, as well as articles published in various periodicals specialising in history and archaeology (partial list in *BIFAO* 97, 1997, p. 376, no. 1), as well as in the film *La Septième Merveille du Monde*, co-produced by Gédéon-France 2-Louvre Museum-Elf Aquitaine-BBC, South-NOVA/WGBM Boston, distributed April 18, 1996. Information can also be found in S. Compoint and W. LaRiche, *Alexandrie, La Septième Merveille du Monde*, Paris, Robert Laffont, 1996 and *Alexandria, the Submerged City*, Weidenfeld & Nicholson, 1996. Lastly, J-Y. Empereur, *Le Phare*, 1998, and *La Gloire*, 1998, p. 98-104, to which we mainly refer, as well as to the more detailed reports from N. Grimal, printed in *BIFAO* 95-98.

The huge granite beams they found were, so they claim, pieces 'recuperated' by the builders in the temples of Heliopolis, and re-employed for the framework of the doors and windows of the lighthouse.[17] A colossal couple in the pharaonic style, representing a Ptolemaic pharaoh and his wife, had been set up in front of the tower gate,[18] just as, for example, Sethos I's two obelisks in Heliopolis were positioned in front of his its entrance,[19] etc.

The removal from Heliopolis would therefore have started at the very outset of the Ptolemaic period, the Greek architects practising at the same time two ways of 'recuperation' which must be distinguished in our context:

On the one hand, a merely technical removal of monoliths, tearing them out of indigenous buildings in order to re-integrate them into new masonry, a re-employment whose only object was utilitarian.

On the other hand, a recovery with an 'ideological' goal of removable items (obelisks, sphinxes), which were destined to maintain their religious and political function and significance in the urban environment of the Hellenistic city.

2. In a short and dense text, Paolo Gallo has suggested an entirely different date and process.[20] In a general way, he suggests, the spoliation of ancient temples in Lower Egypt was due to the Romans, who removed steles, statues, architraves, columns, obelisks, sphinxes, and even slabs of walls weighing dozens of tons, in order to re-install them—not without some changes in significance—in the Serapia and Isia of Alexandria and Rome. This massive export of works of sacral art of ancient Egypt, he declared, was begun immediately on Augustus' annexation of Egypt, but it increased in a formidable way in the 2nd century, following the growing popularity of the Isis cult in the West.

It is undeniable that the numerous transfers of the most varied *pharaonica* into the Roman occident—as, incidentally, into the Graeco-Roman orient—implied a change in the significance of these images of gods, rulers, and other people, once they were installed in temples dedicated to the cult of Isis ... From the end of the 4th, and even more during the 3rd century BC, private communities and even cities in Hellas had developed cults adoring Isis—whom Alexandria herself had adopted as the patron of her ruling dynasty and her sailors, together with Sarapis, one god in one of the city's groups of deities. The Greek environment developed a sort of religion which may for convenience be called 'Isiac'. Its starting-point lay in the mythology of Osiris and rituals proper to the Egyptians. A rather egyptianising piety remodelled a certain number of beliefs and practices to the point where what was initially only magic to promise people eternal life was transformed into a global doctrine of salvation, which was restricted to those initiated into the Egyptian mysteries. As early as the 3rd century BC, often modest imported *pharaonica* may have been present[21] among the cult items of the *Isiea* of Greece, where people of Egyptian origin participated in the rites. Essentially, however, the religion thought and expressed itself in Greek. It built its little sanctuaries and established its deities, priests, and believers according to Greek aesthetics. Obviously, all this leads us to believe that initially the Greek iconography of Isis, as of Sarapis, was created in the Ptolemies' city of Alexandria.

Once worship of the Egyptian gods had taken root in the eastern part of the Mediterranean, it is quickly found also in Italy, and even in Rome.[22] The plastic forms as well as the language of the *Isiaca* are initially Greek, then Graeco-Roman and Latin, while their beliefs spread out over all the western provinces, European as well as African, of the full-grown empire. In Rome, Octavian-Augustus recovers obelisks as signs of his final triumph over Egypt, and as homage to the universal divinity of the sun. On the other hand, like his successor Tiberius, he relegates it to outside the city's walls, and even represses the Isiac religion, deeming it contrary to Roman tradition. Other emperors, however, view the Egyptian gods with sympathy and even active favour: Caius Caligula (37-41) already creates a great Isis temple on the Field of Mars, which lasts until the end of paganism. Hieroglyph scribes in Italy compose hieroglyphic texts for Domitian and Hadrian, the latter building a temple for his dead favourite, Osiris-Antinous, and his sculptors create a 'hadrianic' style to represent this Osiris and the various gods of Egypt.[23] It is this ever-growing fascination with the mysteries of Egypt, together with some sort of 'return to sources', to which specialists in oriental cults throughout the Roman empire attribute the extraordinary abundance of

[17] *'The Ptolemies used Heliopolis like a quarry,'* J-P. Corteggiani in *Libération*, Sept. 28, 1995, p. 32; *'These are mainly pharaonic pieces which the Greek architects 'recuperated' in Heliopolis'*, Id in *Info Matin*, Sept. 27, 1995, p. 24. *'Finally, some pieces strongly resemble corner elements and guardrails such as the lighthouse might contain'...* J-Y. Empereur, *Libération loc. cit.*, p. 31. *'... blocks of a certain size.... made of Aswan granite. These must above all have been the frames of doors and windows.... '*, J-Y. Empereur, *Le Phare*, 1998, p. 41, also p. 93.

[18] The remnants of three couples have been found (J-P. Corteggiani in *BIFAO* 96, 1996, p. 567-570). The crowned masculine colossus, exhibited in front of the Petit Palais in Paris in 1998, is willingly attributed to Ptolemy II, although his face recalls Ptolemy I. The queen of like size, now in the Navy Museum in Alexandria, is said to be Arsinoë II. See also Id. in *La Gloire,* 1998, p. 103-104, nos. 64-65. Virtual reconstitution of the couple, erected in front of the lighthouse in J.Y. Empereur, *Le Phare*, p. 94.

[19] See *BIFAO* 96, 1996, p. 569-570; 97, 1997, p. 376-377.

[20] P. Gallo, *Ostraca*, 1997, p. XXIII-XXV.

[21] Fr. Dunand, *Le culte d'Isis dans le bassin oriental de la Méditerranée* (EPRO VI), XXVI.

[22] M. Malaise, *Les conditions de pénétration et de diffusion des cultes égyptiens en Italie (EPRO* XXII), 1972; S.A. Takács, *Isis & Serapis in the Roman World (EPRO CXXIV)*, 1985.

[23] J-Cl. Grenier, *La décoration statuaire du 'Sérapeum du Canope' de la Villa Adriana*, Rome.

pharaonica in Rome and, to a slightly lesser extent, in Italy, wherever there are traces of *Isea* and Isiac communities.[24] Parallel to this, a certain taste for the exotic from the Nile and Ethiopia prospers in the decorative arts. In view of this fashion for *egyptiaca,* historians often go a little far in attributing a simple 'ornamental' role to the authentic pharaonic works found across the empire. This takes too little account of the religious role which these antique remains, brought from far, must have filled in the temples and in the very hearts of these mystics.

Importation of such a great variety of Egyptian antiques of all periods, including the Ptolemaic, to Rome was manifestly based on purely ideological motives. These objects, which rendered more directly present idols, ritual acts, and the mysteries hidden behind the hieroglyphs, more or less deviated from the original functions which they had had in former times in the temples whence they had been removed. Once brought to Italy, the statues which private Egyptians themselves had once left in various temples throughout the *chôra*, began to represent the attitudes and sacerdotal gestures of Isiac priests, while the hieroglyphic inscriptions which they bore obviously had nothing further to do with this Roman recycling.

P. Gallo assumes a parallel between the *pharaonica* of Rome and those of Alexandria, which would lead to a question of crucial importance: to what extent was Alexandria *ad Aegyptum*, a strange world to Egypt, like Athens, Ephesus, and Rome, a place where Egyptian art introduced an exotic touch, and where certain temples, harbouring in the Greek manner some hellenised figures of the Egyptian pantheon, needed to be belatedly egyptianised in order to serve a spiritual need to plunge back to immemorial origins?

Or did Alexandria *in Aegypto*, residence of the Ptolemaic pharaohs, and later of the prefects representing the Caesar-Pharaoh, accept from the very beginning—at least in the temples and chapels built for her gods—the native arts and rituals as they flourished more than ever in the *chôra* in the Hellenistic era, and up to the age of the Antonine emperors, all of whom took pains to maintain the continuity of Egypt's national past?

The context cannot, in fact, be reduced to a simple choice between these two models. It is well documented that traditional sacred knowledge, arts, and iconography are very much alive in the *chôra* until the end of the 2nd century; and that in Alexandria herself, the famous chapel of Kôm el-Shuqafa, for example, introduces the imagery and graphics of pharaonic temples—not without some re-interpretation—into the funerary architecture of the city. But during the same period of the mature empire, the coins and terracottas indicate the increasing popularity of images displaying native gods dressed in the Graeco-Roman style and the proliferation of *iseia* and *sarapeia* across the provinces.

P. Gallo's assimilation of the two cases of Rome and Alexandria retains the first of the two versions above: as a vehicle of a Hellenism which in its daily display of the arts finally succeeded in conquering the population in the *chôra*, Ptolemaic Alexandria had remained a Greek world parallel to Egypt, and the introduction of things from ancient Egypt had appeared only secondarily, and following the drive of a Graeco-Roman egyptomania.

As well founded as it appears in theory, this answer seems to us not to take into account a noticeable difference between Alexandria and Rome. As the tally stands today, the Roman and Italian *pharaonica* come from the most diverse locations: Saïs, Hermopolis, Xois, Isidospolis near Sebennytos, Heracleopolis, Thebes and Elephantine. Obelisks certainly come from Heliopolis, but only a few sculptures and reliefs. There is a considerable contrast with Alexandria, where, according to the current state of the tally, a large majority of monuments come from Heliopolis. This cannot be considered as simply by chance, but must much rather have been done with a specific intention. To attribute these removals to the imperial period is certainly an attractive working hypothesis. It is indeed known from Strabo that obelisks, already much deteriorated, were taken away from Heliopolis, soon after the conquest (30 BC).[25] We further know that during the 1st and 2nd centuries, the patron saint of Alexandria, often invoked as Zeus-Helios-Sarapis, becomes the universal sun god. Taking relics away preferably from Heliopolis would thus acquire a properly religious significance (without any direct link to the cult of Isis proper?).

It is tempting to try to determine historically as precisely as possible the occasion when transportation from Heliopolis to Alexandria took place. As Strabo discusses the pre-existing Alexandrine temples to be seen in his time,[26] his discourse is clear and must be taken seriously, even if it is difficult to evaluate its significance in the context of the history of religion and monuments. Of all these temples, he only mentions the Serapeum, quite curtly (whereas he broadly discusses the activities of the Serapeum of Canopus).[27] He adds with insistence that '...these very ancient holy enclosures [are] today almost abandoned ... left in abandon ...' In his opinion, the negligence stems from the fact that most of the architectural ventures of the new regime focused on constructions in Nicopolis, a suburban area of concerted

[24] See M. Malaise, *Inventaire préliminaire des documents égyptiens découverts en Italie, (EPRO* XXI), 1972; A. Roullet, *The Egyptian and Egyptianizing Monuments of Imperial Rome, (EPRO* XX), 1972; O. Lollio Barbieri *et al., Le Antichità Egiziane di Roma Imperiale*, 1995.

[25] Strabo, *Geography* XVII, 1. 27.

[26] *Ibid.,* XVII, 1.10. See '*Testimonia'*, no. 28, p. 90.

[27] *Ibid.,* XVII, 1.17.

development planned in the Roman style in honour of Augustus, victor over Mark Anthony.[28] When the same Strabo discusses Heliopolis, on the other hand, he merely mentions the two obelisks removed to be taken to Rome. The inscriptions preserved on the other three obelisks from Heliopolis, the Needles and the *Vaticanus*, admittedly indicate that they had been erected in Alexandria in the time of Augustus, but the first two had been set up with one in front of the temple of Caesar and the other on the Forum. These re-sitings were in line with Roman urbanisation and ideology, and it would be hazardous to let the beginning of the reign of Augustus coincide with the beginning of the massive removal of royal statues and monoliths from the temple of Re, and with the embellishment of the Sarapis temple with *pharaonica* from earlier periods. The first such really plausible opportunity would fall rather into the reign of Caligula, founder of the Iseum on the Field of Mars, importer of the Vatican obelisk, and, what is more, according to Philo,[29] devoured by a passion for Alexandria and the wish to be deified there.

After Strabo, authors hardly ever mention Alexandria's cults and temples. Only at the end of the 2nd, or during the 3rd and 4th centuries, are there again some notable descriptions, particularly Achilles Tatius' and Ammianus Marcellinus' emphatic allusions to the Serapeum and the descriptions in the *Alexander Romance*, in Rufinus and Aphthonius, of the formidable monument in the Graeco-Roman style 'almost as grandiose as the Capitol', and which was to be entirely demolished by Bishop Theophilus. It is true that the major part of ancient architecture which contains *pharaonica* dates from imperial times, but the heterogeneous composition of the deposits which also contain Greek items of the Ptolemaic period must exclude any chronological classification. The few archaeological and epigraphical indices collected at the Serapeum barely permit any attribution to the times of Trajan (98-117) and Hadrian (117-138), the complete redrafting of the hill and the construction of the formidable edifice—an enterprise which may well have sought to remedy the sacking during the Jewish revolt of 115-117 (?). Again, we may suppose the 'despoliation' of Heliopolis and the massive introduction of antique *pharaonica* into a building in the Roman style then took place.

It should be observed in passing that no detrimental inference should be attached to the term *spolia*, even if the disdainful Greek and the brutal Roman acted insolently towards the Egyptian barbarian they dominated. The term of spoliation is certainly appropriate where still intact walls were demolished to recover dressed stones, or even, at a pinch, when the victor took away obelisks as trophies. The transfer and re-employment of furnishings from one ancient holy place to another which is being created—as the Egyptian had repeatedly done themselves[30]—can be motivated by a properly religious motive which implies no lack of piety towards the beliefs attached to these items. Thus, the scouring of temples in the *chôra,* at the time when hieroglyph scribes officiated in Rome, could have been perceived by their colleagues at home as a kind of missionary activity, as it were, rather than sacrilege.

In his admirable *Ptolemaic Alexandria* (1972), P. M. Fraser already wondered to whom should be attributed the installation of the various Egyptian objects brought to Alexandria from Heliopolis and other places.[31] He proposed a qualified answer involving the Ptolemies as well as the Romans, on the basis of a partial but concrete tally of the constructions in the Serapeum, the only great temple in Alexandria whose precise site and approximate extent are known. Having evoked the original identity of the Greek Sarapis, and the Egyptian Osiris-Apis, and having noted the early presence of Greek statues, philosophers, and writers in the Serapeion of Memphis, he then also notes that the *Sarapeia* and *Isea* functioning in Greece during Hellenistic times did occasionally contain some imported Egyptian pieces—with a 'decorative' purpose as much as a ritual one—and suggests very naturally that this could also have been the case in Alexandria. But, he adds, one cannot positively state that most of the pharaonic statues found in the Serapeum were already present in the sanctuary of Ptolemaic times which was too small. Still, Egyptian-style architectural elements were not lacking in that Ptolemaic Serapeum (particularly the use of granite, in a capital that is a '*striking hybrid*'). It would appear, finally, that the great Serapeum contained many more Egyptian statues than the small Ptolemaic structure which it enveloped at the time, and particularly that the area was crossed by a ceremonial road in the Egyptian style, a *dromos* possibly flanked by sphinxes ... In essence, Fraser allowed for a possible Ptolemaic phase, and envisaged a more important Roman one, for the influx of *pharaonica*. This approach, based on a number of details noticed *in situ*, brings out the fact that the architecture of the Hellenistic Serapeum contains elements of native style, built in the time of the Ptolemies.

The attempt to reconstruct in one block the destinies of the Alexandrine temples and their *pharaonica* from rare, well-dated elements which the ancient writers report and from the global image of the religious history of the Graeco-Roman world, is clearly to develop some

[28] P. M. Fraser, *Ptolemaic Alexandria* I, p. 274, noted that the very sporadic interest shown in the god Sarapis by the Ptolemies of the 2nd and 1st centuries BC to explain this neglect.

[29] *Legatio ad Caium,* § 338. See '*Testimonia*', no. 46, p 110.

[30] Transportation of obelisks, statues, sphinxes, naos, columns, from Pi-Ramses to Tanis, some pieces from Pi-Ramses to Bubastis and Leontopolis; transport of statues from the first I'lthom (Tell el-Rabeh) to the new one (Tell el-Maskhoutah), etc.

[31] P. M. Fraser, *Ptolemaic Alexandria*, 1972, I, p. 265-267; II, p. 419-428, notes 621-637.

indispensable patterns of thought. But it does not sufficiently explain the complexity of activities and events, of creations and destructions, which took place over a long period, nor the diversity of meaning and use of the objects of pharaonic style lost in Greek Alexandria. If we want to understand the significance of Alexandria's *pharaonica*, and the place of traditional rituals and native art, it would, in fact, be better to start from the lower end and consider each individual vestige—introducing several criteria into this total—rather than to start from the top, with global models extracted from the general historiography of Graeco-Roman antiquity.

1. We shall thus distinguish the *pharaonica* of ancient dynasties, and those manifestly brought in from elsewhere, from those works which by their material, craftsmanship, postures, clothing, and their hieroglyphic inscriptions, are 'pharaonic' as well, although created in the reign of the Ptolemies or the Roman Emperors.

2. We shall distinguish *royal* works, created in the name of a pharaoh to decorate divine temples, from the *private* works installed for private people, so that they might participate, during their lifetime and after death, in the rituals of these temples. Whatever the king whose name signs and dates a statue or an offering, his image represents the king in front of the god, and carrying out the ritual. These ancient effigies, in addition, indicate the presence of the ancient kings who benefit from the daily rituals in the god's service, and they symbolise dynastic continuity. Sphinxes in particular, with their human heads symbolising the wisdom and their lion bodies the strength of the pharaoh, remain in fashion throughout the imperial period, and even beyond. Any effigy which a commoner may have set up in a sanctuary in his own time could never acquire such religious and political significance.

3. We shall separately consider the *fixed* elements, and the various *movable* categories, the ways to reutilise them, and the subsequent fate of these stones that vary according to their categories. Movable objects of moderate or small size are: statues of kings, divinities, and commoners, royal sphinxes, naos, ritual instruments (offering tables, clepsydrae) relatively easy to transport, and also sarcophagi.[32] Movable objects of great size, always standing in the open air, and difficult to transport, are: obelisks, colossi. Elements of architecture are, by definition, fixed objects: relief-covered blocks forming walls, columns and pillars, architraves, and door posts. These structural elements offer various possibilities for reutilization. A block detached from a wall implies demolition of the wall itself. A section of a column or a block cut out of an architrave requires the cutting up of the original monolith. However, we must assume a different manner of reuse from one temple to another, which has nothing to do with utilitarian vandalism but has on the contrary a conservatory effect: colonnades as well as granite frames are composed like a kit, from monolithic supports and beams, which can be dismantled and rebuilt on another site.[33]

4. This inquiry, item by item, category by category, is further complicated by the well-known fact that very few of the *pharaonica* in Alexandria have been found whole, or even in any adequate state of preservation. Worse, with the sole exception of the Serapeum, where statues and fragments—although manhandled and knocked about—were at least left within the area or at the perimeter of the sacred precinct, there is no way of casually asserting that any stone of some size is still even anywhere near the Alexandrian monument of which it was initially—or even secondarily—a part. The configuration and context of the deposit, as well as the state of the material of certain pieces, open up a confused vista of unending accidental or wilful smashing, of remodelling and even of dispersals, to the extent of carrying the pieces of one single group over considerable distances. And everywhere the *materia aegyptica* is intermingled on the same sites with *materia hellenica*—the latter being generally much more abundant—and in which one finds building segments, Greek inscriptions, and sculptural fragments originating higgledy-piggledy from the early and later Roman empire and the period of the Ptolemies, the whole lying abandoned under or on ground which can be dated to Arab or Ottoman times. Certain groups of Roman columns which appear to have remained on their original site, or to have been utilised in churches or mosques, may lead us to the inference that a temple or basilica once stood there; but they offer little reason to hope for a positive identification of the monument. Left *in situ*, the so-called 'Cleopatra' obelisks identify the facade of the *Caesareum*. Towards Hadra, the remnants of a colossal group,[34] hardly if at all movable, as well as several sphinxes, suggest that a temple of Ptolemaic times was built in the suburban neighbourhood of Eleusis—often cited by ancient historians in the context of major events in the history of the Lagide dynasty. But none of them mention a temple, even if the very name of Eleusis does indeed suggest the notion of its existence.[35]

By and large, scholars were able to put the sites of

[32] Apart from the tank of the monumental coffin of Nekhthorheb, the last native pharaoh, which was used as a basin in the so-called Mosque of Athanasius, of engmatic presence in Alexandria, there is also the sarcophagus of the supreme commander Teïonkhons of Ptolemaic times, which was rediscovered at Moharram-Bey (Graeco-Roman Museum; G. Daressy, *ASAE* 5 (1904), p. 123, §XXI).

[33] Like, for example, the fasciculate granite columns dating from the Middle Empire, and marked in the name of Thutmose III in the bark repository included in the court of Ramses II in Luxor.

[34] Most recently discussed by M. C. Bruwier, *CdE* LXIV (1989), p. 25-43.

[35] Calderini, *Dizionario I*, fasc. 1, 1925, p. 110. Eleusis is mentioned in a trade document of 257 BC. No trace of it, however, in Roman times!

the buildings cited by Greek and Latin authors on the map of present-day Alexandria, but it is fairly rare that any find positively confirms these locations, and the hope of making an exceptional find is slim.

There is one particularly heavy handicap: along the eastern anchorage, the travellers of the 19th century described vast concentrations of large ancient stones, columns, capitals, plinths, and other Graeco-Roman building fragments, pharaonic columns and statues, and hieroglyphic inscriptions, all kinds of rock and all periods intermingled.[36] This constituted, in fact, the kind of jetty, today concealed, which linked the Anfouchy peninsula to the present island of Qa'it-Bey. The same is true for the long band of remains of chaotic appearance covered by the Corniche bordering the royal harbours south-east of the roads. The recent underwater explorations revealed that these fields of large stones extended largely into the submerged parts of the coast, on the outside of Qa'it-Bey, along the jetty, and on the rim of the royal harbours. At first sight at least, the disjointed appearance and the heteroclitic composition of these groups do not resemble what might be buildings which had simply crumbled where they stood. It was quickly supposed that they were big stones removed *en masse* from ancient ruins, and hastily dumped wholesale to build some sort of rough surrounding wall. This interpretation is based on a precise notice by Abd al-Latif of Baghdad. This Arab scholar visited Alexandria in 1200-1201, and heard from the inhabitants that, under the rule of Saladin (1171-1193), the numerous columns which lay about on the site of the Serapeum had been removed and thrown into the sea in order to contain its assaults and to prevent enemy ships from advancing up to the foot of the walls. This circumstance could well account for certain heaps of stone, and we cannot exclude that for military reasons, protection against tidal waves, or to compensate for the consequences of subsidence, some operations of this nature may also have taken place at other times and in other places, before subsequent events flooded part of these enigmatic remains.[37] Various analyses of their configuration, composition, and of the anthropic and geological substrates of such concentrations as are still accessible to underwater exploration, should permit, in time, the solving of this major preliminary problem in Alexandrian archaeology, which is a cause of much perplexity and is difficult to solve with any authority.

The solution of this enigma goes much farther, but it determines the problem of the few Alexandrian *pharaonica*. These have merely shared the erratic destiny of the Greek and Roman elements among which they have been mislaid. That is to say, the spectacular effect of pharaohs and hieroglyphs should no longer deflect our line of thought, which is to define the task of archaeologists specialising in the study of Hellenistic, Roman, and early Christian art. It falls to whom it falls to measure, to define, to date and file thousands of columns, capitals, entablatures, cornices, friezes, pedestals, and sculptures.[38]

5. Noticeably, several of the Egyptian blocks found in the past or recently, are merely remainders of bigger monoliths, showing cutting notches, fitting mortises, drillings, and other traces of resizing.[39] Monuments were visibly cut up at some undetermined date, to become dressed stones or to be recycled for some function different from their original one. One would offhand attribute these later dates of reutilisation to the destruction of the sacred aura of idolatrous temples by Christians or Muslims. It is well established, however, that such resizing for different uses was practised during pagan antiquity ...

Here again, the question is whether Greek and Roman pieces were not cut up and resized in similar manner.[40] It is important to establish whether only the products of indigenous culture had thus become victims to a destructive reuse, and only shared the vicissitudes of dispersion with Greek work. Greek and Roman columns, capitals, friezes, etc., were willingly picked up for use by the Christians, but stones with the so obviously idolatrous images and hieroglyphs could only be reused if they were rehewn and concealed during construction ...

The pharaonic fragments encountered in the Alexandrian areas above or below water are in any case a useful and sometimes original addition to Egyptology, which seeks to date them and determine their function on their original site. Most of the pre-Alexandrian artefacts very usefully enrich our still fragmentary knowledge of Heliopolis. Due its chaotic state, the site where they ended up cannot, until further discovery, contribute anything useful to Alexandrian topography, not even to the initial position of temples dedicated to Egyptian ritual or temples

[36] Bibliography and abstract in Tkaczow, *Topography*, p. 48-49 (Sites 1A and 1B); p. 120 (Site 72), Map A.

[37] Before the 'Arab Wall' was razed at the end of the 19th and the beginning of the 20th century, it was noted that this rampart built in the 11th century and subsequently restored, contained antique columns and fragments, and that the artificial jetty leading to Qa'it-Bey was surely built after antiquity—even if its precise date of building still remains to be established. Crumbled buildings go back far in time in Alexandria. Already the Alexandrian War (48-47 BC) had provoked demolitions (*ruinae*) and the reuse of dressed stones (*quadrato exacto saxo*) to improvise fortifications, erects road blocks, or prevent the approach of hostile ships. See *De bello Alexandrino*, I, III, XIX (*'Testimonia'*, nos. 20, 21, 25, p. 84 *et seq*.).

[38] Particular attention should be paid to the mineralogy of rocks, which for a long time remained very superficial and even absurd in the descriptions of Alexandrine *pharaonica*. See Fraser's reflections in *Ptolemaic Alexandria* I. p. 160, II. p. 861, Note 419. E.g. distinguish granites or granitoides from Aswan from those of *Mons Claudianus* which were really exploited only during the 1st and 2nd centuries AD, following a Roman initiative which had at the same time discovered the porphyry of *Mons Porphyrites*.

[39] Apart from building elements, even monumental sculptures were cut up, as indicated by B. Van de Walle, *CdE* XXIV, Fasc. 47, 1949, p. 19-20, concerning the colossal group at Hadra, and S. Saumeron, *BIFAO* 60 (1960), p. 83 and plate VIII, concerning the monumental triad on Pharos.

[40] Regrettably, in the case of most pharaonic and Greek monuments, writers contented themselves with iconographic descriptions and text copies, without paying any attention to the material state of the support.

partly furnished in the pharaonic style. Some altered blocks, on the other hand, indicate not only strictly utilitarian, but also religious recycling, as shall be seen.

Despite the very summary aspect of existing publications and the consequent enormous gaps in the inventory, some general findings are called for, and several conclusions may be proposed.[41]

A. Private monuments of the Ptolemaic period

Some ten fragments at least of statues of private persons sculpted during the period have been collected, for instance the famous statue of Hor, Cairo CG 697 (Kôm el-Demas), the two statues of the Memphite priest Psherenptah, Graeco-Roman Museum, reg. 17533-34 (Serapeum), and the lady Ptolemaia, British Museum 985. Images of native notables with hieroglyphic texts thus found their way into Alexandrian temples. These notables could easily be passing visitors, like the grand priest from Memphis on his way to meet Ptolemy XII, as well as personalities posted in Alexandria. One begins to perceive that as early as the 3rd century BC, Egyptian priests, some born of a Greek father and an Egyptian mother, maintained close relations with the court. Throughout the entire Greek and Roman period, there is no lack of indications as to the presence of priests and bilingual hieroglyph scribes working in the capital city. From the 2nd century BC on, lettered people who were provincial priests and interested in the religious science of their ethnic group, filled high ministerial posts up to that of finance minister (*dioecetes*) in the central administration. All these people dedicated statues, or had their statues dedicated in the temples of Alexandria and likewise in the sanctuaries of the nomes (statues of people of Greek culture, sculpted in the Greek manner, and dedicated in Greek, then to be installed in the temples of the *chôra*).

The uncommon case of rare Egyptian statues of private people prior to Alexander, like the Basa of the time of Psammetichus I and the chief medical officer Horkheb, a contemporary of Amasis, who has been brought from Sais, could be explained in the same way as similar statues in Italy, as mock likenesses of priests and devotees to Isis. There remains the so-called Metternich stele, a tall stele totally engraved with formulae for healing, which a Mnevis priest had put at the disposal of the people of Heliopolis in the Mnevis temple under the pharaoh Nekhtharhebe.[42] This monument of practically official dimensions and appearance could well have fulfilled its medicinal office for the benefit of those among the Alexandrian population who had been stung by some snake or scorpion.

B. The royal colossi

The sacred precinct of Egyptian temples was closed off by a high wall, but the royal monuments of great size, obelisks, colossi, sphinxes along the access way, were disposed in pairs in front of their facade. In particular the colossi show that the Ptolemies and the Caesars had in no way excluded pharaonic art from the Alexandrian landscape by restricting it to the interior of native temples. Retaining for themselves the hieratic iconography and the gigantic kingly manifestations of their predecessors, they exhibited the superhuman nature of their divinity before the eyes of the people, whether or not they were of Hellenistic statute, taste, and lifestyle.

The rigid attitude, the stance, the stylised musculature, the royal clothing, the added crowns are in the purest pharaonic tradition. The knot with its tails dropping down from the girdle of the queen as Isis is the one concession to modernity. Individualisation of royal faces is not unknown, the only Greek touch to be found here and there are the curls which stand out from under the *nemes*. Obviously, all these statues come from the workshops of Egyptian sculptors of talent. As it is difficult to conceive that the Romans had the Ptolemaic effigies transported from some important provincial town, the Ptolemies must have ordered them to ornament their capital city.

It is not yet certain that the Ptolemaic colossi and sphinxes near Qa'it-Bey were initially placed in front of the lighthouse. The sphinx and the colossal head attributed to Augustus which the IEASM discovered at various points in the royal quarters are without doubt not far removed from their original site. It is reasonable in any case to attribute the Hadra sphinx to an Iseum or an Egyptianised *thesmophorion*. Under these conditions, it may perhaps have been superfluous to search for some far-removed site from which might stem the triad of black granite representing the god Amon, seated between the deified Ptolemy II and Arsinoë II—whose lower part had been picked up in Anfuchi on the very soil of the island of Pharos.[43] This monument unique of its kind found its prototype during the Ramesside period, when certain groups functioned like cult images inside monolithic naosm or of *speos*. Without going as far as to imagine a Zeus-Amon temple built on the island (which Caesar said was peopled by Egyptians), it may still be conceivable that this triad originated from a sanctuary in the Egyptian style,

[41] In view of the vast context of questions enumerated in these reflections, discussion concerning the development of indigenous habits in architecture and funereal rites in Alexandria are excluded.

[42] N. E. Scott in *BMMA*, XX, 9 (1950-51), p. 201-217.

[43] S. Saumeron, *BIFAO* 60 (1960), p. 83-109, plates I-VIII.

dedicated to the joint cult of Arsinoë 'daughter of Amon' and of the supreme god who had promoted her 'into the number of gods on Earth'.

C. The Heliopolis obelisks

From the *Alexander Romance* it can be deducted that two obelisks could be seen in the Serapeum during the 3rd and 2nd centuries.[44] Pliny mentions the two Needles of the Caesareum and indicates that Ptolemy II has supposedly decorated his Arsinoeum with one single obelisk found unfinished in a quarry (Aswan?).[45] As for the remainder, the author repeats a Greco-Egyptian tradition detailing ten great obelisks in Heliopolis and on the basis of a Roman source, he mentions the obelisks on the Field of Mars, in the Circus Maximus, and in the Vatican, all three duly identified in Rome. He does not mention Ramses II's four smaller Heliopolis obelisks, which then decorated the Iseum founded under Caligula;[46] there is no way to know whether this is merely forgetting minor pieces, or whether these obelisks were transported there in the course of decoration after Pliny's time.

Strabo only mentions the two well identified ones removed from Heliopolis directly for Rome, and which were set up in the Circus Maximus at the time of Augustus and as a sundial on the Field of Mars. As the dedication is preserved, we know that the two in the Caesareum of Alexandria were also installed under Augustus, even if another current theory maintains that they were already brought there under Cleopatra with the purpose of deifying Mark Anthony.

The obelisks from Heliopolis which, at the end of their wanderings, came down to us standing in Rome or Alexandria, intact or almost complete, should be considered separate from those of the same origin which, in their final state, were discovered piecemeal under the sea. From the former category we know that significant removals of obelisks from Heliopolis had taken place at the beginning of the Roman seizure, i.e., during the last three decades BC, *but exclusively for the purpose of the conquerors' own projects, and Augustan ideology.*

Nothing leads us to suppose that the imperial departments at that time also engaged in such a costly enterprise in order to erect further obelisks in front of Egyptian temples in Alexandria. These removals must rather have taken place at a later date, under the egyptophile emperors, or much earlier, under the Ptolemies. As regards the Heliopolis obelisk of which one isolated section remains on the royal harbour peninsula, mingled with debris from buildings and statues, this final resting place will assuredly tell us nothing about its first site, nor about the date of its transportation. And as regards the three obelisks of the same king and the same origin, whose remains have been taken out of a similar disorderly deposit at Qa'it-Bey, it remains to be documented that they were really transported in front of the lighthouse under Ptolemy II (see F below).

D. Facts and problems of the Serapeum

The Serapeum is the only temple whose site is clearly documented, and also the only one whose subsoil has preserved datable stratigraphic facts. These are two factors but of difficult context and interpretation, especially since the northern part of the plateau is occupied by the Bâb-Sîdra cemetery. Left outside the walls during the Arab and Ottoman periods, and very carefully protected since, the area had, in addition, been hardly invaded by solid houses, and was rather sparsely built up. There, too, antique objects were nevertheless found mutilated, broken up, dispersed, manhandled, or even recovered and reused in recent shanty lodgings. There, as everywhere else, *pharaonica* of Ptolemaic times and of ancient kings are intermingled with Greek and Graeco-Roman building and sculpture fragments, all in the same lamentably degraded and dilapidated state.

The exemplary conditions leading to this disaster can be reconstructed on the basis of some archaeological evidence, as well as certain events from reliable literary documentation. As late as the last century, chance holes were dug and stones carried away by the population, visiting travellers, and archaeologists on sites which had served as quarries during the Christian and Muslim centuries. In AD 391, bishop Theophilus had condemned, wasted, and allegedly 'totally destroyed' the Serapeum. Still, even in the 12th century, there remained a vast number of fallen and broken granite columns that were subsequently transported to the seashore (where we may dream of one day finding them again!).[47] The vast and beautiful temple destroyed by Theophilus was a work of

[44] See '*Testimonia*', no. 7, p. 64. This *late* romatic work, which manifestly refers to the *Roman* topography and toponymy of Alexandria, deciphers an incredible prophetic message of Greek spirit and expression—without any mention of the hieroglyphic inscriptions of the two obelisks ...

[45] *Hist. Nat. XXXVI*, XIV, p. 67-68 (extract in '*Testimonia*', no. 49 bis, above, p. 111)

[46] On the Egyptian obelisks in Rome, see E. Iversen, *Obelisks In Exile*, Vol. 1, *The Obelisks In Rome*, Copenhagen, 1968.

[47] A dream not easy to put into execution. According to Abd el-Latif, the removal concerned four hundred columns, but his text does not allow to guess at where the seashore was in his time, nor how far from the Arab wall the barrier had been set up. In order to chose among the various heaps of stone brought in, the most reliable criteria would be epigraphic evidence and the close comparison to those elements still present on the site of the Searpeum. It may be doubtful, however, whether the types and units of column shafts and segments (specimens of which can be found in all parts of the city) can be decisive criteria. Until further notice, therre is no reason to recuse the idea that the columns dropped at the foot of Qa'it-Bey stem from the Searapeum, but there is also no reason to consider it definite.

the 2nd century BC in the Graeco-Roman style, built on a vast terrace for which a plateau had to be levelled out, razing in the process almost completely the monuments which Ptolemy III and Ptolemy IV had earlier built on ground which had again been laid out by another levelling that very likely destroyed completely still earlier buildings. Still, this cycle of building and demolition could not have prevented the restorers from endeavouring to remove, if need be, any pre-existing statues and other pieces in order to preserve them.[48] It could further have incited them to integrate into the buildings such pieces of older masonry as they found. Massive concerted, as well as and individual, removals have left only derisory remnants. The repeated, disorderly dismantling and reuse created such havoc that connection between sections found next to each other must be considered accidental, permitting no possible deductions concerning topography, and even less chronology. One is left with the two only examples where the excavation touched on the remnants of superstructures left in place, and are datable with some precision: the 'foundation' deposits discovered in 1943-45, and the 'foundation' of the column of Diocletian.

Doubt still subsists concerning the date at which a first cult building was erected on the natural hill of Rhacotis, dedicated to Osiris-Apis, alias Sarapis.[49] One must take into account the traditions which have the first installation of this god from Memphis—already venerated during the 6th and 5th centuries BC by the Greeks living in the old capital—go back to the two first Ptolemies. At least some errant reminders of Ptolemy II have been collected in the Serapeum, but it is certainly beyond doubt that important buildings were created there in the reign of Ptolemy III Euergetes, thanks to the deposits in the foundations discovered *in situ*.[50] Perhaps the fundamental importance of this discovery has so far been underestimated.

Placed in recesses in the corners of the understructure, these deposits consist of small plaques of gold, silver, glass, and pottery, containing a dedication. The choice of materials compares to the foundation deposits found in various entirely native Ptolemaic temples in the *chôra*.[51] Their originality resides in the fact that the usual hieroglyphic dedication is accompanied by the same text in Greek. The plaques, buried in the SE and SW angles of a great wall surrounding a precinct which is roughly 80 m. large (E-W) and at the very least 150 m. long (N-S)—the northern tip being covered by a cemetery—all contain the same text in two languages. The same bilingual text can also be found on the foundation deposits of a small axial building of 22 by 12 m., situated towards the north on the longitudinal axis of the precinct. This reveals that Ptolemy III 'has made the *tenemos* (Egyptian *pr*) and the naos (Eg. *hwt-ntr*) of Sarapis (Osiris-Apis)'.[52] Another set of such bilingual plaques, under a lateral chapel adjoining the axial building on the east, tells us that the chapel had been dedicated under Ptolemy IV to the god-son Harpocrates 'by order of Sarapis and Isis'; the elegantly engraved hieroglyphic version is written according to a sophisticates system of alphabetical ideograms.[53]

It must also be recalled that one of the gold plaques, a remnant of a deposit of similar kind, has been collected in the centre of the modern city, the bilingual inscription dedicating a foundation to Osiris-Apis, Sarapis, Isis, Ptolemy IV, and Arsinoë Philopator, uniting in one and the same cult the divine and the royal couple.[54]

Would the participation of hierographers and priests in the composition and the deposition of these plaques according to a practice derived from Egyptian concepts of sacred foundations really have been reduced to these sole operations? Their intervention was literally fundamental and would it not much rather also have concerned the conception of the buildings, the organisation of the divine services, and the decoration of the *temenos*? Should we conclude that the Greco-Macedonian pharaoh, having recourse to native theologians when enhancing, on the acropolis of his capital city, the sanctuary of the god patron of his dynasty, needed to make a simple, formal concession to the folklore of the natives, devoid of any deeper implications?

So far effort has gone towards a reconstruction of the Ptolemaic Serapeum in the form of a Greek temple into which had been introduced some Egyptianisms, as if the fundamental idea behind the foundation of the great Serapeum had been to house for the benefit of the Greeks a totally Greek statue—made by Bryaxis—which, according to the writings of Tacitus and Plutarch, Ptolemy I (or II) had sent to be brought from Sinope. Whatever is true about this story, which is difficult to interpret, nothing precludes the theory that the Ptolemy in question, while creating temples for the Olympians beginning with Zeus all over the city, may have from the very start installed in his city also a popular divinity from Memphis, which the

[48] A base dating from the 3rd century BC shows a restoration notice added in the 1st or 2nd century AD; F. Kayser, *Recueil des inscriptions grecques et latines (non funéraires) d'Alexandria impériale, BdE* CVIII (1993), no. 45.

[49] See rectification by P. M. Fraser, *Ptolemaic Alexandria*, 1972, I. p. 267-268, with II, p. 422, notes 638-643.

[50] A. B. Rowe, *Discovery Of The Famous Temple And Enclosure Of Serapis at Alexandria*, *CASAE* 2 (1946).

[51] J. M. Weinstein, *Foundations Deposits In Ancient Egypt*, University of Pennsylvania, *UMI* ed., 1973, p. 351-396, about the deposits of Ptolemaic times.

[52] A.B. Rowe, *op. cit.*, p. 7-8; photo of a glass piece in *La Gloire*, p. 95, no. 51.

[53] E. Drioton, *An Explanation Of The Enigmatical Inscriptions Of The Serapeum Plaques of Ptolemy IV—Plaques bilingues de Ptolémée IV*, in Rowe, *op. cit.*, p. 97-112. Photos in *La Gloire*, p. 95, nos. 50, 52. The formulation of the text leads to the supposition that the chapel of the god son was created by the king following a message received through an oracle or a dream.

[54] A. B. Rowe, *op. cit.*, p. 12-13, with Fig. S. Provenance see B. Tkaczow, *op. cit.*, p. 80 (Site 21).

Greeks of Egypt knew well; and that only later came the identification of this god of the dead and of fecundity with Pluto who presents an image aesthetically closer to Hellenic taste.[55]

A rather paradoxical assumption from research would suppose that the Ptolemaic Serapium was a temple of Egyptian ritual, and included certain added elements of Greek style, similar to the temples in the interior of the country (without prejudice to the obvious existence of purely Greek temples in the remainder of the city of Alexandria). The foundation deposits and the over-abundance of *pharaonica* could lead in that direction.

The small axial building, by its dimensions, its site, and even its disposition, is comparable to the 'sanctuaries' proper of Ptolemaic temples.[56] Wells for cleaning, a 'pool' for officiating priests to purify themselves in, crypts for the storage of idols and Osiris figurines are nothing out of the ordinary in such temples. A fragment of a water clock of a model well known during the 4th and 3rd centuries BC was also found.[57] Clepsydrae were in common use in native ritual, etc. ... In view of the few building elements of one or the other style which can be dated to the Ptolemaic period, one could turn Fraser's sentence round and state that in the Serapeum of Alexandria—as in that of Memphis—elements of the Greek style were not absent.[58]

The Serapeum precinct has revealed a remarkable number of royal pre-Alexandrian sculptures,[59] certainly roughly handled and often damaged, but their presence in the temple in its final version cannot be doubted. It is remarkable that the sphinx was discovered on the southern slope of the hill, as if a *dromos*, a ceremonial passageway, had approached the temple from that side. There are further three kneeling pharaohs, presenting a ritual object (Ramses II, Ramses IX, and Psammetichus I) and four sphinxes (one of Horemheb, one pair of Apries, one of Amasis). Six of these at least come from Heliopolis. We cannot protest with Fraser, that the royal statues were too numerous to be contained in the small axial sanctuary of Ptolemy III. They were not cult figures (the three kings are, in fact, *officiating* figures ...), no more, incidentally, than were the stone images of Egyptian deities, a few of which were also found. The Ptolemaic precinct was easily big enough to house a great number of *pharaonica.* Yet, we find some vestiges of monuments made in Ptolemaic times among the sculptures of Egyptian style: e.g., the statue of a queen and the statue of the Memphite priest Psherenptah, whereas some fragments of Hellenistic statues and some dedications in Greek signify that persons of Greek culture also frequented the same religious precinct of Sarapis. In addition, apart from the sphinx borrowed from prior pharaohs, we find some that were created during Ptolemaic times especially the monumental pair of pink granite, which can still be admired on site. It is not likely that these sphinxes and the private statues, imported ones incidentally, were only introduced to Osiris-Apis during the attempt to 'egyptianise' the Sarapis cult in imperial times.

E. The foundation of Diocletian's column

Under the base of the famous column on top of which a statue of Diocletian was erected in 288-289, there remains a rough assembly of blocks, including granite and quartzite (figs. 17, 18). Rather than a special foundation for the column, this could be the remnant of the platform of a Roman temple that this pile could have protected from quarrymen. In any case, this assembly included at least four pharaonic blocks, cut out, respectively, of a lintel in the name of one of the Sesostris pharaohs,[60] a relief of Seti I,[61] a naos (?) of Ramses II,[62] and two fragments of

[55] From Plutarch, *De Iside*, 20 results that the name of Sarapis did not vome from Sinope and that it was not Ptolemy's dream which had introduced Sarapis to Alexandria. Once the statue arrived in Alexandria, the experts in sacral science agree to acknowledge a figure of Pluto-Hades and to assimilate the god and the funerary Osiris-Apis.

[56] On the reconstructed map by Michael Sabotka (see *La Gloire,* p. 94), one is tempted to raise a little 'hall of offerings', followed by the sanctuary.

[57] Rowe, *op. cit.,* I, p. 41. fig. 10. Of the dedication formula, which normally mentions the place and the temple god, there remains the toponyme 'The Mouth of Houy'. It should be recalled that the region called Houy was the north-western horn of the Delta, with Alexandria well within.

[58] Fraser, *op. cit.,* I, p. 266; 'There are, however, indications that architectural elements of Egyptian style were not lacking'... In fact, only one capital with an Egyptian lotus (*ibid.,* II, p. 421, Note 634), one Corinthian and one Ionian capital (Tkaczow, *op. cit.,* p. 208-209, Obj. 54 and 54A) are so far known as Ptolemaic vestiges. This is meagre for determining whether the Serapeum columns were Ionian or Dorian, referring to the *Serapeia* in Greece.

[59] Tally and bibliography of royal, divine, and private statues of pharaonic style in the Serapeum in *P.M.* IV, p. 3 and Tkaczow, *op. cit.*, p. 187-188 (Obj. 7, 9, 11), p 233-237 (Obj. 1222-136, excluding 124, 126, 134, 135 which have their origins in Tanis, see above Note 1), p. 311-312 (Obj. 334,338). Additions in A. Leahy, *G.M.* 80 (1984), p. 62 and p. 65-66 who indicated that the statue of Psammetichus I, Graeco-Roman Museum, Reg. 20950 and 26532, must be completed by the fragment British Museum 600, offered by W. R. Hamilton in 1840, and no doubt taken by him in 1801.

[60] *Hieroglyphic Texts in the British Museum*, 4 (1913), p. 6, plate VIII (*'... presented by Earl Spencer, 1805').* This block has been drawn in position as early as 1737 by Frederick Norden (see M-L. Buhl, *Les dessins archéologiques et topographiques de l'Egypte ancienne faits par F.L. Norden 1737-1738*, Copenhagen, Royal Academy of Sciences and Letters, 1993, p. 74-75, no. 12). Norden's drawings of 'Pompey's Column' in its environment (*ibid*., p. 73-74, no. 10) and of its 'substructures' (p. 74, no. 11) preserve the best image of the columns state, before certain blocks were taken away around 1801, and before the modern consolidations.

[61] A. Rowe, *BSAA* 35, (1942), p. 12-13 and p. 156, plate XXXIII (B2).

[62] *HTEM* 9 (1970), p. 12-13, plate VII, upper: *'presented by the Duke of York [before 1827]'.* The form of the block and the disposition of the figures and text could lead to infer that the fragment comes from the roof of a monolithic naos.

Fig 17: the base of Diocletian's Column in 1747

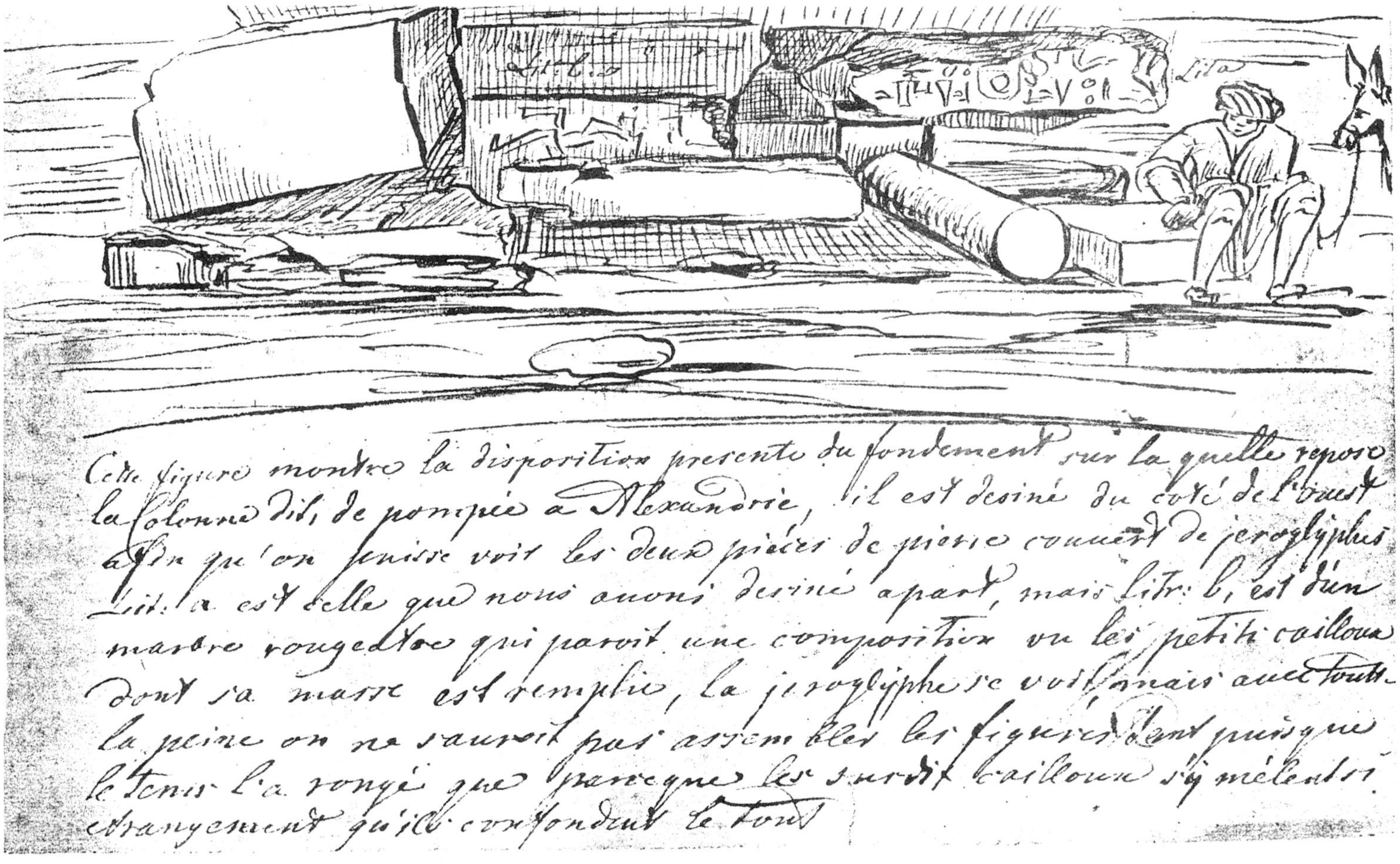

Fig 18: the base of Diocletian's Column in 1747

Psammetichus.[63] All four are of quartzite; two mention gods of Heliopolis.[64] A fifth stone of granite is said to have borne the dedication of a statue of Arsinoë Philadelphia[65] by an Alexandrine citizen.

For once, we find on site, just as they were finally put together in antiquity, a mixture of stone sculpted in various periods, some pre-Alexandrian and brought in from elsewhere, but also one from the period and origin of Alexandria. Whether or not the masons did really incorporate a base dating from the 3rd century BC, the simple assumption is to attribute these reuses to a *Roman reutilisation of rather late dating* of stones found on site, either during the great reconstruction of the Serapeum (around AD 100), or during a partial modification (at the lastest under Diocletian). It is difficult to be more precise: to envisage a possible reuse of a reuse would open the door to the theory that the removal from Heliopolis happened at the time of the Ptolemies—a theory that the evidence from the Serapeum itself does not permit us.

But in any case, the analysis of the base of Diocletian's column provides a useful model to interpret certain mixtures of recut pharaonic stones and Graeco-Roman artefacts that the underwater exploration revealed. Once removed by the quarrymen, this structure would have provided a configuration similar to what the IEASM found on the central part of the island of Antirhodos.[66]

F. The Site of Qa'it-Bey and the supposed remains of the lighthouse

Officially, the broken colossi, sphinxes and obelisks pulled out of the sea between 1992-1995 are said to have been dispersed near the lighthouse and to have then been toppled and then submerged in the course of a great earthquake, while the pre-Alexandrian elements found near them are said to be re-employed elements incorporated in the tower under Ptolemy II, and which had then fallen and broken up during the collapse.

Until further information, these conclusions must be considered problematic and support a number of reservations and even objections which may come to mind, in view of what has been shown and said in the media, or in publications destined for the general public.[67] In particular, it is impossible, on the basis of the images and information distributed, to understand the process of physics by which elements fell off the lighthouse, as well as off other neighbouring installations, and arrived on the bottom in the state and general context in which they were found. A devil's advocate could on the contrary even contest the very site of the lighthouse at Qa'it-Bey.[68]

Finding right below the Mamluk fort remains recognised to stem from this illustrious monument would at last reconcile traditional opinion with the archaeological evidence which is so far still lacking. If such a find implied in addition that Ptolemy II's architects did really take sphinxes from Helipolis, and that they recovered material for his buildings, the expected publication on the findings from the site, and from the objects found (possibly including the fragment of the dedicatory epigram of Posidippus which was announced) would provide a decisive addition to the knowledge of Alexandrine *pharonica*—on the condition that such a publication would truly allow Honor Frost's and J-Y. Empereur's hypotheses to be sustained and answer the objections ... Until this happens, there is no proof whatsoever that the removal and reuse of Heliopolitan monuments already began in the 3rd century BC.

G. The bundled columns of Thutmose IV

In 1845, Lepsius[69] noticed at the southern gate of the Arab wall some monolithic, bundled columns, together with other fluted and smooth ones, obviously dating from Graeco-Roman days. One of them showed cartouches of Ramses II, another, very originally, presented the engraved names of Thutmose IV, Seti I, and Merenptah. In 1869, an Austrian engineer working in Alexandria offered three columns of similar size and type, and showing the same cartouches, to Emperor Francis-Joseph II.[70] These monoliths preserved in the Kunsthistorische Museum in Vienna are intact; the inscriptions are merely more or less eroded, and entirely so from the lower part of the three shafts. The shafts show two bands of hieroglyphic inscriptions: above are the two names of Thutmose IV,

63 A fragment which contains a horizontal titling from Psammetichus, noted by numerous visitors, is published by A. Rowe, *BSAA* 35 (1942), p. 153 and 156, plate XXXIII (B1). Another fragment, containing the beginning of the royal first name, was indicated *in Aegyptiaca or Observations On Certain Antiquities Of Egypt*, according to L. Lepsius, D. *Text I*, p. 1-2.

64 J-Y. Empereur, *Alexandrie recouverte*, Fayard, Stock (1998), p. 100, indicates that an inscription from Thutmose III is currently visible on the base.

65 *OGIS* I, p. 30. There remains, however some doubt concerning the origin of this stone which, according to some, originates in the city itself. See Tkaczow, *op. cit.*, p. 200 (Obj. Nr 37).

66 F. Goddio, see above p. 28.

67 See above, notes 16-19.

68 See above, p. 201.

69 *L.D.*, Text I, p. 127.

70 A. Dedekind, *Geschichte der K. Sammlung Altägyptischer Objekte in Wien*, 1907, p. 24-25; E. von Bergmann dans RT. 7 (1886), p. 177-178; H Satzinger, *Das Kunsthistorische Museum in Wien. Die ägyptisch-orientalische Sammlung...*, Mainz, 1994, p. 98.

surrounded by the complete titles of Seti II, and in their midst the two repeated cartouches of Merenptah. Following a mention of a local form of the god Amon and other indications, the temple of origin must have been Memphis.[71] Whether all three columns remained close to the Alexandrian monument they supported, or were transported over more or less important distances during the Islamic period, one point is certain: they were deposited as they were, and reused intact in support of some edifice in Alexandria.

During the preliminary topographic survey of the western part of the roads, IEASM discovered a long rectangular beam, obviously cut from a bundled column out of the same colonnade, and showing, in addition, notches on both lateral sides (for splitting or calibrating?). On the preserved bundles, we read on top the names of Thutmose IV, Seti II, and of Amon; below, there are two repeated cartouches of a Roman emperor, spelt according to an original alphabetical system: it must be *Nervas-Traianos, Aristos-Sebastos*, in other words Trajan, who was qualified as *optimus* (*aristos* in Greek), from the year 414 up to his death in 417.[72] This addition does not necessarily indicate the date of transfer of our columns, they may well have been set up before Trajan's reign, although it strongly suggests so. It indicates in any case the presence of priests familiar with hieroglyphic culture in an Egyptian or Egyptianising temple in Alexandria in the name and service of the Roman pharaoh.

H. The recycled intercolumnar walls

At several different dates, some very singular slabs of greywacke have been removed from Alexandria. They were all of similar size (around 1.22 m. high) and engraved on both sides, with dedicating texts and images representing the king offering various objects to various divinities.[73] Each slab is crowned with a frieze in high relief, containing a line of *cobras-uraeuses* on one side, a line of falcons on the other, and its base is adorned, front and back with the classical design of a panelled enclosure wall.

[71] E. von Bergmann, *op. cit.,* 'Amon-Re of Khâ-set is known by the titles of a Memphite priest, Serapeum stele, Cat. no. 54 (Libyan period).

[72] With my gratitude to professor Jean-Claude Grenier and his experience for helping me in reading exactly these cartouches.

[73] Bibliography in K. Myšliwiec, *Royal Protraiture of the Dynasties XXI-XXX.* Ph. von Zabern, Mainz (1988), p 4 (A1), 47 (C4), 69 (A1). These monuments are often cited in studies on royal iconography and the 'Egyptian portrait'

a) British Museum 20, brought by Edward Wortley Montagu, 1764[74]

b) British Museum 22, same origin[75]

c) British Museum 398, same origin (?)[76]

d) Vienna, Kunsthistorisches Museum no. 213, donation by the diplomat Joseph von Schwegel, 1869[77]

e) Location unknown; seen by the members of Napoleon Bonaparte's Egyptian Expedition somewhere in Alexandria, 1798-1801[78]

To which must be added the group:

f) Bologna, Museo Civico Ks 1870, found in Rome on the Aventine in 1709[79]

g) Alexandria, Graeco-Roman Museum, Reg. no. 360, found in 1897 in Moharrem-bey, Alexandria[80]

The numerous toponyms, names and terms of gods, the explicit wording of royal declarations, prove to abundance that these stones come from Heliopolis. The proportions and one of the dedication formulae establish beyond doubt that these are *oeices* of a *sebheket*, i.e., one of the 'kiosks' supported by six or eight columns, linked in their lower part by sideboard-like walls or low walls between the columns. The story of the decoration of this

[74] Th. Young, *Hieroglyphics collected by the Egyptian Society,* London, 1823, pl. 7(I), 85 (VI), and 10 (IX); F. Arundale and J. Bonomi, *Gallery of Antiquities Selected From The British Museum,* London, 1844, p. 109, pl. 45, fig. 167. On the evidence of Budge, *A Guide To The Egyptian Gallerie (Sculpture)*, London, British Museum, 1909, p. 222 (no. 800) and p. 250 (no. 926-927), egyptological literature repeats that blocks BM 20 and BM 998 come from Rosetta, whereas block 22 only is said to come from Alexandria. It must be said that the Atum temple which pharaoh Necho founded in Rosetta, and from which also originates the famous *Rosetta Stone* (taken from the French in 1801), is a *phantasy* [verbatim in the original] imagined by Budge between 1902 and 1904; see *The Decrees of Memphis and Canopis, The Rosetta Stone I (Books on Egypt and Chadaea*, Vol. XVII*)*, London, 1904, p. 3. In this instance, the sometimes fanciful curator, embellished on Birch—who attributed the stones with good reason to the Atum temple in Heliopolis—and on Harris—who referred no doubt to a slab mentioning '*Necho, beloved by Atum*' (*ASAE* 42 [1943], p. 379, fig. 100). This last slab is part of the reused stones coming from Sais, which were incorporated in the times of sultan Qa'it-Bey (in 1479) into the fort where the famous trilingual stone was found in 1799. In addition, Budge confused two donations of King George III: part of the archaeological booty taken from the French in 1801 on the one hand, and the deposit of 1766 of the items brought to England by Montagu and offered to the sovereign. It is known that Montagu had been prospecting the ground of Alexandria in 1763-1764. There is thus good reason to keep to Young's indication of '*brought from Egypt by E. Wortley Montagu, Esq.*'

[75] Th. Young, *op. cit.*, pl. 7 (II), o (V,VII); F. Arundale and J. Bonomi, *op. cit.*, p. 110-111, pl. 145, fig. 165.

[76] Only summarily described by Budge, *A Guide To The Egyptian Galleries (Sculpture)*, p. 250 (no. 927)

[77] Description and drawing E. von Bergmann, *R.T.* 9, (1887), p. 53-57, photos K. Myšliwiec, *op. cit.*, pl. LII. H. Satzinger, *op. cit.*, p. 46-47, fig. 30. On the origins see A. Dedekind, *op. cit.*, p. 25.

[78] *Description de l'Egypte Antique* V, pl. 47, fig. 5, with *Explication des Planches*, (1821), p. 542.

[79] Lastly O. Lollio Barberi, G. Parola, M. P. Poti, *Le Antichità Egiziani di roma Imperiale*, Istituto poligraphico e Zeccha dell Stato (1995), p. 189-190.

[80] G. Botti, Catalogue du Musee Graeco-Romain, Alexandrie (1900). p. 382 with photographic partial frontal view p. 382; G. Daressy in *ASAE* S (1904), p. 115-116 (Tkaczow, *op. cit.*, p. 242, obj. 251). According to both descriptions, this slab, including its dimensions, is of the same exceptional kind as the others. However, the stone is identified as grey red siliceous, and not as greywacke!

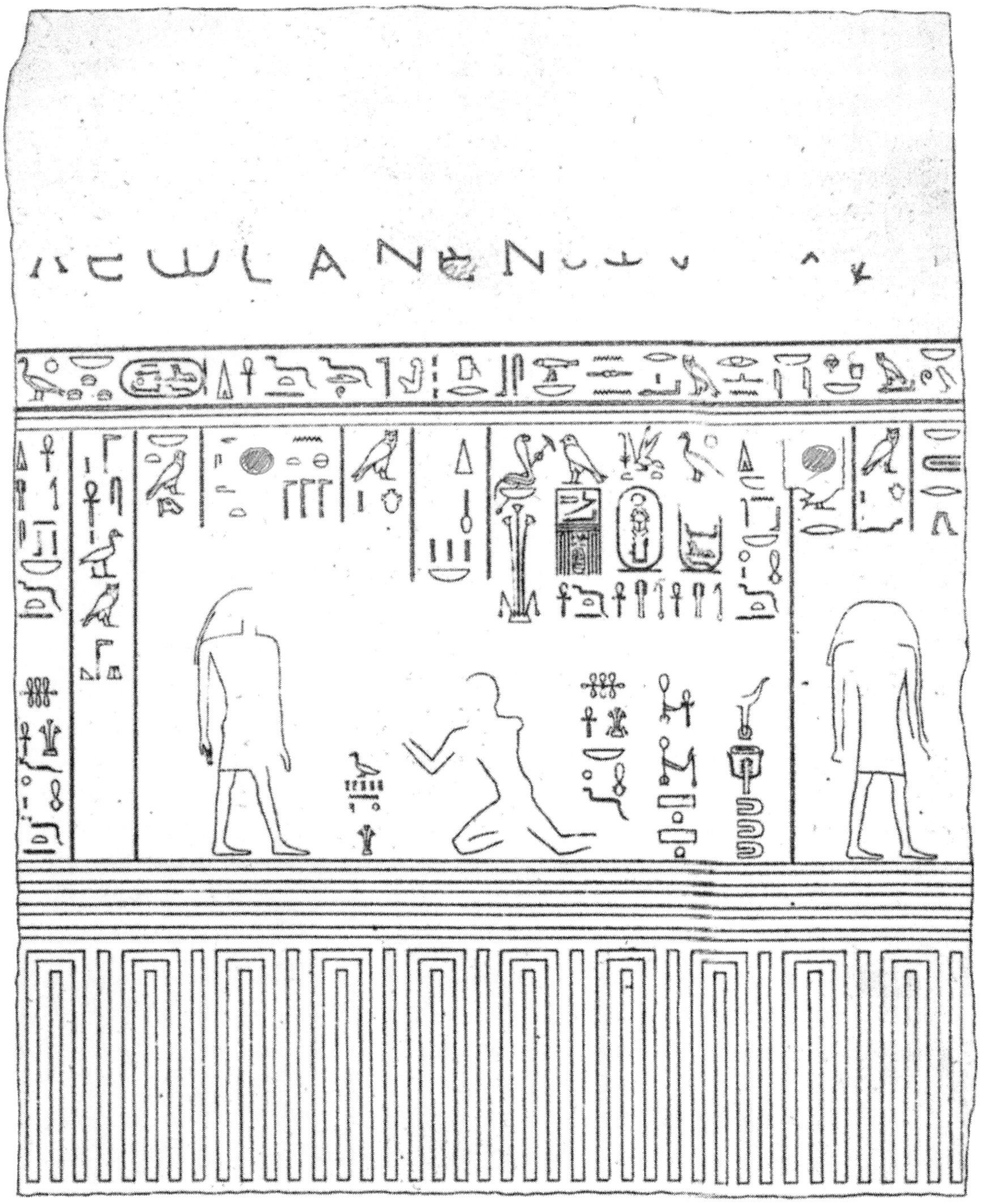

Fig 19: the low wall, British Museum 228 (verso)

Photo 102: the Vienna low wall 213 (recto)

Photo 103: the Vienna low wall 213 (verso)

unusual kiosk, famous because its bas-reliefs contain a set of amazing 'realistic' profiles of Psammetichus I. (*a, d*) and of Nekhtnebef (*b, f*) is a complex one: beginning under Psammetichus I (*a*), added to under Psammetichus II (*d*), the inscriptions were 'renewed' (e.g. *sm3wy*) under Nekhtnebef (*b, c*). But the sequel in Graeco-Roman times is just as complicated.

This type of building consisting of monolithic shafts and walls is theoretically liable to have been dismantled in Heliopolis and set up again in Alexandria. It is to be noted in this context that column blocks in the names of Psammetichus I and of Nekhtnebef have been collected in that city.[81] Whatever may be the case, it appears that one fine day, the low walls were carefully recycled. On one of the blocks, a kind of horizontal channel has been excavated, which follows exactly the border between the image and the surrounding base (*e*). The Vienna wall (*d*), where the left quarter of the external side has intentionally been refaced, and the wall, British Museum 22 (*c*), which is three quarters preserved, show a common characteristic. Very regular, narrow, cylindric conduits, which are very well polished inside, cross the stones horizontally, three on the first, and two in the second, and at roughly the same height on each. These drillings have destroyed some hieroglyphs, but the work did not degrade the images. On one side of the BM wall, the moulding of cobras has been flattened and replaced by a Greek inscription, which is unfortunately reduced to a few letters of its last line. S. Birch recognised in it the remainder of a royal restoration dedication that he dated in the Roman period on the evidence of the lettering.[82] H. Satzinger[83] wondered if these revisions and perforations were not intended to integrate these pharaonic blocks in the construction of a fountain? The idea is attractive, subject to some technical verifications: the rituals concerning water which cleans and renders fruitful and, starting from there, hydraulic installations, were of the utmost importance in the temples of Isis.[84]

Bologna 1870 (*f*), found in Rome in 1709, is a slim rectangular plate containing images and the lower external part of a low wall. The stone is cracked into irregular fragments which almost all fit together, and must have been discovered already broken, the slimming down, the presentation as a picture, and sticking the pieces together with plaster, are attributable to 18th century restorers. The object had been found in the Santa Prisca part of the Aventine, which had been the site of Trajan's private house, and where, under Septimus Severus, an official Mithras temple was supposedly erected around 200 AD. A Sarapis bust stood in that temple; in view of some theological associations of Mithras to Sun-Sarapis, it is accepted that the rearranged wall was part of the accoutrements of this Mithraeum.

The extraordinary affair of the intercolumnar walls reveals an extreme and enigmatic case that can only evoke a surfeit of speculation. One may suppose two simultaneous removals in Heliopolis itself, carried out in the times of Caracalla (211-217), who was devoted both to Sun-Sarapis and to Mithras. One such removal went to Alexandria, the other to Rome. One may just as well imagine that a piece was taken out of a recycled structure in an Egyptian or Egyptianising sanctuary in Alexandria at the time when the authentic witnesses of the Isis mysteries swarmed to the empire's capital. It is very possible to attach the refitted and dismounted kiosk to the 'Isiac' rituals or to the syncretist wanderings of the Mithras cult (in view of the fact that there was a well-known Mithraeum right in Alexandria).

At the end of this essay, in which I have endeavoured to outline a set of problems through a difficult retrospective, the low walls of Psammetichus I and Nekhtnebef, often commented on by pharaonic art historians, but forgotten in Alexandrian archaeology, are very revealing of the complexity of events and the difficult problems which cannot be solved authoritatively with the help of hasty generalities. It is to be hoped and wished that the re-examination of those Alexandrian pharaonica which are so far known but little described, and the scrutiny of subsequent underwater findings, may reveal some of those too rare cases of 'positive' technical alterations (as on our low walls), some epigraphic additions (as on the walls and bundled columns), some examples which will allow us to perceive at least some fleeting instants of Egypto-Alexandrian life and religion.[85]

[81] Lepsius, *I.D.*, Text 1, p. 1 remarked in 1842 a column section deposited in front of the French consul's residence, which bore the name of Ptolemy IV, and another showing the titles of Nekhtnebef. Further, B.M. 964 is a column section inscribed in the name of Psammetichus I which Budge had had brought in as Low Wall 20 of his imaginary Atum temple in Rosetta (*A Guide...*, p. 22, no. 802).

[82] S. Birch in F. Arundale and J. Bonomi, *op. cit.*, p. 111 with Note 1. See also E. Bernand, *Recueil des inscriptions d'Alexandrie ptolémaïque* (in the press), no. 79.

[83] Verbal communication June 1998. It would perhaps not be too hazardous to recall in this context the monumental fountain dedicated to one of the Arsinoë queens, and which was for a long time described in Greek verse by a court poet! Fraser, *op. cit.*, I, p. 609-610 with II, p. 860-862, Notes 411-419, remarked that the simultaneous use of marble imported from Greece and of Aswan granite was 'a mixture of traditionally Greek and native stones'.

[84] B.A. Wild, *Water In The Cultic Worship Of Isis And Serapis* (*EPRO* 87), Leiden (1981).

[85] The objects presenting remodeling and additions are so rare and so vastly dispersed that it would be helpful to syntactically co-ordinate all observations made on the all sectors, above and below water. On the underwater site worked by the Centre d'Etudes Alexandrines East of Qa'it-Bey, for instance, some papyriform columns, recut along their length were discovered, some of which preserve the name of Ramses II (*BIFAO* 95 [1995], p. 588-589. J-Y. Empereur, *Le Phare*, p. 88 and photo p. 25). A shaft of this kind in the name of the king had been seen by Lepsius near a gate in the Arab Wall (*L.D.* Text 1, p. 1). Further, '*a Christian Cross engraved on a papyriform capital*' has been reported among the reused pieces found at the presumed foot of the lighthouse (E. de Roux, *Le Monde*, Sept. 27 1995, p. 25). The case can be compared to the columns of similar kind analysed above: a support of pharaonic origin come down to us abandoned, but which could have been complemented while standing in Alexandria, long after the date of its transportation. Such a case, if confirmed, would be extremely interesting. If the Christians regularly recuperated classical buildings and columns, it may well have happened occasionally to overcome their horror of the demoniacal contents of these Egyptian images and scriptures, and to banish them by adding the sign of the Holy Cross, as happened in the days of Justinian, in 535-537, on the walls of the Isis temple at Philae.

To recapitulate as far as possible observations from facts, the methodological reservations which result from them, and also the working hypotheses which I suggest, let us take up again the problems posed by the *pharaonica* of Alexandria:

What is their significance concerning relations between the culture of the Egyptians and that of the Greeks?

When and with what intentions were monuments of earlier pharaohs removed from Alexandria and introduced into Alexandria?

And, as a subsidiary point, by what random processes were these monuments disseminated throughout Alexandria.

Colossi and sphinxes demonstrate that works of indigenous art, expressing publicly the superhuman quality of the king, were part of the urban landscape of Alexandria. But one must also wonder whether this presence of pharaonic art and ideology in the city founded by Alexander —and which remained a centre of Greek science, thought and aesthetics in the eyes of the world — was restricted to such theologico-political exhibition. In other words, even if the cosmology of the Egyptians exerted no influence whatsoever on the intellectual activities of the Museum and the Library, even if Alexandrian art was purely Hellenistic, would it not appear that in their capital, turned towards the sea and the Greek world as it were, the Ptolemies bestowed importance on the popular divinities of their subjects in the interior, which they themselves honoured in Memphis, that other cosmopolitan capital which they had inherited from previous dynasties. They acknowledged them as they were, in their original names and forms, in temples of Egyptian ritual. They occasionally associated them with their own divinities in temples of Graeco-Macedonian creation. And their entourage of distinguished associates came to frequent Sarapis and Isis and to adopt the images and symbols of a prestigious religion thousands of years old, which had become the religion of their kings and queens. Describing in Greek the rhyton which the engineer Ctesibos offered to Arsinoë-Aphrodite in her temple in Canopus, the poet Hedylus of Samos included the god Bes, 'the Egyptian dancer' who calls the divine waters of the Nile and gives the signal for sacred feasts and drinking bouts. It is the same demon Bes, the joyous trumpeter and drummer who led the drunken feasts in the towns across the *chôra* through which Hathor, in whom the Greeks recognised Aphrodite, was appeased. Thus, from the 3rd century BC on, an object of Hellenistic art and the ceremonial of a Greek sanctuary in the Alexandrian region were intermingled with Egyptian elements.

We must definitely abandon the long-maintained image which presents the first Ptolemies as keeping the native elite at bay, leaving the conquered barbarians locked up in their customs and beliefs, practising some kind of *apartheid*, a segregation which would obviously have excluded all ethnic and cultural pollution of Alexandria which remained in its Hellenistic purity. At Naucratis, the trading post that the Saïte pharaohs had conceded to Greek merchants, temples of various Olympians, built and functioning in the Greek manner, existed long before Alexander, and were right next to an Egyptian temple of Amon. Yet the Alexandrian government went to great expense to enlarge this sanctuary of 'Theban Zeus' to huge proportions. It was extended according to a traditional, strictly native plan and decorated with original hieroglyphic inscriptions in the names of the pharaohs, Ptolemy I and Ptolemy II. Must it therefore not be expected that such a development, contrary to the supposed *apartheid*, could have been extended to Alexandria itself where the Serapeum would have presented the Egyptian aspects of common divinities to the cult and faith of the Greeks.

If we admit the presence of Egyptian temples in Ptolemaic Alexandria, together with the permanent presence of priests in the pharaonic tradition, we may concretely perceive how the hellenised forms of the Egyptian gods came into being. The cult of these gods, with their ritual called 'Isiac', their own theology and mysticism, spread, as we know, from the very beginning throughout the entire Hellenistic period, over all the countries bordering the Aegean, the Black Sea and the Mediterranean. According to a literary tradition passed on by Diodorus Siculus, the first Greek aretology of the goddess Isis is said to have been engraved in the temple of Memphis, which is in no way unlikely in view of the antiquity and the importance of the Greek community there. It must be noted, however, that *Isea* of the Greek type and the popularity of the Sarapis cult are only attested much later in the *chôra*. Let us also add that the figure of Isis Plusia, official protectrix of sailors, and that goddess' ritual navigation towards the open sea, could not readily have come from the heart of Egypt.

It is generally admitted that the exported 'Isiac' religion could just as well be called 'Alexandrian', and that it is out of the great emporium that its theological concepts, its iconographic models, its ritual practices and its pharaonic trappings were exported by Greek sailors. The idea that in Alexandria there were after all so-called indigenous temples and priests permits us to draw a lively picture of the circumstances under which this religion was elaborated amongst the residents of the capital. From the 'new water' of the flooding Nile presented by the priests of Karnak in procession to Amon in ewers and jars covered with lids in the form of heads of rams, falcons or men, through vases in which the gods of the nomes brought the parts of a dismembered Osiris to have them restored to end up with Osiris Canopus, in this, for example, is the substance for a learned re-interpretation of authentic indigenous traditions which the *hierogrammatei* imparted to the Greeks. Intercultural exchanges do not happen through an osmosis between such abstract entities as native 'cultures', but through dialogue between living people. The specific features of the Isiac religion can only result from sustained intercourse between Egyptian priests speaking Greek and Greeks concerned with sacred matters, pursuing a mutual interpretation of their respective pantheons, myths and rituals. Under Ptolemy I, so Plutarch reports, an *ad hoc* commission convened around Manetho of Sebennytus (who related in Greek the history and religion of his nation) and Timotheus of the Eumolpidae, exegete of the Eleusinian mysteries, to identify the extraordinary statue brought from Sinope on the Black Sea. One can easily accept that other such gatherings took place, bringing together personnel from the Serapeum and other sanctuaries established in Alexandria, to treat of Isis and Demeter, Dionysos and Osisris, Apis and the sun, Anubis 'the Guide of Souls' and Thot, and of water and wheat, remodelling the sacred knowledge of Egypt according to Greek thought.

The Chaeremon, encountered by Strabo and the other Chaeremon, the stoic philosopher who was the preceptor of the emperor Nero in Rome and the sacred scribe who had Trajan's hieroglyphic cartouches engraved on a bundled column, illustrate perfectly the continued presence in Alexandria of repositories of ancestral hieratic traditions and the continuation of indigenous rites under Roman domination. Through such 'Egyptian philosophers' elements of the concepts and the representations of pharaonic Egypt passed into Greek astrology and then into the discourse of Hermes Trimegistos and enriched the egyptological knowledge of a Plutarch. The seat of these native scholars must be found in temples of Egyptian ritual and in their libraries which preserved the hieratic and demotic papyri of these 'houses of life'. Those temples of which our *pharaonica* preserve a confused memory …

The visible presence of a number of monuments mostly transported from Heliopolis among the pre-Alexandrine antiquities found dispersed all over Alexandria corresponds to a massive operation of removal to the benefit of only a limited number of temples of Egyptian or Isiac ritual.

The date and, even more so, the modalities and motivations for the removal from Heliopolis of movable and architectural elements (an operation which must not necessarily be linked to the removal of obelisks by Augustus) cannot in the current state of knowledge be determined. A point in Ptolemaic times cannot in theory be excluded (the Centre d'Etudes Alexandrines thesis concerning the lighthouse, regarding which it is preferable to await concrete and convincing proof). A time in the period of the Roman empire cannot be excluded either (P. Gallo's thesis). Several realignments of elements from Heliopolis, and the addition of monuments imported from other sites during imperial times seem clear.

Transportation and serial dispersion since the end of pagan times are such that there is no possibility of deducing from the current state of findings of *pharaonica* the sites and identity of the temples in which they were included. Were the Isis temple in the royal quarter and the Isis temple on the island of Pharos Egyptian or 'Isiac'? The holy place of Eleusis seems rather to have belonged to the second category, even to have been the place where the mysteries of initiation of the goddess were invented and where Osiris-Apis was identified with Pluto?

Particularly rare and ambiguous, the results from the field and the artefacts which could play the role of 'guide fossils' reveal the complexity of the physical and human processes which determined buildings and redevelopments; *at the very best*, they allow us to define the questions.

It is to be hoped that, either in the urban areas in which conservation excavations take place, or during the soundings underground in the flooded areas, some site reveals the remnants of a temple of Ptolemaic times which indubitably contains *pharaonica* originating from Heliopolis.

The deposits immediately accessible to underwater prospecting or excavation only show final sites, more or less posterior to the end of antiquity, but surely prior to the Ottoman period and the ultimate state of the *pharaonica*. We should be happy once we have defined where to situate chronologically the last episode before abandonment and immersion. The *pharaonica* have shared the vicissitudes of the Hellenistic and Graeco-Roman monuments. Research on their sites of origin comes second to the conclusions of the specialists in classical archaeology. A general cartography of the dispersion of Egyptian objects would only be revealing if, among the over-abundance of Greek and Graeco-Roman objects, the coherent remnants of collapsed buildings were identified, if not specifically named, and separated from the mass of elements manifestly torn out of one and the same construction. These contexts will no doubt teach us much about the adventures and mishaps, material and moral, undergone by the *materia aegyptiaca*.

Between the moment of their arrival in Alexandria and that of their rediscovery, pharaonic objects are liable to have undergone all or part of an entire series of tribulations:

—installation in an Alexandrian temple and consecration, whether or not in conformity to their original function and significance

—ritual recycling requiring technical alterations and epigraphic overlay

—reshaping blocks of masonry and cutting them up (which must, in fact, have totally destroyed a number of monuments, or at least their inscriptions). Several successive reuses of blocks are possible.

—individual or collective transportation as to disseminate the various parts of one entity over considerable distances

—all of this being interspersed with breakage and mutilation due to natural causes, to manipulative incidents, or to iconoclastic aggression.

Our inquiries must therefore become increasingly attentive, not only to the original decoration of artefacts, but also to the material state of stones whose alterations and additions preserve the traces of the multiple twists and turns of the building and destruction of ancient Alexandria.

BLOCKS WITH HIEROGLYPHS

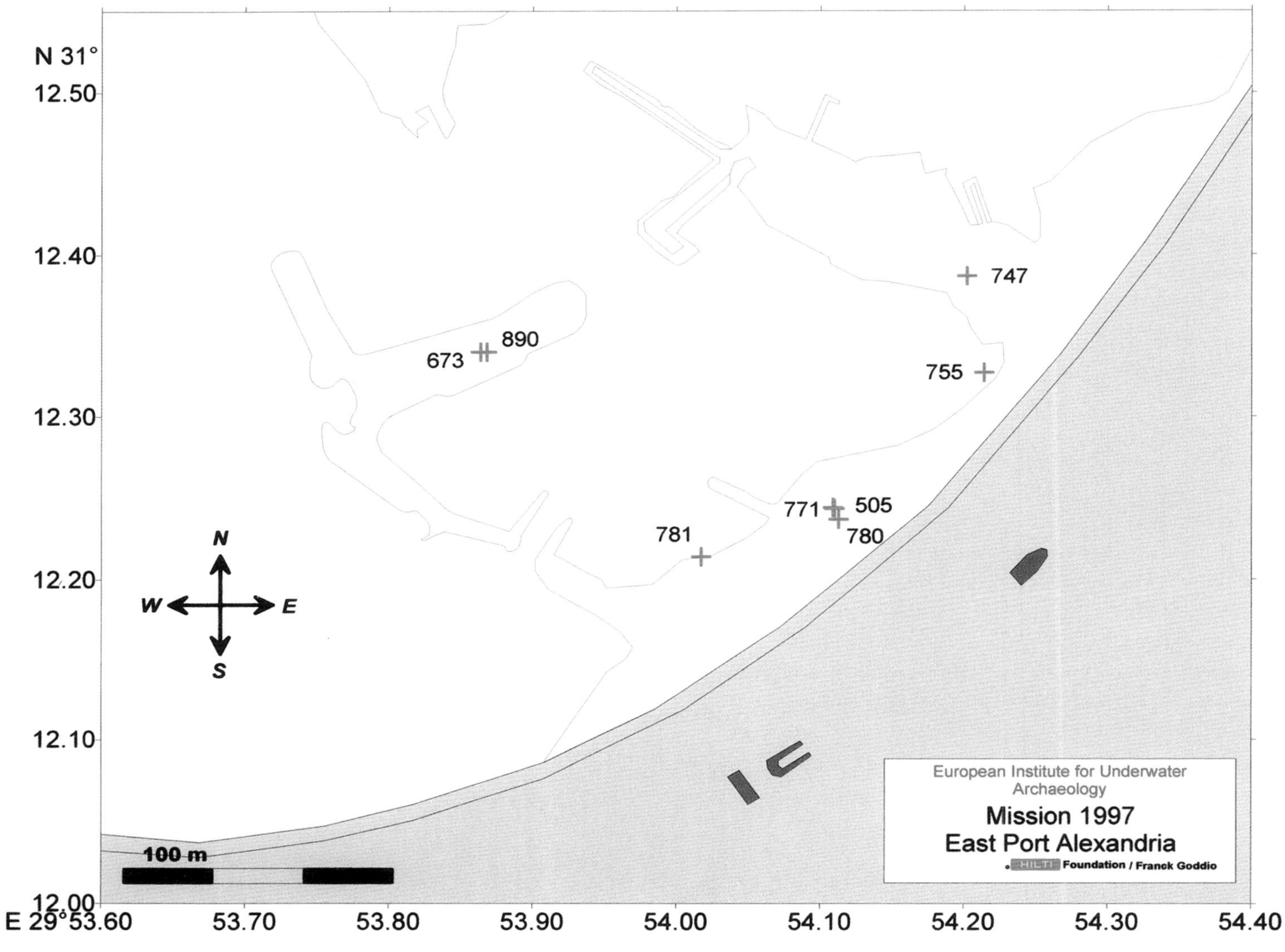
N 31°
12.50
12.40
12.30
12.20
12.10
12.00
E 29°53.60
53.70
53.80
53.90
54.00
54.10
54.20
54.30
54.40
747
890
673
755
771
505
780
781
N
W
E
S
100 m
European Institute for Underwater Archaeology
Mission 1997
East Port Alexandria
HILTI Foundation / Franck Goddio

II. THE EGYPTIAN INSCRIPTIONS

The surveys of 1996 and 1997 produced *pharaonica* of two sorts: Ptolemaic and pre-Alexandrian. This included seven pieces of Egyptian statuary. Five date from the Greek or Roman period. The exceptional monumental falcon's head is certainly from the Late Period, but might be before Alexander. In addition a piece of a statue from the period of Ramesses is datable by its hieroglyphic inscriptions. On the other hand, we have seven blocks with hieroglyphic inscriptions and/or the remains of an Egyptian relief Part of an obelisk is in the name of Sethi I; this seems to have been the monumental base of a statue also from the Ramesside period. Moreover, five architectural elements also come from a monument of the Saite period, whose re-use spared the set of inscriptions. In regard to the latter, it will be remembered that among the numerous large blocks of granite and quartzite that lay at these same sites (see plan p. 220), many of these must have been removed at the demise of native ancient temples, so that we are unable today to be precise about their original nature, much less their dating. In those cases where an examination of such blocks produces traces of some embellishment or primitive decoration or a surface once invisible, now shows texts or pictures, a possible attribution should be sought through study.

The morphological description of the statues and discussion about their dates are to be found in the chapter which Zsolt Kiss has devoted to them.[1]

The present section will offer an initial catalogue of the pharaonica which have retained something of their original decoration with the translation and interpretation of the images and inscriptions. These monuments remain under water and the examination of them is based on the following documentation:

—Scale drawings of the blocks on which was noted the material state of different surfaces and visible edges and sketches to position the reliefs and engraved inscriptions. These sketches were created by the study office in Alexandria of IEASM from measurements, examination and checks made at my request by the divers.[2]

—photographs taking during dives of the accessible decorated surfaces.

—impressions of the engraved surfaces on fabric-backed elastic compound.[3] Without exception the photographs (105, 108, 110) of the excellent impressions published herein show the inscriptions reversed (which does not detract from reading them as Egyptian hieroglyphics are written either left to right or right to left).

Some imprecision, in spite of cleaning, remains in their identification or the petrographical identification of some stones.[4]

1 Block no. 747: section of obelisk of Sethi I (*c.* 1297-1291BC) grey granite (p. 223).

Position: Peninsula

Dimensions: height 0.55 m, approx., width 2 m. approx., deep 0.7 m.

Condition: only face A is preserved. Faces B and C, missing a band 0.7 m. wide; the depth of the block has been reduced by re-dressing to about 1.3 m. Three notches are cut into the edge.

It is possible to deduce the original type of decoration of the obelisk from this fragment which belonged to the inner part of the shaft. Below this column, divided into two, is the picture of a king (kneeling rather that in the form of a sphinx) in the presence of a standing divinity. Above the king in a frame are his two cartouches faced by an epithet, the so-called 'beloved' of this divinity.

Face A

Central column: [→] 'Sethi-Merenptah'

To the right, the king: [←] '*Lord of the Two Lands Menmare, lord of the crowns Sethi-Merenptah, beloved of Amon-Re, lord of the Thrones of the Two Lands.*'

To the left, the god: [→] '*Amon-Re, lord of the Thrones of the Two Lands*'

Face B

Central column: [→] '*beloved of the lords of the Great Castle.*'

[1] Above, p. 169 *et seq*.

[2] I must thank fellow team members from the Supreme Council for Antiquities for having enabled the egyptological identification of the monuments through their dives.

[3] Above, F. Goddio, p. 7.

[4] 'Limestone' should be amended to quartzite in J-Y. Empereur, *Le Phare*, 1998, p. 88; *Alexandrie redécouverte*, p. 75 and 79. On the geological and egyptological definitions of the rocks, cf. Th. De Putter and Chr. Karlshauser, *Les pierres utilisées dans la sculpture et l'architecture de l'Egypt pharaonique. Guide pratique illlustré* (Connaissance de l'Egypte ancienne. Etude no. 4), Brussels, 1992.

Photo 104: section of obelisk, no. 747, *in situ*: Face A

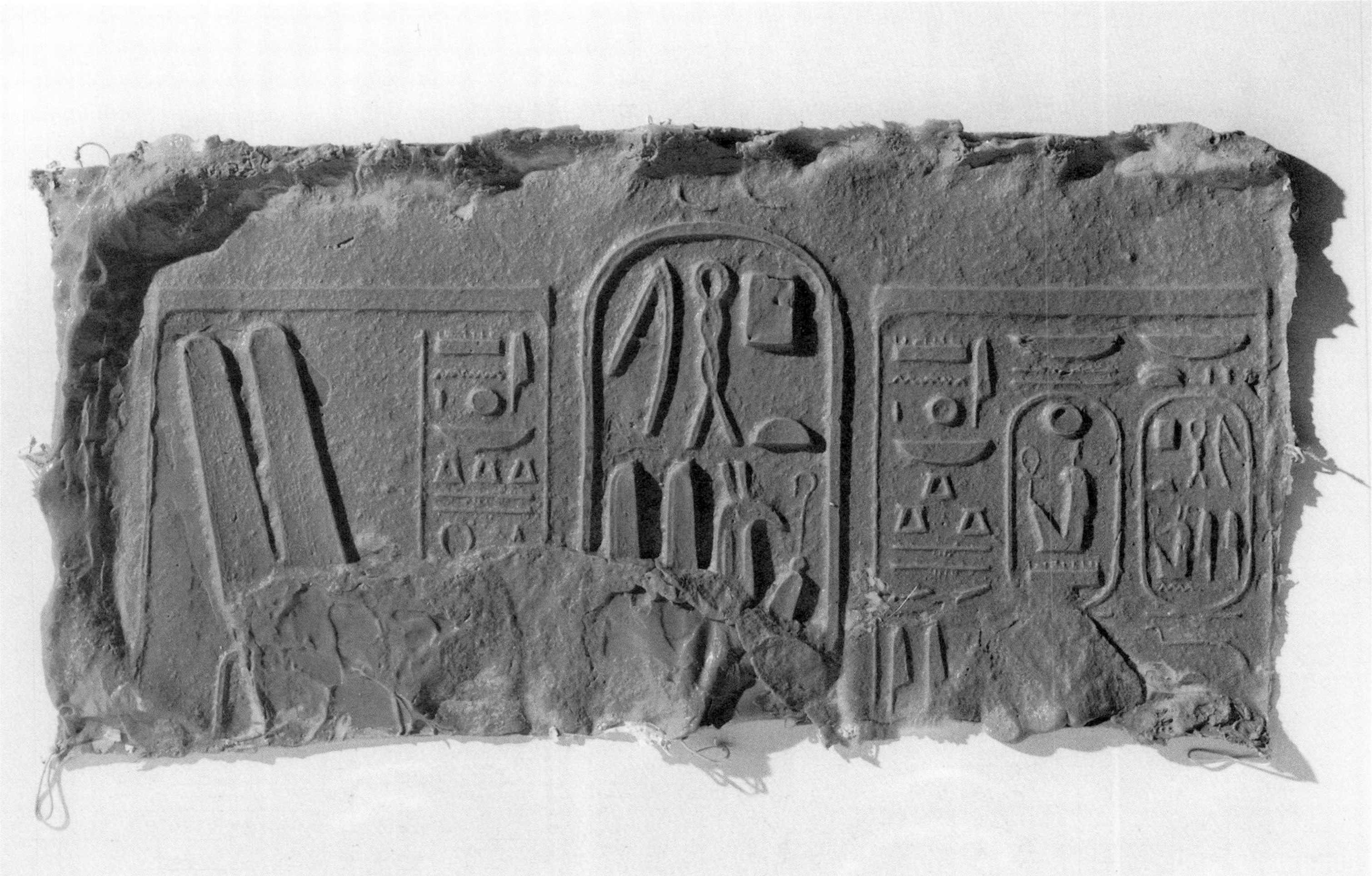

Photo 105: section of obelisk, no. 747, impression: Face A

BLOCK DB4 N° 747
Peninsula
Grey Granite
Lat : 31° 12' 3863 N
Long : 29° 54' 2023 E
Depth : 4,8 m.

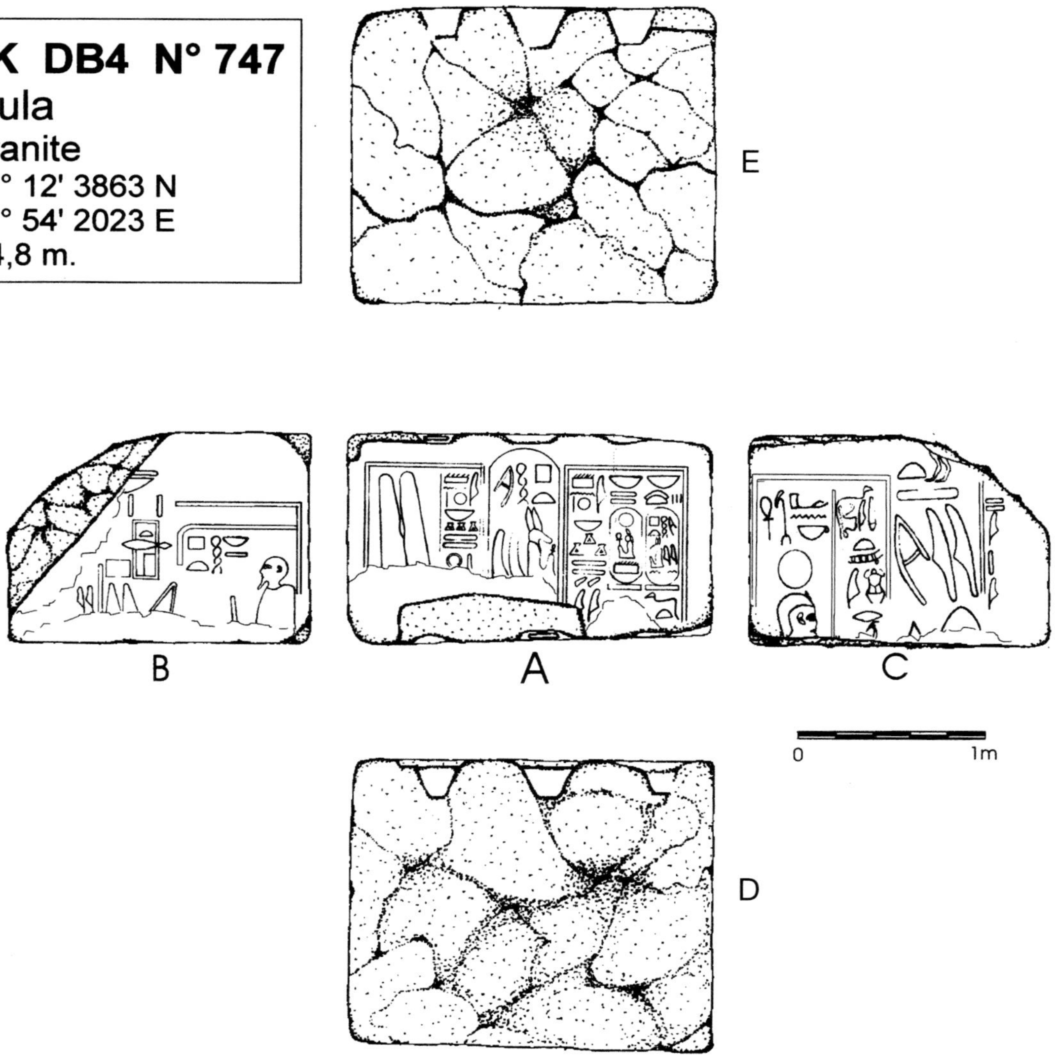

Photo 106: section of obelisk, no. 747, Face C

Photo 107: section of obelisk, no. 747, *in situ*: Face C

Photo 108: section of obelisk, no. 747, impression: Face C

Photo 109: section of obelisk, no. 747, *in situ*: Face B

Photo 110: section of obelisk, no. 747, impression: Face B

To the left the king. Only the adjective remains, [→] *'beloved of [Ptah in] Heliopolis.'*

To the right, the god Ptah in his chapel: [←] *'Ptah, lord of Maat'*

Face C

Central column: [←] *'beloved of [Re-Hor]akhti, endowed with life [...]'*

To the right, the king: only the adjective remains: [→] *'beloved of Atum-Khepri, the great god.'*

To the left, the god Atum with a human face, wearing on his head the solar disk: [→] *'Words spoken by Atum-Khepri: I give you life.'*

Neither the iconography, nor the designation of Atum were current any longer. Whilst the god is most often shown with the *pschent* in his hair, here he wears a wig topped by a solar disk which distinguishes certain images of Re-Horakhti. The appellation which confirms the identity of the sun in the evening and the renewed son in the morning is attested very rarely.[5] The second example I know of is given in a table of offerings that Sethi I dedicated in Heliopolis to *'Atum-Khperi who comes into being from himself'* (Cairo CG 23090, below, n. 18).

The three images thus present three of the four major gods of the Ramesside state, Theban Amon, the Heliopolitan sun in the form of Atum-Khepri and Ptah of Memphis (a fourth would have been either Seth or another form of the sun on the missing face). In every case the crucial mention of Re-Horakhti and the divinities of the Great Castle, that is to say the main temple of Heliopolis, allows us to regard this block as a further testimony to the monumental work of Sethi I in this city.

Actually we know at present of obelisks from Heliopolis by this king, two obelisks of quartzite making a pair[6] and a pink granite obelisk, pieces of which were fished out by Qa'it-Bey,[7] as well as the obelisk of the Piazza del Popolo, removed in about 29 for Rome and which was the work of Ramesses II.[8] One should add the greywacke pair which is mentioned by the dedicatrix of the famous model of the monumental doorway from Heliopolis, Brooklyn Museum 49.185.[9]

Few relics of Sethi I have been gathered from the ravaged site of the central temple of the Sun: a small piece from the base of a statue,[10] and more significantly, small fragments of rose granite from which it has been possible to reconstruct an important cuboid naos, now Torino Suppl. 2676.[11] On the other hand, several important remains of buildings from Heliopolis under Sethi I have been found spread about in Alexandria. Apart from the obelisks already referred to, we should note the wall fragment in quartzite re-used under the 'Column of Pompey',[12] the large door upright of quartzite in the Graeco-Roman Museum, no. 420 (Labbane),[13] the block of granite seen by Brugsch, place des Consuls in 1853,[14] the enormous granite lintel in Brussels which served as a threshold in an Arab house[15] and a naos (?) which was located by Botti in 1896 (Gheninah).[16] Other pieces were removed from Heliopolis for other places: thus the beautiful granite statue featuring Sethi in a great pleated robe which ended up in the Roman period in a villa or Isiac temple in Tusculum;[17] or even the big offering tables in the same material, dedicated to various members of the Ennead, and of which two were dug up in Fatimid Cairo.[18]

On our lower fragment from the obelisk the ideogram of the god Seth in the name Sethi is intact as is the figure of the sphinx with the head of a Sethian animal on the granite obelisk of Qa'it-Bey. The accursed god is hammered off the offering table CG 23090.[19] Verification of the other original items remains to be done.[20]

2. Block no. 755: fragment of a quartzite base (?) (p. 227).

Position: south coast.

Dimensions: height 0.5 m; width 1.1 m; depth 1.75 m.

Condition: triangular shape cut from a large block. Severe chipping on faces A, D and C, apparently due to accident damage leaving only small areas of initial decoration engraved.

To identify the original nature, the date, recyclings and misfortunes of this fragment where the remains of decoration are particularly corroded are highly conjectural.

5 It is not listed as such in the monograph of K. My(liwiec, *Studien zum Gott Atum II* (*HÄB* 8, 1979), p. 175, which deals with the affinities between Atum and Khepri.

6 J. P. Corteggiani in *BIFAO* 96 (1996), p. 564 and 97 (1997), p. 376-377; J-Y. Empereur, *Le Phare*, 1998, p. 87b and 118, cf. p. 124; *Alexandrie redécouverte*, Paris, 1998, p. 75 and 79.

7 J. P. Corteggiani, *op. cit.*, p. 564, and *La gloire d'Alexandrie*, Paris, Petit Palais 1998, p. 102, n. 63, J-Y. Empereur, *Alexandrie redécouverte*, p. 69 and 75.

8 PM VII, p. 409 (2); E. Iverson, *Obelisks in Exile 1 The Obelisks of Rome*, Copenhagen, 1969, p. 65-75, fig. 35-36. Texts K*RI*, 118-120.

9 A. Badawy, 'A monumental gateway for a temple of Sety I. An ancient model restored', in *Miscellanea Wilbouriana* I (1972), p. 1-23.

10 M. E. Petrie, 'Heliopolis, Kafr Ammarr and Shurafa', BSAE XVIII, 1912, p. 7, §16, pl. VIII, fig. 3.

11 *Passato e futuro del Museo egizio di Torini*, Turin, 1989, p. 27-28.

12 A. Rowe, *BSA Alex* 35 (1942), p. 153-154 and 156, pl. XXXIII (B2).

13 G. Daressy, *ASAE* 5 (1904), p. 120-121, §XXIII. On the find site, see B. Tkaczow, *Topography*, p. 282-283 (obj. 121)

14 H. Brugsch, *Reiseberichte aus Aegypten*, Leipzig, 1855, p. 10.

15 J. Capart, *Recueil de Monuments égyptiens*, 1ère serie, Brussels, 1902, pl. XXXIX.

16 G Botti, *Plan de la ville d'Alexandrie,* Alexandrie, 18, p. 114, no. XCIX. Cf. B Tlcaczow, *op. cit.*, p. 238 (obj. 140).

17 S Bosticco, 'Frammento di statua di Sethos I a Grottaferrata' dans *Aegyptus* 36 (1956), p. 18-23, fig. 1-4.

18 Caire CG 23090. A Kamal, *Tables d'offrandes* (CGC), Le Caire 1, p. 73-74, pl. 19; *KRI* I, 121, no. 60 (dédiée à Atoum-Khépi) New York MMA 22.2.22, Badowi, *op .cit.*, p. 11-12, fig. 14; *KRI* I, 324-325, no. 103 (dedicated to Seth and Nephthys); Copenhague, Glyptothèque Ny Carlsberg E 115, M Mogensen, *La Glyptothèque Ny Carlsberg. La collection égyptienne* (1930), p. 102, pl. 110 (dedicated to Blue-Horus-the Great-Castle).

19 G Botti, cited above n. 16 notes that the name of Seth was hammered out on the naos.

20 We know that the figures of Seth were destroyed on the ancient monuments no doubt from the 9th century BC, but this proscription was not a general one for all. The preservation of these images of Typhon can be explained by not being re-used visibly or by the tolerance of local theologians.

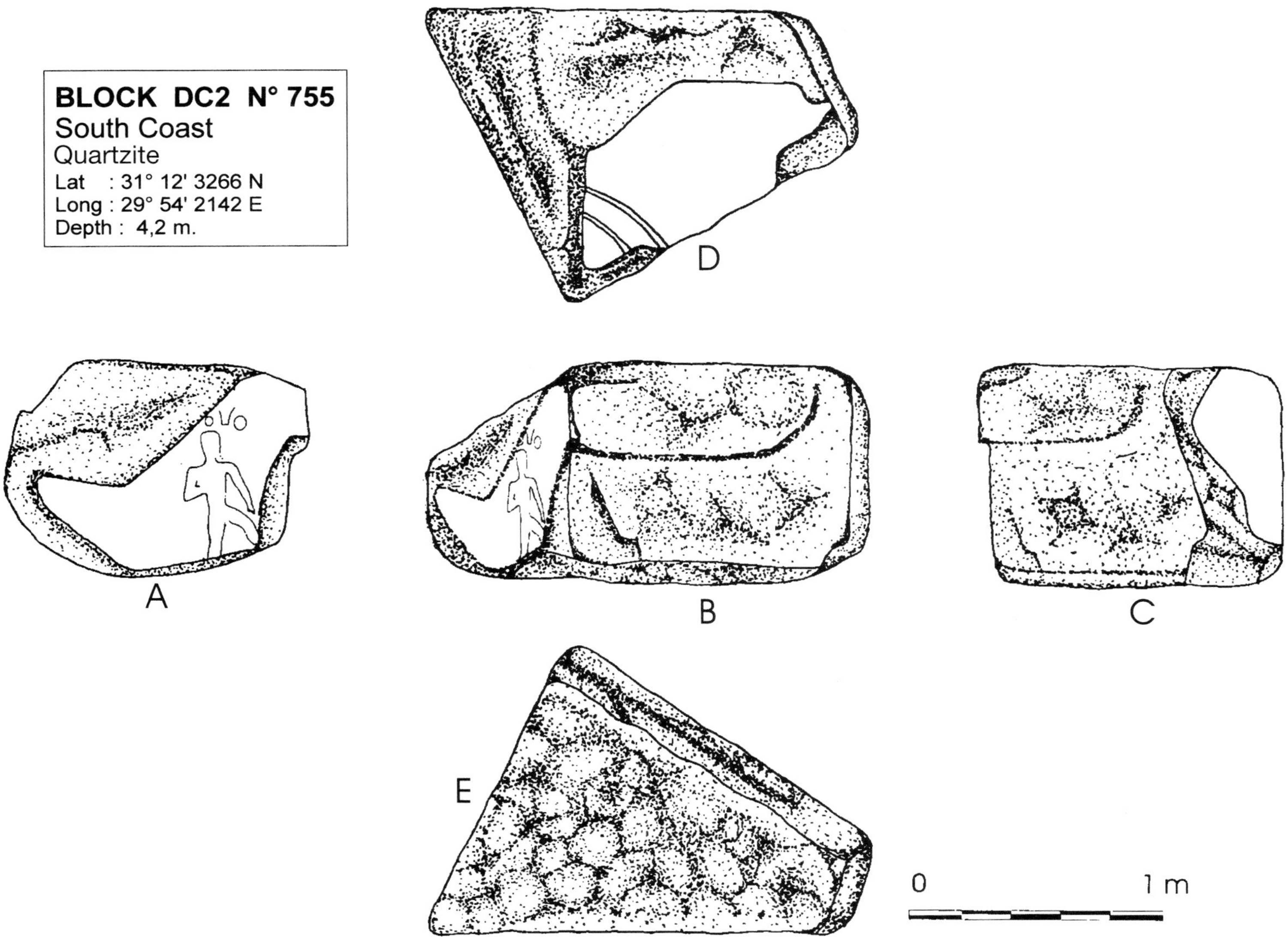

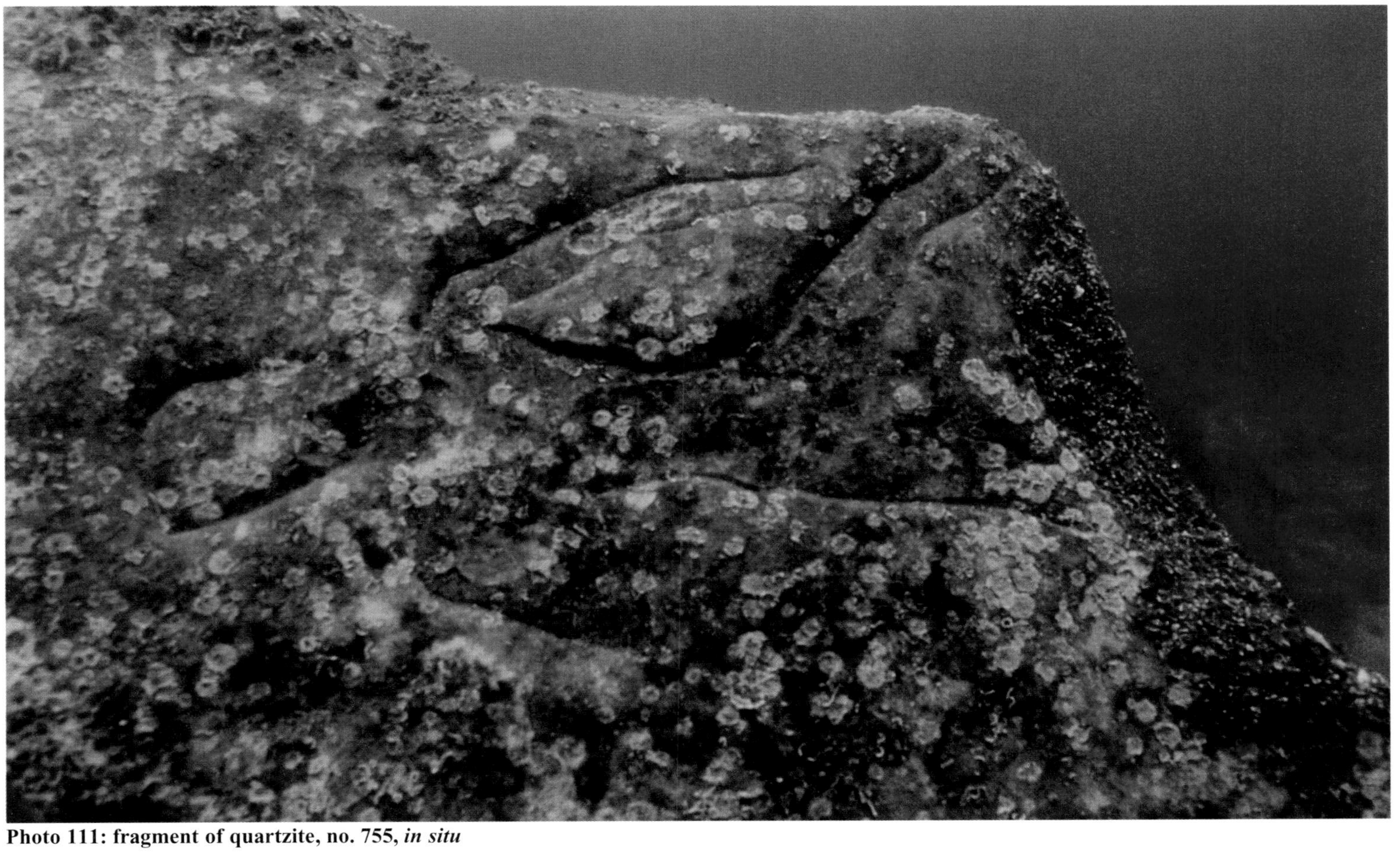

Photo 111: fragment of quartzite, no. 755, *in situ*

The person visible on face A, which was found facing the sky, allows us to determine which were the vertical faces of the block when it was first used in a pharaonic monument.

The rest of the engraving which remains on horizontal plane D—which is parallel to plane E—denotes an upper face which must therefore be visible from above. We might thus have the remains of a socle decorated on its vertical faces (at least on the front side) and on the ledge, like the bases of statues (compare fragment 3). However, it does not seem complete in width (actually 1.10 m.). In effect, as will be seen, the posture of the person requires iconographically, in all likelihood, that the scene in which it played a part is extended to the right for a distance which has yet to be determined. Thus it seems that the block, crudely rectangular—planes A and C being parallel—was later sawn diagonally to give the roughly triangular shape it now shows.

On what is left of the upper face (D) of the block, a neatly engraved line drawing is repeated five times (p. 227). This drawing makes one immediately think of the schematic figure of a bow, according to hieroglyphic style and Egyptian iconography. Here one would readily see the left half of five bows which the sawing cut towards the middle, causing the right half to disappear. The bows were set out parallel to the front side (A) of the block.

Moreover, one notices that inharmonious incisions cut the bows (figure 20). The double line bending to the inside of the third bow (from the edge of A) resembles an outline or a repeat of the design of a bow. The large spindle-shaped cavity and the triple spindle of lines which cut obliquely the fourth and fifth bows does not seem part of the initial design (was the block used as a grindstone?). Now it is well known the design of Nine Bows, a symbol for all the foreign populations that the pharaoh had to keep 'beneath his sandals', is sometimes engraved on the flat surfaces of royal statue bases showing the king marching or enthroned; through an artistic device the two halves of the bows are divided beneath the feet of the king (figure 21).[21] This may be the case here, in so far as the surface of our block allows us to put back the four bows lost when it was broken.

On the front face (A) in spite of the strong corrosion of the rock which has obliterated all the details of the picture, the figure of a standing person is clearly distinguishable. It is without doubt a king, indicated by the hairstyle he wears, the *khepresh* being perfectly recognisable and the loincloth, although seriously degraded, can only be the expected *shendjyt*. The posture of this pharaoh is, however, strange. One leg is raised, as if striding forward, the other being firmly planted on the ground. One arm, the fist clenched, is brought back to the centre of the chest; the other arm, the fist likewise clenched, is carried forward towards the knee of the raised leg. At once, these movements recall the manner how Egyptian style renders the gesture of a man about to pull on a rope to tighten a knot. It is rather like what is seen in the scenes of slaughter from the Old Kingdom, where a butcher is shown who holds the rope tying the rear legs of a bullock to help topple it onto the ground.[22] More exactly it is just the stance of two persons who, symmetrically knot around the *sema* sign the long stems of the heraldic plants of the Two Lands (*taouy*), a common device in the iconography of every age.[23] This theme of the Union of the Two Lands (*sema-taouy*) is frequently sculpted in bas–relief on the walls of the throne where the pharaoh sits. Perhaps the image might be reduced to a static panel with the two bouquets of plants tied to the *sema* signs.[24] Elsewhere on the sides of the seat, two divine beings, most often two 'figures of fecundity' are busy pulling on the stems (figure 22).[25] On the statues of the king standing, it happens sometimes that the representation of the *sema-taouy* is drawn in the centre of the front face of the base (photo 114).[26] Having observed that the mark of the stems has been rubbed off the outer layer of stone, one might gladly reconstruct a picture of the *sema-taouy* occupying the centre of our presumed base, the supposed axis of the row of bows, or rather the crotch of the striding sovereign, coming right over the central *sema*. This hypothetical fixing of the axis of the original monument lets us represent it as a plaque about 22.10 m. by 1.75 m. and 50 cm. thick and the socle or base for a colossus. The destroyed surface to the left of the preserved figures as well as on the surface might be filled with vertical columns of hieroglyphic inscriptions containing royal legends or

21 Alexandria, Musée Greco-romain, reg. no. 426 (Serapeum) + G 901(garden): seated statue of Ramesses I brought from Tamis in 1825 by Rifaud, *Voyage en Egypte,* 1930, bl. 125, fig. 12. Other examples Cairo CG 42053, Legrain, *Statues et statuettes* II, p. 33, pl. XXIX (Thoutmosis III marching); Louvre AF 795 bis, Vandiex, *Manuel d'Archéologie égyptienne* III Album,pl. CI, fig. 1 (Thoutmosis II seated); New York MMA 14.3.17, *ibid.*, pl. LIX, fig. 3. J. Baines, cited *infra* n.c, fig. 66-68 (Sesostris I seated); Index PM2 II, p. 346, 'Sur les bronzes des IVè époques récentes, les Neuf Arcs sont semblablement déssinés sous les pieds des dieux', J. Leclant, in *Mélanges Mospero* I, 4ème fascicule (*MIFAO* C XVI/4, 1961), p. 86-91.

22 For example in the tomb of Ti, cf. Vandier, *Manuel* V, 2ème partie, p. 135, fig. 73,2. And on the scene p. 146-147.

23 On the *sema-taouy*, important documentation and interpretation in John Baines, *Fecundity Figures. Egyptian Personifications and the Iconology as a Genre*, Warminster 1984, p. 50, 69-72, 226-225.

24 Thus, Baines, p. 86, fig. 48 (Mycérinos); p. 100, fig. 66 (Sesoshis I); p. 274, fig. 165 (Anenemmes I), etc.

25 Thus in the Middle Empire, Baines, p. 190, fig. 107, after Rifaud (Sesostris II ?); p. 232, fig. 132 (Sesostris I); p. 233, fig. 133 (Ammenemes III) and in the Ramesside era, the colossi of Abu Simbel, *PM* VII, 100 (25) et (26), et de Louqsor, *PM* II 2, p. 313, (70)-(71), etc.

26 Statues of Darius, Susa, (Tehran Museum), J. Yoyotte in *Cahiers de la Délégation archéologique francaise en Iran IV* (1974), pl. XXX, fig. 1 et 2. Also in the late period, the same image before or behind bronzes depicting divinities, Baines, *op. cit.*, p. 190, fig. 110 ; p. 267, fig. 159.

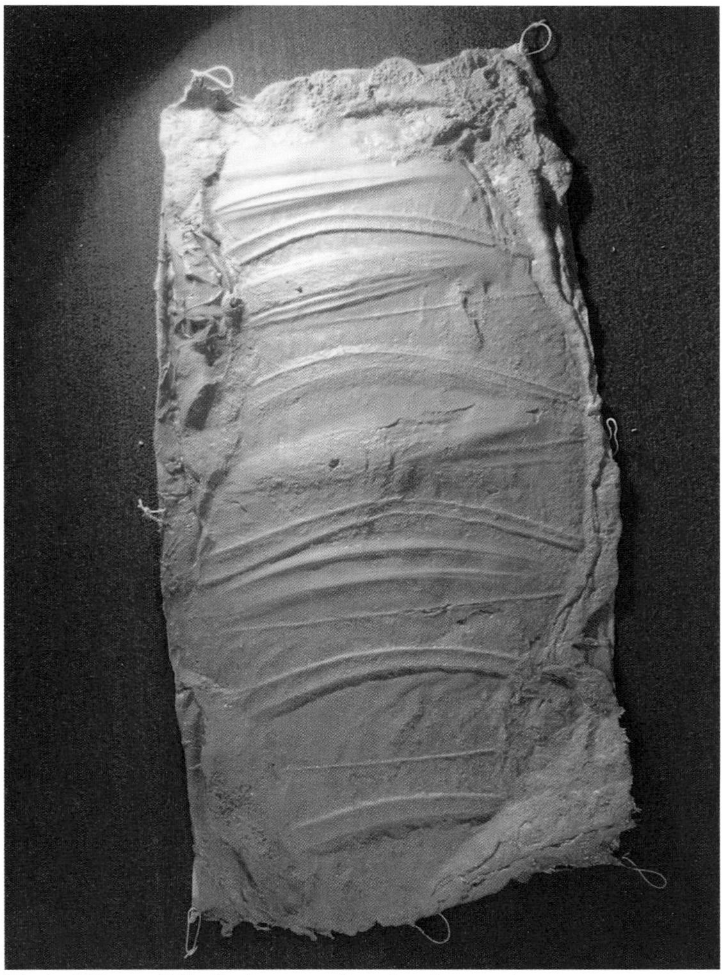
Photo 112: no. 755: the bows on the edge, impression

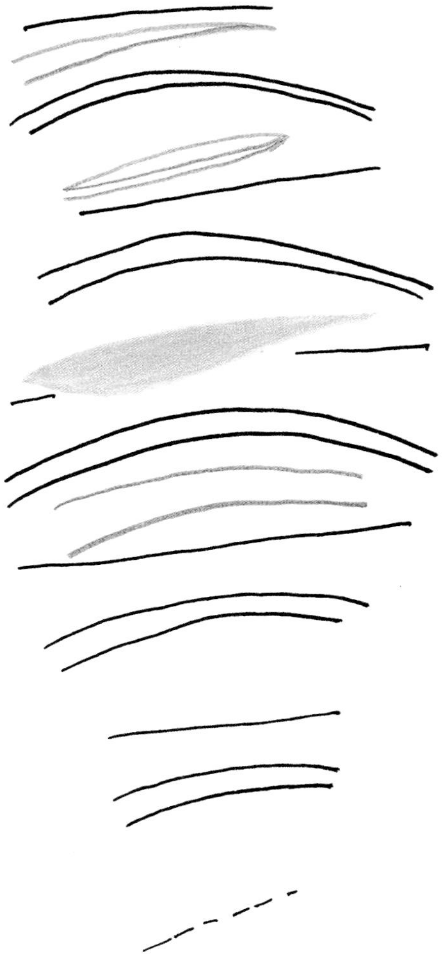
Figure 20: no. 755: edge, engraving, amended

Photo 113: fragment of quartzite, no. 755, front face, impression

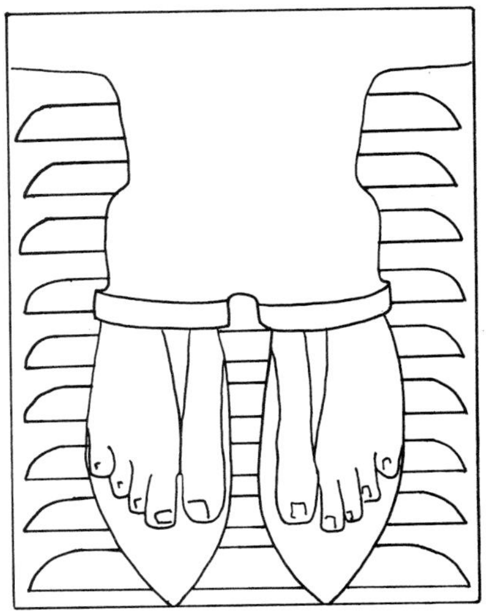
Figure 21: the Nine Bows under the feet of Ramesses II

Photo 114: *sema-taoui* on the base of a statue of Darius

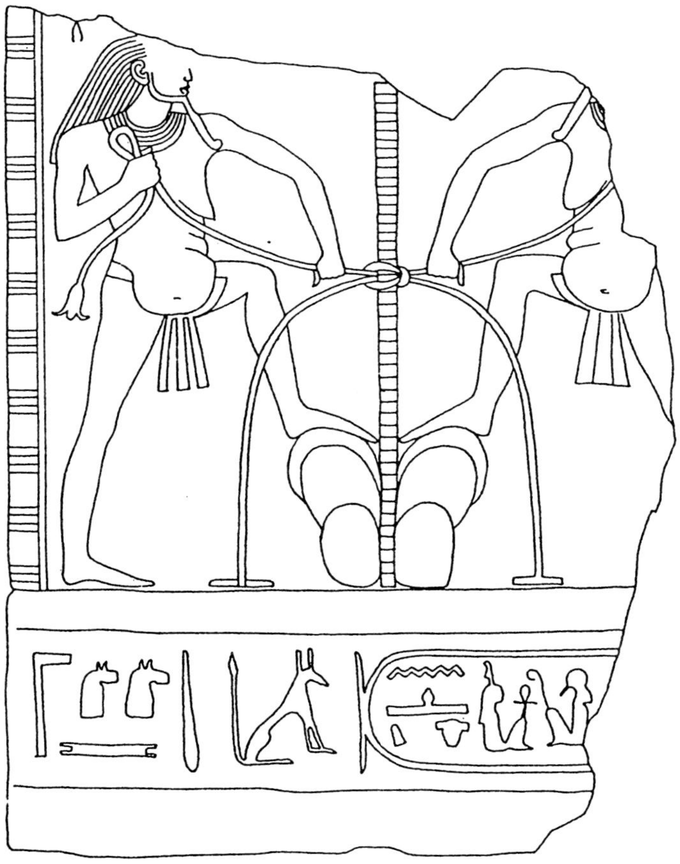

Fig 22: the *sema-taoui* on the throne of Sesostris I

divine discourse. Anyway, the fairly frequent association at the base of royal statues of the *sema-taouy* and keeping foreigners under the feet of the king is again found here.[27] This nice chain of reasoning runs up against a notable problem: at the bottom of royal effigies and others is a pair of major gods (Horus and Seth), or more often a pair of familiar spirits, personifying fecundity, who make the Union of the Two Lands. Here it would be the king himself, a case where I do not know of any other examples.

Finally, it will have been noted above the king, on face A, the presence of a line of three large hieroglyphic signs which seem to underline in a certain light a ghostly horizontal line which leads us to deduce that a horizontal text runs across the top of the scene. Normally, writing above a person turned to the right, runs from the left. The first sign clearly is Re. The second, which a large hole has destroyed in the upper part, resembles an ideogram showing a seated divinity. The third, aligned towards the back, appears to be an oblong. Since a Re sign, central and alone is characteristic of royal cartouches, we may surmise that the identity of the sovereign has been preserved under this debris and even go so far as to guess at the *prenomen* 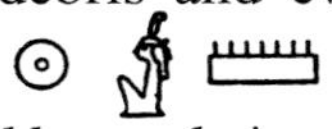 of Sethi I. The elongated form of the *khepresh*, in any case, suggests the Ramesside period.

[27] Baines, *op.cit.*, p. 245-250.

3. Block no. 781: front part of the base of a statue with the names of Merenptah (*c.* 1213-1204 BC); grey granite.

Position: south coast.

Dimensions: height approx. 0.60 m; width approx. 0.5 m; depth 0.52 m.

Condition: a secondary chip on the corner at the angle A-B-E; corrosion fairly widespread in places.

In form, this block is a paralellopiped, representing almost the quarter of a statue base of a masculine figure marching. The absence of the rest prevents us from saying any more about this type of Ramesside figure.[28]

On the front face (D) on either side of the axis, the two names of the king Merenptah are set on the ideogram signifying 'gold' and surmounted by the sign for the heavens.

To the right, the forename [←] *'the lord of the Two Lands, Ba-en-Re, beloved of the gods.'*

To the left, the birth name [→] *' the lord of crowns, Merenptah who is in peace in accordance with Maat.'*

Either side of the central panel are two titles, written horizontally, which follow the lateral sides. Only the beginning remains, containing the forename introduced by *'Long live the King of Upper and Lower Egypt, he lord of*

[28] On the sculpting of the feet, Z Kiss, p. 178.

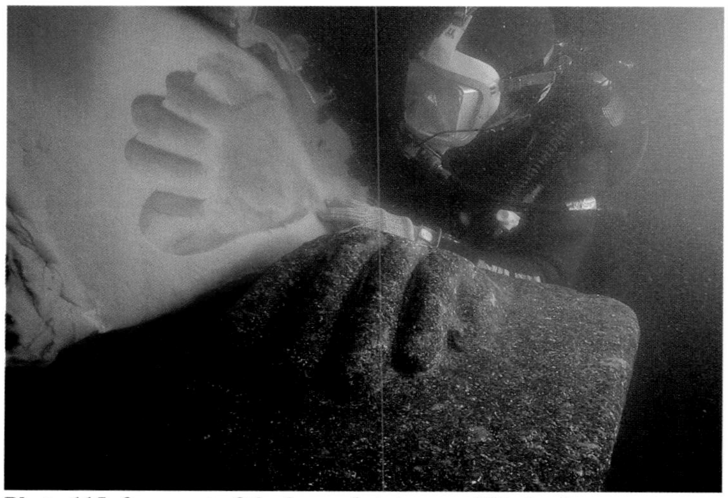

Photo 115: fragment of the base of statue, no. 781, *in situ*

BLOCK DE9 N° 781
South Coast
Grey Granite
Lat : 31° 12' 2137 N
Long : 29° 54' 0176 E
Depth : 4,8 m.

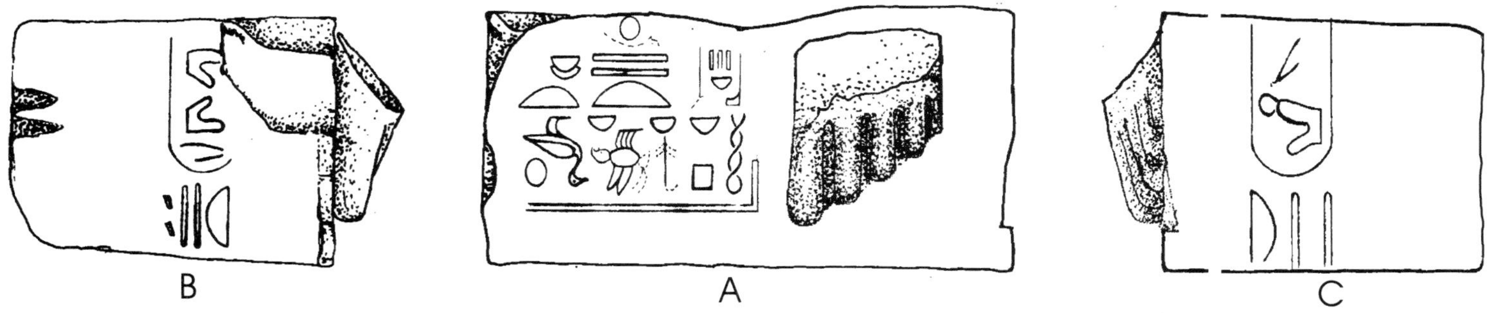

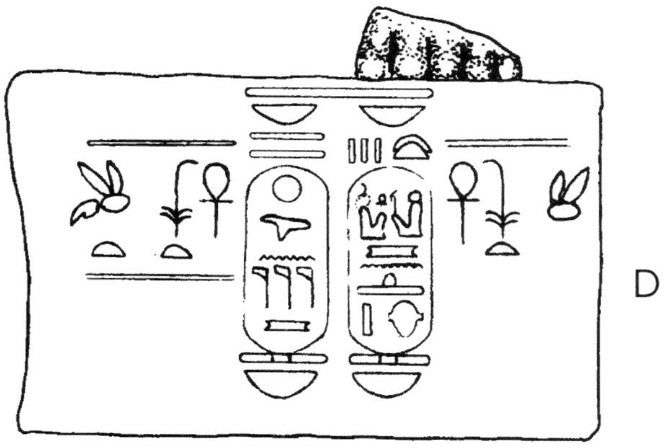

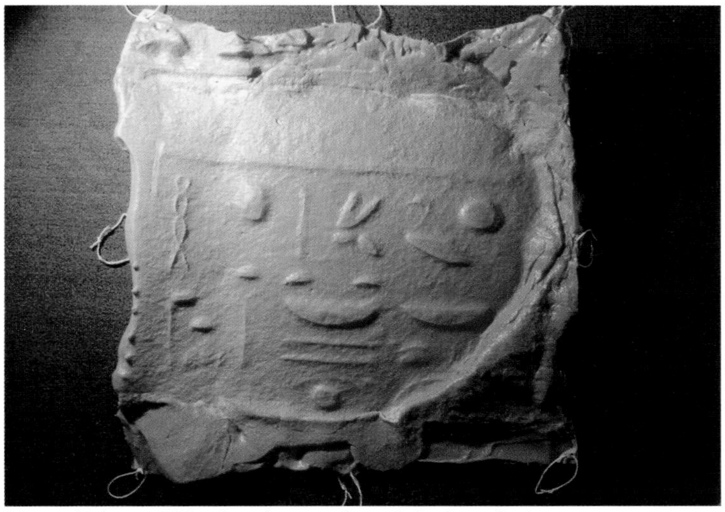

Photo 116: no. 781, edge, impression of the inscription

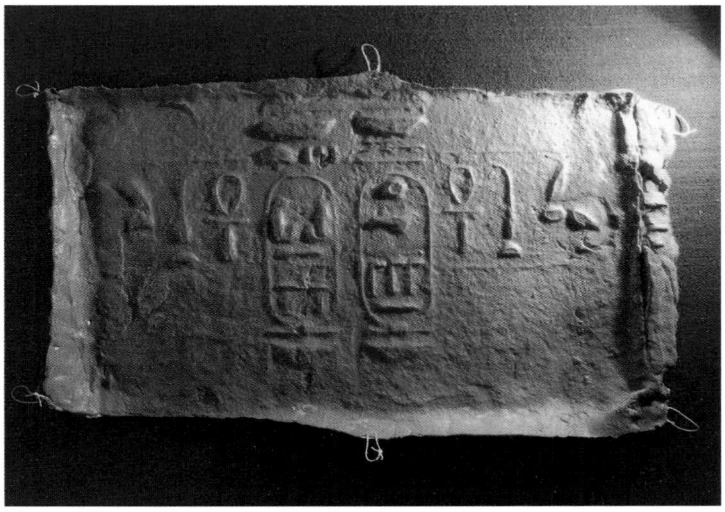

Photo 117: no. 781, forward surface, impression

Photo 118: no. 781, surface right side, impression

Photo 119: no. 781, surface left side, impression

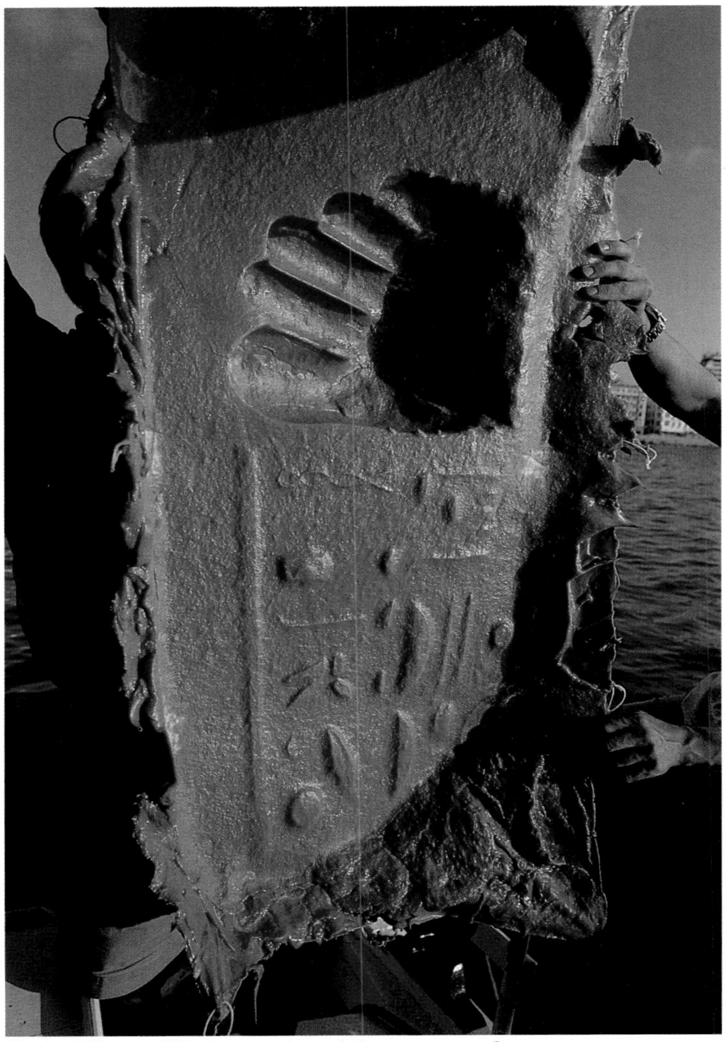

Photo 120: no. 781, impression of the upper surface

[→]; here the king is *'[beloved of ...] Ptah king of gods.'* The adjective current for Amon-Re from Thebes is only rarely given to Ptah of Memphis,[29] so this must be a form or idol peculiar to the latter. Also, unusually this text, instead of being turned as is normal on the bases of royal statues to be read by the viewer, is here turned towards the back of the statue. It is not inconceivable that the statue represents not Ptah, but a non-mummiform of Ptah (Ptah-Tatenem? Ptah-Hapy?). We have here a new document to include in the corpus of statuary for the reign of Merenptah.[30] The mention of Ptah suggests a provenance from Memphis where the son of Ramesses II was particularly active, but another origin, including Heliopolis cannot be excluded.[31] The provenance of another statue

the Two Lands.' One notes the existence of the two variants of this forename: in C *'Ba-en-Re [beloved of] Amon'*; and in B *'Ba-en-Re [beloved of the gods].'*

On surface A, a rectangular picture surmounted by the 'sky', encloses in three columns, two cartouches [←] preceded by the usual titles facing the titulature of a god

[29] M. Sandman-Holmberg, *The God Ptah*, Lund, 1946, p.113, §5, cites only 'Louvre Wb 35 unpublished'.

[30] H. Sourouzian, *Les Monuments du roi Merenptah* (SDAIK 22, 1989), *passim*.

[31] On the presence and forms of Ptah in this town, E. El-Banna, *BIFAO* 84 (1984), p. 111-120; J. Yoyotte, *Annuaire du Collège de France* 95 (1995), p. 665-666.

Photo 121: discovery of the base of no. 781

Photo 122: fragment no. 781, sections *in situ*

recently dug up in Alexandria and inscribed with the names of Merenptah[32] *'beloved of Osiris'*, is not clear, but an origin from Heliopolos is no less likely. There is an argument thus: a colossus recovered from Canopus among the *pharaonica* brought onto this Graeco-Roman site and which depicts Ramesses II bearing symbols doubtless comes from Heliopolis as the sacred baton is topped by the image of Re in which *'Atoum lord of Heliopolis and the Two Lands'* is mentioned.[33] So Merenptah has set on the shaft of his baton an inscription with his name followed by the epithet *'beloved of Osiris'*. It is known that outside Abydos and the royal tombs this epithet is rare which makes this combination significant.

All together few momentoes of Merenptah have turned up in ancient Alexandria,[34] much fewer than those of Sethe I and Ramesses II. The percentage, compared to the percentage of the monumental inheritance of his father and grandfather, is in the same proportion as for the whole of Egypt.

4-8: architectural elements from a work by Apries (589-570 BC), pink granite.

These five blocks were scattered between the south shore and the centre of the Island and belonged originally to the same monument. Their general form and proportion remain recognisable in spite of the large fractures and breakages, obviously from secondary events which mutilated them. They retain the second (*nebty* **7**), the fourth (the coronation forename **5** and **7**) and the fifth (birth name **6**) of Apries and the rest of the engraved hieroglyphic inscriptions, all from the same output and module, date the original construction to the reign of this XXVth dynasty Saite king (589-570 BC).

4. Block no 505, p. 236

Position: south coast.

Dimensions: height 1.5 m; width 0.60 m; depth 0.60 m.

Condition: two notches or mortises on edge A-B. Secondary fractures. Matches block 5 face for face.[35]

Photo 123: 4-5 broken sections of upright nos. 505 et 890 with the name of Apries

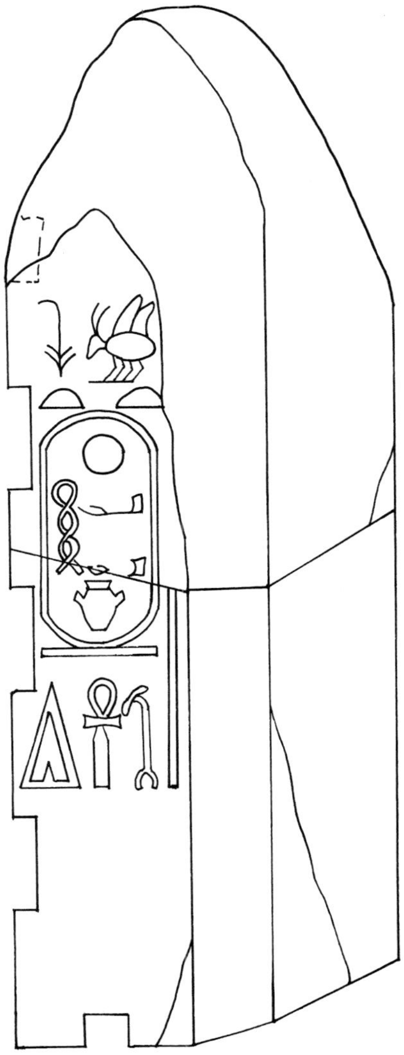

Fig 23: 4-5 the Apries upright broken in two, nos. 505 and 890: sketch made *in situ*

[32] A. Abdel Fâltah and P. Gallo, *Aegyptiaca Alexandrina* II. *Un fragment de statue au nom de pharaon Merenptah,* in press, *BIFAO* 98. Dressed in an ordinary loincloth and holding the sign of life, is the person a god (Osiris king non-mummiform) rather than the king himself?

[33] Caire CG 574, Abûqic, 1885, L. Borchurdt, *Statuen und Statuetten (CGC)* II, p. 122-123, pl. 98; textes *KRI* IV, p. 51, no. 23B.

[34] Papyriform bundled columns of the XVIIIth dynasty (above p. 214) were covered by this king. Brugsch, *Reiseberichte*, p. 14, says he saw in Alexandria in 1852 an inscription of Merenptah, but gives no details. We should be cautious about the two fragments on a torso of Seostris I covered by Merenhap, Caire CG 384 (PM IV, 3; *KRI* IV, 51 no. 23A), found separately at two places in Alexandria and reported in Cairo in 1889 to have been brought from Tanis by J. J. Rifaud in 1825.

[35] Reconciliation is confirmed by provisionally transferring block no. 505 to the island and taking an impression of the whole, then the block was put back *in situ*.

Photo 124: fragment no. 890 *in situ*

BLOCK N° 505
South Coast
Red Granite
Lat : 31° 12' 2434 N
Long : 29° 54' 1103 E
Depth : 4,3 m.

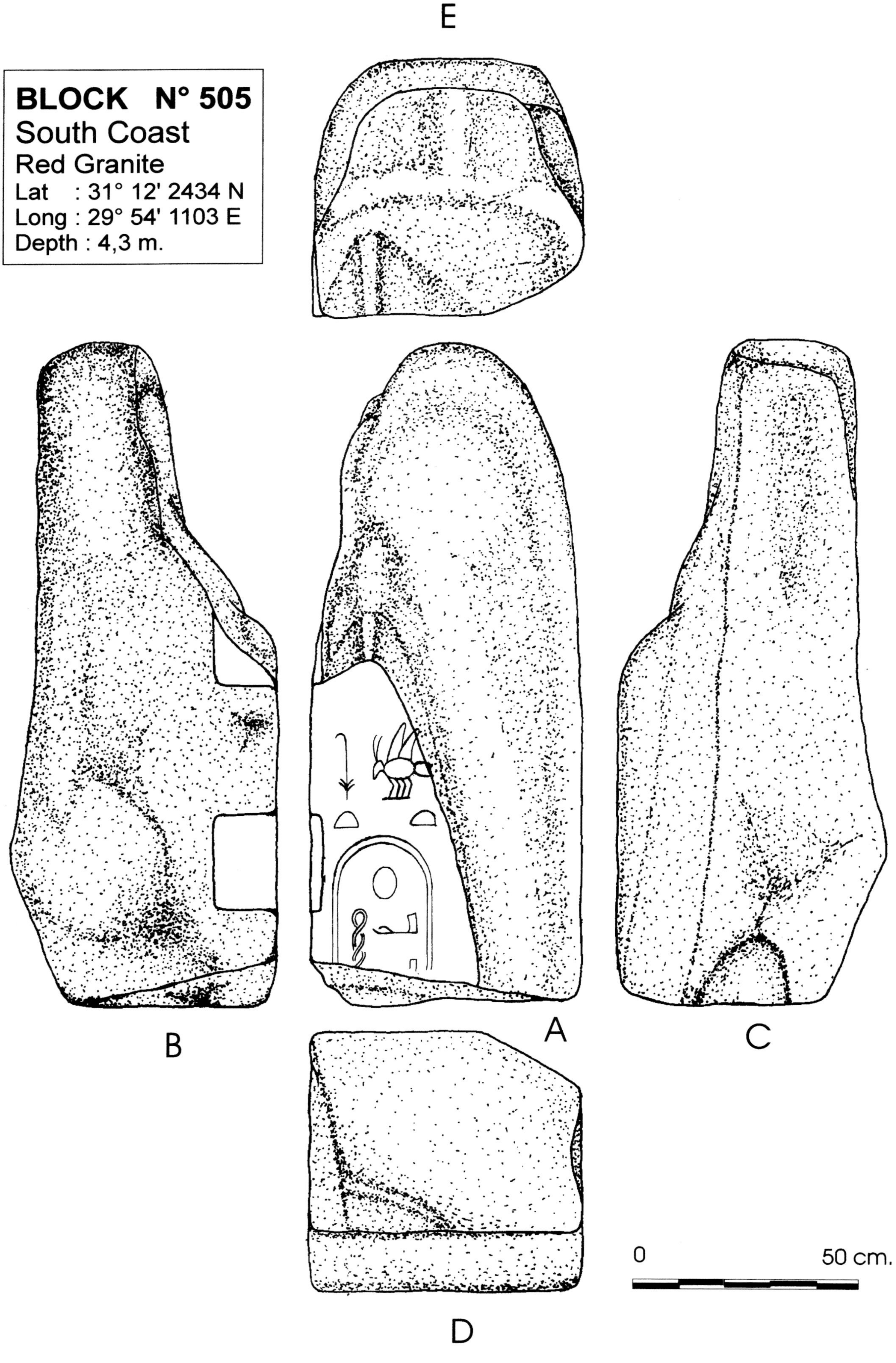

BLOCK RD4 N° 890
Centre Island
Red Granite
Lat : 31° 12'3395 N
Long : 29° 53'8684 E
Depth : 4,6 m.

D

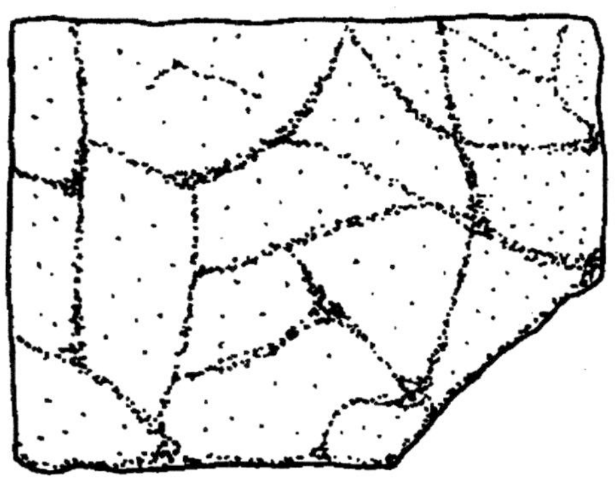

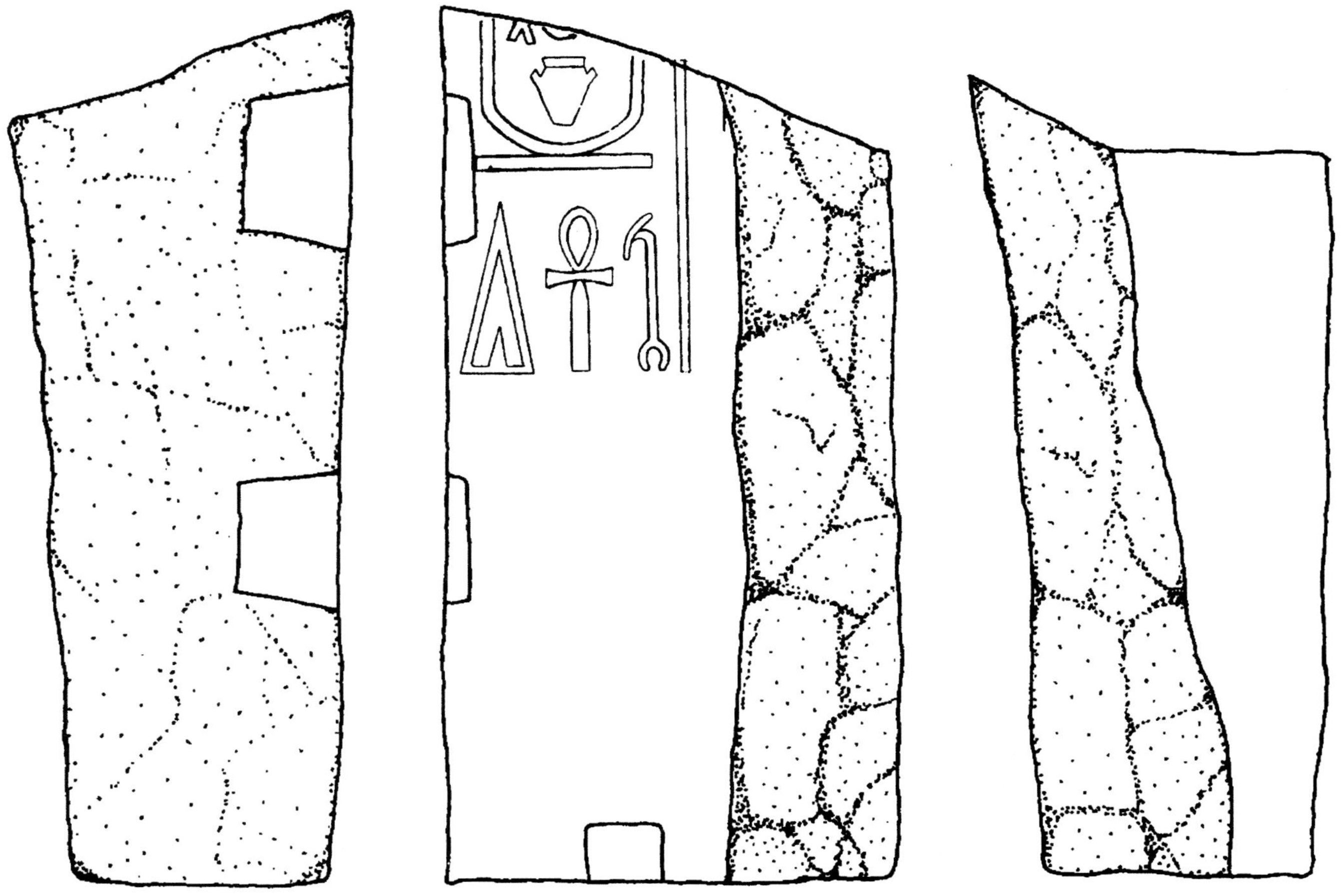

B A C

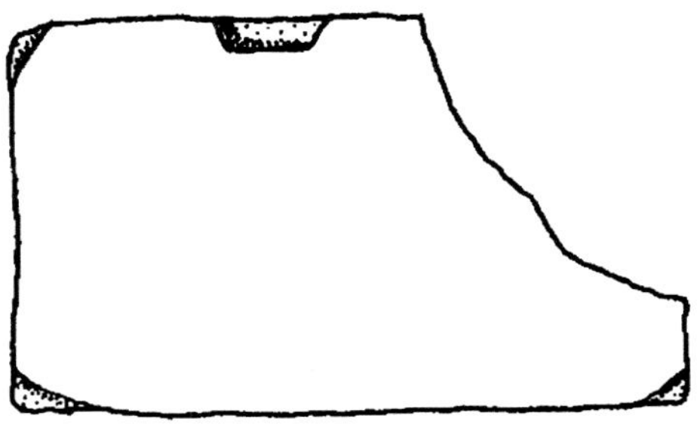

E

0 50 cm.

5. Block no. 890, p. 237.
Position: centre Island
Dimensions: height 1,.15m. approx.; width 0.60 m; depth 0.45 m.
Condition: two notches or mortises on edge A-B; one on the lower part. Secondary fractures. Matches block 4 face for face.

This match gives an oblong block 2.50 m. high, with a near square section (p. 237), which was cut for a pillar or rather the upright of a door. When it was re-used the pillar or upright was cut in two along its length to obtain a sort of post or beam; the notches visible on the edge and the base originate from this re-cutting or an adjustment when used in the new structure.

On face A, remains of a column of hieroglyphics (0.35 wide).

[←] *'The king of Upper and Lower Egypt Haa-ib-Re, endowed with life and power.'*

By comparison with block 6, we can deduce that a facing parallel column disappeared with the other half.

6. Block DD9, no. 771.

Position: south coast DD9

Dimensions: height 1.67 m; width 0.77 m; depth 0.50 m.

Condition: secondary fractures. Lateral cut right B, front face A and inner face C preserved. Groove of an uncertain nature in D. The module of the original block and the sizes of the inscription are the same as in 4 and 5.

On face A, remains of two columns of hieroglyphs (0.35 wide) facing each other:

[←] *'[The Son of Re] Apries, endowed [with life and power], (_) beloved of the [gods], lord of Kher-Aha.'*

Photo 125: fragment of an upright of Apries, no. 771 *in situ*

Photo 126: fragment no. 771, impression (photo reveresed)

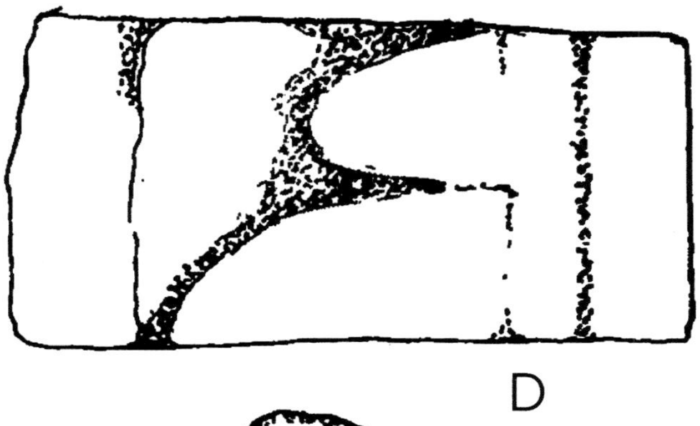

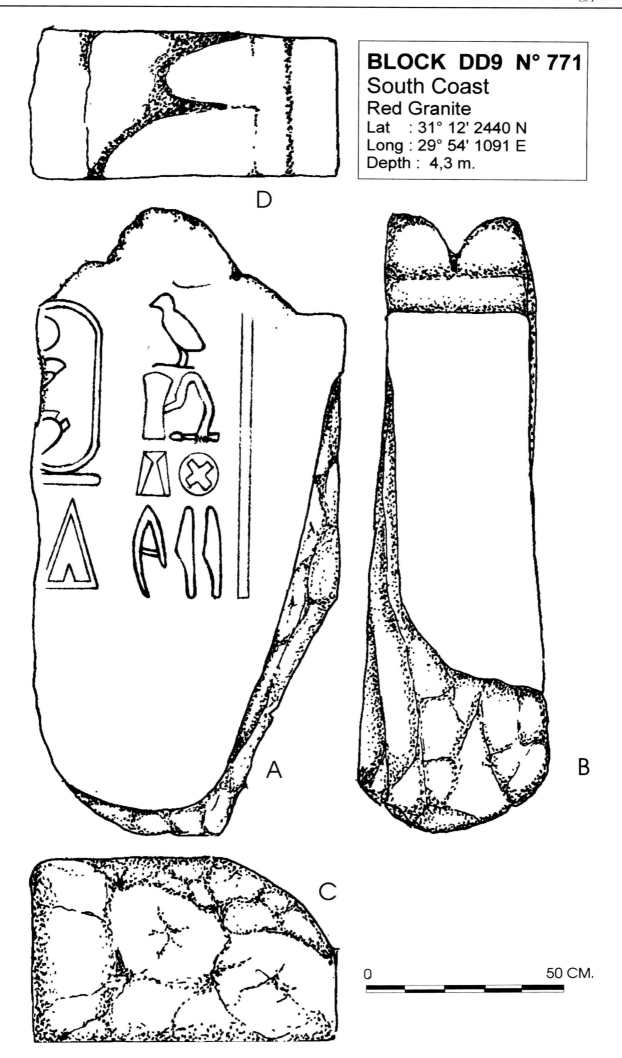

BLOCK DD9 N° 771
South Coast
Red Granite
Lat : 31° 12' 2440 N
Long : 29° 54' 1091 E
Depth : 4,3 m.

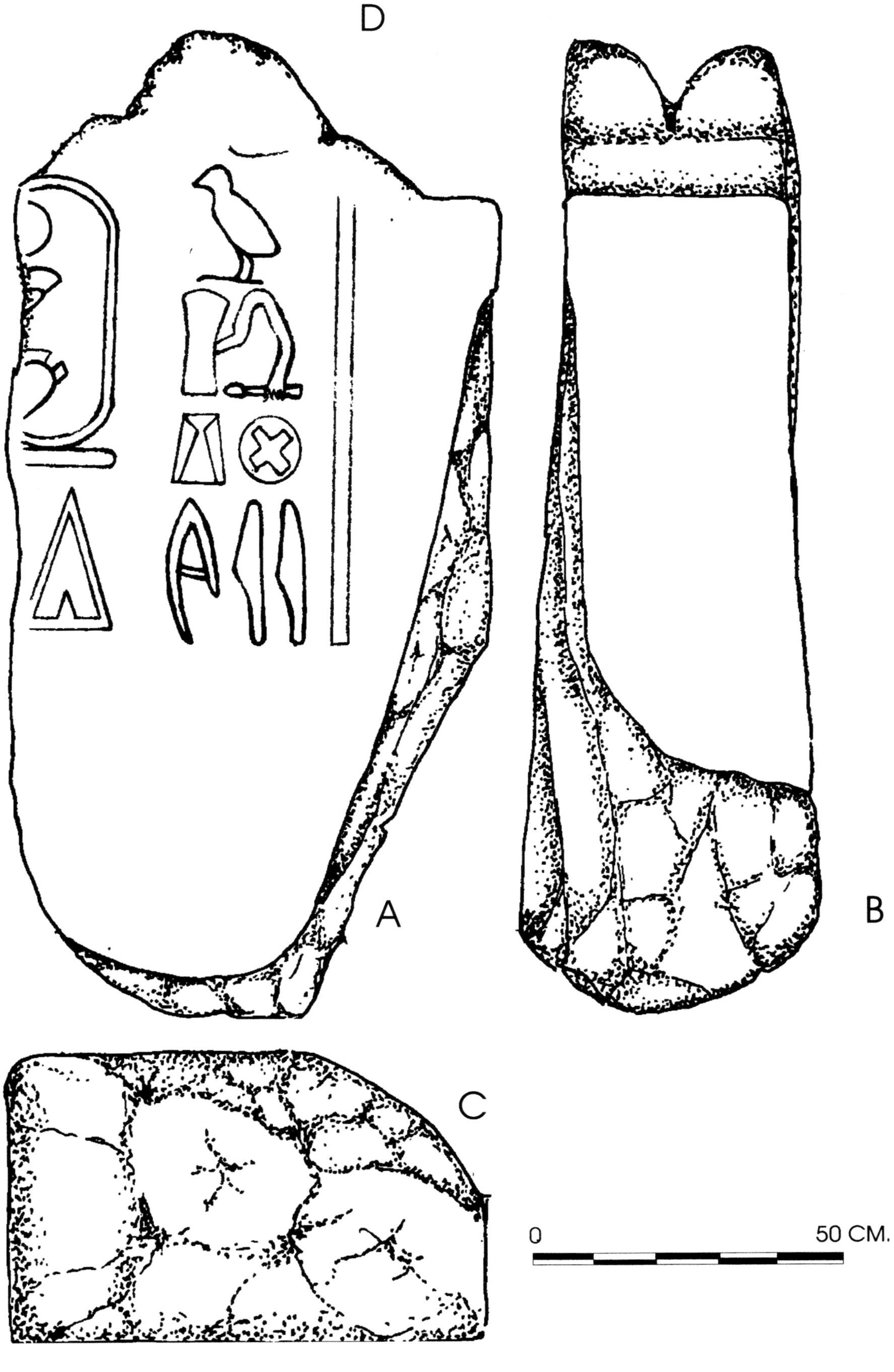

BLOCK N° 673
Centre Island
Red Granite
Lat : 31° 12' 3396 N
Long : 29° 53' 8639 E
Depth : 4,7 m.

B

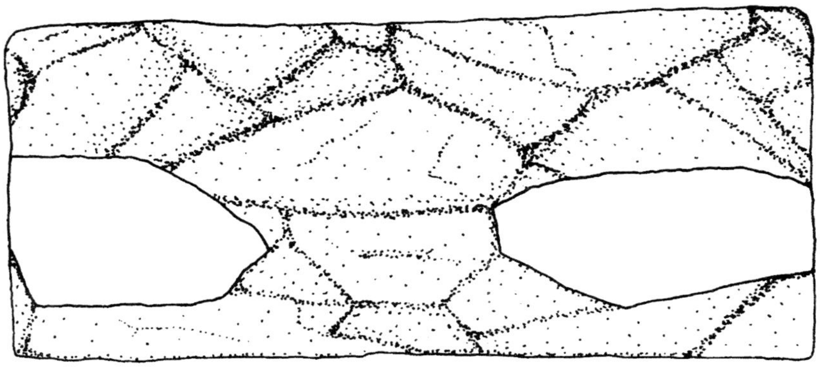

D

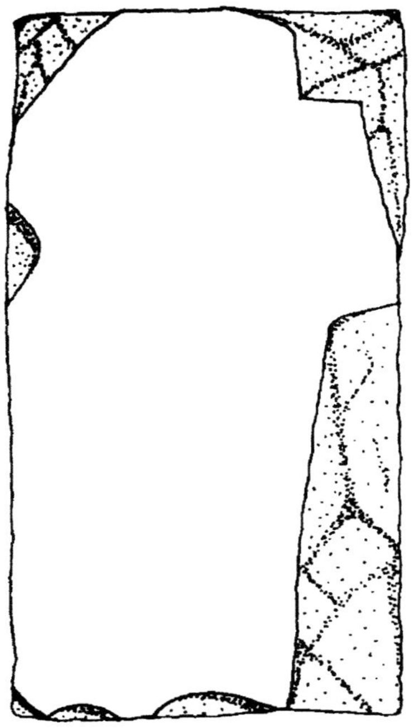

A

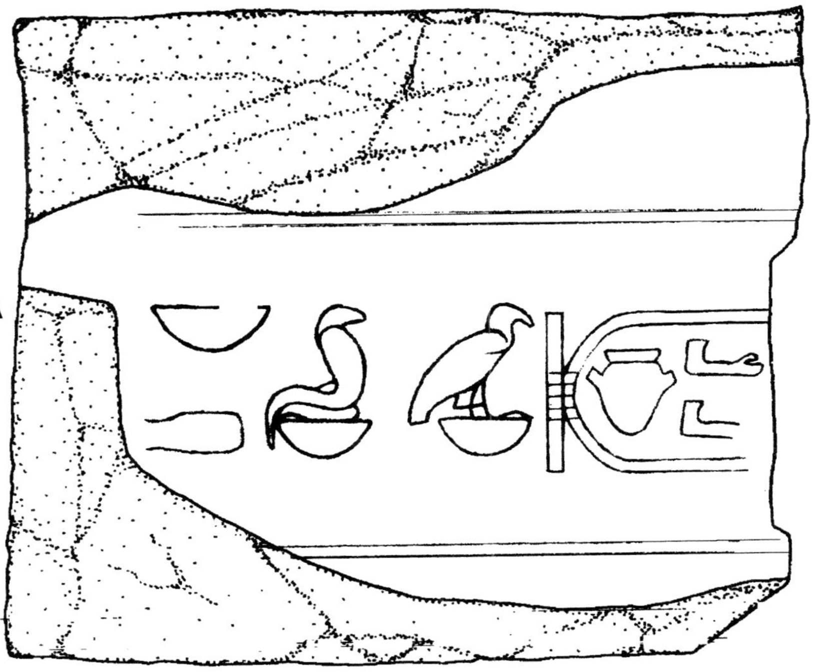

C

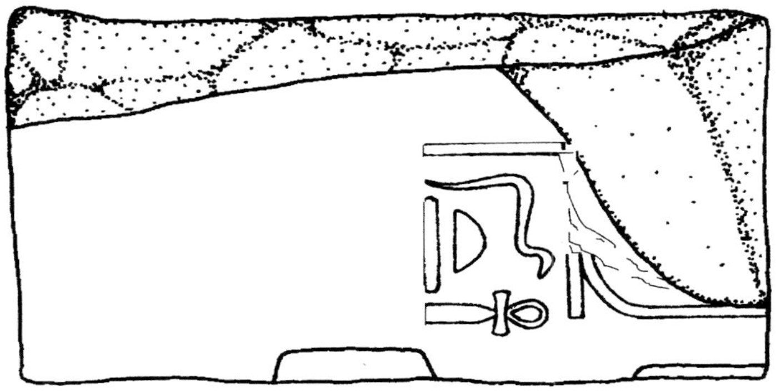

7. Block no. 673.

Position: centre Island

Dimensions: height 1.20 m. approx.; width 1.30 m. approx.; depth 0.60 m. approx.

Condition: secondary fractures on all faces. The plan of the original surface is preserved on A, B, C and D. Two notches on edge A-C.

This piece has the appearance of an architrave or a door lintel with the horizontal inscription of A corresponding to the visible vertical face of the face of the stone when in place, the vertical inscription on C, apparently from the same break, decorating the inner face (?).

In C vertical we can read: the end of a cartouche, [→] followed by *'living eternally'*; the rest of the well polished bottom area, 0.60 m x 0.60 m, remains untouched. In A horizontal: [→] *'[...] Haab-ib-[Re], he of the Two Ladies, the lord of Bras (khepesh)'*. The fourth name of the king, his coronation cartouche, is curiously followed by his second name (*nebty*). This unusual arrangement of the royal titulature finds an exact parallel on a monument of this same Apries, on one of the blocks of quartzite from Sais, re-used in the Mamluk fort at Rosetta (figure 24), '[...] *Haa-ib-Re, the Horus Ouah-ib,*' where the first name follows the fourth.[36]

[36] L. Habachi, *ASAE* 42 (1943), p. 383, fig. 104.

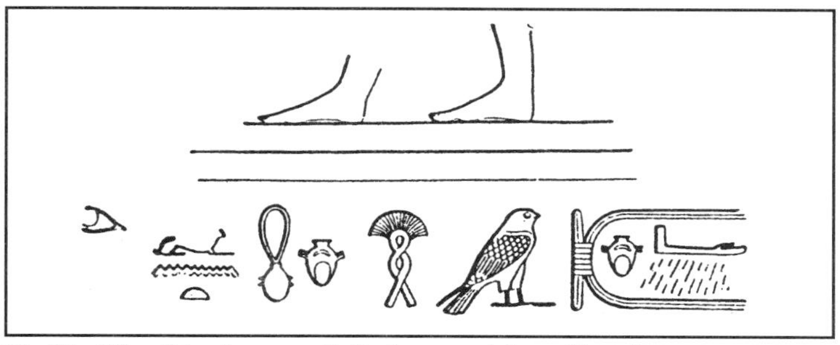

Fig 24: title of Apries on a Saite fragment from Rosetta

Photo 127: fragment of a beam in the name of Apries, no. 673, lower face

Photo 128: no. 673, lower face, impression

Photo 129: no. 673, lower face, *in situ*

Photo 130: no. 673, vertical face, impression

Photo 131: no. 673, vertical face, detail *in situ*

8. Block no. 780.

Position: south coast DE 8.

Dimensions: height 1.05 m, max. width 1.40 m, depth 0.55 m.

Condition: secondary fractures on all edges. The plan of the original surfaces is preserved on A and apparently on D; the inner face E is mutilated. Notch on edge D-E and perhaps a man-made gash on F running from B to C. On the vertical face A there remains a horizontal line of hieroglyphics (height 0.55/0.66): [→] *'Son of Atoum, [his] beloved'* (restored according to the parallel at Memphis, from the Decree of Apries, 1.1, p. 243: *'Son of Ptah, his beloved'*).[37]

The mention of Atoum takes us back to Heliopolis as does the allusion to the gods of Kher-Aha. In effect, the place named, situated on the site of Old Cairo itself, and which was known to the Greeks under the name of Babylon of Egypt, was administratively a dependency of Heliopolis and theoretically directly linked to the temple of Re.[38]

The Heliopolitan origin of these five fragments invite us to wonder whether a block of pink granite discovered in submerged deposits of Qa'it-Bey did not come from the same construction by Apries. On this block, 'a piece of an architrave or lintel' (2.42 m. bu 0.90 m.) a horizontal inscription is engraved naming '[He of the Two Ladies] lord of Bras Apries, *beloved of the powers of Heliopolis.*'[39]

The monumental works of Apries in the temples of Heliopolis are not unknown.[40] Their importance is seen notably in the reading of the autobiography inscribed by his great major-domo, Peftaouneit, on the statue that he placed in the temple of Atoum.[41] *In situ*, in the ruins of the *secos* of the bull Mnevis (Arab el-Hisn), a piece of stone links the name of Apries to that of Osiris-Mnevis.[42] Lastly but not least, a *dromos* of the Serapeum in Alexandria incorporated among other sphinxes, a magnificent pair of quartzite sphinxes made for Apries, *'beloved of the God of the Souls of Heliopolis'* and of the *'Souls of Heliopolis'*.[43]

Whether they had been part of a hall of square pillars, or rather a door frame, the large monoliths removed from a building in Heliopolis which had been embellished under Apries were deposited—and perhaps set up again—in a temple in Alexandria. At an unknown date they were cut up for use as material in some construction. We must imagine that the latter itself was used as a quarry for the benefit of two new buildings. In effect, of the five remains of Apries, two (5 and 7) lay on the paved esplanade at the centre of the Island, 5 m. away from each other, in a field of Roman column segments of which two carried votive inscriptions from the beginning of the 3rd century.[44] The three others, 4, 6, 8, lay on the south coast of the royal harbour, as if face to face in a paved area, in a great jumble of blocks of stone and Roman column shafts. Much better (or worse), both halves of the same total, neatly broken by an earthquake or damaged in transit, have ended up one (no. 4) on the south coast of the harbour (p. 236), the other (no. 5) on the Island (p. 237). In photo 125, it is seen that the surface and the inscription of the first are very much corroded, whilst the second seems as new. One plausible hypothesis would be as follows: the blocks of Apries from Heliopolis were set up again or already cut up into masonry blocks in an Alexandrian structure. During the period of reconstruction in the Roman or Byzantine period, this building served as a communal quarry for several new constructions. This would have caused an uncertain and savage allocation in the different and more or less contemporary construction sites and the dispersal of our stones from Heliopolis which are found in the deserted places of the last demolition sites which flooding has preserved in their state of abandon.[45] The case is an example of the enigmatic misadventures of stone so often displaced, recycled and roughly handled.[46]

---

[37] B. Gunn, *ASAE* 27 (1927), p. 216-217.

[38] See J. Yoyotte, 'Prêtres et sanctuaires du nome héliopolitaine à la Basse-Epoque', in *BIFAO* 54 (1954).

[39] J. P. Corteggiani in *BIFAO* 95 (1995), p. 600; 96 (1996) p. 567.

[40] One should without doubt add to the Alexandrian dossier of Apries the unrecorded block, Musée Greco-romain reg. no. 27821, a square granite flag found in Toussoun street (0.90 x 0.87 x 0.21), inscribed at the edge with the titles and names of this pharaoh, with a square indentation noted by B. Tlcaczow, *Topography*, p. 239 (obj. 141). Among the *pharaonica* of Alexandria, we can attribute to Apries the greywacke capital of Hathor in the Musée Greco-romain (dépôt de Kom el-Shuqafa), G. Botti, *Catalogue* (1900), p. 350.7, which is identical to a completely preserved column, Cairo Museum (Daressy, *ASAE* 2 [1901], p. 239); photograph G. Jéquier, '*Des temples temples ramessides et saïtes,* pl.78, fig. 5, which comes from the temple of Neitta of Saïs, name of Héliopolis. See Gauthier, *Livre des Rois* IV/1 (*BIS*), p.103 §XVII et no. 4.

[41] British Museum 83, Texts K. Piehl, *ZÄS* 31 (1893), p. 88-89; photograph E. Brunner . Crant, *ZÄS* 82 (1937), pl. 4, cf. p. 84.

[42] F. Ll. Griffith, *The Antiquities of Tell el-Yahûdîyeh (EEF* VII 1888-9), London, 1890 pl. XXI, fig. 22, cf. p.67.

[43] Musée gréco-romain *P* 2136-2137, found in 1899 on the south slope of the plateau. Text: G. Daressy, *ASAE* 5 (1904), p. 127 §XI; photograph: J. Leclant *et alii, d'Egypte du Crépuscule* (l'Univers des Formes), 1980, fig. 286.

[44] Above, E. Bernand, p. 147-148, nos. 1-2. The five other dedications found on the Island are in honour of Caracalla (died 217), which fixes a wide *terminus port quem* for the date of the final use of the blocks!

[45] Cf. p. 214, the case of bundled columns of the New Empire which complicates their re-use and dissemination in the Islamic period.

[46] If the block of Qa'it-Bey, the presumed last resting place of the Pharos of Ptolemy II belonged to the same monument of Apries ... (!)

BLOCK DE8 N° 780
South Coast
Red Granite
Lat : 31° 12' 2368 N
Long : 29° 54' 1130 E
Depth : 4,5 m.

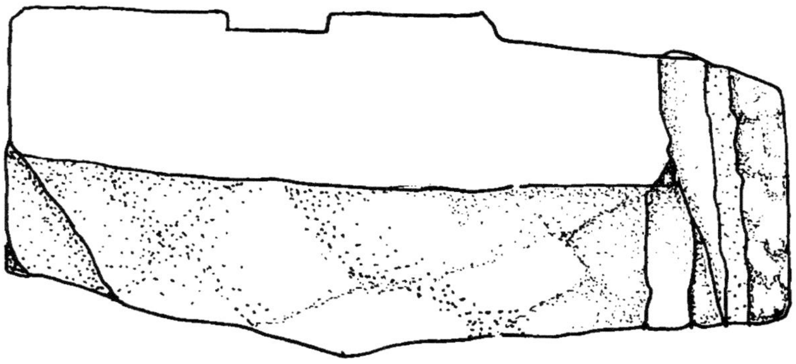

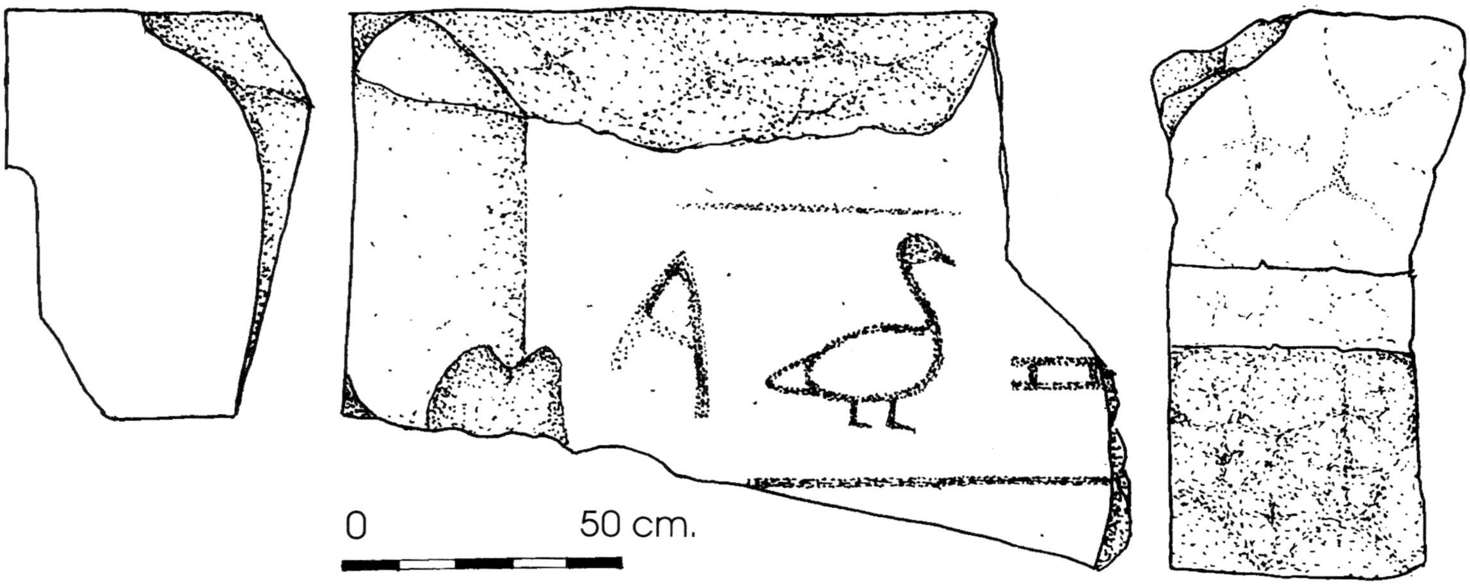

Fig 25: title of the king in the Decree of Apries at Memphis

Photo 132: no. 780, impression

Photo 133: no. 780, removing the moulding

Photo 134: fragment of a beam with the name of Apries, no. 780

EPILOGUE

Franck Goddio and Jean Yoyotte

In 1992, the European Institute of Underwater Archaeology (IEASM) obtained permission from the authorities of the Organisation of Egyptian Antiquities to put its team of experienced divers, sophisticated equipment, and working methods at the disposal of Alexandrian archaeological research. Developed during the search and excavation of several wrecks from 1985-91, and fine-tuned during work on the *San Diego* (1991-1994), the procedure was the following: collection and analysis of all available information concerning the submerged object, topographical definition from the surface of the object's exact situation in its underwater surroundings, dives for precise siting and first visual appreciation, excavation proper, and removal of artefacts. This is then followed by the study and publication, by scholars specialising in the different categories of objects, using the various techniques of material analysis, and the necessary instruments of knowledge, since it is the IEASM's aim—as that of all centres of archaeology, under water or on *terra firma*—to provide material for the historians.

When applied to the submerged parts of the Hellenistic metropolis in Egypt, this chain of procedures underwent a change of scale. Apart from wrecks proper, which were momentary and habitual targets, inevitably to be found somewhere off the antique shoreline, we were going to take care of an entirely different kind of wreck, i.e. huge jumbles of massive stones difficult to manipulate, and spread over a wide surface. It followed that in this mission, we had to abandon the idea of removing the items from their site, and had thus to invent special procedures for registering and interpreting inscriptions. Working conditions also would surely not be the same in an area subjected to intense natural sedimentation, and polluted by all the refuse of a megapolis, than in the clear waters of the Pacific. If our search, contrary to the operations off the coasts of the Philippines, required us to dive in shallow waters only (average 5, maximum 15 m.), then this represented a formidable change in conditions. All documentary research in preparation of the IEASM's previous missions in Europe and in the Pacific started from European books and archives of the 16th to 18th centuries. Now, however, preliminary information for this mission in the waters of Alexandria had to be gleaned from classical authors, Greek as well as Latin and—which was much worse—from the total mass of observations and archaeological material which had been assembled in the neighbouring areas, submerged or not, of the Alexandrian coast, over two hundred years of a prolific bibliography. The existing 'archaeological' charts noting the sites of antique vestiges most often turn out to be 'historical', rather, indicating the sites and monuments of Graeco-Roman Alexandria, and frequently repeat each other, to the extent of producing the impression that they reflect realities definitely acquired. As the fruit of a more methodical and rigorous work than many others, the 'Map of Ancient Alexandria and its Suburbs' (Fig. 1), created in 1866 by the astronomer Mahmud el-Falaki, is today used as the basis for many published plans of the city.[1] Over long periods of time, Alexandrian archaeologists and their public displayed an enthusiastic imagination for hasty interpretations of ancient authors and errant fragments picked up around the town, orienting their research and demonstrations according to event-related and romantic tendencies in the writing of history. The objectives were to find again, at last, the sites which had made, and continue to make, the glory of Alexandria, such as the tomb of Alexander the Great, the palace of Cleopatra, the residence of Mark Antony, the Library, the Museum, the remnants of the Lighthouse itself. This romantic and fictional way, well away from the preoccupations of modern historians, did not hesitate to plunge into the sensational in order to cater to the needs, real or imagined, of the public, to the cults of great men, of great deeds … and of great archaeologists.

This mediatic approach is and will remain necessary and legitimate. Alexandria, in its time the Mecca of Hellenistic culture, and the capital of the Graeco-Macedonian pharaohs remains, through all its adventures related by antique literature, and which nourished our own legends and writings, a high-profile reference, both for Egypt, and for the international community. *'We dream of this submerged Alexandria and its history, its tales: the royal city of Cleopatra on the island of Antirrhodos, the Timoneum built by Mark Antony to house his despair and his bitter reflections, the royal harbour where the galleys accosted on quaysides which line basins hewn into solid rock, the palaces built by the Ptolemies and maybe also—who would know—the mausoleum of Cleopatra. And then, no doubt, temples, quays, moles, the embankments of the*

[1] Most recently the plans and perspective renderings by J. Cl. Golvin, 'Alexandrie, lumière du monde antique', in *Dossiers d'Archéologie* no. 201, March 1995, p. 58-61; *La gloire d'Alexandrie*, 1998, p. 84-85.

trade *harbour...*'[2] Alexandria's seduction, the dreams of Alexandria, must be counted among the motivations which brought the IEASM to sail along her shores and drop anchor, let alone the anticipating pleasure of coming to meet in her waters a Greek work of art from the times of the Ptolemies and Cleopatra, or even some hieroglyphic inscriptions.[3]

Following the magnetometric survey and some promising visual prospecting carried out in 1992, it was decided to start off in the east part of the Eastern Harbour, a more accessible and readable area, where the foundered parts of the royal quarters of Ptolemaic times were commonly supposed to be situated.

Once we went into detail, the scholarly literature of the 19th and early 20th centuries turned out to be rather perplexing, and provided a documentary support which must be called vague and limited as far as the submerged parts of Alexandria are concerned. Many writers hardly considered in any way the phenomena that had affected the configuration of shorelines and sea bottoms. They had, in fact, reduced them to a few tectonic catastrophes known from classical and Arab writings. The sites of monuments which were said to have disappeared under the sea—even those which were commonly accepted as pure fact—resulted in reality from speculative ideas without foundation, and hardly ever verified on the supposed site. The list of critical and well-defined queries which have been published more recently, are apt to dissipate some aberrations and point out the uncertainties,[4] but they are rather short on the submerged areas, as if the authors were clearly conscious of the rarity and weakness of the available information.

The lovely discoveries and underwater surveys in the Eastern Harbour which were carried out by the Egyptian Navy, by Kamal Abu el-Sadat, and by Mrs Honor Frost, were situated around Fort Qa'it-Bey, which is far removed from the area chosen for our first extensive survey. In 1986-7, the recovery of some vestiges of the armament and the cargo of the *Patriote*, stranded disastrously in 1798, took place on a site even further removed in time and space. An American television crew is said to have carried out some prospecting in 1979-80, at the tip of Silsileh Point, but to our knowledge, they have not left any trace except for the press release claiming to have discovered the 'palaces of Cleopatra ... and Mark Antony'.[5]

Still, the consensus of preceding cartographers appeared well-founded in a general way, at least as far as our first objective was concerned, and to the extent that the oriental part of the Eastern Harbour with its current shoreline was indeed the site of what can be called the Royal Quarters of antique Alexandria.

The band of submerged land which the IEASM was going to survey, and which we shall henceforth call 'antique South coast' is the extension of the band of land above water which is covered with debris and which has been described several times, although too summarily: columns and capitals in disorder, kilns and basins, some of which described as the so-called 'Baths of Cleopatra', big limestone blocks cut to measure, statues of Egyptian divinities, and even walls; the borders of these deposits visibly continuing into and under the waters.[6] The commentators believed to recognise in some of these structures what they called 'port installations of Ptolemaic times, and buildings of Roman times above them'. Soundings carried out by M. Rodkiewicz and Ahmed Abd el-Fattah have produced late Ptolemaic and early Roman ceramics.[7] The construction of the fairway and the buildings bordering the Corniche have unfortunately covered this archaeological area between land and sea. All scholars have unanimously agreed that the part of Alexandrian shoreline between the Caesareum and the beginnings of Cape Silsileh corresponded to the area where, according to Strabo, one after another of the Ptolemies had built new residences, the Basileia.[8]

The surveyed and explored area covers the underwater surroundings of Cape Silsileh, where the ancient Cape Lochias, as Strabo had clearly positioned it, was unanimously recognised. Similar vestiges were indicated on the surface of today's Cape.[9] Beyond the tip, the presence of submerged debris had been seen from the shore. The sites on this peninsula of a temple of an 'Isis of Lochias'[10] and of the burial monument which was the last residence, and then became the mausoleum of Cleopatra VII,[11] are entirely uncertain.

On the basis of the same Strabo, it is established that the waters of the current Eastern Harbour must cover the installations of a port which directly served the royal palaces, and that on the island which he calls Antirhodos, there was a *basileion* in his time. Some stones perceived on

[2] F. Goddio, *A la recherche de Cléopâtre*, Paris, Robert Laffont, 1996, p. 12.

[3] F. Goddio, *Le Mystère du San Diego ... (L'aventure continue)*, Paris, Robert Laffont, 1994, p. 186-188; *A la recherche de Cléopâtre*, Paris, Robert Laffont, 1996, p. 14-15, 183-203.

[4] P. M. Fraser, *Ptolemaic Alexandria*, Oxford 1972, 3 volumes, see vol. I, text, p. 17-25 on the harbours and royal quarters.

[5] Information collected by J. Leclant, *Orientalia*, NS 51, fax I, p. 52 (6c), pointing in turn to the major Egyptian press.

[6] Bibliography and short analysis in B. Tkaczow, *Topography* (1993), p.120-124, sites nos. 72-73, map A.

[7] Recent discoveries in the Royal Quarter of Alexandria', in *BSAA* 44 (1991), p. 131-150.

[8] *'Testimonia'* no. 28, see above p. 91. References to recent authors can be found in A. Calderini, *Dizionarie dei nomi geografici dell'Egitto Greco-Romano*, vol. I, Cairo (1935), p. 97-100.

[9] B. Tkaczow, *ibid*., p.124-126; Sites 76 B-E.

[10] See above, F. Goddio, p. 16, and E. Bernand, p. 145.

[11] The exact site of Cleopatra's mausoleum, inside the area of the *basileia*, and close to the pre-existing temple of Isis cannot be deducted from the texts of Plutarch (*'Testimonia'* no. 56), and Cassius Dio (*ibid*., no. 64), see Calderini, *op. cit*., p. 122-123.

a shoal were taken for traces of that island,[12] but neither position nor shape were certain, much less the reality of its installations.

Franck Goddio began in 1992 to survey and map the Eastern Harbour and its surroundings with very sophisticated equipment (...). Awaiting his first results and the continued mapping, it is already established that he was able to define with great precision the contours of installations and buildings which were once established near the royal palaces: the royal port, the Timoneum, Antirhodos Island, antique moles, etc ...[13]

As early as autumn 1992, magnetometric survey and exploratory diving had, indeed, permitted to formulate some definite hypotheses concerning the sites and monuments mentioned in the antique sources, and to publish a new, if preliminary, chart.

The operations of 1996 and 1997, which are the object of this report, consisted of:

—Measuring and charting topographic reliefs, paved surfaces, sedimentation levels, depths, etc.

—Create an inventory of stone artefacts, their positioning, nature, and material.

—List the most outstanding archaeological objects: sculptures, inscriptions.

—Carry out soundings of the grounds, which were above water level in ancient times.

The great number of dives necessary to carry out this programme confirmed that the sunken palaces and harbours of the Ptolemies and of Cleopatra had been located. They also established that these sites of so many dreams turned out merely to be mysterious collections of debris.

The intense joys of discovery were continued by the pleasure of almost detective-like inquiries aiming at establishing indices liable to offer the keys to the problems. What did the sculptures and inscriptions which we found represent in their days? How, when, and for what reasons, by what act of nature or man were these eminent places of Ptolemy kingship reduced to the disastrous condition in which we found them?

The campaign of 1997 was able to recruit the help and co-operation of several specialist scholars, philologists, archaeologists, engineers capable of interpreting the problems raised by the situations and objects found, to redefine questions and methods, and to study the documents relating to their speciality.

The map (after p. 252) reveals that the results which we obtained and added to the maps which were established and generally accepted prior to our surveys, radically changed knowledge of the topography of this essential part of antique Alexandria, i.e., the ports installed for, and used by, the *basileia*.

The port installations do not present the aspect imagined. Technically, their disposition is more coherent. Entrance to the harbour basins is better protected from waves and swell. The long dyke pencilled in, and siting the Timoneum at its end, does in no way correspond to reality. Such a construction, incidentally, would not have resisted to one single winter, exposed to the main aperture and passage as it has been drawn on these fictitious maps.

The shoal, which was interpreted as the emerging island of Antirhodos, is merely the peninsula with the dyke on which might have stood the Timoneum. The island, of a very different shape from the one it was allotted, does indeed include the magnificent Little Harbour, the perfect haven. If the Poseidion temple must be sited, then it will have to be on the peninsula. And as regards the 'private harbour of the kings', its site and installation are much more functional, and indeed much lovelier, than on any of the fictitious reconstitutions.

The new and added topographical information can be considered as definite. The map not only results directly from the measurements carried out with minute precision, but it also corresponds perfectly to the descriptions of the ancient writers. From there, it was easy to examine the choice of sites and the antique architecture of the ports with the eyes of the engineers. The presence or absence of a sap line allows us to conclude to the rocky levels which either emerged or merely shoaled in antique days.

If this work has certainly determined the geographical sites of these Ptolemaic palaces and temples related by Strabo, we cannot claim to have found these memorable monuments themselves.

To this day, we have identified the abandoned vast grounds, once built over, which their immersion has protected from the rebuilding and new demolition to which the apparent surfaces of the city were subjected in mediaeval, recent, and current times. Much is still lacking before we can date with precision the installations and transformations of each sector without a long effort of analysis, before we can attribute and identify buildings which may once have existed, and determine the dates and circumstances which finally ended up leaving only chaotic fields of rubble.

One pertinent fact has been established, however, in our four areas, the western slope of Lochias, the antique coastline, the peninsula, and the twin- branched island, the ground remained covered with limestone pavements which preserved their continuity and their coherence, except for some limited spots where they suffered from marginal collapse or local smashing. These esplanades, however, only carry ruins strewn about, great remnants of architecture interspersed with the fragments of sculptures, sometimes in concentrated heaps, sometimes vastly dispersed. The immersed grounds of the antique shoreline, including the two peninsular extensions, are covered with

[12] B. Tkaczow, *ibid.*, p. 126, Site 76A.

[13] J-Y. Empereur, 'Fouilles et découvertes récentes', in *Dossiers d'Archaeologie'*, no. 1, p. 87

an almost uninterrupted series of confused deposits of blocks: entire or fragmented shafts of columns of various types and segments, errant capitals and bases, pieces of entablature, blocks which must once have been integrated into walls, etc. ...

The rocks from which these building elements were hewn are limestone, marble, red granite, granitoids, and quartzite. Here and there can be found a monolith from pre- Alexandrian pharaonic temples, visibly re-employed in walls. At one point, what looks like the remnants of a stone-cutter's workshop. Among the deposits could be identified a few structures still standing, like huge limestone walls still fitted together, and very rarely, the remnants of a red brick wall. Our antique coastline thus is in the same state as the adjacent emerging band of shore which has remained continental, and which the visitors of Napoleon's Egyptian Expedition and of last century were able to describe. It corresponds to the continuation under water which these visitors could observe themselves. Although this part is now covered by the Corniche, some of their observations may still be helpful, same as the punctual soundings carried out in preparation of the anchorage's construction.

We know that the buildings created in Alexandria under the Ptolemies and the Caesars have undergone terrible upheavals, already in antique times, as well as since then. These were direct or indirect consequences of tectonic phenomena which periodically crumbled or smashed them, but there was also the hands of man:

—reutilisation on site, or after removal of the columns, in churches and later in mosques.

—blocks taken from earlier buildings and integrated into constructions of Roman if not Ptolemaic times.

—massive removal and transport to different sites of big stone objects during Arab times, particularly to serve in defensive constructions, as documented, for example in the great Tulunid wall, or in Abd el-Latif's famous text describing how the columns of the Serapeum were removed for defence of the coast in Saladin's time.

—and from there, successive dispersals of elements stemming originally from one monument, toward sites which are sometimes far removed from each other.

The available indications which would permit to rebuild a stratigraphic chronology of the vicissitudes of the area of the *basileia* are still scarce.

The fact of the broken statues leads to place the present state as dating posterior to the iconoclastic vandalising which accompanied the spread of Christianity in the 4th century AD.

Some groups of rubble may transmit the impression that a building on columns crumbled in place; still it must be confirmed that the remaining elements of the upper part, capitals, entablatures, cornices, lintels and roofings confirm this thesis.

The cases of dispersal, like that of the monoliths of Apries, found both on the coast and on the island, suggest that the buildings, crumbled or not on their original site, must have served as a quarry at some time, which is further confirmed by the traces of workshop activity.

The numerous sleek columns and the walls of red brick positively point to Roman times and can be inventoried. It was suggested that the big coastal limestone constructions represent moles, quaysides, and harbour installations from Ptolemaic times.[14] Plausible hypothesis which needs to be confirmed.

For the time being, we ignore the date at which the vast pavements as well as their subsoil were created, except for some spots where mortar could be found, which was dated to the 3rd century BC.

It may be considered probable that one of the masses of debris on the island represents the remnants of the Poseidon temple, but not the Ptolemaic one which Strabo saw around 27 BC, and we shall not venture as far as to declare the rubble along the antique coastline as being 'the palaces' of the Ptolemies. Even if the *temenos* must have continued in Roman times to house the divinity to which its founders had dedicated it, if some of the *basileia* were affected to the service of the prefect of Egypt, and became basilicas, the great programmes of urban and monument renovation are likely to have modified the use of space, and to have destroyed some of the buildings of the earlier Hellenistic dynasty (*vide* the Serapeum).

On the condition of being able to separate what might be a lovely motion picture scenario and what does not belong within the framework of the local archaeological drama, one can see from the chart that the palace which Strabo saw on Antirhodos three years after Cleopatra's death—and which may very well have housed her before she removed into her mausoleum—is sited to face the Timoneum, the palace which a defeated Mark Antony built to lock up his derelictions. The ghosts of the two lovers shall continue to haunt these sunken places, especially as the residences they used have become phantoms themselves. But the ground provides some evidence of what became of them.

On the island of Antirhodos, our excavations have brought to light a chronology of the successive occupations and activities.

The jetty on the eastern tip is dated by the C14 method to the 5th-4th century BC, which is a surprising date as long as one clings to the simplistic and schematic view of presence on the coast during the dynasties

[14] B. Tkaczow, *Topography*, p. 120-126: 'remains of Ptolemaic waterfront ...'

preceding Alexander, on reading Homer, Herodotus, and Strabo. The XXIXth and XXth dynasties (398-341) indubitably maintained the rigorous police and excise control established by the Saite and Persian kings against the Greek navigators and traders. We know, on the other hand, that the pharaohs recruited the help of mercenaries imported from Greece. Reception of these auxiliaries could not possibly be limited to quarantining them upon arrival on the island of Pharos, like so many pirates or smugglers; the protection offered by the inside cove, i.e. the current anchorage could well have been prepared for their arrival, using imported wood (elm).[15]

The pavement of the esplanade was started under the first Ptolemies, since the wooden casing which served to build the sill dates from the 3rd century BC, according to C14 analysis.

On the east-west branch of Antirhodos, a band of paved land is covered with more or less dense groups of sleek granite columns and some blocks of various hard rock material, including some reused pharaonic ones. These deposits seem to point at a quarry abandoned at the end of its exploitation. In three different places there, we found granite pedestals with Greek inscriptions, seven of which date from Caracalla's reign (and more precisely from AD 213).

[15] Following this thought: a village to the south-east of Lake Mareotis kept the memory of an establishment created by the Athenian *condottiere* Chabrias around 360 (Strabo, XVII, 1.22).

In the absence of any building elements from Ptolemaic times on this site, where there was once 'Cleopatra's Palace', we must conclude to an edifice built in the times of the emperors, which was decorated in honour of the emperor at the beginning of the 3rd century AD.

On the south-west branch, at the tip of the pavement that is still in place, where there is a small rock slide, three sculptures were extracted from under small building debris. They were manhandled but still in good condition: two sphinxes (p. 170, 171) and the statue of a priest (p. 179). Together with them, ceramics that could be dated between the 1st century BC and the 2nd century AD were found smashed under heavier blocks.

The three sculptures visibly escaped early Christian iconoclasm. This was either because the ground on which they lay had already sunk under the surface of the sea in AD 360-391 (iconoclasm, incidentally, continued intermittently until the end of the 5th century, when Christians again smashed idols with a vengeance). This is a timespan in which can be situated the earthquake of which provoked the collapse of Antirhodos' shoreline. A homogenous group of fifty tall columns that disintegrated in their fall was found on a sunken slope on the eastern flank of the same south-western branch of the island. These building debris are most likely the result of the same brutal upheaval.

It is of some interest to be able to place the ruins and

Photo 135: View of the wreck during its uncovering.

collapse provoked by such an upheaval, even approximately, in history. We felt that it was indeed important to try to distinguish among the causes of the foundering of Alexandria's shores, on one hand the brutal and formidable catastrophes of the historical earthquakes accompanied by tidal waves, and apart from these other instances where slow phenomena of subsidence or elevation of the sea level progressively but also discreetly submerged monument which were already shattered and ruined.[16]

As our reflections continued, they also refined and qualified in other ways our models of interpretation of the literary sources on one hand, and the field results on the other. We need, for example, to make some distinctions between the various 'descriptions' of the classical authors, Greek, Latin or Arab, for example, between Strabo on one side, who is a true eye-witness, and Pliny on the other, who is an often too succinct compiler, mostly of book knowledge, and thirdly the Romance of Alexander which transcribes the images of the city of its time (2nd of 3rd century AD), wrapping them into legends which had formed through the ages.

It is better to refrain from hasty, definite conclusions on the basis of fragments of inscriptions or works of art which came the excavator's way, to identify and date sites and monuments. There is the dedication of 'Pompey's Column', the one and only column of the Serapeum which is still standing on its pedestal, and visible. There are two of the four foundation deposits at the levelled-off Ptolemaic wall of this temple, and one of the four deposits of its little sanctuary, which were found where they had been put in the times of Ptolemy III. And there is the dedication which allows to date precisely at 13-12 BC the raising of the two 'Needles of Cleopatra', and which allow—with the help of a cross-reference in Pliny—to place the facade of the Caesareum; a dedication which is preserved on only one of the pincers of the four bronze crabs which supported the one obelisk which remained standing ... These are practically the only three epigraphic finds which are certainly still in situ, in all the archaeology over two centuries in the vast expanse of Alexandria. The hope of finding an Egyptian foundation deposit in its original place, or the dedicatory inscription engraved on the pediment of a Greek temple is practically zero. When extracting a fragment of inscription from the rubble, one would be wise—before peremptorily fixing an identification and dating, often at the price of too learned deductions—to make certain, in view of the context and the state of the stone, that the object has not been moved over some more or less important distance.[17] It is the same with the remains of figurines representing divinities or attributable to sovereigns. There was very little chance to ever find Cleopatra's signature somewhere on Antirhodos, and no better one to find the wreck of the splendid swimming palace which in 41 BC had carried the queen all the way to Cilicia to join Mark Antony. The preservation, dispersed but on the same ground, of eight inscriptions of one single short period, and most of them complete—accidental result of the complex adventures of the site—is a miraculous piece of luck, and a most precious contribution to our knowledge of emperor Caracalla's tempestuous relations with the city.

Despite this piece of luck, and especially of the decisive results of the topographic surveys, we chose to formulate our own reservations in the outline of our interpretation of the findings, and of the remarkable objects found.

Three fragments of an obelisk, a pedestal, the fragment of a statue dating from Ramesside times (1291-1204 BC), and eight elements of a building constructed by the Saite king Apries (589-570 BC) constitute the last re-uses of elements of monuments built by dynasties prior to Alexander's coming. They confirm the idea that most of the items of pharaonic antiquity found in Graeco-Roman Alexandria had been removed from the temples of Heliopolis, as numerous pieces found over the last century on the *terra firma* parts of the city indicated.

Some remarkable remnants of statues in the pharaonic style, as well as the Hellenistic and the Graeco-Roman one, were discovered on various sites. The beauty of the marble female head attributable to a roman empress (photo 89) is touching, plunged into the murky depths as she was. The torso of the god Hermes (photo 88) is a magnificent sample of the talent of the Hellenistic sculptors. Almost entirely preserved, the image of the priest clutching the jar which contains the remains of Osiris seems to express a sentiment of almost tender piety for the saviour god who resurrects the initiated of Isis. In the vast area of the *basileia* facing the sea, a royal colossus and two classical sphinxes are works of pharaonic style hewn from granite it Graeco-Roman times. In front of community or religious buildings, they displayed the divine power of the ruler.

In the same area, there remains the gigantic head of a monumental sphinx with the head of a predator (photo 100), an image representing in all probability a universal protector god specially appealed to by theologians and invoked by the magicians of roman Egypt.

A little further, two animal statues, a granite Hellenistic serpent (photo 84) and a typically Egyptian limestone ibis (photo 87) which may be supposed very little away from their original position, represent two gods especially venerated by the Alexandrians, the Good Spirits on whom depended the city's destiny in the first instance,

[16] Some sedimentation strata may indicate the passage of a tidal wave.

[17] These distances were often considerable, e.g., the Apries blocks shared between the coast and the island, at the latest in Roman times (see above, p. 234). Dispersal went even further: the segment of a bundled column found in a deposit at the edge of the north-western shore of the Eastern Harbour belonged to a colonnade of which three columns were found at the south gate of the Arab walls.

and the master of knowledge and wisdom who was Thot, alias Hermes Trismegistos in the other one. These finds must, of course, be put into relation with other divine effigies which were noted earlier in adjacent areas which are now covered by the Corniche: such as a small statue of Harpocrates,[18] and the statues of Isis, and of Sekhmet with a lion's head.[19] These finds, however, do not allow us to extrapolate as many temples as there were gods in question. The patron of each major temple, whether in the Egyptian or in the Greek tradition, housed the images and the cult of other related gods. These 'resident' gods could even institute a secondary cult or *synnaoi*, and some were offered for the devotion of the lay and uninitiated. We can readily imagine the falcon-sphinx with the benevolently listening ears, the city's Good Spirit, or the Master Thot-Hermes taking their place in the open areas of the great buildings or the secondary chapels.

[18] G. Wilkinson, *Modern Egypt and Thebes*, vol. 1., London, 1848, p.157.
[19] P. de Vaujany, *Recherches sur les anciens monuments situés sur le Grand Port d'Alexandrie,* Paris, 1888, cited by B. Tkaczow, *Topography*, p.120, note 148.

Three sculptures found in the ruins of a single place on Antirhodos led to a very acceptable assumption.[20] The two sphinxes (no. 1185 and no. 1198) and the so lovely granite priest presenting Osiris in the form of the Canopic Jar (no. 1199) could have taken their place in a chapel comparable, for example, to the small Serapeion built under Hadrian in front of the facade of the temple in Luxor.

The achievements of the campaigns of 1992, 1996, and 1997 promise several years of work under water and of concerted research in the libraries. Already the campaign of 1998, on which we shall report in due course, has undertaken some verifications, gathered additional information, and made new discoveries. In the small harbour of Antirhodos, in particular, an antique boat was discovered which contained, among other things, a small religious motive mounted on a gold ring.

The study of the harbour basins should be pushed further in order to determine their depths, and the type of sedimentation, to find eventual wrecks, to draw a detailed

[20] Z. Kiss, F. Dunand and J. Yoyotte independently arrived at this same thesis.

Photo 136: Reconstruction: the priest of Canopus before the chapel.

Photo 137: head no. 889, Antonia Minor

map of their quaysides, and possibly to find subterranean channels coming from beneath the city.

An overview and study of the numerous and repetitive elements of architecture (which can be labelled), which cover the areas of the palaces, shall be accompanied by soundings underneath the pavement in order to establish a chronology of the development and the following destruction of that area.[21]

The topographical survey and visual exploration, finally, should be extended to the western part of the roadstead. Strabo,[22] walking from East to West, described the royal quarter and harbour, and the pursued: '.... *then comes the Kaisarion, the the Emporion, and the warehouses which are followed by the arsenals which stretch forward unto the Heptastadion'*, the artificial dyke which closed the roadstead to the west and served as a road to reach Pharos. An emporion, a landing stage, is a place of trade, and Strabo tells us elsewhere that the one in Alexandria is the biggest emporion in the inhabited world.[23] A little further follow the shipyards where the fleets were built which trade all over the Mediterranean in Ptolemaic times, and those which went to feed the Roman people with wheat ... The sober catalogue of the geographer would have a great need for some elaboration from more concrete knowledge of the major facts on which it only touches with one word here or there ... The area will not be easy to survey. It serves today as an anchorage for the fishermen's boats and its waters and bottom are darkened by an abundant sludgy sedimentation. Cartography of that part, with the same methods and technologies which have given the results here presented, would first allow to evaluate more closely how the tectonic

[21] A mineralogical identification of the various specimens of stone might serve to identify the different quarries from which the Egyptians and then the Romans had extracted them.

[22] Strabo, XVII, I.9, '*Testimonia'* no. 28.

[23] *Ibid.*, XVII, I, 13, 253.

movements have modified the Alexandrian coastline. Also, they will no doubt reveal the presence of further monuments. Crucial points of very memorable events could be made clear: prospecting the western part of the roads will let us meet Julius Caesar, blocked down together with the young Cleopatra between land and water, fraying his way from the royal quarter to Pharos; we will see the uncertain battles unwind between land and sea, and still, we would perhaps be able to know more about the powerful devices created by the Ptolemies and maintained by the Caesars, arsenals and warehouses, which despite other reefs and across other passages guaranteed the orderly functioning of the great international trade which made the prosperity and glory of Alexandria in Egypt.

CHRONOLOGICAL OUTLINE

This table places in time the personalities and events which mark the history of Alexandria and the circumstance known from the literary tradition which contributed to the destruction of the city's monuments and the sinking underwater of its shores. It should not be forgotten that often this destruction took place in circumstances not reported by the texts, especially the circumstances of the flooding which may have been the result of numerous landslides and subsidence.

PHARAOHS
whose monuments have been rediscovered in Alexandria

XIIth dynasty	
Sesostris I	1971-1926 BC
Sesostris II	1897-1878
Sesostris III	1878-1843
XVIIIth dynasty	
Thoutmosis III	1478-1426
Thoutmosis IV	1401-1391
Amenhotep III	1391-1353
Horemheb	1323-1293
XIXth dynasty	
Sethi I	1291-1279
Ramesses II	1279-1213
Merenptah	1213-1204
Sethi II	1204-1192
XXth dynasty	
Ramesses IX	1120-1103
XXVIth dynasty (Sais)	
Psammetichus I	664-610
Nechao	610-595
Psammetichus II	595-589
Apries	589-570
Amasis	570-526
XXVIIth dynasty (Persian)	525-404
XXVIIIth dynasty (Sais)	404-399
XXIXth dynasty (Mendes)	
Hakoris	393-380
XXXth dynasty (Sebennytus)	
Nekhtnebef (Nectanebo I)	380-363
Nekhthorheb (Nectanebo II)	360-343

Second Persian Domination	343-332
THE HELLENISTIC ERA	
Alexander the Great in Egypt	**332**
The Lagide dynasty	
Ptolemy I Soter	305-283
Ptolemy II Philadelphos	285-246
Ptolemy III Evergetes	246-221
Ptolemy IV Philopator	221-204
Ptolemy V Epiphanos	204-180
Ptolemy VI Philometor	180-145
Ptolemy VIII Evergetes II	145-116
Ptolemy IX Soter II Lathyros	116-80
Ptolemy X Alexander I, concurrent	110-88
Ptolemy XI Alexander II	80
Ptolemy XII called Auletes	80-51
Cleopatra VII	51-30
with Ptolemy XIII	52-47
with Ptolemy XIV	47-44
with Ptolemy XV Caesar	43-30
Julius Caesar in Egypt	**48-46**
Mark Antony in Egypt	**41/30**
Octavian in Alexandria	30
THE ROMAN ERA	
Augustus (= Octavian Caesar)	28-14 AD
Tiberius	14-37
Caius Caligula	37-41
Claudius	41-54
Nero	54-68
Domitian	81-96
Trajan	98-117
Hadrian	117-138
Septimus Severus	193-211
Caracalla	211-217
Diocletian	284-305
CHRISTIANITY	
Conversion of Constantine the Great	**324/332**
Constantius II	337-361
Bishop George: destruction of the Mithraeum c. *360*	
Julien, called the Apostate	361-363
Valens	364-378
Tidal wave at Alexandria	*365*
Theodosius the Great	379-395

Destruction of the Serapium by Bishop Theophilus	391
Continued elimination of pagan temples and building of churches	c. *360-414*
Closing of the temple of Isis at Menouthis	c. *485*

THE ARAB-ISLAMIC ERA

Capture of Alexandria by Amr ibn al-As	**641**
The *Rashidun* caliphs	641-661
Umayyad caliphs	661-750
Abbasid caliphs	750-969
Earthquake at Alexandria	*796*
Tulunid sultans	850-905
Earthquake in Alexandria as far as Fustat	*950, 956*
Fatimid caliphs	969-1171
Ayyubid sultans	1174-1250
Saladin	1174-1195
The Mamluks	1251-1517
Earthquake in Alexandria as far as Upper Egypt	*1258, 1268*
Baybars el-Muzaffar	1294-1310
Earthquake from Alexandria and all of Egypt, restoration	*1303-1304*
Earthquake in Alexandria	*1341*
Qa'it-Bey	1468-1496
Conquest of Egypt by the Ottoman Selim I	1517

ABBREVIATIONS

ANRW	*Aufstieg und Niedergang des römischen Welt*, éd. H Temporini et W Haase, Berlin, W De Gruyter.
ASAE	*Annales du Service des Antiquités de l'Egypte*
BCH	*Bulletin de correspondance hellénique.*
BdE	*Bibliothèque d'Etudes* (IFAO)
BIFAO	*Bulletin de l'Institut français d'archéologie orientale,* Le Caire.
BMMA	*Bulletin of the Metropolitan Museum of Art* (New York)
BSA Alex	*Bulletin de la Société Archéologique d'Alexandrie.*
BSAE	*British School of Archaeology in Egypt*
CdE	*Chronique d'Egypte*, Bruxelles.
CGC	*Catalogue Général du Musée du Louvre*
Descr.	Description de l'Egypte
Dizionario	A. Calderini, *Dizionario dei nomi geografici e topografici dell' Egitto greco-romano*
EEF	*Egyptian Exploration Fund*
EPRO	*Etudes préliminaires aux religions orientales dans l'Empire romain*
HÄB	*Hildesheimer ägyptologische Beiträge*
IGRR	*Inscriptiones Graecae ad res Romanas pertinentes*, ed. R Cagnat *et alii.*
JEA	*Journal of Egyptian Archaeology*, Londres.
JRS	*Journal of Roman Studies*, Londres.
K*RI*	Kitchen, *Ramesside Inscriptions*
LÄ	*Lexikon der Ägyptologie*
LD	Lepsius, *Denkmäler aus Aegypten und Aethiopien*
LIMC	*Lexicon iconographicum mythologiae classicae*
MDAIK	*Mitteilungen des deutschen archäologischen Instituts. Abteilung Kairo*
MEFRA	*Mélanges de l'Ecole Française de Rome, Antiquité.*
NC	*Numismatic Chronicle*, Londres.
OGI	W Dittenberger, *Orientis Graeci Inscriptiones selectae,* Leipzig, 1903-1905.
OLA	*Orientalia Lovaniensia analecta*
OMS	L Robert, *Opera minora selecta*, Amsterdam, Hakkert, 1969 *sqq.*
PM	B. Porter and R Moss, *Topographical Bibliography of Ancient Egyptian Hieroglyphics Texts, Reliefs and Painting.*
REA	*Revue des Etudes anciennes*
REG	*Revue des Etudes grecques*, Paris.
RT	*Recueil de travaus relatifs à la philologie et à l'archéologie égyptiennes et assyriennes*
SB	*Sammelbuch griechischer Urkunden aus Aegypten*, F Preisigke *et alii*, 1918 *sqq.*
SDAIK	*Sonderschrift des deutschen archäologischen Instituts. Abteiliung Kairo*
SEG	*Supplementum epigraphicum Graecum*, La Haye.
ZÄS	*Zeitschrift für ägyptische Sprache und Altertumskunde*
ZPE	*Zeitschrift für Papyrologie und Epigraphik*, Bonn.

Monographs

J-Y. Empereur, *Le Phare* = *Le Phare d'Alexandrie*, Paris, 1998.

P. Gallo, *Ostraca* = *Ostrace demoticí e sieratici dall' archivio bilingue di Narmouthis*, Pisa, Edizioni ETS, 1997.

La Gloire = *La Gloire d'Alexandrie*, Paris, Paris-Musées, éd. 1998

B. Tkaczow, *Topography* = *Topography of Ancient Alexandria (An Archaeological Map)*, Varsovie. 1993.

J. Vandier, *Manuel* = *Manuel d'Archéologie égyptienne*, 6 tomes, Paris, Picard éd., 1952-1978.

SELECTED BIBLIOGRAPHY

This bibliography is restricted to a number of recent monographs and specialist articles which provide general information on Egypt for the Ptolemaic and Roman periods and on the current exploration of the underwater sites at Alexandria. References and details are given in the notes on the appropriate pages.

ADAM, J. P., *La construction romaine, matériaux et techniques*, éd. Picard, Paris, 1984.

ADRIANI, A., *Repertorio d'Arte dell'Egitto Greco-Romano*, Serie C, vol. I-II, Tavole (1963), Testo (1966), Palerme.

Alessandria e il mondo ellenistico-romano, Studi in onore di A. Adriani, Rome, L'Erma, 1983.

Alessandria e il mondo hellenistico-romano, I centenario del Museo Greco-Romano (Atti del Congresso Internazionale Italo-Egiziano), Rome, l'Erma di Bretschneider, 1995(cf. CdF LXXI (1996) 368-374).

Alexandria and Alexandrianism. Papers delivered at a Symposium organized by the J. Paul Getty Museum ..., Getty Museum, 1996.

Alexandrie, IIIe siècle av. J.-C.: tous les savoirs du monde ou le rêve d'universalité des Ptolémées, Éd. Autrement, Séries Mémoires, no 19, nov. 1992.

Alexandrien (Aegyptica Treverensia. Trierer Studien zum griechisch-römischen Ägypten, Band I), Mainz, 1981.

'Alexandrie, lumière du monde antique', *Les dossiers de l'archéologie*, no 201, 1995.

Aufstieg und Niedergang der römischen Welt. Geschichte und Kultur Roms im Spiegel der neuesten Forschung. Teil II: Principat, Band 10, (Halbband 1-2). Politische Geschichte (Provinzen und Randvölker: Afrika und Ägypten), Ed. H. Temporini. Walter de Gruyter, Berlin-New York, 1982-1988.

BADEL, C., and BÉRENGER, A., *L'Empire romain au IIIe siècle après J.C., Textes et documents,* Ed.. Sedes, 1998.

BARRY, W. D., 'Popular Violence and the Stability of Roman Alexandria, 30 BC-1D 215', dans *BSA Alex*.. 45 (1993) 19-33.

BASCH, L., *Le musée imaginaire de la marine antique*, Institut hellénique pour la préservation de la tradition nautique, Athènes, 1987, (disponible au Musée de la Marine de Paris).

BENOÎT, P. and SCHWARTZ, J., 'Caracalla et les troubles d'Alexandrie en 215 ap. J.C.', dans *Etudes de Papyrologie*, VII (1948) 17-33 (IFAO).

BERNAND, A. and E. and GODDIO, Fr., 'L'épigraphie sous-marine dans le port oriental d'Alexandrie', *ZPE* 121 (1998), 131-144, Taf. XIII-XVI.

BERNAND, A., *Alexandrie des Ptolémées*, éd. Du CNRS, Paris, 1995.

BERNAND, A., *Alexandrie la Grande,* 1ère éd. Arthaud, 1966; new enlarged edition, Hachette, 1998.

BERNAND, A., and E., *Les inscriptions grecques et latines du Colosse de Memnon*, IFAO, 1960.

BERNAND, E, *Inscriptions grecques d'Egypte et de Nubie Répertoire bibliographique des IGRR*, Les Belles Lettres 1983.

BERNAND, E *Inscriptions métriques de l'Egypte gréco-romaine*, Annales littéraires de l'Université de Besançon, vol. 98, Les Belles Lettres 1969.

BERNAND, E, *Inscriptions grecques d'Egypte et de Nubie*, *Répertoire bibliographique des OGIS*, Les Belles Lettres 1982.

BERNAND, E., *Recueil des inscriptions grecques du Fayoum,* I, Leiden, Brill, 1975, 2 and 3, IFAO, 1981.

BERNAND, E.*, Inscriptions grecques d'Alexandrie ptolémaïque*, in the press, IFAO.

BERNAND, E.*, Inscriptions grecques et latines d'Akôris,* IFAO, 1988.

BESNIER, M., *Histoire romaine*, t. IV, Ière partie (Hist. générale de G. Glotz, PUF, 1937*): L'Empire romain de l'avènement des Sévères au concile de Nicée.*

BIRLEY, A., *Septimius Severus: the African Emperor*, New Haven, Yale University Press,, 1989 (1st ed.. Garden City, NY, Doubleday, 1971).

BLACKMAN, D., 'Ancient harbours in the Mediterranean', *International Journal of Nautical Archeology and Underwater Exploration,* 11.2 (pp. 79-104) and 11.3 (pp. 185-211), 1982.

BOWMAN, A. K., *Egypt after the Pharaohs: 332 BC-AD 641, from Alexander to the Arab Conquest*, British Museum Publications Ltd., London, 1986.

BRECCIA E., *Iscrizioni Greche e Latine,* Catalogue général des antiquités égyptiennes du Musée d'Alexandrie, IFAO, 1911.

BRECCIA, E., *Alexandrea ad Aegyptum,* Bergame, 1914.

BURASELIS, K., 'Zu Caracallas Strafmassnahmen in Alexandrien (215/6), Die Frage der Leinenweber in P. GISS. 4O, II und der syssitia in Cass. Dio 77 (78) 23.3', in *ZPE* 108 (1995) 166-188.

CALDERINI, A., *Dizionario dei nomi geographici e topographici dell'Egitto greco-romano*, vol. I-V (1935-1987) e *Supplemento* I (1998).

CASSON, L., *Ships and Seafaring in Ancient Times*, The British Museum Press, London, 1994

CASSON, L., *Ships and Seamanship in the Ancient World*, Princeton, 1971.

CHAUVEAU, M., *L'Egypte au temps de Cléopâtre, 180-30 av. J.C.* (Coll. *La vie quotidienne*), Paris, Hachette Littératures éd., 1997.

CHRISTOL, M., *L'Empire romain du IIIe siècle, Histoire politique, 192-235 après J.C.*, Ed. Errance, Paris, 1997.

CHUVIN, P., *Chronique des derniers païens. La disparition du paganisme dans l'Empire romain du règne de Constantin à celui de Justinien*, Paris, des Belles Lettres/Fayard, 1990.

CLAUSS, M., *Kleopatra*, Verlag C. H. Beck, München, 1989.

Cleopatra's Egypt, Age of the Ptolemies, The Brooklyn Museum, 1989.

COOK, S. A., *et alii*, *The Cambridge Ancient History,* XII: *The Imperial Crisis and Recovery, AD 193-324*, Cambridge, 1939; rééd. 1971.

DELIA, D., 'Alexandrian Citizenship During the Roman Principate', *American Classical Studies*, 23, Scholars Press, Atlanta, Georgia, 1991.

DEVIJVER, H., 'The Roman Army in Egypt', *ANRW* II, I, p. 452-492.

DION CASSIUS, *Dio's Roman History*, ed. And trans., E. Cary, 9 vol., Harvard Univ. Press, Loeb Classical Library, Cambridge (Mass.), 1927.

DION CASSIUS, *Histoire romain e,* éd. U. P. Boissevain, Berlin, 1895-1910.

DION CASSIUS, *Histoire romaine,* éd. et trad. E Gros et V Boissée, 10 vol., Didot Paris, 1845-1870.

DOUGLAS, B., 'Global sea level rise', *J. of Geophysical Research*, vol. 96, N° C4, pp. 6981-6992, April 1991.

DUNAND, Fr., and ZIVIE-COCHE, C., *Dieux et hommes en Égypte, 3000 av. J.-C., 395 ap. J.-C., Anthropologie religieuse* (U, Histoire ancienne), Paris Armand Colin, 1991.

Égypte romaine, l'autre Égypte, catalogue de l'exposition réalisée par le Musée d'Archéologie méditerranéenne, avril-juillet 1997, éd. A. Durand, Marseille, RMN et Musées de Marseille.

EMPEREUR, J-Y., *A Short Guide to the Graeco-Roman Museum of Alexandria*, Sarapis Publishing, Alexandria, 1995.

EMPEREUR, J-Y., *Alexandrie redécouverte*, Paris, Fayard/Stock, 1998.

EMPEREUR, J-Y., *Le Phare d'Alexandrie. La Merveille retrouvée*, (Découvertes Gallimard, no 352), Paris, 1998.

FLEMMING, N. 'Archéologie des côtes de la Crète', *Les Dossiers de l'Archéologie*, N° 50, février 1981.

FORSTER, E.-M., *Alexandria: a History and a Guide*, trad. Claude Blanc, *Alexandrie, une histoire et un guide*, éd. 10/18, Paris, 1990.

FRANCO, L., 'Ancient Mediterranean harbours: a heritage to preserve', *Ocean & Coastal Management*, vol. 30, nos. 2-3, pp. 115-151, Elsevier Science Ltd, 1996.

FRASER, P. M., *Ptolemaic Alexandria*, 3 vol., Oxford, Clarendon Press, 1972.

GAGÉ, J., *'Basiléia', Les Césars, les rois d'Orient et les 'Mages'*, Paris, les Belles Lettres, 1968

GERACI, G., *Genesi della Provincia Romana d'Egitto*, Bologne, 1983

GODDIO, Fr., *À la recherche de Cléopâtre*, Paris, Robert Laffont, éd., 1996.

GODDIO, Fr., *et alii*, *Le San Diego. Un trésor sous la mer*, Catalogue de l'Exposition à la Grande Halle de la Villette, 14 septembre-8 janvier 1995, Paris, RMN-AFAA, 1994.

GODDIO, Fr., *et alii*, *Weisses Gold*, Catalogue of the Exhibition at Frankfurt, September-December 1997, Göttingen, éd. Steidel, 1997.

GODDIO, Fr., *Le mystère du San Diego*, Paris, Robert Laffont, éd., 1994.

GRAINDOR, P., *Bustes et statues-portraits d'Egypte romaine*, Le Caire, 1937.

GRIMM, G., *Kunst und Ptolemäer und Römerzeit im Ägyptischen Museum Kairo*, Aufnahmen D. Johannes, Verlag Philipp von Zabern, Mainz, 1975.

GUILLERM, A., *La marine dans l'antiquité*, Que sais-je? N° 2995, éd. Presses Universitaires de France, 1995.

HABACHI, L., *The Obelisks of Egypt, Skyscrapers of the Past*, Cairo, The American University Press, 1984.

HALFMANN, H., *Itinera Principum*, Stuttgart, 1986.

HERODIEN, *Histoire des empereurs romains*: ed. C. R. Whittaker, 2 vol. (London, 1969-1970), used by Denis Roques, *Hérodien* Belles Lettres, Paris, 1990, tran. and comment., with postscript by Luciano Canfora, 'Hérodien et Rostovtseff'.

HERZ, P., 'Der *dies imperii* unter den Severen', in *ZPE* 31 (1978) 285-290.

HILL, P. V., 'Notes on the coinage of Septimius Severus and his Family, A.D. 193-217', *NC* 1964, 169-188, pl. XV.

HILL, P. V., 'The Coin-Portraiture of Severus and his Family from the Mint of Rome', *NC* 1979, 36-46, pl. 6-7.

HILL, P. V., 'The Issues of Severus and his Sons in A.D. 211', *NC* 1978, 33-37 and pl. II.

Histoire Auguste, Chastagnol (André), *Histoire Auguste, les empereurs romains des IIe et IIIe siècless*, éd. bilingue, éd. Robert Laffont, coll. Bouquins, Paris, 1994.

HUSSON, G. and VALBELLE, D., *L'État et les institutions en Égypte, des premiers pharaons aux empereurs romains* (U, Histoire ancienne), Paris, Armand Colin, 1992.

HUZAR, E. G., 'Alexandria ad Aegyptum in the Julio-Claudian Age', *ANRW*, II, 10, I (1988), p. 619-668.

IVERSEN, E., *Obelisks in Exile.* Vol. I, *The Obelisks of Rome*, Copenhagen, 1968.

IVERSEN, E., *Obelisks in Exile.* Vol. II, *The Obelisks of Istanbul and England*, Copenhagen, 1972.

JOHNSON, A. C., *Egypt and the Roman Empire*, Ann Arbor, University of Michigan Press, 1951.

KAYSER, Fr., *Recueil des inscriptions grecques et latines (non funéraires) d'Alexandrie impériale* [BdE T. CVIII], Le Caire, IFAO, 1994.

KISS, Z., *Etudes sur le portrait impérial romain en Egypte* (Travaux du Centre d'Archéologie Méditerranéenne de l'Académie polonaise des sciences, t. 23), Varsovie, 1984.

KISS, Z., *Sculptures des fouilles polonaises à Kôm el-Dikka (1960-1982)* [Alexandrie IV], Varsovie, Centre d'Archéologie méditerranéenne de l'Académie polonaise des Sciences et Centre polonais d'Archéologie méditerranéenne de l'Université de Varsovie au Caire, 1988.

KOLB, F., *Literarische Beziehungen zwischen Cassius Dio, Herodian und der Historia Augusta,* Bonn, 1972.

KYRIELEIS, H., *Bildniss der Ptolemäer* (*DAI. Archäologischen Forschungen*, Band 2), Gebr. Mann Verlag, Berlin, 1975.

La Gloire d'Alexandrie, Catalogue de l'Exposition au Musée du Petit Palais, 7 mai-26 juillet 1998, Paris, Musée éd. 1998.

LE BOHEC, Y., *L'Armée romaine sous le Haut-Empire*, Paris, Picard, 1989.

LE GALL, J., and LE GLAY, M., *L'Empire romain*, tome I: *Le Haut-Empire, de la bataille d'Actium* (*31 av. J.C.*) *à l'assassinat de Sévère Alexandre (235 ap. J.C.),* PUF, 1987; 2e éd. 1992.

LE GLAY, M., VOISIN, J-L., LE BOHEC, Y, *Histoire romaine*, PUF, 1991.

LESQUIER,, 'L'Armée romaine d'Egypte d'Auguste à Dioclétien', Le Caire, IFAO, 1918.

LETRONNE, J-A., *Recueil des inscriptions grecques et latines de l'Egypte*, t. I, 1842; t. 2, Paris, 1848.

LEWIS, N., *Greeks in Ptolemaic Egypt. Case Studies in the Social History of the Hellenistic World,* Clarendon Press, Oxford, 1986.

LEWIS, N., *Life in Egypt under Roman Rule*, Oxford, Clarendon Press, 1983; trad. P. Chuvin, *La mémoire des Sables, La vie en Egypte sous la domination romaine*, Paris, Armand Colin, 1988.

Life in a Multi-cultural Society, Egypt from Cambyses to Constantine and Beyond, Johnson, J. H., ed., SAOC, no. 51, Chicago, 1992.

LUKASCZEWICZ, A., *Aegyptica Antoniana*, Varsovie, 1993.

LUKASZEWICZ, A., 'Alexandrie sous les Sévères et l'historiographie', in *Egitto e Storia Antica* (Actes de Bologne, 1989), 491-496.

MACMULLEN, R., *Le Paganisme dans l'Empire Romain*, trad., PUF, 1987.

MARICQ, A., 'La chronologie des dernières années de Caracalla', in *Syria* 34 (1957) 297-302.

MASTINO, A., *Le titolature di Caracalla e Geta attraverso le iscrizioni*, Bologne, CLUEB, 1981.

MELÈZE-MODRZEJEWSKI, J., 'L'Egypte, dans Rome et l'intégration de l'Empire 44 av. J.C.-260 ap. J.C.' (dir.Claude Lepelley), Tome 2 (PUF, 1998), chap.. X, 435-493.

MÉLÈZE-MODRZEJEWSKI, J., *Les Juifs d'Egypte de Ramsès II à Hadrien*, Paris, Armand Colin, 1991.

MILLAR, F., *The Emperor in the Roman World,* London, 1977; 2nd ed. 1992.

MILLAR, F., *The Roman Near East, 31 B.C.-AD 337*, Harvard Univ. Press, 1993.

MILNE, J. G., *A History of Egypt under Roman Rule*, Oxford, OUP, 1924.

MOMMSEN, Th., *Histoire romaine*, 2 vol. éd. Cl. Nicolet, éd. Robert Laffont, coll. Bouquins, 1985.

MUSTAFA EL ABBADI, 'The Problem of the Council of Alexandria: Can a Solution be Found?' in *BSA Alex*., 45 (1993) I-6.

NICOLET, C., *L'Inventaire du Monde, géographie et politique aux origines de l'Empire romain*, Paris, Fayard, 1988.

PERRIN, Y., and BAUZOU, Th.., *De la Cité à l'Empire: histoire de Rome*, éd. Ellipses, Paris, 1997.

PETIET, C., *Ces Messieurs de la religion; l'ordre de Malte au dix-huitième siècle ou le crépuscule d'une épopée*, éd. France-Empire, 1992.

POIDEBARD, A., *Un grand port disparu, TYR. Recherches aériennes et sous-marines,* Librairie orientaliste Paul Geuthner, Paris, 1939.

POMEY, P., dir., *La navigation dans l'Antiquité*, Aix en Provence, Edisud, 1997.

PRADA, J. and DE LA PENA, J., 'Maritime engineering during the Roman Republic and the early Empire', Medcoast Conference, Tarragona, 1995.

RABAN, A., 'Coastal processes and ancient harbour engineering', *Proc. Int. Symp. OnCities on the Sea—Past and Present,* BAR International Series, 404, pp. 185-207, 1988.

REDDE, M., *Mare Nostrum*, Ecole française de Rome, Palais Farnèse, 1986 (disponible au Musée de la Marine de Paris).

RÉMONDON, R., *La crise de l'Empire romain, de Marc Aurèle à Anastase,* PUF, 1964.

ROWE, A., 'Excavations of the Graeco-Roman Museum at Kôm el-Shukafa during the Season 1941-1942', in *BSA Alex*. 35 (1942) 3-45, pl. I-XV.

ROWE, A., 'Short Report on Excavation of the Graeco Roman Museum at 'Pompey's Pillar' Site', *ibid*., 35 (1942) 124-161, pl. XXVII-XLIV.

SARTRE, M., *L'Orient Romain, Provinces et sociétés provinciales en Méditerranée orientale d'Auguste aux Sévères (Collection UH)*, éd. du Seuil, 1991.

SCARRE, C., *Chronicle of the Roman Emperors,* Thames and Hudson, 1995; repr. 1997

SCHULZ, O. Th., *Der röm. Kaiser Caracalla, Genie, Wahnsinn oder Verbrechen*, Leipzig, 1909.

SCHUWARTZ, J., 'Note sur le séjour de Caracalla en Egypte', dans *CdE* 67 (1959) 120-123.

SOLOVIEV, S., 'Tsunamigenic zones in the Mediterranean Sea', *Natural Hazards* 3: 183-202, Kluwer Academic Publ., 1990.

SYME, R.,,*Emperors and Biography, Studies in the Historia Augusta*, Oxford, 1971.

The Acts of the Pagan Martyrs, ed., trans. and comment., H. A. Musurillo, Clarendon Press, Oxford, 1954.

THELAMON, F., *Païens et Chrétiens au IVe siècle, L'apport de l'Histoire ecclésiastique' de Rufin d'Aquilée*, Etudes Augustiniennes, Paris, 1981.

THOMSON, D. J., *Memphis under the Ptolemies*, Princeton University Press, 1988.

TKACZOW, B., *Topography of Ancient Alexandria (An Archaeological Map)*, Travaux du Centre d'Archéologie méditerranéenne de l'Académie polonaise des Sciences, tome 32, Varsovie, 1993.

TURCAN, R., *Les cultes orientaux dans le monde romain*, Les Belles Lettres, 1989.

VERNUS, P. and YOYOTTE, J., *Dictionnaire des Pharaons*, 3ème éd. complétée, Paris, Editions Noêsis, 1998.

VEYNE, P., *Le Pain et le Cirque, Sociologie historique d'un pluralisme politique*, Paris, éd. du Seuil, 1976.

VITRUVE, M., *De Architectura*, (écrit vers 30 av. J.-C. et traduit en français par C. Perrault en 1684), Pierre Mardaga Editeur, Liège, 1988.

WHITEHORNE, J. E. G., 'Did Caracalla intend to return to Egypt?', in *CdE* 113 (1982) 132-135.

WHITEHORNE, J., *Cleopatras*, Routledge, London and New York, 1994.

YOYOTTE, J., CHARVET, P., and GOMPERTZ, S., *Strabon. Le Voyage en Egypte*, Paris, NiL éditions, 1997.

PHOTOGRAPHIC CREDITS

Prudence Cummings: 105, 108, 110

Jérome de la Fosse: photo 19, 27, 28, 30, 35, 36, 37, 40, 56, 57, 58, 59, 60, 61, 62, 63, 64, 65, 69, 70, 71, 72, 73, 74, 75, 76, 79, 80, 82, 84, 85, 88, 93, 94, 95, 96, 97, 98, 99, 101, 106, 111, 115, 116, 118, 119, 120, 121, 122, 125, 126, 128, 129, 130, 131

Christoph Gerigk: photo 7, 8, 9, 10, 11, 83, 92, 100, 112, 113, 123, 124, 132, 133, 134, 135, 136

Frédéric Osada: photo 2, 3, 6, 12, 13, 14, 15, 18, 20, 21, 22, 23, 24, 25, 26, 31, 32, 33, 34, 41, 42, 43, 44, 45, 46, 47, 48, 49, 50, 77, 78, 81, 87, 89, 90, 91, 104, 107, 109, 117, 127, 137

M. Psaïla: 1

© *Roger Viollet:* photo 38, 39

Cabinet des Medailles à Marseilles: page 59

© *DAFI:* photo 114

Département des Antiquités Égyptiennes, Musée du Louvre, Paris: photo 86

© *Kunsthistorische Museum, Vienna:* photo 102, 103

Musée du Caire: photo 66

Musée Gréco-Romain d'Alexandrie: photo 68

Museum of the University of Philadelphia: photo 67

Palais des Conservateurs, Rome: photo 55

Staatliche Museen, Berlin: photo 54

Decorative motif from the tomb at Mafrusa, Repertorio d'Arte dell' Egitto greco-romano, *Palermo, 1966, n. 93:* p. 60 et seq.

LIST OF ILLUSTRATIONS, FIGURES AND MAPS

Photos

Photo 1: survey equipment on the research vessel 3
Photo 2: Fort of Qa'it-Bey from the eastern harbour 3
Photo 3: the 'Corniche' along the eastern harbour 3
Photo 4: the magnetic detectors seen from the research vessel 4
Photo 5: GPS magnetic reference and positioning beacon on the fort of Qa'it-Bey 4
Photo 6: the DGPS location equipment under water 6
Photo 7: the fabric covering is passed to the divers 7
Photo 8: applying the fabric over the surface to take the moulding 7
Photo 9: after being positioned the fabric is covered by a lead sheet 7
Photo 10: removing the impression from the moulding 7
Photo 11: the moulded impression 7
Photo 12: the support vessel *Oceanex* 8
Photo 13: a diver cleaning an area of paving 9
Photo 14: paving after the removal of concretions 9
Photo 15: measuring an architectural feature 9
Photo 16: one of 'Cleopatra's Needles' being removed in 1879. This obelisk is today in Central Park, New York. 10
Photo 17: one of 'Cleopatra's Needles' being removed. The building behind still stands today. 11
Photo 18: removing the deposits from an architectural feature 11
Photo 19: paving stones after cleaning 17
Photo 20: lead ingots *in situ* after cleaning 22
Photo 21: limestone paving 25
Photo 22: underwater photo of the block 25
Photo 23: a diver holds the marble head 25
Photo 24: section of a brick and mortar wall 26
Photo 25: sarcophagus fragment 26
Photo 26: pile and timber base 29
Photo 27: a red granite block with a hieroglyphic inscription 31
Photo 28: another block found on the island 31
Photo 29: limestone paving in the column area 33
Photo 30: a red granite base with a Greek inscription 33
Photo 31: a timber section seen on the surface of the block and small limestones 33
Photo 32: wood from the shuttering under a mortar block 35
Photo 33: the important accumulation of columns at the south-west end 37
Photo 34: the field of columns 39
Photo 35: discovery of the grey granite statue no. 1199 41
Photo 36: small sphinx with diver 42
Photo 37: large sphinx with diver under water 42
Photo 38: the shoreline by the site of Cleopatra's Needle 43
Photo 39: the coast with one of Cleopatra's Needles about 1860-1870 45
Photo 40: the ibis with a diver under water 45
Photo 41: the red granite column field 47
Photo 42: red granite column and capital 47
Photo 43: red granite capital 47
Photo 44: a fluted column shaft in red granite 47
Photo 45: limestone paving 49
Photo 46: red granite block with hieroglyphs 50

Photo 47: head of a statue with *nemes* 50
Photo 48: releasing the grey granite statue 50
Photo 49: diver taking notes 50
Photo 50: amphorae on the bottom of the harbour 52
coin Aegypto-Capta 59
coin of Ptolemy I 138
Photo 51: André and Etienne Bernand 142
Photo 52: applying a moulding *in situ* 142
Photo 53: removing a moulding *in situ* 142
Photo 54: the Emperor Septimus Severus with his wife Julia Domma and their sons, Caracalla et Geta 146
Photo 55: Caracalla 146
Photo 56: fragment of white marble 147
Photo 57: moulding C116 147
Photo 58: moulding C129 148
Photo 59: C308, lines 1-5 149
Photo 60: C308, lines 5-8 149
Photo 61: C309 149
Photo 62: C310, lines 1-4 150
Photo 63: C310, lines 5-7 150
Photo 64: C1174 151
Photo 65: C347 151
Photo 66: Caracalla as Pharaoh 153
Photo 67: colossal head of Caracalla in red grantie, found at Koptos on the steps of the temple of Isis. Musée de l'Université de Philidelphie (CE 976) 160
Photo 68: Caracalla 166
Photo 69: sphinx no. 1198, diorite, *in situ*, right side 170
Photo 70: sphinx no. 1198 diorite, *in situ*, left side 170
Photo 71: sphinx no. 1185, grey granite, from the front 171
Photo 72: sphinx no. front part, from the front 171
Photo 73: sphinx no. 1185, left profile 171
Photo 74: sphinx no. 1185, right profile 172
Photo 75: sphinx no. 1185, *in situ* 172
Photo 76: face of no. 1185 174
Photo 77: sphinx no. 778, basalt, *in situ* 175
Photo 78: sphinx no. 900, basalt, *in situ* 175
Photo 79: head of a royal colossus, no. 1015 176
Photo 80: head of no. 1015 from the front 176
Photo 81: head of no. 1015, left profile 177
Photo 82: giant head of a falcon no. 795 178
Photo 83: priest bearing an 'Osisris-Canopus', no. 1199 179
Photo 84: huge coiled serpent, Agathodaïmon, no. 1182 180
Photo 85: small statute of ibis: Thot-Hermes. no. 1181 182
Photo 86: ibis, Louvre E. 17375 182
Photo 87: ibis no. 1181, right side, *in situ* 183
Photo 88: torso of the god Hermes, no. 1204 184
Photo 89: head of a woman: Antonia minos (?), no. 889 186
Photo 90: head of a woman no. 889, left profile 187
Photo 91: head of a woman no. 889, from the back 187
Photo 92: head of a woman no. 889 188
Photo 93: priest bearing an 'Osisris-Canopus', no. 1199 190
Photo 94: profile of same 190
Photo 95: no. 1199, back 191
Photo 96: no. 1199, detail: face and the god Canopus 192
Photo 97: no. 1199, detail: the shaved head 192
Photo 98: no. 1199, detail: fracture at the ankles 192
Photo 99: no. 1199, detail: face and the god Canopus 193

Photo 100: colossal falcon-headed sphinx, no. 795 196
Photo 101: colossal falcon-headed sphinx, no. 795, seen from front, *in situ* 197
Photo 102: the Vienna low wall 213 (recto) 216
Photo 103: the Vienna low wall 213 (verso) 216
Photo 104: section of obelisk, no. 747, *in situ*: Face A 222
Photo 105: section of obelisk, no. 747, impression: Face A 222
Photo 106: section of obelisk, no. 747, Face C 223
Photo 107: section of obelisk, no. 747, *in situ*: Face C 224
Photo 108: section of obelisk, no. 747, impression: Face C 224
Photo 109: section of obelisk, no. 747, *in situ*: Face B 225
Photo 110: section of obelisk, no. 747, impression: Face B 225
Photo 111: fragment de quartzite, no. 755, *in situ* 227
Photo 112: no. 755: the bows on the edge, impression 229
Photo 113: fragment of quartzite, no. 755, front face, impression 229
Photo 114: *sema-taoui* on the base of a statue of Darius 230
Photo 115: fragment of the base of statue, no. 781, *in situ* 230
Photo 116: no. 781: edge, impression of the inscription 231
Photo 117: no. 781: forward surface, impression 231
Photo 118: no. 781: surface right side, impression 232
Photo 119: no. 781: surface left side, impression 232
Photo 120: no. 781: impression of the upper surface 232
Photo 121: discovery of the base of no. 781 233
Photo 122: fragment no. 781, sections *in situ* 233
Photo 123: 4-5 broken sections of upright nos. 505 et 890 with the name of Apries 234
Photo 124: fragment no. 890 *in situ* 235
Photo 125: fragment of an upright of Apries, no. 771 *in situ* 238
Photo 126: fragment no. 771, impression (photo reveresed) 238
Photo 127: fragment of a beam in the name of Apries, no. 673, lower face 241
Photo 128: no. 673, lower face, impression 241
Photo 129: no. 673, lower face, *in situ* 241
Photo 130: no. 673, vertical face, impression 241
Photo 131: no. 673, vertical face, detail *in situ* 241
Photo 132: no. 780, impression 243
Photo 133: no. 780, removing the moulding 244
Photo 134: fragment of a beam with the name of Apries, no. 780 244
Photo 135: view of the wreck during its uncovering 249
Photo 136: reconstruction: the priest of Canopus before the chapel 251
Photo 137: head no. 889, Antonia Minor 252

Figures

Fig 1: map of Mahmoud el-Falaki 2
Fig 2: modern map of the eastern harbour 2
Fig 3: diagram of the detection process 4
Fig 4: Plate XII: 1738. Map and plan of the New Harbour of Alexandria. From *Travels in Egypt and Nubia*, by Frederick Lewis 19
Fig 5: Plate XXXIII: 1841. Plan of Alexandria and its neighbourhood in 1841, by E. Napier 20
Fig 6: sonar side scan image from the north-west jetty 22
Fig 7: colour drawing by Dejuine showing the obelisk 44
Fig 8: side scan sonar image at the entrance to the third harbour 52
Fig 9: general plan 54
Fig 10: floating caisson 56
Fig 11: ancient quay 57
Fig 12: hand sketch made under water. 196
Fig 13: Amenhotep II as a hieracocephalic sphinx 197
Fig 14: Horus-Hekenou pictured as a hieracocephalic sphinx 197

Fig 15: the Horus of Sohag, after a 'magical' statue 198
Fig 16: the Horus of Sohag, after the Borgia torso 198
Fig 17: the base of Diocletian's Column in 1747 213
Fig 18: the base of Diocletian's Column in 1747 213
Fig 19: the low wall, British Museum 228 (verso) 216
Fig 20: no. 755: edge, engraving, amended 229
Fig 21: the Nine Bows under the feet of Ramesses II 229
Fig 22: the *sema-taoui* on the throne of Sesostris I 230
Fig 23: 4-5 the Apries upright broken in two, nos. 505 and 890: sketch made *in situ* 234
Fig 24: title of Apries on a Saite fragment from Rosetta 241
Fig 25: title of the king in the Decree of Apries at Memphis 243

Maps

The Island, bathymetry 1997 5
The Eastern Harbour of Alexandria 7
The outer reefs 13
The great central reef 13
The main channel 15
Cape Lochias 17
The inner harbour 18
The Peninsula 21
The breakwater 22
Section of the large breakwater 23
The great south-west mole 24
The second harbour 27
Antirhodos Island 28
The Island, sites I1, I3, I4, S2 29
The Island, wooden remains at the extreme north-east 30
The Island, location of the column shafts and red granite blocks 32
The Island, excavation no. 1 34
Stratigraphy I4 36
The Island, column field to the south-west 38
The ancient coast 44
The ancient coast, excavation no. 2 46
The ancient coast, excavation no. 1 48
The third harbour 51
Antirhodos Island, remains with Greek inscriptions 144
Statuary 168
Block DB no. 747 223
Block DC2 no. 755 227
Block DE9 no. 781 231
Block no. 505 236
Block RD4 no. 890 237
Block DD9 no. 771 239
Block no. 673 240
Block DE8 no. 890 243

The submerged royal quarters facing p. 1
The Peninsula, bathymetry 1997 between p. 4 and 5
The submerged royal quarters between p. 12 and 13
The Peninsula between p. 20 and 21
The Island between p. 28 and 29
The ancient coast between p. 42 and 43
Artifacts around the Third Harbour between p. 50 and 51
The submerged royal quarters and position of various artefacts between p. 245 and 246
The submerged royal quarters, comparison of discoveries with ancient hypotheses between p. 250 and 251